THE RANDOM HOUSE Biographical DICTIONARY

THE RANDOM HOUSE Biographical DICTIONARY

RANDOM HOUSE
NEW YORK

 All inquiries should be addressed to: Reference and Electronic Publishing Division, Random House, Inc., 201 East 50th Street, New York, NY 10022. Published in the United States by Random House, Inc., New York, and simultaneously in Canada by Random House of Canada, Limited, Toronto.

Library of Congress Cataloging-in-Publication Data

The Random House biographical dictionary.
p. cm.
ISBN 0-679-41580-7
1. Biography—Dictionaries. I. Random House (Firm)
CT103.R2 1992
920.02—dc20
[B] 92-23953
CIP

Manufactured in the United States of America

1 2 3 4 5 6 7 8 9

First Edition

Contents

Staff

Enid Pearsons, *Editor*
Sol Steinmetz, *Executive Editor*
Mia McCroskey, *Managing Editor*

Alice Kovac Somoroff, *Project Editor*
Constance Baboukis Padakis, *Associate Editor*
Judy Kaplan Johnson, *Supervising Copyeditor*
Lani Mysak, Maria Padilla, *Editorial Assistants*
Stephen Weinstein, *Research Assistant*

Patricia W. Ehresmann, *Production Director*
Rita E. Rubin, *Production Associate*
Charlotte Staub, *Designer*

Publisher, Michael Mellin
Associate Publishers, Catherine Fowler,
John L. Hornör III

Preface

The Random House Biographical Dictionary is designed to provide a convenient source of authoritative, essential information about the most notable and influential personalities of the past and present. Here, in a handy, portable format, are listings for the famous and notorious alike—the authors, artists, scientists, philosophers, rulers, political leaders, soldiers, athletes, entertainers, and others who have helped make this world what it is.

More than 6,000 men and women, culled from every important field, are identified, their names listed in convenient alphabetical order. Each boldface entry is divided into syllables to show end-of-line hyphenation, although such hyphenation for proper names should be avoided whenever possible. Each name is followed by a parenthesized pronunciation. Every entry offers the birth year, death year (if applicable), nationality, and occupation or status of the person described. Difficult or foreign given names are also syllabified and pronounced, and titles, nicknames, and birth or real names are cited in italics within parentheses. Nobel Prizes and other special achievements are also indicated.

Based on Random House's constantly updated "Living Dictionary" database, the entries include the names of most prominent figures of the 20th century, making this the most up-to-date pocket-size biographical reference book available.

Pronunciation Key

STRESS

Pronunciations are marked for stress to reveal the relative differences in emphasis between syllables. In words of two or more syllables, a primary stress mark (**ʹ**), as in **mother** (muŧħʹər), follows the syllable having greatest stress. A secondary stress mark (ʹ), as in **grandmother** (grand**ʹ** muŧħʹər), follows a syllable having slightly less stress than primary but more stress than an unmarked syllable.

ENGLISH SOUNDS

a act, bat, marry
ā age, paid, say
â(r) air, dare, Mary
ä ah, part, balm
b back, cabin, cab
ch child, beach
d do, madder, bed
e edge, set, merry
ē equal, bee, pretty
ēr ear, mere
f fit, differ, puff
g give, trigger, beg
h hit, behave
hw which, nowhere
i if, big, mirror
ī ice, bite, deny
j just, tragic, fudge
k keep, token, make
l low, mellow, bottle (botʹl)
m my, summer, him
n now, sinner, button (butʹn)
ng sing, Washington
o ox, bomb, wasp
ō over, boat, no
ô order, ball, raw

oi oil, joint, joy
o͝o book, tour
o͞o ooze, fool, too
ou out, loud, cow
p pot, supper, stop
r read, hurry, near
s see, passing, miss
sh shoe, fashion, push
t ten, matter, bit
th thin, ether, path
th̸ that, either, smooth
u up, sun
û(r) urge, burn, cur
v voice, river, live
w witch, away
y yes, onion
z zoo, lazy, those
zh treasure, mirage
ə used in unaccented syllables to indicate the sound of the reduced vowel in *a*lone, syst*e*m, eas*i*ly, gall*o*p, circ*u*s
ᵊ used between ī and r and between ou and r to show triphthongal quality, as in fire(fīᵊr), hour (ouᵊr)

NON-ENGLISH SOUNDS

A as in French *ami* (A mē′)
KH as in Scottish *loch* (lôKH)
N as in French *bon* (bôN) [used to indicate that the preceding vowel is nasalized.]
Œ as in French *feu* (fŒ)
R [a symbol for any non-English *r*, including a trill or flap in Italian and Spanish and a sound in French and German similar to KH but pronounced with voice]
Y as in French *tu* (tY)
ᵊ as in French *Bastogne* (bA stôn′yᵊ)

Abbreviations
Used in this Book

Arab.	Arabic
Brit.	British
Ch.	Chinese
Dan.	Danish
Du.	Dutch
esp.	especially
fl.	flourished
Fr.	French
Ger.	German
Japn.	Japanese
Norw.	Norwegian
Rom.	Romanian
Russ.	Russian
Sp.	Spanish
Sw.	Swedish

THE RANDOM HOUSE Biographical DICTIONARY

Aal•to (äl′tō), **Al•var** (äl′vär), 1898–1976, Finnish architect and furniture designer.

Aar•on (âr′ən, ar′-), **Henry Louis** (*"Hank"*), born 1934, U.S. baseball player.

A•bai•lard (A bā LAR′), **Pierre,** ABÉLARD.

Ab•ba•do (ə bâ′dō), **Claudio,** born 1933, Italian symphony and opera conductor.

Ab•bey (ab′ē), **Edwin Austin,** 1852–1911, U.S. painter and illustrator.

Ab•bot (ab′ət), **Charles Greeley,** 1872–1973, U.S. astrophysicist.

Ab•bott (ab′ət), **1. Berenice,** 1898–1991, U.S. photographer. **2. Bud,** 1895–1974, U.S. comedian. **3. Edith,** 1876–1957, and her sister **Grace,** 1878–1939, U.S. social reformers. **4. Jacob,** 1803–79, and his son, **Lyman,** 1835–1922, U.S. clergymen and writers. **5. Robert Sengstake,** 1868–1940, U.S. newspaper publisher.

Abd-el-Ka•dir (äb′del kä′dēr) also **Abd-al-Ka•dir** (äb′-dal-), 1807?–83, Algerian leader.

Abd-el Krim (äb′del krēm′, krim′), 1881?–1963, Moroccan chief: leader of the Riff revolts 1921, 1924.

Ab•der•hal•den (*Ger.* äp′dəʀ häl′dn), **Emil,** 1877–1950, Swiss chemist and physiologist.

Abd-er-Rah•man Khan or **Abd•ur•rah•man Khan** (äb′dər rə män′ KHän′), 1830?–1901, emir of Afghanistan 1880–1901.

Ab•dul-A•ziz (äb′dŏŏl ä zēz′), 1830–76, sultan of Turkey 1861–76 (brother of Abdul-Mejid I).

Ab•dul-Ha•mid II (äb′dŏŏl hä mēd′), 1842–1918, sultan of Turkey 1876–1909.

Ab•dul-Jab•bar (äb dŏŏl′jə bär′, ab-), **Kareem** (*Ferdinand Lewis Alcindor, Jr.*), born 1947, U.S. basketball player.

Ab•dul-Me•jid I or **Ab•dul-Me•djid I** (äb′dŏŏl me jēd′), 1823–61, sultan of Turkey 1839–61 (brother of Abdul-Aziz).

Ab•dul Rah•man (äb′dŏŏl rä′män), **Tunku,** 1903–73, Malaysian political leader: first prime minister of Malaya 1957–63; prime minister of Malaysia 1963–70.

A•bel (ā′bəl; *for 3 also Norw.* ä′bəl), **1. Sir Frederick Augustus,** 1827–1902, English chemist: inventor of cordite. **2. I. W.,** 1908–87, U.S. labor leader: president of the United Steelworkers of America 1965–77. **3. Niels Henrik,** 1802–29, Norwegian mathematician.

Ab•é•lard (ab′ə lärd′; *Fr.* A bā LAR′), **Pierre,** 1079–1142, French philosopher, teacher, and theologian: love affair with Heloïse. English, **Peter Abelard.**

Ab•er•crom•bie (ab′ər krom′bē, -krum′-), **Sir (Leslie) Patrick,** 1879–1957, English architect and town planner.

Ab•er•nath•y (ab′ər nath′ē), **Ralph (David),** 1926–90, U.S. clergyman and civil-rights leader.

A•bruz•zi (ə bro͞ot′sē), **Duke of the** (*Prince Luigi Amedeo of Savoy-Aosta*), 1873–1933, Italian naval officer, mountain climber, and Arctic explorer.

A•bu-Bakr (ə bo͞o′bak′ər) also **A•bu-Bekr** (-bek′-), A.D. 573–634, Muhammad's father-in-law and successor: first caliph of Mecca 632–634.

A•bu Ha•ni•fa (ä bo͞o′ ha nē′fə), A.D. 699–767, Islamic scholar: founder of one of the four schools of Islamic law.

A•bu•me•ron (ə bo͞o′mə ron′), AVENZOAR.

Ab•zug (ab′zo͝og), **Bella (Savitzky),** born 1920, U.S. politician and women's-rights activist: congresswoman 1971–76.

Ac•ci•us (ak′shē əs) also **Attius, Lucius,** c170–c90 B.C., Roman poet and prose writer.

A•chae•me•nes (ə kē′mə nēz′, ə kem′ə-), fl. 7th century B.C., Persian king: traditional founder of the Achaemenid dynasty.

A•che•be (ä chā′bā), **Chin•ua** (chin′wä), born 1930, Nigerian writer.

Ach•e•son (ach′ə sən), **1. Dean (Gooderham),** 1893–1971, U.S. statesman: Secretary of State 1949–53. **2. Edward Goodrich,** 1856–1931, U.S. chemist.

Ac•ton (ak′tən), **Lord** (*John Emerich Edward Dalberg-Acton,* 1st Baron), 1834–1902, English historian.

A•cuff (ā′kuf), **Roy (Claxton),** born 1903, U.S. country-and-western singer and composer.

Ad•am (ad′əm *for 2;* A däN′ *for 1, 3),* **1. Adolphe Charles** 1803–56, French composer of comic opera and ballet music. **2. James,** 1730–94, and his brother **Robert,** 1728–92, English architects and furniture designers. **3. Lambert Sigisbert,** 1700–59, and his brother **Nicholas Sébastien,** 1705–78, French sculptors.

Ad•ams (ad′əmz), **1. Ansel,** 1902–84, U.S. photographer. **2. Brooks,** 1848–1927, U.S. historian (son of Charles Francis Adams). **3. Charles Francis,** 1807–86, U.S. statesman (son of John Quincy Adams). **4. Franklin P(ierce)** (*"F.P.A."*), 1881–1960, U.S. author and columnist. **5. Henry (Brooks),** 1838–1918, U.S. historian and writer (son of Charles Francis Adams). **6. James Truslow,** 1878–1949, U.S. historian. **7. John,** 1735–1826, 2nd president of the U.S. 1797–1801: a leader in the American Revolution. **8. John Quincy**, 1767–1848, 6th president of the U.S. 1825–29 (son of John Adams). **9. Maude** (*Maude Kiskadden*), 1872–1953, U.S. actress. **10. Samuel,** 1722–1803, a leader in the American Revolution. **11. Samuel Hopkins,** 1874–1958, U.S. journalist and novelist.

Ad•dams (ad′əmz), **1. Charles (Samuel),** 1912–88, U.S. cartoonist. **2. Jane,** 1860–1935, U.S. social worker and writer: Nobel peace prize 1931.

Ad•di•son (ad′ə sən), **1. Joseph,** 1672–1719, English essayist and poet. **2. Thomas,** 1793–1860, English physician.

Ade (ād), **George,** 1866–1944, U.S. humorist.

A•de•nau•er (ad′n ouᵊr, -ou′ər, äd′-), **Konrad,** 1876–1967, chancellor of West Germany 1949–63.

Ad•ler (ad′lər; *for 1–3 also* äd′lər), **1. Alfred,** 1870–1937, Austrian psychiatrist and psychologist. **2. Cyrus,** 1863–1940, U.S. religious leader and Jewish scholar. **3. Felix,** 1851–1933, U.S. educator, reformer, and writer. **4. Lawrence Cecil** (*"Larry"*), born 1914, U.S. harmonica player. **5. Mortimer (Jerome),** 1902–91, U.S. philospher and educator.

A•dou•la (ä do͞o′lə), **Cy•rille** (sē ril′), 1922–78, African statesman: premier of the Democratic Republic of the Congo (now Zaire) 1961–64.

A•dri•an (ā′drē ən), **Edgar Douglas,** 1889–1977, English physiologist: Nobel prize for medicine 1932.

Adrian (or **Hadrian**) **IV,** (*Nicholas Breakspear*), c1100–59, pope 1154-59: the only English pope.

Æ or **AE** or **A.E.,** pen name of George William Russell.

Æl•fric (al′frik), (*"Ælfric Grammaticus"; "Ælfric the Grammarian"*) A.D. c955–c1020, English abbot and writer.

Aes•chi•nes (es′kə nēz′; *esp. Brit.* ē′skə-), 389–314 B.C., Athenian orator; rival of Demosthenes.

Aes•chy•lus (es′kə ləs; *esp. Brit.* ē′skə-), 525–456 B.C., Greek poet and dramatist.

Ae•sop (ē′səp, ē′sop), c620–c560 B.C., Greek writer of fables.

Aeth•el•stan (ath′əl stan′) ATHELSTAN.

A•ga Khan III (ä′gə kän′, kan′), 1877–1957, leader of the Isma'ili sect of Muslims in India 1885–1957.

Aga Khan IV, (*Shah Karim al-Husainy*), born 1936, leader of the Isma'ili sect of Muslims in India since 1957.

Ag•as•siz (ag′ə sē), **1. Alexander,** 1835–1910, U.S. oceanographer and marine zoologist, born in Switzerland. **2.** his father, **(Jean) Louis (Rodolphe)** (zhäɴ), 1807–73, U.S. zoologist and geologist, born in Switzerland.

Ag•a•thon (ag′ə thon′), c450–c400 B.C., Greek poet and dramatist.

A•gee (ā′jē), **James,** 1909–55, U.S. author and film critic.

A•ges•i•la•us II (ə jes′ə lā′əs), 444?–c360 B.C., king of Sparta c400–c360.

Ag•nes (ag′nis), **Saint,** A.D. 292?–304?, Roman Catholic child martyr.

Ag•new (ag′no͞o, -nyo͞o), **Spi•ro T(heodore)** (spēr′ō), born 1918, U.S. vice president 1969–73; resigned 1973.

Ag•non (ag′non), **Shmuel Yosef** (*Samuel Josef Czaczkes*), 1888–1970, Israeli novelist and short-story writer, born in Poland: Nobel prize 1966.

A•gric•o•la (ə grik′ə lə), **1. Geor•gi•us** (jôr′jē əs, jē ôr′-), (*Georg Bauer*), 1494–1555, German historian, physician, and pioneer in mineralogy. **2. Gnae•us Julius** (nē′əs), A.D. 37–93, Roman general: governor of Britain.

A•grip•pa (ə grip′ə), **Marcus Vipsanius,** 63–12 B.C., Roman general and statesman.

Ag•rip•pi•na II (ag′rə pī′nə, -pē′-), A.D. 16?–59?, mother of the Roman emperor Nero and sister of Caligula.

A•gui•nal•do (ä′gē näl′dô), **Emilio,** 1869–1964, Filipino leader during the Spanish-American war: opposed to U.S. occupation.

Ah•mose I (ä′mōs), 1580–1557 B.C., founder of the New Kingdom of ancient Egypt.

Ai•ken (ā′kən), **Conrad (Potter),** 1889–1973, U.S. poet.

Ai•ley (ā′lē), **Alvin,** 1931–89, U.S. dancer and choreographer.

A•i•sha (ä′ē shä′), A.D. 613?–678, favorite wife of Muhammad (daughter of Abu-Bakr).

Ak•bar (ak′bär), (*"the Great"*) (*Jalal-ud-Din Mohammed*), 1542–1605, Mogul emperor of India 1556–1605.

A•khe•na•ton or **A•khe•na•ten** (äk nät′n, ä′kə-), also **Akh•na•ton** (äk nät′n), (*Amenhotep IV*) died 1357? B.C., king of Egypt 1375?-1357?: reformer of ancient Egyptian religion.

Akh•ma•to•va (äKH mä′tə və), **Anna** (*Anna Andreyevna Gorenko*), 1889–1966, Russian poet.

A•ki•ba ben Jo•seph (ä kē′bä ben jō′zəf, -səf, ə kē′və), A.D. c50–c135, rabbi and scholar. Also called **A•ki′ba.**

A•ki•hi•to (ä′ki hē′tō), (*"Heisei"*), born 1933, emperor of Japan since 1989 (son of Hirohito).

A•kins (ā′kinz), **Zoë,** 1886–1958, U.S. playwright.

A•lar•cón (ä′lär kōn′), **Pedro Antonio** (*Pedro Antonio Alarcón y Ariza*), 1833–91, Spanish writer and diplomat.

Al•a•ric (al′ər ik), A.D. c370–410, king of the Visigoths: captured Rome 410.

Al•ba (al′bə; *Sp.* äl′vä), **Duke of,** ALVA, Fernando Alvarez de Toledo.

Al•ban (ôl′bən, al′-), **Saint,** 3rd century A.D., first English martyr.

Al•ba•teg•ni•us (al′bə teg′nē əs), Latin name of BATTANI.

Al-Bat•ta•ni (al bə tä′nē), BATTANI.

Al•bee (ôl′bē), **Edward,** born 1928, U.S. playwright.

Al•bé•niz (äl bā′nēs, al-), **Isaac,** 1860–1909, Spanish composer and pianist.

Al•be•ro•ni (äl′be Rô′nē), **Giulio,** 1664–1752, Italian cardinal and statesman: prime minister of Spain 1715–19.

Al•bert (al′bərt), **1. Carl (Bert),** born 1908, U.S. politician: Speaker of the House 1971–77. **2. Prince** (*Albert Francis Charles Augustus Emanuel, Prince of Saxe-Coburg-Gotha*), 1819–61, consort of Queen Victoria.

Albert I, 1875–1934, king of the Belgians 1909–34.

Al•ber•ti (äl beR′tē), **Leon Battista,** 1404–72, Italian architect, artist, musician, and poet.

Al•ber•tus Mag•nus (al bûr′təs mag′nəs), **Saint** (*Count von Bollstädt*), 1193?–1280, German scholastic philosopher: teacher of Saint Thomas Aquinas.

Al•bi•nus (al bī′nəs), ALCUIN.

Al•bi•zu Cam•pos (äl bē′so͞o käm′pôs), **Pedro,** 1891–1964, Puerto Rican political leader.

Al•boin (al′boin, -bō in), died A.D. 573?, king of the Lombards 561?–573?.

Al•bright (ôl′brīt), **1. Ivan (Le Lorraine),** 1897–1983, U.S. painter. **2. Tenley (Emma),** born 1935, U.S. figure skater. **3. William Foxwell,** 1891–1971, U.S. archaeologist and biblical historian.

Al•bu•quer•que (al′bə kûr′kē), **Affonso de,** 1453–1515, founder of the Portuguese empire in the East.

Al•cae•us (al sē′əs), fl. c600 B.C., Greek poet of Mytilene.

Al•ci•bi•a•des (al′sə bī′ə dēz′), 450?–404 B.C., Athenian politician and general.

Al•cott (ôl′kət, -kot), **1. (Amos) Bronson,** 1799–1888, U.S. educator and philosopher. **2.** his daughter **Louisa May,** 1832–88, U.S. author.

Al•cuin (al′kwin), (*Ealhwine Flaccus*) A.D. 735–804, English theologian and scholar: teacher and adviser of Charlemagne.

Al•da (äl′də, ôl′-, al′-), **Frances,** 1885–1952, U.S. operatic singer.

Al•den (ôl′dən), **John,** 1599?–1687, Pilgrim settler in Plymouth, Massachusetts, 1620.

Al•der (äl′dər), **Kurt,** 1902–58, German chemist: Nobel prize 1950.

Al•ding•ton (ôl′ding tən), **Richard,** 1892–1962, English poet, novelist, and composer.

Al•drich (ôl′drich), **Thomas Bailey,** 1836–1907, U.S. short-story writer, poet, and novelist.

Al•drin (ôl′drin), **Edwin Eugene, Jr.** (*"Buzz"*), born 1930, U.S. astronaut: second person to walk on the moon, 1969.

Al•dus Ma•nu•ti•us (ôl′dəs mə no͞o′shē əs, -nyo͞o′-, al′-dəs), MANUTIUS, Aldus.

A•le•ar•di (ä′le äʀ′dē), **Count Aleardo,** 1812–78, Italian poet and patriot.

A•lei•chem (ä lā′ᴋʜem), **Sho•lom** (shô′ləm), (pen name of *Solomon Rabinowitz*), 1859–1916, Russian author of Yiddish novels, plays, and short stories; in the U.S. from 1906.

A•lei•xan•dre (ä′lā ksän′dʀe), **Vicente,** 1898–1984, Spanish poet: Nobel prize 1977.

A•le•mán (ä′lā män′), **1. Mateo,** 1547?–1610, Spanish novelist. **2. Miguel,** born 1902, president of Mexico 1946–52.

A•lem•bert, d' (dal′əm bâr′), **Jean Le Rond** (zhäɴ), 1717?–83, French mathematician, philosopher, and writer: associate of Diderot.

A•les•san•dri (ä′le sän′dʀē), **1. Jorge,** 1896–1986, Chilean engineer and statesman: president 1958–64. **2. Arturo,** 1868–1950, Chilean lawyer and statesman: president 1920–24, 1925, 1932–38.

Al•ex•an•der[1] (al′ig zan′dər, -zän′-), **1.** ALEXANDER THE GREAT. **2. Franz,** 1891–1964, U.S. psychoanalyst, born in Hungary. **3. Grover Cleveland,** 1887–1950, U.S. baseball player. **4. Sir Harold R. L. G.** (*1st Earl Alexander of Tunis*), 1891–1969, British general: governor general of Canada

1946–52. **5. Samuel,** 1859–1938, British philosopher. **6. William,** 1726–83, general in the American Revolution.

Al•ex•an•der² (al′ig zan′dər, -zän′-), **1. Alexander I,** (*Aleksandr Pavlovich*) 1777–1825, czar of Russia 1801–25. **2. Alexander II,** (*Aleksandr Nikolaevich*) 1818–81, czar of Russia 1855–81. **3. a. Alexander III,** died 1181, Italian ecclesiastic: pope 1159–81. **b.** (*Aleksandr Aleksandrovich*) 1845–94, czar of Russia 1881–94. **4. Alexander VI,** (*Rodrigo Borgia*) 1431?–1503, Italian ecclesiastic: pope 1492–1503 (father of Cesare and Lucrezia Borgia).

Alexan′der Nev′sky (nev′skē, nef′-, nyef′-), (*Aleksandr Nevski*) 1220?–63, Russian prince, national hero, and saint.

Alexan′der Se•ve′rus (sə vēr′əs), A.D. 208?–235, Roman emperor 222–235.

Alexan′der the Great′, 356–323 B.C., king of Macedonia 336–323: conqueror of Greek city-states and of the Persian Empire from Asia Minor and Egypt to India.

Al•ex•an•dra (al′ig zan′drə, -zän′-), 1844–1925, queen consort of Edward VII of England.

A•lex•is Mi•khai•lo•vich (ə lek′sis mi kī′lə vich), (*Aleksei Mikhailovich*), 1629–76, czar of Russia 1645–76 (father of Peter I).

Alex′is Ni•ko•la′ye•vich (nik′ə lī′ə vich) (*Aleksei Nikolayevich*), 1904–18, son of Nicholas II of Russia, heir apparent to the Russian throne: executed in the Russian Bolshevik Revolution.

A•lex•i•us I (ə lek′sē əs), (*Alexius Comnenus*) 1048–1118, emperor of the Byzantine Empire 1081–1118.

Al Fa•ra•bi (al′ fä rä′bē) also **Al′fa•ra′bi•us** (-fə rā′bē-əs), died A.D. 950, Arab philosopher. Also called **Al•fa•ra•bi•us** (al′fə rā′bē əs).

Al•fa•ro (äl fä′rô), **(Flavio) Eloy,** 1864–1912, Ecuadorian political leader: president 1897–1901, 1907–11.

Al•fie•ri (äl fye′rē), **Count Vittorio,** 1749–1803, Italian dramatist and poet.

Al•fon•so (al fon′sō, -zō), **1. Alfonso I** (*Alfonso Henriques*), 1109?–85, first king of Portugal 1139–85. **2. Alfonso X** ("*Alfonso the Wise*"), 1221–84, king of Castile 1252–84. **3. Alfonso XII,** 1857–85, king of Spain 1886–85. **4. Alfonso XIII,** 1886–1941, king of Spain 1886–1930.

Al′fred the Great′ (al′frid, -fred), A.D. 849–899, king of the West Saxons 871–899.

Alf•vén (äl vān′, al-), **Hannes (Olof Gösta),** born 1908, Swedish physicist: Nobel prize 1970.

Al-Ga•zel (al′gə zel′), GHAZZALI.

Al•ger (al′jər), **Horatio, Jr.,** 1834–99, U.S. novelist: author of a series of books for boys.

Al-Ghaz•za•li (al′ga zä′lē), GHAZZALI.

Al•gren (ôl′grin), **Nelson,** 1909–81, U.S. novelist and short-story writer.

A•li (ä′lē, ä lē′ *for 1;* ä lē′ *for 2*), **1.** (*'Alī ibn-abu-Talib*), A.D. c600-61, fourth caliph of Islam 656-661 (cousin and son-in-law of Muhammad): considered the first caliph by Shi'ites. **2. Muhammad** (*Cassius Marcellus Clay, Jr.*), born 1942, U.S. boxer: world heavyweight champion 1964–67, 1974–78, 1978–79.

A′li Muham′mad of Shiraz′, BAB ED-DIN.

A′li Pa′sha (ä′lē, ä lē′), (*Arslan*) 1741–1822, Turkish pasha and ruler of Albania 1787?–1820.

Al•len (al′ən), **1. (Charles) Grant (Blairfindie),** (*"Cecil Power," "J. Arbuthnot Wilson"*), 1848–99, British philosophical writer and novelist. **2. Ethan,** 1738–89, American soldier in the Revolutionary War: leader of the "Green Mountain Boys" of Vermont. **3. Fred** (*John Florence Sullivan*), 1894–1956, U.S. comedian. **4. Frederick Lewis,** 1890–1954, U.S. historian and editor. **5. Gracie** (*Grace Ethel Cecile Rosalie Allen*), 1905–64, U.S. comedian (partner and wife of George Burns). **6. Richard,** 1760–1831, U.S. clergyman: a founder of the African Methodist Episcopal Church. **7. Steve,** born 1921, U.S. entertainer and comedian. **8. (William) Hervey,** 1889–1949, U.S. novelist, poet, and biographer. **9. Woody** (*Allen Stewart Konigsberg*), born 1935, U.S. comedian, author, actor, and filmmaker.

Al•len•by (al′ən bē), **Edmund Henry Hyn•man** (hin′mən), **1st Viscount,** 1861–1936, British field marshal: commander of British forces in Egypt in World War I.

Al•ling•ham (al′ing əm), **Margery,** 1904–66, English mystery writer.

Al•li•son (al′ə sən), **Donald** (*Donnie*), born 1939, and his brother, **Robert** (*Bobby*), born 1937, U.S. racing-car drivers.

All•port (ôl′pôrt, -pōrt), **Gordon W(illard),** 1897–1967, U.S. psychologist and educator.

All•ston (ôl′stən), **Washington,** 1799–1843, U.S. painter, novelist, and poet.

Al•ma-Tad•e•ma (al′mə tad′ə mə), **Sir Lawrence,** 1836–1912, English painter, born in the Netherlands.

Al•mei•da (äl mā′də), **Francisco de,** 1450?–1510, Portuguese military leader: first Portuguese viceroy in India.

A•lon•so (ə lon′zō), **1. Alicia** (*Alicia Ernestina de la Caridad del Cobre Martínez Hoyo*), born 1921, Cuban ballerina. **2. Dámaso,** 1898–1990, Spanish poet, critic, and philologist.

Alt•dor•fer (ält′dôr′fər), **Albrecht,** c1480–1538, German painter.

Alt•geld (ôlt′geld), **John Peter,** 1847–1902, U.S. politician, born in Germany: governor of Illinois 1892–96; made controversial decision to pardon those convicted in Haymarket Riot.

Al•va (äl′vä) also **Alba, Fernando Alvarez de Toledo, Duke of,** 1508–82, Spanish general who suppressed a Protestant rebellion in the Netherlands in 1567.

Al•va•ra•do (äl′vä rä′dō), **1. Alonso de,** c1490–1554, Spanish soldier in the conquests of Mexico and Peru. **2.**

Pedro de, 1495–1541, Spanish soldier: chief aide of Cortés in the conquest of Mexico.

Al•va•rez (al′və rez′), **Luis Walter,** 1911–88, U.S. physicist: Nobel prize 1968.

Ál•va•rez Quin•te•ro (äl′vä reth′ kēn te′rô), **Joa•quín** (hwä kēn′), 1873–1944, and his brother **Se•ra•fín** (se′rä-fēn′), 1871–1938, Spanish dramatists and coauthors.

Al•va•ro (äl vä′rô), **Corrado,** c1890–1956, Italian journalist and novelist.

Al•y•at•tes (al′ē at′ēz), king of Lydia c617–560 B.C.

A•ma•do (ə mä′dō, -do͞o), **Jor•ge** (zhôr′zhə), born 1912, Brazilian novelist.

A•ma•dor Guer•re•ro (ä′mə dôr′ gə râr′ô), **Manuel,** 1833–1909, Panamanian political leader: first president of Panama 1904–08.

A•ma•ti (ä mä′tē), **Nicolò,** 1596–1684, Italian violinmaker, one of a family of 16th- and 17th-century violinmakers: teacher of Antonio Stradivari.

A•ma•to (ə mä′tō), **Pasquale** 1879–1942, Italian operatic baritone.

Am•bed•kar (äm bed′kär), **Bhim•rao Ram•ji** (bēm′rou räm′jē), 1893–1956, Indian politician and jurist.

Am•bler (am′blər), **Eric,** born 1909, English suspense novelist.

Am•brose (am′brōz), **Saint,** A.D. 340?–397, bishop of Milan 374–397.

Amenhotep IV, original name of AKHENATON.

A•me•ri•go Ves•puc•ci (ə mer′i gō′ ve spo͞o′chē, -spyo͞o′-), VESPUCCI, Amerigo.

Am•herst (am′ərst), **Jeffrey, Baron,** 1717–97, British field marshal: governor general of British North America 1760–63.

A•min (ä mēn′), **I•di** (ē′dē), (*Idi Amin Dada*), born 1925?, Ugandan dictator: president 1971–79; in exile from 1979.

A•mis (ā′mis), **Kingsley,** born 1922, English novelist.

Am•ma•na•ti (ä′mə nä′tē), **Bartolommeo,** 1511–92, Italian architect and sculptor.

Am•mi•a•nus (am′ē ā′nəs), **Marcellinus,** A.D. c325–c398, Roman historian.

A•mund•sen (ä′mənd sən, ä mən-), **Ro•ald** (rō′äl), 1872–1928, Norwegian explorer: discovered the South Pole in 1911.

An•a•cle•tus (an′ə klē′təs), fl. 1st century A.D., pope 76–88. Also called **Cletus.**

A•nac•re•on (ə nak′rē ən), c570–c480 B.C., Greek writer, esp. of love poems and drinking songs.

A•nan•da (ä′nən də), fl. early 5th century B.C., favorite disciple of Gautama Buddha.

An•a•sta•sia (an′ə stā′zhə, ä′nə stä′shə), **Nikolaievna Romanov, Grand Duchess,** 1901–?, daughter of Nicholas II: believed executed by the Bolsheviks in 1918 with other members of the Romanov family.

An•ax•ag•o•ras (an′ak sag′ər əs), 500?–428 B.C., Greek philosopher.

A•nax•i•man•der (ə nak′sə man′dər), 611?–547? B.C., Greek astronomer and philosopher.

An•der•sen (an′dər sən), **Hans Christian,** 1805–75, Danish author, esp. of fairy tales.

An•der•son (an′dər sən), **1. Carl David,** 1905–91, U.S. physicist. **2. Dame Judith,** 1898–1991, Australian actress in the U.S. **3. Marian,** born 1902, U.S. contralto. **4. Maxwell,** 1888–1959, U.S. dramatist. **5. Philip Warren,** born 1923, U.S. physicist: developer of solid-state circuitry; Nobel prize 1977. **6. Sherwood,** 1876–1941, U.S. author.

An•dra•da e Sil•va (an drä′də ā sēl′və), **José Bonifacio de,** 1763–1838, Brazilian statesman and scientist: architect of Brazilian independence.

An•drás•sy (an dras′ē; *Hung.* on′drä shē), **Count Julius,** 1823–90, Hungarian statesman.

An•dré (än′drā, an′drē), **John,** 1751–80, British major hanged as a spy by the Americans in the Revolutionary War.

An•dre•a del Sar•to (än drā′ə del sär′tō), (*Andrea Domenico d'Annolo di Francesco*) 1486–1531, Italian painter.

An•dret•ti (an dret′ē), **Mario (Gabriel),** born 1940, U.S. racing-car driver.

An•drew (an′dro͞o), *n.* one of the 12 apostles of Jesus.

An•drewes (an′dro͞oz), **Lancelot,** 1555–1626, English theologian: one of the translators of the Authorized Version of the Bible.

An′drew of Crete′ (an′dro͞o), A.D. c650–730, Greek poet and Orthodox archbishop of Crete.

An•drews (an′dro͞oz), **1. Charles McLean,** 1863–1943, U.S. historian and author. **2. Julie** (*Julia Elizabeth Wells*), born 1935, British singer and actress. **3. Roy Chapman,** 1884–1960, U.S. naturalist, explorer, and author.

An′drews Sis′ters, a family of U.S. singers, including **LaVerne,** 1915–67, **Maxine,** born 1918, and **Patricia** (*Patty*), born 1920.

An•dre•yev (än drā′əf), **Leonid Nikolaevich,** 1871–1919, Russian novelist, short-story writer, and playwright.

An•drić (än′drich), **I•vo** (ē′vô), 1892–1975, Yugoslavian novelist and short-story writer: Nobel prize 1961.

An•dros (an′drəs), **Sir Edmund,** 1637–1714, British governor in the American colonies.

An•fin•sen (an′fin sən), **Christian Boeh•mer** (bā′mər, bō′-), born 1916, U.S. biochemist: Nobel prize for chemistry 1972.

An•ge•la Me•ri•ci (än′je lä me rē′chē), **Saint,** 1474–1540, Italian ecclesiastic, founder of the Ursuline order.

An•ge•li•co (an jel′i kō′), **Fra** (*Guido di Pietro*) (*Giovanni da Fiesole*), 1387–1455, Italian painter.

An•gell (ān′jəl), **1. James Rowland,** 1869–1949, U.S. educator. **2. Norman** (*Sir Ralph Norman Angell Lane*), 1874–1967, English pacifist, economist, and writer: Nobel peace prize 1933.

An•guier (äɴ gyā′), **François,** 1604–69, and his brother **Michel,** 1614–86, French sculptors.

An•i•ce•tus (an′ə sē′təs), **Saint,** pope A.D. 155?–166?.

An•ka (ang′kə), **Paul,** born 1941, Canadian singer and composer.

An•na I•va•nov•na (ä′nə ē vä′nəv nə), 1693–1740, empress of Russia 1730–40.

Anne (an), 1665–1714, queen of England 1702–14 (daughter of James II of England).

Anne′ Boleyn′, Boleyn, Anne.

An•nen•sky or **An•nen•ski** (ə nen′skē), **Innokenty Fyodorovich,** 1856–1909, Russian poet.

Anne′ of Aus′tria, 1601–66, queen consort of Louis XIII of France: regent during the minority of her son Louis XIV.

Anne′ of Bohe′mia, 1366–94, queen consort of Richard II of England.

Anne′ of Cleves′, 1515–57, fourth wife of Henry VIII of England.

Anne′ of Den′mark, 1574–1619, queen consort of James I of England.

Anne′ of France′, (*Anne de Beaujeu*) 1460–1522, daughter of Louis XI of France: regent during the minority of her brother Charles VIII 1483–91.

An•nun•zio, d′ (dän nōōn′tsyô), **Gabriele,** D'Annunzio, Gabriele.

A•nouilh (ᴀ nōō′yᵊ; *Eng.* än wē′), **Jean** (zhäɴ), 1910–87, French dramatist.

An•selm (an′selm), **Saint,** 1033–1109, archbishop of Canterbury: scholastic theologian and philosopher.

Ans•gar (ans′gär) also **Ans•kar** (an′skär), **Saint,** 801–865, French Benedictine priest and missionary: patron saint of Scandinavia.

An•ter•us (an′tər əs) also **An′te•ros** (-tə ros′), **Saint,** pope A.D. 235–236.

An•theil (an′til), **George,** 1900–59, U.S. composer.

An•tho•ny (an′tə nē, -thə- *for 1, 2;* an′thə nē *for 3*), **1. Mark,** Antony, Mark. **2. Saint,** A.D. 251?–356?, Egyptian hermit: founder of Christian monasticism. **3. Susan Brownell,** 1820–1906, U.S. reformer and suffragist.

An′tho•ny of Pad′ua (an′tə nē, -thə-), **Saint,** 1195–1231, Franciscan monk and preacher in Italy and France.

An•tig•o•nus (an tig′ə nəs), **1. Antigonus I,** (*Cyclops*) 382?–301 B.C., Macedonian general under Alexander the Great: king of Macedonia 306–301 B.C. **2. Antigonus II,** (*Gonatus*) c319–239 B.C., king of Macedonia 283–239 (son of Demetrius I).

An•tim•a•chus (an tim′ə kəs), fl. c410 B.C. Greek poet.

An•ti•o•chus (an tī′ə kəs), **1. Antiochus III,** (*"the Great"*) 241?–187 B.C., king of Syria 223–187. **2. Antiochus IV,** (*Antiochus Epiphanes*) died 164? B.C., king of Syria 175–164?.

An•tip•a•ter (an tip′ə tər), 398?–319 B.C., Macedonian statesman and general: regent of Macedonia 334–323.

An·tis·the·nes (an tis′thə nēz′), 444?–365? B.C., Greek philosopher: founder of the Cynic school.

An·toine (an′twän), **1. André,** 1858–1943, French theatrical director, manager, and critic. **2. Père,** (*Francisco Ildefonso Mareno*), 1748–1829, Roman Catholic priest in Louisiana: tried to establish an Inquisition.

An·toi·nette (an′twə net′, -tə-), **Marie,** 1755–93, queen of France 1774–93: wife of Louis XVI.

An·to·nel·lo da Mes·si·na (än′tə nel′ō dä mə sē′nə), 1430?–79, Sicilian painter.

An·to·ni·nus (an′tə nī′nəs), **Marcus Aurelius,** MARCUS AURELIUS.

Antoni′nus Pi′us (pī′əs), A.D. 86–161, emperor of Rome 138–161.

An·to·nio·ni (än′tōn yō′nē, an tō′nē ō′nē), **Michelangelo,** born 1912, Italian film director.

An·to·ni·us (an tō′nē əs), **Marcus,** ANTONY, Mark.

An·to·ny (an′tə nē), **Mark** (*Marcus Antonius*), 83?–30 B.C., Roman general: friend of Caesar; rival of Augustus Caesar.

An·za (än′sä), **Juan Bautista de,** 1735–88, Spanish frontiersman and army officer, born in Mexico: explored western coast of U.S., founded San Francisco in 1776.

An·zen·gru·ber (än′tsən grōō′bər), **Ludwig,** 1839–89, Austrian playwright and novelist.

A·o·ki (ä ō′kē), **Shuzo,** 1844–1914, first Japanese ambassador to U.S., 1905–09.

A·pel·les (ə pel′ēz), 360?–315? B.C., Greek painter.

Ap·gar (ap′gär), **Virginia,** 1909–74, U.S. physician: developed test to evaluate health of newborns.

A·pol·li·naire (ə pol′ə nâr′), **Guil·laume** (gē yōm′), (*Wilhelm Apollinaris de Kostrowitzky*), 1880–1918, French poet.

Ap·ol·lo·ni·us Dys·co·lus (ap′ə lō′nē əs dis′kə ləs), died A.D. c140, Greek grammarian.

Ap·ple·seed (ap′əl sēd′), **Johnny** (*John Chapman*), 1774–1845, American pioneer and orchardist: prototype for character in American folklore.

Ap·ple·ton (ap′əl tən), **Sir Edward Victor,** 1892–1965, British physicist: Nobel prize 1947.

Ap·u·le·ius (ap′yə lē′əs), **Lucius,** born A.D. 125?, Roman philosopher and satirist.

A·qui·nas (ə kwī′nəs), **Saint Thomas,** 1225?–74, Italian scholastic philosopher.

A·qui·no (ä kē′nō), **Corazon C.,** born 1933, Philippine president 1986–92.

Ar·a·fat (ar′ə fat′, är′ə fät′), **Ya·sir** (yä′sər, yas′ər), born 1929, Palestinian leader.

A·ra·gon (ar′ə gon′), **Louis,** 1897–1982, French novelist, poet, and journalist.

A·ram·bu·ru (ä′räm bōō′rōō), **Pedro Eugenio,** 1903–70, president of Argentina 1955–58.

A•ra•nha (ä rän′yä), **Oswaldo,** 1894–1960, Brazilian politician.

Ar•blay, d' (där′blā), **Madame Frances,** BURNEY, Frances.

Ar•buth•not (är buth′nət, är′bəth not′), **John,** 1667–1735, Scottish author and physician.

Ar•ca•ro (är kâr′ō), **Edward** (*Eddie*), born 1916, U.S. jockey.

Arc, d' (DARK), **Jeanne** (zhän), JOAN OF ARC.

Ar•ces•i•la•us (är ses′ə lā′əs), 316–241 B.C., Greek philosopher.

Ar•cher (är′chər), **William,** 1856–1924, Scottish playwright, drama critic, and translator.

Ar•chil•o•chus (är kil′ə kəs), fl. c650 B.C., Greek poet.

Ar•chi•me•des (är′kə mē′dēz), 287?–212 B.C., Greek mathematician, physicist, and inventor.

Ar•chi•pen•ko (är′kə peng′kō), **Aleksander Porfirievich,** 1887–1964, U.S. sculptor, born in Russia.

Ar•cim•bol•di (är′chim bōl′dē), **Giuseppe,** 1527–93, Italian painter.

Ar•den (är′dn), **Elizabeth,** 1891–1966, U.S. cosmetician, born in Canada.

Ar•endt (âr′ənt, är′-), **Hannah,** 1906–75, U.S. author and political scientist, born in Germany.

A•ren•sky (ə ren′skē), **Anton Stepanovich,** 1861–1906, Russian composer.

A•re•ti•no (är′i tē′nō), **Pietro,** 1492–1556, Italian satirist.

Ar•gall (är′gôl, -gəl), **Sir Samuel,** 1572–1639, British explorer: colonial governor of Virginia 1617–19.

Ar•güe•das (äR gwe′thäs), **Alcides,** 1879–1946, Bolivian author, sociologist, and statesman.

A•ri•as Sán•chez (ä′Rē äs sän′ches), **Oscar,** born 1941, Costa Rican political leader: president 1986–90; Nobel peace prize 1987.

A•ri•on (ə rī′ən), fl. 7th century B.C., Greek poet: inventor of the dithyramb.

A•ri•os•to (är′ē os′tō), **Ludovico,** 1474–1533, Italian poet.

A•ris•ta (ə rē′stə), **Mariano,** 1802–55, Mexican general: president of Mexico 1851–53.

Ar•is•tar•chus (ar′ə stär′kəs), **1. of Samos,** late 3rd century B.C., Greek astronomer. **2. of Samothrace,** c216–144 B.C., Greek philologist and critic.

Ar•is•ti•des (ar′ə stī′dēz), ("*the Just*") 530?–468? B.C., Athenian statesman and general.

Ar•is•toph•a•nes (ar′ə stof′ə nēz′), 448?–385? B.C., Athenian comic dramatist.

Ar•is•tot•le (ar′ə stot′l), 384–322 B.C., Greek philosopher: pupil of Plato; tutor of Alexander the Great.

A•ri•us (ə rī′əs, âr′ē-), died A.D. 336, Christian priest at Alexandria: founder of Arianism.

Ark•wright (ärk′rīt′), **Sir Richard,** 1732–92, English inventor of the spinning jenny.

Ar•len (är′lən), **1. Harold** (*Hymen Arluck*), 1905–86, U.S.

songwriter. **2. Michael** (*Dikran Kouyoumdjian*), 1895–1956, English novelist, born in Bulgaria.

Ar•liss (är′lis), **George,** 1868–1946, English actor.

Ar•min•i•us (är min′ē əs), **1.** (*Hermann*) 17? B.C.–A.D. 21, Germanic hero who defeated Roman army A.D. 9. **2. Jacobus,** (*Jacob Harmensen*), 1560–1609, Dutch Protestant theologian.

Ar•mi•tage (är′mi tij), **Kenneth,** born 1916, English sculptor.

Ar•mour (är′mər), **Philip Danforth,** 1832–1901, U.S. meat-packing industrialist.

Arm•strong (ärm′strông′), **1. Edwin Howard,** 1890–1954, U.S. electrical engineer: developed frequency modulation. **2. Henry** (*Henry Jackson*), 1912–88, U.S. boxer: world featherweight champion 1937–38; world lightweight champion 1938–39; world welterweight champion 1938–40. **3. Louis (Daniel)** (*"Satchmo"*), 1900–71, U.S. jazz trumpeter. **4. Neil A.,** born 1930, U.S. astronaut: first person to walk on the moon, July 20, 1969.

Arndt (ärnt), **Ernst Moritz,** 1769–1860, German poet and historian.

Arne (ärn), **Thomas Augustine,** 1710–78, English composer of operas.

Ar•no (är′nō), **Peter** (*Curtis Arnoux Peters*), 1904–68, U.S. cartoonist and author.

Ar•nold (är′nld), **1. Benedict,** 1741–1801, American general in the Revolutionary War who became a traitor. **2. Sir Edwin,** 1832–1904, English poet and journalist. **3. Henry H.** (*"Hap"*), 1886–1950, U.S. general. **4. Matthew,** 1822–88, English poet and literary critic. **5.** his father, **Thomas,** 1795–1842, English clergyman, educator, and historian. **6. Thurman Wesley,** 1891–1969, U.S. lawyer and writer.

Ar•nold•son (är′nld sən), **Klas Pontus,** 1844–1916, Swedish author and politician: Nobel peace prize 1908.

Ar•nulf (är′no͝olf), A.D. 850?–899, emperor of the Holy Roman Empire 887–899: crowned 896.

Arp (ärp), **Hans** or **Jean** (zhäN), 1888?–1966, French painter and sculptor; one of the founders of dadaism.

Ár•pád (är′päd), died A.D. 907, Hungarian national hero.

Ar•pi•no (är pē′nō), **Gerald (Peter),** born 1928, U.S. choreographer.

Ar•rau (ə rou′), **Claudio,** 1903–91, Chilean pianist.

Ar•rhe•ni•us (ä rā′nē əs), **Svante August,** 1859–1927, Swedish physicist and chemist: Nobel prize for chemistry 1903.

Ar•row (ar′ō), **Kenneth Joseph,** born 1921, U.S. economist: Nobel prize 1972.

Ar•sa•ces I (är′sə sēz′, är sā′sēz), founder of the Parthian empire c250 B.C.

Ar•taud (är tō′), **Antonin,** 1896–1948, French actor, poet, and drama critic.

Ar•ta•xerx•es (är′tə zûrk′sēz), **1. Artaxerxes I,** (*"Longimanus"*), died 424 B.C., king of Persia 464–24. **2.**

Artaxerxes II, (*"Mnemon"*), died 359? B.C., king of Persia 404?–359?

Ar•te•veld (är′tə velt′) also **Ar•te•vel•de** (-vel′də), **1. Jacob van,** 1290?–1345, Flemish statesman. **2.** his son, **Philip van,** 1340?–82, Flemish revolutionist.

Ar•thur (är′thər), **Chester Alan,** 1830–86, 21st president of the U.S. 1881–85.

Ar•ti•gas (är tē′gäs), **José Gervasio,** 1764–1850, Uruguayan soldier and patriot.

Ar•tzy•ba•sheff (ärt′si bä′shif), **Boris Mikhailovich,** 1899–1965, U.S. illustrator and writer, born in Russia.

Ar•tzy•ba•shev or **Ar•tsy•ba•shev** (ärt′si bä′shif), **Mikhail,** 1878–1927, Russian writer.

As•björn•sen (äs′byûrn sən), **Peter Christen,** 1812–85, Norwegian naturalist and folklorist.

As•bur•y (az′bə rē), **Francis,** 1745–1816, English missionary: first bishop of the Methodist Church in America.

Asch (ash), **Sho•lom** or **Sho•lem** (shô′ləm), 1880–1957, U.S. author, born in Poland.

As•cham (as′kəm), **Roger,** 1515–68, English scholar and writer: tutor of Queen Elizabeth I.

A•se•yev (ä sā′ev, -ef), **Nikolay Nikolaevich,** 1889–1963, Russian poet.

Ash•croft (ash′krôft, -kroft), **Dame Peggy** (*Edith Margaret Emily Ashcroft*), 1907–91, English actress.

Ashe (ash), **Arthur (Robert, Jr.),** born 1943, U.S. tennis player.

A•shi•ka•ga (ä′shē kä′gä), a member of a powerful family in Japan that ruled as shoguns 1338–1573.

Ash•ke•na•zy (äsh′kə nä′zē), **Vladimir (Davidovich),** born 1937, Russian pianist in W Europe since 1963.

Ash•ton (ash′tən), **Sir Frederick** (*William*), born 1906, English dancer and choreographer, born in Ecuador.

A•shur•ba•ni•pal (ä′sho͝or bä′nē päl′) also **Assurbanipal,** died 626? B.C., king of Assyria 668?–626? B.C.

As•i•mov (az′ə môf′, -mof′), **Isaac,** 1920–92, U.S. science and science-fiction writer, born in Russia.

A•so•ka (ə sō′kə), died 232 B.C., Buddhist king in India 269?–232? B.C.

As•pa•sia (a spā′shə, -zhə), c470–410 B.C., Athenian courtesan: mistress of Pericles.

As•quith (as′kwith), **Herbert Henry** (*1st Earl of Oxford and Asquith*), 1852–1928, British statesman: prime minister 1908–16.

As•sad (ä säd′), **Hafez al,** born 1928?, Syrian military and political leader: president since 1971.

As•ser (ä′sər), **Tobias,** 1838–1913, Dutch jurist and statesman: Nobel peace prize 1911.

As•sur•ba•ni•pal (ä′so͝or bä′nē päl′), ASHURBANIPAL.

A•staire (ə stâr′), **Fred** (*Frederick Austerlitz*), 1899–1987, U.S. dancer and actor.

As•ton (as′tən), **Francis William,** 1877–1945, English physicist and chemist: Nobel prize for chemistry 1922.

As·tor (as′tər), **1. John Jacob,** 1763–1848, U.S. capitalist and fur merchant. **2. Nancy (Langhorne), Viscountess,** 1879–1964, first woman member of Parliament in England.

As·tu·ri·as (a sto͝or′ē əs, a styo͝or′-), **Miguel Ángel,** 1899–1974, Guatemalan writer: Nobel prize 1967.

A·ta·hual·pa (ä′tə wäl′pə) c1500–33, last Incan king of Peru (son of Huayna Capac). Also called **A′ta·ba′li·pa** (-bä′lē pə).

A·ta·türk (at′ə tûrk′, ä′tə-), KEMAL ATATÜRK.

Ath·a·na·sius (ath′ə nā′shəs), **Saint,** A.D. 296?–373, bishop of Alexandria: opponent of Arianism.

Ath·el·stan (ath′əl stan′), A.D. 895?–940, king of England 925–940.

Ath·e·nae·us (ath′ə nē′əs, -nā′-), late 2nd century A.D., Greek philosopher and rhetorician at Naucratis in Egypt.

Athenae′us of At·ta·lei′a (at′l i′ə), Greek physician in Rome, fl. A.D. c40–65.

Ath·e·nag·o·ras I (ath′ə nag′ər əs), (*Aristocles Spyrou*) 1886–1972, Archbishop Ecumenical of Constantinople and Ecumenical Patriarch of the Greek Orthodox Church 1948–72.

Ath·er·ton (ath′ər tən), **Gertrude (Franklin)** (*Gertrude Franklin Horn*), 1857–1948, U.S. novelist.

At·kins (at′kinz), **Chester** (*"Chet"*), born 1924, U.S. country-and-western singer and musician.

At·kin·son (at′kin sən), **(Justin) Brooks,** 1894–1984, U.S. drama critic, journalist, and author.

At·las (at′ləs), **Charles** (*Angelo Siciliano*), 1894–1972, U.S. body-building advocate, born in Italy.

At·ta·lus (at′l əs), **1. Attalus I** (*Soter*), king of Pergamum 241–197 B.C. **2. Attalus II** (*Philadelphus*), king of Pergamum c159–138 B.C. **3. Attalus III** (*Philometor*), king of Pergamum 138–133 B.C.

At·ti·la (at′l ə, ə til′ə), (*"Scourge of God"*) A.D. 406?–453, king of the Huns who invaded Europe: defeated by the Romans and Visigoths in 451.

At·ti·us (at′ē əs), **Lucius,** ACCIUS, LUCIUS.

Att·lee (at′lē), **Clement (Richard),** 1883–1967, British prime minister 1945–51.

At·tucks (at′əks), **Crispus,** 1723?–70, American patriot, probably a fugitive slave, killed in the Boston Massacre.

At·wood (at′wo͝od′), **Margaret (Eleanor),** born 1939, Canadian poet and novelist.

Au·ber (ō bâr′), **Daniel François Esprit,** 1782–1871, French composer.

Au·chin·closs (ô′kin klôs′, -klos′), **Louis,** born 1917, U.S. novelist and short-story writer.

Au·den (ôd′n), **W(ystan) H(ugh),** 1907–73, English poet in the U.S.

Au·du·bon (ô′də bon′, -bən), **John James,** 1785–1851, U.S. naturalist who painted and wrote about the birds of North America.

Auel (oul), **Jean,** born 1936, U.S. novelist.

Au•er (ou′ər), **Leopold,** 1845–1930, Hungarian violinist and teacher.

Au•er•bach (ou′ər bäk′, our′-; *for 2 also Ger.* ou′əʀ-bäкн′), **1. Arnold** (*"Red"*), born 1917, U.S. basketball coach and manager. **2. Berthold,** 1812–82, German novelist.

Au•gier (ō zhyā′), **Guillaume Victor Émile,** 1820–89, French dramatist.

Au•gus•tine (ô′gə stēn′, ô gus′tin, ə gus′-), **1. Saint,** A.D. 354–430, one of the Latin fathers in the early Christian Church; bishop of Hippo in N Africa. **2. Saint,** (*Austin*) died A.D. 604, Roman monk: headed group of missionaries who landed in England A.D. 597; first archbishop of Canterbury 601–604.

Au•gus•tus (ô gus′təs, ə gus′-), (*Gaius Julius Caesar Octavianus, Augustus Caesar*), 63 B.C.–A.D. 14, first Roman emperor 27 B.C.–A.D. 14: heir and successor to Julius Caesar. Also called **Octavian.**

Au•lard (ō lär′), **François Victor Alphonse,** 1849–1928, French historian.

Aung San Suu Kyi (oung′ sän′ so͞o′ kē′), Burmese opposition leader: Nobel peace prize 1990.

Au•rang•zeb or **Au•rung•zeb** (ôr′əng zeb′), 1618–1707, Mogul emperor of Hindustan 1658–1707.

Au•re•li•an (ô rē′lē ən, ô rēl′yən), (*Lucius Domitius Aurelianus*) A.D. 212?–275, Roman emperor 270–275.

Au•riol (ôr′ē ōl′, -ôl′), **Vincent,** 1884–1966, French statesman: president 1947–54.

Au•ro•bin•do (ôr′ə bin′dō), **Sri** (*Sri Aurobindo Ghose*), 1872–1950, Indian scholar and spiritual leader.

Au•rung•zeb (ôr′əng zeb′), AURANGZEB.

Aus•ten (ô′stən), **Jane,** 1775–1817, English novelist.

Aus•tin (ô′stən), **1. Alfred,** 1835–1913, English poet: poet laureate 1896–1913. **2. John,** 1790–1859, English writer on law. **3. John Lang•shaw** (lang′shô), 1911–60, British philosopher. **4. Mary (Hunter),** 1868–1934, U.S. novelist, playwright, and short-story writer. **5. Stephen Fuller,** 1793–1836, American colonizer in Texas. **6. Warren Robinson,** 1877–1962, U.S. diplomat. **7.** AUGUSTINE, Saint (def. 2).

Au•try (ô′trē), **Gene,** born 1907, U.S. singer and movie actor.

Av•e•don (av′i don′), **Richard,** born 1923, U.S. photographer.

Av•en•zo•ar (av′ən zō′ər, -zō är′), 1091?–1162, Arab physician and writer in Spain: founder of Almohad dynasty. Also called **Abumeron.**

A•ver•ro•ës or **A•ver•rho•ës** (ə ver′ō ēz′), 1126?–98, Arab philosopher in Spain.

A•ver•y (ā′və rē), **Milton,** 1893–1965, U.S. painter.

A•vi•ce•brón (ä′vē the bʀôn′, -se-), (*Solomon ben Judah ibn-Gabirol*) 1021?–58, Jewish poet and philosopher in Spain.

Av•i•cen•na (av′ə sen′ə), A.D. 980–1037, Islamic physician and philosopher, born in Persia.

A•vi•la Ca•ma•cho (ä′vē lä′ kə mä′chō), **Manuel,** 1897–1955, president of Mexico 1940–46.

A•vo•ga•dro (ä′və gä′drō), **Count Amadeo,** 1776–1856, Italian physicist and chemist.

Ax (aks), **Emmanuel,** born 1949, U.S. pianist, born in Austria.

Ax•el•rod (ak′səl rod′), **Julius,** born 1912, U.S. biochemist and pharmacologist: Nobel prize for medicine 1970.

Ay•de•lotte (ād′l ot′), **Frank,** 1880–1956, U.S. educator.

Ayer (âr), **Sir A(lfred) J(ules),** 1910–89, English philosopher.

A•ye•sha (ä′ē shä′), AISHA.

Ayl•win (āl′win), **Patricio,** born 1918, president of Chile since 1990.

Ay•mé (e mā′), **Marcel,** 1902–67, French novelist and short-story writer.

A•yub Khan (ä yo͝ob′ kän′), **Mohammed,** 1908–74, Pakistani army officer and political leader: president 1958–69.

A•za•ña (ä sä′nyä), **Manuel,** (*Manuel Azaña y Diez*), 1880–1940, Spanish statesman: prime minister 1931–33, 1936; president 1936–39.

A•zi•ki•we (ä′zē kē′wā), **Nnamdi** ("*Zik*"), born 1904, Nigerian statesman: president 1963–66.

Az•na•vour (az′nə vo͝or′), **Charles,** born 1924, French singer.

A•zo•rín (ä′sô rēn′), (*José Martínez Ruiz*), 1873–1967, Spanish novelist and critic.

A•zue•la (ä swā′lə), **Mariano,** 1873–1952, Mexican physician and novelist.

B

Baal Shem Tov (bäl′ shem′ tôv′), (*Israel ben Eliezer*), c1700–60, Jewish religious leader in Poland: founder of the Hasidic movement.

Bāb or **Bab** (bäb), often, **the Bab,** Bab ed-Din.

Ba•bar (bä′bər), Baber.

Bab•bage (bab′ij), **Charles,** 1792–1871, English mathematician: invented the precursor of the modern computer.

Bab•bitt (bab′it), **1. Irving,** 1865–1933, U.S. educator and critic. **2. Milton Byron,** born 1916, U.S. composer.

Bab ed-Din (bäb′ ed dēn′), (*the Bab, Ali Muhammad of Shiraz*), 1819–50, Persian religious leader: founder of Bābi.

Ba•bel (bab′əl), **Isaak Emmanuilovich,** 1894–1941, Russian author.

Ba•ber or **Ba•bar** or **Ba•bur** (bä′bər), (*Zahir ed-Din Mohammed*), 1483–1530, founder of the Mogul Empire.

Ba•beuf (bA bœf′), **François Noël** (*Gracchus Babeuf*), 1760–97, French revolutionary.

Bab•son (bab′sən), **Roger Ward,** 1875–1967, U.S. statistician and businessman.

Ba•bur (bä′bər), Baber.

Ba•call (bə kôl′), **Lauren** (*Betty Joan Perske*), born 1924, U.S. actress.

Bac•chyl•i•des (bə kil′i dēz′), fl. 5th century B.C., Greek poet.

Bach (bäKH), **1. Johann Sebastian,** 1685–1750, German organist and composer. **2.** his sons, **Carl Philipp Emanuel,** 1714–88, and **Johann Christian,** 1735–82, German organists and composers.

Ba•con (bā′kən), **1. Francis** (*Baron Verulam, Viscount St. Albans*), 1561–1626, English essayist, philosopher, and statesman. **2. Francis,** born 1910, English painter, born in Ireland. **3. Henry,** 1866–1924, U.S. architect. **4. Nathaniel,** 1647–76, American colonist, born in England: leader of a rebellion in Virginia 1676. **5. Roger,** 1214?–94?, English philosopher and scientist.

Ba•den-Pow•ell (bād′n pō′əl), **Robert Stephenson Smyth** (smith), **1st Baron,** 1857–1941, British general: founded the Boy Scouts and, with his sister Lady Agnes, the Girl Guides.

Ba•do•glio (bä dōl′yō), **Pietro,** 1871–1956, Italian general.

Bae•da (bē′də), **Saint,** Bede, Saint.

Baeke•land (bāk′land′, bä′kə länt′), **Leo Hendrik,** 1863–1944, U.S. chemist, born in Belgium: developed Bakelite.

Baer (bâr), **1. Karl Ernst von,** 1792–1876, Estonian zoologist and pioneer embryologist. **2. Max,** 1909–59, U.S. boxer: world heavyweight champion 1934.

Bae•yer (bā′ər), **(Johann Friedrich Wilhelm) Adolf von,** 1835–1917, German chemist: Nobel prize 1905.

Ba•ez (bī ez′, bī′iz), **Joan,** born 1941, U.S. folk singer.

Baf•fin (baf′in), **William,** 1584?–1622, English navigator who explored arctic North America.

Bage•hot (baj′ət), **Walter,** 1826–77, English economist, political journalist, and critic.

Bag•ley (bag′lē), **William Chandler,** 1874–1946, U.S. educator and writer.

Bag•nold (bag′nəld), **Enid,** 1889–1981, English novelist and playwright.

Ba•ha•ul•lah (bä hä′ōōl lä′), (*Husayn 'Ali*), 1817–92, Persian religious leader: founder of Baha'i.

Bahr (bär), **Hermann,** 1863–1934, Austrian playwright and critic.

Bai•ley (bā′lē), **1. Liberty Hyde,** 1858–1954, U.S. botanist, horticulturist, and writer. **2. Nathan** or **Nathaniel,** died 1742, English lexicographer. **3. Pearl,** 1918–90, U.S. singer.

Baj•er (bī′ər), **Fredrik,** 1837–1922, Danish politician and author: Nobel peace prize 1908.

Ba Jin (bä′ jin′), (*Li Feigan*), born 1904, Chinese writer and novelist.

Ba•ker (bā′kər), **1. George Pierce,** 1866–1935, U.S. critic, author, and professor of drama. **2. James A(ddison), III,** born 1930, U.S. Secretary of State since 1989. **3. Josephine,** 1906–75, French entertainer, born in the U.S. **4. Newton Diehl** (dēl), 1871–1937, U.S. lawyer: Secretary of War 1916–21. **5. Ray Stannard** (*"David Grayson"*), 1870–1946, U.S. author. **6. Russell (Wayne),** born 1925, U.S. newspaper columnist.

Bakst (bäkst), **Léon Nikolaevich,** 1866–1924, Russian painter and designer.

Ba•ku•nin (bə kōō′nin, -kōōn′yin), **Mikhail Aleksandrovich,** 1814–76, Russian anarchist and writer.

Ba•la•guer (bä′lä gâr′), **Joaquin** (*Joaquin Balaguer y Ricardo*), born 1907, Dominican political leader: president 1960–62, 1966–78, and since 1986.

Bal•an•chine (bal′ən chēn′), **George,** 1904–83, U.S. choreographer, born in Russia.

Bal•bo (bal′bō), **Italo,** 1896–1940, Italian aviator, general, and statesman.

Bal•bo•a (bal bō′ə), **Vasco Núñez de,** 1475?–1517, Spanish explorer who discovered the Pacific Ocean in 1513.

Bal•bue•na (bäl bwā′nə), **Bernardo de,** 1568–1627, Mexican poet and priest, born in Spain.

Balch (bôlch), **Emily Greene,** 1867–1961, U.S. economist, sociologist, and author: Nobel peace prize 1946.

Bald•win (bôld′win), **1. James (Arthur),** 1924–87, U.S. writer. **2. James Mark,** 1861–1934, U.S. psychologist. **3. Loammi,** 1740–1807, U.S. civil engineer and developer of the Baldwin apple. **4. Matthias William,** 1795–1866, U.S. inventor, manufacturer, and philanthropist. **5. Roger,** 1884–1981, U.S. advocate of constitutional rights. **6. Stanley** (*1st Earl Baldwin of Bewdley*), 1867–1947, British prime minister 1923–24, 1924–29, 1935–37.

Baldwin I, 1058–1118, king of Jerusalem 1100–18: fought in the first crusade.

Ba•len•ci•a•ga (bə len′sē ä′gə), **Cristóbal,** 1895–1972, French fashion designer, born in Spain.

Ba•le•wa (bä′lā wä′), **Sir Abubakar Tafawa,** 1912–66, Nigerian statesman: prime minister 1957–66.

Bal•four (bal′fŏŏr, -fər), **Arthur James** (*1st Earl of Balfour*), 1848–1930, British statesman and writer: prime minister 1902–05.

Bal•iol (bāl′yəl, bā′lē əl), **John de,** 1249–1315, king of Scotland 1292–96.

Ball (bôl), **1. John,** died 1381, English priest: one of the leaders of Wat Tyler's peasants' revolt in 1381. **2. Lucille,** 1911–89, U.S. comedienne and actress.

Bal•la (bäl′ə), **Giacomo,** 1871?–1958, Italian painter.

Bal•lance (bal′əns), **John,** 1839–93, New Zealand statesman, born in Ireland: prime minister 1891–93.

Bal•main (bAl maN′), **Pierre (Alexandre),** 1914–82, French fashion designer.

Bal•ti•more (bôl′tə môr′, -mōr′), **1. David,** born 1938, U.S. microbiologist: Nobel prize for medicine 1975. **2. Lord,** CALVERT, Sir George.

Bal•zac (bôl′zak, bal′-), **Honoré de,** 1799–1850, French novelist.

Ban•croft (ban′krôft, -kroft, bang′-), **1. George,** 1800–91, U.S. historian and statesman. **2. Hubert Howe,** 1832–1918, U.S. publisher and historian.

Ban•da (ban′də), **Hastings Kamuzu,** born 1905, president of Malawi since 1966.

Ban•del•lo (ban del′ō), **Matteo,** 1485–1561, Italian ecclesiastic and author.

Ban•di•nel•li (ban′də nel′ē), **Baccio** or **Bartolommeo,** 1493–1560, Italian sculptor.

Ba•ner•jea (ban′ər jē′), **Sir Su•ren•dra•nath** (sŏŏ ren′drə nät′), 1848–1925, Indian political leader.

Bangs (bangz), **John Kendrick,** 1862–1922, U.S. humorist.

Bank•head (bangk′hed), **1. Tallulah (Brockman),** 1903–68, U.S. actress (daughter of William Brockman Bankhead). **2. William Brockman,** 1874–1940, U.S. politician: Speaker of the House 1936–40.

Banks (bangks), **1. Sir Joseph,** 1734–1820, English naturalist. **2. Nathaniel Pren•tiss** (pren′tis), 1816–94, U.S. army officer and politician: Speaker of the House 1856–57.

Ban•ne•ker (ban′i kər), **Benjamin,** 1731–1806, U.S. mathematician, natural historian, and astronomer.

Ban•nis•ter (ban′ə stər), **Sir Roger (Gilbert),** born 1929, English track and field athlete: first to run a mile in less than four minutes.

Ban•ting (ban′ting), **Sir Frederick Grant,** 1891–1941, Canadian physician: one of the discoverers of insulin; Nobel prize 1923.

Bao Dai (bou′ dī′), (*Nguyen Vinh Thuy*), born 1913, emperor of Annam 1925–45, chief of state of Vietnam 1949–55.

Bar•a (bar′ə), **The•da** (thē′də), (*Theodosia Goodman*), 1890–1955, U.S. actress.

Ba•ra•ka (bə rä′kə), **Imamu Amiri** (*Everett LeRoi Jones*), born 1934, U.S. dramatist, poet, and political activist.

Ba•ra•nov (bə rä′nôf, -nof), **Aleksandr Andreyevich,** 1747–1819, Russian fur trader in Alaska.

Bá•rány (bä′Rän′y^{ə}), **Robert,** 1876–1936, Austrian physician: Nobel prize 1914.

Bar•ba•ros•sa (bär′bə ros′ə), **1. Frederick,** FREDERICK I (def. 1a). **2.** (*Khair ed-Din*), c1466–1546, Barbary pirate, born in Greece.

Bar•ber (bär′bər), **1. Walter Lanier** (*"Red"*), born 1908, U.S. sports broadcaster. **2. Samuel,** 1910–81, U.S. composer.

Bar•bi•rol•li (bär′bə rō′lē, -rol′ē), **Sir John,** 1899–1970, English conductor.

Bar•busse (bär byo͞os′), **Henri,** 1873?–1935, French journalist and author.

Bar•clay de Tol•ly (bər klī′ də tōl′yē), **Prince Mikhail Bogdanovich,** 1761–1818, Russian field marshal: commander in chief against Napoleon I in 1812.

Bar•deen (bär dēn′), **John,** 1908–91, U.S. physicist: Nobel prize 1956, 1972.

Bard′ of A′von, William Shakespeare: so called from his birthplace, Stratford-on-Avon.

Bar•dot (bär dō′), **Brigitte** (*Camille Javal*), born 1934, French actress.

Ba•re•a (bə rā′ə), **Arturo,** 1897–1957, Spanish author, critic, lecturer, and broadcaster.

Bar•en•boim (bar′ən boim′), **Daniel,** born 1932, Israeli conductor and pianist, born in Argentina.

Bar•ents (bar′ənts, bär′-), **Willem,** died 1597, Dutch navigator and explorer.

Bar•ing (bâr′ing), **1. Alexander, 1st Baron Ashburton,** 1774–1848, British statesman. **2. Evelyn, 1st Earl of Cromer,** 1841–1917, British statesman and diplomat.

Bark•la (bärk′lə), **Charles Glover,** 1877–1944, English physicist: Nobel prize 1917.

Bark•ley (bärk′lē), **Alben William,** 1877–1956, vice president of the U.S. 1949–53.

Bar Kok•ba (bär′ kôKH′bä, -vä), **Simon,** died A.D. 135, Hebrew leader of insurrection against the Romans A.D. 132–135.

Bar•lach (bär′läk), **Ernst Heinrich,** 1870–1938, German sculptor and playwright.

Bar•low (bär′lō), **Joel,** 1754–1812, U.S. poet and diplomat.

Bar•nard (bär′nərd), **1. Christiaan N(eethling),** born 1922, South African surgeon: performed first successful human-heart transplant 1967. **2. Frederick Augustus Porter,** 1809–89, U.S. educator and advocate of higher education for women: president of Columbia University

1864–89. **3. George Gray,** 1863–1938, U.S. sculptor. **4. Henry,** 1811–1900, U.S. educator.

Bar•nar•do (bär när′dō, bər-), **Thomas John,** 1845–1905, English physician, social reformer, and philanthropist, born in Ireland.

Bar•ne•veldt (bär′nə velt′), **Jan van Olden,** 1547–1619, Dutch statesman and patriot.

Bar•num (bär′nəm), **P(hineas) T(aylor),** 1810–91, U.S. showman and circus impresario.

Ba•ro•ja (bə rō′hä), **Pío,** 1872–1956, Spanish novelist.

Ba•ron (bA RôN′), **Michel** (*Michel Boyron*), 1653–1729, French actor.

Bar•rault (bA Rō′), **Jean-Louis** (zhäN lwē′), born 1910, French actor and director.

Bar•rès (ba res′), **Maurice,** 1862–1923, French novelist, politician, and political writer.

Bar•rett (bar′it), **Elizabeth,** BROWNING, Elizabeth Barrett.

Bar•rie (bar′ē), **Sir James M(atthew),** 1860–1937, Scottish novelist, short-story writer, and playwright.

Bar•rios (bäR′Ryôs), **Justo Rufino,** 1835–85, Guatemalan statesman: president of Guatemala 1873–85.

Bar•ron (bar′ən), **Clarence Walker,** 1855–1928, U.S. financial publisher.

Bar•ros (bär′o͝osh), **João de** (*"the Portuguese Livy"*), 1496–1570, Portuguese historian.

Bar•ry (bar′ē), **1. Sir Charles,** 1795–1860, English architect. **2. John,** 1745–1803, American naval commander in the Revolution. **3. Leonora Marie Kearney** (*"Mother Lake"*), 1849–1930, U.S. labor leader and social activist, born in Ireland. **4. Philip,** 1896–1949, U.S. playwright.

Bar•ry•more (bar′ə môr′, -mōr′), **1. Maurice** (*Herbert Blythe*), 1847–1905, U.S. actor. **2.** his children: **Ethel,** 1879–1959, **John,** 1882–1942, and **Lionel,** 1878–1954, U.S. actors.

Barth (bärt, bärth), **1. John (Simmons),** born 1930, U.S. novelist. **2. Karl,** 1886–1968, Swiss theologian.

Bar•thé (bär tā′), **Richmond,** born 1901, U.S. sculptor.

Bar•thol•di (bär thol′dē, -tol′-), **Frédéric Auguste,** 1834–1904, French sculptor: designed Statue of Liberty.

Bar•thol•o•mew (bär thol′ə myo͞o′), *n.* one of the 12 apostles: sometimes called Nathanael.

Bartholomew I, (*Dimitrios Archontonis*), born 1940, Archbishop of Constantinople and Ecumenical Patriarch of the Eastern Orthodox Church since 1991.

Bar•thou (bär to͞o′), **(Jean) Louis,** 1862–1934, French statesman and author.

Bart•lett (bärt′lit), **1. John,** 1820–1905, U.S. publisher. **2. John Russell,** 1805–86, U.S. editor and bibliographer of early Americana. **3. Josiah,** 1729–95, U.S. physician and statesman. **4. Paul Wayland,** 1865–1925, U.S. sculptor. **5. Robert Abram,** 1875–1946, U.S. arctic explorer, born in Newfoundland. **6. Vernon,** born 1894, English writer.

Bar•tók (bär′tok, -tôk), **Béla,** 1881–1945, Hungarian composer.

Bar•to•lom•me•o (bär tol′ə mā′ō), **Fra,** (*Baccio della Porta*), 1475–1517, Italian painter.

Bar•to•loz•zi (bäʀ′tô lôt′tsē), **Francesco,** 1725?–1815?, Italian engraver.

Bar•ton (bär′tn), **1. Clara,** 1821–1912, U.S. philanthropist who organized the American Red Cross in 1881. **2. Derek H(arold) R(ichard),** born 1918, English chemist: Nobel prize 1969. **3. Sir Edmund,** 1849–1920, Australian jurist and statesman: prime minister 1901–03.

Bar•tram (bär′trəm), **John,** 1699–1777, U.S. botanist.

Bar•uch (bə ro͞ok′), **Bernard M(annes),** 1870–1965, U.S. statesman and financier.

Ba•rye (ba rē′), **Antoine Louis,** 1795–1875, French sculptor and painter.

Ba•rysh•ni•kov (bə rish′ni kôf′, -kof′), **Mikhail,** born 1948, Russian ballet dancer, in the U.S. since 1974.

Bar•zun (bär′zun), **Jacques (Martin),** born 1907, U.S. historian, educator, and writer, born in France.

Ba•sho (bä shô′), (*Basho Matsuo*), 1644?–94, Japanese poet.

Ba•sie (bā′sē), **William** (*"Count"*), 1904–84, U.S. jazz pianist, bandleader, and composer.

Bas•il (baz′əl, bas′-, bā′zəl, -səl), **Saint** (*"the Great"*), A.D. 329?–379, bishop of Caesarea in Asia Minor (brother of Saint Gregory of Nyssa). Also called **Basilius.**

Ba•sil•i•us (bə sil′ē əs, -zil′-), **Saint,** BASIL, Saint.

Bas•ker•ville (bas′kər vil′), **John,** 1706–75, English typographer.

Bas•kin (bas′kin), **Leonard,** born 1922, U.S. sculptor and artist.

Ba•sov (bä′səf), **Nikolai Gennadiyevich,** born 1922, Russian physicist: Nobel prize 1964.

Bass (bas), **Sam,** 1851–78, U.S. outlaw: bank and train robber in the West.

Bas•sa•no (bə sä′nō), **1. Jacopo** (*Giacomo da Ponte*), 1510–92, Italian painter. **2.** his sons, **Francesco,** 1549–92; **Giambattista da Ponte,** 1533–?; **Girolamo da Ponte** 1566–1621; **Leandro,** 1557–1623, Italian painters.

Bas•so (bas′ō), **Hamilton,** 1904–64, U.S. journalist and novelist.

Ba•sti•an (bäs′tē än′), **Adolf,** 1826–1905, German anthropologist.

Bates (bāts), **Katherine Lee,** 1859–1929, U.S. educator and author.

Ba•tis•ta (bə tē′stə), **Fulgencio,** 1901–73, Cuban military leader: president 1940–44, 1952–59.

Bat•lle y Or•dó•ñez (bät′ye ē ôr ᵺô′nyes), **José,** 1856–1929, Uruguayan statesman: president of Uruguay 1903–07, 1911–15.

Bat•ta•ni (bə tä′nē), **Al-,** c850–929, Arab astronomer. Also called **Albategnius.**

Ba•tu Khan (bä′to͞o kän′), died 1255, Mongol conqueror: grandson of Genghis Khan and leader of the Golden Horde.

Bau•de•laire (bōd′l âr′), **Charles Pierre,** 1821–67, French poet.

Bau•douin I (*Fr.* bō dwaɴ′), born 1930, king of Belgium since 1951.

Baudouin′ de Cour•te•nay′ (də ko͝or′tə nā′), **Jan Ig•na•cy Nie•cis•ław** (yän ig nä′tsi nye′tsis läf′), 1845–1929, Polish linguist: pioneer in modern phonology.

Baum (bôm, bäm), **1. L(yman) Frank,** 1856–1919, U.S. playwright and author of children's books. **2. Vicki,** 1888–1960, U.S. novelist, born in Austria.

Bau•meis•ter (bou′mī′stər), **Willi,** 1889–1955, German painter.

Bax (baks), **Sir Arnold Edward Trevor,** 1883–1953, English composer.

Bax•ter (bak′stər), **Richard,** 1615–91, English Puritan preacher, scholar, and writer.

Ba•yar (bä yär′), **Ce•lâl** (je läl′), 1884–1986, Turkish statesman: president 1950–60.

Ba•yard (bā′ərd; *Fr.* ʙᴀ ʏᴀʀ′), **Pierre Terrail, Seigneur de,** (*"the knight without fear and without reproach"*), 1473–1524, heroic French soldier.

Bayle (bāl), **Pierre,** 1647–1706, French philosopher and critic.

Bay•liss (bā′lis), **Sir William Maddock,** 1860–1924, English physiologist.

Ba•zaine (ba zen′), **François Achille,** 1811–88, French general and marshal.

Ba•zin (ba zaɴ′), **René François Nicolas Marie,** 1853–1932, French novelist.

Baz•i•o•tes (baz′ē ō′tēz), **William,** 1912–63, U.S. painter.

Beach (bēch), **1. Moses Yale,** 1800–68, U.S. newspaper publisher. **2. Rex Ellingwood,** 1877–1949, U.S. novelist and short-story writer.

Bea•cons•field (bē′kənz fēld′, bek′ənz-), **Earl of,** Dɪsʀᴀᴇʟɪ, Benjamin.

Bea•dle (bēd′l), **George Wells,** 1903–89, U.S. biologist and educator: Nobel prize for medicine 1958.

Bea•mon (bē′mən), **Robert** (*Bob*), born 1946, U.S. track-and-field athlete.

Bean (bēn), **1. Alan L(aVern),** born 1932, U.S. astronaut. **2. Roy** (*"Judge"*), 1825?–1903, U.S. frontiersman and justice of the peace.

Beard (bērd), **1. Charles Austin,** 1874–1948, and his wife **Mary,** 1876–1958, U.S. historians. **2. Daniel Carter,** 1850–1941, U.S. artist and naturalist: organized the Boy Scouts of America in 1910.

Beards•ley (bērdz′lē), **Aubrey Vincent,** 1872–98, English illustrator.

Bea•tles (bēt′lz), **the,** British rock group (1962–70) including **George Harrison** (born 1943), **John (Winston) Len•non** (len′ən) (1940–80), **Paul (James) Mc•Cart•ney**

(mə kärt′nē) (born 1942), and **Ringo Starr** (stär) (*Richard Starkey*) (born 1940).

Bea•ton (bēt′n), **Sir Cecil (Walter Hardy)**, 1904–80, English photographer, writer, and theatrical designer.

Be•a•trix (bā′ə triks, bē′-), (*Beatrix Wilhelmina Armgard*), born 1938, queen of the Netherlands since 1980 (daughter of Juliana).

Beat•tie (bē′tē), **1. Ann,** born 1947, U.S. novelist. **2. James,** 1735–1803, Scottish poet.

Beat•ty (bē′tē), **David** (*1st Earl of the North Sea and of Brooksby*), 1871–1936, British admiral.

Beau Brum•mell (bō′ brum′əl), (*George Bryan Brummell*), 1778–1840, an Englishman who set the fashion in men's clothes.

Beau•har•nais (bō′är nā′), **1. Eugénie Hortense de,** 1782–1837, queen of Holland: wife of Louis Bonaparte. **2. Joséphine de,** 1763–1814, empress of France 1804–09; first wife of Napoleon I.

Beau•mar•chais (bō′mär shā′), **Pierre Augustin Caron de,** 1732–99, French dramatist.

Beau•mont (bō′mont), **1. Francis,** 1584–1616, English dramatist who collaborated with John Fletcher. **2. William,** 1785–1853, U.S. surgeon.

Beau•re•gard (bō′ri gärd′), **Pierre Gustave Toutant,** 1818–93, Confederate general in the Civil War.

Beau•voir (bōv wär′), **de, Simone,** DE BEAUVOIR, Simone.

Bea•ver•brook (bē′vər bro͝ok′), **William Maxwell Aitken, Lord** (*1st Baron*), 1879–1964, English publisher, born in Canada.

Be•bel (bā′bəl), **Ferdinand August,** 1840–1913, German socialist and writer.

Be•chet (bə shā′), **Sidney,** 1897–1959, U.S. jazz soprano saxophonist and clarinetist.

Beck•er (bek′ər), **1. Carl Lotus,** 1873–1945, U.S. historian. **2. George Ferdinand,** 1847–1919, U.S. scientist and mathematician. **3. Howard Paul,** 1899–1960, U.S. sociologist.

Beck•et (bek′it), **Saint Thomas à,** 1118?–70, archbishop of Canterbury: murdered because of his opposition to Henry II's policies toward the church.

Beck•ett (bek′it), **Samuel,** 1906-89, Irish playwright and novelist: Nobel prize for literature 1969.

Beck•ford (bek′fərd), **William,** 1759–1844, English writer.

Beck•mann (bek′män), **Max,** 1884–1950, German painter.

Beck•nell (bek′nl), **William,** c1790–1865, U.S. frontier trader: opened Santa Fe Trail 1822.

Béc•quer (bek′ər), **Gustavo Adolfo,** 1836–70, Spanish poet.

Bec•que•rel (bek′ə rel′), **1. Alexandre Edmond,** 1820–91, French physicist (son of Antoine César). **2. Antoine César,** 1788–1878, French physicist. **3. Antoine**

Henri, 1852–1908, French physicist (son of Alexandre Edmond): Nobel prize 1903.

Bed•does (bed′ōz), **Thomas Lovell,** 1803–49, English dramatist and poet.

Bede (bēd) also **Baeda, Saint** (*"the Venerable Bede"*), A.D. 673?–735, English monk, historian, and theologian.

Bed•ford (bed′fərd), **John of Lancaster, Duke of,** 1389–1435, English regent of France.

Bee•be (bē′bē), **(Charles) William,** 1877–1962, U.S. naturalist, explorer, and writer.

Bee•cham (bē′chəm), **Sir Thomas,** 1879–1961, English conductor and impresario.

Bee•cher (bē′chər), **1. Catharine Esther,** 1800–78, U.S. educator: advocated educational rights for women. **2. Edward,** 1803–95, U.S. clergyman, educator, and abolitionist. **3. Henry Ward,** 1813–87, U.S. preacher and writer. **4. Lyman,** 1775–1863, U.S. preacher and theologian (father of Harriet Beecher Stowe and Henry Ward Beecher).

Beer (bēr), **Thomas,** 1889–1940, U.S. author.

Beer•bohm (bēr′bōm), **Sir Max,** 1872–1956, English essayist, critic, and caricaturist.

Beer•naert (bâr′närt), **Auguste Marie François,** 1829–1912, Belgian statesman: Nobel peace prize 1909.

Beers (bērz), **Clifford Whittingham,** 1876–1943, U.S. pioneer in mental hygiene.

Bee•tho•ven (bā′tō vən), **Ludwig van,** 1770–1827, German composer.

Be•gin (bā′gin), **Menachem,** 1913–92, Israeli political leader, born in Poland: prime minister 1977–83: Nobel peace prize 1978.

Be•han (bē′ən), **Brendan (Francis),** 1923–64, Irish playwright.

Behn (bān), **Aphra,** 1640–89, English writer.

Beh•rens (bâr′ənz), **Peter,** 1868–1940, German architect.

Beh•ring (bâr′ing), **Emil von,** 1854–1917, German physician and bacteriologist: Nobel prize for medicine 1901.

Behr•man (bâr′mən), **S(amuel) N(athan),** 1893–1973, U.S. dramatist.

Bei•der•becke (bī′dər bek′), **Leon Bismarck** (*"Bix"*), 1903–31, U.S. jazz cornetist.

Bé•jart (bā zhAR′), **Maurice** (*Maurice Berger*), born 1927, French ballet dancer and choreographer.

Bel•a•fon•te (bel′ə fon′tā, -tē), **Harry (George),** born 1927, U.S. singer.

Be•las•co (bə las′kō), **David,** 1854–1931, U.S. playwright and producer.

Bel•gra•no (bel grä′nō), **Manuel,** 1770–1820, Argentine general.

Bel•i•sar•i•us (bel′ə sâr′ē əs), A.D. 505?-565, Byzantine general.

Bell (bel), **1. Acton,** pen name of Anne BRONTË. **2. Alexander Graham,** 1847–1922, U.S. scientist, born in Scotland: inventor of the telephone. **3. (Arthur) Clive (How-**

ard), 1881–1964, English critic of literature and art. **4. Currer,** pen name of Charlotte BRONTË. **5. Ellis,** pen name of Emily BRONTË. **6. John,** 1797–1869, U.S. political leader: Speaker of the House 1834–35.

Bel•la•my (bel′ə mē), **Edward,** 1850–98, U.S. author.

Bel•lay (be lā′), **Joachim du,** c1525–60, French poet.

Bel•lings•hau•sen (bel′ingz hou′zən), **Fabian Gottlieb von** (*Faddey Faddeyevich Bellingshauzen*), 1778–1852, Russian naval officer and explorer.

Bel•li•ni (bə lē′nē), **1. Gentile,** 1427?–1507, and **Giovanni,** 1430?–1516, Venetian painters (sons of Jacopo). **2. Jacopo,** 1400?–70, Venetian painter. **3. Vincenzo,** 1801?–35, Italian composer.

Be•llo (be′yô), **Andrés,** 1781–1865, Venezuelan poet, philologist, and educator.

Bel•loc (bel′ək, -ok), **Hi•laire** (hi lâr′), 1870–1953, English author, born in France.

Bel•lot•to (bə lot′ō), **Bernardo** (*Canaletto*), 1720–80, Italian painter.

Bel•low (bel′ō), **Saul,** born 1915, U.S. novelist, born in Canada: Nobel prize for literature 1976.

Bel•lows (bel′ōz), **George Wesley,** 1882–1925, U.S. painter.

Bel•mont (bel′mont), **1. Alva Ertskin Smith Vanderbilt,** 1853–1933, U.S. women's-rights activist and socialite. **2. August,** 1816–90, U.S. financier, diplomat, and horse-racing enthusiast, born in Germany.

Bel•tra•mi (bel trä′mē), **Eugenio,** 1835–1900, Italian mathematician.

Be•ly (bye′lē), **Andrei,** (*Boris Nikolayevich Bugayev*), 1880–1934, Russian writer.

Be•mel•mans (bē′məl mənz, bem′əl-), **Ludwig,** 1898–1962, U.S. humorous satirist and painter; born in Austria: author and illustrator of children's books.

Be•na•ven•te y Mar•tí•nez (ben′ə ven′tē ē mär tē′nez), **Jacinto,** 1866–1954, Spanish dramatist: Nobel prize 1922.

Ben Bel•la (ben bel′lä, bel′ə), **Ahmed,** born 1916, Algerian statesman: premier 1962–65; president 1963–65.

Ben•bow (ben′bō′), **John,** 1653–1702, English admiral.

Bench•ley (bench′lē), **Robert (Charles),** 1889–1945, U.S. humorist.

Ben•e•dict[1] (ben′i dikt), **1. Ruth (Fulton),** 1887–1948, U.S. anthropologist. **2. Saint,** A.D. 480?–543?, Italian monk: founded Benedictine order. **3. Stanley Rossiter,** 1884–1936, U.S. biochemist.

Ben•e•dict[2] (ben′i dikt), **1. Benedict I,** died A.D. 579, pope 575–79. **2. Benedict II, Saint,** died A.D. 685, pope 684–85. **3. Benedict III,** died A.D. 858, pope 855–58. **4. Benedict IV,** died A.D. 903, pope 900–03. **5. Benedict V,** died A.D. 966, pope 964. **6. Benedict VI,** died A.D. 974, pope 973–74. **7. Benedict VII,** died A.D. 983, pope 974–83. **8. Benedict VIII,** died 1024, pope 1012–24. **9. Benedict IX,** died 1056?, pope 1032–44; 1045; 1047–48. **10. Benedict XI,** (*Niccolò Boccasini*) 1240–1304, Italian ecclesiastic: pope 1303–04. **11. Benedict XII,** (*Jacques Fournier*) died 1342, French ecclesiastic: pope 1334–42. **12. Benedict XIII,** (*Pietro Francesco Orsini*) 1649–1730, Italian ecclesiastic: pope 1724–30. **13. Benedict XIV,** (*Prospero Lambertini*) 1675–1758, Italian ecclesiastic: pope 1740–58. **14. Benedict XV,** (*Giacomo della Chiesa*) 1854–1922, Italian ecclesiastic: pope 1914–22.

Be•neš (be′nesh), **Eduard,** 1884–1948, Czech patriot and statesman: president of Czechoslovakia 1935–38, 1945–48.

Be•nét (bi nā′), **1. Stephen Vincent,** 1898–1943, U.S. poet. **2.** his brother **William Rose,** 1886–1950, U.S. poet and critic.

Ben-Gu•rion (ben go͝or′ē ən, ben′go͝or yôn′), **David,** 1886–1973, Israeli statesman, born in Poland: prime minister of Israel 1948–53, 1955–63.

Ben•ja•min (ben′jə mən), **1. Asher,** 1773–1845, U.S. architect and writer. **2. Judah Philip,** 1811–84, Confederate statesman.

Ben•nett (ben′it), **1. (Enoch) Arnold,** 1867–1931, English novelist. **2. James Gordon,** 1795–1872, U.S. journalist. **3. Richard Bedford,** 1870–1947, prime minister of Canada 1930–35. **4. Robert Russell,** 1894–1981, U.S. composer and conductor. **5. William A(ndrew) C(ecil),** 1900–79, Canadian political leader: premier of British Columbia 1952–72.

Ben•ny (ben′ē), **Jack** (*Benjamin Kubelsky*), 1894–1974, U.S. comedian.

Ben•tham (ben′thəm, -təm), **Jeremy,** 1748–1832, English jurist and philosopher.

Ben•tinck (ben′tingk), **William Henry Cavendish, Duke of Portland,** 1738–1809, British statesman: prime minister 1783; 1807–09.

Bent•ley (bent′lē), **1. Eric (Russell),** born 1916, U.S. critic, editor, and translator; born in England. **2. Richard,** 1662–1742, English scholar and critic.

Ben•ton (ben′tn), **1. Thomas Hart** (*"Old Bullion"*), 1782–1858, U.S. political leader. **2.** his grandnephew **Thomas Hart,** 1889–1975, U.S. painter and lithographer.

Ben Ye•hu•dah (ben′ yə ho͞o′də), **Eliezer,** 1858–1922, Jewish scholar, born in Lithuania.

Benz (bents; *Eng.* benz), **Karl,** 1844–1929, German automotive engineer and manufacturer.

Ben-Zvi (ben tsvē′), **It•zhak** (it′säk), 1884?–1963, Israeli statesman, born in Russia: president of Israel 1952–63.

Ber•dya•ev (bər dyä′yef), **Nikolai Aleksandrovich,** 1874–1948, Russian theologian and philosopher: in France after 1922.

Ber•en•son (ber′ən sən), **Bernard** or **Bernhard,** 1865–1959, U.S. art critic, born in Lithuania.

Berg (berg), **1. Al•ban** (äl′bän), 1885–1935, Austrian composer. **2. Patricia Jane** (*Patty*), born 1918, U.S. golfer.

Ber•gen (bûr′gən), **Edgar,** 1903–78, U.S. ventriloquist.

Ber•ge•rac (bûr′zhə rak′), **Savinien Cyrano de,** 1619–55, French soldier, swordsman, and writer: hero of play by Rostand.

Bergh (bûrg), **Henry,** 1811–88, U.S. social reformer: founder of A.S.P.C.A.

Ber•gi•us (ber′gē əs, -ŏŏs), **Friedrich,** 1884–1949, German chemist: Nobel prize 1931.

Berg•man (bûrg′mən), **1. Ingmar,** born 1918, Swedish filmmaker. **2. Ingrid,** 1915–82, Swedish-born film actress.

Bergs•ma (bûrgz′mə), **William,** born 1921, U.S. composer.

Berg•son (bûrg′sən, berg′-), **Henri,** 1859–1941, French philosopher and writer: Nobel prize for literature 1927.

Be•ri•a (ber′ē ə), **Lavrenti Pavlovich,** 1899–1953, Soviet secret-police chief.

Ber•ing (bēr′ing, bâr′-), **Vitus,** 1680–1741, Danish navigator: explorer of the N Pacific.

Berke•ley (bûrk′lē; *for 2, 3 also Brit.* bärk′-), **1. Busby** (*William Berkeley Enos*), 1895–1976, U.S. choreographer and musical-film director. **2. George,** 1685?–1753, Irish bishop and philosopher. **3. Sir William,** 1610–77, British colonial governor of Virginia 1642–76.

Berle (bûrl), **Milton** (*Milton Berlinger*), born 1908, U.S. television performer.

Ber•lin (bər lin′), **Irving,** 1888–1989, U.S. songwriter.

Ber•li•ner (bûr′lə nər), **Emile,** 1851–1929, U.S. inventor, born in Germany.

Ber•li•oz (ber′lē ōz′), **Louis Hector,** 1803–69, French composer.

Ber•na•dette (bûr′nə det′), **Saint,** (*Marie Bernarde Soubirous*), 1844–79, French nun. Also called **Bernadette′ of Lourdes′.**

Ber•na•dotte (bûr′nə dot′), **Jean Baptiste Jules,** 1764–1844, French marshal under Napoleon; as Charles XIV, king of Sweden and Norway 1818–44.

Ber•na•nos (bᴇʀ nᴀ nôs′), **Georges,** 1888–1948, French novelist and pamphleteer.

Ber•nard (ber när′), **Claude,** 1813–78, French physiologist.

Ber•nard of Clair•vaux (bûr närd′ əv klâr vō′), **Saint,** 1090–1153, French Cistercian monk and writer.

Bern•har•di (bern här′dē), **Friedrich A. J. von,** 1849–1930, German general.

Bern•hardt (bûrn′härt), **Sarah** (*Rosine Bernard*), 1845–1923, French actress.

Ber•ni•ni (bər nē′nē), **Giovanni** or **Gian Lorenzo,** 1598–1680, Italian sculptor, architect, and painter.

Ber•noul•li or **Ber•nouil•li** (bər nōō′lē), **1. Daniel,** 1700–82, Swiss physicist and mathematician born in the Netherlands (son of Johann Bernoulli). **2. Jakob** or **Jacques,** 1654–1705, Swiss mathematician and physicist. **3. Johann** or **Jean** (zhäɴ), 1667–1748, Swiss mathematician (brother of Jakob Bernoulli).

Bern•stein (bûrn′stin, -stēn), **Leonard,** 1918–90, U.S. conductor and composer.

Bern•storff (bûrn′stôrf, -stôrf), **Count Johann-Heinrich,** 1862–1939, German diplomat.

Ber•ry (ber′ē), **Charles Edward Anderson** ("*Chuck*"), born 1926, U.S. rock-'n'-roll singer, musician, and composer.

Ber•ry•man (ber′ē mən), **John,** 1914–72, U.S. poet.

Ber•til•lon (bûr′tl on′; *Fr.* ber tē yôn′), **Alphonse,** 1853–1914, French anthropologist.

Ber•ze•li•us (bər zē′lē əs), **Jöns Jakob, Baron,** 1779–1848, Swedish chemist.

Bes•ant (bez′ənt), **1. Annie (Wood),** 1847–1933, English theosophist. **2. Sir Walter,** 1836–1901, English novelist.

Bes•sel (bes′əl), **Friedrich Wilhelm,** 1784–1846, German astronomer.

Bes•se•mer (bes′ə mər), **Sir Henry,** 1813–98, English engineer.

Best (best), **Charles Herbert,** 1899–1978, Canadian physiologist, born in the U.S.: one of the discoverers of insulin.

Bet•an•court (bet′n ko͝or′, -kôr′), **Rómulo,** 1908–81, Venezuelan journalist and political leader: president of Venezuela 1945–48 and 1959–64.

Be•the (bā′tə), **Hans Albrecht,** born 1906, U.S. physicist, born in Alsace; Nobel prize 1967.

Beth•mann-Holl•weg (bāt′män hôl′vāk), **Theobald von,** 1856–1921, German statesman: chancellor 1909–17.

Be•thune (bə thyo͞on′, -tho͞on′), **Mary McLeod,** 1875–1955, U.S. educator.

Bet•je•man (bech′ə mən), **Sir John,** 1906–84, English poet.

Bet•tel•heim (bet′l hīm′), **Bruno,** 1903–90, U.S. psychologist, educator, and writer, born in Austria.

Bet•ter•ton (bet′ər tən), **Thomas,** 1635?–1710, English actor and dramatist.

Bet•ti (bet′ē), **Ugo,** 1892–1953, Italian poet and dramatist.

Bev•an (bev′ən), **A•neu•rin** (ə nī′rən), 1897–1960, British political leader: minister of health 1945–50.

Bev•er•idge (bev′ər ij, bev′rij), **1. Albert Jeremiah,** 1862–1927, U.S. senator and historian. **2. Sir William Henry,** 1879–1963, English economist.

Bev•in (bev′in), **Ernest,** 1881–1951, British labor leader: foreign minister 1941–51.

Bew•ick (byo͞o′ik), **Thomas,** 1753–1828, English wood engraver.

Beyle (bāl), **Marie Henri,** Stendhal.

Bha•bha (bä′bä), **Ho•mi J(e•han•gir)** (hō′mē jə hän gēr′), 1909–1966, Indian physicist and government official.

Bhar•tri•ha•ri (bur′tri hur′ē), A.D. 570?–650?, Indian grammarian and poet.

Bha•va•bhu•ti (buv′ə bo͞o′tē), fl. 8th century, Indian dramatist.

Bha•ve (bä′vā), **Vi•no•ba** (vē nō′bə), 1895–1982, Indian religious leader and mystic.

Bhu•mi•bol A•dul•ya•dej (po͞o′mē pôn′ ä do͞on′yä ded′), RAMA IX.

Bia•lik (byä′lik), **Chaim Nachman,** 1873–1934, Hebrew poet, born in Russia.

Bi•as (bi′əs), fl. 570 B.C., Greek philosopher, born in Ionia.

Bi•chat (bē shä′), **Marie François Xavier,** 1771–1802, French physician.

Bi•dault (bē dō′), **Georges,** 1899–1983, French statesman.

Bid•dle (bid′l), **1. Francis,** 1886–1968, U.S. attorney general 1941–45. **2. John,** 1615–62, English theologian: founder of English Unitarianism. **3. Nicholas,** 1786–1844, U.S. financier.

Bien•ville (byaN vēl′), **Jean Baptiste Le Moyne, Sieur de,** 1680–1768, French governor of Louisiana.

Bierce (bērs), **Ambrose (Gwinnett),** 1842–1914?, U.S. journalist and short-story writer.

Bier•stadt (bēr′stat), **Albert,** 1830–1902, German-born U.S. painter.

Biggs (bigz), **E(dward George) Power,** 1906–77, English organist in the U.S.

Bih•zad (bē′zäd), **Ka•mal ad-Din** (kā′mäl äd dēn′), c1440–c1527, Persian painter and calligrapher.

Bi•ki•la (bi kē′lə), **A•be•be** (ä bā′bā), 1932–73, Ethiopian track-and-field athlete.

Bil•bo (bil′bō), **Theodore Gilmore,** 1877–1947, U.S. Southern populist politician: senator 1935–47.

Bil•lings (bil′ingz), **Josh,** pen name of Henry Wheeler SHAW.

Bil′ly the Kid′, (*William H. Bonney*) 1859–81, U.S. outlaw.

Bi•net (bi nā′), **Alfred,** 1857–1911, French psychologist.

Bing (bing), **Sir Rudolf,** born 1902, English opera impresario born in Austria; in the U.S. since 1949.

Bing•ham (bing′əm), **George Caleb,** 1811–79, U.S. painter.

Bing Xin (bing′ shin′), (*Xie Wanying*), born 1900, Chinese writer.

Bi•on (bi′on), fl. c100 B.C., Greek pastoral poet.

Birds•eye (bûrdz′ī′), **Clarence,** 1886–1956, U.S. inventor and businessman: developer of food-freezing process.

Bish•op (bish′əp), **1. Elizabeth,** 1911–79, U.S. poet. **2. John Peale,** 1892–1944, U.S. poet and essayist. **3. Morris** (*Gilbert*), 1893–1973, U.S. humorist, poet, and biographer. **4. William Avery** (*"Billy"*), 1894–1956, Canadian aviator: helped to establish Canadian air force.

Bis•marck (biz′märk), **Otto von,** 1815–98, German statesman: first chancellor of modern German Empire 1871–90.

Bi·zet (bē zā′), **Georges** (*Alexandre César Léopold*), 1838–75, French composer.

Bjoer·ling or **Björ′ling** (byœʀ′ling), **Jus·si** (yo͝os′ē), 1911–60, Swedish tenor.

Björn·son (byûrn′sən), **Björn·stjer·ne** (byûrn′styer nə), 1832–1910, Norwegian poet, novelist, and playwright: Nobel prize 1903.

Black (blak), **1. Hugo Lafayette,** 1886–1971, associate justice of the U.S. Supreme Court 1937–71. **2. Joseph,** 1728–99, Scottish physician and chemist. **3. Shirley Temple,** TEMPLE, Shirley.

Black·beard (blak′bērd′), pseudonym of Edward TEACH.

Black·ett (blak′it), **Patrick Maynard Stuart,** 1897–1974, English physicist: Nobel prize 1948.

Black′ Hawk′, 1767–1838, American Indian chief of the Sauk tribe; leader in the Black Hawk War 1831–32.

Black·more (blak′môr, -mōr), **Richard Doddridge,** 1825–1900, English novelist.

Black·mun (blak′mən), **Harry A(ndrew),** born 1908, associate justice of the U.S. Supreme Court since 1970.

Black·mur (blak′mər), **R(ichard) P(almer),** 1904–65, U.S. critic and poet.

Black′ Prince′, EDWARD[1].

Black·stone (blak′stōn′, -stən), **Sir William,** 1723–80, English jurist and writer on law.

Black·well (blak′wəl, -wel′), **1. Antoinette Louisa (Brown),** 1825–1921, U.S. clergywoman, abolitionist, and women's-rights activist. **2. Elizabeth,** 1821–1910, first woman physician in the U.S., born in England. **3. Henry Brown,** 1825?–1909, U.S. editor, abolitionist, and suffragist, born in England (husband of Lucy Stone).

Black·wood (blak′wo͝od′), **William,** 1776–1834, English publisher.

Blaeu or **Blaeuw** or **Blaew** (blou), **Willem Janszoon,** 1571–1638, Dutch cartographer, geographer, astronomer, and mathematician.

Blaine (blān), **James Gillespie,** 1830–93, U.S. statesman.

Blais (blā), **Marie-Claire,** born 1939, Canadian poet and novelist.

Blake (blāk), **1. James Hubert** (*"Eubie"*), 1883–1983, U.S. jazz pianist and composer. **2. Robert,** 1599–1657, British admiral. **3. William,** 1757–1827, English poet, engraver, and painter.

Blanc (bläN), **Jean Joseph Charles Louis** (zhäN), 1811–82, French socialist and historian.

Blan·co-Fom·bo·na (bläng′kô fôm bô′nä), **Ru·fi·no** (ʀo͞o fē′nô), 1874–1944, Venezuelan author.

Bland (bland), **James A(llen),** 1854–1911, U.S. songwriter and minstrel performer.

Blas·co I·bá·ñez (bläs′kō ē bän′yes), **Vicente,** 1867–1928, Spanish novelist, journalist, and politician.

Bla·vat·sky (blə vat′skē), **Madame** (*Elena Petrovna Blavatskaya,* nee *Hahn*), 1831–91, Russian theosophist.

Blé•riot (blâr′ē ō′), **Louis,** 1872–1936, French aviator, pioneer aeronautical engineer, and inventor.

Bleu•ler (bloi′lər), **Eugen,** 1857–1939, Swiss psychiatrist and neurologist.

Bligh (blī), **William,** 1754–1817, British naval officer: captain of H.M.S. *Bounty,* the crew of which mutinied 1789.

Bliss (blis), **1. Sir Arthur (Edward Drummond),** 1891–1975, English composer. **2. Tas•ker** (tas′kər) **Howard,** 1853–1930, U.S. general.

Blitz•stein (blits′stīn), **Marc,** 1905–64, U.S. composer.

Blix•en (blik′sən), **Karen,** DINESEN, Isak.

Bloch (blok), **1. Ernest,** 1880–1959, U.S. composer, born in Switzerland. **2. Felix,** 1905–83, Swiss physicist in the U.S.: Nobel prize 1952. **3. Konrad E.,** born 1912, U.S. biochemist, born in Germany: Nobel prize for medicine 1964.

Block (blok), **Herbert Lawrence** (*"Herblock"*), born 1909, U.S. cartoonist.

Blok (blok; *Russ.* blôk), **Alexander Alexandrovich,** 1880–1921, Russian poet.

Blon•del (blôN del′), **François,** (*Sieur des Croisettes*), 1618–86, French architect.

Blood′y Mar′y, MARY².

Bloo•mer (blōō′mər), **Amelia Jenks,** 1818–94, U.S. social reformer and women's-rights leader.

Bloom•field (blōōm′fēld′), **Leonard,** 1887–1949, U.S. linguist.

Blü•cher (blōō′kər, -chər), **Geb•hart Le•be•recht von** (gep′härt lā′bə reKHt′ fən), 1742–1819, Prussian field marshal.

Blum (blōōm), **Léon,** 1872–1950, French socialist: premier of France 1936–37, 1938, 1946–47.

Blum•berg (blum′bûrg), **Baruch S(amuel),** born 1925, U.S. physician: Nobel prize 1976.

Blume (blōōm), **Judy,** born 1938, U.S. novelist.

Bly (blī), **1. Nellie** (*Elizabeth Cochrane Seaman*), 1867–1922, U.S. journalist and social reformer. **2. Robert,** born 1926, U.S. poet.

Bo•ab•dil (bō′əb dil), (*abu-Abdallah*) (*"El Chico"*), died 1533?, last Moorish king of Granada 1482–83, 1486–92.

Bo•ad•i•ce•a (bō ad′ə sē′ə), BOUDICCA.

Bo•as (bō′az), **Franz,** 1858–1942, U.S. anthropologist, born in Germany.

Bo•ba•di•lla (bô′vä thē′lyä, -thē′yä), **Francisco de,** died 1502, Spanish colonial governor in the West Indies: sent Columbus back to Spain in chains.

Boc•cac•ci•o (bə kä′chō, -chē ō′), **Giovanni,** 1313–75, Italian writer: author of the *Decameron.*

Boc•che•ri•ni (bok′ə rē′nē, bō′kə-), **Luigi,** 1743–1805, Italian composer.

Boc•cio•ni (bə chō′nē), **Umberto,** 1882–1916, Italian painter and sculptor.

Bo•danz•ky (bō dänts′kē), **Artur,** 1877–1939, Austrian opera director and orchestra conductor, in the U.S. after 1915.

Bo•den•heim (bōd′n hīm′), **Maxwell,** 1892–1954, U.S. poet and novelist.

Bod•go Ge•gen (bōd′gō gā′gān), a former Buddhist leader of the Mongols.

Bo•dhi•dhar•ma (bō′di dur′mə), died A.D. c530, Indian Buddhist philosopher and missionary: founder of Ch'an in China, which was later called Zen in Japan.

Bod•ley (bod′lē), **George Frederick,** 1827–1907, English architect.

Bo•do•ni (bə dō′nē), **Giambattista,** 1740–1813, Italian painter and printer.

Bo•e•thi•us (bō ē′thē əs), **Anicius Manlius Severinus,** A.D. 475?–525?, Roman philosopher and statesman.

Bo•gan (bō gan′, bō′gən), **Louise,** 1897–1970, U.S. poet.

Bo•gart (bō′gärt), **Humphrey (DeForest)** (*"Bogey"*), 1900–57, U.S. film actor.

Boh•len (bō′lin), **Charles Eustis** (*"Chip"*), 1904–74, U.S. diplomat.

Böhm (bœm), **Karl,** 1894–1981, Austrian conductor.

Böh•me (bā′mə, bō′-), **Jakob,** 1575–1624, German theosophist and mystic.

Bohr (bôr, bōr), **1. Aage Niels,** born 1922, Danish physicist. **2.** his father, **Niels Henrik David,** 1885–1962, Danish physicist.

Bo•iar•do (boi är′dō), **Matteo Maria,** 1434–94, Italian poet.

Boi•el•dieu (bwA el dyœ′), **François Adrien,** 1775–1834, French composer.

Boi•leau-Des•pré•aux (bwä lō′də prā′ō), **Nicolas,** 1636–1711, French critic and poet.

Boi•ta•no (boi tä′nō), **Brian,** born 1963, U.S. figure skater.

Bo•i•to (boi′tō, bō ē′tō), **Arrigo,** 1842–1918, Italian opera composer, poet, and novelist.

Boj•er (boi′ər), **Johan,** 1872–1959, Norwegian novelist and playwright.

Bok (bok), **Edward William,** 1863–1930, U.S. editor and writer, born in the Netherlands.

Bol•den (bōl′dən), **Charles** (*"Buddy"*), 1868?–1931, U.S. cornet player: early pioneer in jazz.

Bol•eyn (bo͝ol′in, bo͝o lin′), **Anne,** 1507–36, second wife of Henry VIII of England: mother of Queen Elizabeth I.

Bol•ger (bōl′jər), **Ray,** 1904–87, U.S. dancer and actor.

Bol•ing•broke (bol′ing bro͝ok′; *older* bo͝ol′-), **Henry St. John** (sin′jən), **1st Viscount,** 1678–1751, British statesman, writer, and orator.

Bol•i•var (bol′ə vər, bə lē′vär), **Simón** (*"El Libertador"*), 1783–1830, Venezuelan statesman: leader of revolt of South American colonies against Spanish rule.

Böll (bœl), **Heinrich (Theodor),** 1917–85, German novelist and short-story writer: Nobel prize 1972.

Bol•land (bol′ənd; *Fr.* bô läɴ′; *Flemish* bol′änt), **Jean de** (*Fr.* zhäɴ də) or **Jo•han van** (*Flemish.* yō hän′ vän) or **John,** 1596–1665, Belgian Jesuit hagiographer. Also called **Bol•lan•dus** (bō lan′dəs).

Bo•lo•gna (bə lōn′yə), **Giovanni da** (*Jean de Boulogne, Giambologna*), c1525–1608, Italian sculptor, born in France.

Boltz•mann (bôlts′män′; *Eng.* bōlts′mən), **Ludwig,** 1844–1906, Austrian physicist.

Bo•lyai (bô′lyoi), **Já•nos** (yä′nôsh), 1802–60, Hungarian mathematician.

Bo•na•parte (bō′nə pärt′), **1. Charles Louis Napoleon,** Napoleon (def. 3). **2. François Charles Joseph,** Napoleon (def. 2). **3. Jérôme,** 1784–1860, king of Westphalia 1807 (brother of Napoleon I). **4. Joseph,** 1768–1844, king of Naples 1806–08; king of Spain 1808–13 (brother of Napoleon I). **5. Louis,** 1778–1846, king of Holland 1806–10 (brother of Napoleon I). **6. Lucien,** 1775–1840, prince of Canino, a principality in Italy (brother of Napoleon I). **7. Napoleon,** Napoleon (def. 1). Italian, **Buonaparte.**

Bon•a•ven•ture (bon′ə ven′cher, bon′ə ven′-) also **Bon′a•ven•tu′ra** (-chŏŏr′ə), **Saint** (*"the Seraphic Doctor"*), 1221–74, Italian scholastic theologian.

Bond (bond), **1. Carrie** (nee **Jacobs**), 1862–1946, U.S. songwriter and author. **2. Julian,** born 1940, U.S. civil-rights leader and politician.

Bon•heur (bo nûr′), **Rosa** (*Maria Rosalie Bonheur*), 1822–99, French painter.

Bon•i•face[1] (bon′ə fis, -fās′), **Saint** (*Wynfrith*), A.D. 680?–755?, English monk who became a missionary in Germany.

Bon•i•face[2] (bon′ə fis, -fās′), **1. Boniface I, Saint,** died A.D. 422, pope 418–422. **2. Boniface VIII** (*Benedetto Caetani*), c1235–1303, Italian ecclesiastic: pope 1294–1303.

Bon•ing•ton (bon′ing tən), **Richard Parkes,** 1801–28, English painter.

Bon•nard (bô när′), **Pierre,** 1867–1947, French painter.

Bon•net (bô nā′), **Georges,** 1889–1973, French statesman.

Bo•non•ci•ni (bô′nôn chē′nē), **Giovanni Maria,** 1640–78, and his sons **Giovanni Battista,** 1670–1747, and **Marc Antonio,** 1675–1726, Italian composers.

Bon•tem•pel•li (bôn′tem pel′lē), **Massimo,** 1878–1960, Italian novelist.

Boole (bo͞ol), **George,** 1815–64, English mathematician and logician.

Boone (bo͞on), **Daniel,** 1734–1820, American pioneer, esp. in Kentucky.

Booth (bo͞oth; *Brit.* bo͞oth), **1. Ballington,** 1859–1940, founder of the Volunteers of America, 1896 (son of William Booth). **2. Edwin Thomas,** 1833–93, U.S. actor (brother of John Wilkes Booth). **3. Evangeline Cory,** 1865?–1950, general of the Salvation Army 1934–39 (daughter of William Booth). **4. John Wilkes,** 1838–65, U.S. actor: assassin of Abraham Lincoln (brother of Edwin Thomas Booth). **5. Junius Brutus,** 1796–1852, English actor (father of Edwin Thomas and John Wilkes Booth). **6. William** (*"General Booth"*), 1829–1912, English religious leader: founder of the Salvation Army 1865. **7. William Bram•well** (bram′wel′, -wəl), 1856–1929, general of the Salvation Army (son of William Booth).

Bopp (bop; *Ger.* bôp), **Franz,** 1791–1867, German philologist.

Bo•rah (bôr′ə, bōr′ə), **William Edgar,** 1865–1940, U.S. senator from Idaho 1906–40.

Bor•den (bôr′dn), **1. Gail,** 1801–74, U.S. inventor: developed technique for condensing milk. **2. Lizzie (Andrew),** 1860–1927, defendant in U.S. 1893 trial: acquitted of ax murder of father and stepmother. **3. Sir Robert Laird** (lârd), 1854–1937, Canadian statesman: prime minister 1911–20.

Bor•det (bôr dā′; *Fr.* bôʀ de′), **Jules Jean Baptiste Vincent,** 1870–1961, Belgian physiologist and bacteriologist: Nobel prize for medicine 1919.

Bo•rel (bô rel′, bə-), **Félix Édouard Émile,** 1871–1956, French mathematician.

Bo•rel•li (bô rel′ē, bə-), **Giovanni Alfonso,** 1608–79, Italian astronomer, physicist, and physiologist.

Borg (bôrg), **Björn,** born 1956, Swedish tennis player.

Bor•ges (bôr′hās), **Jorge Luis,** 1899–1986, Argentine poet, short-story writer, and essayist.

Bor•gia (bôr′jə, -zhə), **1. Cesare,** 1476?–1507, Italian cardinal, military leader, and politician. **2. Lucrezia** (*Duchess of Ferrara*), 1480–1519, sister of Cesare Borgia: patron of the arts. **3.** their father, **Rodrigo,** ALEXANDER[2] (def. 4).

Bor•glum (bôr′gləm), **John Gutzon,** 1867–1941, U.S. sculptor.

Boris III, 1894–1943, king of Bulgaria 1918–43.

Bor•laug (bôr′lôg, -log), **Norman Ernest,** born 1914, U.S. agronomist: Nobel peace prize 1970.

Bor•man (bôr′mən), **Frank,** born 1928, U.S. astronaut.

Bor•mann (bôr′mən), **Martin Ludwig,** 1900–45, German Nazi official.

Born (bôrn), **Max,** 1882–1970, German physicist: Nobel prize 1954.

Bo•ro•din (bôr′ə dēn′, bor′-), **Aleksandr Porfirevich,** 1833–87, Russian composer and chemist.

Bor•ro•mi•ni (bôr′ə mē′nē, bor′-), **Francesco,** 1599–1667, Italian architect and sculptor.

Bor•row (bor′ō, bôr′ō), **George,** 1803–81, English traveler, writer, and student of languages, esp. Romany.

Bo•san•quet (bō′zən ket′, -kit), **Bernard,** 1848–1923, English philosopher and writer.

Bosch (bosh), **1. Carl** or **Karl,** 1874–1940, German chemist: Nobel prize 1931. **2. Hieronymus** (*Hieronymus van Aeken*), 1450?–1516, Dutch painter. **3. Juan** (*Juan*

Bosch Gaviño), born 1909, Dominican writer and political leader: president 1963.

Bose (bōs), **Sir Jagadis Chandra**, 1858–1937, Indian physicist and plant physiologist.

Bos•suet (bô swā′), **Jacques Bénigne**, 1627–1704, French bishop, writer, and orator.

Bos•well (boz′wel′, -wəl), **James**, 1740–95, Scottish author: biographer of Samuel Johnson.

Bo•tha (bō′tə), **1. Louis**, 1862–1919, South African statesman. **2. Pieter Willem**, born 1916, president of South Africa 1984–89.

Bo•the (bō′tə), **Walther**, 1891–1957, German physicist: Nobel prize 1954.

Both•well (both′wel′, -wəl, bo*th*′-), **James Hepburn, Earl of**, 1536?–78, third husband of Mary, Queen of Scots.

Bot•kin (bot′kin), **Benjamin Albert**, 1901–75, U.S. folklorist, editor, and essayist.

Bött•ger (bet′gər), **Johann Friedrich**, 1682–1719, German chemist.

Bot•ti•cel•li (bot′i chel′ē), **Sandro** (*Alessandro di Mariano del Filipepi*), 1444?–1510, Italian painter.

Bot•vin•nik (bot vē′nik, -vin′ik), **Mikhail (Moiseevich)**, born 1911, Russian chess master.

Bou•chard (bo͞o shär′), **(Louis) Henri**, 1875–1960, French sculptor.

Bou•ché (bo͞o shā′), **Louis**, 1896–1969, U.S. painter.

Bou•cher (bo͞o shā′), **François**, 1703–70, French painter.

Boucher′ de Crève•coeur′ de Perthes′ (də krev-kœr′ də pert′), **Jacques**, 1788–1868, French archaeologist and writer.

Bou•ci•cault (bo͞o′sē kôlt′, -kō′), **Dion**, 1822–90, Irish playwright and actor, in the U.S. after 1853.

Bou•dic•ca (bo͞o dik′ə), died A.D. 62, ancient British Celtic queen: leader of an unsuccessful revolt against the Romans in Britain. Also called **Boadicea.**

Bou•gain•ville (bo͞o′gən vil′, bo͞o gən vēl′), **Louis Antoine de**, 1729–1811, French navigator.

Bou•gue•reau (bo͞og° rō′), **Adolphe William**, 1825–1905, French painter.

Bou•lan•ger (bo͞o′län jā′, -län zhā′), **Nadia (Juliette)**, 1887-1979, French composer and teacher.

Bou•lez (bo͞o lez′), **Pierre**, born 1925, French composer and conductor.

Boult (bōlt), **Sir Adrian Cedric**, 1889–1983, English conductor.

Bou•me•dienne (bo͞o′mə dyen′, -dē en′), **Houari** (*Mohammed Boukharouba*), 1925?–78, Algerian military and political leader: president 1965–78.

Bour•bon (bo͝or′bən, bo͝or bôn′), **1.** a member of a French royal family that ruled in France 1589–1792, Spain 1700–1931, and Naples 1735–1806, 1815–60. **2. Charles**, ("*Constable de Bourbon*"), 1490–1527, French general.

Bour•geois (bo͝or zhwä′, bo͝or′zhwä), **Léon Victor Au-**

guste, 1851–1925, French statesman: Nobel peace prize 1920.

Bour•get (bo͝or zhā′), **Paul,** 1852–1935, French novelist and critic.

Bour•gui•ba (bo͝or gē′bə), **Habib ben Ali,** born 1903, president of Tunisia 1957-87.

Bourke-White (bûrk′hwīt′, -wīt′), **Margaret,** 1906–71, U.S. photographer and author.

Bour•non•ville (bo͝or′nən vil′), **Auguste,** 1805–79, Danish ballet dancer and choreographer.

Bo•vet (bō vā′, -vet′), **Daniel,** born 1907, Italian pharmacologist, born in Switzerland: Nobel prize for medicine 1957.

Bow (bō), **Clara,** 1905–65, U.S. film actress: known as the "It Girl."

Bow•ditch (bou′dich), **Nathaniel,** 1773–1838, U.S. mathematician, astronomer, and navigator.

Bow•ell (bō′əl), **Sir Mackenzie,** 1823–1917, Canadian statesman, born in England: prime minister 1894–96.

Bow•en (bō′ən), **1. Catherine (Shober) Drinker,** 1897–1973, U.S. biographer and essayist. **2. Elizabeth (Dorothea Cole),** 1899–1973, Anglo-Irish novelist and short-story writer.

Bow•ers (bou′ərz), **Claude Gernade,** 1878–1958, U.S. diplomat and historian.

Bow•ie (bō′ē, bo͞o′ē), **1. James,** 1799–1836, U.S. soldier and pioneer. **2. William,** 1872–1940, U.S. geodesist.

Bowles (bōlz), **1. Chester,** 1901–86, U.S. statesman and author: special adviser on Afro-Asian and Latin-American affairs; ambassador to India 1951–53, 1963–69. **2. Paul (Frederic),** born 1910?, U.S. novelist and composer. **3. Samuel,** 1826–78, U.S. journalist.

Boyd Orr (boid′ ôr′), **John** (*1st Baron Boyd Orr of Brechin Mearns*), 1880–1971, Scottish nutritionist and writer: Nobel peace prize 1949.

Boy•er (bwa yā′), **1. Charles,** 1899–1978, French actor. **2. Jean Pierre,** 1776–1850, Haitian political leader: president 1818–43.

Boyle (boil), **1. Kay,** born 1903, U.S. novelist, short-story writer, and poet. **2. Robert,** 1627–91, English chemist and physicist.

Boz (boz), pen name of Charles DICKENS.

Boz•za•ris (bō zar′is, -zär′-), **Marco,** 1788?–1823, Greek patriot.

Brab•ham (brab′əm), **Sir John Arthur** (*"Jack"*), born 1926, Australian racing-car driver.

Brad•bur•y (brad′bə rē), **Ray (Douglas),** born 1920, U.S. science-fiction writer.

Brad•dock (brad′ək), **Edward,** 1695–1755, British general in America.

Brad•ford (brad′fərd), **1. Barbara Taylor,** born 1933, U.S. novelist, born in England. **2. Gamaliel,** 1863–1932, U.S. biographer and novelist. **3. Roark,** 1896–1948, U.S. novelist and short-story writer. **4. William,** 1590–1657, second governor of Plymouth Colony 1621–56. **5. William,** 1663–1752, American printer, born in England.

Brad•ley (brad′lē), **1. Bill** (*William Warren*), born 1943, U.S. politician: senator from New Jersey since 1979. **2. Francis Herbert,** 1846–1924, English philosopher. **3. Henry,** 1845–1923, English lexicographer and philologist. **4. Omar Nelson,** 1893–1981, U.S. general. **5. Thomas** (*Tom*), born 1917, U.S. politician: mayor of Los Angeles since 1973.

Brad•street (brad′strēt′), **1. Anne (Dudley),** 1612?–72, American poet. **2.** her husband, **Simon,** 1603–97, governor of the Massachusetts colony 1679–86, 1689–92.

Bra•dy (brā′dē), **1. James Buchanan** (*"Diamond Jim"*), 1856–1917, U.S. financier, noted for conspicuously extravagant living. **2. Mathew B.,** 1823?–96, U.S. photographer, esp. of the Civil War.

Brag•don (brag′dən), **Claude,** 1866–1946, U.S. architect, stage designer, and author.

Bragg (brag), **1. Braxton,** 1817–76, Confederate general in the U.S. Civil War. **2. Sir William Henry,** 1862–1942, and his son, **Sir William Lawrence,** 1890–1971, English physicists: Nobel prize winners 1915.

Brahe (brä, brä′hē), **Tycho,** 1546–1601, Danish astronomer.

Brahms (brämz), **Johannes,** 1833–97, German composer.

Braille (brāl), **Louis,** 1809–52, French teacher of the blind.

Brai•low•sky (brī lôf′skē, brā-, -lof′-), **Alexander,** 1896–1976, Russian pianist.

Bram•ah (bram′ə, brä′mə), **Joseph,** 1748–1814, English engineer and inventor.

Bra•man•te (brə män′tā), **Donato d'Agnolo,** 1444–1514, Italian architect and painter.

Bran•cu•si (bräng ko͞o′zē), **Constantin,** 1876–1957, Romanian sculptor.

Brand (brand), **Oscar,** born 1920, U.S. folk singer, born in Canada.

Bran•deis (bran′dīs), **Louis Dembitz,** 1856–1941, associate justice of the U.S. Supreme Court 1916–39.

Bran•des (brän′des), **Georg Morris** (*Georg Morris Cohen*), 1842–1927, Danish historian and literary critic.

Bran•do (bran′dō), **Marlon,** born 1924, U.S. actor.

Brandt (brant), **Willy,** born 1913, chancellor of West Germany 1969–74: Nobel peace prize 1971.

Brant (brant), **Joseph** (*Thayendanegea*), 1742–1807, Mohawk chief: fought for the British in the American Revolution.

Bran•ting (bran′ting, brän′-), **Karl Hjalmar,** 1860–1925, Swedish statesman: prime minister 1920, 1921–23, 1924–25; Nobel peace prize 1921.

Braque (bräk), **Georges,** 1882–1963, French painter.

Brat•tain (brat′n), **Walter Houser,** 1902–87, U.S. physicist: Nobel prize 1956.

Brau•del (brō del′), **Fernand,** 1902–85, French historian.

Braun (broun), **1. Eva,** 1912–45, mistress of Adolf Hitler. **2. Karl Ferdinand,** 1850–1918, German physicist and specialist in wireless telegraphy: Nobel prize in physics 1909. **3. Wernher von,** 1912–77, German rocket engineer, in U.S. after 1945.

Braz•za (*Fr.* BRA ZA′), **Pierre Paul François Camille Savorgnan de,** 1852–1905, French explorer in Africa, born in Italy.

Bream (brēm), **Julian (Alexander),** born 1933, English guitarist and lutanist.

Breas•ted (bres′tid), **James Henry,** 1865–1935, U.S. archaeologist and historian of ancient Egypt.

Brecht (brekt, breKHt), **Bertolt,** 1898–1956, German dramatist and poet.

Breck•in•ridge (brek′ən rij′), **John Cabell,** 1821–75, vice president of the U.S. 1857–61; Confederate general.

Brel (brel), **Jacques,** 1929–78, Belgian composer and singer.

Bren•nan (bren′ən), **William Joseph, Jr.,** born 1906, associate justice of the U.S. Supreme Court 1956–90.

Bren•ta•no (bren tä′nō), **Franz,** 1838–1917, German philosopher and psychologist.

Bresh•kov•sky (bresh kôf′skē, -kof′-), **Catherine,** 1844–1934, Russian revolutionary of noble birth: called "the little grandmother of the Russian Revolution."

Bre•ton (brə tôN′), **André,** 1896–1966, French poet and critic.

Breu•er (broi′ər), **1. Josef,** 1842–1925, Austrian neurologist: pioneer in psychoanalytic techniques. **2. Marcel Lajos,** 1902–81, Hungarian architect and furniture designer, in the U.S. after 1937.

Breu•ghel or **Breu•gel** or **Brue•ghel** (broi′gəl, broo͞′-, brœ′-), **1. Pieter the Elder,** c1525–69, Flemish genre and landscape painter. **2.** his sons, **Jan,** 1568–1625, and **Pieter the Younger,** 1564–1637?, Flemish painters.

Brew•ster (broo͞′stər), **William,** 1560?–1644, Pilgrim settler: leader of the colonists at Plymouth.

Brezh•nev (brezh′nef), **Leonid Ilyich,** 1906–82, president of the Soviet Union 1960–64, 1977–82, general secretary of the Soviet Communist Party 1966–82.

Bri•an Bo•ru or **Bri•an Bo•roimhe** (brī′ən bô rō′, -roo͞′, brēn′), 926–1014, king of Ireland 1002–14.

Bri•and (brē änd′), **Aristide,** 1862–1932, French statesman: minister of France 11 times; Nobel peace prize 1926.

Brice (brīs), **Fanny** (*Fannie Borach*), 1891–1951, U.S. singer and comedian.

Bride (brīd), **Saint,** BRIGID, Saint.

Bridg•es (brij′iz), **1. Calvin Blackman,** 1889–1938, U.S. geneticist. **2. Harry (Alfred Bryant Renton),** 1900–90, U.S. labor leader, born in Australia. **3. Robert (Seymour),** 1884–1930, English poet and essayist: poet laureate 1913–30.

Bridg•et (brij′it), **Saint,** BRIGID, Saint.

Bridg•man (brij′mən), **Percy Williams,** 1882–1961, U.S. physicist: Nobel prize 1946.

Bri•eux (bʀē œ′), **Eugène,** 1858–1932, French playwright, journalist, and editor.

Briggs (brigz), **Henry,** 1561–1630, English mathematician.

Bright (brīt), **1. John,** 1811–89, British statesman and economist. **2. Richard,** 1789–1858, English physician.

Brig•id (brij′id, brē′id) also **Brig•it** (-it), **Bridget, Saint,** A.D. 453–523, Irish abbess: a patron saint of Ireland. Also called **Bride.**

Brill (bril), **A(braham) A(rden),** 1874–1948, U.S. psychoanalyst and author, born in Austria.

Bril•lat-Sa•va•rin (bʀē ya sa va ʀaɴ′), **Anthelme,** 1755–1826, French jurist and gastronome.

Brink•ley (bringk′lē), **David,** born 1920, U.S. news broadcaster and commentator.

Bris•bane (briz′bān, -bən), **Arthur,** 1864–1936, U.S. journalist.

Brit•ten (brit′n), **(Edward) Benjamin,** 1913–76, English composer and pianist.

Brit•ton (brit′n), **Nathaniel Lord,** 1859–1934, U.S. botanist.

Broad (brôd), **C(harlie) D(unbar),** 1887–1971, English philosopher.

Bro•ca (brō′kə), **Paul,** 1824–80, French surgeon and anthropologist.

Brod•sky (brod′skē), **Joseph,** born 1940, U.S. lyric poet, born in U.S.S.R.

Brom•field (brom′fēld′), **Louis,** 1896–1956, U.S. novelist.

Bron•të (bron′tē), **1. Anne** (*"Acton Bell"*), 1820–49, English novelist. **2.** her sister **Charlotte** (*"Currer Bell"*), 1816–55, English novelist. **3.** her sister **Emily Jane** (*"Ellis Bell"*), 1818–48, English novelist.

Bron•zi•no Agnolo (di Cosimo di Mariano), 1502–72, Italian painter.

Brooke (bro͝ok), **Rupert,** 1887–1915, English poet.

Brook•ings (bro͝ok′ingz), **Robert Somers,** 1850–1932, U.S. merchant and philanthropist.

Brooks (bro͝oks), **1. Gwendolyn,** born 1917, U.S. poet and novelist. **2. Mel** (*Melvin Kaminsky*), born 1926, U.S. filmmaker and comedian. **3. Phillips,** 1835–93, U.S. Protestant Episcopal bishop and orator. **4. Van Wyck** (wīk), 1886–1963, U.S. author and critic.

Broun (bro͞on), **(Matthew) Heywood (Campbell),** 1888–1939, U.S. journalist, essayist, and novelist.

Brou•wer (brou′ər), **1. Adriaen,** 1606?–38, Flemish painter. **2. Luitzen Egbertus Jan,** 1881–1966, Dutch mathematician and philosopher.

Brow•der (brou′dər), **Earl Russell,** 1891–1973, U.S. Communist party leader 1930–45.

Brown (broun), **1. Charles Brockden,** 1771–1810, U.S. novelist. **2. Edmund Gerald, Jr.** (*Jerry*), born 1938, U.S. politician: governor of California 1975–83. **3. James,** born

1928, U.S. singer. **4. James Nathaniel** (*Jimmy*), born 1936, U.S. football player and actor. **5. John** (*"Old Brown of Osawatomie"*), 1800–59, U.S. abolitionist: leader of the attack at Harpers Ferry. **6. Olympia,** 1835–1926, U.S. women's-rights activist and Universalist minister: first American woman ordained by a major church. **7. William Wells,** 1815–84, U.S. novelist.

Browne (broun), **1. Charles Farrer** (*"Artemus Ward"*), 1834–67, U.S. humorist. **2. Sir Thomas,** 1605–82, English physician and author.

Brown•ing (brou′ning), **1. Elizabeth Barrett,** 1806–61, English poet. **2. John Moses,** 1885–1926, U.S. designer of firearms. **3. Robert,** 1812–89, English poet.

Broz (*Serbo-Croatian.* brôz), **Josip,** Tito, Marshal.

Bru•beck (bro͞o′bek), **David Warren** (*Dave*), born 1920, U.S. jazz pianist and composer.

Bruce (bro͞os), **1. Blanche Kelso,** 1841–98, U.S. politician: first black to serve a full term as U.S. senator 1875–81. **2. Sir David,** 1855–1931, Australian physician. **3. Robert,** Robert I (def. 2). **4. Stanley Melbourne** (*1st Viscount Bruce of Melbourne*), 1883–1967, prime minister of Australia 1923–29.

Bruch (bro͝ok), **Max,** 1838–1920, German composer and conductor.

Bruck•ner (bro͝ok′nər, bruk′-), **Anton,** 1824–96, Austrian composer.

Brue•ghel or **Brue•gel** (broi′gəl, bro͞o′-, brœ-), Breughel.

Bruhn (bro͞on), **Erik** (*Belton Evers*), 1928–86, Danish ballet dancer.

Brum•mell (brum′əl), **George Bryan II,** Beau Brummell.

Brundt•land (bro͝ont′län), **Gro Harlem,** born 1939, prime minister of Norway since 1986.

Bru•nel (bro͞o nel′), **1. Isambard Kingdom,** 1806–59, English civil engineer and naval architect. **2.** his father, **Sir Marc Isambard,** 1769–1849, English civil engineer, born in France: chief engineer of New York City 1793–99.

Bru•nel•les•chi (bro͞on′l es′kē) also **Bru•nel•les•co** (-kō), **Filippo,** 1377?–1446, Italian architect.

Brun•ner (bro͝on′ər), **Emil,** 1889–1966, Swiss Protestant theologian.

Bru•no (bro͞o′nō), **1. Giordano,** 1548?–1600, Italian philosopher. **2. Saint,** c1030–1101, German ecclesiastical writer: founder of the Carthusian order.

Brush (brush), **Katharine,** 1902–52, U.S. novelist and short-story writer.

Bru•tus (bro͞o′təs), **Marcus Junius,** 85?–42 B.C., Roman statesman: one of the assassins of Julius Caesar.

Bry•an (brī′ən), **William Jennings,** 1860–1925, U.S. political leader.

Bry•ant (brī′ənt), **1. Gridley,** 1789–1867, U.S. engineer and inventor. **2. William Cullen,** 1794–1878, U.S. poet and journalist.

Bryce (bris), **James, 1st Viscount,** 1838–1922, British diplomat, historian, and jurist, born in Ireland.

Bu•ber (bo͞o′bər), **Martin,** 1878–1965, Jewish philosopher, theologian, and scholar, born in Austria.

Buch•an (buk′ən), **John** (*Baron Tweedsmuir*), 1875–1940, Scottish novelist and historian: governor general of Canada 1935–40.

Bu•chan•an (byo͞o kan′ən, bə-), **James,** 1791–1868, 15th president of the U.S. 1857–61.

Buck (buk), **Pearl (Sydenstricker),** 1892–1973, U.S. novelist: Nobel prize 1938.

Buck•ing•ham (buk′ing əm, -ham′), **1. George Villiers, 1st Duke of,** 1592–1628, English lord high admiral 1617. **2.** his son, **George Villiers, 2nd Duke of,** 1628–87, English courtier and author.

Buck•ner (buk′nər), **1. Simon Bolivar,** 1823–1914, U.S. Confederate general and politician. **2.** his son, **Simon Bolivar, Jr.,** 1886–1945, U.S. general.

Bud•dha (bo͞o′də, bo͝od′ə), (*Prince Siddhāttha* or *Siddhartha*) 566?–c480 B.C., Indian religious leader: founder of Buddhism. Also called **Gautama, Gautama Buddha.**

Bu•dën•ny (bo͞o den′ē), **Semën Mikhailovich,** 1883–1973, Russian general in 1917 revolution and World War II.

Budge (buj), **(John) Donald,** born 1915, U.S. tennis player.

Bu•ell (byo͞o′əl), **Don Carlos,** 1818–98, Union general in the U.S. Civil War.

Buf′falo Bill′, CODY, William Frederick.

Buf•fon (bʏ fôɴ′), **Georges Louis Leclerc, Comte de,** 1707–88, French naturalist.

Bu•kha•rin (bo͞o ᴋʜär′in), **Nikolai Ivanovich,** 1888–1938, Russian editor, writer, and Communist leader.

Bul•finch (bo͝ol′finch′), **1. Charles,** 1763–1844, U.S. architect. **2.** his son, **Thomas,** 1796–1867, U.S. author and mythologist.

Bul•ga•nin (bo͝ol gä′nin, -gan′in), **Nikolai Aleksandrovich,** 1895–1975, Russian political leader: premier of the Soviet Union 1955–58.

Bul•litt (bo͝ol′it), **William C(hristian),** 1891–1967, U.S. diplomat and journalist.

Bü•low (bʏ′lō), **1. Prince Bernhard von,** 1849–1929, chancellor of Germany 1900–09. **2. Hans (Guido, Freiherr) von,** 1830–94, German pianist and conductor.

Bult•mann (bo͝olt′män′), **Rudolf,** 1884–1976, German theologian.

Bul•wer (bo͝ol′wər), **Sir Henry** (*William Henry Lytton Earle Bulwer; Baron Dalling and Bulwer*), 1801–72, British diplomat and author.

Bul•wer-Lyt•ton (bo͝ol′wər lit′n), **1st Baron,** LYTTON, Edward George.

Bunche (bunch), **Ralph (Johnson),** 1904–71, U.S. diplomat, at the United Nations 1946–71: Nobel peace prize 1950.

Bu•nin (bo͞o′nyin), **Ivan Alekseevich,** 1870–1953, Russian poet and novelist: Nobel prize 1933.

Bun•sen (bun′sən), **Robert Wilhelm,** 1811–99, German chemist.

Bu•ñuel (bo͞on wel′), **Luis,** 1900–83, Spanish film director.

Bun•yan (bun′yən), **John,** 1628–88, English preacher: author of *The Pilgrim's Progress.*

Buo•na•par•te (*It.* bwô′nä pär′te), BONAPARTE.

Buo•nar•ro•ti (*It.* bwô′när rô′tē), MICHELANGELO.

Bur•bage (bûr′bij), **Richard,** 1567?–1619, English actor: associate of Shakespeare.

Bur•bank (bûr′bangk′), **Luther,** 1849–1926, U.S. horticulturist and plant breeder.

Bur•bidge (bûr′bij), **(Eleanor) Margaret (Peachey),** born 1919, U.S. astronomer, born in England.

Burch•field (bûrch′fēld′), **Charles Ephraim,** 1893–1967, U.S. painter.

Burck•hardt (bûrk′härt), **Jakob,** 1818–97, Swiss historian.

Bur•ger (bûr′gər), **Warren Earl,** born 1907, U.S. jurist: Chief Justice of the U.S. 1969–86.

Bur•gess (bûr′jis), **1. (Frank) Gelett,** 1866–1951, U.S. illustrator and humorist. **2. Thornton Waldo,** 1874–1965, U.S. author.

Burgh•ley (bûr′lē), **1st Baron,** CECIL, William.

Bur•goyne (bər goin′), **John,** 1722–92, British general: surrendered at Saratoga in the American Revolution.

Burke (bûrk), **1. Billie** (*Mary William Ethelbert Appleton Burke*), 1886–1970, U.S. actress. **2. Edmund,** 1729–97, Irish statesman, orator, and writer.

Bur•leigh (bûr′lē), **1. 1st Baron.** CECIL, William. **2. Henry Thacker,** 1866–1949, U.S. singer: early collector and arranger of spirituals.

Bur•lin•game (bûr′lin gām′, -ling gām′), **Anson** (an′sən), 1820–70, U.S. diplomat.

Burne-Jones (bûrn′jōnz′), **Sir Edward Coley,** 1833–98, English painter and designer.

Bur•net (bər net′, bûr′nit), **Sir (Frank) Macfarlane,** 1899–1985, Australian physician: Nobel prize for physiology 1960.

Bur•nett (bər net′), **1. Carol,** born 1933, U.S. comedienne and actress. **2. Frances Hodgson,** 1849–1924, U.S. novelist, born in England.

Bur•ney (bûr′nē), **1. Charles,** 1726–1814, English organist, composer, and music historian. **2. Fanny** or **Frances** (*Madame D'Arblay*), 1752–1840, English novelist and diarist.

Burns (bûrnz), **1. Arthur F(rank),** born 1904, U.S. economist, born in Austria: chairman of the Federal Reserve Board 1970–78. **2. George** (*Nathan Birnbaum*), born 1896, U.S. comedian (partner and husband of Gracie Allen). **3. Robert,** 1759–96, Scottish poet. **4. Tommy** (*Noah Brusso*), 1881–1955, U.S. boxer: world heavyweight champion 1906–08.

Burn•side (bûrn′sīd′), **Ambrose E.,** 1824–81, Union general in the Civil War.

Burr (bûr), **Aaron,** 1756–1836, vice president of the U.S. 1801–05.

Bur•roughs (bûr′ōz, bur′-), **1. Edgar Rice,** 1875–1950, U.S. novelist. **2. John,** 1837–1921, U.S. naturalist and essayist. **3. William Seward,** 1855–98, U.S. inventor of the adding machine. **4.** his grandson **William S(eward),** born 1914, U.S. novelist.

Burt (bûrt), **William Austin,** 1792–1858, U.S. surveyor and inventor.

Bur•ton (bûr′tn), **1. Harold Hitz,** 1888–1964, associate justice of the U.S. Supreme Court 1945–58. **2. Sir Richard Francis,** 1821–90, English explorer, Orientalist, and writer. **3. Richard** (*Richard Jenkins*), 1925–84, British actor, born in Wales. **4. Robert** (*"Democritus Junior"*), 1577–1640, English clergyman and author.

Busch (bo͝osh), **Fritz** (frits), 1890–1951, German conductor.

Bush (bo͝osh), **1. George (Herbert Walker),** born 1924, vice president of the U.S. 1981–89; 41st president since 1989. **2. Van•ne•var** (və nē′vär, -vər), 1890–1974, U.S. electrical engineer: education and research administrator.

Bush•man (bo͝osh′mən), **Francis X(avier),** 1883–1966, U.S. film actor.

Bush•nell (bo͝osh′nl), **David,** 1742?–1824, U.S. inventor: pioneered in submarine construction.

Bu•so•ni (byo͞o sō′nē, -zô′-), **Ferruccio (Benvenuto),** 1866–1924, Italian composer and pianist.

Bus•ta•man•te (bo͞os′tə män′tā), **1. Anastasio,** 1780–1853, Mexican military and political leader: president 1830–32, 1837–41. **2. Sir (William) Alexander,** 1884–1977, Jamaican political leader: prime minister 1962–67.

Bu•te•nandt (bo͞ot′n änt′), **Adolf Friedrich Johann,** born 1903, German chemist: declined 1939 Nobel prize on the demand of the Nazi government.

But•ler (but′lər), **1. Benjamin Franklin,** 1818–93, U.S. politician and Union general in the Civil War. **2. Joseph,** 1692–1752, English bishop, theologian, and author. **3. Nicholas Murray,** 1862–1947, U.S. educator: president of Columbia University 1902–45; Nobel peace prize 1931. **4. Pierce,** 1866–1939, U.S. jurist: associate justice of the U.S. Supreme Court 1923–39. **5. Samuel,** 1612–80, English poet. **6. Samuel,** 1835–1902, English novelist and satirist.

But•ton (but′n), **Richard Totten,** (*Dick*), born 1929, U.S. figure skater.

Bux•te•hu•de (bo͝ok′stə ho͞o′də), **Dietrich,** 1637–1707, Danish organist and composer, in Germany after 1668.

Byng (bing), **Julian Hedworth George,** (*Viscount Byng of Vimy*), 1862–1935, English general: governor general of Canada 1921–26.

Byrd (bûrd), **1. Richard Evelyn,** 1888–1957, rear admiral in the U.S. Navy: polar explorer. **2. Robert C(arlyle),** born

1917, U.S. politician: senator since 1959. **3. William,** c1540–1623, English composer.

Byrnes (bûrnz), **1. James Francis,** 1879–1972, U.S. statesman and jurist: Secretary of State 1945–47. **2. Joseph Wellington,** 1869–1936, U.S. lawyer: Speaker of the House 1935–36.

C

Ca•ba•llé (kä′bä yā′, -bäl yā′), **Montserrat,** born 1933, Spanish soprano.

Cab•ell (kab′əl), **James Branch,** 1879–1958, U.S. novelist and critic.

Ca•bet (KA be′), **Étienne,** 1788–1856, French socialist who established a utopian community in the U.S.

Ca•be•za de Va•ca (kə bā′zä də vä′kä), **Álvar Núñez,** c1490–1557?, Spanish explorer in the Americas.

Ca•ble (kā′bəl), **George Washington,** 1844–1925, U.S. writer.

Cab•ot (kab′ət), **1. John** (*Giovanni Caboto*), c1450–98?, Italian navigator for England: discoverer of North American mainland 1497. **2.** his son, **Sebastian,** 1474?–1557, English navigator and explorer.

Ca•bral (kə BRÔL′), **Pedro Álvares,** c1460–c1520, Portuguese navigator.

Ca•bri•ni (kə brē′nē), **Saint Frances Xavier** ("*Mother Cabrini*"),1850–1917, U.S. nun, born in Italy; founder of the Missionary Sisters of the Sacred Heart of Jesus.

Cac•ci•ni (kät chē′nē), **Giulio,** c1546–1618, Italian singer and composer.

Cad•il•lac (kad′l ak′; *Fr.* KA dē YAK′), **Antoine de la Mothe** (môt′), 1657?–1730, French colonial governor in North America: founder of Detroit.

Cad•mus (kad′məs), **Paul,** born 1904, U.S. painter and etcher.

Cæd•mon (kad′mən), fl. A.D. c670, Anglo-Saxon religious poet.

Cae•sar (sē′zər), **1. Gaius Julius,** c100–44 B.C., Roman general, statesman, and historian. **2. Sid,** born 1922, U.S. comedian.

Cage (kāj), **John,** born 1912, U.S. composer.

Ca•glios•tro (kal yō′strō), **Count Alessandro di,** (*Giuseppe Balsamo*), 1743–95, Italian adventurer and impostor.

Cag•ney (kag′nē), **James,** 1899–1986, U.S. film actor.

Cain (kān), **James M.,** 1892–1977, U.S. novelist.

Caine (kān), **(Sir Thomas Henry) Hall,** 1853–1931, English novelist.

Ca•ius (kā′əs), **Saint,** died A.D. 296, pope 283–296.

Calam′ity Jane′, (*Martha Jane Canary Burke*) 1852?–1903, U.S. frontier markswoman.

Cal•der (kôl′dər), **Alexander,** 1898–1976, U.S. sculptor; originator of mobiles.

Cal•de•rón de la Bar•ca (käl′də rōn′ del′ə bär′kə), **Pedro,** 1600–81, Spanish dramatist and poet.

Cald•well (kôld′wel, -wəl), **1. Erskine,** born 1903, U.S. novelist. **2. Sarah,** born 1924, U.S. conductor and opera producer.

Cal•houn (kal ho͞on′, kəl-), **John Caldwell,** 1782–1850, vice president of the U.S. 1825–32.

Ca•lig•u•la (kə lig′yə lə), (*Gaius Caesar*), A.D. 12–41, emperor of Rome 37–41.

Cal•ish•er (kal′ə shər), **Hortense,** born 1911, U.S. novelist and short-story writer.

Ca•lix•tus (kə lik′stəs), **1. Calixtus I, Saint,** A.D. c160–222, Italian ecclesiastic: pope 218–222. **2. Calixtus II,** died 1124, French ecclesiastic: pope 1119–24. **3. Calixtus III** (*Alfonso de Borja* or *Alfonso Borgia*), 1378–1458, Spanish ecclesiastic: pope 1455–58.

Cal•la•ghan (kal′ə han′ *or, esp. Brit.*, -hən, -gən), **1. (Leonard) James,** born 1912, British political leader: prime minister 1976–79. **2. Morley Edward,** 1903–90, Canadian novelist.

Cal•las (kal′əs), **Maria Meneghini,** 1923–77, U.S. operatic soprano.

Ca•lles (kä′yes), **Plutarco Elías,** 1877–1945, Mexican general and statesman: president of Mexico 1924–28.

Cal•lic•ra•tes (kə lik′rə tēz′), fl. mid-5th century B.C., Greek architect who together with Ictinus designed the Parthenon.

Cal•lim•a•chus (kə lim′ə kəs), c310–c240 B.C., Greek poet, grammarian, and critic.

Cal•lip•pus (kə lip′əs), fl. 4th century B.C., Greek astronomer.

Cal•lis•the•nes (kə lis′thə nēz′), c360–327 B.C., Greek philosopher: chronicled Alexander the Great's conquests.

Cal•lot (KA lō′), **Jacques,** 1592?–1635, French engraver and etcher.

Cal•lo•way (kal′ə wā′), **Cab(ell),** born 1907, U.S. jazz bandleader and singer.

Cal•pur•ni•a (kal pûr′nē ə), fl. 1st century B.C., third wife of Julius Caesar 59–44.

Cal•vert (kal′vərt), **1. Charles** (*3rd Baron Baltimore*), 1637–1715, English colonial administrator in America: governor (1661–75) and proprietor (1675–89) of Maryland (grandson of George Calvert). **2. Sir George** (*1st Baron Baltimore*), c1580–1632, British founder of the colony of Maryland. **3.** his son, **Leonard,** 1606–47, first colonial governor of Maryland 1634–47.

Cal•vin (kal′vin), **1. John** (*Jean Chauvin* or *Caulvin*), 1509–64, French theologian and reformer in Switzerland: leader in the Protestant Reformation. **2. Melvin,** born 1911, U.S. chemist: Nobel prize 1961.

Cam•by•ses (kam bī′sēz), died 522 B.C., king of Persia 529–522 (son of Cyrus the Great).

Cam•er•on (kam′ər ən, kam′rən), **1. Julia Margaret,** 1815–79, English photographer, born in India. **2. Richard,** 1648?–80, Scottish Covenanter.

Cam•maerts (kä′märts), **Émile,** 1878–1953, Belgian poet.

Cam•o•ëns (kam′ō ens′) also **Ca•mões** (kə moiNSH′), **Luis Vaz de** (väzh), 1524?–80, Portuguese poet.

Camp (kamp), **Walter Chauncey,** 1859–1925, U.S. football coach and author.

Camp•bell (kam′bəl, kam′əl), **1. Alexander,** 1788–1866, U.S. religious leader, born in Ireland: a founder of the Disciples of Christ Church. **2. Colen** or **Colin,** died 1729, Scottish architect and author. **3. Colin** (*Baron Clyde*), 1792–1863, Scottish general. **4. Sir John,** 1779–1861, English jurist and writer: Lord Chancellor of England 1859–61. **5. Sir Malcolm,** 1885–1948, English automobile and speedboat racer. **6. Mrs. Patrick** (*Beatrice Stella Tanner*), 1865–1940, English actress. **7. Thomas,** 1763–1854, Irish religious leader, in the U.S. after 1807: cofounder with his son, Alexander, of the Disciples of Christ Church. **8. Thomas,** 1777–1844, Scottish poet and editor.

Camp′bell-Ban′ner•man (ban′ər mən), **Sir Henry,** 1836–1908, British statesman, born in Ireland: prime minister 1905–08.

Cam•pi•on (kam′pē ən), **Thomas,** 1567–1620, English songwriter and poet.

Ca•mus (KA MY′; *Eng.* ka mōō′), **Albert,** 1913–60, French novelist, playwright, and essayist: Nobel prize 1957.

Ca•na•let•to (kan′l et′ō), **Antonio,** (*Canale*), 1697–1768, Italian painter.

Can•by (kan′bē), **Henry Seidel,** 1878–1961, U.S. author and critic.

Can•dolle (käN dôl′), **Augustin Pyrame de,** 1778–1841, Swiss botanist.

Can•ning (kan′ing), **1. Charles John, 1st Earl,** 1812–62, British statesman: governor general of India 1856–62. **2. George,** 1770–1827, British statesman: prime minister 1827.

Can•niz•za•ro (kan′ə zär′ō), **Stanislao,** 1826–1910, Italian chemist.

Can•non (kan′ən), **1. Annie Jump** (jump), 1863–1941, U.S. astronomer. **2. Joseph Gurney,** (*"Uncle Joe"*), 1836–1926, U.S. legislator.

Ca•non•chet (kə non′chet, -chit), (*Nanuntenoo*), died 1676, Narragansett leader: executed by colonists.

Ca•non•i•cus (kə non′i kəs), c1565–1647, Narragansett leader: yielded Rhode Island to Roger Williams 1636.

Ca•no•va (kə nō′və), **Antonio,** 1757–1822, Italian sculptor.

Can•ro•bert (käN RÔ BER′), **François Certain,** 1809–95, French marshal.

Can•til•lon (käN tē yôN′), **Richard,** c1680–1734, French economist, born in Ireland.

Can•tor (kan′tôr, kän′-), **Ge•org** (gā ôrk′), 1845–1918, German mathematician, born in Russia.

Ca•nute (kə nōōt′, -nyōōt′), A.D. 994?–1035, Danish king of England 1017–35; of Denmark 1018–35; and of Norway 1028–35.

Cao Yu (tsou′ yōō′), (*Wan Jiabao*) born 1910, Chinese playwright.

Cap•a (kap′ə), **Robert** (*Andrei Friedmann*), 1913–54, U.S. photographer, born in Hungary.

Ca•pa•blan•ca (kä′pə bläng′kə), **José Raoul,** 1888–1942, Cuban chess master.

Ča•pek (chä′pek), **Karel,** 1890–1938, Czech playwright, novelist, and producer.

Ca•pet (kā′pit, kap′it, ka pā′), **Hugh** or *Fr.* **Hugues** (yg), A.D. 938?–996, king of France 987–996.

Ca•pone (kə pōn′), **Al(phonse)** ("*Scarface*"), 1899–1947, U.S. gangster and Prohibition-era bootlegger, probably born in Italy.

Ca•po•te (kə pō′tē), **Truman,** 1924–84, U.S. novelist and playwright.

Capp (kap), **Al** (*Alfred Gerald Caplin*), 1909–79, U.S. comic-strip artist: creator of "Li'l Abner."

Cap•ra (kap′rə), **Frank,** 1897–1991, U.S. film director and producer, born in Italy.

Cap′tain Jack′, (*Kintpuash*), 1837?–73, Modoc leader.

Car•a•cal•la (kar′ə kal′ə), (*Marcus Aurelius Antoninus Bassianus*) A.D. 188–217, Roman emperor 211–217.

Ca•rac•ta•cus (kə rak′tə kəs) also **Ca•rat′a•cus** (-rat′ə-kəs), fl. A.D. c50, British chieftain who opposed the Romans. Also called **Ca•rad′oc** (-rad′ək).

Ca•ra•vag•gio (kar′ə vä′jō, kär′ə-), **Michelangelo Merisi da,** c1565–1609?, Italian painter.

Cár•de•nas (kär′dn äs′), **Lázaro,** 1895–1970, president of Mexico 1934–40.

Car•do•zo (kär dō′zō), **Benjamin Nathan,** 1870–1938, associate justice of the U.S. Supreme Court 1932–38.

Car•duc•ci (kär do͞o′chē; *It.* kär do͞ot′chē), **Gio•suè** (jô-swe′), ("*Enotrio Romano*"), 1835–1907, Italian poet and critic: Nobel prize 1906.

Ca•rew (kə ro͞o′; *sometimes* kâr′o͞o), **Thomas,** 1598?–1639?, English poet.

Car•ey (kâr′ē, kar′ē), **George,** born 1935, English clergyman: archbishop of Canterbury since 1991.

Carl XVI Gustaf (kärl), (*Charles XVI Gustavus*) born 1946, king of Sweden since 1973.

Car•lisle (kär līl′, kär′līl), **John Grif•fin** (grif′in), 1835–1910, U.S. politician: Speaker of the House 1883–89.

Car•los (kär′lōs, -ləs), **Don** (*Carlos María Isidro de Borbón*), 1788–1855, pretender to the Spanish throne.

Car′los de Aus′tri•a (dā ous′trē ə), **Don,** 1545–68, eldest son of Philip II of Spain: died during imprisonment for conspiracy against his father.

Car•lo•ta (kär lō′tə, -lot′ə), 1840–1927, wife of Maximilian: empress of Mexico 1864–67.

Carl•son (kärl′sən), **1. Anton Julius,** 1875–1956, U.S. physiologist, born in Sweden. **2. Chester Floyd,** 1906–68, U.S. inventor of xerographic copying process. **3. Evans Fordyce,** 1896–1947, U.S. Marine Corps general in World War II.

Carls•son (kärl′sən), **Ingvar,** born 1934, prime minister of Sweden 1986–91.

Car•lyle (kär līl′), **Thomas,** 1795–1881, Scottish essayist and historian.

Car•man (kär′mən), **(William) Bliss,** 1861–1929, Canadian poet and journalist in the U.S.

Car•mi•chael (kär′mī kəl), **1. Hoagland Howard** (*"Hoagy"*), 1899–1981, U.S. songwriter. **2. Stokely,** born 1941, U.S. civil-rights leader, born in Trinidad.

Car•nap (kär′nap), **Rudolf P.,** 1891–1970, U.S. philosopher, born in Germany.

Car•né (kär nā′), **Marcel,** born 1909, French film director.

Car•ne•a•des (kär nē′ə dēz′), 214?–129? B.C., Greek philosopher.

Car•ne•gie (kär′ni gē, kär nā′gē, -neg′ē), **1. Andrew,** 1835–1919, U.S. steel manufacturer and philanthropist, born in Scotland. **2. Dale,** 1888–1955, U.S. author and teacher of self-improvement techniques.

Car•ney (kär′nē), **Art(hur),** born 1918, U.S. actor.

Car•not (kär nō′), **1. Lazare Nicolas Marguerite,** 1753–1823, French general and statesman. **2. (Ma•rie François) Sa•di** (mə rē′ fran swä′ sad′ē; *Fr.* MA RĒ′ FRÄN SWA′ SA dē′), 1837–94, French statesman: president of the Republic 1887–94. **3. Nicolas Léonard Sadi,** 1796–1832, French physicist.

Car•ol II (kar′əl, kär′-), 1893–1953, king of Romania 1930–40.

Ca•roth•ers (kə ruth′ərz), **Wallace Hume,** 1896–1937, U.S. chemist.

Car•pac•cio (kär pä′chō, -chē ō′), **Vittore,** c1450–1525, Venetian painter.

Car•peaux (kär pō′; *Fr.* KAR pō′), **Jean Baptiste** (zhäN), 1827–75, French sculptor.

Car•pen•ter (kär′pən tər), **1. John Alden,** 1876–1951, U.S. composer. **2. (Malcolm) Scott,** born 1925, U.S. astronaut and oceanographer.

Carr (kär), **John Dickson,** 1906–77, U.S. mystery writer.

Car•rac•ci (kə rä′chē, kär-), **1. Agostino,** 1557–1602, and his brother, **Annibale,** 1560–1609, Italian painters. **2.** their cousin, **Ludovico,** 1555–1619, Italian painter.

Car•ran•za (kə raŋ′zə, -rän′-), **Venustiano,** 1859–1920, Mexican revolutionary and political leader: president 1915–20.

Car•rel (kə rel′, kar′əl), **Alexis,** 1873–1944, French surgeon and biologist, in U.S. 1905–39: Nobel prize 1912.

Car•re•ra (kə râr′ə), **José Miguel de,** 1785–1821, Chilean revolutionary and political leader: dictator 1811–13.

Car•re•ras (kə râr′əs), **José Maria,** born 1946, Spanish tenor.

Car•rère (kə râr′), **John Merven,** 1858–1911, U.S. architect.

Car•roll (kar′əl), **1. Charles,** 1737–1832, American patriot and legislator. **2. Lewis,** pen name of Charles Lutwidge DODGSON.

Car•son (kär′sən), **1. Christopher** (*"Kit"*), 1809–68, U.S. frontiersman and scout. **2. Sir Edward Henry** (*Baron Car-*

son), 1854–1935, Irish public official. **3. Johnny,** born 1925, U.S. television entertainer. **4. Rachel Louise,** 1907–1964, U.S. marine biologist and author.

Carte (kärt), **Richard d'Oyly,** 1844–1901, English theatrical producer.

Car•ter (kär′tər), **1. Bennett Lester** (*Benny*), born 1907, U.S. jazz saxophonist and composer. **2. Don(ald James),** born 1926, U.S. bowler. **3. Elliott (Cook, Jr.),** born 1908, U.S. composer. **4. Hodding,** 1907–72, U.S. journalist and publisher. **5. Howard,** 1873–1939, English Egyptologist. **6. James Earl, Jr.** (*Jimmy*), born 1924, 39th president of the U.S. 1977–81. **7. Mrs. Leslie** (*Caroline Louise Dudley*), 1862–1937, U.S. actress. **8. Maybelle** (*"Mother Maybelle Carter"*), 1909–78, U.S. country-and-western singer and guitarist.

Car•ter•et (kär′tər it), **John, Earl of Granville,** 1690–1763, British statesman and orator.

Car•tier (kär′tē ā′, kär tyā′), **1. Sir George Étienne,** 1814–73, Canadian prime minister 1857–62, defense minister 1867–73. **2. Jacques,** 1491–1557, French navigator: discovered the St. Lawrence River.

Car•tier-Bres•son (kär tyā′ bre sôɴ′), **Henri,** born 1908, French photographer.

Cart•land (kärt′lənd), **Barbara,** born 1904, English novelist.

Cart•wright (kärt′rīt′), **1. Edmund,** 1743–1822, English clergyman: inventor of the power-driven loom. **2.** his brother, **John,** 1740–1824, English parliamentary reformer.

Ca•ru•so (kə ro͞o′sō), **Enrico,** 1873–1921, Italian tenor.

Car•ver (kär′vər), **1. George Washington,** 1864?–1943, U.S. botanist and chemist. **2. John,** 1575?–1621, Pilgrim leader: first governor of Plymouth Colony 1620–21. **3. Raymond,** 1938–88, U.S. poet and short-story writer.

Car•y (kâr′ē, kar′ē), **1. Alice,** 1820–71, U.S. poet (sister of Phoebe Cary). **2. (Arthur) Joyce (Lunel),** 1888–1957, English novelist. **3. Henry Francis,** 1772–1844, British writer and translator. **4. Phoebe,** 1824–71, U.S. poet (sister of Alice Cary).

Ca•sa•bian•ca (kaz′ə byäng′kə), **Louis de,** c1755–98, French naval officer.

Ca•sa•de•sus (kä′sə dā′səs, -dā so͞os′), **Robert,** 1899–1972, French pianist and composer.

Ca•sals (kə sälz′, -salz′), **Pablo,** 1876–1973, Spanish cellist, conductor, and composer.

Cas•a•no•va (kaz′ə nō′və, kas′-), **Giovanni Jacopo,** 1725–98, Italian adventurer and writer.

Ca•sas (kä′säs), **Bartolomé de las,** Las Casas, Bartolomé de.

Ca•sau•bon (kə sô′bən, kaz′ō bôɴ′), **Isaac,** 1559–1614, French classical scholar and theologian.

Case•ment (kās′mənt), **(Sir) Roger (David),** 1864–1916, Irish patriot: hanged by the British for treason.

Cash (kash), **John** (*Johnny*), born 1932, U.S. country-and-western singer, musician, and songwriter.

Cas•lon (kaz′lən), **William,** 1692–1766, English type founder.

Cass (kas), **Lewis,** 1782–1866, U.S. statesman.

Cas•san•der (kə san′dər), c354-297 B.C., king of Macedonia 301-297 (son of Antipater).

Cas•satt (kə sat′), **Mary,** 1845–1926, U.S. painter.

Cas•sa•vet•es (kas′ə vet′ēz), **John,** 1929–89, U.S. actor, director, and screenwriter.

Cas•sin (KA SAN′), **René,** 1887–1976, French diplomat and human-rights advocate: at the United Nations 1946–68; Nobel peace prize 1968.

Cas•si•ni (kə sē′nē, kä-), **Oleg** (*Oleg Cassini-Loiewski*), born 1913, U.S. fashion designer and businessman, born in France.

Cas•si•o•do•rus (kas′ē ə dôr′əs, -dōr′-), **Flavius Magnus Aurelius,** died A.D. 575, Roman statesman and writer.

Cas•si•rer (kä sēr′ər, kə-), **Ernst,** 1874–1945, German philosopher.

Cas•sius Lon•gi•nus (kash′əs lon jī′nəs), **Gaius,** died 42 B.C., Roman general: leader of the conspiracy against Julius Caesar.

Cas•ta•gno (kə stä′nyō), **Andrea del** (*Andrea di Bartolo di Bargilla*), c1423–57, Florentine painter.

Cas•te•lla•nos (kä′stə yä′nōs), **Julio,** 1905–47, Mexican painter.

Cas•tel•nuo•vo-Te•des•co (kä′stəl nwō′vō tə des′kō), **Mario,** 1895–1968, U.S. composer, born in Italy.

Cas•te•lo Bran•co (kä stel′o͞o brän′ko͞o), **Humberto de Alencar,** 1900–67, Brazilian general and statesman: president 1964–67.

Cas•tel•ve•tro (kas′tl ve′trō), **Lodovico,** 1505–71, Italian philologist and literary critic.

Cas•ti•glio•ne (kas′tēl yō′nā), **Baldassare,** 1478–1529, Italian diplomat and author.

Cas•ti•lla (kä stē′yä), **Ramón,** 1797–1867, Peruvian general and statesman: president of Peru 1845–51 and 1855–62.

Cas•ti•llo (kä stēl′yō, -stē′yō), **Antonio** (*Antonio Cánovas del Castillo del Rey*), born 1908, Spanish fashion designer.

Cas•tle (kas′əl, kä′səl), **Irene (Foote),** 1893–1969, born in the U.S., and her husband and partner **Vernon** (*Vernon Castle Blythe*), 1887–1918, born in England, U.S. ballroom dancers.

Cas•tle•reagh (kas′əl rā′, kä′səl-), **Robert Stewart, Viscount** (*2nd Marquess of Londonderry*), 1769–1822, British statesman.

Cas•tro (kas′trō), **1. Cipriano,** 1858?–1924, Venezuelan military and political leader: president 1901–08; exiled 1908. **2. Fidel** (*Fidel Castro Ruz*), born 1927, Cuban revolutionary leader: prime minister 1959–76; president since 1976.

Cath•er (kath′ər; *often* kath′-), **Willa (Sibert),** 1876–1947, U.S. novelist.

Cath•er•ine (kath′ər in, kath′rin), **1. Catherine I,** (*Marfa Skavronskaya*) 1684?–1727, Lithuanian wife of Peter the Great: empress of Russia 1725–27. **2. Catherine II,** (*Sophia Augusta of Anhalt-Zerbst*) (*"Catherine the Great"*) 1729–96, empress of Russia 1762–96.

Cath′erine de Mé•di•cis′ (də mā dē sēs′) also **Cath′erine de′** (or **de**) **Med′i•ci** (də med′i chē), (*Caterina de' Medici*) 1518–89, queen of Henry II of France.

Cath′erine How′ard, 1520?–42, fifth queen of Henry VIII of England.

Cath′erine of Alexan′dria, Saint, A.D. c310, Christian martyr.

Cath′erine of Ar′agon 1485–1536, first wife of Henry VIII of England.

Cath′erine Parr′ (pär), 1512–48, sixth wife of Henry VIII of England.

Cat•i•line (kat′l in′), (*Lucius Sergius Catilina*) 108?–62 B.C., Roman politician and conspirator.

Cat•lin (kat′lin), **George,** 1796–1872, U.S. painter.

Ca•to (kā′tō), **1. Marcus Porcius,** (*"the Elder"* or *"the Censor"*), 234–149 B.C., Roman statesman, soldier, and writer. **2.** his great-grandson, **Marcus Porcius** (*"the Younger"*), 95–46 B.C., Roman statesman, soldier, and Stoic philosopher.

Catt (kat), **Carrie Chapman (Lane),** 1859–1947, U.S. leader in women's suffrage movements.

Cat•tell (kə tel′), **James McKeen,** 1860–1944, U.S. psychologist, educator, and editor.

Cat•ton (kat′n), **(Charles) Bruce,** 1899–1978, U.S. historian.

Ca•tul•lus (kə tul′əs), **Gaius Valerius,** 84?–54? B.C., Roman poet.

Cau•chy (kō shē′), **Augustin Louis,** 1789–1857, French mathematician.

Ca•va•fy (kä vä′fē), **Constantine** (*Konstantinos Kavafis*), 1863–1933, Greek poet in Egypt.

Cav•ell (kav′əl), **Edith Louisa,** 1865–1915, English nurse: executed by the Germans in World War I.

Cav•en•dish (kav′ən dish), **1. Henry,** 1731–1810, English chemist and physicist. **2. William, 4th Duke of Devonshire,** 1720–64, British statesman: prime minister 1756–57.

Cav•ill (kav′əl), **1. Frederick,** 1839–1927, Australian swimmer and coach, born in England: developed the Australian crawl. **2.** his son **Sydney St. Leonards,** died 1945, Australian-American swimmer and coach: developed the butterfly stroke.

Ca•vour (kä vo͝or′), **Camillo Benso di,** 1810–61, Italian statesman.

Cax•ton (kak′stən), **William,** 1422?–91, English printer: established first printing press in England 1476.

Cay•ley (kā′lē), **Arthur,** 1821–95, English mathematician.

Ceau•şes•cu (chou shes′ko͞o), **Nicolae,** 1918–89, Romanian political leader and dictator; president 1967–89.

Cec•il (ses′əl, sis′-), **1. (Edgar Algernon) Robert** (*1st Viscount Cecil of Chelwood*), 1864–1958, British statesman: Nobel peace prize 1937. **2. Robert Arthur Talbot Gascoyne,** SALISBURY. **3. William** (*1st Baron Burghley* or *Burleigh*), 1520–98, British statesman: adviser to Elizabeth I.

Ce•cil•ia (si sēl′yə), **Saint,** died A.D. 230?, Roman martyr: patron saint of music.

Ce•la (the′lä), **Camilo José,** born 1916, Spanish writer.

Cel•es•tine (sel′ə stīn′, si les′tin, -tīn), **1. Celestine I, Saint,** died A.D. 432, Italian ecclesiastic: pope 422–432. **2. Celestine II** (*Guido di Castello*), fl. 12th century, Italian ecclesiastic: pope 1143–44. **3. Celestine III** (*Giacinto Bobone*), died 1198, Italian ecclesiastic: pope 1191–98. **4. Celestine IV** (*Godfrey Castiglione*), died 1241, Italian ecclesiastic: pope 1241. **5. Celestine V, Saint** (*Pietro di Murrone* or *Morone*), 1215–96, Italian ascetic: pope 1294.

Cé•line (sā lēn′), **Louis-Ferdinand,** (*Louis F. Destouches*), 1894–1961, French novelist and physician.

Cel•li•ni (chə lē′nē), **Benvenuto,** 1500–71, Italian metalsmith, sculptor, and autobiographer.

Cen•ci (chen′chē), **Beatrice,** 1577–1599, Italian parricide whose life is the subject of various novels and poems.

Ce•ren•kov or **Che•ren•kov** (chə reng′kôf, -kof, -ren′-), **Pavel A.,** born 1904, Russian physicist: Nobel prize 1958.

Cerf (sûrf), **Bennett (Alfred),** 1898–1971, U.S. book publisher.

Cer•nan (sûr′nən), **Eugene Andrew,** born 1934, U.S. astronaut.

Cer•nu•da (sər no͞o′də, -nyo͞o′-), **Luis,** 1902–63, Spanish poet, in England after 1939.

Cer•van•tes (sər van′tēz, -vän′tās), **Miguel de,** (*Miguel de Cervantes Saavedra*), 1547–1616, Spanish novelist.

Cé•saire (sā zeʀ′), **Aimé Fernand,** born 1913, West Indian poet.

Ces•ti (ches′tē), **Marcantonio,** 1623–69, Italian composer.

Cé•zanne (sā zan′, -zän′), **Paul,** 1839–1906, French painter.

Cha•bri•er (shä′brē ā′), **Alexis Emmanuel,** 1841–94, French composer.

Chad•wick (chad′wik), **1. Florence (May),** born 1918, U.S. long-distance swimmer. **2. George Whitefield,** 1854–1931, U.S. composer. **3. James,** 1891–1974, English physicist: discoverer of the neutron; Nobel prize 1935.

Cha•gall (shə gäl′), **Marc,** 1887–1985, Russian painter in France.

Chai•kov•ski (chī kôf′skē, -kof′-), **Pëtr Ilich,** TCHAIKOVSKY, Pëtr Ilich.

Chain (chān), **Sir Ernst Boris,** 1906–79, English biochemist, born in Germany: Nobel prize for medicine 1945.

Cha•lia•pin (shəl yä′pin), **Fëdor Ivanovich,** 1873–1938, Russian operatic bass.

Chal•mers (chä′mərz, chal′-), **Alexander,** 1759–1834, Scottish biographer, editor, and journalist.

Cham•ber•lain (chām′bər lin), **1. (Arthur) Neville,** 1869–1940, British prime minister 1937–40. **2. Joseph,** 1836–1914, British statesman (father of Sir Austen and Neville Chamberlain). **3. Sir (Joseph) Austen,** 1863–1937, British statesman: Nobel peace prize 1925. **4. Owen,** born 1920, U.S. physicist: Nobel prize 1959. **5. Wilt(on Norman)** (*"Wilt the Stilt"*), born 1936, U.S. basketball player.

Cham•bers (chām′bərz), **1. Robert,** 1802–71, Scottish publisher and editor. **2. Robert William,** 1865–1933, U.S. novelist and illustrator. **3. Whittaker** (*Jay David Chambers*), 1901–61, U.S. journalist, Communist spy, and accuser of Alger Hiss.

Cha•mi•nade (sham′i näd′), **Cécile Louise Stéphanie,** 1857–1944, French pianist and composer.

Cha•mor•ro (chə môr′ō, chä-), **Violeta Barrios de,** born 1929, president of Nicaragua since 1990.

Cham•plain (sham plān′), **Samuel de,** 1567–1635, French explorer: founder of Quebec; first colonial governor 1633–35.

Cham•pol•lion (shän pô lyôn′), **Jean François** (zhän), 1790–1832, French Egyptologist.

Chan•dler (chand′lər, chänd′-), **1. Charles Frederick,** 1836–1925, U.S. scientist, educator, and public-health expert. **2. Raymond (Thornton),** 1888–1959, U.S. writer of detective novels.

Chan•dra•gup•ta (chun′drə gŏŏp′tə), (*Chandragupta Maurya*) died 286? B.C., king of northern India 322?–298 B.C.: founder of the Maurya empire.

Cha•nel (shə nel′, sha-), **Gabrielle,** (*"Coco"*), 1882–1971, French fashion designer.

Cha•ney (chā′nē), **Lon,** 1883–1930, U.S. film actor.

Chang Tso-lin (jäng′ tsō′lin′), 1873–1928, Chinese general: military ruler of Manchuria 1918–28.

Chan•ning (chan′ing), **1. Carol,** born 1923, U.S. actress and singer. **2. William Ellery,** 1780–1842, U.S. Unitarian clergyman and writer.

Chao K'uang-yin (jou′ kwäng′yin′), (*T'ai Tsu*) 927–976 A.D., Chinese emperor 960–976: founder of the Sung dynasty.

Chap•lin (chap′lin), **Sir Charles Spencer** (*Charlie*), 1889–1977, English film actor, producer, and director; in the U.S. 1910–52.

Chap•man (chap′mən), **1. Frank Michler,** 1864–1945, U.S. ornithologist, museum curator, and author. **2. George,** 1559–1634, English poet, dramatist, and translator. **3. John,** APPLESEED, Johnny.

Char (shär), **René,** born 1907, French poet.

Char•cot (shär kō′), **1. Jean Baptiste Étienne Auguste**

(zhäN), 1867–1936, French explorer. **2. Jean Martin** (zhäN), 1825–93, French neuropathologist.

Char•din (SHAR daN′), **1. Jean Baptiste Siméon** (zhäN), 1699–1779, French painter. **2. Pierre Teilhard de,** TEILHARD DE CHARDIN, Pierre.

Char•don•net (shär′dn ā′; *Fr.* SHAR dô ne′), **Hilaire Bernigaud, Comte de,** 1839–1924, French chemist and inventor.

Char•le•magne (shär′lə mān′), (*"Charles the Great"*) A.D. 742–814, king of the Franks 768–814; as Charles I, first emperor of the Holy Roman Empire 800–814.

Charles[1] (chärlz), **1.** (*Prince of Edinburgh and of Wales*) born 1948, heir apparent to the throne of Great Britain (son of Elizabeth II). **2. Ray,** born 1930, U.S. singer and songwriter.

Charles[2] (chärlz), **1. Charles I, a.** CHARLEMAGNE. **b.** (*"the Bald"*) A.D. 823–877, king of France 840–877; as Charles II, emperor of the Holy Roman Empire 875–877. **c.** 1500–58, king of Spain 1516–56; as Charles V, emperor of the Holy Roman Empire 1519–56. **d.** 1600–49, king of England, Scotland, and Ireland 1625–49 (son of James I). **e.** 1887–1922, emperor of Austria 1916–18; as Charles IV, king of Hungary 1916–18. **2. Charles II, a.** CHARLES I (def. 1b). **b.** 1630–85, king of England, Scotland, and Ireland 1660–85 (son of Charles I). **3. Charles IV, a.** (*"Charles the Fair"*) 1294–1328, king of France 1322–28. **b.** (*Charles of Luxembourg*) 1316–78, king of Germany 1347–78 and Bohemia 1346–78; emperor of the Holy Roman Empire 1355–78. **c.** CHARLES I (def. 1e). **4. Charles V, a.** (*"Charles the Wise"*) 1337–81, king of France 1364–80. **b.** CHARLES I (def. 1c). **5. Charles VI** (*"Charles the Mad"* or *"Charles the Well-beloved"*), 1368–1422, king of France 1380–1422. **6. Charles VII** (*"Charles the Victorious"*), 1403–61, king of France 1422–61 (son of Charles VI). **7. Charles IX,** 1550–74, king of France 1560–74. **8. Charles X,** 1757–1836, king of France 1824–30. **9. Charles XIV,** BERNADOTTE, Jean Baptiste Jules.

Charles′ Ed′ward Stu′art, STUART, Charles Edward.

Charles′ Lou′is, (*Karl Ludwig Johann*) 1771–1847, archduke of Austria.

Charles′ Mar•tel′ (mär tel′), *n.* A.D. 690?–741, ruler of the Franks 714–741 (grandfather of Charlemagne).

Charles′ the Great′, CHARLEMAGNE.

Char•lot (shär′lō; *Fr.* SHAR lō′), **Jean** (zhäN), born 1898, U.S. painter, lithographer, and illustrator; born in France.

Char•pen•tier (shär′päN tyā′), **1. Gustave,** 1860–1956, French composer. **2. Marc Antoine,** 1634–1704, French composer.

Chase (chās), **1. Mary Ellen,** 1887–1973, U.S. educator, novelist, and essayist. **2. Sal•mon Portland** (sal′mən), 1808–73, Chief Justice of the U.S. 1864–73. **3. Samuel,** 1741–1811, U.S. jurist and leader in the American Revolution. **4. Stuart,** 1888–1985, U.S. economist and writer.

Chasles (shäl), **Mi•chel** (mē shel′), 1793–1880, French mathematician.

Châ•teau•bri•and (sha tō′brē äN′), **1. François René, Vicomte de,** 1768–1848, French author and statesman. **2. Vicomte de,** 1768–1848, French author and statesman.

Chat•ham (chat′əm), **1st Earl of,** PITT, William, 1st Earl of Chatham.

Cha•tri•an (sha′trē äN′), **Alexandre,** ERCKMANN-CHATRIAN.

Chat•ter•ji or **Chat•ter•jee** (chä′tər jē), **Bankim Chandra,** 1838–94, Indian novelist in the Bengali language.

Chat•ter•ton (chat′ər tən), **Thomas,** 1752–70, English poet.

Chau•cer (chô′sər), **Geoffrey,** 1340?–1400, English poet.

Chaus•son (shō sôN′), **Ernest,** 1855–99, French composer.

Chau•temps (shō täN′), **Camille,** 1885–1963, French politician: premier 1930, 1933–34, 1937–38.

Cha•vannes (shA VAN′), **Puvis de,** PUVIS DE CHAVANNES, Pierre.

Cha•vez (chä′vez, -ves *or, for 2,* shä′-, shə vez′), **1. Carlos,** 1899–1978, Mexican composer and conductor. **2. Cesar (Estrada),** born 1927, U.S. labor leader: organizer of migrant farmworkers.

Chay•ef•sky (chī ef′skē), **Paddy,** 1923–1981, U.S. playwright and director.

Chee•ver (chē′vər), **John,** 1912–82, U.S. novelist and short-story writer.

Che•khov (chek′ôf, -of), **Anton (Pavlovich),** 1860–1904, Russian dramatist and short-story writer.

Chen Du•xiu (jun′ do͞o′shyo͞o′), 1879–1942, Chinese intellectual, journalist, and cofounder of the Chinese Communist party.

Che•ney (chā′nē), **Richard,** born 1940, Secretary of Defense since 1989.

Ch'eng Tsu (chung′ dzo͞o′) also **Cheng Zu** (zo͞o′), YUNG LO.

Ché•nier (shā nyā′), **André Marie de,** 1762–94, French poet.

Chen•nault (shə nôlt′), **Claire Lee,** 1890–1958, U.S. Air Force general.

Che•ops (kē′ops), fl. early 26th century B.C., king of Egypt: builder of the great pyramid at Giza. Also called **Khufu.**

Cheph•ren (kef′rən), KHAFRE.

Che•ren•kov (chə reng′kôf, -kof, -ren′-), **Pavel A.,** CERENKOV, Pavel A.

Che•ru•bi•ni (ker′o͝o bē′nē), **Maria Luigi Carlo Zenobio Salvatore,** 1760–1842, Italian composer, esp. of opera.

Ches•nutt (ches′nət, -nut), **Charles Wad•dell** (wo del′), 1858–1932, U.S. short-story writer and novelist.

Ches•ter•field (ches′tər fēld′), **Philip Dormer Stanhope, 4th Earl of,** 1694–1773, British statesman and author.

Ches•ter•ton (ches′tər tən), **G(ilbert) K(eith),** 1874–1936, English essayist, critic, and novelist.

Che•va•lier (shə val′yā, -väl′-; *Fr.* shə VA lyā′), **Maurice (Auguste),** 1888–1972, French actor and singer.

Chey•ne (chā′nē, chān), **Thomas Kelly,** 1841–1915, English clergyman and Biblical scholar.

Chiang Ching-kuo (jyäng′ jing′gwô′), 1910–88, Chinese political leader: president of the Republic of China 1978–88 (son of Chiang Kai-shek).

Chiang Kai-shek (chang′ kī shek′, jyäng′), (*Chiang Chung-cheng*) 1886?–1975, president of the Republic of China 1950–75.

Ch'ien Lung (chyen′ lŏŏng′), (*Kao Tsung*) 1711–99, Chinese emperor of the Ch'ing dynasty 1736–96.

Chif•ley (chif′lē), **Joseph Benedict,** 1885–1951, Australian statesman: prime minister 1945–49.

Chi•ka•ma•tsu (chē′kä mä′tsōō), **Mon•za•e•mon** (môn′-zä e môn′), 1653–1724, Japanese playwright.

Child (chīld), **1. Julia** (*Julia McWilliams*), born 1912, U.S. cookbook author. **2. Lydia Maria (Francis),** 1802–80, U.S. author, abolitionist, and social reformer.

Childe (chīld), **Vere Gordon** (vēr), 1892–1957, English anthropologist, archaeologist, and writer; born in Australia.

Chi•lon (kī′lon) also **Chi′lo** (-lō), fl. 556 B.C., Greek sage and ephor at Sparta.

Chip•pen•dale (chip′ən dāl′), **Thomas,** 1718?–79, English cabinetmaker and furniture designer.

Chi•rac (shē RäK′), **Jacques (René),** born 1932, French political leader: prime minister 1986–88.

Chi•ri•co (kēr′i kō′), **Giorgio de,** 1888–1978, Italian painter.

Chis•holm (chiz′əm), **Shirley (Anita St. Hill),** born 1924, first black woman elected to the U.S. House of Representatives 1969–83.

Ch'iu Ch'u-chi (chyōō′ chōō′jē′), (*Ch'ang Ch'un*) 1148–1227, Chinese Taoist philosopher and author.

Chlod•wig (klōt′VIKH), German name of CLOVIS I.

Choate (chōt), **1. Joseph Hodges,** 1832–1917, U.S. lawyer and diplomat. **2. Rufus,** 1799–1859, U.S. lawyer and orator.

Chom•sky (chom′skē), **(Avram) Noam,** born 1928, U.S. linguist and political writer.

Cho•pin (shō′pan; *also Fr.* shō PAN′ *for 1*), **1. Frédéric François,** 1810–49, Polish composer and pianist, in France after 1831. **2. Kate O'Flaherty,** 1851–1904, U.S. short-story writer and novelist.

Chou En-lai (jō′ en′lī′), ZHOU ENLAI.

Chré•tien de Troyes or **Chres•tien de Troyes** (KRā-tyaN′ də TRWä′), fl. 1160–90, French poet.

Chris•tian (kris′chən), **1. Christian IX,** 1818–1906, king of Denmark 1863–1906. **2. Christian X,** 1870–1947, king of Denmark 1912–47.

Chris•tie (kris′tē), **Agatha,** 1891–1976, English writer of detective fiction.

Chris•ti•na (kri stē′nə), 1626–89, queen of Sweden 1632–54.

Chris•tophe (krē stôf′), **Henri** (*"Henri I"*), 1767–1820, Haitian revolutionary general: king 1811–20.

Chris•to•pher (kris′tə fər), **Saint,** died A.D. c250, Christian martyr.

Chris•ty (kris′tē), **1. Edwin P.,** 1815–62, U.S. minstrel-show performer and producer. **2. Howard Chandler,** 1873–1952, U.S. artist.

Chry•sip•pus (krī sip′əs, kri-), 280–209? B.C., Greek Stoic philosopher.

Chrys•ler (krīs′lər), **Walter Percy,** 1875–1940, U.S. automobile manufacturer.

Chrys•os•tom (kris′ə stəm, kri sos′təm), **Saint John,** A.D. 347?–407, ecumenical patriarch of Constantinople.

Chuang-tzu or **Chwang-tse** (jwäng′dzu′), fl. 4th century B.C., Chinese mystic and philosopher.

Chu Hsi (jo͞o′ shē′), 1130–1200, Chinese philosopher.

Chun Doo Hwan (jœn′ dō′ hwän′), born 1931, South Korean political leader: president 1980–88.

Church (chûrch), **Frederick Edwin,** 1826–1900, U.S. painter: a member of the Hudson River school of landscape painting.

Church•ill (chûr′chil, -chəl), **1. John, 1st Duke of Marlborough,** (*"Corporal John"*), 1650–1722, British military commander. **2. Lord Randolph (Henry Spencer),** 1849–95, British statesman (father of Winston L. S. Churchill). **3. Winston,** 1871–1947, U.S. novelist. **4. Sir Winston (Leonard Spencer),** 1874–1965, British statesman and author: prime minister 1940–45, 1951–55; Nobel prize for literature 1953.

Ch'ü Yüan (chʏ′ yʏän′), 343–289 B.C., Chinese poet: author of the *Li-sao.*

Cia•no (chä′nō, -nô), **Count Galeazzo** (*Ciano di Cortellazzo*), 1903–44, Italian Fascist statesman: minister of foreign affairs 1936–43.

Ciar•di (chär′dē), **John,** 1916–86, U.S. poet.

Cib•ber (sib′ər), **Colley,** 1671–1757, English actor and dramatist: poet laureate 1730–57.

Cic•e•ro (sis′ə rō′), **Marcus Tullius,** (*"Tully"*), 106–43 B.C., Roman statesman, orator, and writer.

Cid (sid), **The,** (*"El Cid Campeador"*) (*Rodrigo Díaz de Bivar*), c1040–99, Spanish soldier: hero of the wars against the Moors.

Ci•ma•bu•e (chē′mə bo͞o′ā), **Giovanni,** (*Cenni di Pepo*), c1240–1302?, Italian painter and mosaicist.

Ci•ma•ro•sa (chē′mə rō′zə), **Domenico,** 1749–1801, Italian conductor and composer.

Ci•mon (sī′mən), c. 510–450 B.C., Athenian military leader, naval commander, and statesman (son of Miltiades).

Cin•cin•na•tus (sin′sə nā′təs, -nat′əs), **Lucius Quinctius,** 519?–439? B.C., Roman general and statesman.

Clair (klâr), **René,** 1898–1981, French motion-picture director and writer.

Clai•raut (klâ rō′), **Alexis Claude,** 1713–65, French mathematician.

Claire (klâr), **Ina,** 1892–1985, U.S. actress.

Clar•en•don (klar′ən dən), **Edward Hyde, 1st Earl of,** 1609–74, British statesman and historian.

Clare′ (or **Clar′a**) **of As•si′si** (klâr *or* klar′ə; ə sē′zē), **Saint,** 1194–1253, Italian nun: founder of the Franciscan order of nuns.

Clark (klärk), **1. Alvan,** 1804–87, and his son **Alvan Graham,** 1832–97, U.S. astronomers and telescope-lens manufacturers. **2. Champ** (*James Beauchamp*), 1850–1921, U.S. political leader: Speaker of the House 1911–19. **3. (Charles) Joseph** (*Joe*), born 1939, Canadian political leader: prime minister 1979–80. **4. George Rogers,** 1752–1818, U.S. soldier. **5. John Bates,** 1847–1938, U.S. economist and educator. **6. Kenneth B(ancroft),** born 1914, U.S. psychologist, born in the Panama Canal Zone. **7. Mark Wayne,** 1896–1984, U.S. general. **8. Thomas Campbell** (*Tom*), 1899–1977, associate justice of the U.S. Supreme Court 1949–67. **9. Walter Van Tilburg,** 1909–71, U.S. author. **10. William,** 1770–1838, U.S. explorer: on expedition with Meriwether Lewis.

Clarke (klärk), **Arthur C(harles),** born 1917, English science-fiction writer.

Claude (klôd; *Fr.* klōd), **Albert,** 1899–1983, U.S. biologist, born in Belgium: Nobel prize for medicine 1974.

Clau•del (klō del′), **Paul (Louis Charles),** 1868–1955, French diplomat, poet, and dramatist.

Claude Lor•rain (klōd lô RAN′), (*Claude Gellée*), 1600–82, French painter.

Clau•di•us (klô′dē əs), **1. Claudius I,** 10 B.C.–A.D. 54, Roman emperor A.D. 41–54. **2. Claudius II,** (*"Gothicus"*) A.D. 214–270, Roman emperor 268–270.

Clau•se•witz (klou′zə vits), **Karl von,** 1780–1831, German military officer and author of books on military science.

Clau•si•us (klou′zē əs), **Rudolf Julius Emanuel,** 1822–88, German mathematical physicist: pioneer in the field of thermodynamics.

Clay (klā), **1. Bertha M.** (*Charlotte Monica Braeme*), 1836–84, English author: originator of a long series of romantic novels. **2. Cassius Marcellus,** 1810–1903, U.S. antislavery leader. **3. Cassius Marcellus, Jr.,** original name of Muhammad ALI. **4. Henry,** 1777–1852, U.S. statesman and orator. **5. Lucius (DuBignon),** 1897–1978, U.S. general.

Clay•ton (klāt′n), **John Middleton,** 1796–1856, U.S. jurist and politician: senator 1829–36, 1845–49, 1853–56; Secretary of State 1849–50.

Cle•an•thes (klē an′thēz), c300–232? B.C., Greek Stoic philosopher.

Cle•ar•chus (klē är′kəs), died 401 B.C., Spartan general.

Cleis•the•nes (klīs′thə nēz′), active c515–c495 B.C., Athenian statesman.

Cle•men•ceau (klem′ən sō′; *Fr.* kle mäN sō′), **Georges Eugène Benjamin,** 1841–1929, French premier 1906–09, 1917–20.

Clem•ens (klem′ənz), **Samuel Langhorne,** ("*Mark Twain*"), 1835–1910, U.S. author and humorist.

Clem•ent (klem′ənt), **1. Clement I, Saint** (*Clement of Rome*), A.D. c30–c100, first of the Apostolic Fathers: pope 88?–97? **2. Clement II** (*Suidger*), died 1047, pope 1046–47. **3. Clement III** (*Paolo Scolari*), died 1191, Italian ecclesiastic: pope 1187–91. **4. Clement IV** (*Guy Foulques*), died 1268, French ecclesiastic: pope 1265–68. **5. Clement V** (*Bertrand de Got*), 1264–1314, French ecclesiastic: pope 1305–14. **6. Clement VI** (*Pierre Roger*), 1291–1352, French ecclesiastic: pope 1342–52. **7. Clement VII** (*Giulio de' Medici*), 1478–1534, Italian ecclesiastic: pope 1523–34. **8. Clement VIII** (*Ippolito Aldobrandini*), 1536–1605, Italian ecclesiastic: pope 1592–1605. **9. Clement IX** (*Giulio Rospigliosi*), 1600–69, Italian ecclesiastic: pope 1667–69. **10. Clement X** (*Emilio Altieri*), 1590–1676, Italian ecclesiastic: pope 1670–76. **11. Clement XI** (*Giovanni Francesco Albani*), 1649–1721, Italian ecclesiastic: pope 1700–21. **12. Clement XII** (*Lorenzo Corsini*), 1652–1740, Italian ecclesiastic: pope 1730–40. **13. Clement XIII** (*Carlo della Torre Rezzonico*), 1693–1769, Italian ecclesiastic: pope 1758–69. **14. Clement XIV** (*Giovanni Vincenzo Antonio Ganganelli* or *Lorenzo Ganganelli*), 1705–74, Italian ecclesiastic: pope 1769–74.

Cle•men•ti (klə men′tē), **Muzio,** 1752–1832, Italian pianist and composer in England.

Clem′ent of Alexan′dria, *(Titus Flavius Clemens)* A.D. c150–c215, Greek Christian theologian and writer.

Cle•o•bu•lus (klē′ō byo͞o′ləs, klē′ə-, klē ob′yə ləs), fl. 560 B.C., Greek sage and lyric poet, a native and tyrant of Lindus, Rhodes.

Cle•om•e•nes III (klē om′ə nēz′), died c220 B.C., king of Sparta c235–c220.

Cle•on (klē′on), died 422 B.C., Athenian general and political opponent of Pericles.

Cle•o•pa•tra (klē′ə pa′trə, -pä′-, -pā′-), 69–30 B.C., queen of Egypt 51–49, 48–30.

Clerc (klâr), **Laurent,** 1785–1869, French educator of the deaf, in the U.S. after 1816.

Cle•tus (klē′təs), ANACLETUS.

Cle•ve (klā′və), **Per Teodor,** 1840–1905, Swedish chemist.

Cleve•land (klēv′lənd), **(Stephen) Grover,** 1837–1908, 22nd and 24th president of the U.S. 1885–89, 1893–97.

Cli•burn (klī′bərn), **Van,** (*Harvey Lavan Cliburn, Jr.*), born 1934, U.S. pianist.

Clif•ford (klif′ərd), **William Kingdon,** 1845–79, English mathematician and philosopher.

Clin•ton (klin′tn), **1. De Witt,** 1769–1828, U.S. statesman. **2. George,** 1739–1812, vice president of the U.S. 1805–12. **3. Sir Henry,** 1738?–95, commander of the British forces in the American Revolutionary War. **4. James,** 1733–1812, American general in the Revolutionary War (brother of George Clinton). **5. William Jefferson** (*Bill*), born 1946, U.S. politician: governor of Arkansas 1979–81 and since 1983.

Clive (klīv), **Robert** (*Baron Clive of Plassey*), 1725–74, British general and statesman in India.

Cloe•te (klo͞o′tē), **Stuart,** 1897–1976, South African novelist, born in France.

Cloots (klōts), **Jean Baptiste du Val-de-Grâce, Baron de** (*"Anacharsis Clootz"*), 1755–94, Prussian leader in the French Revolution.

Clough (kluf), **Arthur Hugh,** 1819–61, English poet.

Clo•vis I (klō′vis), A.D. c465–511, king of the Franks 481–511. German, **Chlodwig.**

Clur•man (klûr′mən), **Harold (Edgar),** 1901–80, U.S. theatrical director, author, and critic.

Cnut (kə no͞ot′, -nyo͞ot′), CANUTE.

Co•an•da (kō äɴ dä′), **Henri Marie,** 1885–1972, French engineer and inventor.

Coates (kōts), **1. Eric,** 1886–1957, English violist and composer. **2. Joseph Gordon,** 1878–1943, New Zealand statesman: prime minister 1925–28.

Coats•worth (kōts′wûrth′), **Elizabeth,** 1893–1986, U.S. writer, esp. of children's books.

Cobb (kob), **1. Howell,** 1815–68, U.S. politician: Speaker of the House 1849–51. **2. Irvin S(hrewsbury),** 1876–1944, U.S. humorist and writer. **3. Ty(rus Raymond)** (*"the Georgia Peach"*), 1886–1961, U.S. baseball player.

Cob•bett (kob′it), **William** (*"Peter Porcupine"*), 1763–1835, English political essayist and journalist.

Cob•den (kob′dən), **Richard,** 1804–65, English merchant, economist, and statesman.

Cob•ham (kob′əm), **Sir John,** OLDCASTLE, Sir John.

Co•chise (kō chēs′), c1815–74, a chief of the Apaches.

Coch•ran (kok′rən), **Jacqueline,** 1910?–80, U.S. aviator.

Cock•croft (kok′krôft, -kroft), **Sir John Douglas,** 1897–1967, English physicist: Nobel prize 1951.

Coc•teau (kok tō′), **Jean** (zhäɴ), 1889–1963, French author and painter.

Co•dy (kō′dē), **William Frederick** (*"Buffalo Bill"*), 1846–1917, U.S. Army scout and showman.

Coeur de Li•on (kûr′ də lē′ən; *Fr.* kœʀ də lyôɴ′), RICHARD (def. 1).

Cof•fin (kô′fin, kof′in), **1. Levi,** 1798–1877, U.S. abolitionist leader. **2. Robert P(eter) Tristram,** 1892–1955, U.S. poet, essayist, and biographer.

Cog•gan (kog′ən), **(Frederick) Donald,** born 1909, English clergyman: archbishop of Canterbury 1974–80.

Co•han (kō han′, kō′han), **George M(ichael),** 1878–1942, U.S. actor, playwright, and songwriter.

Co•hen (kō′ən), **1. Morris Raphael,** 1880–1947, U.S. philosopher and educator, born in Russia. **2. Octavus Roy,** 1891–1959, U.S. short-story writer and novelist.

Cohn (kōn), **1. Edwin Joseph,** 1892–1953, U.S. chemist and researcher on blood proteins. **2. Ferdinand Julius,** 1828–98, German botanist and bacteriologist.

Coke (ko͝ok), **Sir Edward,** 1552–1634, English jurist.

Col•bert (kôl ʙᴇʀ′), **Jean Baptiste** (zhäɴ), 1619–83, French statesman and finance minister under Louis XIV.

Col•den (kōl′dən), **Cadwallader,** 1688–1776, Scottish physician, botanist, and public official in America, born in Ireland.

Cole (kōl), **1. Nat "King"** (*Nathaniel Adams Coles*), 1919–65, U.S. singer and pianist. **2. Thomas,** 1801–48, U.S. painter, born in England.

Cole•man (kōl′mən), **Ornette,** born 1930, U.S. jazz saxophonist and composer.

Cole•ridge (kōl′rij, kō′lə-), **Samuel Taylor,** 1772–1834, English poet, critic, and philosopher.

Cole•ridge-Tay•lor (kōl′rij tā′lər), **Samuel,** 1875–1912, English composer.

Col•et (kol′it), **John,** 1467?–1519, English educator and clergyman.

Co•lette (kō let′, kô-, kə-), (*Sidonie Gabrielle Claudine Colette*) 1873–1954, French author.

Col•fax (kōl′faks), **Schuyler,** 1823–85, U.S. political leader: vice president of the U.S. 1869–73.

Co•li•gny (kô lē nyē′), **Gaspard de,** 1519–72, French admiral and Huguenot leader.

Col•lier (kol′yər), **Jeremy,** 1650–1726, English clergyman and author.

Col•lins (kol′inz), **1. Edward Trowbridge** (*Eddie*), 1887–1951, U.S. baseball player. **2. Michael,** 1890–1922, Irish revolutionist and patriot. **3. Michael,** born 1930, U.S. astronaut. **4. William,** 1721–59, English poet. **5. (William) Wilkie,** 1824–89, English novelist.

Col•lo•di (kə lō′dē; *It.* kôl lô′dē), **Carlo** (*Carlo Lorenzini*), 1826–90, Italian writer: creator of the story of Pinocchio.

Col•lor de Mel•lo (kol′ər də mel′ō), **Fernando,** born 1949, president of Brazil since 1990.

Colt (kōlt), **Samuel,** 1814–62, U.S. inventor of the Colt revolver.

Col•trane (kōl′trān), **John (William),** 1926–67, U.S. jazz saxophonist and composer.

Col•um (kol′əm), **Pa•draic** (pô′drik), 1881–1972, Irish poet and dramatist, in the U.S. from 1914.

Co•lum•ba (kə lum′bə), **Saint,** A.D. 521–597, Irish missionary in Scotland.

Co•lum•bus (kə lum′bəs), **Christopher** (Sp. *Cristóbal Colón;* It. *Cristoforo Colombo*), 1446?–1506, Italian navigator in Spanish service: traditionally considered the discoverer of America 1492.

Co•ma•neci (kō′mə nēch′; *Rom.* kô′mä nech′), **Nadia,** born 1961, Romanian gymnast.

Co•me•ni•us (kə mē′nē əs), **John Amos** (*Jan Amos Komenský*), 1592–1670, Moravian educational reformer and bishop.

Co•mines or **Com•mines** (kô mēn′), **Philippe de,** 1445?–1511?, French historian and diplomat.

Com•ma•ger (kom′ə jər), **Henry Steele,** born 1902, U.S. historian, author, and teacher.

Com•mo•dus (kom′ə dəs), **Lucius Aelius Aurelius,** A.D. 161–192, Roman emperor 180–192 (son of Marcus Aurelius).

Com•ne•nus (kom nē′nəs), a dynasty of Byzantine emperors that ruled at Constantinople, 1057?–1185, and at Trebizond in Asia Minor, 1204–1461?.

Comp•ton (komp′tən), **1. Arthur Holly,** 1892–1962, U.S. physicist: Nobel prize 1927. **2.** his brother, **Karl Taylor** (kärl), 1887–1954, U.S. physicist. **3. Spencer, Earl of Wilmington,** 1673?–1743, British statesman: prime minister 1742–43.

Com•stock (kum′stok, kom′-), **Anthony,** 1844–1915, U.S. reformer.

Comte (kôɴt), **(Isidore) Auguste (Marie François),** 1798–1857, French founder of philosophical positivism.

Co•nant (kō′nənt), **James Bryant,** 1893–1978, U.S. chemist and educator.

Con•dé (kôɴ dā′), **Louis II de Bourbon, Prince de,** (*Duc d'Enghien*) (*"the Great Condé"*) 1621–86, French general.

Con•dil•lac (kôɴ dē yak′), **Étienne Bonnot de,** 1715–80, French philosopher.

Con•don (kon′dən), **Edward Uhler,** 1902–74, U.S. physicist.

Con•dor•cet (kôɴ dôʀ se′), **Marie Jean Antoine Nicolas Caritat, Marquis de,** 1743–94, French mathematician and philosopher.

Con•fu•cius (kən fyo͞o′shəs), 551?–478? B.C., Chinese philosopher and teacher. Chinese, **K'ung Fu-tzu.**

Con•greve (kon′grēv, kong′-), **1. William,** 1670–1729, English dramatist. **2. Sir William,** 1772–1828, English engineer and inventor.

Conk•ling (kong′kling), **Roscoe,** 1829–88, U.S. lawyer and politician: senator 1867–81.

Con•nel•ly (kon′l ē), **Marc(us Cook),** 1890–1980, U.S. dramatist.

Con•ner•y (kon′ə rē), **Sean** (*Thomas Connery*), born 1930, Scottish actor.

Con•nol•ly (kon′l ē), **Maureen** (*Maureen Catherine Connolly Brinker*) (*"Little Mo"*), 1934–69, U.S. tennis player.

Con•nor (kon′ər), **Ralph** (*Charles William Gordon*), 1860–1937, Canadian novelist and clergyman.

Co•non (kō′non), died A.D. 687, pope 686–687.

Con•rad[1] (kon′rad), **1. Charles, Jr.,** born 1930, U.S. astronaut. **2. Joseph** (*Teodor Jozef Konrad Korzeniowski*), 1857–1924, English novelist, born in Poland.

Con•rad[2] (kon′rad), **1. Conrad I,** died A.D. 918, king of Germany 911–918. **2. Conrad II,** c990–1039, king of

Germany 1024–39 and emperor of the Holy Roman Empire 1027–39. **3. Conrad III,** 1093–1152, king of Germany 1138–52; uncrowned emperor of the Holy Roman Empire: founder of the Hohenstaufen dynasty. **4. Conrad IV,** 1228–54, king of Germany 1237–54 and Sicily 1251–54; uncrowned emperor of the Holy Roman Empire (son of Frederick II).

Con•sta•ble (kun′stə bəl, kon′-), **John,** 1776–1837, English painter.

Con•stans I (kon′stanz), (*Flavius Julius Constans*) A.D. c323–350, emperor of Rome 337–350 (son of Constantine I).

Con•stant (kôɴ stäɴ′), **Jean Joseph Benjamin,** 1845–1902, French painter.

Con•stant de Re•becque (kôɴ stäɴ′ də ʀə bek′), **Henri Benjamin** (*Benjamin Constant*), 1767–1830, French statesman and author, born in Switzerland.

Con•stan•tine (kon′stən tēn′, -tīn′), **1. Constantine I, a.** (*Flavius Valerius Aurelius Constantinus*) (*"the Great"*), A.D. 288?–337, Roman emperor 324–337: named Constantinople as the new capital, legally sanctioned Christian worship. **b.** 1868–1923, king of Greece 1913–17, 1920–22. **2. Constantine II, a.** (*Flavius Claudius Constantinus*), A.D. 317–40, emperor of Rome 337–40 (son of Constantine I). **b.** born 1940, king of Greece 1964–74.

Constantine XI Pa•lae•ol•o•gus (pā′lē ol′ə gəs, pal′-ē-), (*Dragases*), 1404–53, last Byzantine emperor 1449–53.

Con•verse (kon′vûrs), **Frederick Shepherd,** 1871–1940, U.S. composer.

Con•way (kon′wā), **Thomas,** 1735–1800?, Irish soldier of fortune in America and India.

Cook (ko͝ok), **1. Frederick Albert,** 1865–1940, U.S. physician and polar explorer. **2. Captain James,** 1728–79, English explorer of the S Pacific, Antarctica, and the coasts of Australia and New Zealand. **3. Sir Joseph,** 1860–1947, Australian statesman, born in England: prime minister 1913–14.

Cooke (ko͝ok), **1. Jay,** 1821–1905, U.S. financier. **2. Terence (James), Cardinal,** 1921–83, U.S. Roman Catholic clergyman: archbishop of New York 1968–83.

Coo•ley (ko͞o′lē), **Charles Horton,** 1864–1929, U.S. author and pioneer in the field of sociology.

Cool•idge (ko͞o′lij), **Calvin,** 1872–1933, 30th president of the U.S. 1923–29.

Coo•per (ko͞o′pər, ko͝op′ər), **1. Gary** (*Frank James Cooper*), 1901–61, U.S. actor. **2. James Fenimore,** 1789–1851, U.S. novelist. **3. Leon N.,** born 1930, U.S. physicist: Nobel prize 1972. **4. Peter,** 1791–1883, U.S. inventor and philanthropist.

Co•per•ni•cus (kō pûr′ni kəs, kə-), **Nicolaus** (*Mikołaj Kopernik*), 1473–1543, Polish astronomer who promulgated the theory that the earth and the other planets move around the sun.

Cop•land (kōp′lənd), **Aaron,** 1900–90, U.S. composer.

Cop•ley (kop′lē), **John Singleton,** 1738–1815, U.S. painter.

Cop•po•la (kop′ə lə), **Francis Ford,** born 1939, U.S. film director and screenwriter.

Co•que•lin (kôk lan′), **Benoît Constant,** 1841–1909, French actor.

Cor•bett (kôr′bit), **James John** (*"Gentleman Jim"*), 1866–1933, U.S. boxer: world heavyweight champion 1892–97.

Cor•bin (kôr′bin), **Margaret (Cochran),** 1751–1800, American Revolutionary military heroine.

Cor•day d'Ar•mont (kôr dā′ där môn′), **(Marie Anne) Charlotte,** 1768–93, French Revolutionary heroine who assassinated Marat.

Co•rel•li (kô rel′ē, kō-), **1. Arcangelo,** 1653–1713, Italian violinist and composer. **2. Marie** (*Mary Mackay*), 1854?–1924, English novelist.

Co•ri (kôr′ē, kōr′ē), **Carl Ferdinand,** 1896–1984, and his wife, **Gerty Theresa,** 1896–1957, U.S. biochemists, born in Czechoslovakia: Nobel prize for medicine 1947.

Cor•i•o•la•nus (kôr′ē ə lā′nəs, kor′-), **Gaius Marcius,** fl. late 5th century B.C., legendary Roman military hero.

Cor•liss (kôr′lis), **George Henry,** 1817–88, U.S. engineer and inventor.

Cor•neille (kôr nā′), **Pierre,** 1606–84, French dramatist and poet.

Cor•nel•ia (kôr nēl′yə), **1.** fl. 2nd century B.C., Roman matron: mother of Gaius and Tiberius Gracchus. **2.** fl. 1st century B.C., first wife of Julius Caesar 83–67?.

Cor•ne•li•us (kôr nēl′yəs, -nē′lē əs), **Saint,** died A.D. 253, Italian ecclesiastic: pope 251–253.

Cor•nell (kôr nel′), **1. Ezra,** 1809–74, U.S. capitalist and philanthropist. **2. Katharine,** 1898–1974, U.S. stage actress.

Corn•forth (kôrn′fərth, -fôrth′, -fōrth′), **Sir John Warcup,** born 1917, British chemist, born in Australia: Nobel prize 1975.

Corn•wal•lis (kôrn wô′lis, -wol′is), **Charles, 1st Marquis,** 1738–1805, British general and statesman.

Co•ro•na•do (kôr′ə nä′dō, kor′-), **Francisco Vásquez de,** 1510–54?, Spanish explorer in North America.

Co•rot (kô rō′, kə-) **Jean Baptiste Camille,** 1796–1875, French painter.

Cor•reg•gio (kə rej′ō, -rej′ē ō′), **Antonio Allegri da,** 1494–1534, Italian painter.

Cor•ri•gan (kôr′i gən, kor′-), **Mai•read** (mə rād′), born 1944, Northern Irish peace activist: Nobel peace prize 1976.

Cor•tá•zar (kôr tä′sär), **Julio,** 1914–84, Argentine novelist and short-story writer.

Cor•tel•you (kôr′tl yōō′), **George Bruce,** 1862–1940, U.S. cabinet officer and public utility director.

Cor•tés or **Cor•tez** (kôr tez′), **Hernando** or **Hernán,** 1485–1547, Spanish conqueror of Mexico.

Cor•ti (kôr′tē), **Alfonso,** 1822–76, Italian anatomist.

Cor•to•na (kôʀ tô′nä), **Pietro da** (*Pietro Berrettini*), 1596–1669, Italian painter and architect.

Cor•win (kôr′win), **Norman (Lewis),** born 1910, U.S. dramatist and novelist.

Cor•y•ate or **Cor•y•at** (kôr′ē it, kôr′yit), **Thomas,** 1577–1617, English traveler and author.

Cor•yell (kôr yel′), **John Russell,** 1848–1924, U.S. author of detective and adventure stories.

Cos•by (koz′bē), **Bill** (*William Henry*), born 1937, U.S. comedian and actor.

Co•sell (kō sel′), **Howard** (*Howard William Cohen*), born 1920, U.S. sports broadcaster.

Cos•grave (koz′grāv′), **William Thomas,** 1880–1965, Irish political leader: president of the executive council of the Irish Free State 1922–32.

Cos•tain (kos′tān), **Thomas Bertram,** 1885–1965, U.S. novelist, historian, and editor, born in Canada.

Cos•tel•lo (kos′tl ō′, ko stel′ō *for 1;* ko stel′ō *for 2*), **1. John Aloysius,** 1891–1976, prime minister of the Republic of Ireland 1948–51, 1954–57. **2. Lou** (*Louis Cristillo*), 1906–59, U.S. comedian.

Cot•ton (kot′n), **John,** 1584–1652, U.S. clergyman, colonist, and author (grandfather of Cotton Mather).

Co•ty (kō tē′), **René Jules Gustave,** 1882–1962, president of France 1954–59.

Cou•é (ko͞o ā′), **Émile,** 1857–1926, French psychotherapist.

Cough•lin (kôg′lin, kog′-), **Charles Edward** (*"Father Coughlin"*), 1891–1979, U.S. Roman Catholic priest and activist, born in Canada.

Cou•lomb (ko͞o′lom, -lōm, ko͞o lom′, -lōm′), **Charles Augustin de,** 1736–1806, French physicist and inventor.

Coul•ter (kōl′tər), **John Merle,** 1851–1928, U.S. botanist.

Cou•pe•rin (ko͞opᵉ ʀᴀɴ′), **François,** 1668–1733, French composer.

Cou•pe•rus (ko͞o pā′rəs), **Louis,** 1863–1923, Dutch novelist.

Cour•bet (ko͝or bā′), **Gustave,** 1819–77, French painter.

Cour•nand (ko͝or′nand, -nənd; *Fr.* ko͞oʀ näɴ′), **André Frédéric,** 1895–1988, U.S. physiologist, born in France: Nobel prize for medicine 1956.

Court (kôrt, kōrt), **Margaret Smith,** born 1942, Australian tennis player.

Cou•sin (ko͞o zᴀɴ′), **Victor,** 1792–1867, French philosopher and educational reformer: founder of the method of eclecticism in French philosophy.

Cous•ins (kuz′ənz), **Norman,** 1915–90, U.S. editor and writer.

Cous•teau (ko͞o stō′), **Jacques Yves,** born 1910, French author and underseas explorer.

Cou•sy (ko͞o′zē), **Robert Joseph** (*Bob*), born 1928, U.S. basketball player.

Co•var•ru•bias (kō′və ro͞o′bē əs; *Sp.* kô′vär ro͞o′byäs), **Miguel,** 1904–57, Mexican caricaturist, illustrator, and painter.

Cov•er•dale (kuv′ər dāl′), **Miles,** 1488–1569, English cleric: translator of the Bible into English 1535.

Cow•ard (kou′ərd), **Noel,** 1899–1973, English playwright, author, actor, and composer.

Cow•ell (kou′əl), **Henry (Dixon),** 1897–1965, U.S. composer.

Cow•ley (kou′lē, ko͞o′-), **1. Abraham,** 1618–67, English poet. **2. Malcolm,** 1898–1989, U.S. writer, critic, and editor.

Cow•per (ko͞o′pər, kou′-), **William,** 1731–1800, English poet and hymnologist.

Cox (koks), **James Middleton,** 1870–1957, U.S. journalist and politician.

Cox•ey (kok′sē), **Jacob Sechler,** 1854–1951, U.S. political reformer: led unemployed marchers to petition Congress 1894.

Coz•zens (kuz′ənz), **James Gould,** 1903–78, U.S. novelist.

Crabb (krab), **George,** 1778–1851, English author and philologist.

Craig (krāg), **Edward Gordon,** 1872–1966, English stage designer, producer, and author.

Craig•a•von (krāg ā′vən, -av′ən), **James Craig,** 1st Viscount, 1871–1940, first prime minister of Northern Ireland 1921–40.

Crai•gie (krā′gē), **Sir William (Alexander),** 1867–1957, Scottish lexicographer and philologist.

Cram (kram), **Ralph Adams,** 1863–1942, U.S. architect and writer.

Cra•nach (krä′näкн) **1. Lucas** (*"the Elder"*), 1472–1553, German artist. **2.** his son, **Lucas the Younger,** 1515–86, German painter and graphic artist.

Cran•dall (kran′dl), **Prudence,** 1803–90, U.S. educator and civil-rights activist.

Crane (krān), **1. (Harold) Hart,** 1899–1932, U.S. poet. **2. Stephen,** 1871–1900, U.S. novelist and short-story writer.

Cran•mer (kran′mər), **Thomas,** 1489–1556, first Protestant archbishop of Canterbury.

Crash•aw (krash′ô), **Richard,** 1613–49, English poet.

Cras•sus (kras′əs), **Marcus Licinius,** c115–53 B.C., Roman politician: member of the first triumvirate.

Cra•ter (krā′tər), **Joseph Force,** 1889–?, a judge of the New York State Supreme Court: his mysterious disappearance on August 6, 1930, has never been solved.

Craw•ford (krô′fərd), **1. Cheryl,** 1902–86, U.S. stage director and producer. **2. Francis Marion,** 1854–1909, U.S. novelist, in Italy after 1885. **3. Joan** (*Lucille LeSueur*), 1908–77, U.S. film actress. **4. William Harris,** 1772–1834,

U.S. political leader: senator 1807–13, Secretary of the Treasury 1816–25.

Cra′zy Horse′, (*Tashunca-Uitco*), c1849–77, Lakota Indian leader: defeated General George Custer.

Cre•mer (krē′mər), **Sir William Randal,** 1838–1908, English union organizer: Nobel peace prize 1903.

Cres•cas (kres′kəs), **Hasdai,** 1340–1412?, Jewish philosopher and theologian, born in Spain.

Crève•coeur (krev kûr′, -ko͝or′, krēv-), **Michel Guillaume Jean de,** (zhäɴ), (*"J. Hector St. John"*), 1735–1813, U.S. essayist and agriculturalist, born in France.

Crich•ton (krīt′n), **James** (*"the Admirable Crichton"*), 1560?–82, Scottish scholar and linguist.

Crick (krik), **Francis Harry Compton,** born 1916, English biophysicist: Nobel prize for medicine 1962.

Crile (krīl), **George Washington,** 1864–1943, U.S. surgeon.

Cripps (krips), **Sir Stafford,** 1889–1952, British statesman and socialist leader.

Cris•pin (kris′pin), **Saint,** martyred A.D. c285, Roman Christian missionary in Gaul: patron saint of shoemakers.

Cris•tia•ni (kris′tē ä′nē, -tyä′-), **Alfredo,** born 1947, president of El Salvador since 1989.

Cro•ce (krō′chā), **Benedetto,** 1866–1952, Italian statesman, philosopher, and historian.

Crock•ett (krok′it), **David** (*Davy*), 1786–1836, U.S. frontiersman, politician, and folklore hero.

Croe•sus (krē′səs), (-sī). died 546 B.C., king of Lydia 560–546: noted for his great wealth.

Cromp•ton (kromp′tən), **Samuel,** 1753–1827, English inventor of the spinning mule.

Crom•well (krom′wəl, -wel, krum′-), **1. Oliver,** 1599–1658, English general and statesman: Lord Protector of England, Scotland, and Ireland 1653–58. **2.** his son, **Richard,** 1626–1712, Lord Protector of England 1658–59. **3. Thomas, Earl of Essex,** 1485?–1540, English statesman.

Cro•nin (krō′nin), **A(rchibald) J(oseph),** 1896–1981, Scottish novelist and physician in the U.S.

Cron•jé (kron′yā), **Piet Arnoldus,** 1835?–1911, Boer general.

Cron•kite (krong′kīt), **Walter (Leland, Jr.),** born 1916, U.S. news broadcaster and commentator.

Cro•nyn (krō′nin), **Hume,** born 1911, Canadian actor in the U.S.

Crookes (kro͝oks), **Sir William,** 1832–1919, English chemist and physicist.

Cros•by (krôz′bē, kroz′-), **Bing** (*Harry Lillis Crosby*), 1904–77, U.S. singer and film actor.

Cross (krôs, kros), **Wilbur Lucius,** 1862–1948, U.S. educator: governor of Connecticut 1931–39.

Crouse (krous), **Russel,** 1893–1966, U.S. dramatist.

Cruik•shank (kro͝ok′shangk′), **George,** 1792–1878, English illustrator, caricaturist, and painter.

Cue•vas (kwā′vəs), **José Luis,** born 1934, Mexican painter, graphic artist, and illustrator.

Cuf•fe (kuf′ē), **Paul,** 1759–1817, U.S. merchant, seaman, and philanthropist: advocated U.S. black emigration to Africa.

Cu•i (kwē), **César Antonovich,** 1835–1918, Russian composer.

Cu•kor (ko͞o′kər, -kôr, kyo͞o′-), **George,** 1899–1983, U.S. film director.

Cul•bert•son (kul′bərt sən), **Ely,** 1893–1955, U.S. authority on contract bridge.

Cul•len (kul′ən), **Countee,** 1903–46, U.S. poet.

Cul•pep•er (kul′pep′ər), **Thomas** (*2nd Baron Culpeper of Thoresway*), 1635–89, English colonial governor of Virginia 1680–83.

Cum•mings (kum′ingz), **Edward Estlin,** (*"e e cummings"*), 1894–1962, U.S. poet.

Cun•ning•ham (kun′ing ham′), **1. Glenn** (*"Kansas Ironman"*), born 1909, U.S. track-and-field athlete. **2. Merce,** born 1919?, U.S. dancer and choreographer.

Cuo•mo (kwō′mō), **Mario (Matthew),** born 1932, U.S. political leader: governor of New York since 1982.

Cu•rie (kyo͝or′ē, kyo͝o rē′), **1. Irène,** JOLIOT-CURIE. **2. Marie,** 1867–1934, Polish physicist and chemist in France: codiscoverer of radium 1898: Nobel prize for physics 1903, for chemistry 1911. **3.** her husband, **Pierre,** 1859–1906, French physicist and chemist: codiscoverer of radium: Nobel prize for physics 1903.

Cur•ley (kûr′lē), **James M(ichael),** 1874–1958, U.S. politician.

Cur•ri•er (kûr′ē ər, kur-), **Nathaniel,** 1813–88, U.S. lithographer: with James Merritt Ives produced prints showing American life.

Cur•ry (kûr′ē, kur′ē), **1. John (Anthony),** born 1949, British figure skater. **2. John Steuart,** 1897–1946, U.S. painter.

Cur•tin (kûr′tin), **John,** 1885–1945, prime minister of Australia 1941–45.

Cur•tis (kûr′tis), **1. Benjamin Robbins,** 1809–74, U.S. jurist: associate justice of the U.S. Supreme Court 1851–57; resigned in dissent over Dred Scott case. **2. Charles,** 1860–1936, vice president of the U.S. 1929–33. **3. Cyrus Hermann Kotzschmar,** 1850–1933, U.S. publisher. **4. George Ticknor,** 1812–94, U.S. attorney and writer. **5. George William,** 1824–92, U.S. essayist, editor, and reformer.

Cur•tiss (kûr′tis), **Glenn Hammond,** 1878–1930, U.S. inventor: pioneer in the field of aviation.

Cur•ti•us (ko͝or′tsē əs), **Ernst,** 1814–96, German archaeologist and historian.

Cur•zon (kûr′zən), **George Nathaniel, 1st Marquis Curzon of Kedleston,** 1859–1925, British viceroy of India 1899–1905.

Cush•ing (ko͝osh′ing), **1. Caleb,** 1800–79, U.S. statesman and diplomat. **2. Harvey (Williams),** 1869–1939, U.S. surgeon. **3. Richard James,** 1895–1970, U.S. Roman Catholic clergyman: cardinal 1958–70; archbishop of Boston 1944–70.

Cus•ter (kus′tər), **George Armstrong,** 1839–76, U.S. general: killed at the battle of Little Bighorn.

Cuth•bert (kuth′bərt), **Saint,** A.D. c635–687, English monk and bishop.

Cut•ler (kut′lər), **Manasseh,** 1742–1823, U.S. Congregational clergyman and scientist: promoted settlement of Ohio; congressman 1801–05.

Cu•vi•er (kyōō′vē ā′, kōōv yā′), **Georges Léopold Chrétien Frédéric Dagobert, Baron,** 1769–1832, French naturalist, pioneer in the fields of paleontology and comparative anatomy.

Cuyp or **Kuyp** (koip, kip), **Aelbert,** 1620–91, Dutch painter.

Cyn•e•wulf (kin′ə wŏŏlf′) also **Cyn′wulf** (-wŏŏlf), fl. 9th century A.D., Anglo-Saxon poet.

Cyp•ri•an (sip′rē ən), **Saint** (*Thascius Caecilius Cyprianus*), A.D. c200–258, early church father, bishop, and martyr.

Cyr•a•no de Ber•ge•rac (sir′ə nō′ də bûr′zhə rak′), BERGERAC, Savinien Cyrano de.

Cyr•il (sir′əl), **Saint** (*"Apostle of the Slavs"*), A.D. 827–869, Greek missionary to the Moravians.

Cy•rus (sī′rəs), **1.** (*"the Great"*) c600-529 B.C., king of Persia c550-529: founder of the Persian Empire. **2.** (*"the Younger"*) 424-401 B.C., Persian prince and satrap.

Czer•ny (cher′nē), **Carl,** 1791–1857, Austrian pianist and composer.

D

Da•ché (da shā′), **Lilly,** 1895?–1989, U.S. hat designer, born in France.

Dack•o (dak′ō, dä′kō), **David,** born 1930, African statesman: president of the Central African Republic (now Central African Empire) 1960–66.

Dad•dah (dad′ə, dä′dä), **Mokhtar Ould,** born 1924, Mauritanian statesman: president of the Republic of Mauritania 1961–78.

Da•fydd ap Gwi•lym (dä′viŧħ äp gwi′lim), c1340–c1400, Welsh poet.

da Ga•ma (də gam′ə, gä′mə), **Vasco,** GAMA, Vasco da.

Dag•o•bert I (dag′ə bərt, -ō bâr′), A.D. 602?–639, Merovingian king of the Franks 628–639.

Da•guerre (də gâr′), **Louis Jacques Mandé,** 1789–1851, French painter and inventor of the daguerreotype.

Dahl (däl), **Roald,** born 1916, British short-story and children's book writer.

Dahl•gren (dal′grən), **John Adelphus Bernard,** 1809–70, U.S. naval officer and inventor.

Daim•ler (dīm′lər; *Ger.* dīm′lər), **Gottlieb (Wilhelm),** 1834–1900, German automotive engineer, inventor, and manufacturer.

Da•la•dier (də lä′dē ā′, də läd yā′), **Édouard,** 1884–1970, premier of France 1933, 1934, 1938–40.

Da•lai La•ma (dä′lī lä′mə), (*Tenzin Gyatso*), born 1935, Tibetan religious and political leader, in exile since 1959: the Dalai Lama since 1940; Nobel peace prize 1989.

Dal•croze (dal krōz′), JAQUES-DALCROZE, Émile.

Dale (dāl), **1. Sir Henry Hallett,** 1875–1968, English physiologist: Nobel prize for medicine 1936. **2. Sir Thomas,** died 1619, British colonial governor of Virginia 1614–16.

Da•lén (də lān′, da-), **Gustaf,** 1869–1937, Swedish inventor: Nobel prize for physics 1912.

Da•ley (dā′lē), **Richard J(oseph),** 1902–76, U.S. politician: mayor of Chicago 1955–76.

Dal•hou•sie (dal hōō′zē, -hou′-), **1. George Ramsay, Earl of,** 1770–1838, British governor of Canadian colonies 1819–28. **2. James Andrew Broun Ramsay, 1st Marquis and 10th Earl of,** 1812–60, British viceroy of India 1848–56.

Da•li (dä′lē), **Salvador,** 1904–89, Spanish surrealist painter.

Dal•la•pic•co•la (dä′lä pē′kō lə), **Luigi,** 1904–75, Italian composer.

Dal•las (dal′əs), **George Mifflin,** 1792–1864, vice president of the U.S. 1845–49.

Dal•lin (dal′in), **Cyrus Earle,** 1861–1944, U.S. sculptor.

Dal•rym•ple (dal rim′pəl, dal′rim-), **Sir James, 1st Viscount Stair,** 1619–95, Scottish jurist.

Dal•ton (dôl′tn), **1. John,** 1766–1844, English chemist and physicist. **2. Robert,** 1867–92, U.S. outlaw in the West.

Da•ly (dā′lē), **(John) Augustin,** 1838–99, U.S. playwright, critic, and theatrical manager.

Dam (dam, däm), **(Carl Peter) Henrik,** 1895–1976, Danish biochemist: Nobel prize for medicine 1943.

Dam•a•sus (dam′ə səs), **1. Damasus I, Saint,** pope A.D. 366–384. **2. Damasus II,** died 1048, pope 1048.

d'Am•boise (*Fr.* däɴ bwaz′), **Jacques (Joseph),** born 1934, U.S. ballet dancer and choreographer.

Da•mien (dā′mē ən; *Fr.* da myaɴ′), **Father (Joseph de Veuster),** 1840–89, Belgian Roman Catholic missionary to the lepers of Molokai.

Dam•pi•er (dam′pē ər, damp′yər), **William,** 1652–1715, English explorer and buccaneer.

Dam•rosch (dam′rosh), **1. Leopold,** 1832–85, German conductor and violinist, in the U.S. after 1871. **2. Walter Johannes,** 1862–1950, U.S. conductor, born in Germany.

Da•na (dā′nə), **1. Charles Anderson,** 1819–97, U.S. newspaper publisher. **2. James Dwight,** 1813–95, U.S. geologist and mineralogist. **3. Richard Henry, Jr.,** 1815–82, U.S. jurist and author.

Dan•cer (dan′sər, dän′-), **Stanley,** born 1927, U.S. harness racer and trainer.

Dan•iel (dan′yəl), **Samuel,** 1562–1619, English poet and historian: poet laureate 1599–1619.

Dan•iels (dan′yəlz), **1. Jonathan Worth,** 1902–81, U.S. journalist, editor, and author. **2. Josephus,** 1862–1948, U.S. editor and statesman.

Da•ni•lo•va (də nē′lə və, -nyē′-), **Alexandra,** born 1904?, Russian ballet dancer.

D'An•nun•zio (də no͞on′sē ō′, dä no͞on′-), **Gabriele,** (*Duca Minimo*), 1863–1938, Italian soldier, novelist, and poet.

Dan•te (dän′tā, -tē, dan′tē,), (*Dante Alighieri*), 1265–1321, Italian poet: author of the *Divine Comedy.*

Dan•ton (däɴ tôɴ′), **Georges Jacques,** 1759–94, French Revolutionary leader.

Da Pon•te (də pon′tē), **Lorenzo** (*Emanuele Conegliano*), 1749–1838, Italian librettist and teacher of Italian, in the U.S. after 1805.

Dare (dâr), **Virginia,** 1587–?, first child born of English parents in America.

Da•rí•o (də rē′ō), **Rubén,** (*Félix Rubén García Sarmiento*), 1867–1916, Nicaraguan poet and diplomat.

Da•ri•us (də rī′əs), **1. Darius I** (*Darius Hystaspes*) (*"the Great"*), 558?–486? B.C., king of Persia 521–486. **2. Darius II** (*Ochus*), died 404 B.C., king of Persia 424–404 (son of Artaxerxes I). **3. Darius III** (*Codomannus*), died 330 B.C., king of Persia 336–330.

Dar•lan (dar läɴ′), **Jean Louis Xavier François,** 1881–1942, French naval officer and politician.

Dar•ling (där′ling), **Jay Norwood** (*"Ding"*), 1876–1962, U.S. cartoonist.

Darn•ley (därn′lē), **Lord Henry Stewart** or **Stuart,** 1545–67, Scottish nobleman: second husband of Mary Queen of Scots (father of James I of England).

Dar•row (dar′ō), **Clarence (Seward),** 1857–1938, U.S. lawyer.

Dar•win (där′win), **1. Charles (Robert),** 1809–82, English naturalist. **2.** his grandfather, **Erasmus,** 1731–1802, English naturalist and poet.

Das•sin (das′in, da san′), **Jules,** born 1911, French motion-picture director, born in the U.S.

Dau•bi•gny (dō bē nyē′), **Charles François,** 1817–78, French painter.

Dau•det (dō dā′, dô-), **1. Alphonse,** 1840–97, French writer. **2.** his son, **Léon,** 1867–1942, French writer.

Dau•mier (dō myā′), **Honoré,** 1808–79, French painter, cartoonist, and lithographer.

D'Av•e•nant or **Dav•e•nant** (dav′ə nənt), **Sir William,** 1606–68, English dramatist and producer: poet laureate 1638–68.

Dav•en•port (dav′ən pôrt′, -pōrt′), **John,** 1597–1670, Puritan clergyman: one of the founders of New Haven.

Da•vid (dā′vid *for 1; Fr.* dᴀ vēd′ *for 2*), **1. Saint,** A.D. c510–601?, Welsh bishop: patron saint of Wales. **2. Jacques Louis,** 1748–1825, French painter.

Da•vid I (dā′vid), 1084–1153, king of Scotland 1124–53.

Da•vid•son (dā′vid sən), **Jo** (jō), 1883–1952, U.S. sculptor.

Da•vies (dā′vēz), **1. Arthur Bowen,** 1862–1928, U.S. painter. **2. (William) Robertson,** born 1913, Canadian novelist, playwright, and essayist.

da Vin•ci (də vin′chē, dä), **Leonardo,** Leonardo da Vinci.

Da•vis (dā′vis), **1. Benjamin Oliver,** 1877–1970, U.S. military officer: first black Army brigadier general. **2.** his son, **Benjamin Oliver, Jr.,** born 1912, U.S. military officer: first black Air Force lieutenant general. **3. Bet•te** (bet′ē) (*Ruth Elizabeth Davis*), 1908-89, U.S. film actress. **4. Dwight F(illey),** 1879–1945, U.S. tennis player and public official: donor of the Davis Cup (1900), an international tennis trophy; Secretary of War 1925–29. **5. Elmer (Holmes),** 1890–1958, U.S. radio commentator and author. **6. Jefferson,** 1808–89, president of the Confederate States of America 1861–65. **7. John,** c1550–1605, English navigator and explorer. **8. Miles (Dewey, Jr.),** 1926–91, U.S. jazz trumpeter. **9. Owen,** 1874–1956, U.S. playwright. **10. Richard Harding,** 1864–1916, U.S. journalist, novelist, and playwright. **11. Sammy, Jr.,** 1925–90, U.S. singer and actor. **12. Stuart,** 1894–1964, U.S. painter and illustrator.

Da•vis•son (dā′və sən), **Clinton Joseph,** 1881–1958, U.S. physicist: Nobel prize 1937.

Da•vout (da vo͞o′), **Louis Nicolas, Duke of Auerstadt, Prince of Eckmühl,** 1770–1823, marshal of France: one of Napoleon's leading generals.

Da•vy (dā′vē), **Sir Humphry,** 1778–1829, English chemist.

Dawes (dôz), **Charles Gates,** 1865–1951, U.S. financier and diplomat: vice president of the U.S. 1925–29; Nobel peace prize 1925.

Daw•son (dô′sən), **1. Sir John William,** 1820–99, Canadian geologist. **2. William Levi,** born 1899, U.S. composer and conductor.

Day (dā), **1. Clarence (Shepard),** 1874–1935, U.S. author. **2. Doris** (*Doris von Kappelhoff*), born 1924, U.S. singer and actress.

Da•yan (dä yän′), **Moshe,** 1915–81, Israeli politician and military leader: defense minister 1967–74, foreign minister 1977–79.

Day-Lew•is (dā′lo͞o′is), **C(ecil),** 1904–72, British poet, born in Ireland: poet laureate 1968–72.

Day•ton (dāt′n), **Jonathan,** 1760–1824, U.S. politician, Speaker of the House 1795–99.

Dea•kin (dē′kin), **Alfred,** 1856–1919, Australian statesman: prime minister 1903–04; 1905–08; 1909–10.

Dean (dēn), **1. Christopher,** born 1959, British ice dancer. **2. Jay Hanna** ("*Dizzy*"), 1911–74, U.S. baseball pitcher.

Dear•born (dēr′bərn, -bôrn), **Henry,** 1751–1829, U.S. soldier and diplomat.

De Ba•key (də bā′kē), **Michael Ellis,** born 1908, U.S. physician: pioneer in heart surgery.

de Beau•voir (də bōv wär′), **Simone,** 1908–86, French writer.

de Bro•glie (də brō glē′, brō′glē, broi), **Louis Victor,** 1892–1987, French physicist: Nobel prize 1929.

Debs (debz), **Eugene Victor,** 1855–1926, U.S. labor leader: Socialist candidate for president 1900–20.

De•bus•sy (deb′yo͝o sē′, dā′byo͝o-, də byo͞o′sē), **Claude Achille,** 1862–1918, French composer.

De•bye (de bī′), **Peter Joseph Wilhelm,** 1884–1966, Dutch physicist, in the U.S. after 1940: Nobel prize for chemistry 1936.

De•ca•tur (di kā′tər), **Stephen,** 1779–1820, U.S. naval officer.

De•cius (dē′shəs, desh′əs), (*Gaius Messius Quintus Trajanus Decius*) A.D. c201–251, emperor of Rome 249–251.

Deck•er (dek′ər), **Thomas,** DEKKER, Thomas.

Dee (dē), **John,** 1527–1608, English mathematician and astrologer.

Deere (dēr), **John,** 1804–86, U.S. inventor and manufacturer of farm implements.

De•foe or **De Foe** (di fō′), **Daniel,** 1659?–1731, English novelist and political journalist.

De For•est (di fôr′ist, for′-), **Lee,** 1873–1961, U.S. inventor of radio, telegraphic, and telephonic equipment.

De•gas (dā gä′, də-), **Hilaire Germain Edgar,** 1834–1917, French impressionist painter.

De Gas•pe•ri (de gäs′pe rē), **Alcide,** 1881–1954, Italian statesman: premier 1945–53.

de Gaulle (də gōl′, gôl′), **Charles André Joseph Marie,** 1890–1970, French general: president 1959–69.

de Groot (də KHRōt′), **Huig** (hœIKH), GROTIUS, Hugo.

de Haas (də häz′), **Jacob,** 1872–1937, English Zionist leader, in U.S. after 1902.

de Kalb (di kalb′), **Baron,** KALB, Johann.

Dek•ker or **Deck•er** (dek′ər), **Thomas,** 1572?–1632?, English dramatist.

de Klerk (də klârk′), **Frederik Willem,** born 1937, president of South Africa since 1989.

de Koo•ning (də ko͞o′ning), **Willem,** born 1904, U.S. painter, born in the Netherlands.

De Ko•ven (di kō′vən), **(Henry Louis) Reginald,** 1861–1920, U.S. composer, conductor, and music critic.

de Kruif (də krīf′), **Paul,** 1890–1971, U.S. bacteriologist and author.

De•la•croix (del′ə krwä′), **(Ferdinand Victor) Eugène,** 1798–1863, French painter.

de la Ma•drid Hur•ta•do (də lä mə drid′ hər tä′dō), **Miguel,** born 1934, Mexican political leader: president 1982–88.

de la Mare (də lə mâr′, del′ə mâr′), **Walter (John),** 1873–1956, English poet, novelist, and playwright.

Del•a•ma•ter (del′ə mä′tər), **Cornelius Henry,** 1821–89, U.S. mechanical engineer and shipbuilder.

De Lan•cey (də lan′sē), **James,** 1703–60, American jurist and politician in New York.

De•land (də land′), **Margaret** (*Margaretta Wade Campbell Deland*), 1857–1945, U.S. novelist.

De•lan•noy (də LA NWA′), **Marcel,** born 1898, French composer.

De•la•ny (də lā′nē), **Martin Robinson,** 1812–85, U.S. physician and army officer: leader of black nationalist movement.

de la Ren•ta (də lə ren′tə, del′ə, dē′ lə), **Oscar,** born 1932, U.S. fashion designer, born in the Dominican Republic.

de la Roche (də lə rôsh′), **Mazo,** 1885–1961, Canadian novelist.

De•la•roche (də lä rōsh′, -rôsh′), **(Hippolyte) Paul,** 1797–1856, French historical and portrait painter.

de la Rue (del′ə ro͞o′, del′ə ro͞o′), **Warren,** 1815–89, English astronomer and inventor.

De•lau•nay (də lô ne′), **Ro•bert** (RŌ BER′), 1885–1941, French painter.

De•la•vigne (də lä vēn′yə), **(Jean François) Casimir,** 1793–1843, French poet and dramatist.

De La Warr or **Del•a•ware** (del′ə wâr′), **12th Baron** (*Thomas West*), 1577–1618, 1st English colonial governor of Virginia.

Del•brück (del′bro͝ok), **Max,** 1906–81, U.S. biologist, born in Germany: Nobel prize for medicine 1969.

Del•cas•sé (del KA sä′), **Théophile,** 1852–1923, French statesman.

De•led•da (de led′dä), **Grazia,** 1875–1936, Italian novelist: Nobel prize 1926.

de Les•seps (də les′eps), **Vicomte Ferdinand Marie,** LESSEPS, Ferdinand Marie, Vicomte de.

De•libes (də lēb′), **(Clément Philibert) Léo,** 1836–91, French composer.

De•li•us (dē′lē əs, dēl′yəs), **Frederick,** 1862–1934, English composer.

del•la Rob•bia (del′ə rō′bē ə), ROBBIA.

Del•lo Joi•o (del′ō joi′ō), **Norman,** born 1913, U.S. composer and pianist.

Del•mon•i•co (del mon′i kō′), **Lorenzo,** 1813–81, U.S. restaurateur, born in Switzerland.

De•lorme (də lôRM′), **Philibert,** 1515?–70, French architect.

de los An•ge•les (dā los an′jə ləs; *Sp.* de lôs än′he les), **Victoria,** born 1923?, Spanish operatic soprano.

del Sar•to (del sär′tō), **Andrea,** ANDREA DEL SARTO.

De•me•tri•us I (di mē′trē əs) (*Poliorcetes*), 337?–283 B.C., king of Macedonia 294–286.

De Mille (də mil′), **1. Agnes (George),** born 1908, U.S. choreographer and dancer. **2.** her uncle, **Cecil B(lount),** 1881–1959, U.S. motion-picture producer and director.

De•moc•ri•tus (di mok′ri təs), (*"the Laughing Philosopher"*), c460–370 B.C., Greek philosopher.

de Moi•vre (də mwäv′, mwä′vrə, moi′vər), **Abraham,** 1667–1754, French mathematician in England.

De Mor•gan (di môr′gən), **1. Augustus,** 1806–71, English mathematician and logician. **2. William Frend** (frend), 1839–1917, English novelist and ceramist.

De•mos•the•nes (di mos′thə nēz′), 384?–322 B.C., Athenian statesman and orator.

Demp•sey (demp′sē), **Jack** (*William Harrison Dempsey*), 1895–1983, U.S. boxer: world heavyweight champion 1919–26.

Demp•ster (demp′stər, dem′-), **Arthur Jeffrey,** 1886–1950, U.S. physicist.

De•muth (di mo͞oth′), **Charles,** 1883–1935, U.S. painter.

Deng Xiao•ping (dung′ shou′ping′), born 1904, Chinese Communist leader.

Den•ham (den′əm), **Sir John,** 1615–69, English poet and architect.

De•ni•ker (de nē KER′), **Joseph,** 1852–1918, French anthropologist and naturalist.

De Ni•ro (də nēr′ō), **Robert,** born 1943, U.S. actor.

Den•is or **Den•ys** (den′is; *Fr.* də nē′), **Saint,** died A.D. c280, 1st bishop of Paris: patron saint of France.

Den•nis (den′is), **John,** 1657–1734, English dramatist and critic.

De Quin•cey (di kwin′sē), **Thomas,** 1785–1859, English essayist.

De•rain (də RAN′), **André,** 1880–1954, French painter.

Der•leth (dûr′leth, -ləth), **August (William),** 1909–71, U.S. novelist, poet, and short-story writer.

Der•ri•da (der′ē dä′), **Jacques,** born 1930, French philosopher and literary critic, born in Algiers.

De•sargues (dā zärg′), **Gérard,** 1593–1662, French mathematician.

Des•cartes (dā kärt′), **René,** 1596–1650, French philosopher and mathematician.

Des•mou•lins (de mo͞o lan′), **(Lucie Simplice) Camille (Benoit),** 1760–94, journalist and pamphleteer in the French Revolution.

De So•to (də sō′tō), **Hernando** or **Fernando,** c1500–42, Spanish explorer in America.

Des Prés (də prā′), **Josquin,** c1445–1521, Flemish composer.

Des•sa•lines (dā SA lēn′), **Jean Jacques** (zhäN zhäk), 1758–1806, Haitian revolutionary: emperor of Haiti as Jacques I 1804–06.

De•us•ded•it (dē′əs ded′it, -dē′dit), **Saint,** died A.D. 618, Italian ecclesiastic: pope 615–618.

De•us Ra•mos (de′o͝osh rä′mo͝osh), **João de,** 1830–96, Portuguese poet.

Deutsch (doich), **Babette,** 1895–1982, U.S. poet, novelist, and critic.

Deut•scher (doi′chər), **Isaac,** 1907–1967, English journalist and author, born in Poland.

De Va•le•ra (dev′ə lâr′ə, -lēr′ə), **Ea•mon** (ā′mən), 1882–1975, Irish political leader and statesman, born in the U.S.: prime minister of the Republic of Ireland 1932–48, 1951–54, 1957–59; president 1959–73.

de Val•ois (də val′wä), **Dame Ninette** (*Edris Stannus*), born 1898, British ballet dancer, choreographer, teacher, and director: founder of the Royal Ballet (originally the Sadler's Wells Ballet).

de Ve•ga (də vā′gə), **Lope,** (*Lope Félix de Vega Carpio*), 1562–1635, Spanish dramatist and poet.

Dev•e•reux (dev′ə ro͞o′), **Robert, 2nd Earl of Essex,** 1566–1601, English statesman, soldier, and courtier of Queen Elizabeth I.

De Vo•to (də vō′tō), **Bernard (Augustine),** 1897–1955, U.S. novelist and critic.

De Vries (də vrēs′), **1. Hugo,** 1848–1935, Dutch botanist. **2. Peter,** born 1910, U.S. novelist and humorist.

Dew•ar (do͞o′ər, dyo͞o′-), **Sir James,** 1842–1923, Scottish chemist and physicist.

De Wet (də wet′), **Christian Rudolph,** 1854–1922, Boer general and politician.

Dew•ey (do͞o′ē, dyo͞o′ē), **1. George,** 1837–1917, U.S. admiral during the Spanish-American War. **2. John,** 1859–1952, U.S. philosopher and educator. **3. Melvil,** (*Melville Louis Kossuth Dewey*), 1851–1931, U.S. educator and innovator in library science. **4. Thomas E(dmund),** 1902–71, U.S. lawyer and political leader.

De Witt (də wit′), **Jan** (yän), 1625–72, Dutch statesman.

Dia•bel•li (dē′ä bel′ē), **Antonio,** 1781–1858, Austrian composer and music publisher.

Dia•ghi•lev (dē ä′gə lef′, -lif), **Sergei Pavlovich,** 1872–1929, Russian ballet producer.

Di•an•a (dī an′ə), (*Princess of Wales*) (*Lady Diana Spencer*), born 1961, wife of Charles, Prince of Wales.

Di•as or **Di•az** (dē′əs, -əsh), **Bartholomeu,** c1450–1500, Portuguese navigator: discovered Cape of Good Hope.

Dí•az (dē′äs), **(José de la Cruz) Porfirio,** 1830–1915, president of Mexico 1877–80, 1884–1911.

Dí•az de Bi•var or **Dí•az de Vi•var** (dē′äth the vē vär′), **Rodrigo** or **Ruy,** Cid, The.

Dí•az del Cas•til•lo (dē′äth thel käs tē′lyô), **Bernal,** 1492–1581, Spanish soldier-historian of the conquest of Mexico.

Dí•az Mi•rón (dē′äs mē rōn′), **Salvador,** 1853–1928, Mexican poet.

Dí•az Or•daz (dē′äs ôr thäs′), **Gustavo,** 1911–79, Mexican teacher, jurist, and public official: president 1964–70.

Dí•az Ro•drí•guez (dē′äs rō drē′ges), **Manuel,** 1868–1927, Venezuelan author.

Di•be•li•us (di bā′lē əs), **Martin,** 1883–1947, German theologian.

Dick (dik), **1. George Frederick,** 1881–1967, U.S. internist. **2. Philip K.,** 1928–82, U.S. science-fiction writer.

Dick•ens (dik′inz), **Charles (John Huffam)** (*"Boz"*), 1812–70, English novelist.

Dick•ey (dik′ē), **James,** born 1923, U.S. poet, novelist, and critic.

Dick•in•son (dik′in sən), **1. Edwin (Walter),** 1891–1978, U.S. landscape and still-life painter. **2. Emily (Elizabeth),** 1830–86, U.S. poet. **3. John,** 1732–1808, U.S. statesman and publicist.

Did•dley (did′lē), **Bo** (*Elias McDaniel*), born 1928, U.S. rock-'n'-roll singer, guitarist, and songwriter.

Di•de•rot (dē′də rō′), **Denis,** 1713–84, French encyclopedist.

Did•i•on (did′ē ən), **Joan,** born 1934, U.S. novelist and journalist.

Did•rik•son (did′rik sən), **Mildred,** Zaharias, Mildred Didrikson.

Die•fen•ba•ker (dē′fən bā′kər), **John George,** 1895–1979, prime minister of Canada 1957–63.

Diels (dēlz), **Otto,** 1876–1954, German chemist: Nobel prize 1950.

Die•sel (dē′zəl, -səl), **Rudolf,** 1858–1913, German automotive engineer.

Die•trich (dē′trik, -trikh), **Mar•le•ne** (mär lā′nə), 1904–92, U.S. actress and singer, born in Germany.

Dig•by (dig′bē), **Sir Kenelm,** 1603–65, English writer, naval commander, and diplomat.

Dil•lin•ger (dil′in jər), **John,** 1902–34, U.S. bank robber and murderer.

Dil•lon (dil′ən), **C(larence) Douglas,** born 1909, U.S. lawyer and government official, born in Switzerland: Secretary of the Treasury 1961–65.

Di•Mag•gi•o (də mä′jē ō′, -maj′ē ō′), **Joseph Paul** (*Joe*), born 1914, U.S. baseball player.

Di•mi•tri•os I (di mē′trē əs), (*Dimitrios Papadopoulos*), 1914–91, Archbishop of Constantinople and Ecumenical Patriarch of the Eastern Orthodox Church 1972–91.

d'In•dy (daɴ dē′), **Vincent,** Indy, d'.

Dine (dīn), **James** (*Jim*), born 1935, U.S. painter.

Din•e•sen (din′ə sən, dē′nə-), **Isak,** (pen name of *Baroness Karen Blixen*), 1885–1962, Danish author.

Ding Ling (ding′ ling′), (*Jiang Bingzhi*) 1904–86, Chinese author.

Din•wid•die (din wid′ē, din′wid ē), **Robert,** 1693–1770, British colonial administrator in America.

Di•o•cle•tian (dī′ə klē′shən), (*Gaius Aurelius Valerius Diocletianus*), A.D. 245–316, emperor of Rome 284–305.

Di•o•do•rus Sic•u•lus (dī′ō dôr′əs sik′yə ləs, -dōr′-), late 1st century B.C., Greek historian.

Di•og•e•nes (dī oj′ə nēz′), 412?–323 B.C., Greek Cynic philosopher.

Di•o•ny•si•us (dī′ə nish′ē əs, -nis′-, -nish′əs, -nī′sē əs), **1.** (*"the Elder"*), 431?–367 B.C., Greek soldier: tyrant of Syracuse 405–367. **2. Saint,** died A.D. 268, pope 259–268.

Diony′sius Ex•ig′u•us (eg zig′yo͞o əs, ek sig′-), died A.D. 556?, Scythian monk, chronologist, and scholar: devised the current system of reckoning the Christian era.

Diony′sius of Alexan′dria, Saint (*"the Great"*), A.D. c190–265, patriarch of Alexandria 247?–265?.

Diony′sius of Halicarnas′sus, died 7? B.C., Greek rhetorician and historian in Rome.

Diony′sius the Areop′agite, 1st century A.D., Athenian scholar: converted to Christianity by Saint Paul c50.

Diony′sius Thrax′ (thraks), c100 B.C., Greek grammarian.

Di•or (dē ôr′), **Christian,** 1905–57, French fashion designer.

Di•rac (di rak′), **Paul Adrien Maurice,** 1902–84, British physicist, in the U.S. after 1971: Nobel prize 1933.

Dis•ney (diz′nē), **Walt(er E.),** 1901–66, U.S. creator and producer of animated cartoons, motion pictures, etc.

Dis•rae•li (diz rā′lē), **Benjamin, 1st Earl of Beaconsfield** (*"Dizzy"*), 1804–81, British prime minister 1868, 1874–80.

Dit•mars (dit′märz), **Raymond Lee,** 1876–1942, U.S. zoologist.

Dit•ters•dorf (dit′ərz dôrf′), **Karl Ditters von,** 1739–99, Austrian violinist and composer.

Dix (diks), **Dorothea Lynde,** 1802–87, U.S. educator and social reformer.

Dix•on (dik′sən), **Jeremiah,** died 1777, English astronomer and surveyor.

Dji•las (jil′äs), **Milovan,** born 1911, Yugoslavian political leader and author.

Do•bie (dō′bē), **(James) Frank,** 1888–1964, U.S. folklorist, educator, and author.

Dö•blin (dœ′blēn), **Alfred,** 1878–1957, German physician and novelist.

Do•bry•nin (dō brē′nin, -brin′in), **Anatoly F(edorovich),** born 1919, Russian diplomat.

Dob•son (dob′sən), **(Henry) Austin,** 1840–1921, English poet, biographer, and essayist.

Dob•zhan•sky (dob zhän′skē), **Theodosius (Grigorievich),** 1900–75, U.S. geneticist, born in Russia.

Doc•to•row (dok′tə rō′), **E(dgar) L(awrence),** born 1931, U.S. novelist.

Dodd (dod), **William Edward,** 1869–1940, U.S. historian and diplomat.

Dodds (dodz), **Warren** (*"Baby"*), 1898–1959, U.S. jazz drummer.

Dodge (doj), **Mary Elizabeth,** 1831–1905, U.S. editor and author of children's books.

Dodg•son (doj′sən), **Charles Lutwidge** (*"Lewis Carroll"*), 1832–98, English mathematician and writer.

Doe•nitz (dœ′nits), **Karl,** 1891–1980, German admiral.

Doi•sy (doi′zē), **Edward Adelbert,** 1893–1986, U.S. biochemist: Nobel prize for medicine 1943.

Dole (dōl), **1. Robert J(oseph),** born 1923, U.S. politician: senator since 1969. **2. Sanford Ballard,** 1844–1926, U.S. politician and jurist in Hawaii: president of Republic of Hawaii 1894–98; first territorial governor 1900–03.

Do•lin (dō′lin), **Sir Anton** (*Patrick Healey-Kay*), 1904–83, English ballet dancer.

Do•magk (dō′mäk), **Gerhard,** 1895–1964, German physician: declined 1939 Nobel prize at demand of Nazi government.

Do•min•go (də ming′gō), **Placido,** born 1941, Spanish operatic tenor, in the U.S.

Do•min•guín (dô′mēng gēn′), **Luis Miguel** (*Luis Miguel González Lucas*), born 1926, Spanish bullfighter.

Dom•i•nic (dom′ə nik), **Saint,** 1170–1221, Spanish priest: founder of the Dominican order.

Dom•i•no (dom′ə nō′), **Antoine** (*"Fats"*), born 1928, U.S. rhythm-and-blues pianist, singer, and songwriter.

Do•mi•tian (də mish′ən, -ē ən), (*Titus Flavius Domitianus Augustus*), A.D. 51–96, Roman emperor 81–96.

Don•a•tel•lo (don′ə tel′ō), (*Donato di Niccolo di Betto Bardi*), 1386?–1466, Italian sculptor.

Do•na•tus (dō nā′təs), **1.** early-4th-century bishop of Casae Nigrae in N Africa: leader of a heretical Christian group. **2. Aelius.** 4th century A.D., Roman grammarian.

Don•i•zet•ti (don′i zet′ē), **Gaetano,** 1797–1848, Italian operatic composer.

Donn-Byrne (don′bûrn′), **Brian Oswald** (*"Donn Byrne"*), 1889–1928, U.S. novelist and short-story writer.

Donne (dun), **John,** 1573–1631, English poet and clergyman.

Don•o•van (don′ə vən), **William Joseph** (*"Wild Bill"*), 1883–1959, U.S. lawyer and military officer: organizer and director of the OSS 1942–45.

Do•nus (dō′nəs), died A.D. 678, pope 676–678.

Doo•lit•tle (do͞o′lit′l), **1. Hilda** (*"H.D."*), 1886–1961, U.S. poet. **2. James Harold,** born 1896, U.S. aviator and general.

Do•ra•ti (dô rä′tē, dō-; *Hung.* dô′RO ti), **Antal,** 1906–88, Hungarian conductor, in the U.S.

Do•ré (dô rā′), **(Paul) Gustave,** 1832?–83, French painter, illustrator, and sculptor.

Dor•set (dôr′sit), **1st Earl of,** SACKVILLE, Thomas.

Dor•ti•cós (dôR′tē kôs′), **Osvaldo** (*Osvaldo Dorticós Torrado*), 1919–83, Cuban lawyer and statesman: president 1959–76.

Dos Pas•sos (dōs pas′ōs), **John (Roderigo),** 1896–1970, U.S. novelist.

Dos•to•ev•sky or **Dos•to•yev•sky** (dos′tə yef′skē, dus′-), **Fyodor Mikhailovich,** 1821–81, Russian novelist.

Dou or **Douw** (dou), **Gerard,** 1613–75, Dutch painter.

Dou•ble•day (dub′əl dā′), **Abner,** 1819–93, U.S. army officer: sometimes credited with inventing baseball.

Dough•ty (dou′tē), **Charles Montagu,** 1843–1926, English traveler and writer.

Doug•las (dug′ləs), **1. Sir James** (*"the Black Douglas"*), 1286–1330, Scottish military leader. **2. James, 2nd Earl of,** 1358?–88, Scottish military leader. **3. Lloyd C(assel),** 1877–1951, U.S. novelist and clergyman. **4. Stephen A(rnold),** 1813–61, U.S. political leader. **5. William O(rville),** 1898–1980, associate justice of the U.S. Supreme Court 1939–75.

Doug•las-Home (dug′ləs hyo͞om′), **Alexander Frederick, (Baron Home of the Hirsel),** born 1903, British statesman and politician: prime minister 1963–64.

Doug•lass (dug′ləs), **Frederick,** 1817–95, U.S. abolitionist.

Dou•mergue (do͞o meRg′), **Gaston,** 1863–1937, French statesman: president of France 1924–31.

Douw (dou), **Gerrard,** Dou, Gerard.

Dov•zhen•ko (dəv zheng′kō), **Alexander P.,** 1894–1956, Russian motion-picture director.

Dow (dou), **Herbert Henry,** 1866–1930, U.S. chemist, inventor, and industrialist.

Dow•den (doud′n), **Edward,** 1843–1913, Irish critic and poet.

Dow•land (dou′lənd), **John,** 1563–1626, English lutenist and composer.

Down•ing (dou′ning), **Andrew Jackson,** 1815–52, U.S. landscape architect.

Dow•son (dou′sən), **Ernest (Christopher),** 1867–1900, English poet.

Doyle (doil), **Sir Arthur Conan,** 1859–1930, British physician, novelist, and detective-story writer.

D'Oy•ly Carte (doi′lē kärt′), **Richard,** CARTE, Richard d'Oyly.

Drab•ble (drab′əl), **Margaret,** born 1939, English novelist and critic.

Dra•co (drā′kō) also **Dra•con** (-kon), fl. late 7th century B.C., Athenian lawgiver: noted for the severity of his code of laws.

Drake (drāk), **1. Sir Francis,** c1540–96, English admiral and buccaneer. **2. Joseph Rodman,** 1795–1820, U.S. poet.

Dra•peau (dra pō′; *Fr.* DRA pō′), **Jean** (zhäN), born 1916, Canadian lawyer and politician: mayor of Montreal 1954–57 and 1960–86.

Dra•per (drā′pər), **1. Henry,** 1837–82, U.S. astronomer. **2.** his father, **John William,** 1811–82, U.S. chemist, physiologist, historian, and writer; born in England. **3. Ruth,** 1884–1956, U.S. diseuse and writer of character sketches.

Dray•ton (drāt′n), **1. Michael,** 1563–1631, English poet. **2. William Henry,** 1742–1779, American member of Continental Congress, 1778–79.

Drei•ser (drī′sər, -zər), **Theodore,** 1871–1945, U.S. novelist.

Dress•ler (dres′lər), **Marie** (*Leila Koerber*), 1869–1934, U.S. actress, born in Canada.

Drew (dro͞o), **1. Charles Richard,** 1904–50, U.S. physician: developer of blood-bank technique. **2. John,** 1827–62, U.S. actor, born in Ireland.

Drey•fus (drā′fəs, drī′-), **Alfred,** 1859–1935, French army officer of Jewish descent: wrongfully convicted of treason; acquitted 1906.

Drink•wa•ter (dringk′wô′tər, -wot′ər), **John,** 1882–1937, English poet, playwright, and critic.

Dru•sus (dro͞o′səs), **Nero Claudius** (*"Germanicus"*), 38–9 B.C., Roman general.

Dry•den (drīd′n), **John,** 1631–1700, English dramatist and critic.

Duar•te Fuen•tes (dwäR′te fwen′tes), **José Napoleón,** 1926–90, Salvadoran political leader: president 1980–82, 1984–89.

Du Bar•ry (do͞o bar′ē, dyo͞o), **Comtesse** (*Marie Jeanne Bécu*), 1746–93, mistress of Louis XV.

Dub•ček (do͞ob′chek, do͞op′-), **Alexander,** born 1921, Czechoslovakian political leader.

du Bel•lay (do͞o be lā′), **Joachim,** BELLAY, Joachim du.

Du•bin•sky (do͞o bin′skē), **David,** 1892–1982, U.S. labor leader, born in Poland: president of the ILGWU 1932–66.

Du Bois (do͞o bois′), **W(illiam) E(dward) B(urghardt),** 1868–1963, U.S. educator and writer.

Du•bois (dʏ bwä′), **(Marie) Eugène (François Thomas),** 1858–1941, Dutch physical anthropologist and anatomist.

Du•bos (do͞o bōs′), **René Jules,** 1901–82, U.S. bacteriologist, born in France: early advocate of ecological concern.

Du•buf•fet (do͞o′bə fā′, dyo͞o′-), **Jean** (zhäɴ), 1901–85, French painter.

Du•casse (dʏ kas′), **Jean Jules Amable Roger-** (zhäɴ), Roger-Ducasse, Jean Jules Amable.

Duc•cio di Buo•nin•se•gna (do͞ot′chô dē bwô′nēn se′nyä), c1255–1319?, Italian painter.

Du Chail•lu (do͞o shi′yo͞o, shal′-, dyo͞o; *Fr.* dʏ sha yʏ′), **Paul Belloni,** 1835–1903, U.S. explorer in Africa, traveler, and writer; born in France.

Du•champ (dʏ shäɴ′), **Marcel,** 1887–1968, French painter, in U.S. after 1915.

Du•champ-Vil•lon (dʏ shäɴ vē yôɴ′), **Raymond,** 1876–1918, French sculptor (brother of Jacques Villon and Marcel Duchamp).

Du•com•mun (dʏ kô mœɴ′), **Élie,** 1833–1906, Swiss author: Nobel peace prize 1902.

Du•de•vant (*Fr.* dʏdᵊ väɴ′), **Madame Amandine Lucile Aurore,** Sand, George.

Dud•ley (dud′lē), **1. Robert, 1st Earl of Leicester,** 1532?–88, British statesman and favorite of Queen Elizabeth I. **2. Thomas,** 1576–1653, English governor of Massachusetts Bay Colony, 1634–35, 1640–41, 1645–46, 1650–51.

Du•fay (do͞o fi′; *Fr.* dʏ fā′), **Guillaume,** c1400–74, Flemish composer.

Duf•fy (duf′ē), **Sir Charles Gavan,** 1816–1903, Irish and Australian politician.

Du•fy (dʏ fē′), **Raoul,** 1877–1953, French painter.

Du Gues•clin (dʏ ge klaɴ′), **Bertrand** (*"the Eagle of Brittany"*), c1320–80, French military leader: constable of France 1370–80.

Du•ha•mel (do͞o′ə mel′, dyo͞o′-), **Georges,** 1884–1966, French novelist, physician, and poet.

Du•ka•kis (do͝o kä′kis), **Michael,** born 1933, U.S. politician.

Du•kas (dʏ ka′), **Paul (Abraham),** 1865–1935, French composer.

Duke (do͞ok, dyo͞ok), **Benjamin Newton,** 1855–1929, and his brother, **James Buchanan,** 1856–1925, U.S. industrialists.

Dul•bec•co (dul bek′ō, do͞ol-), **Renato,** born 1914, U.S. biologist, born in Italy: Nobel prize for medicine 1975.

Dul•les (dul′əs), **John Foster,** 1888–1959, U.S. secretary of state 1953–59.

Dull′ Knife′, (*Tah-me-la-pash-me*), died 1883, leader of the Northern Cheyenne.

Du•luth (də lo͞oth′; *Fr.* dʏ lʏt′), **Daniel Greysolon, Sieur,** 1636–1710, French trader and explorer in Canada and Great Lakes region.

Du•mas (do͞o mä′, dyo͞o-), **1. Alexandre** (*"Dumas père"*), 1802–70, and his son, **Alexandre** (*"Dumas fils"*),

1824–95, French dramatists and novelists. **2. Jean-Baptiste André,** 1800–84, French chemist.

Du Mau•ri•er (do͞o môr′ē ā′, dyo͞o), **1. Dame Daphne** (*Lady Browning*), 1907-89, English novelist. **2.** her grandfather, **George Louis Palmella Busson,** 1834–96, English illustrator and novelist.

Du•mont d'Ur•ville (dʏ môɴ dʏʀ vēl′), **Jules Sébastien César,** 1790–1842, French naval officer: explored South Pacific and Antarctic.

Du•nant (do͞o näɴ′, dyo͞o-), **Jean Henri** (zhäɴ), 1828–1910, Swiss banker and philanthropist: founder of the Red Cross; Nobel peace prize 1901.

Dun•bar (dun′bär *for 1;* dun bär′ *for 2*), **1. Paul Laurence,** 1872–1906, U.S. poet. **2. William,** c1460–c1520, Scottish poet.

Dun•can (dung′kən), **Isadora,** 1878–1927, U.S. dancer.

Duncan I, died 1040, king of Scotland 1030–40: murdered by Macbeth.

Dun•ham (dun′əm), **Katherine,** born 1910?, U.S. dancer and choreographer.

Dun•lap (dun′lap), **William,** 1766–1839, U.S. dramatist, theatrical producer, and historian.

Dun•more (dun môr′, -mōr′; dun′môr, -mōr), **John Murray, 4th Earl of,** 1732–1809, Scottish colonial governor in America.

Du•nois (dʏ nwa′), **Jean** (zhäɴ), **Comte de,** (*"Bastard of Orleans"*), 1403?–68; French military leader: relieved by Joan of Arc and her troops when besieged at Orleans.

Dun•sa•ny (dun sā′nē), **Edward John Moreton Drax Plunkett, 18th Baron** (*"Lord Dunsany"*), 1878–1957, Irish dramatist, poet, and essayist.

Duns Sco•tus (dunz skō′təs), **John** (*"Doctor Subtilis"*), 1265?–1308, Scottish scholastic theologian.

Dun•sta•ble (dun′stə bəl), **John,** c1390–1453, English composer.

Dun•stan (dun′stən), **Saint,** A.D. c925–988, English archbishop of Canterbury 961–978.

Du•pleix (dʏ pleks′), **Joseph François, Marquis,** 1697–1763, French colonial governor of India 1724–54.

Du•ples•sis-Mor•nay (do͞o ple sē′ môr nā′, dyo͞o-), **Philippe,** MORNAY, Philippe de.

Du•Pont or **Du Pont** (do͞o pont′, dyo͞o-, do͞o′pont, dyo͞o′-), **1. Eleuthère Irénée,** 1771–1834, U.S. industrialist, born in France. **2. Pierre Samuel,** 1739–1817, French economist and statesman (father of Eleuthère Irénée). **3. Samuel Francis,** 1803–65, Union admiral in the U.S. Civil War.

Du•pré (dʏ pʀā′), **1. Jules,** 1812–89, French painter. **2. Marcel,** 1886–1971, French organist and composer.

Du•quesne (do͞o kān′, dyo͞o-), **Abraham,** 1610–88, French naval commander.

Du•rand (də rand′), **Asher Brown,** 1796–1886, U.S. engraver and landscape painter of the Hudson River School.

Du•rant (də rant′), **Ariel,** 1898–1981, and her husband, **Will(iam James),** 1885–1981, U.S. authors and historians.

Du•ran•te (də ran′tē), **James Francis** (*Jimmy*), 1893–1980, U.S. comedian.

Du•ran•ty (də ran′tē), **Walter,** 1884–1957, English journalist and author in the U.S.

Dü•rer (do͝or′ər, dyo͝or′-), **Albrecht,** 1471–1528, German painter and engraver.

D'Ur•fey (dûr′fē), **Thomas,** 1653–1723, English dramatist.

Durk•heim (dûrk′hīm, dûr kem′), **Émile,** 1858–1917, French sociologist and philosopher.

Dur•rell (do͝or′əl, dur′-), **Lawrence (George),** 1912–90, English novelist and poet.

Dür•ren•matt (do͝or′ən mät′, dyo͝or′-; *Ger.* dʏʀ′ən mät′), **Friedrich,** 1921–90, Swiss dramatist and novelist.

Dur•yea (do͝or′yā, do͝or′ē ā′), **Charles Edgar,** 1861–1938, U.S. inventor and manufacturer of automobiles and automotive devices.

Du Sa•ble (do͞o sä′blə, säb′, dyo͞o; *Fr.* dʏ sä′blᵊ), **Jean Baptiste Pointe,** 1745?–1818, U.S. pioneer trader, born in Haiti: early settler of Chicago.

Du•se (do͞o′zā), **Eleonora,** 1859–1924, Italian actress.

Du•va•lier (do͞o′val yā′, do͞o val′yā), **1. François,** ("*Papa Doc*"), 1907–71, Haitian dictator: president 1957–71. **2.** his son **Jean-Claude** (zhäɴ klōd′), ("*Baby Doc*"), born 1951, Haitian political leader: president 1971–86.

Du•ve (dʏ′və), **Christian René de,** born 1917, Belgian biologist, born in England: Nobel prize for medicine 1974.

Du•ve•neck (do͞o′və nek′), **Frank** (*Frank Decker*), 1848–1919, U.S. painter and teacher.

du Vi•gneaud (do͞o vēn′yō, dyo͞o), **Vincent,** 1901–78, U.S. biochemist: Nobel prize for chemistry 1955.

Dvo•řák (dvôr′zhäk, -zhak), **Antonín,** 1841–1904, Czech composer.

Dy•er (dī′ər), **1. John,** 1700–58, British poet. **2. Mary,** died 1660, American Quaker religious martyr, born in England.

Dyl•an (dil′ən), **Bob** (*Robert Zimmerman*), born 1941, U.S. folk-rock singer, guitarist, and songwriter.

Eads (ēdz), **James Buchanan,** 1820–87, U.S. engineer and inventor.

Ea•kins (ā′kinz), **Thomas,** 1844–1916, U.S. painter.

Eames (ēmz), **Charles,** 1907–78, U.S. designer and architect.

Ear•hart (âr′härt), **Amelia (Mary),** 1897–1937, U.S. aviator.

Ear•ly (ûr′lē), **Jubal Anderson,** 1816–94, Confederate general in the U.S. Civil War.

Earp (ûrp), **Wyatt (Berry Stapp),** 1848–1929, U.S. law officer.

East•lake (ēst′lāk′), **Sir Charles Locke,** 1836–1906, English architect, designer, and author.

East•land (ēst′lənd), **James O(liver),** 1904–86, U.S. politician: senator 1941, 1943–78.

East•man (ēst′mən), **1. George,** 1854–1932, U.S. philanthropist and inventor in the field of photography. **2. Max Forrester,** 1883–1969, U.S. editor and writer.

East•wood (ēst′wo͝od), **Clint,** born 1930, U.S. actor and director.

Ea•ton (ēt′n), **Theophilus,** 1590–1658, English colonist and colonial administrator in America.

E•ban (ē′bən), **Abba** (*Aubrey Solomon Eban*), born 1915, Israeli political leader, born in South Africa.

E•ber•hart (ā′bər härt′, eb′ər-), **Richard,** born 1904, U.S. poet.

E•bert (ā′bərt), **Friedrich,** 1871–1925, first president of Germany 1919–25.

Ec•cles (ek′əlz), **1. Sir John Carew,** born 1903, Australian physiologist: Nobel prize for medicine 1963. **2. Marriner Stoddard,** 1890–1977, U.S. economist and banker.

E•ce•vit (e je vēt′), **Bülent,** born 1925, Turkish journalist and political leader: prime minister 1974, 1977, 1978–79.

E•che•ga•ray (e′che gä rī′), **José** (*José Echegaray y Eizaguirre*), 1832–1916, Spanish dramatist and statesman: Nobel prize 1904.

E•che•ver•ri•a Ál•va•rez (ech′ə və rē′ə al′və rez′; *Sp.* e′che ver rē′ä äl′vä res′), **Luis** born 1922, Mexican political leader: president 1970–76.

Eck (ek), **Johann** (*Johann Mayer*), 1486–1543, German Roman Catholic theologian.

Eck•er•mann (ek′ər män′), **Johann Peter,** 1792–1854, German writer and literary assistant to Goethe.

Eck•hart (ek′ärt), **Johannes,** (*"Meister Eckhart"*), c1260–1327?, Dominican theologian: founder of German mysticism.

Ed•ding•ton (ed′ing tən), **Sir Arthur (Stanley),** 1882–1944, English astronomer, physicist, and writer.

Ed•dy (ed′ē), **Mary (Morse) Baker** (*Mrs. Glover; Mrs.*

Patterson), 1821–1910, U.S. founder of the Christian Science Church.

Ed•el•man (ed′l mən), **Gerald Maurice,** born 1929, U.S. biochemist: Nobel prize for medicine 1972.

E•den (ēd′n), **(Robert) Anthony, Earl of Avon,** 1897–1977, British prime minister 1955–57.

Edge•worth (ej′wûrth), **Maria,** 1767–1849, English novelist.

Ed•in•burgh (ed′n bûr′ə, -bur′ə; *esp. Brit.* -brə), **Duke of,** PHILIP[1] (def. 4).

Ed•i•son (ed′ə sən), **Thomas Alva,** 1847–1931, U.S. inventor, esp. of electrical devices.

Ed•man (ed′mən), **Irwin,** 1896–1954, U.S. philosopher and essayist.

Ed•mund (ed′mənd), **1. Edmund I,** A.D. 921?–946, English king 940–946. **2. Edmund II** (*"Ironside"*) A.D. c980–1016, English king 1016: defeated by Canute.

Ed•munds (ed′məndz), **George Franklin,** 1828–1919, U.S. lawyer and politician: senator 1866–91.

Ed•ward[1] (ed′wərd), **Prince of Wales** and **Duke of Cornwall** (*"The Black Prince"*), 1330–76, English military leader (son of Edward III).

Ed•ward[2] (ed′wərd), **1. Edward I,** (*"Edward Longshanks"*) 1239–1307, king of England 1272–1307 (son of Henry III). **2. Edward II,** 1284–1327, king of England 1307–27 (son of Edward I). **3. Edward III,** 1312–77, king of England 1327–77 (son of Edward II). **4. Edward IV,** 1442–83, king of England 1461–70, 1471–83: 1st king of the house of York. **5. Edward V,** 1470–83, king of England 1483 (son of Edward IV). **6. Edward VI,** 1537–53, king of England 1547–53 (son of Henry VIII and Jane Seymour). **7. Edward VII,** (*Albert Edward*) (*"the Peacemaker"*) 1841–1910, king of Great Britain and Ireland 1901–10 (son of Queen Victoria). **8. Edward VIII,** (*Duke of Windsor*) 1894–1972, king of Great Britain 1936: abdicated (son of George V; brother of George VI).

Ed•wards (ed′wərdz), **Jonathan,** 1703–58, American theologian.

Ed′ward the Confes′sor, 1. Saint, 1002?–66, English king 1042–66: founder of Westminster Abbey. **2.** 1002?–66, English king 1042–66: founder of Westminster Abbey.

Ed•win (ed′win), A.D. 585?–633, king of Northumbria 617–633.

Eg•bert (eg′bərt), A.D. 775?–839, king of the West Saxons 802–839; 1st king of the English 828–839.

Eg•gle•ston (eg′əl stən), **Edward,** 1837–1902, U.S. author.

Eg•lev•sky (i glef′skē, eg′ləf skē), **André,** 1917–77, U.S. ballet dancer, born in Russia.

Eh•ren•burg (er′ən bûrg′, -bŏŏrg′), **Ilya Grigorievich,** 1891–1967, Russian novelist and journalist.

Ehr•lich (âr′likн, -lik), **Paul,** 1854–1915, German physician, bacteriologist, and chemist: Nobel prize for medicine 1908.

Eich•mann (ik′mən, ikh′-; *Ger.* ikh′män′), **Adolf,** 1906–62, German Nazi official: executed for war crimes.

Eif•fel (ī′fəl; *Fr.* e fel′), **Alexandre Gustave,** 1832–1923, French civil engineer and pioneer aerodynamic researcher.

Ei•gen (ī′gən), **Manfred,** born 1927, German chemist: Nobel prize 1967.

Eijk•man (ik′män), **Christiaan,** 1858–1930, Dutch physician: Nobel prize 1929.

Ein•stein (īn′stīn), **1. Albert,** 1879–1955, U.S. physicist, born in Germany: formulator of the theory of relativity; Nobel prize 1921. **2. Alfred,** 1880–1952, German musicologist in U.S.

Eint•ho•ven (īnt′hō′vən), **Willem,** 1860–1927, Dutch physiologist: Nobel prize for medicine 1924.

Ei•sen•how•er (ī′zən hou′ər), **Dwight David,** 1890–1969, U.S. general: 34th president of the U.S. 1953–61.

Ei•sen•staedt (ī′zən stat′), **Alfred,** born 1898, U.S. news photographer, born in Germany.

Ei•sen•stein (ī′zən stīn′), **1. Ferdinand Gotthold Max,** 1823–52, German mathematician. **2. Sergei Mikhailovich,** 1898–1948, Russian theatrical and motion-picture director.

El•a•gab•a•lus (el′ə gab′ə ləs, ē′lə-), Heliogabalus.

El Cid Cam•pe•a•dor (*Sp.* el thēd′ käm′pe ä thôr′, sēd′), Cid, The.

El Cor•do•bés (el kôr′thô ves′), (*Manuel Benítez Pérez*), born 1936, Spanish bullfighter.

El•dridge (el′drij), **(David) Roy,** 1911–89, U.S. jazz trumpeter.

El′ea•nor of Aq′uitaine (el′ə nər, -nôr′), 1122?–1204, queen of Louis VII of France 1137–52; queen of Henry II of England 1154–89.

El•eu•the•ri•us (el′yo͞o thēr′ē əs), **Saint,** pope A.D. 175–189.

El•gar (el′gər, -gär), **Sir Edward,** 1857–1934, English composer.

El Gre•co (el grek′ō, grā′kō), (*Domenikos Theotocopoulos*), 1541–1614, Spanish painter, born in Crete.

E•li•a (ē′lē ə), pen name of Charles Lamb.

Eli′jah Muham′mad, (*Elijah Poole*) 1897–1975, U.S. religious leader of the Black Muslims 1934–75.

El•i•ot (el′ē ət, el′yət), **1. Charles William,** 1834–1926, U.S. educator: president of Harvard University 1869–1909. **2. George** (*Mary Ann Evans*), 1819–80, English novelist. **3. John** (*"the Apostle of the Indians"*), 1604–90, American colonial missionary. **4. T(homas) S(tearns),** 1888–1965, British poet and critic, born in the U.S.: Nobel prize 1948.

E•liz•a•beth[1] (i liz′ə bəth), **1.** (*Elizaveta Petrovna*) 1709–62, empress of Russia 1741–62 (daughter of Peter the Great). **2.** (*Pauline Elizabeth Ottilie Luise, Princess of Wied*) (*"Carmen Sylva"*) 1843–1916, queen of Romania 1881–1914 and author. **3.** (*Elizabeth Angela Marguerite*

Bowes-Lyon) born 1900, queen consort of George VI of Great Britain (mother of Elizabeth II). **4. Saint,** 1207–31, Hungarian princess and religious mystic.

E•liz•a•beth[2] (i liz′ə bəth), **1. Elizabeth I,** (*Elizabeth Tudor*) 1533–1603, queen of England 1558–1603 (daughter of Henry VIII and Anne Boleyn). **2. Elizabeth II,** (*Elizabeth Alexandra Mary Windsor*) born 1926, queen of Great Britain since 1952 (daughter of George VI).

El•let (el′it), **Charles, Jr.,** 1810–62, U.S. civil engineer: builder of suspension bridges.

El•ling•ton (el′ing tən), **Edward Kennedy** (*"Duke"*), 1899–1974, U.S. jazz musician and composer.

El•lis (el′is), **1. Alexander John** (*Alexander John Sharpe*), 1814–90, English phonetician and mathematician. **2. (Henry) Havelock,** 1859–1939, English psychologist and writer.

El•li•son (el′ə sən), **Ralph (Waldo),** born 1914, U.S. novelist.

Ells•worth (elz′wûrth), **1. Lincoln,** 1880–1951, U.S. polar explorer. **2. Oliver,** 1745–1807, U.S. jurist and statesman: Chief Justice of the U.S. 1796–1800.

El•man (el′mən), **Mischa,** 1891–1967, U.S. violinist, born in Russia.

É•lu•ard (ā ly ar′), **Paul,** (*Eugène Grindel*), 1895–1952, French poet.

El•ze•vir or **El•ze•vier** (el′zə vēr′, -vər, -sə-), **Louis,** c1540–1617, Dutch printer.

Em•er•son (em′ər sən), **Ralph Waldo,** 1803–82, U.S. essayist and poet.

E•mi•ne•scu (ye′mē ne′sko͞o), **Mihail** (*Mihail Iminovici*), 1850–89, Romanian poet.

Em•mett (em′it), **Daniel Decatur,** 1815–1904, U.S. songwriter and minstrel-show performer and producer: composer of "Dixie."

Em•ped•o•cles (em ped′ə klēz′), c490–c430 B.C., Greek philosopher and statesman.

Emp•son (emp′sən), **William,** 1906–84, English critic and poet.

En•ci•na (en thē′nä, -sē′), **Juan del,** 1468?-1529?, Spanish poet, composer, and playwright.

En•de•cott or **En•di•cott** (en′di kət, -kot′), **John,** 1588?–1665, colonial governor of Massachusetts 1644–65, born in England.

En•ders (en′dərz), **John Franklin,** 1897–1985, U.S. bacteriologist: Nobel prize for medicine 1954.

E•nes•co (e nes′kō) also **E•nes•cu** (-ko͞o), **Georges,** 1881–1955, Romanian violinist, composer, and conductor.

En•gel (eng′gəl), **Lehman,** born 1910, U.S. conductor and composer.

En•gels (eng′gəlz), **Friedrich,** 1820–95, German socialist in England: collaborated with Karl Marx in systematizing Marxism.

En•ghien, d' (dän gan′), **Duc,** (*Louis Antoine Henry de*

Bourbon-Condé), 1772–1804, French prince: executed by Napoleon I.

En•gle (eng′gəl), **Paul (Hamilton),** 1908–91, U.S. poet and educator.

En•ni•us (en′ē əs), **Quintus,** 239–169? B.C., Roman poet.

En•sor (en′sôr), **James,** 1860–1949, Belgian painter.

En•ver Pa•sha (en ver′ pä shä′), 1881–1922, Turkish soldier and statesman.

E•pam•i•non•das (i pam′ə non′dəs), 418?–362 B.C., Theban general and statesman.

Eph•ron (ef′rən), **Nora,** born 1941, U.S. novelist.

Ep•ic•te•tus (ep′ik tē′təs), A.D. c60–c120, Greek Stoic philosopher, mainly in Rome.

Ep•i•cu•rus (ep′i kyo͝or′əs), 342?–270 B.C., Greek philosopher.

Ep•stein (ep′stīn), **Sir Jacob,** 1880–1959, British sculptor, born in the U.S.

Er•a•sis•tra•tus (er′ə sis′trə təs), c300–250 B.C., Greek physician and physiologist.

E•ras•mus (i raz′məs), **Desiderius,** 1466?–1536, Dutch humanist, scholar, and theologian.

E•ras•tus (i ras′təs), **Thomas,** 1524–83, Swiss-German theologian.

Er•a•tos•the•nes (er′ə tos′thə nēz′), 276?–195? B.C., Greek mathematician and astronomer at Alexandria.

Er•cel•doune (ûr′səl do͞on′), **Thomas of,** THOMAS OF ERCELDOUNE.

Er•ci•lla (er thē′lyä, -sē′yä), **Alonso de,** 1533–94, Spanish epic poet; soldier in the conquest of Chile.

Erck•mann-Cha•tri•an (erk′man sha′trē än′), joint pen name of **Émile Erckmann,** 1822–99, and **Alexandre Chatrian,** 1826–90, collaborating French novelists and dramatists.

Er•hard (âr′härt; *Ger.* er′härt), **Ludwig,** 1897–1977, West German economist and government official: chancellor 1963–66.

Er•ic•son or **Er•ics•son** (er′ik sən), **Leif,** fl. A.D. c1000, Norse mariner (son of Eric the Red).

Er•ics•son (er′ik sən), **John,** 1803–89, Swedish engineer and inventor; in the U.S. after 1839.

Er′ic the Red′ (er′ik), born A.D. c950, Norse mariner: explorer and colonizer of Greenland c985.

E•rig•e•na (i rij′ə nə), **Johannes Scotus,** A.D. c810–c877, Irish philosopher and theologian.

Er•ik•son (er′ik sən), **Erik (Homburger),** born 1902, U.S. psychoanalyst, born in Germany.

Er•lan•der (er′län dər), **Tage (Fritiof),** 1901–85, Swedish statesman: prime minister 1946–69.

Er•lan•ger (ûr′lang ər), **Joseph,** 1874–1965, U.S. physiologist: Nobel prize for medicine 1944.

Ernst (ûrnst, ernst), **Max,** 1891–1976, German painter.

Er•skine (ûr′skin), **1. John** (*Erskine of Carnock*), 1695–

1768, Scottish writer on law. **2. John,** 1879–1951, U.S. novelist and essayist.

Er•vin (ûr′vin), **Samuel James, Jr.** (*Sam*), 1896–1985, U.S. jurist and politician: senator 1954–74.

Er•vine (ûr′vin), **St. John Greer** (grēr), 1883–1971, Irish dramatist and novelist.

Er•ving (ûr′ving), **Julius Winfield** (*"Dr. J"*), born 1950, U.S. basketball player.

E•sa•ki (i sä′kē), **Leo,** born 1925, Japanese physicist, in the U.S. since 1960: Nobel prize 1973.

Es•cof•fier (es kô fyā′), **Georges Auguste,** 1846–1935, French chef and author of cookbooks.

Es•cu•de•ro (es′ko͞o ᵺe′rô), **Vicente,** 1892?–1980, Spanish dancer.

Esh•kol (esh′kôl, esh kôl′), **Levi** (*Levi Shkolnik*), 1895–1969, Israeli statesman, born in Russia: prime minister 1963–69.

Es•pron•ce•da (es′prôn the′ᵺä, -se′-), **José de,** 1808–42, Spanish poet.

Es•sex (es′iks), **2nd Earl of,** Devereux, Robert.

Es•ter•há•zy or **Es•ter•ha•zy** (es′tər hä′zē), **Prince Miklós József,** 1714–90, Hungarian patron of the arts.

Es•tienne (es tyen′) also **Étienne,** a family of French printers, book dealers, and scholars, including **Henri,** died 1520; his son, **Robert,** 1503?–59; **Henri** (son of Robert), 1531?–98.

Es•tra•da Ca•bre•ra (es trä′ᵺä kä vre′rä), **Manuel,** 1857–1924, Guatemalan politician: president 1898–1920.

Eth•el•bert (eth′əl bûrt′), A.D. 552?–616, king of Kent 560–616.

Eth•el•red II (eth′əl red′), (*"the Unready"*) A.D. 968?–1016, king of the English 978–1016.

Eth•er•ege (eth′ər ij, eth′rij), **Sir George,** 1635?–91, English dramatist.

Euck•en (oi′kən), **Rudolph Christoph,** 1846–1926, German philosopher: Nobel prize for literature 1908.

Eu•clid (yo͞o′klid), fl. c300 B.C., Greek geometrician and educator at Alexandria.

Eu•gène (œ zhen′), **Prince** (*François Eugène de Savoie-Carignan*), 1663–1736, Austrian general, born in France.

Eu•gé•nie (œ zhā nē′), **Comtesse de Teba** (*Marie Eugénie de Montijo de Guzmán*), 1826–1920, wife of Napoleon III, born in Spain: Empress of France 1853–71.

Eu•ge•ni•us (yo͞o jē′nē əs), **1. Eugenius I, Saint,** died A.D. 657, pope 654–657. **2. Eugenius II,** died A.D. 827, Italian ecclesiastic: pope 824–827. **3. Eugenius III** (*Bernardo Pignatelli* or *Paganelli*), died 1153, Italian ecclesiastic: pope 1145–53. **4. Eugenius IV** (*Gabriele* or *Gabriel Condolmieri* or *Condulmer*), 1383–1447, Italian ecclesiastic: pope 1431–47.

Eu•he•mer•us (yo͞o hē′mər əs, -hem′ər-), fl. c300 B.C., Greek mythographer.

Eu•ler (oi′lər), **1. Leonhard,** 1707–83, Swiss mathematician. **2. Ulf Svante von,** 1905–83, Swedish physiologist: Nobel prize for medicine 1970.

Eu•ler-Chel•pin (oi′lər kel′pin), **Hans Karl August Simon von,** 1873–1964, German chemist in Sweden: Nobel prize 1929.

Eu•men•es (yo͞o men′ēz), **1. Eumenes I,** king of Pergamum. 263–241 B.C. **2. Eumenes II,** king of Pergamum. 197–c159 B.C.

Eu•rip•i•des (yo͝o rip′i dēz′, yə-), c480–406? B.C., Greek dramatist.

Eu•se•bi•us (yo͞o sē′bē əs), pope A.D. 309 or 310.

Euse′bius of Caes•a•re′a (sē′zə rē′ə, sez′ə-), (*Pamphili*) A.D. 263?–c340, Christian theologian and historian.

E•u•sta•chio (e′o͞o stä′kyô), **Bartolommeo,** 1524?–1574, Italian anatomist. Latin, **Eu•sta•chi•us** (yo͞o stā′kē əs).

Eu•tych•i•a•nus (yo͞o tik′ē ā′nəs) also **Eu•tych′i•an** (-ən), **Saint,** died A.D. 283, pope 275–283.

Ev•ans (ev′ənz), **1. Sir Arthur John,** 1851–1941, English archaeologist. **2. Dame Edith,** 1888–1976, English actress. **3. Herbert McLean,** 1882–1971, U.S. embryologist and anatomist. **4. Mary Ann,** ELIOT, George. **5. Maurice,** 1901–1989, U.S. actor and producer, born in England. **6. Oliver,** 1755–1819, U.S. inventor: constructed the first high-pressure steam engine in the U.S. 1801?. **7. Walker,** 1903–75, U.S. photographer.

Ev•a•ris•tus (ev′ə ris′təs), **Saint,** died A.D. 105, pope 97–105.

Ev•arts (ev′ərts), **William Maxwell,** 1818–1901, U.S. lawyer and statesman.

Ev•att (ev′ət), **Herbert Vere** (vēr), 1894–1966, Australian lawyer and statesman: president of the General Assembly of the United Nations 1948–49.

Eve•lyn (ēv′lin), **John,** 1620–1706, English diarist.

Ev•er•ett (ev′ər it, ev′rit), **Edward,** 1794–1865, U.S. statesman, orator, and writer.

Ev•er•good (ev′ər go͝od′), **Philip** (*Philip Blashki*), 1901–73, U.S. painter.

Ev•ers (ev′ərz), **(James) Charles,** born 1922, and his brother **Medgar (Wiley),** 1925–63, U.S. civil-rights leaders.

Ev•ert (ev′ərt), **Chris(tine Marie),** born 1954, U.S. tennis player.

Ev•tu•shen•ko (yev′to͝o sheng′kō), **Evgenii Alexandrovich,** YEVTUSHENKO, Yevgeny Alexandrovich.

Ew•ell (yo͞o′el), **Richard Stoddert,** 1817–72, Confederate lieutenant general in the U.S. Civil War.

Eyck (īk), **Hubert van** or **Huybrecht van,** 1366–1426, and his brother **Jan van** (*Jan van Brugge*), 1385?–1440: Flemish painters.

Ey•senck (ī′sengk), **Hans J(urgen),** born 1916, British psychologist, born in Germany.

E•ze•ki•el (i zē′kē əl), **1.** a Major Prophet of the 6th century B.C. **2. Moses Jacob,** 1844–1917, U.S. sculptor.

Ez•ra (ez′rə), a Jewish scribe and prophet of the 5th century B.C.

Fa•ber•gé (fab′ər zhā′), **(Peter) Carl Gustavovich,** 1846–1920, Russian goldsmith and jeweler.

Fa•bi•us Max•i•mus (fā′bē əs mak′sə məs), (*Quintus Fabius Maximus Verrucosus*) ("*Cunctator*") 275–203 B.C., Roman general.

Fa•bre (fä′bər), **Jean Henri** (zhäɴ), 1823–1915, French entomologist and popular writer on insect life.

Fa•bri•ti•us (fə brēt′sē əs), **Carel,** 1622–54: Dutch painter: pupil of Rembrandt.

Fa•de•yev or **Fa•de•ev** (fə dā′ef, -ev; *Russ.* fu dye′yif), **Aleksandr Aleksandrovich,** 1901–56, Russian novelist.

Fag•gi (fä′jē), **Al•fe•o** (al fā′ō), 1885–1966, U.S. sculptor, born in Italy.

Fahd (fäd), (*Fahd ibn Abdul-Aziz al Saud*), born 1922, king of Saudi Arabia since 1982 (son of ibn-Saud and brother of Khalid).

Fahr•en•heit (far′ən hīt′), **Gabriel Daniel,** 1686–1736, German physicist.

Fair•banks (fâr′bangks′), **1. Charles Warren,** 1852–1918, vice president of the U.S. 1905–09. **2. Douglas,** 1883–1939, U.S. actor.

Fair•fax (fâr′faks), **1. Thomas** (*3rd Baron Fairfax of Cameron*), 1612–71, British general: commander in chief of the parliamentary army 1645–50. **2. Thomas** (*6th Baron Fairfax of Cameron*), 1692–1782, English colonist in Virginia.

Fai•sal[1] (fī′səl), 1904–75, king of Saudi Arabia 1964–75.

Fai•sal[2] (fī′səl), **1. Faisal I,** 1885–1933, king of Syria 1920; king of Iraq 1921–33. **2. Faisal II,** 1935–58, king of Iraq 1939–58 (grandson of Faisal I).

Fa•lie•ri (*It.* fä lye′ʀē) also **Fa•lie•ro** (-ʀô), **Marino,** 1278?–1355, Venetian army commander: doge of Venice 1354–55.

Fal•ken•hayn (fäl′kən hīn′), **Erich von,** 1861–1922, German general of World War I.

Fall (fôl), **Albert Bacon,** 1861–1944, U.S. politician: senator 1912–21; Secretary of the Interior 1921–23; convicted in Teapot Dome scandal.

Fal•la (fä′yə, fäl′yä), **Manuel de,** 1876–1946, Spanish composer.

Fal•well (fôl′wel), **Jerry L.,** born 1933, U.S. evangelist and political activist.

Fan•euil (fan′l, -yəl; *formerly* fun′l; *spelling pron.* fan′yōō-əl), **Peter,** 1700–43, American merchant: builder of Faneuil Hall.

Fan•fa•ni (fän fä′nē), **Amintore,** born 1908, Italian statesman: premier 1954, 1958–59, 1960–63.

Fa•non (fan′ən; *Fr.* fa nôɴ′), **Frantz (Omar),** 1925–61, West Indian psychiatrist and political theorist, born in Martinique; in Algeria after 1953.

Fan•tin-La•tour (fäN taN lä to͞or′), **(Ignace) Henri (Joseph Théodore),** 1836–1904, French painter.

Far•a•day (far′ə dē, -dā′), **Michael,** 1791–1867, English physicist.

Far•go (fär′gō), **William George,** 1818–81, U.S. businessman: pioneered in express shipping and banking.

Fa•ri•nel•li (far′ə nel′ē; *It.* fä′rē nel′lē), **Carlo** (*Carlo Broschi*), 1705–82, Italian operatic male soprano.

Far•mer (fär′mər), **Fannie (Merritt),** 1857–1915, U.S. authority on cooking.

Far•ne•se (fär ne′ze), **Alessandro, Duke of Parma,** 1545–92, Italian general, statesman, and diplomat.

Farns•worth (färnz′wûrth′), **Philo Taylor,** 1906–71, U.S. physicist and inventor: pioneer in the field of television.

Fa•rouk I (fä ro͞ok′, fə-), FARUK I.

Far•quhar (fär′kwər, -kwär, -kər), **George,** 1678–1707, English playwright, born in Ireland.

Far•ra•gut (far′ə gət), **David Glasgow,** 1801–70, U.S. admiral for the Union in the U.S. Civil War.

Far•rar (fə rär′), **Geraldine** (*Mrs. Lou Tellegen*), 1882–1967, U.S. operatic soprano.

Far•rell (far′əl), **1. Eileen,** born 1920, U.S. soprano. **2. James T(homas),** 1904–79, U.S. novelist.

Fa•ruk I or **Fa•rouk I** (fə ro͞ok′, fä-), 1920–65, king of Egypt from 1936 until his abdication in 1952.

Fast (fast), **Howard,** born 1914, U.S. novelist and screenwriter.

Fat•i•ma (fat′ə mə, fä′tē mä′), A.D. 606?–632, daughter of Muhammad and wife of Ali.

Faulk•ner (fôk′nər), **William,** 1897–1962, U.S. novelist and short-story writer: Nobel prize 1949.

Fau•ré (fô rā′, fō-), **Gabriel Urbain,** 1845–1924, French composer.

Faust (foust), **Johann,** c1480–c1538, German magician, alchemist, and astrologer.

Fawkes (fôks), **Guy,** 1570–1606, English conspirator: leader of the Gunpowder Plot 1605.

Fear•ing (fēr′ing), **Kenneth (Flexner),** 1902–61, U.S. poet and novelist.

Fech•ner (feKH′nər), **Gustav Theodor,** 1801–87, German physicist, psychologist, and philosopher.

Fe•din (fye′dyin), **Konstantin Aleksandrovich,** 1892–1977, Russian novelist and short-story writer.

Fein•ing•er (fī′ning ər), **1. Andreas (Bernhard Lyonel),** born 1906, U.S. photographer, born in France. **2. Lyonel (Charles Adrian),** 1871–1956, U.S. painter.

Fe•lix (fē′liks), **1. Felix I, Saint,** died A.D. 274, pope 269–274. **2. Felix III, Saint,** died A.D. 492, pope 483–492. **3. Felix IV, Saint,** died A.D. 530, pope 526–530.

Fel•ler (fel′ər), **Robert William Andrew** (*Bob*), born 1918, U.S. baseball player.

Fel•li•ni (fə lē′nē), **Federico,** born 1920, Italian filmmaker.

Fé•ne•lon (fān^e lôn′), **François de Salignac de La Mothe,** 1651–1715, French theologian and writer.

Feng Yu-hsiang or **Feng Yu•xiang** (fung′ yoo′-shyäng′), (*"Christian General"*) 1880–1948, Chinese general.

Fer•ber (fûr′bər), **Edna,** 1887–1968, U.S. writer.

Fer•di•nand (fûr′dn and′), **1. Ferdinand I, a.** (*"Ferdinand the Great"*) died 1065, king of Castile 1033–65, king of Navarre and Leon 1037–65, emperor of Spain 1056–65. **b.** 1503–64, Holy Roman emperor 1558–64 (brother of Emperor Charles V). **c.** (*Maximilian Karl Leopold Maria*) 1861–1948, king of Bulgaria 1908–18. **2. Ferdinand II, a.** (*"the Catholic"*) 1452–1516, king of Sicily 1468–1516, king of Aragon 1479–1516; as Ferdinand III, king of Naples 1504–16; as King Ferdinand V, joint sovereign (with Isabella I) of Castile 1474–1504. **b.** 1578–1637, Holy Roman emperor 1620–37. **3. Ferdinand III, a.** Ferdinand II (def. 2a). **b.** 1608–57, Holy Roman emperor 1637–57 (son of Ferdinand II).

Fer•lin•ghet•ti (fûr′ling get′ē), **Lawrence,** born 1920?, U.S. poet associated with the Beat Generation.

Fer•mat (fer ma′; *Eng.* fer mä′), **Pierre de,** 1601–65, French mathematician.

Fer•mi (fûr′mē, fâr′-), **Enrico,** 1901–54, Italian physicist, in the U.S. after 1939: Nobel prize 1938.

Fer•nan•dez (fer nan′dez, fər-), **Juan,** 1536?–1602?, Spanish navigator: explorer in South America and the Pacific.

Fer•nan•do I (*Sp.* fer nän′dô), Ferdinand I (def. 1a).

Fer•ra•ro (fə rär′ō), **Geraldine Anne** ("Gerry"), born 1935, U.S. politician: congresswoman 1978–84; first woman chosen as the vice-presidential nominee of a major political party 1984.

Feucht•wang•er (foikht′väng′ər), **Lion,** 1884–1958, German novelist and dramatist.

Feu•er•bach (foi′ər bäkh′, -bäk′), **Ludwig Andreas,** 1804–72, German philosopher.

Feyn•man (fīn′mən), **Richard Phillips,** 1918–88, U.S. physicist: Nobel prize 1965.

Fi•bi•ger (fē′bē gər), **Johannes Andreas Grib,** 1867–1928, Danish pathologist: Nobel prize for medicine 1926.

Fich•te (fikh′tə), **Johann Gottlieb,** 1762–1814, German philosopher.

Fied•ler (fēd′lər), **Arthur,** 1894–1979, U.S. symphony conductor.

Field (fēld), **1. Cyrus West,** 1819–92, U.S. financier. **2. David Dudley, Jr.,** 1805–94, U.S. jurist (brother of Cyrus West and Stephen Johnson Field). **3. Eugene,** 1850–95, U.S. poet and journalist. **4. Marshall,** 1834–1906, U.S. merchant and philanthropist. **5. Stephen Johnson,** 1816–99, U.S. jurist: associate justice of the U.S. Supreme Court 1863–97 (brother of Cyrus West and David Dudley Field).

Field•ing (fēl′ding), **Henry,** 1707–54, English novelist.

Fields (fēldz), **W. C.** (*William Claude Dukenfield*), 1880–1946, U.S. vaudeville and motion-picture comedian.

Fie•so•le (fyā′zə lē), **Giovanni da,** ANGELICO, Fra.

Fi•gue•res (fē ge′RES), **José,** 1906–90, Costa Rican businessman and political leader: president 1953–58, 1970–74.

Fi•lene (fi lēn′, fi-), **Edward Albert,** 1860–1937, U.S. retail merchant.

Fill•more (fil′môr, -mōr), **Millard,** 1800–74, 13th president of the United States 1850–53.

Fin•lay (fin′lā, -lē, fin li′), **Carlos Juan,** 1833–1915, U.S. physician, born in Cuba: first to suggest mosquito as carrier of yellow fever.

Finn•bo•ga•dót•tir (fin′bō gə dô′tər), **Vigdís,** born 1930, president of Iceland since 1980.

Fin•ney (fin′ē), **Charles Grandison,** 1792–1875, U.S. clergyman and educator.

Fin•sen (fin′sən), **Niels Ryberg,** 1860–1904, Danish physician: Nobel prize 1903.

Fir•dau•si or **Fir•dou•si** (fər dou′sē), also **Fir•du•si** (-do͞o′-), (*Abul Qasim Mansu* or *Hasan*), 932–1020, Persian poet.

Fire•stone (fiᵊr′stōn′), **Harvey Samuel,** 1868–1938, U.S. industrialist and rubber manufacturer.

Firth (fûrth), **John Rupert,** 1890–1960, English linguist.

Fisch•er (fish′ər), **1. Emil,** 1852–1919, German chemist: Nobel prize 1902. **2. Ernst Otto,** born 1918, German chemist. **3. Hans,** 1881–1945, German chemist: Nobel prize 1930. **4. Robert James** ("*Bobby*"), born 1943, U.S. chess player.

Fisch•er-Dies•kau (fish′ər dē′skou), **Dietrich,** born 1925, German baritone.

Fisch•er von Er•lach (fish′ər fən âr′läKH), **Johann Bernhard,** 1656–1723, Austrian architect.

Fish (fish), **Hamilton,** 1808–93, U.S. secretary of state 1869–77.

Fish•er (fish′ər), **1. Andrew,** 1862–1928, Australian statesman, born in Scotland: prime minister 1908–09, 1910–13, 1914–15. **2. Avery,** born 1906, U.S. designer. **3. Dorothy Canfield** (*Dorothea Frances Canfield Fisher*), 1879–1958, U.S. novelist. **4. Saint John** ("*John of Rochester*"), c1469–1535, English Roman Catholic prelate and humanist: executed for treason.

Fisk (fisk), **James,** 1834–72, U.S. financier and stock speculator.

Fiske (fisk), **John** (*Edmund Fisk Green; John Fisk*), 1842–1901, U.S. philosopher and historian.

Fitch (fich), **1. John,** 1743–98, U.S. inventor: pioneer in development of the steamboat. **2. (William) Clyde,** 1865–1909, U.S. playwright.

Fitz•ger•ald (fits jer′əld), **1. Ella,** born 1918, U.S. jazz singer. **2. F(rancis) Scott (Key),** 1896–1940, U.S. novelist and short-story writer.

Fitz•Ger•ald (fits jer′əld), **1. Edward,** 1809–83, English poet: translator of Omar Khayyám. **2. George Francis,** 1851–1901, Irish physicist.

Flagg (flag), **James Montgomery,** 1877–1960, U.S. painter and illustrator.

Flag•stad (flag′stad), **Kirsten Marie,** 1895–1962, Norwegian soprano.

Fla•her•ty (fla′ər tē, flä′-), **Robert Joseph,** 1884–1951, U.S. pioneer in the production of documentary motion pictures.

Fla•min•i•us (flə min′ē əs), **Gaius,** died 217 B.C., Roman statesman and general who was defeated by Hannibal.

Flam•ma•rion (flə mâr′ē yôN′), **(Nicolas) Camille,** 1842–1925, French astronomer.

Flam•steed (flam′stēd), **John,** 1646–1719, English astronomer.

Flan•a•gan (flan′ə gən), **Edward Joseph** (*"Father Flanagan"*), 1886–1948, U.S. Roman Catholic priest, born in Ireland.

Flau•bert (flō bâr′), **Gustave,** 1821–80, French novelist.

Flax•man (flaks′mən), **John,** 1755–1826, English sculptor and draftsman.

Flem•ing (flem′ing), **1. Sir Alexander,** 1881–1955, Scottish bacteriologist: discoverer of penicillin; Nobel prize for medicine 1945. **2. Ian (Lancaster),** 1908–64, British writer. **3. Peggy (Gale),** born 1948, U.S. figure skater.

Flem•ming (flem′ing), **Walther,** 1843–1905, German cell biologist.

Fletch•er (flech′ər), **1. John,** 1579–1625, English dramatist: collaborated with Francis Beaumont. **2. John Gould,** 1886–1950, U.S. poet.

Fleu•ry (flœ Rē′), **1. André Hercule de,** 1653–1743, French cardinal and statesman. **2. Claude,** 1640–1723, French ecclesiastical historian.

Flin•ders (flin′dərz), **Matthew,** 1774–1814, English navigator and explorer: surveyed coast of Australia.

Flint (flint), **Austin,** 1812–86, U.S. physician: founder of Bellevue and Buffalo medical colleges.

Flo•rey (flôr′ē, flōr′ē), **Sir Howard Walter,** 1898–1968, Australian pathologist in England: Nobel prize for medicine 1945.

Flo•ri•o (flôr′ē ō′, flōr′-), **John,** 1553?–1625, English lexicographer and translator.

Flo•ry (flôr′ē, flōr′ē), **Paul John,** 1910–85, U.S. chemist: pioneer in research on polymers; Nobel prize 1974.

Flo•tow (flō′tō), **Friedrich von,** 1812–83, German composer.

Floyd (floid), **Carlisle (Sessions, Jr.),** born 1926, U.S. composer, esp. of operas.

Flynn (flin), **Erroll,** 1909–59, U.S. actor.

Foch (fosh, fôsh), **Ferdinand,** 1851–1929, French marshal.

Fo•gar•ty (fō′gər tē), **Anne,** 1919–80, U.S. fashion designer.

Fo•kine (fō kēn′), **Michel Mikhaylovich,** 1880–1942, Russian choreographer and ballet dancer.

Fok•ker (fok′ər), **Anthony Herman Gerard,** 1890–1939, Dutch airplane designer and builder.

Fon•da (fon′də), **1. Henry,** 1905–82, U.S. actor. **2. Jane,** born 1937, U.S. actress.

Fong (fông, fong), **Hiram L(eong),** born 1907, U.S. lawyer and senator from Hawaii 1959–77.

Fon•tan•a (fon tan′ə), **Domenico,** 1543–1607, Italian architect.

Fon•tanne (fon tan′), **Lynn,** 1887–1983, U.S. actress, born in England (wife of Alfred Lunt).

Fon•teyn (fon tān′), **Dame Margot,** (*Margaret Hookham*), 1919–91, English ballerina.

Forbes (fôrbz), **1. Esther,** 1894?–1967, U.S. novelist. **2. George William,** 1869–1947, New Zealand statesman: prime minister 1930–35.

Forbes-Rob•ert•son (fôrbz′rob′ərt sən), **Sir Johnston,** 1853–1937, English actor and theatrical manager.

Ford (fôrd, fōrd), **1. Ford Madox** (*Ford Madox Hueffer*), 1873–1939, English critic and editor. **2. Gerald R(udolph, Jr.)** (*Leslie Lynch King, Jr.*), born 1913, 38th president of the U.S. 1974–77. **3. Henry,** 1863–1947, U.S. automobile manufacturer. **4. John** (*Sean O'Feeney*), 1895–1973, U.S. film director.

For•est•er (fôr′ə stər, for′-), **C(ecil) S(cott),** 1899–1966, English novelist.

For•mo•sus (fôr mō′səs), A.D. c816–896, Italian ecclesiastic: pope 891–896.

For•rest (fôr′ist, for′-), **1. Edwin,** 1806–72, U.S. actor. **2. Nathan Bedford,** 1821–77, U.S. Confederate general.

For•res•tal (fôr′ə stl, -stôl′, for′-), **James Vincent,** 1892–1949, U.S. financier, secretary of Defense 1947–49.

Forss•man (fôrs′män, -mən, fōrs′-), **Werner,** 1904–70, German surgeon: Nobel prize for medicine 1956.

For•ster (fôr′stər), **E(dward) M(organ),** 1879–1970, English novelist.

For•tas (fôr′təs), **Abe,** 1910–1982, U.S. lawyer, government official, and jurist: associate justice of the U.S. Supreme Court 1965–69.

Fos•dick (foz′dik), **Harry Emerson,** 1878–1969, U.S. preacher and author.

Foss (fos), **Lukas,** born 1922, U.S. pianist, conductor, and composer; born in Germany.

Fos•ter (fô′stər, fos′tər), **1. Stephen (Collins),** 1826–64, U.S. songwriter. **2. William Z(ebulon),** 1881–1961, U.S. labor organizer: leader in the Communist party.

Fou•cault (fo͞o kō′), **Jean Bernard Léon** (zhäɴ), 1819–68, French physicist.

Fou•ji•ta (fo͞o′jē tä′), **Tsugouharu,** 1886–1968, Japanese painter in France.

Fou•qué (fo͞o kā′), **Friedrich Heinrich Karl, Baron de la Motte-,** 1777–1843, German romanticist: poet and novelist.

Fou•quet (fo͞o kā′), **Nicolas** (*Marquis de Belle-Isle*), 1615–80, French statesman.

Fou•quier-Tin•ville (fo͞o kyā taɴ vēl′), **Antoine Quentin,** 1747?–95, French revolutionist: prosecutor during the Reign of Terror.

Fou•rier (fo͝or′ē ā′, -ē ər), **1. François Marie Charles,** 1772–1837, French socialist and reformer. **2. Jean Baptiste Joseph,** 1768–1830, French mathematician and physicist.

Fow•ler (fou′lər), **Henry Watson,** 1858–1933, English lexicographer.

Fowles (foulz), **John,** born 1926, English novelist.

Fox (foks), **1. Charles James,** 1749–1806, British statesman. **2. George,** 1624–91, English religious leader: founder of the Society of Friends. **3. Margaret,** 1833–93, and her sister **Katherine** (*"Kate"*), 1839–92, U.S. spiritualist mediums, born in Canada. **4. Sir William,** 1812–93, New Zealand statesman, born in England: prime minister 1856, 1861–62, 1869–72, 1873.

Foyt (foit), **A(nthony) J(oseph, Jr.),** born 1935, U.S. racing-car driver.

Fra Fi•lip•po Lip•pi (frä fi lip′ō lip′ē; *It.* fʀä fē lēp′pô lēp′pē). Lippi, Fra Filippo.

Fra•go•nard (fʀa gô naʀ′), **Jean Honoré** (zhäɴ), 1732–1806, French painter.

Fran•çaix (fʀäɴ se′), **Jean** (zhäɴ), born 1912, French composer.

France (frans, fräns), **Anatole** (*Jacques Anatole Thibault*), 1844–1924, French author: Nobel prize 1921.

Fran•ces•ca (fran ches′kə, frän-), **Piero della** (*Piero dei Franceschi*), c1420–92, Italian painter.

Fran•ces•ca da Rim•i•ni (fran ches′kə də rim′ə nē, frän-), died 1285?, Italian noblewoman: immortalized in Dante's *Divine Comedy.*

Fran•cia (frän′sē ə; *Sp.* fʀän′syä), **José Gaspar Rodríguez de** (*"El Supremo"*), 1766–1840, Paraguayan political leader: dictator 1814–40.

Fran•cis I (fran′sis), **1.** 1494–1547, king of France 1515–47. **2.** 1768–1835, first emperor of Austria 1804–35; as **Francis II,** last emperor of the Holy Roman Empire 1792–1806.

Fran′cis Fer′dinand, 1863–1914, archduke of Austria: his assassination precipitated the outbreak of World War I.

Francis Joseph I, 1830–1916, emperor of Austria 1848–1916; king of Hungary 1867–1916. German, **Franz Josef.**

Fran′cis of As•si′si (ə sē′zē), **Saint** (*Giovanni Francesco Bernardone*), 1182?–1226, Italian friar: founder of the Franciscan order.

Fran′cis of Pau′la (pou′lə, -lä), **Saint,** 1416–1507, Italian monk: founder of the order of Minims.

Fran′cis of Sales′ (sālz; *Fr.* sal), **Saint,** 1567–1622, French ecclesiastic and writer on theology: bishop of Geneva 1602–22.

Fran′cis Xa′vier, Saint, Xavier, Saint Francis.

Franck (frängk), **1. César (Auguste),** 1822–90, French composer, born in Belgium. **2. James,** 1882–1964, U.S. physicist, born in Germany: Nobel prize 1925.

Fran•co (frang′kō), **Francisco,** 1892–1975, Spanish dictator: head of Spain 1939–75.

Frank (frangk, frängk), **1. Anne,** 1929–45, German Jewish girl who died in Belsen concentration camp in Germany: her diaries about her family hiding from Nazis in Amsterdam (1942–44) published in 1947. **2. Ilya Mikhailovich,** 1908–90, Russian physicist: Nobel prize 1958. **3. Leonhard,** 1882–1961, German novelist.

Frank•en•tha•ler (frang′kən thô′lər, -thä′-), **Helen,** born 1928, U.S. painter.

Frank•furt•er (frangk′fər tər), **Felix,** 1882–1965, U.S. jurist, born in Austria: associate justice of the U.S. Supreme Court 1939–62.

Frank•land (frangk′lənd), **Sir Edward,** 1825–99, English chemist: developed theory of valence.

Frank•lin (frangk′lin), **1. Aretha,** born 1942, U.S. singer. **2. Benjamin,** 1706–90, American statesman and inventor. **3. Sir John,** 1786–1847, English Arctic explorer.

Fran•ko (frän kô′), **Ivan,** 1856–1916, Ukrainian writer.

Franz Jo•sef (*Ger.* fränts′ yō′zef), Francis Joseph I.

Franz Jo•seph II (frants′ jō′zəf, -səf; *Ger.* fränts′ yō′-zef), 1906–89, prince of Liechtenstein 1938–89.

Fra•ser (frā′zər), **1. James Earle,** 1876–1953, U.S. sculptor. **2. (John) Malcolm,** born 1930, Australian political leader: prime minister 1975–83. **3. Peter,** 1884–1950, New Zealand statesman, born in Scotland: prime minister 1940–49. **4. Simon,** 1776–1862, Canadian explorer and fur trader, born in the U.S.

Fraun•ho•fer (froun′hō′fər, frou′ən hof′ər), **Joseph von,** 1787–1826, German optician and physicist.

Fra•zer (frā′zər), **Sir James George,** 1854–1941, Scottish anthropologist.

Fra•zier (frā′zhər), **E(dward) Franklin,** 1894–1962, U.S. sociologist.

Fré•chet (frā she′), **René Maurice,** 1878–1973, French mathematician.

Fred•er•ick (fred′rik, -ər ik), **1. Frederick I, a.** (*"Frederick Barbarossa"*) 1123?–90, emperor of the Holy Roman Empire 1152–90. **b.** 1194–1250, king of Sicily 1198–1212: as Frederick II, emperor of the Holy Roman Empire 1215–50. **c.** 1657–1713, king of Prussia 1701–13 (son of Frederick William, the Great Elector). **2. Frederick II, a.** Frederick I (def. 1b). **b.** (*"Frederick the Great"*) 1712–86, king of Prussia 1740–86 (son of Frederick William I). **3. Frederick III, a.** 1415–93, emperor of the Holy Roman Empire 1452–93; as Frederick IV, king of Germany 1440–93. **b.** (*"the Wise"*) 1463–1525, elector of Saxony 1486–1525: protector of Martin Luther.

Fred′erick Wil′liam, 1. (*"the Great Elector"*) 1620–88, elector of Brandenburg who increased the power and importance of Prussia. **2.** 1882–1951, German general:

crown prince of Germany 1888–1918 (son of William II of Germany). **3. Frederick William I,** 1688–1740, king of Prussia 1713–40. **4. Frederick William II,** 1744–97, king of Prussia 1786–97. **5. Frederick William III,** 1770–1840, king of Prussia 1797–1840. **6. Frederick William VI,** 1795–1861, king of Prussia 1840–61 (brother of William I of Prussia).

Fre•de•rik IX (fʀe′thə ʀēk), 1899–1972, king of Denmark 1947–72 (son of Christian X).

Free•man (frē′mən), **Douglas Southall,** 1886–1953, U.S. journalist and biographer.

Fre•ge (fʀā′gə), **(Friedrich Ludwig) Gottlob,** 1848–1925, German mathematician and logician.

Frei (frā), **Eduardo,** born 1911, Chilean statesman: president 1964–70.

Fré•mont (frē′mont), **John Charles,** 1813–90, U.S. general and explorer: first Republican presidential candidate, 1856.

French (french), **Daniel Chester,** 1850–1931, U.S. sculptor.

Fre•neau (fri nō′), **Philip,** 1752–1832, U.S. poet and editor.

Fres•co•bal•di (fres′kō bäl′dē), **Girolamo,** 1583–1643, Italian composer.

Freud (froid), **1. Anna,** 1895–1982, British psychoanalyst, born in Austria (daughter of Sigmund Freud). **2. Sigmund,** 1856–1939, Austrian neurologist: founder of psychoanalysis.

Frey•re (fʀā′ʀə), **Gilberto,** 1900–87, Brazilian sociologist and anthropologist.

Frey•tag (fʀī′täk), **Gustav,** 1816–95, German novelist, playwright, and journalist.

Frick (frik), **Henry Clay,** 1849–1919, U.S. industrialist and art patron.

Fried (frēd; *Ger.* fʀēt), **Alfred Hermann,** 1864–1921, Austrian writer and journalist: Nobel peace prize 1911.

Frie•dan (fri dan′), **Betty (Naomi Goldstein),** born 1921, U.S. women's-rights leader and writer.

Fried•man (frēd′mən), **Milton,** born 1912, U.S. economist: Nobel prize 1976.

Frie•drich (frē′drik, -drikʜ), **Caspar David,** 1774–1840, German painter.

Friml (frim′əl), **Rudolf,** 1881–1972, U.S. composer and pianist, born in Czechoslovakia.

Frisch (frish), **1. Karl von,** born 1886, Austrian zoologist: Nobel prize for physiology 1973. **2. Max (Rudolf),** 1911–91, Swiss novelist and playwright. **3. Ragnar,** 1895–1973, Norwegian economist: Nobel prize 1969.

Fro•bish•er (frō′bi shər, frob′i-), **Sir Martin,** 1535?–94, English explorer.

Froe•bel (fʀœ′bəl), **Friedrich,** 1782–1852, German educational reformer: founder of the kindergarten system.

Froh•man (frō′mən), **Charles,** 1860–1915, U.S. theatrical producer.

Frois•sart (froi′särt; *Fr.* FRWA SAR′), **Jean** (zhäN), 1333?–c1400, French chronicler.

Fro•men•tin (FRô män taN′), **Eugene,** 1820–76, French painter, critic, and author.

Fromm (from), **Erich,** 1900–80, U.S. psychoanalyst and author, born in Germany.

Fron•di•zi (fron dē′zē, -sē), **Arturo,** born 1908, Argentine lawyer and political leader: president of Argentina 1958–62.

Fron•te•nac (fron′tn ak′; *Fr.* FRôNTᵊ NAK′), **Louis de Buade de,** c1620–98, French governor of Canada 1672–82, 1689–98.

Frost (frôst, frost), **Robert (Lee),** 1874–1963, U.S. poet.

Froude (fro͞od), **James Anthony,** 1818–94, English historian.

Fru•men•ti•us (fro͞o men′shē əs), **Saint,** A.D. c300–c380, founder of the Ethiopian Church.

Fry (frī), **Christopher,** born 1907, English playwright.

Frye (frī), **(Herman) Northrop,** 1912–91, Canadian literary critic and educator.

Fu•ad I (fo͞o äd′), (*Ahmed Fuad Pasha*) 1868–1936, king of Egypt 1922–36.

Fuen•tes (fwen′tās), **Carlos,** born 1928, Mexican writer.

Fuer•tes (fyo͝or′tēz, -tēs), **Louis Agassiz,** 1874–1927, U.S. painter and naturalist.

Fu•gard (fyo͞o′gärd, fo͞o′-), **Athol (Harold),** born 1932, South African playwright and actor.

Fug•ger (fo͝og′əR), **Ja•kob II** (yä′kôp), (*"the Rich"*), 1459–1525, German financier, a member of a German family of bankers and merchants of the 14th to 17th centuries.

Fu•ji•mo•ri (fo͞o′jē môr′ē), **Alberto,** born 1938, president of Peru since 1990.

Ful•bright (fo͝ol′brīt′), **(James) William,** born 1905, U.S. senator 1945–74.

Ful•ler (fo͝ol′ər), **1. Melville Wes•ton** (wes′tən), 1833–1910, Chief Justice of the U.S. 1888–1910. **2. R(ichard) Buckminster,** 1895–1983, U.S. engineer, designer, and architect. **3. (Sarah) Margaret** (*Marchioness Ossoli*), 1810–50, U.S. author and literary critic.

Ful•ton (fo͝ol′tn), **Robert,** 1765–1815, U.S. engineer and inventor: builder of the first profitable steamboat.

Funk (fo͝ongk, fungk), **Casimir,** 1884–1967, U.S. biochemist, born in Poland: discovered thiamine, the first vitamin isolated.

Fur•ness (fûr′nis), **Horace Howard,** 1833–1912, and his son **Horace Howard,** 1865–1930, U.S. Shakespearean scholars and editors.

Fur•ni•vall (fûr′nə vəl), **Frederick James,** 1825–1910, English philologist and editor.

Furt•wäng•ler (fo͝oRt′veng′ləR), **Wilhelm,** 1886–1954, German orchestral conductor.

Fu•se•li (fyo͞o′zə lē), **(John) Henry** (*Johann Heinrich*

Füssli), 1741–1825, English painter, illustrator, and essayist; born in Switzerland.

Fu•ta•ba•tei (fo͞o tä′bä tā′), **Shimei** (*Tatsunosuke Hasegawa*), 1864–1909, Japanese author.

G

Ga•ble (gā′bəl), **(William) Clark,** 1901–60, U.S. film actor.

Ga•bo (gä′bə, -bō), **Naum** (noum), (*Naum Pevsner*), 1890–1977, U.S. sculptor, born in Russia.

Ga•bor (gä′bôr, gə bôr′), **Dennis,** 1900–79, British physicist, born in Hungary: inventor of holography; Nobel prize 1971.

Ga•bo•riau (gᴀ bô ʀyō′), **Émile,** 1835–73, French author of detective stories.

Ga•bri•e•li or **Ga•bri•el•li** (gä′brē el′ē, gab′rē-), **1. Andrea,** 1510–86, Italian organist and composer. **2. Giovanni,** 1557–1612, Italian organist and composer.

Ga•bri•lo•witsch (gä′bri luv′ich), **Ossip,** 1878–1936, Russian pianist and conductor, in America.

Gad•di (gäd′dē), **Taddeo,** 1300–66, Italian painter and architect.

Gad•dis (gad′is), **William,** born 1922, U.S. novelist.

Gads•den (gadz′dən), **James,** 1788–1858, U.S. railroad promoter and diplomat.

Ga•ga•rin (gä gär′in, gə-), **Yuri Alekseyevich,** 1934–68, Russian astronaut: first person to make an orbital space flight (1961).

Gage (gāj), **Thomas,** 1721–87, British general in America 1763–76.

Gaines (gānz), **Edmund Pendleton,** 1777–1849, U.S. general.

Gains•bor•ough (gānz′bûr′ō, -bur′ō; *Brit.* -bər ə), **Thomas,** 1727–88, English painter.

Gai•ser•ic (gī′zə rik), Genseric.

Ga•ius (gā′əs), a.d. c110–c180, Roman jurist and writer on civil law.

Gaj•du•sek (gī′do͝o shek′, -də-), **D(aniel) Carleton,** born 1923, U.S. medical researcher, esp. on viral diseases: Nobel prize 1976.

Gal•ba (gal′bə), **Servius Sulpicius,** 5? b.c.–a.d. 69, Roman emperor a.d. 68–69.

Gal•braith (gal′brāth), **John Kenneth,** born 1908, U.S. economist, born in Canada.

Gale (gāl), **Zona,** 1874–1938, U.S. novelist, short-story writer, playwright, and poet.

Ga•len (gā′lən), **Claudius,** a.d. c130–c200, Greek physician and writer. Latin, **Ga•le•nus** (gə lē′nəs).

Gal•i•le•o (gal′ə lā′ō, -lē′ō), (*Galileo Galilei*), 1564–1642, Italian physicist and astronomer.

Gall (gôl), (*Pizi*), 1840?–94, leader of the Hunkpapa Sioux: a major chief in the battle of Little Bighorn.

Gal•la•tin (gal′ə tin), **Albert,** 1761–1849, U.S. statesman: Secretary of the Treasury 1801–13.

Gal•lau•det (gal′ə det′), **Thomas Hopkins,** 1787–1851, U.S. educator of the deaf.

Ga•lle•gos (gä ye′gôs), **Rómulo,** 1884–1969, Venezuelan educator, statesman, and novelist: president of Venezuela 1948.

Gal•li-Cur•ci (gal′i kûr′chē; *It.* gäl′lē kōōr′chē), **A•me•li•ta** (ä′me lē′tä), 1889–1964, Italian soprano in the U.S.

Gal•li•e•nus (gal′ē ē′nəs), (*Publius Licinius Egnatius*) died A.D. 268, emperor of Rome 253–268 (son of Valerian).

Gal•lo (gal′ō), **Robert (Charles),** born 1937, U.S. scientist, specializing in cancer and AIDS research.

Gal•lup (gal′əp), **George Horace,** 1901–84, U.S. statistician.

Gals•wor•thy (gôlz′wûr′thē, galz′-), **John,** 1867–1933, English novelist and dramatist: Nobel prize 1932.

Gal•ton (gôl′tn), **Sir Francis,** 1822–1911, English scientist.

Ga•lup•pi (gä lōōp′pē), **Baldassare** (*"Il Buranello"*), 1706–85, Italian composer.

Gal•va•ni (gäl vä′nē), **Luigi,** 1737–98, Italian physiologist and physicist.

Gal•way (gôl′wā), **James,** born 1939, Irish flutist.

Ga•ma (gam′ə, gä′mə), **Vasco da,** c1460–1524, Portuguese navigator: first to sail from Europe to India.

Gam•bet•ta (gam bet′ə), **Léon,** 1838–82, French statesman.

Gam•ow (gam′ôf, -of), **George,** 1904–68, U.S. nuclear physicist, born in Russia.

Gan•dhi (gän′dē, gan′-), **1. Indira,** 1917–84, prime minister of India 1966–77 and 1980–84 (daughter of Jawaharlal Nehru). **2. Mohandas Karamchand** (*"Mahatma"*), 1869–1948, Hindu religious leader, nationalist, and social reformer. **3. Rajiv,** 1944–91, prime minister of India 1984–1989 (son of Indira).

Gan•nett (gan′it), **Henry,** 1846–1914, U.S. geographer and cartographer.

Ganse•voort (ganz′vôrt, -vōrt), **Peter,** 1749–1812, U.S. general: soldier in the American Revolutionary War.

Gar•and (gar′ənd, gə rand′), **John C(antius),** 1888–1974, U.S. inventor of M-1 semiautomatic rifle, born in Canada.

Gar•bo (gär′bō), **Greta** (*Greta Lovisa Gustaffson*), 1905–90, U.S. film actress, born in Sweden.

Gar•cí•a Lor•ca (gär sē′ə lôr′kə), **Federico,** 1899–1936, Spanish poet and dramatist.

Gar•cí′a Már′quez (mär′kes), **Gabriel,** born 1928, Colombian novelist and short-story writer: Nobel prize 1982.

Gar•cí′a Mo•re′no (mô rā′nō), **Gabriel,** 1821–75, Ecuadorian journalist and political leader: president of Ecuador 1861–65, 1869–75.

Garcí′a Rob′les (rō′blās), **Alfonso,** 1911–91, Mexican diplomat: Nobel peace prize 1982.

Gar•den (gär′dn), **Mary,** 1877–1967, U.S. soprano.

Gar•di•ner (gärd′nər, gär′dn ər), **Samuel Rawson,** 1829–1902, English historian.

Gard•ner (gärd′nər), **1. Ava,** 1922–90, U.S. actress. **2. Erle Stanley,** 1889–1970, U.S. writer. **3. John W(illiam),** born 1912, U.S. educator and author.

Gar•field (gär′fēld′), **James Abram,** 1831–81, 20th president of the U.S., 1881.

Gar•i•bal•di (gar′ə bôl′dē), **Giuseppe,** 1807–82, Italian patriot and general.

Gar•land (gär′lənd), **1. Hamlin,** 1860–1940, U.S. writer. **2. Judy** (*Frances Gumm*), 1922–69, U.S. singer and actress.

Gar•neau (*Fr.* GAR nō′), **François Xavier,** 1809–66, Canadian historian.

Gar•ner (gär′nər), **1. Erroll,** 1921–77, U.S. jazz pianist and composer. **2. John Nance,** 1868–1967, vice president of the U.S. 1933–41.

Gar•net (gär′nit), **Henry Highland,** 1815–82, U.S. clergyman and abolitionist.

Gar•nett (gär′nit, gär net′), **Constance Black,** 1862–1946, English translator from Russian.

Gar•rick (gar′ik), **David,** 1717–79, English actor and theatrical manager.

Gar•ri•son (gar′ə sən), **William Lloyd,** 1805–79, U.S. leader in the abolition movement.

Gar•vey (gär′vē), **Marcus (Moziah),** 1887–1940, Jamaican black-rights activist in the U.S. 1916–27.

Gar•y (gâr′ē, gar′ē), **Elbert Henry,** 1846–1927, U.S. financier and lawyer.

Gas•coigne (gas′koin), **George,** 1525?–77, English poet.

Gas•kell (gas′kəl), **Mrs.** (*Elizabeth Cleghorn Stevenson Gaskell*), 1810–65, English novelist.

Gas•sen•di (GA SÄN dē′), **Pierre,** 1592–1655, French philosopher and scientist.

Gas•ser (gas′ər), **Herbert Spencer,** 1888–1963, U.S. physiologist: Nobel prize for medicine 1944.

Gates (gāts), **1. Horatio,** 1728–1806, American Revolutionary general, born in England. **2. William Henry** (*Bill*), born 1955, U.S. computer software entrepreneur.

Gau•dí i Cor•net (gou dē′ ē kôR′net), **Antoni,** 1852–1926, Spanish architect and designer.

Gau•guin (gō GAN′), **(Eugène Henri) Paul,** 1848–1903, French painter.

Gaunt (gônt, gänt), **John of,** JOHN OF GAUNT.

Gauss (gous), **Karl Friedrich,** 1777–1855, German mathematician and astronomer.

Gau•ta•ma or **Go•ta•ma** (gô′tə mə), BUDDHA. Also called **Gau′tama Bud′dha.**

Gau•tier (gō tyā′), **Théophile,** 1811–72, French poet, novelist, and critic.

Gay (gā), **John,** 1685–1732, English poet and dramatist.

Gay-Lus•sac (gā′lə sak′), **Joseph Louis,** 1778–1850, French chemist and physicist.

Ge•ber (jē′bər), (*Jabir ibn Hayyan*) 8th-century A.D. Arab alchemist. Also, **Jabir.**

Ged•da (ged′ə), **Nikolai,** born 1925, Swedish tenor.

Ged•des (ged′ēz), **1. Norman Bel** (bel), 1893–1958, U.S. industrial and stage designer and architect. **2. Sir Patrick,** 1854–1932, Scottish biologist, sociologist, and town planner.

Geh•rig (ger′ig), **Henry Louis** (*"Lou"*), 1903–41, U.S. baseball player.

Gei•ger (gī′gər), **Hans,** 1882–1947, German physicist.

Gei•kie (gē′kē), **Sir Archibald,** 1835–1924, Scottish geologist.

Gei•sel (gī′zəl), **Theodor Seuss** (sōōs), (*"Dr. Seuss"*), 1904–91, U.S. humorist, illustrator, and author of children's books.

Ge•la•si•us I (jə lā′shē əs, -zhē-, -zē-), **Saint,** died A.D. 496, pope 492–496.

Gel•lée (zhə lā′), **Claude,** CLAUDE LORRAIN.

Gell-Mann (gel män′, -man′), **Murray,** born 1929, U.S. physicist: devised a system for classifying elementary particles and postulated theory of quarks; Nobel prize 1969.

Ge•mi•nia•ni (je′mē nyä′nē), **Francesco,** c1680–1762, Italian violinist and composer.

Ge•net (zhə nā′), **Jean** (zhäɴ), 1910–86, French playwright and novelist.

Ge•nêt (zhə nā′), **Edmond Charles Edouard** (*"Citizen Genêt"*), 1763–1834, French minister to the U.S. in 1793.

Gen•e•vieve (jen′ə vēv′) also **Gene•viève** (*Fr.* zhənᵊ-vyev′), **Saint,** A.D. 422–512, French nun: patron saint of Paris.

Gen•ghis Khan (jeng′gis kän′ *or, often,* geng′-), 1162–1227, Mongol conqueror.

Gen•na•ro (jə när′ō), **San,** JANUARIUS.

Gen•ser•ic (jen′sər ik, gen′-) also **Gaiseric,** A.D. c390-477, king of the Vandals 428-477: conqueror in N Africa and Italy.

Geof′frey of Mon′mouth (jef′rē), 1100?–1154, English chronicler.

George[1] (jôrj), **1. David Lloyd,** LLOYD GEORGE, David. **2. Henry,** 1839–97, U.S. economist. **3. Saint,** died A.D. 303?, Christian martyr: patron saint of England. **4. Stefan Anton,** 1868–1933, German poet.

George[2] (jôrj), **1. George I, a.** 1660–1727, king of England 1714–27. **b.** 1845–1913, king of Greece 1863–1913. **2. George II, a.** 1683–1760, king of England 1727–60 (son of George I). **b.** 1890–1947, king of Greece 1922–23 and 1935–47. **3. George III,** 1738–1820, king of England 1760–1820 (grandson of George II). **4. George IV,** 1762–1830, king of England 1820–30 (son of George III). **5. George V,** 1865–1936, king of England 1910–36 (son of Edward VII). **6. George VI,** 1895–1952, king of England 1936–1952 (son of George V).

Gé•rard (zhā RÄR′), **Comte Étienne Maurice,** 1773–1852, French marshal under Napoleon.

Gé•ri•cault (zhā Rē kō′), **(Jean Louis André) Théodore** (zhäɴ), 1791–1824, French painter.

Ger•man′i•cus Cae′sar (jər man′i kəs), 15 B.C.–A.D. 19, Roman general.

Gé•rôme (zhā rōm′), **Jean Léon,** 1824–1904, French painter and sculptor.

Ge•ron•i•mo (jə ron′ə mō′), (*Goyathlay*), 1829–1909, American Apache Indian chief.

Ger•ry (ger′ē), **Elbridge,** 1744–1814, U.S. vice president 1813–14.

Gersh•win (gûrsh′win), **1. George,** 1898–1937, U.S. composer. **2.** his brother, **Ira,** 1896–1983, U.S. lyricist.

Ge•sell (gə zel′), **Arnold Lucius,** 1880–1961, U.S. psychologist.

Ges•ner (ges′nər), **Konrad von,** 1516–65, Swiss physician and naturalist.

Ge•su•al•do (je′zo͞o äl′dô), **Don Carlo, Prince of Venosa,** c1560–1613, Italian composer.

Get•ty (get′ē), **J(ean) Paul,** 1892–1976, U.S. oil magnate.

Getz (gets), **Stan(ley),** 1927–91, U.S. jazz saxophonist.

Geu•lincx (*Flem.* gœ′lingks), **Arnold,** 1624?–69, Belgian philosopher.

Ghaz•za•li or **Gha•za•li** (ga zä′lē), **Al-,** 1058–1111, Arab philosopher. Also called **Al-Gazel.**

Ghi•ber•ti (gē ber′tē), **Lorenzo,** 1378–1455, Florentine sculptor, goldsmith, and painter.

Ghir•lan•da•io or **Ghir•lan•da•jo** (gēr′lən dä′yō), (*Domenico di Tommaso Curradi di Doffo Bigordi*) 1449–94, Italian painter.

Gia•co•met•ti (jä′kə met′ē), **Alberto,** 1901–66, Swiss sculptor and painter.

Giae•ver (yā′vər), **Ivar,** born 1929, U.S. physicist, born in Norway: Nobel prize 1973.

Gi•auque (jē ōk′), **William Francis,** 1895–1982, U.S. chemist: Nobel prize 1949.

Gib•bon (gib′ən), **Edward,** 1737–94, English historian.

Gib•bons (gib′ənz), **1. Grinling,** 1648–1720, English woodcarver and sculptor, born in the Netherlands. **2. Orlando,** 1583–1625, English composer.

Gibbs (gibz), **1. James,** 1682–1754, Scottish architect and author. **2. Josiah Willard,** 1839–1903, U.S. physicist. **3. Oliver Wolcott,** 1822–1908, U.S. chemist and educator. **4. Sir Philip,** 1877–1962, English journalist and writer.

Gib•ran (ji brän′), **Kah•lil** (kä lēl′), 1883–1931, Lebanese poet, dramatist, and artist; in the U.S. after 1910.

Gib•son (gib′sən), **1. Althea,** born 1927, U.S. tennis player. **2. Charles Dana,** 1867–1944, U.S. artist and illustrator. **3. Josh(ua),** 1911–47, U.S. baseball player.

Gide (zhēd), **André (Paul Guillaume),** 1869–1951, French writer: Nobel prize 1947.

Giel•gud (gil′go͝od, gēl′-), **Sir (Arthur) John,** born 1904, English actor and director.

Gie•rek (gēr′ek; *Pol.* gye′rek), **Edward,** born 1913, Polish political leader: first secretary of the Polish Communist party 1970–80.

Gie•se•king (gē′zə king, -sə-), **Walter (Wilhelm),** 1895–1956, German pianist and composer.

Gi•gli (jē′lyē), **Beniamino,** 1890–1957, Italian operatic tenor.

Gil•bert (gil′bərt), **1. Cass,** 1859–1934, U.S. architect. **2. Henry Franklin Belknap,** 1868–1928, U.S. composer. **3. Sir Humphrey,** 1509?–83, English navigator and colonizer in America. **4. John** (*John Pringle*), 1895–1936, U.S. film actor. **5. William,** 1544–1603, English physician and physicist: pioneer experimenter in magnetism and electricity. **6. Sir William Schwenck,** 1836–1911, English dramatist and poet: collaborator with Sir Arthur Sullivan.

Gi•lels (gi lelz′), **Emil (Grigoryevich),** 1916–85, Russian pianist.

Giles (jīlz), **Saint,** 8th century A.D., Athenian hermit in France.

Gil•les•pie (gi les′pē), **John Birks,** (*"Dizzy"*), born 1917, U.S. jazz trumpeter and composer.

Gil•lette (ji let′), **1. King Camp,** 1855–1932, U.S. businessman: inventor of the safety razor. **2. William (Hooker),** 1855–1937, U.S. actor and dramatist.

Gil•man (gil′mən), **1. Arthur,** 1837–1909, U.S. educator. **2. Daniel Coit** (koit), 1831–1908, U.S. educator.

Gil•son (zhēl sôɴ′), **Étienne Henry,** 1884–1978, French historian.

Gim•bel (gim′bəl), **Jacob,** 1850–1922, U.S. retail merchant.

Gi•nas•te•ra (hē′näs te′rä), **Alberto,** 1916–83, Argentine composer.

Gins•berg (ginz′bûrg), **Allen,** born 1926, U.S. poet.

Ginz•berg (ginz′bûrg), **Asher,** (*Achad Ha-Am, Ahad Ha-am*), 1856–1927, Hebrew philosophical writer and editor, born in Russia.

Gio•no (jə nō′), **Jean** (zhäɴ), 1895–1970, French novelist.

Gior•da•no (jôr dä′nō), **1. Luca** (*"Luca Fapresto"*), 1632–1705, Italian painter. **2. Umberto,** 1867–1948, Italian composer of operas.

Gior•gio•ne (jôr jō′nē), (*Giorgione de Castelfranco, Giorgio Barbarelli*) 1478?–1511, Italian painter.

Giot•to (jot′ō), (*Giotto di Bondone*) 1266?–1337, Florentine painter, sculptor, and architect.

Gi•rard (jə rärd′), **Stephen,** 1750–1831, U.S. merchant, banker, and philanthropist, born in France.

Gi•raud (zhē rō′), **Henri Honoré,** 1879–1949, French general.

Gi•rau•doux (zhē rō do͞o′), **Jean** (zhäɴ), 1882–1944, French writer.

Gir•tin (gûr′tin), **Thomas,** 1775–1802, English painter.

Gis•card d'Es•taing (zhēs kar des taɴ′; *Eng.* zhē skär′ de stang′), **Valéry,** born 1926, French political leader: president 1974–81.

Gish (gish), **Dorothy,** 1898–1968, and her sister **Lillian,** born 1896, U.S. film actresses.

Gis•sing (gis′ing), **George (Robert),** 1857–1903, English novelist.

Giu•lio Ro•ma•no (jo͞ol′yō rə mä′nō), (*Giulio Pippi de' Giannuzzi*), 1492?–1546, Italian painter and architect.

Gi•ven•chy (zhi väɴ′shē), **Hubert de,** born 1927, French fashion designer.

Gjel•le•rup (gel′ə ro͝op), **Karl,** 1857–1919, Danish novelist: Nobel prize 1917.

Gla•ber (glä′bər), **Raoul** or **Rudolphe,** c990–c1050, French ecclesiastic and chronicler.

Glack•ens (glak′ənz), **William James,** 1870–1938, U.S. painter and illustrator.

Glad•stone (glad′stōn′, -stən), **William Ew•art** (yo͞o′ərt), 1809–98, British prime minister four times between 1868 and 1894.

Gla•ser (glā′zər), **Donald A.,** born 1926, U.S. physicist: Nobel prize 1960.

Glas•gow (glas′gō, -kō), **Ellen (Anderson Gholson),** 1874–1945, U.S. novelist.

Glas•pell (glas′pel), **Susan,** 1882–1948, U.S. novelist and dramatist.

Glass (glas, gläs), **Carter,** 1858–1946, U.S. statesman.

Gla•zer (glā′zər), **Nathan,** born 1923, U.S. sociologist.

Gla•zu•nov (glaz′ə nôf, -nof′), **Alexander Konstantinovitch,** 1865–1936, Russian composer.

Glea•son (glē′sən), **Jackie,** 1916–87, U.S. comedian and actor.

Glen•dow•er (glen dou′ər, glen′dou ər), **Owen,** 1359?–1416?, Welsh rebel against Henry IV of England.

Glenn (glen), **John (Herschel),** born 1921, U.S. astronaut and politician: first U.S. orbital space flight 1962; U.S. senator since 1975.

Glid•den (glid′n), **Charles Jasper,** 1857–1927, U.S. businessman: a pioneer in the telephone industry.

Glière (glyâr), **Reinhold Moritzovich,** 1875–1956, Russian composer.

Glin•ka (gling′kə), **Mikhail Ivanovich,** 1803–57, Russian composer.

Glov•er (gluv′ər), **John,** 1732–97, American general.

Glubb (glub), **Sir John Bagot** (*"Glubb Pasha"*), 1897–1986, British army officer: commander of the Arab Legion in Jordan 1939–56.

Gluck (glo͝ok), **1. Alma** (*Reba Fiersohn, Mme. Efrem Zimbalist*), 1884–1938, U.S. operatic soprano, born in Romania. **2. Christoph Willibald von,** 1714–87, German operatic composer.

Glyn (glin), **Elinor,** 1864–1943, English writer.

Go•bat (*Fr.* gô ʙᴀ′), **Albert,** 1843–1914, Swiss lawyer and statesman: Nobel peace prize 1902.

Go•dard (gō därd′, -där′), **Jean-Luc,** born 1930, French filmmaker.

God•dard (god′ərd), **Robert Hutchings,** 1882–1945, U.S. physicist: pioneer in rocketry.

God•den (god′n), **(Margaret) Rumer,** born 1907, English novelist and writer of children's books.

Go•de•froy de Bouil•lon (gôd° frwä′ də bo͞o yôɴ′), c1060–1100, French crusader.

Gö•del (gœd′l), **Kurt,** 1906–78, U.S. mathematician and logician, born in Czechoslovakia.

Go•dey (gō′dē), **Louis Antoine,** 1804–78, U.S. publisher: founded the first women's magazine in the U.S. 1830.

Go•di•va (gə dī′və), (*"Lady Godiva"*), died 1057, an English noblewoman who, according to legend, rode naked through the streets of Coventry to win relief for the people from a burdensome tax.

Go•dol•phin (gō dol′fin, gə-), **Sidney, 1st Earl of,** 1645–1712, English statesman and financier.

Go•dow•sky (gə dôf′skē, gô-), **Leopold,** 1870–1938, U.S. composer and pianist, born in Poland.

Go•du•nov (god′n ôf′, -of′, go͝od′-), **Boris Fedorovich,** 1552–1605, czar of Russia 1598–1605.

God•win (god′win), **1.** Also, **God′wi•ne** (-wi nə). **Earl of the West Saxons,** died 1053, English statesman. **2. Mary Wollstonecraft,** 1759–97, English writer. **3. William,** 1756–1836, English political philosopher and writer.

Goeb•bels (gœ′bəlz, -bəls), **Joseph Paul,** 1897–1945, Nazi German offical: served as propaganda director.

Goe•ring (gâr′ing, gûr′-), **Hermann Wilhelm,** Göring, Hermann Wilhelm.

Goes (go͞os), **Hugo van der,** c1440–82, Flemish painter.

Goe•thals (gō′thəlz), **George Washington,** 1858–1928, U.S. major general and chief engineer of the Panama Canal.

Goe•the (gœ′tə), **Johann Wolfgang von,** 1749–1832, German poet and dramatist.

Goetz (gets; *Ger.* gœts), **Hermann,** Götz, Hermann.

Gogh (gō, gôᴋʜ; *Du.* ᴋʜôᴋʜ), **Vincent van,** van Gogh, Vincent.

Go•gol (gō′gəl, -gôl), **Nikolai Vasilievich,** 1809–52, Russian novelist and playwright.

Gold (gōld), **Thomas,** born 1920, U.S. astronomer, born in Austria: formulated the steady-state theory of the universe.

Gold•berg (gōld′bûrg), **1. Arthur Joseph,** 1908–90, U.S. jurist, statesman, and diplomat: associate justice of the U.S. Supreme Court 1962–65; ambassador to the U.N. 1965–68. **2. Reuben Lucius** (*"Rube"*), 1883–1970, U.S. cartoonist. **3. Whoopi** (*Caryn E. Johnson*), born 1949, U.S. actress and comedienne.

Gold•ber•ger (gōld′bûr gər), **Joseph,** 1874–1929, U.S. physician, born in Austria: discovered the cause of and treatment for pellagra.

Gol•ding (gōl′ding), **1. Louis,** 1895–1958, English novelist and essayist. **2. William Gerald,** born 1911, British novelist: Nobel prize 1983.

Gold•man (gōld′mən), **1. Edwin Franko,** 1878–1956,

U.S. composer and bandmaster. **2. Emma,** 1869–1940, U.S. anarchist leader, born in Russia.

Gold•mark (gōld′märk′), **Karl,** 1830–1915, Hungarian composer.

Gol•do•ni (gôl dō′nē), **Carlo,** 1707–93, Italian dramatist.

Gol•dov•sky (gōl dôf′skē, -dof′-), **Boris,** born 1908, U.S. conductor, pianist, and opera director, born in Russia.

Gold•smith (gōld′smith′), **Oliver,** 1730?–74, Irish writer.

Gold•wa•ter (gōld′wô′tər, -wot′ər), **Barry Morris,** born 1909, U.S. politician: U.S senator 1953–64 and 1968–87.

Gold•wyn (gōld′win), **Samuel** (*Samuel Goldfish*), 1882–1974, U.S. movie producer, born in Poland.

Gol•gi (gôl′jē), **Camillo,** 1843?–1926, Italian physician and histologist: Nobel prize for medicine 1906.

Golsch•mann (gōlsh′män), **Vladimir,** 1893–1972, French orchestra conductor in the U.S.

Goltz (gôlts), **Baron Kolmar von der,** 1843–1916, German field marshal.

Gom•berg (gom′bûrg), **Moses,** 1866–1947, U.S. chemist, born in Russia.

Gó•mez (gō′mez; *Sp.* gô′mes), **Juan Vicente,** 1857?–1935, Venezuelan soldier and political leader: commander in chief and dictator of Venezuela 1908–35; president of Venezuela 1908–15, 1922–29, 1931–35.

Gó•mez de la Ser•na (gô′meth *th*e lä seʀ′nä, -mes), **Ramón** (*"Ramón"*), 1888–1963, Spanish novelist, dramatist, biographer, and critic.

Gom•pers (gom′pərz), **Samuel,** 1850–1924, U.S. labor leader, born in England.

Go•mul•ka (gə mo͝ol′kə), **Wladyslaw,** 1905–82, Polish political leader: first secretary of the Polish Communist party 1956–70.

Gon•cha•rov (gon′chə rôf′, -rof′), **Ivan Alexandrovich,** 1812–91, Russian novelist.

Gon•court (gôɴ ko͞oʀ′), **Edmond Louis Antoine Huot de,** 1822–96, and his brother **Jules Alfred Huot de,** 1830–70, French art critics, novelists, and historians.

Gon•do•mar (gon′dō mär′), **Diego Sarmiento de Acuña, Count of,** 1567–1626, Spanish diplomat.

Gón•go•ra y Ar•go•te (gong′gō rä′ ē är gō′tā), **Luis de,** 1561–1627, Spanish poet.

Gon•zal•es (gən zä′lis), **Richard Alonzo** (*"Pancho"*), born 1928, U.S. tennis player.

Gooch (go͞och), **George Peabody,** 1873–1968, English historian.

Good•hue (go͝od′hyo͞o), **Bertram Grosvenor,** 1869–1924, U.S. architect.

Good•man (go͝od′mən), **Benjamin David** (*"Benny"*), 1909–86, U.S. jazz clarinetist and bandleader.

Good•rich (go͝od′rich), **Samuel Griswold** (*"Peter Parley"*), 1793–1860, U.S. author and publisher.

Good•speed (go͝od′spēd′), **Edgar Johnson,** 1871–1962, U.S. Biblical scholar and translator.

Good•year (go͝od′yēr′), **Charles,** 1800–60, U.S. inventor.

Goos•sens (go͞o′sənz), **Sir Eugene,** 1893–1962, English composer and conductor.

Gor•ba•chev (gôr′bə chôf′, -chof′), **Mikhail S(ergeyevich),** born 1931, president of the Soviet Union 1988–91: Nobel peace prize 1990.

Gor•cha•kov (gôr′chə kôf′, -kof′), **Prince Aleksander Mikhailovich,** 1798–1883, Russian diplomat and statesman.

Gor•di•mer (gôr′də mər), **Nadine,** born 1923, South African novelist and short-story writer: Nobel prize 1991.

Gor•don (gôr′dn), **1. Charles George** ("*Chinese Gordon*", "*Gordon Pasha*"), 1833–85, British administrator in China and Egypt. **2. Lord George,** 1751–93, English politician. **3. Mary,** born 1949, U.S. novelist. **4. Ruth** (*Ruth Gordon Jones*), 1896–1985, U.S. actress and screenwriter.

Gor•en (gôr′ān), **Charles Henry,** 1901–91, U.S authority and writer on contract bridge.

Gor•gas (gôr′gəs), **William Crawford,** 1854–1920, U.S. physician and epidemiologist: chief sanitary officer of the Panama Canal 1904–13; surgeon general of the U.S. Army 1914–18.

Gor•gi•as (gôr′jē əs), c483–c375 B.C., Greek philosopher.

Gö•ring or **Goe•ring** (gâr′ing, gûr′-), **Hermann Wilhelm,** 1893–1946, German field marshal and Nazi party leader.

Gor•ki or **Gor•ky** (gôr′kē), **Maxim** (*Aleksey Maksimovich Pyeshkov*), 1868–1936, Russian novelist and dramatist.

Gor•ky (gôr′kē), **1. Arshile** (*Vosdanig Adoian*), 1904–48, U.S. painter, born in Armenia. **2. Maxim,** GORKI, Maxim.

Gor•ton (gôr′tn), **John Grey,** born 1911, Australian political leader: prime minister 1968–71.

Go•sa•la (gō sä′lə), died c484 B.C., Indian religious leader: founder of the Ajivaka sect.

Gos•saert or **Gos•sart** (go särt′), **Jan,** MABUSE, Jan.

Gosse (gôs, gos), **Sir Edmund William,** 1849–1928, English poet, biographer, and critic.

Go•ta•ma (gô′tə mə), GAUTAMA. Also called **Go′tama Bud′dha.**

Gott•lieb (got′lēb), **Adolph,** 1903–74, U.S. painter.

Gott•schalk (got′shôk), **Louis Moreau,** 1829–69, U.S. pianist and composer.

Gott•wald (gôt′vält), **Klement,** 1896–1953, Czech Communist leader: prime minister 1946–48; president 1948–53.

Götz or **Goetz** (gets; *Ger.* gœts), **Hermann,** 1840–76, German composer.

Gou•dy (gou′dē), **Frederic William,** 1865–1947, U.S. designer of printing types.

Gou•jon (go͞o zhôɴ′), **Jean** (zhäɴ), c1510–c1568, French sculptor.

Gould (go͞old), **1. Chester,** 1900–85, U.S. cartoonist: creator of the comic strip "Dick Tracy." **2. Glenn Herbert,** 1932–82, Canadian pianist and composer. **3. Jay,** 1836–92, U.S. financier. **4. Morton,** born 1913, U.S. composer and pianist. **5. Stephen Jay,** born 1941, U.S. paleontologist.

Gou•nod (gōō′nō, gōō nō′), **Charles François,** 1818–93, French composer.

Gour•mont (gōōr môɴ′), **Remy de,** 1858–1915, French critic and novelist.

Gow•er (gou′ər, gôr, gōr), **John,** 1325?–1408, English poet.

Go•ya (goi′ə), **Francisco de** (*Francisco José de Goya y Lucientes*), 1746–1828, Spanish painter.

Go•yen (goi′ən), **Jan van,** 1596–1656, Dutch painter.

Grac•chus (grak′əs), **Gaius Sempronius,** 153–121 B.C., and his brother, **Tiberius Sempronius,** 163–133 B.C., Roman reformers and orators: known as **the Gracchi** (grak′ī).

Grace (grās), **William Russell,** 1832–1904, U.S. financier and shipping magnate, born in Ireland: mayor of New York City 1880–88.

Gra•ham (grā′əm, gram), **1. Martha,** 1894–1991, U.S. dancer and choreographer. **2. Thomas,** 1805–69, Scottish chemist. **3. William Franklin** (*"Billy"*), born 1918, U.S. evangelist.

Gra•hame (grā′əm), **Kenneth,** 1859–1932, Scottish writer.

Grain•ger (grān′jər), **Percy Aldridge,** 1882–1961, Australian pianist and composer, in the U.S. after 1915.

Gra•mont (ɢʀᴀ môɴ′), **Philibert, Comte de,** 1621–1707, French courtier, soldier, and adventurer.

Gram•sci (gräm′shē), **Antonio,** 1891–1937, Italian political leader and Socialist theoretician.

Gra•na•dos (grə nä′dōs), **Enrique,** 1867–1916, Spanish composer.

Grand•gent (gran′jənt), **Charles Hall,** 1862–1939, U.S. philologist and essayist.

Grand′ma Mo′ses, Mᴏsᴇs, Anna Mary Robertson.

Grange (grānj), **Harold** (*"Red"*), 1903–91, U.S. football player.

Gra•nit (*Sw.* ɢʀä nēt′), **Ragnar Arthur,** born 1900, Swedish physiologist, born in Finland: Nobel prize for medicine 1967.

Grant (grant, gränt), **1. Cary** (*Archibald Leach*), 1904–86, U.S. actor, born in England. **2. Heber Jedediah,** 1856–1945, U.S. president of the Mormon Church 1918–45. **3. Ulysses S(impson),** 1822–85, Union general: 18th president of the U.S. 1869–77.

Gran•ville (gran′vil), **Earl of,** Cᴀʀᴛᴇʀᴇᴛ, John.

Gran′ville-Bar′ker (bär′kər), **Harley,** 1877–1946, English dramatist, actor, and critic.

Grass (gräs), **Günter (Wilhelm),** born 1927, German author.

Grasse (ɢʀäs), **François Joseph Paul, Comte de** (*Marquis de Grasse-Tilly*), 1722–1788, French admiral.

Grass•man (gräs′mən, -män), **Hermann Günther,** 1809–77, German mathematician and linguist.

Gras•so (gras′ō, grä′sō), **Ella T(ambussi),** 1919–81, U.S. politician: congresswoman 1971–75; governor of Connecticut 1975–80.

Gra•ti•an (grā′shē ən, -shən), (*Flavius Gratianus*) A.D. 359–383, Roman emperor 375–383.

Grat•tan (grat′n), **Henry,** 1746–1820, Irish statesman and orator.

Grau (grou), **Shirley Ann,** born 1929, U.S. short-story writer and novelist.

Grave•ly (grāv′lē), **Samuel L(ee), Jr.,** born 1922, U.S. naval officer: first black admiral.

Graves (grāvz), **Robert (Ranke),** 1895–1985, English author.

Gray (grā), **1. Asa,** 1810–88, U.S. botanist. **2. Thomas,** 1716–71, English poet.

Gre•co (grek′ō, grā′kō), **1. José,** born 1918, U.S. dancer and choreographer, born in Italy. **2. El,** EL GRECO.

Gree•ley (grē′lē), **Horace,** 1811–72, U.S. journalist, editor, and political leader.

Gree•ly (grē′lē), **Adolphus Washington,** 1844–1935, U.S. general and arctic explorer.

Green (grēn), **1. Henrietta Howland Robinson** (*"Hetty"*), 1835–1916, U.S. financier. **2. Henry** (*Henry Vincent Yorke*), 1905–73, English novelist. **3. John Richard,** 1837–83, English historian. **4. Julian,** born 1900, U.S. writer, born in France. **5. Paul Eliot,** 1894–1981, U.S. writer. **6. William,** 1873–1952, U.S. labor leader.

Green•a•way (grēn′ə wā′), **Kate** (*Catherine*), 1846–1901, English painter and illustrator of children's books.

Green•berg (grēn′bûrg), **Henry B.** (*Hank*), 1911–86, U.S. baseball player.

Greene (grēn), **1. Graham,** 1904–91, English novelist and journalist. **2. Nathanael,** 1742–86, American Revolutionary general. **3. Robert,** 1558–92, English dramatist and poet.

Green•ough (grē′nō), **Horatio,** 1805–52, U.S. sculptor.

Gregg (greg), **John Robert,** 1864–1948, U.S. educator: inventor of a system of shorthand.

Greg•o•ry[1] (greg′ə rē), **1. Lady Augusta** (*Isabella Augusta Persse*), 1852–1932, Irish dramatist. **2. Horace,** 1898–1982, U.S. poet and critic. **3. James,** 1638–75, Scottish mathematician.

Greg•o•ry[2] (greg′ə rē), **1. Gregory I, Saint** (*"Gregory the Great"*), A.D. c540–604, Italian pope 590–604. **2. Gregory II, Saint,** died A.D. 731, pope 715–731. **3. Gregory III, Saint,** died A.D. 741, pope 731–741. **4. Gregory IV,** died A.D. 844, pope 827–844. **5. Gregory V,** (*Bruno of Carinthia*) died A.D. 999, German ecclesiastic: pope 996–999. **6. Gregory VI,** (*Johannes Gratianus*) died 1048, German ecclesiastic: pope 1045–46. **7. Gregory VII, Saint** (*Hildebrand*) c1020–85, Italian pope 1073–85. **8. Gregory VIII,** (*Alberto de Mora* or *Alberto di Morra*) died 1187, Italian ecclesiastic: pope 1187. **9. Gregory IX,** (*Ugolino di Segni* or *Ugolino of Anagni*) c1143–1241, Italian ecclesiastic: pope 1227–41. **10. Gregory X,** (*Teobaldo Visconti*) c1210–76, Italian ecclesiastic: pope 1271–76. **11. Gregory XI,** (*Pierre Roger de Beaufort*) 1330–78, French ecclesiastic: pope 1370–78. **12. Gregory XII,** (*Angelo Correr, Corrario,* or *Corraro*) c1327–1417, Italian ecclesiastic: installed as pope in 1406 and resigned office in 1415. **13. Gregory XIII,** (*Ugo Buoncompagni*) 1502–85, Italian pope 1572–85. **14. Gregory XIV,** (*Niccolò Sfandrati*) 1535–91, Italian ecclesiastic: pope 1590–91. **15. Gregory XV,** (*Alessandro Ludovisi*) 1554–1623, Italian ecclesiastic: pope 1621–23. **16. Gregory XVI,** (*Bartolommeo Alberto Cappellari*) 1765–1846, Italian ecclesiastic: pope 1831–46.

Greg′ory of Nys′sa (nis′ə), **Saint,** A.D. c330–395?, Christian bishop and theologian in Asia Minor (brother of Saint Basil).

Greg′ory of Tours′, Saint, A.D. 538?–594, Frankish bishop and historian.

Gren•fell (gren′fel), **Sir Wilfred Thomason,** 1865–1940, English physician and medical missionary in Labrador.

Gren•ville (gren′vil), **1. George,** 1712–70, British prime minister 1763–65. **2.** Also, **Greynville. Sir Richard,** 1541?–91, English naval commander. **3. William Wyndham, Baron,** 1759–1834, British statesman: prime minister 1806–07 (son of George Grenville).

Gresh•am (gresh′əm), **Sir Thomas,** 1519?–79, English financier.

Gré•try (GRā tRē′), **André Ernest Modeste,** 1741–1813, French operatic composer.

Greuze (GRœz), **Jean Baptiste** (zhäN), 1725–1805, French painter.

Grev•ille (grev′il), **Fulke** (fŏŏlk), **1st Baron Brooke,** 1554–1628, English poet and statesman.

Grey (grā), **1. Charles, 2nd Earl,** 1764–1845, British prime minister 1830–34. **2. Sir Edward** (*Viscount Fallodon*), 1862–1933, British statesman. **3. Sir George,** 1812–98, British statesman and colonial administrator: prime minister of New Zealand 1877–79. **4. Lady Jane** (*Lady Jane Dudley*), 1537–54, descendant of Henry VII of England; executed as a rival to Mary I for the throne. **5. Zane,** 1875–1939, U.S. novelist.

Greyn•ville (grān′vil, gren′-), **Sir Richard.** GRENVILLE, Sir Richard.

Grieg (grēg), **Edvard,** 1843–1907, Norwegian composer.

Grif•fes (grif′əs), **Charles Tomlinson,** 1884–1920, U.S. composer.

Grif•fith (grif′ith), **D(avid Lewelyn) W(ark),** 1875–1948, U.S. film director and producer.

Gri•gnard (grēn yärd′), **(François Auguste) Victor,** 1871–1935, French organic chemist: Nobel prize 1912.

Grill•par•zer (gril′pärt′sər), **Franz,** 1791–1872, Austrian poet and dramatist.

Gri•mal•di (gri mäl′dē, -môl′-), **Joseph,** 1779–1837, English actor, mime, and clown.

Grim•ké (grim′kē), **Sarah Moore,** 1792–1873, and her

sister **Angelina Emily,** 1805–79, U.S. abolitionists and women's-rights leaders.

Grimm (grim), **Jakob Ludwig Karl,** 1785–1863, and his brother **Wilhelm Karl,** 1786–1859, German philologists and folklorists.

Gris (grēs), **Juan** (*José Vittoriano Gonzáles*), 1887–1927, Spanish painter in France.

Gris•wold (griz′wôld, -wəld), **Erwin Nathaniel,** born 1904, U.S. lawyer and educator: dean of Harvard University Law School 1950–67.

Groe•te (*Du.* KHrōō′tə; *Eng.* grōt), **Gerhard,** GROOTE, Gerhard.

Gro•fé (grō′fā, grə fā′), **Fer•de** (fûr′dē), (*Ferdinand Rudolf von Grofé*), 1892–1972, U.S. composer.

Gro•lier de Ser•vières (GRÔ lyā də SER vyER′), **Jean** (zhäN), 1479–1565, French bibliophile.

Gro•my•ko (grə mē′kō, grō-), **Andrei Andreevich,** 1909–1989, Russian diplomat: foreign minister of the Soviet Union 1957–85, president 1985–88.

Gron•chi (grong′kē; *It.* GRÔN′kē), **Giovanni,** 1887–1978, Italian statesman: president 1955–62.

Groot (*Du.* KHRŌt; *Eng.* grōt), **1. Huig de** or **van,** GROTIUS, Hugo. **2. Gerhard,** GROOTE, Gerhard.

Groo•te or **Groe•te** (*Du.* KHRŌ′tə; *Eng.* grōt) also **Groot, Gerhard** (*Gerardus Magnus*), 1340–84, Dutch religious reformer, educator, and author: founder of the order of Brethren of the Common Life.

Gro•pi•us (grō′pē əs), **Walter,** 1883–1969, German architect, in the U.S. after 1937.

Grop•per (grop′ər), **William,** 1897–1977, U.S. painter.

Gros (GRŌ′), **Antoine Jean, Baron,** 1771–1835, French painter.

Gross (grōs), **Chaim,** born 1904, U.S. sculptor and graphic artist, born in Austria.

Gros•ve•nor (grōv′nər), **Gilbert Hovey,** 1875–1966, U.S. geographer, writer, and editor.

Grosz (grōs), **George,** 1893–1959, U.S. painter and graphic artist, born in Germany.

Grote (grōt), **George,** 1794–1871, English historian.

Gro•ti•us (grō′shē əs), **Hugo** (*Huig De Groot*), 1583–1645, Dutch jurist and statesman.

Grou•chy (grōō shē′), **Emmanuel, Marquis de,** 1766–1847, French general.

Grove (grōv), **1. Sir George,** 1820–1900, English musicologist. **2. Robert Moses** (*"Lefty"*), 1900–75, U.S. baseball player.

Groves (grōvz), **Leslie Richard,** 1896–1970, U.S. general.

Grow (grō), **Galusha Aaron,** 1822–1907, U.S. political leader: Speaker of the House 1861–63.

Gru•en•berg (grōō′ən bûrg′), **Louis,** 1884–1964, U.S. pianist and composer, born in Russia.

Grun•dy (grun′dē), **Felix,** 1777–1840, American politician: senator 1829–38, 1839–40; attorney general 1838–39.

Grü•ne•wald (gro͞o′nə vält′), **Mathias,** (*Mathias Neithardt-Gothardt*), c1470–1528, German painter and architect.

Gru•nit•sky (grə nit′skē), **Nicolas,** 1913–69, African statesman: president of the Republic of Togo 1963–67.

Guar•di (gwär′dē), **Francesco,** 1712–93, Italian painter.

Gua•ri•ni (gwä rē′nē), **Guarino,** 1624–83, Italian architect.

Guar•ne•ri (gwär nâr′ē), **Giuseppe Antonio,** (*Joseph Guarnerius*), 1683–1745, Italian violinmaker.

Gu•de•a (go͞o dē′ə), fl. c2250 B.C., Sumerian ruler.

Gud•munds•son (gʏd′mo͝on son), **Kristmann,** born 1902, Icelandic novelist.

Gue•rick•e (gâr′ə kē, -kə, gwâr′-), **Otto von,** 1602–86, German physicist.

Guesde (ged), **Jules,** (*Mathieu Basile*), 1845–1922, French socialist leader, editor, and writer.

Guest (gest), **Edgar A(lbert),** 1881–1959, U.S. journalist and writer of verse, born in England.

Gue•va•ra (gə vär′ə, gā-), **Ernesto,** ("*Che*"), 1928–67, Cuban revolutionary leader, born in Argentina.

Gug•gen•heim (go͝og′ən him′, go͞o′gən-), **Daniel,** 1856–1930, U.S. industrialist and philanthropist.

Gui•do d'A•rez•zo (gwē′dō də ret′sō), (*Guido Aretinus*) ("*Fra Guittone*"), c995–1049?, Italian monk and music theorist.

Guil•laume (*Fr.* gē yōm′), **Charles Édouard,** 1861–1938, Swiss physicist: Nobel prize 1920.

Guil•laume de Ma•chaut (gē yōm də mᴀ shō′), 1300–77, French poet and composer.

Guille•min (gē′ə man′; *Fr.* gēyᵉ mᴀɴ′), **Roger (Charles Louis),** born 1924, U.S. physiologist, born in France: Nobel prize for medicine 1977.

Gui•llén (gēl yen′), **Jorge,** 1893–1984, Spanish poet, in the U.S. 1940–75.

Guin•ness (gin′is), **Sir Alec,** 1914–89, English actor.

Guis•card (*Fr.* gēs kᴀʀ′), **Robert,** (*Robert de Hauteville*) c1015–85, Norman conqueror in Italy.

Guise (gēz), **1. François de Lorraine, 2nd Duc de,** 1519–63, French general and statesman. **2.** his son, **Henri I de Lorraine, Duc de,** 1550–88, French leader of opposition to the Huguenots.

Gui•try (gē′trē), **Sacha,** 1885–1957, French actor and dramatist, born in Russia.

Gui•zot (gē zō′), **François Pierre Guillaume,** 1787–1874, French historian and statesman.

Gull•strand (gul′strand′; *Swed.* go͞ol′stʀänd′), **Allvar,** 1862–1930, Swedish oculist: Nobel prize for medicine 1911.

Gun•ter (gun′tər), **Edmund,** 1581–1626, English mathematician and astronomer: inventor of various measuring instruments and scales.

Gun•ther (gun′thər), **John,** born 1901, U.S. journalist and author.

Guo Mo•ruo (gwô′ mô′ʀwô′, -zhwô′), 1892–1978, Chinese intellectual, writer, poet, scholar, and government official.

Gür•sel (gʏʀ sel′), **Ce•mal** (je mäl′), 1895–1966, Turkish army officer and statesman: president 1961–66.

Gus•ta•vus (gu stā′vəs, -stä′-), **1. Gustavus I** (*Gustavus Vasa*), 1496–1560, king of Sweden 1523–60. **2. Gustavus II** (*Gustavus Adolphus*) (*"Lion of the North"*), 1594–1632, king of Sweden 1611–32: national military hero (grandson of Gustavus I). **3. Gustavus III,** 1746–92, king of Sweden 1771–92: economic and legal reformer. **4. Gustavus IV** (*Gustavus Adolphus*), 1778–1837, king of Sweden 1792–1809 (son of Gustavus III). **5. Gustavus** (or **Gus•taf** or **Gus•tav**) **V** (gus′täv), 1858–1950, king of Sweden 1907–50: advocate of Swedish neutrality during World Wars I and II. **6. Gustavus** (or **Gustav**) **VI** (*Gustaf Adolf*), 1882–1973, king of Sweden 1950–73 (son of Gustavus V).

Gu•ten•berg (go͞ot′n bûrg′), **Johannes,** (*Johann Gensfleisch*), c1400–68, German printer: first to print with movable type.

Guth•rie (guth′rē), **1. Sir (William) Tyrone,** 1900–71, English stage director and producer. **2. Woodrow Wilson** (*"Woody"*), 1912–67, U.S. folk singer.

Gu•tiér•rez Ná•je•ra (go͞o tyâr′res nä′hə rä′), **Manuel,** (*"El Duque Job"*), 1859–95, Mexican poet, short-story writer, and editor.

Guy•on (gwē yôɴ′), **Madame** (*Jeanne Marie Bouvier de la Matte*), 1648–1717, French writer.

Guz•mán (go͞os män′), **Martín Luis,** 1887–1976, Mexican novelist, journalist, and soldier.

Gwin•nett (gwi net′), **Button,** 1735?–77, American Revolutionary leader, born in England.

Gwyn or **Gwynne** (gwin), **Eleanor** (*"Nell"*), 1650–87, English actress: mistress of Charles II.

Haa•kon VII (hô′ko͝on), (*Prince Carl of Denmark*) 1872–1957, king of Norway 1905–57.

Ha•ber (hä′bər), **Fritz,** 1868–1934, German chemist: Nobel prize 1918.

Ha•da•mard (ä′dä mär′), **Jacques Salomon,** 1865–1963, French mathematician.

Ha•das (had′əs, hä′dəs), **Moses,** 1900–66, U.S. classical scholar, teacher, and author.

Had•don (had′n), **Alfred Cort,** 1855–1940, English ethnologist, anthropologist, and writer.

Had•field (had′fēld′), **Sir Robert Abbott,** 1858–1940, English metallurgist and industrialist.

Had•ley (had′lē), **Henry Kimball,** 1871–1937, U.S. composer and conductor.

Ha•dri•an (hā′drē ən), (*Publius Aelius Hadrianus*) A.D. 76–138, Roman emperor 117–138.

Hadrian IV, ADRIAN IV.

Haeck•el (hek′əl), **Ernst Heinrich,** 1834–1919, German biologist and philosopher of evolution.

Ha•fiz (hä fiz′), (*Shams ud-din Mohammed*) c1320–89?, Persian poet.

Hag•gard (hag′ərd), **(Sir) H(enry) Rider,** 1856–1925, English novelist.

Hahn (hän), **Otto,** 1879–1968, German physical chemist: Nobel prize 1944.

Hah•ne•mann (hä′nə mən), **(Christian Friedrich) Samuel,** 1755–1843, German physician: founder of homeopathy.

Hai•dar (or **Hy•der**) **A•li** (hī′dər ä′lē, ä lē′), 1722–82, Islamic prince and military leader of India: ruler of Mysore 1759–82.

Haig (hāg), **Douglas, 1st Earl,** 1861–1928, British field marshal: commander in chief of the British forces in France 1915–18.

Hai•le Se•las•sie I (hī′lē sə las′ē, -lä′sē), (*Ras Tafari*), 1891–1975, emperor of Ethiopia 1930–74: in exile 1936–41.

Hak•luyt (hak′lit), **Richard,** 1552?–1616, English geographer and editor of explorers' narratives.

Hal•as (hal′əs), **George Stanley,** 1895–1983, U.S. football coach and team owner.

Hal•dane (hôl′dān), **1. John Burdon Sanderson,** 1892–1964, English geneticist and writer. **2.** his father, **John Scott,** 1860–1936, Scottish physiologist and writer. **3. Richard Burdon** (*Viscount Haldane of Cloan*), 1856–1928, Scottish jurist and writer (brother of John Scott).

Hale (hāl), **1. Edward Everett,** 1822–1909, U.S. clergyman and author. **2. George Ellery,** 1868–1938, U.S. astronomer. **3. Sir Matthew,** 1609–76, British jurist: Lord Chief Justice 1671–76. **4. Nathan,** 1755–76, American soldier hanged as a spy by the British during the American Revolution. **5. Sarah Josepha,** 1788–1879, U.S. editor and author.

Ha•lé•vy (A lā vā′), **1. Fromental** (*Jacques François Fromental Élie Lévy*), 1790–1862, French composer. **2.** his nephew, **Ludovic,** 1834–1908, French novelist and playwright: librettist in collaboration with Henri Meilhac.

Ha•ley (hā′lē), **Alex,** 1921–92, U.S. author.

Hal•i•fax (hal′ə faks′), **Earl of** (*Edward Frederick Lindley Wood*), 1881–1959, British statesman.

Hall (hôl), **1. Asaph,** 1829–1907, U.S. astronomer: discovered the satellites of Mars. **2. Charles Francis,** 1821–71, U.S. Arctic explorer. **3. Charles Martin,** 1863–1914, U.S. chemist and metallurgist. **4. Granville Stanley,** 1846–1924, U.S. psychologist and educator. **5. James Norman,** 1887–1951, U.S. novelist. **6. Prince,** 1748–1807, U.S. clergyman and abolitionist, born in Barbados: fought at Bunker Hill.

Hal•lam (hal′əm), **Henry,** 1777–1859, English historian.

Hal•leck (hal′ik, -ək), **1. Fitz-Green** (fits′grēn′, fits-grēn′), 1790–1867, U.S. poet. **2. Henry Wager,** 1815–72, Union general in the U.S. Civil War and writer on military subjects.

Hal•ler (hä′lər), **Albrecht von,** 1708–77, Swiss physiologist, botanist, and writer.

Hal•ley (hal′ē *or, sometimes,* hā′lē), **Edmund** or **Edmond,** 1656–1742, English astronomer.

Hals (häls), **Frans,** 1581?–1666, Dutch portrait and genre painter.

Hal•sey (hôl′zē), **William Frederick,** 1882–1959, U.S. admiral.

Hal•sted (hôl′stid, -sted), **William Stewart** ("*Brill*"), 1852–1922, U.S. surgeon and educator.

Ha•mil•car Bar•ca (hə mil′kär bär′kə, ham′əl kär′), c270–228 B.C., Carthaginian general and statesman (father of Hannibal).

Ham•ill (ham′əl), **Dorothy (Stuart),** born 1956, U.S. figure-skater.

Ham•il•ton (ham′əl tən), **1. Alexander,** 1757–1804, first U.S. Secretary of the Treasury 1789–97. **2. Edith,** 1867–1963, U.S. classical scholar and writer. **3. Lady Emma** (*Amy,* or *Emily, Lyon*), 1765?–1815, mistress of Viscount Nelson. **4. Sir Ian Standish Monteith,** 1853–1947, British general. **5. Sir William,** 1788–1856, Scottish philosopher. **6. Sir William Rowan,** 1805–65, Irish mathematician and astronomer.

Ham•lin (ham′lin), **Hannibal,** 1809–91, U.S. political leader: vice president of the U.S. 1861–65.

Ham•mar•skjöld (ham′ər shəld, -shœld′), **Dag Hjalmar,** 1905–61, Swedish statesman: Secretary General of the U.N. 1953–61: Nobel peace prize 1961.

Ham•mer (ham′ər), **Armand,** 1898–1990, U.S. businessman and art patron.

Ham•mer•stein (ham′ər stīn′), **1. Oscar,** 1847?–1919,

U.S. theatrical manager, born in Germany. **2.** his grandson, **Oscar II,** 1895–1960, U.S. lyricist and librettist.

Ham•mett (ham′it), **(Samuel) Da•shiell** (də shēl′, dash′ēl, -əl), 1894–1961, U.S. writer of detective stories.

Ham•mon (ham′ən), **Jupiter,** c1720–c1800, American poet.

Ham•mond (ham′ənd), **John Hays** (hāz), 1855–1936, U.S. engineer.

Ham•mu•ra•bi (hä′mo͝o rä′bē, ham′o͝o-) also **Ham•mu•ra•pi** (-rä′pē), 18th century B.C. or earlier, king of Babylonia: instituted a legal code.

Hamp•ton (hamp′tən), **1. Lionel,** born 1913, U.S. jazz vibraphonist. **2. Wade,** 1818–1902, Confederate general: U.S. senator 1879–91.

Ham•sun (häm′so͝on), **Knut,** 1859–1952, Norwegian novelist: Nobel prize 1920.

Han•cock (han′kok), **1. John,** 1737–93, American statesman: first signer of the Declaration of Independence. **2. Winfield Scott,** 1824–86, Union general in the Civil War.

Hand (hand), **Lear•ned** (lûr′nid), 1872–1961, U.S. jurist.

Han•del (han′dl), **George Frideric** (*Georg Friedrich Händel*), 1685–1759, German composer in England after 1712.

Han•dy (han′dē), **W(illiam) C(hristopher),** 1873–1958, U.S. blues composer.

Han•na (han′ə), **Marcus Alonzo** ("*Mark*"), 1837–1904, U.S. merchant and politician.

Han•ni•bal (han′ə bəl), 247–183 B.C., Carthaginian general who crossed the Alps and invaded Italy (son of Hamilcar Barca).

Han•no (han′ō), fl. 3rd century B.C., Carthaginian statesman.

Ha•no•taux (A nô tō′), **(Albert Auguste) Gabriel,** 1853–1944, French statesman and historian.

Hans•ber•ry (hanz′ber ē), **Lorraine,** 1930–65, U.S. playwright.

Han•sen (hän′sən), **Peter Andreas,** 1795–1874, Danish astronomer.

Han•son (han′sən), **1. Duane,** born 1925, U.S. artist and sculptor. **2. Howard** (*Harold*), 1896–1981, U.S. composer.

Han Wu Ti (or **Di**) (hän′ wo͞o′ dē′), (*Liu Ch'e, Liu Che*) 156–87 B.C., emperor of China 140–87.

Han Yü (or **Yu**) (hän′ yʏ′), (*Han Wen-kung, Han Wengong*) A.D. 768–824, Chinese writer, poet, and philosopher.

Ha•rald V (har′əld), born 1937, king of Norway since 1991.

Har•de•ca•nute (här′də kə no͞ot′, -nyo͞ot′), 1019?–42, king of Denmark 1035–42, king of England 1040–42 (son of Canute).

Har•den (här′dn), **Sir Arthur,** 1865–1940, English biochemist: Nobel prize 1929.

Har•din (här′dn), **John Wesley,** 1853–95, U.S. outlaw in the West.

Har•ding (här′ding), **1. Chester,** 1792–1866, U.S. painter. **2. Warren G(amaliel),** 1865–1923, 29th president of the U.S. 1921–23.

Har•dy (här′dē), **1. Godfrey Harold,** 1877–1947, English mathematician. **2. Oliver,** 1892–1957, U.S. motion-picture comedian. **3. Thomas,** 1840–1928, English novelist and poet.

Har•greaves (här′grēvz), **James,** died 1778, English inventor of spinning machinery.

Har•kins (här′kinz), **William Draper,** 1873–1951, U.S. chemist.

Hark•ness (härk′nis), **Edward Stephan,** 1874–1940, U.S. philanthropist.

Har•lan (här′lən), **1. John Marshall,** 1833–1911, U.S. jurist: associate justice of the U.S. Supreme Court 1877–1911. **2. John Marshall,** 1899–1971, associate justice of the U.S. Supreme Court 1955–71.

Har•low (här′lō), **Jean,** 1911–37, U.S. motion-picture actress.

Harms•worth (härmz′wûrth), **1. Alfred Charles William, Viscount Northcliffe,** 1865–1922, English journalist, publisher, and politician. **2.** his brother, **Harold Sidney, 1st Viscount Rothermere,** 1868–1940, English publisher and politician.

Har•nack (här′nak), **Adolf von,** 1851–1930, German Protestant theologian, born in Estonia.

Har•nett (här′nit), **William Michael,** 1848–92, U.S. painter.

Har•non•court (här′nən kôrt′, -kōrt′), **Nikolaus,** born 1929, Austrian conductor.

Har•old (har′əld), **1. Harold I** (*"Harefoot"*), died 1040, king of England 1035–40 (son of Canute). **2. Harold II,** 1022?–66, king of England 1066: defeated at Hastings (son of Earl Godwin).

Har•per (här′pər), **James,** 1795–1869, and his brothers **John,** 1797–1875, **(Joseph) Wesley,** 1801–70, and **Fletcher,** 1806–77, U.S. printers and publishers.

Har•ri•man (har′ə mən), **1. Edward Henry,** 1848–1909, U.S. financier and railroad magnate. **2.** his son, **W(illiam) A•ve•rell** (ā′vər əl), 1891–1986, U.S. statesman.

Har•ris (har′is), **1. Benjamin,** c1660–c1720, English journalist who published the first newspaper in America 1690. **2. Emmylou,** born 1947, U.S. singer and songwriter. **3. Joel Chandler,** 1848–1908, U.S. writer. **4. Julie,** born 1925, U.S. actress. **5. Louis,** born 1921, U.S. public-opinion pollster and columnist. **6. Roy,** 1898–1979, U.S. composer. **7. Thaddeus William,** 1795–1856, U.S. entomologist: pioneer in applied entomology.

Har•ri•son (har′ə sən), **1. Benjamin,** 1726?–91, American political leader (father of William Henry Harrison). **2. Benjamin,** 1833–1901, 23rd president of the U.S. 1889–93 (grandson of William Henry Harrison). **3. Peter,** 1716–75, English architect in the U.S. **4. Rex** (*Reginald Carey*),

1908–90, English actor. **5. William Henry,** 1773–1841, 9th president of the U.S. 1841.

Hart (härt), **1. Albert Bushnell,** 1854–1943, U.S. editor, historian, and educator. **2. Gary (Warren),** born 1936, U.S. politician: senator 1975–87. **3. Lo•renz** (lôr′ənts, lōr′-), 1895–1943, U.S. lyricist. **4. Moss,** 1904–61, U.S. playwright and librettist. **5. William S(urrey),** 1872–1946, U.S. film actor.

Har•tack (här′tak), **William John, Jr.** (*"Bill"*), born 1932, U.S. jockey.

Harte (härt), **(Francis) Bret,** 1839–1902, U.S. author.

Hart•ford (härt′fərd), **(George) Huntington, 2nd,** born 1911, U.S. businessman and patron of the arts.

Hart•line (härt′līn), **Haldan Keffer,** 1903–83, U.S. physiologist: Nobel prize for medicine 1967.

Hart•mann (härt′män, -mən), **1. (Karl Robert) Eduard von,** 1842–1906, German philosopher. **2. Nicolai,** 1882–1950, German philosopher, born in Latvia.

Ha•run al-Ra•shid (hä ro͞on′ äl′rä shēd′) A.D. 764?–809, caliph of Baghdad 786–809: made a legendary hero in *The Arabian Nights.*

Ha•ru•no•bu (här′o͝o nō′bo͞o), **Suzuki,** 1720?–70, Japanese painter and printmaker.

Har•vard (här′vərd), **John,** 1607–38, English clergyman in the U.S.: benefactor of Harvard College.

Har•vey (här′vē), **William,** 1578–1657, English physician.

Ha•san (hä′sən, ha san′), (*al-Hasan*), A.D. 624?–669?, Arabian caliph: son of Ali and Fatima (brother of Hussein).

Has•dru•bal (haz′dro͝o bəl, haz dro͞o′-), died 207 B.C., Carthaginian general (brother of Hannibal).

Ha•šek (hä′shek), **Ja•ro•slav** (yär′ə släf′), 1883–1923, Czech writer.

Has•sam (has′əm), **(Frederick) Childe,** 1859–1935, U.S. painter.

Has•san II (hä′sən, ha san′), born 1929, king of Morocco since 1961.

Has•sel (hä′səl), **Odd,** 1897–1981, Norwegian chemist: Nobel prize 1969.

Has•tie (hā′stē), **William Henry,** 1904–76, U.S. jurist: first black judge of the U.S. Circuit Court of Appeals.

Has•tings (hā′stingz), **1. Thomas,** 1860–1929, U.S. architect. **2. Warren,** 1732–1818, first British governor general of India 1773–85.

Hath•a•way (hath′ə wā′), **Anne,** 1557–1623, the wife of William Shakespeare.

Hat•shep•sut (hat shep′so͞ot) also **Hat•shep•set** (-set), queen of Egypt c1503–c1482 B.C.

Hat•ta (hat′ə), **Mohammed,** born 1902, Indonesian political leader: vice president of the Republic of Indonesia 1945–49, 1950–56; prime minister 1948, 1949–50.

Haupt•mann (houpt′män′), **Gerhart,** 1862–1946, German dramatist, novelist, and poet: Nobel prize 1912.

Haus•ho•fer (hous′hō fər), **Karl,** 1860–1946, German geographer and general: political adviser to Hitler.

Hauss•mann (hous′mən), **Georges Eugène, Baron,** 1809–91, French administrator who improved the landscaping, street designs, and utilities systems of Paris.

Ha•vel (hä′vel), **Vá•clav** (väts′läf), born 1936, Czech dramatist: president of Czechoslovakia since 1989.

Hav•i•land (hav′ə lənd), **John,** 1792–1852, English architect, in the U.S.

Hawke (hôk), **Robert (James Lee),** born 1929, Australian political leader: prime minister since 1983.

Haw•king (hô′king), **Stephen William,** born 1942, English physicist.

Haw•kins (hô′kinz), **1. Sir Anthony Hope** (*"Anthony Hope"*), 1863–1933, English novelist and playwright. **2. Coleman,** 1904–69, U.S. jazz saxophonist. **3.** Also, **Hawkyns. Sir John,** 1532–95, English slave trader and rear admiral.

Hawks (hôks), **Howard (Winchester),** 1896–1977, U.S. film director.

Hawks•moor (hôks′mŏŏr′), **Nicholas,** 1661–1736, English architect.

Ha•worth (hä′wərth, hô′-), **Sir Walter Norman,** 1883–1950, English chemist: Nobel prize 1937.

Haw•thorne (hô′thôrn′), **Nathaniel,** 1804–64, U.S. writer.

Hay (hā), **John Milton,** 1838–1905, U.S. statesman and author.

Ha•ya•ka•wa (hä′yə kä′wə), **1. S(amuel) I(chiye),** 1906–92, U.S. semanticist, educator, and politician, born in Canada: senator 1977–83. **2. Sessue,** 1889–1973, Japanese film actor.

Hay•dn (hīd′n), **Franz Joseph,** 1732–1809, Austrian composer.

Ha•yek (hä′yek), **Friedrich August von,** 1899–1992, British economist, born in Austria: Nobel prize 1974.

Hayes (hāz), **1. Carlton J(oseph) H(untley),** 1882–1964, U.S. historian, educator, and diplomat. **2. Helen** (*Helen Hayes Brown MacArthur*), born 1900, U.S. actress. **3. Roland,** 1887–1976, U.S. tenor. **4. Rutherford B(irchard),** 1822–93, 19th president of the U.S. 1877–81.

Haynes (hānz), **Elwood,** 1857–1925, U.S. inventor.

Hays (hāz), **Will (Harrison),** 1879–1954, U.S. lawyer, politician, and official of the motion-picture industry.

Hay•ward (hā′wərd), **Leland,** 1902–71, U.S. theatrical producer.

Hay•wood (hā′wŏŏd′), **William Dudley** (*"Big Bill"*), 1869–1928, U.S. labor leader.

Hay•worth (hā′wûrth), **Rita** (*Margarita Carmen Cansino*), 1918–87, U.S. actress.

Haz•litt (haz′lit), **William,** 1778–1830, English essayist.

Hea•ly (hē′lē), **Timothy Michael,** 1855–1931, Irish nationalist politician.

Hearn (hûrn), **Lafcadio** (*"Koizumi Yakumo"*), 1850–1904, U.S. writer, born in Greece; in Japan after 1894.

Hearst (hûrst), **1. William Randolph,** 1863–1951, U.S.

editor and publisher. **2.** his son, **William Randolph, Jr.,** born 1908, U.S. publisher and editor.

Heath (hēth), **Edward (Richard George),** born 1916, British prime minister 1970–74.

Heav•i•side (hev′ē sīd′), **Oliver,** 1850–1925, English physicist.

Heb•bel (heb′əl), **(Christian) Friedrich,** 1813–63, German lyric poet and playwright.

He•ber (hē′bər), **Reginald,** 1783–1826, British bishop and hymn writer.

Hé•bert (ā bers′), **Jacques René** (*"Père Duchesne"*), 1755–94, French journalist and revolutionary leader.

He•din (he dēn′), **Sven Anders,** 1865–1952, Swedish geographer and explorer.

Hef•fel•fin•ger (hef′əl fing′gər), **William Walter** (*"Pudge"*), 1867–1954, U.S. football player.

He•gel (hā′gəl), **Georg Wilhelm Friedrich,** 1770–1831, German philosopher.

Hei•deg•ger (hī′deg ər, -di gər), **Martin,** 1889–1976, German philosopher.

Hei•den (hīd′n), **Eric,** born 1958, U.S. speed skater.

Hei•den•stam (hā′dən stäm′), **Verner von,** 1859–1940, Swedish poet and novelist: Nobel prize 1916.

Hei•fetz (hī′fits), **Ja•scha** (yä′shə), 1901–87, U.S. violinist, born in Russia.

Hei•ne (hī′nə), **Heinrich,** 1797–1856, German poet.

Hein•lein (hīn′līn), **Robert A(nson),** 1907–88, U.S. science-fiction writer.

Heinz (hīnz), **H(enry) J(ohn),** 1844–1919, U.S. businessman: founder of food-processing company.

Hei•sen•berg (hī′zən bûrg′), **Werner Karl,** 1901–76, German physicist: Nobel prize 1932.

Heiss (hīs), **Carol E(lizabeth),** born 1940, U.S. figure skater.

Held (held), **John, Jr.,** 1889–1958, U.S. cartoonist, illustrator, and writer.

Hel•e•na (hel′ə nə), **Saint,** c247–c330, mother of Constantine I.

He•li•o•gab•a•lus (hē′lē ə gab′ə ləs) also **Elagabalus,** (*Varius Avitus Bassianus*) A.D. 204–222, Roman emperor 218–222.

Hel•ler (hel′ər), **Joseph,** born 1923, U.S. novelist.

Hell•man (hel′mən), **Lillian Florence,** 1905–84, U.S. playwright.

Helm•holtz (helm′hōlts), **Hermann Ludwig Ferdinand von,** 1821–94, German physiologist and physicist.

Hel•mont (hel′mont), **Jan Baptista van,** 1579–1644, Flemish chemist and physician.

Hé•lo•ïse (el′ō ēz′), 1101?–64, French abbess: pupil of and secretly married to Pierre Abélard.

Help•mann (help′mən), **Sir Robert (Murray),** 1909–86, Australian dancer, choreographer, and actor.

Hel•vé•tius (hel vē′shəs), **Claude Adrien,** 1715–71, French philosopher.

Hem•ans (hem′ənz, hē′mənz), **Felicia Dorothea (Browne),** 1793–1835, English poet.

Hem•ing•way (hem′ing wā′), **Ernest (Miller),** 1899–1961, U.S. novelist, short-story writer, and journalist: Nobel prize 1954.

Hé•mon (ā môɴ′), **Louis,** 1880–1913, Canadian novelist, born in France.

Hem•pel (hem′pəl), **Carl Gustav,** born 1905, U.S. philosopher, born in Germany.

Hench (hench), **Philip Showalter,** 1896–1965, U.S. physician: Nobel prize for medicine 1950.

Hen•der•son (hen′dər sən), **1. Arthur,** 1863–1935, British statesman and labor leader: Nobel peace prize 1934. **2. David Bremner,** 1840–1906, U.S. political leader: Speaker of the House 1899–1903. **3. Fletcher** (*"Smack"*), 1898–1952, U.S. jazz pianist, arranger, and bandleader.

Hen•dricks (hen′driks), **Thomas Andrews,** 1819–85, vice president of the U.S. 1885.

Hen•drix (hen′driks), **Jimi** (*James Marshall Hendrix*), 1942–70, U.S. singer and guitarist.

Hen•gist or **Hen•gest** (heng′gist, hen′jist), died A.D. 488?, chief of the Jutes: with his brother Horsa led invasion of S Britain c440.

Hen•ie (hen′ē), **Sonja,** 1912–69, U.S. figure skater and film actress, born in Norway.

Hen•ley (hen′lē), **William Ernest,** 1849–1903, English poet, critic, and editor.

Hen•ne•pin (hen′ə pin), **Louis,** 1640?–1701?, Belgian Roman Catholic missionary and explorer in America.

Hen•ri (hen′rē), **Robert,** 1865–1929, U.S. painter.

Hen•ry[1] (hen′rē), **1. Joseph,** 1797–1878, U.S. physicist. **2. O.,** pen name of William Sidney PORTER. **3. Patrick,** 1736–99, American patriot and orator.

Hen•ry[2] (hen′rē), **1. Henry I, a.** 1068–1135, king of England 1100–35 (son of William the Conqueror). **b.** 1008–60, king of France 1031–60. **2. Henry II, a.** 1133–89, king of England 1154–89: first king of the Plantagenets. **b.** 1519–59, king of France 1547–59. **3. Henry III, a.** 1207–72, king of England 1216–72 (son of John). **b.** 1551–89, king of France 1574–89 (son of Henry II). **4. Henry IV, a.** (*Bolingbroke*) (*"Henry of Lancaster"*) 1367–1413, king of England 1399–1413 (son of John of Gaunt). **b.** (*"Henry of Navarre"*) 1553–1610, king of France 1589–1610: first of the Bourbon kings. **5. Henry V,** 1387–1422, king of England 1413–22 (son of Henry IV of Bolingbroke). **6. Henry VI,** 1421–71, king of England 1422–61, 1470–71 (son of Henry V). **7. Henry VII,** (*Henry Tudor*) 1457–1509, king of England 1485–1509: first king of the house of Tudor. **8. Henry VIII,** (*"Defender of the Faith"*) 1491–1547, king of England 1509–47 (son of Henry VII).

Hen′ry of Por′tugal, (*"the Navigator"*) 1394–1460, prince of Portugal: sponsor of geographic explorations.

Hen•sen (hen′sən), **Jim,** 1936–90, U.S. puppeteer and TV producer.

Hens•lowe (henz′lō), **Philip,** died 1616, English theater manager.

Hen•son (hen′sən), **Matthew Alexander,** 1866–1955, U.S. arctic explorer: accompanied Peary to North Pole 1909.

Hen•ty (hen′tē), **George Alfred,** 1832–1902, English journalist and novelist.

Hen•ze (hen′tsə), **Hans Werner,** born 1926, German composer.

Hep•burn (hep′bûrn′), **1. Audrey** (*Audrey Hepburn-Ruston*), born 1929, U.S. actress, born in Belgium. **2. Katharine,** born 1909, U.S. actress.

Hep•ple•white (hep′əl hwīt′, -wīt′), **George,** died 1786, English furniture designer.

Her•a•cli•tus (her′ə klī′təs), (*"the Obscure"*) c540–c470 B.C., Greek philosopher.

Her•a•cli•us (her′ə klī′əs, hi rak′lē əs), A.D. 575?–641, Byzantine emperor 610–641.

Her•bart (hâr′bärt), **Johann Friedrich,** 1776–1841, German philosopher and educator.

Her•bert (hûr′bərt), **1. George,** 1593–1633, English cleric and poet. **2. Victor,** 1859–1924, U.S. composer, born in Ireland.

Her•der (hâr′dər), **Johann Gottfried von,** 1744–1803, German philosopher.

He•re•di•a (e rā′dē ə), **José María de,** 1842–1905, French poet, born in Cuba.

Her•ges•hei•mer (hûr′gəs hī′mər), **Joseph,** 1880–1954, U.S. novelist.

He•ring (hā′ʀing), **Ewald,** 1834–1918, German physiologist and psychologist.

Her•ki•mer (hûr′kə mər), **Nicholas,** 1728–77, American Revolutionary general.

Her•man (hûr′mən), **Woodrow** (*"Woody"*), born 1913, U.S. jazz saxophonist, clarinetist, and bandleader.

Her•mite (hər mēt′), **Charles,** 1822–1901, French mathematician.

Her•nán•dez (eʀ nän′des), **José,** 1834–86, Argentine poet.

Hern•don (hûrn′dən), **William Henry,** 1818–91, U.S. law partner and biographer of Abraham Lincoln.

Herne (hûrn), **1. James A(hern), 2.** 1839–1901, U.S. actor and playwright.

He•ro (hēr′ō) also **Heron,** (*Hero of Alexandria*) fl. 1st century A.D., Greek scientist.

Her•od (her′əd), (*"the Great"*) 73?–4 B.C., king of Judea 37–4.

Her′od A•grip′pa (ə grip′ə), (*Julius Agrippa*) c10 B.C.–A.D. 44, king of Judea 41–44 (grandson of Herod the Great).

Her′od An′ti•pas (an′ti pas′), died after A.D. 39, ruler of Galilee A.D. 4–39.

He•ro•di•as (hə rō′dē əs), the second wife of Herod Antipas; mother of Salome.

He•rod•o•tus (hə rod′ə təs), 484?–425? B.C., Greek historian.

Hé•rold (ā rôld′), **Louis Joseph,** 1791–1833, French composer.

He•ron (hēr′on), HERO.

Her•re•ra (ə râr′ə), **Francisco de** (*"el Viejo"*), 1576–1656, Spanish painter and etcher.

Her•rick (her′ik), **1. Robert,** 1591–1674, English poet. **2. Robert,** 1868–1938, U.S. novelist.

Her•ri•ot (er yō′), **Édouard,** 1872–1957, French statesman, political leader, and author.

Herr•mann (hûr′mən), **Bernard,** 1911–75, U.S. conductor and composer.

Her•schel (hûr′shəl, hâr′-), **1. Sir John Frederick William,** 1792–1871, English astronomer. **2.** his father, **Sir William** (*Friedrich Wilhelm Herschel*), 1738–1822, English astronomer, born in Germany.

Her•sey (hûr′sē, -zē), **John Richard,** born 1914, U.S. journalist, novelist, and educator.

Her•shey (hûr′shē), **1. Alfred Day,** born 1908, U.S. biologist: helped lay the foundation of modern molecular genetics; Nobel prize for medicine 1969. **2. Lewis B(laine),** 1893–1977, U.S. Army general: director of the Selective Service System 1941–70. **3. Milton Snave•ly** (snāv′lē), 1857–1945, U.S. businessman: founder of chocolate manufacturing company.

Her•sko•witz (hûr′skə vits), **Melville (Jean),** 1895–1963, American anthropologist.

Her•ter (hûr′tər), **Christian Archibald,** 1895–1966, U.S. politician: Secretary of State 1959–61.

Hertz (hûrts, hârts), **1. Gustav,** 1887–1975, German physicist: Nobel prize 1925. **2. Heinrich Rudolph,** 1857–94, German physicist.

Her•tzog (*Du.* heʀ′tsôкн), **James Barry Munnik,** South African statesman and general: prime minister 1924–39.

Herz•berg (hûrts′bûrg), **Gerhard,** born 1904, Canadian physicist, born in Germany: Nobel prize for chemistry 1971.

Her•zl (hûrt′səl, hârt′-), **Theodor,** 1860–1904, Hungarian-born Austrian Jewish writer and Zionist.

Her•zog (hûrt′sog, hûr′zog), **Maurice,** born 1919, French mountaineer: climbed Annapurna 1950.

He•si•od (hē′sē əd, hes′ē-), fl. 8th century B.C., Greek poet.

Hess (hes), **1. Dame Myra,** 1890–1965, English pianist. **2. Victor Francis,** 1883–1964, U.S. physicist, born in Austria: Nobel prize 1936. **3. Walter Rudolf,** 1881–1973, Swiss physiologist: Nobel prize for medicine 1949. **4. (Walther Richard) Rudolf,** 1894–1987, German Nazi official.

Hes•se (hes′ə), **Hermann,** 1877–1962, German writer: Nobel prize 1946.

He•ve•li•us (hə vā′lē əs), **Johannes** (*Johann Hewel* or *Hewelke*), 1611–87, Polish astronomer: charted the moon's surface and discovered four comets.

He•ve•sy (he′ve shē), **Georg von,** 1885–1966, Hungarian chemist: Nobel prize 1943.

Hew•ish (hyōō′ish *or, often,* yōō′-), **Antony,** born 1924, British astronomer: discovered pulsars; Nobel prize for physics 1974.

Hew•lett (hyōō′lit *or, often,* yōō′-), **Maurice Henry,** 1861–1923, English novelist, poet, and essayist.

Hey•er•dahl (hā′ər däl′), **Thor,** born 1914, Norwegian ethnologist and author.

Hey•mans (hī′mənz), **Corneille,** 1892–1968, Belgian physiologist: Nobel prize for medicine 1938.

Hey•rov•ský (hā′rôf skē), **Ja•ro•slav** (yär′ə släf′), 1890–1967, Czech chemist: Nobel prize 1959.

Hey•se (hī′zə), **Paul (Johann von),** 1830–1914, German playwright, novelist, poet, and short-story writer: Nobel prize 1910.

Hey•ward (hā′wərd), **Du•Bose** (də bōz′), 1885–1940, U.S. playwright, novelist, and poet.

Hey•wood (hā′wŏŏd), **1. John,** 1497?–1580?, English dramatist and epigrammatist. **2. Thomas,** 1573?–1641, English dramatist, poet, and actor.

Hich•ens (hich′ənz), **Robert Smythe** (smīth, smith), 1864–1950, English novelist.

Hick•ok (hik′ok), **James Butler** (*"Wild Bill"*), 1837–76, U.S. frontiersman.

Hicks (hiks), **1. Edward,** 1780–1849, U.S. painter. **2. Sir John Richard,** 1904–89, British economist: Nobel prize 1972.

Hi•dal•go (hi dal′gō), **Juan,** c1600–85, Spanish composer and harpist.

Hi•dal•go y Cos•til•la (ē thäl′gô ē kôs tē′yä), **Miguel,** 1753–1811, Mexican priest, patriot, and revolutionist.

Hi•de•yo•shi (hē′de yô′shē), **Toyotomi,** 1536–98, Japanese general and statesman: prime minister and dictator of Japan 1585–98.

Hi•er•on•y•mus (hī′ə ron′ə məs, hī ron′-), **Eusebius,** JEROME, Saint.

Hig•gin•son (hig′in sən), **Thomas Wentworth Storrow,** 1823–1911, U.S. clergyman, author, and social reformer.

Hi•lar•i•us (hi lâr′ē əs) also **Hil•a•rus** (hil′ər əs) or **Hil′a•ry** (-ə rē), **Saint,** died A.D. 468, pope 461–468.

Hil′ary of Poi•tiers′ (pwä tyā′), **Saint,** A.D. c300–368, French bishop and theologian. French, **Hi•laire de Poi•tiers** (ē leʀ′ də pwa tyā′).

Hil•bert (hil′bərt), **David,** 1862–1943, German mathematician.

Hil•de•brand (hil′də brand′), GREGORY VII, Saint.

Hill (hil), **1. Ambrose Powell,** 1825–65, Confederate general in the U.S. Civil War. **2. Archibald Vivian,** 1886–

1977, English physiologist: Nobel prize for medicine 1922. **3. James Jerome,** 1838–1916, U.S. railroad builder and financier, born in Canada.

Hil•la•ry (hil′ə rē), **Sir Edmund P.,** born 1919, New Zealand mountain climber who scaled Mount Everest 1953.

Hil•lel (hil′el, -āl, hi lāl′), c60 B.C.–A.D. 9?, Palestinian rabbi and interpreter of Biblical law.

Hil•ler (hil′ər), **Dame Wendy,** born 1912, British actress.

Hil•lis (hil′is), **Margaret,** born 1921, U.S. conductor.

Hill•man (hil′mən), **Sidney,** 1887–1946, U.S. labor leader, born in Lithuania.

Hill•yer (hil′yər), **Robert (Silliman),** 1895–1961, U.S. poet and critic.

Hil•ton (hil′tn), **1. Conrad (Nicholson),** 1887–1979, U.S. hotel owner and developer. **2. James,** 1900–54, English novelist.

Himm•ler (him′lər), **Heinrich,** 1900–45, German Nazi leader and chief of the secret police.

Hin•de•mith (hin′də mith, -mit), **Paul,** 1895–1963, U.S. composer, born in Germany.

Hin•den•burg (hin′dən bûrg′), **Paul von** (*Paul von Beneckendorff und von Hindenburg*), 1847–1934, German field marshal; 2nd president of Germany 1925–34.

Hin•dus (hin′dəs), **Maurice Gerschon,** 1891–1969, U.S. writer, born in Russia.

Hines (hīnz), **1. Earl** ("*Fatha*"), 1905–83, U.S. jazz pianist. **2. Jerome,** born 1921, U.S. basso.

Hin•shel•wood (hin′shəl wo͝od′), **Sir Cyril Norman,** 1897–1967, English chemist: Nobel prize 1956.

Hin•ton (hin′tn, -tən), **1. Christopher, Baron Hinton of Bankside,** born 1901, British nuclear engineer. **2. William Augustus,** 1883–1959, U.S. medical researcher and educator.

Hip•par•chus (hi pär′kəs), **1.** died 514 B.C., tyrant of Athens 527–514. **2.** c190–c125 B.C., Greek astronomer.

Hip•pi•as (hip′ē əs), fl. 6th century B.C., tyrant of Athens (brother of Hipparchus, son of Pisistratus).

Hip•poc•ra•tes (hi pok′rə tēz′), ("*Father of Medicine*") c460–c377 B.C., Greek physician.

Hi•ra•nu•ma (hē rä′no͞o mä′), **Baron Kiichiro,** 1867?–1952, Japanese statesman.

Hi•ro•hi•to (hēr′ō hē′tō), 1901–89, emperor of Japan 1926–89.

Hi•ro•shi•ge (hēr′ō shē′gā), **Ando,** 1797–1858, Japanese painter.

Hirsch (hûrsh), **John Stephen,** 1930–89, Canadian stage director, born in Hungary.

Hiss (his), **Alger,** born 1904, U.S. public official, accused of espionage 1948 and imprisoned for perjury 1950–54.

Hitch•cock (hich′kok), **1. Sir Alfred (Joseph),** 1899–1980, U.S. film director, born in England. **2. Thomas, Jr.** (*Tommy*), 1900–44, U.S. polo player.

Hit•ler (hit′lər), **Adolf,** ("*der Führer*"), 1889–1945, Nazi dictator of Germany, born in Austria: chancellor 1933–45; dictator 1934–45.

Hoad (hōd), **Lew(is A.),** born 1934, Australian tennis player.

Hoare (hôr, hōr), **Sir Samuel John Gurney, 1st Viscount Templewood,** 1880–1959, British statesman.

Ho•ban (hō′bən), **James,** c1762–1831, U.S. architect, born in Ireland: designed the White House.

Ho•bart (hō′bərt, -bärt), **Garret Augustus,** 1844–99, U.S. lawyer and politician: vice president of the U.S. 1897–99.

Hob•be•ma (hob′ə mə), **Meindert,** 1638–1709, Dutch painter.

Hobbes (hobz), **Thomas,** 1588–1679, English philosopher and author.

Hob•by (hob′ē), **Oveta Culp,** born 1905, U.S. newspaper publisher and government official: first director of Women's Army Corps 1942–45; first Secretary of Health, Education, and Welfare 1953–55.

Hob•son (hob′sən), **Richmond Pearson,** 1870–1937, U.S. naval officer and politician.

Hoc•cleve (hok′lēv) also **Occleve, Thomas,** 1370–1450, English poet.

Ho Chi Minh (hō′ chē′ min′), 1890?–1969, president of North Vietnam 1954–69.

Hock•ing (hok′ing), **William Ernest,** 1873–1966, U.S. philosopher.

Hock•ney (hok′nē), **David,** born 1937, British artist.

Hodg•kin (hoj′kin), **1. Sir Alan Lloyd,** born 1914, English biophysicist: Nobel prize for medicine 1963. **2. Dorothy Mary Crowfoot,** born 1910, English chemist: Nobel prize 1964.

Hoe (hō), **1. Richard,** 1812–86, U.S. inventor and manufacturer of printing-press equipment. **2.** his father, **Robert,** 1784–1833, U.S. manufacturer of printing presses.

Ho•fer (hō′fər), **Andreas,** 1767–1810, Tyrolese patriot.

Hof•fa (hof′ə), **James Riddle** (*"Jimmy"*), 1913–75?, U.S. labor leader: president of the International Brotherhood of Teamsters 1957–71; disappeared 1975.

Hoff•man (hof′mən), **1. Dustin,** born 1937, U.S. actor. **2. Malvina,** 1887–1966, U.S. sculptor.

Hoff•mann (hof′mən), **1. Ernst Theodor Amadeus Wilhelm,** 1776–1822, German author and composer. **2. Josef,** 1870–1956, Viennese architect and designer, born in Czechoslovakia. **3. Roald,** born 1937, U.S. chemist, born in Poland: Nobel prize 1981.

Hof•mann (hof′mən), **1. August Wilhelm von,** 1818–92, German chemist. **2. Hans,** 1880–1966, U.S. painter, born in Germany. **3. Josef (Casimir),** 1876–1957, U.S. pianist, born in Poland.

Hof•manns•thal (hof′məns täl′, hôf′-), **Hugo von,** 1874–1929, Austrian poet and playwright.

Hof•stadt•er (hof′stat′ər, -stä′tər), **1. Richard,** 1916–70, U.S. historian. **2. Robert,** 1915–90, U.S. physicist: Nobel prize 1961.

Ho•gan (hō′gən), **Ben,** born 1912, U.S. golfer.

Ho•garth (hō′gärth), **William,** 1697–1764, English painter and engraver.

Hogg (hog), **James,** 1770–1835, Scottish poet.

Hog•wood (hôg′wo͝od′, hog′-), **Christopher,** born 1941, English conductor and harpsichordist.

Ho•kin•son (hō′kin sən), **Helen,** 1893–1949, U.S. cartoonist.

Ho•ku•sai (hō′ko͞o sī′, hō′ko͞o sī′), **Katsushika,** 1760–1849, Japanese artist.

Hol•bein (hōl′bīn), **1. Hans** (*"the Elder"*), 1465?–1524, German painter. **2.** his son, **Hans** (*"the Younger"*), 1497?–1543, German painter, chiefly in England.

Höl•der•lin (hœl′dəʀ lēn′), **Johann Christian Friedrich,** 1770–1843, German poet.

Hol•i•day (hol′i dā′), **Billie** (*"Lady Day"*), 1915–59, U.S. jazz singer.

Hol•ins•hed (hol′inz hed′, hol′in shed′) also **Hol•lings•head** (-ingz hed′), **Raphael,** died c1580, English chronicler.

Hol•land (hol′ənd), **1. John Philip,** 1840–1914, Irish inventor in the U.S. **2. Sir Sidney (George),** 1893–1961, New Zealand political leader: prime minister 1949–57.

Hol•ley (hol′ē), **Robert William,** born 1922, U.S. biochemist: Nobel prize for medicine 1968.

Hol•ly (hol′ē), **Buddy** (*Charles Holley*), 1936–59, U.S. singer and guitarist.

Holm (hōlm), **Han•ya** (hän′yə), born 1895?, U.S. dancer, choreographer, and teacher; born in Germany.

Hol•man (hōl′mən), **Nathan** (*"Nat"*), born 1896, U.S. basketball player and coach.

Holmes (hōmz, hōlmz), **1. John Haynes,** 1879–1964, U.S. clergyman. **2. Oliver Wendell,** 1809–94, U.S. poet, essayist, and physician. **3.** his son, **Oliver Wendell,** 1841–1935, U.S. jurist.

Holst (hōlst), **Gustav Theodore,** 1874–1934, English composer.

Holt (hōlt), **Harold Edward,** 1908–67, Australian political leader: prime minister 1966–67.

Hol•yoake (hōl′yōk, hō′lē ōk′), **Sir Keith Jack•a** (jak′ə), 1904–83, New Zealand political leader: prime minister 1957, 1960–72; governor general 1977–80.

Ho•mer (hō′mər), **1.** 9th-century B.C. Greek epic poet: reputed author of the *Iliad* and *Odyssey.* **2. Winslow,** 1836–1910, U.S. artist.

Ho•neck•er (hō′ni kər, -nek ər), **Erich,** born 1912, East German Communist leader: chairman of the Council of State 1976–89.

Ho•neg•ger (hon′i gər, hō′neg ər), **Arthur,** 1892–1955, Swiss composer, born in France.

Ho•no•ri•us¹ (hō nôr′ē əs, -nōr′-), **Flavius,** A.D. 384–423, Roman emperor of the West 395–423.

Ho•no•ri•us² (hō nôr′ē əs, -nōr′-), **1. Honorius I,** died A.D. 638, Italian ecclesiastic: pope 625–638. **2. Honorius**

II, (*Lamberto Scannabecchi*) died 1130, Italian ecclesiastic: pope 1124–30. **3. Honorius III,** (*Cencio Savelli*) died 1227, Italian ecclesiastic: pope 1216–27. **4. Honorius IV,** (*Giacomo Savelli*) 1210–87, Italian ecclesiastic: pope 1285–87.

Hooch (ho͞och; *Du.* hōᴋʜ) also **Hoogh** (*Du.* hōᴋʜ), **Pieter de,** 1629?–88?, Dutch painter.

Hood (ho͝od), **1. John Bell,** 1831–79, Confederate general. **2. Raymond Mathewson,** 1881–1934, U.S. architect. **3. Thomas,** 1799–1845, English poet and humorist.

Hooke (ho͝ok), **Robert,** 1635–1703, English physicist.

Hook•er (ho͝ok′ər), **1. Joseph,** 1814–79, Union general in the U.S. Civil War. **2. Richard,** 1554?–1600, English author and clergyman. **3. Thomas,** 1586?–1647, English Puritan: founder of Connecticut.

Hooks (ho͝oks), **Benjamin Lawson,** born 1925, U.S. lawyer, clergyman, and civil-rights advocate: executive director of the NAACP since 1977.

Hoo•ton (ho͞ot′n), **Earnest Albert,** 1887–1954, U.S. anthropologist and writer.

Hoo•ver (ho͞o′vər), **1. Herbert (Clark),** 1874–1964, 31st president of the U.S. 1929–33. **2. J(ohn) Edgar,** 1895–1972, director of the U.S. FBI 1924–72.

Hope (hōp), **1. Anthony,** pen name of Sir Anthony Hope Hawkins. **2. Bob** (*Leslie Townes Hope*), born 1903, U.S. comedian, born in England. **3. John,** 1868–1936, U.S. educator.

Hop•kins (hop′kinz), **1. Sir Frederick Gowland,** 1861–1947, English physician and biochemist: Nobel prize for medicine 1929. **2. Gerard Manley,** 1844–89, English poet. **3. Harry Lloyd,** 1890–1946, U.S. government administrator and social worker. **4. Johns,** 1795–1873, U.S. financier and philanthropist. **5. Mark,** 1802–87, U.S. educator.

Hop•kin•son (hop′kin sən), **Francis,** 1737–91, American statesman and satirist.

Hop•pe (hop′ē), **Willie (William Frederick),** 1887–1959, U.S. billiards player.

Hop•per (hop′ər), **1. Edward,** 1882–1967, U.S. painter. **2. Grace Murray,** 1906–92, U.S. naval officer and computer scientist. **3. (William) De Wolf,** 1858–1935, U.S. actor.

Hor•ace (hôr′is, hor′-), (*Quintus Horatius Flaccus*) 65–8 B.C., Roman poet and satirist.

Hor•mis•das (hôr miz′dəs), **Saint,** died A.D. 523, pope 514–523.

Horne (hôrn), **1. Lena,** born 1917, U.S. singer. **2. Marilyn,** born 1934, U.S. mezzo-soprano.

Hor•ney (hôr′nī), **Karen,** 1885–1952, U.S. psychiatrist and author, born in Germany.

Horns•by (hôrnz′bē), **Rogers,** 1896–1963, U.S. baseball player and manager.

Hor•o•witz (hôr′ə wits, hor′), **Vladimir,** 1904–89, U.S. pianist, born in Russia.

Hor•sa (hôr′sə), died A.D. 455, Jute chief. Compare HENGIST.

Hor•ta (hôr′tə), **Baron Victor,** 1861?–1947, Belgian architect.

Hor•tense′ de Beauharnais′ (*Fr.* ôR täNs′), BEAUHARNAIS, Eugénie Hortense de.

Hor•thy (hôr′tē), **Miklós von Nagybánya,** 1863–1957, Hungarian admiral: regent of Hungary 1920–44.

Hou•di•ni (ho͞o dē′nē), **Harry** (*Erich Weiss*), 1874–1926, U.S. magician.

Hou•don (o͞o dôN′), **Jean Antoine,** 1741–1828, French sculptor.

Hough (huf), **Emerson,** 1857–1923, U.S. novelist.

Hou•phouet-Boi•gny (*Fr.* o͞o fwā′bwä nyē′), **Félix,** born 1905, Ivory Coast political leader: president since 1960.

House (hous), **Edward Mandell** (*"Colonel House"*), 1858–1938, U.S. diplomat.

House•lan•der (hous′lən dər), **Caryll,** 1901–54, English writer on Roman Catholicism.

Hous•man (hous′mən), **A(lfred) E(dward),** 1859–1936, English poet and classical scholar.

Hous•say (o͞o sī′), **Bernardo Alberto,** 1887–1971, Argentine physiologist: Nobel prize for medicine 1947.

Hous•ton (hyo͞o′stən), **Sam(uel),** 1793–1863, U.S. soldier: president of the Republic of Texas 1836–38.

Hov•ey (huv′ē), **Richard,** 1864–1900, U.S. poet.

Ho•vha•ness (hō vä′nis), **Alan,** born 1911, U.S. composer.

How•ard (hou′ərd), **1. Catherine,** CATHERINE HOWARD. **2. Sir Ebenezer,** 1850–1928, English town planner. **3. Henry,** SURREY, Henry Howard, Earl of. **4. Leslie** (*Leslie Stainer*), 1893–1943, English actor. **5. Roy Wilson,** 1883–1964, U.S. newspaper publisher. **6. Sidney (Coe),** 1891–1939, U.S. playwright and short-story writer.

Howe (hou), **1. Elias,** 1819–67, U.S. inventor of the sewing machine. **2. Gordon** (*Gordie*), born 1928, Canadian ice-hockey player. **3. Julia Ward,** 1819–1910, U.S. writer and reformer. **4. Richard** (*Earl Howe*) (*"Black Dick"*), 1726–99, British admiral (brother of William Howe). **5. Samuel Gridley,** 1801–76, U.S. surgeon and humanitarian. **6. William, 5th Viscount,** 1729–1814, British general in the American Revolutionary War.

How•ells (hou′əlz), **William Dean,** 1837–1920, U.S. author, critic, and editor.

Hox•ha (hô′jä), **Enver,** 1908–85, Albanian political leader: premier 1944–54, First Secretary of the Central Committee 1954–1985.

Hoyle (hoil), **1. Edmond,** 1672–1769, English authority and writer on card games. **2. Sir Fred,** born 1915, British astronomer and mathematician.

Hrd•lič•ka (hûrd′lich kə), **Aleš,** 1869–1943, U.S. anthropologist, born in Czechoslovakia.

Hrot•svi•tha or **Hrot•swi•tha** (hrōt svē′tä), c935–c1000, German nun, poet, and dramatist.

Hsüan Tsung (shyän′ dzŏŏng′), A.D. 685–762, Chinese emperor of the Tang dynasty 712–756.

Hua Guo•feng (hwä′ gwô′fung′), born 1920?, Chinese Communist leader: premier 1976–80.

Huás•car (wäs′kär), 1495?–1533, Inca prince of Peru (half brother of Atahualpa; son of Huayna Capac).

Huay•na Ca•pac (wī′nä kä′päk), c1450–1527?, Inca ruler of Peru 1493?–1527? (father of Atahualpa and Huascar).

Hub•bard (hub′ərd), **Elbert Green,** 1856–1915, U.S. author, editor, and printer.

Hub•ble (hub′əl), **Edwin Powell,** 1889–1953, U.S. astronomer.

Hud•dle•ston (hud′l stən), **(Ernest Urban) Trevor,** born 1913, English Anglican bishop and missionary in Africa.

Hud•son (hud′sən), **1. Henry,** died 1611?, English navigator and explorer. **2. William Henry,** 1841–1922, English naturalist and author.

Hü•gel (hyōō′gəl *or, often,* yōō′-), **Baron Friedrich von,** 1852–1925, English theologian and writer.

Hug•gins (hug′inz), **Charles Brenton,** born 1901, U.S. surgeon and medical researcher, born in Canada: Nobel prize 1966.

Hugh′ Ca′pet (hyōō *or, often,* yōō), CAPET, Hugh.

Hughes (hyōōz), **1. Charles Evans,** 1862–1948, Chief Justice of the U.S. 1930–41. **2. Howard (Robard),** 1905–76, U.S. businessman. **3. (James) Langston,** 1902–67, U.S. novelist and poet. **4. Rupert,** 1872–1956, U.S. novelist and biographer. **5. Ted,** born 1930, English poet: poet laureate since 1984. **6. Thomas,** 1822–96, English novelist, reformer, and jurist. **7. William Morris,** 1864–1952, Australian statesman, born in Wales: prime minister 1915–23.

Hu•go (hyōō′gō *or, often,* yōō′-), **Victor (Marie, Viscount)** 1802–85, French poet, novelist, and dramatist.

Hu Han-min (or **Han•min**) (hōō′ hän′min′), 1879–1936, Chinese nationalist revolutionary.

Hui•do•bro (wē ᵺô′vrô), **Vicente,** 1893–1948, Chilean poet.

Hui Tsung (hwē′ dzŏŏng′) also **Hui Zong** (hwē zông′), 1082–1135, emperor of China 1101–26: painter and patron of art.

Hull (hul), **1. Cordell,** 1871–1955, U.S. statesman: Secretary of State 1933–44; Nobel peace prize 1945. **2. Robert Marvin** (*Bobby*), born 1939, Canadian ice-hockey player. **3. William,** 1753–1825, U.S. general.

Hu•ma•yun (hōō mä′yōōn), 1508–56, Mogul emperor of Hindustan 1530–56 (son of Baber).

Hum•bert I (hum′bərt), (*Umberto I*) 1844–1900, king of Italy 1878–1900.

Hum•boldt (hum′bōlt, hŏŏm′-), **1. Friedrich Heinrich Alexander, Baron von,** 1769–1859, German naturalist and statesman. **2.** his brother, **(Karl) Wilhelm, Baron von,** 1767–1835, German philologist and diplomat.

Hume (hyo͞om; *often* yo͞om), **David,** 1711–76, Scottish philosopher and historian.

Hum•per•dinck (hum′pər dingk′), **Engelbert,** 1854–1921, German composer.

Hum•phrey (hum′frē), **1.** (*Duke of Gloucester*) 1391–1447, English soldier and statesman (youngest son of Henry IV). **2. Doris,** 1895–1958, U.S. dancer, choreographer, and teacher. **3. Hubert H(oratio),** 1911–78, U.S. vice president 1965–69.

Hun•e•ker (hun′i kər), **James (Gibbons),** 1860–1921, U.S. music critic and writer.

Hung-wu (ho͝ong′wo͞o′), (*Chu Yüan-chang*) 1328–98, emperor of China 1368–98: founder of the Ming dynasty.

Hunt (hunt), **1. (James Henry) Leigh,** 1784–1859, English essayist, poet, and editor. **2.** 1784–1859, English essayist, poet, and editor. **3. Richard Morris,** 1828–95, U.S. architect. **4. (William) Holman,** 1827–1910, English painter. **5. William Morris,** 1824–79, U.S. painter (brother of Richard Morris Hunt).

Hun•ter (hun′tər), **1. John,** 1728–93, Scottish surgeon, physiologist, and biologist. **2. Robert Mercer Tal•ia•ferro** (tol′ə vər), 1809–87, U.S. political leader: Speaker of the House 1839–41.

Hun•ting•ton (hun′ting tən), **1. Collis Potter,** 1821–1900, U.S. railroad developer. **2. Samuel,** 1731–96, U.S. statesman: governor of Connecticut 1786–96.

Hu•nya•di or **Hu•nya•dy** (ho͝on′yod ē), **János,** 1387?–1456, Hungarian soldier and national hero.

Hu•rok (hyo͝or′ok *or, often,* yo͝or′-), **Sol(omon),** 1888–1974, U.S. impresario, born in Russia.

Hurst (hûrst), **Fannie,** 1889–1968, U.S. novelist and short-story writer.

Hus (ho͝os, hus), **Jan** (yän), 1369?–1415, Czech religious reformer and martyr.

Hu•sák (ho͞o′sak, -säk), **Gustáv,** 1913–91, Czechoslovak political leader: first secretary of the Communist party 1969–87; president 1975–89.

Hu•sein ibn-A•li (ho͝o sin′ ib′ən ä′lē, -ä lē′; ho͝o sān′), 1856–1931, 1st king of Hijaz 1916–24.

Hu Shih (or **Shi**) (ho͞o′ shœ′), 1891–1962, Chinese scholar and diplomat.

Hus•kis•son (hus′kə sən), **William,** 1770–1830, British statesman and financier.

Huss (hus, ho͝os), **John,** Hus, Jan.

Hus•sein (ho͝o sān′), **1.** (*al-Husayn*), A.D. 629?–680, Arabian caliph, the son of Ali and Fatima and the brother of Hasan. **2. Sad•dam** (sä′dəm, sə däm′), (*at-Takriti*), born 1937, president of Iraq since 1979.

Hussein I, born 1935, king of Jordan since 1953.

Hus•serl (ho͝os′ərl), **Edmund (Gustav Albrecht),** 1859–1938, German philosopher, born in Austria.

Hus•ton (hyo͞o′stən *or, often,* yo͞o′-), **1. John,** 1906–87, U.S. film director and writer. **2.** his father, **Walter,** 1884–1950, U.S. actor, born in Canada.

Hutch•ins (huch′inz), **Robert Maynard,** 1899–1977, U.S. educator.

Hutch•in•son (huch′in sən), **1. Anne Marbury,** 1591–1643, American religious liberal, born in England. **2. Thomas,** 1711–80, American colonial administrator of Massachusetts 1769–74.

Hux•ley (huks′lē), **1. Aldous (Leonard),** 1894–1963, English novelist, essayist, and critic. **2. Sir Andrew Fielding,** born 1917, English physiologist: (half brother of Aldous and Sir Julian Sorell): Nobel prize for medicine 1963. **3. Sir Julian Sorell,** 1887–1975, English biologist and writer (brother of Aldous). **4. Thomas Henry,** 1825–95, English biologist and writer (grandfather of Aldous and Sir Julian Sorell).

Hu Yao•bang (hʏ′ you′bäng′), 1915–89, Chinese Communist leader: general secretary of the Chinese Communist Party 1980–87.

Huy•gens or **Huy•ghens** (hī′gənz, hoi′-), **Christian,** 1629–95, Dutch mathematician, physicist, and astronomer.

Huys•mans (wēs mäns′), **Joris Karl** (*Charles Marie Georges Huysmans*), 1848–1907, French novelist.

Hyde (hīd), **1. Douglas,** 1860–1949, president of Ireland 1938–45. **2. Edward,** CLARENDON, Edward Hyde.

Hy•gi•nus (hī jī′nəs), **Saint,** died A.D. 140, pope 136–140.

I

I•a•coc•ca (ī′ə kō′kə), **Lee** (*Lido Anthony Iacocca*), born 1924, U.S. industrialist.

I•bá•ñez (ē vä′nyeth, -nyes), **Vicente Blasco,** BLASCO IBÁÑEZ, Vicente.

I•bert (ē bᴇʀ′), **Jacques François Antoine,** 1890–1962, French composer.

I•ber•ville, d' (dē bᴇʀ vēl′), **Pierre le Moyne, Sieur,** 1661–1706, French-Canadian founder of the first French settlement in Louisiana, 1699.

ibn Han•bal (ib′ən han′bal), **Ahmad,** A.D. 780–855, Islamic legist and traditionist: founder of the Hanbali school of law, one of four such schools in Islam.

ibn Khal•dun (ib′ən ᴋʜäl do͞on′), **Abd-al-Rahman,** 1332–1406, Arab historian and philosopher.

ibn Rushd (ib′ən ʀo͝osht′), Arabic name of AVERROËS.

ibn Sa•ud (ib′ən sä o͞od′), **Abdul-Aziz,** 1880–1953, king of Saudi Arabia 1932–53.

ibn Si•na (ib′ən sē′nä), Arabic name of AVICENNA.

Ib•sen (ib′sən), **Henrik,** 1828–1906, Norwegian dramatist and poet.

Ib•y•cus (ib′i kəs), fl. c540 B.C., Greek poet.

Ick•es (ik′ēz), **Harold (Le Claire),** 1874–1952, U.S. lawyer and statesman.

Ic•ti•nus (ik tī′nəs), fl. mid-5th century B.C., Greek architect: a designer of the Parthenon.

I•dris I (ī′dris, i drēs′), (*Mohammed Idris Senussi*), 1890–1983, king of Libya 1951–69.

Ig•na•tius (ig nā′shəs), **1. Saint** (*Ignatius Theophorus*), A.D. c40–107?, bishop of Antioch and Apostolic Father. **2. Saint** (*Nicetas*), A.D. 799?–878, patriarch of Constantinople 846–858, 867–878.

Igna′tius of Loyo′la, Saint, LOYOLA, Saint Ignatius.

I•ke•da (ē ke′dä), **Hayato,** 1899–1965, Japanese statesman: prime minister 1960–64.

Ikh•na•ton (ik nät′n), AKHENATON.

Il•i•es•cu (il′ē es′ko͞o), **Ion,** born 1930, president of Romania since 1989.

I•llí•a (ē yē′ä), **Arturo,** 1900–83, Argentine physician and statesman: president 1963–66.

In•di•an•a (in′dē an′ə), **Robert** (*Robert Clarke*), born 1928, U.S. painter of pop art.

In•dy, d' (dᴀɴ dē′), **Vincent,**1851–1931, French composer.

In•dy, d' (dᴀɴ dē′), **Vincent,** 1851–1931, French composer.

Inge (inj *for 1;* ing *for 2*), **1. William (Motter),** 1913–73, U.S. playwright. **2. William Ralph,** 1860–1954, English clergyman and scholar.

In•ge•low (in′jə lō′), **Jean,** 1820–97, English poet and novelist.

In•ger•soll (ing′gər sôl′, -sol′), **Robert Green,** 1833–99, U.S. lawyer, political leader, and orator.

In•gres (aɴ′gʀᵊ), **Jean Auguste Dominique,** (zhäɴ), 1780–1867, French painter.

In•ness (in′is), **George,** 1825–94, and his son **George,** 1854–1926, U.S. painters.

In•no•cent (in′ə sənt), **1. Innocent I, Saint,** died A.D. 417, Italian pope 401–417. **2. Innocent II,** (*Gregorio Papareschi*) died 1143, Italian pope 1130–43. **3. Innocent III,** (*Giovanni Lotario de' Conti*) 1161?–1216, Italian pope 1198–1216. **4. Innocent IV,** (*Sinbaldo de Fieschi*) c1180–1254, Italian pope 1243–54. **5. Innocent V,** (*Pierre de Tarentaise*) c1225–76, French ecclesiastic: pope 1276. **6. Innocent VI,** (*Étienne Aubert*) died 1362, French jurist and ecclesiastic: pope 1352–62. **7. Innocent VII,** (*Cosimo de' Migliorati*) 1336–1406, Italian ecclesiastic: pope 1404–06. **8. Innocent VIII,** (*Giovanni Battista Cibò*) 1432–92, Italian ecclesiastic: pope 1484–92. **9. Innocent IX,** (*Giovanni Antonio Facchinetti*) 1519–91, Italian ecclesiastic: pope 1591. **10. Innocent X,** (*Giambattista Pamfili*) 1574–1655, Italian ecclesiastic: pope 1644–55. **11. Innocent XI,** (*Benedetto Odescalchi*) 1611–89, Italian pope 1676–89. **12. Innocent XII,** (*Antonio Pignatelli*) 1615–1700, Italian ecclesiastic: pope 1691–1700. **13. Innocent XIII,** (*Michelangelo Conti*) 1655–1724, Italian ecclesiastic: pope 1721–24.

I•nö•nü (i nœ ny′), **Ismet** (*Ismet Paşa*), 1884–1973, president of Turkey 1938–50; prime minister 1923–24, 1925–37, 1961–65.

In•sull (in′səl), **Samuel,** 1859–1938, U.S. public utilities magnate, born in England.

Io•nes•co (yə nes′kō, ē ə-), **Eugène,** born 1912, French playwright, born in Romania.

Ip•po•li•tov-I•va•nov (ip′ə lē′tôf ē vä′nôf, -nof, -tof-), **Mikhail Mikhailovich,** 1857–1935, Russian composer.

Iq•bal (ik bäl′), **Sir Muhammad,** 1873–1938, Pakistani poet.

Ire•dell (īᵊr′del), **James,** 1751–99, associate justice of U.S. Supreme Court, 1790–99.

Ire•land (īᵊr′lənd), **John,** 1838–1918, U.S. Roman Catholic clergyman and social reformer, born in Ireland: archbishop of St. Paul, Minn., 1888–1918.

Ir•ving (ûr′ving), **1. John,** born 1942, U.S. novelist. **2. Sir Henry** (*John Henry Brodribb*), 1838–1905, English actor. **3. Washington,** 1783–1859, U.S. essayist, story writer, and historian.

Ir•win (ûr′win), **1. Wallace,** 1875–1959, U.S. journalist and humorist. **2.** his brother **William Henry** (*"Will"*), 1873–1948, U.S. novelist, short-story writer, and journalist.

I•saacs (ē säks′), **1. Sir Isaac Alfred,** 1855–1948, Australian jurist: governor general of Australia 1931–36. **2. Jorge,** 1837–95, Colombian novelist.

Is•a•bel•la I (iz′ə bel′ə), (*"the Catholic"*), 1451–1504, wife of Ferdinand V: queen of Castile 1474–1504; joint ruler of Aragon 1479–1504.

Ish•er•wood (ish′ər wŏŏd′), **Christopher (William Bradshaw),** 1904–86, English poet, novelist, and playwright; in the U.S. after 1938.

Is′i•dore of Seville′ (iz′i dôr′, -dōr′; sə vil′), **Saint** (*Isidorus Hispalensis*), A.D. c570–636, Spanish archbishop, historian, and encyclopedist.

Is•ma•il Pa•sha (is mä′ēl pä′shä), 1830–95, viceroy and khedive of Egypt 1863–79.

I•soc•ra•tes (ī sok′rə tēz′), 436–338 B.C., Athenian orator.

Is•to•min (is′tə min), **Eugene,** born 1925, U.S. concert pianist.

I•to (ē′tô′), **Prince Hirobumi,** 1841–1909, Japanese statesman.

I•tur•bi (i tûr′bē, i tŏŏr′-), **José,** 1895–1980, U.S. pianist, conductor, and composer; born in Spain.

I•túr•bi•de (ē tōōʀ′vē t͟he), **Agustín de,** 1783–1824, Mexican soldier and revolutionary: as Agustín I, emperor of Mexico 1822–23.

I•van (ī′vən, ē vän′), **1. Ivan III,** (*"Ivan the Great"*) 1440–1505, grand duke of Muscovy 1462–1505. **2. Ivan IV,** (*"Ivan the Terrible"*) 1530–84, first czar of Russia 1547–84.

I•va•nov (ē vä′nəf), **Vsevolod Vyacheslavovich,** 1895–1963, Russian playwright.

Ives (īvz), **1. Burl (Icle Ivanhoe),** born 1909, U.S. actor and folk singer. **2. Charles Edward,** 1874–1954, U.S. composer. **3. Frederic Eugene,** 1856–1937, U.S. inventor. **4. James Merritt,** 1824–95, U.S. lithographer. Compare CURRIER.

I•ye•ya•su or **I•e•ya•su** (ē′ye yä′sōō), **Tokugawa,** 1542–1616, Japanese general and public servant.

Iz•ard (iz′ərd), **Ralph,** 1742–1804, U.S. diplomat and politician.

J

Ja•bir (jä′bir), GEBER.

Jab•o•tin•sky (yab′ə tin′skē, yä′bə-), **Vladimir,** 1880–1940, Russian Zionist leader in Palestine.

Jack•son (jak′sən), **1. Andrew** (*"Old Hickory"*), 1767–1845, U.S. general: 7th president of the U.S. 1829–37. **2. Helen Hunt** (*Helen Maria Fiske*), 1830–85, U.S. novelist and poet. **3. Jesse L(ouis),** born 1941, U.S. Baptist minister and political activist. **4. Mahalia,** 1911–72, U.S. gospel singer. **5. Michael (Joseph),** born 1958, U.S. singer and entertainer. **6. Robert Hough•wout** (hou′ət), 1892–1954, associate justice of the U.S. Supreme Court 1941–54. **7. Shirley,** 1919–65, U.S. short-story writer and novelist. **8. Thomas Jonathan** (*"Stonewall Jackson"*), 1824–63, Confederate general.

Ja•cob (zhᴀ kôb′), **François,** born 1920, French geneticist: Nobel prize for medicine 1965.

Ja•cob ben Ash•er (jā′kəb ben ash′ər), c1269–c1340, Hebrew commentator on the Bible and codifier of Jewish law.

Ja•co•bi (jə kō′bē; *for 2 also Ger.* yä kō′bē), **1. Abraham,** 1830–1919, U.S. pediatrician, born in Germany. **2. Karl Gustav Jakob,** 1804–51, German mathematician. **3. Mary Corinna (Putnam),** 1842–1906, U.S. physician (wife of Abraham Jacobi).

Ja•cobs (jā′kəbz), **1. Helen Hull,** born 1908, U.S. tennis player. **2. Hirsch(el),** 1904–70, U.S. thoroughbred horse trainer.

Ja•cob•sen (yä′kôp sən), **Jens Peter,** 1847–85, Danish novelist.

Ja•han•gir or **Je•han•gir** (jə hän′gēr, yə-), 1569–1627, 4th Mogul emperor in India 1605–27 (son of Akbar).

Ja•kob•son (yä′kəb sən), **Roman,** 1896–1982, U.S. linguist and scholar, born in Russia.

Ja•lal ud-din Ru•mi (ja läl′ o͞od dēn′ ʀo͞o′mē, o͝od-), 1207–73, Persian poet and mystic.

Ja•mal ud-Din (ja mäl′ o͞od dēn′, o͝od-), (*Jamal ud-Din al-Afghani*), 1838–97, Muslim educator and political leader, born in Persia: founder of modern Pan-Islamism.

James[1] (jāmz), **1.** Also called **James′ the Great′.** one of the 12 apostles, brother of the apostle John. **2.** Also called **James′ the Less′.** (*"James the son of Alphaeus"*) one of the 12 apostles. **3. Daniel, Jr.** (*"Chappie"*), 1920–78, U.S. Air Force officer: first black general. **4. Henry,** 1811–82, U.S. philosopher (father of Henry and William James). **5. Henry,** 1843–1916, U.S. writer in England. **6. Jesse (Woodson),** 1847–82, U.S. outlaw and legendary figure. **7. Will,** 1892–1942, U.S. author and illustrator. **8. William,** 1842–1910, U.S. psychologist and pragmatist philosopher.

James[2] (jāmz), **1. James I,** 1566–1625, king of England and Ireland 1603–25; as **James VI,** king of Scotland 1567–1625 (son of Mary Stuart). **2. James II,** 1633–1701, king of England, Ireland, and Scotland 1685–88 (son of Charles I of England). **3. James III,** STUART, James Francis Edward.

Jame•son (jām′sən), **Sir Leander Starr** (*"Doctor Jameson"*), 1853–1917, Scottish physician and statesman: colonial administrator in South Africa.

Ja•ná•ček (yä′nə chek′), **Leoš,** 1854–1928, Czech composer.

Ja•net (zhä nā′), **Pierre Marie Félix,** 1859–1947, French psychologist and neurologist.

Jan•sen (jan′sən, yän′-), **Cornelis Otto** (*Cornelius Jansenius*), 1585–1638, Dutch Roman Catholic theologian.

Jan•sky (jan′skē), **Karl Guthe,** 1905–50, U.S. engineer: pioneer in radio astronomy.

Jan•u•ar•i•us (jan′yo͞o âr′ē əs), **Saint,** A.D. 272?–305?, Italian ecclesiastic and martyr: patron saint of Naples. Italian, **San Gennaro.**

Jaques-Dal•croze (zhäk′dal krōz′), **Émile,** 1865–1950, Swiss composer and teacher: created eurhythmics.

Jar•rell (jar′əl, jə rel′), **Randall,** 1914–65, U.S. poet and critic.

Jar•ry (zhA Rē′), **Alfred,** 1873–1907, French poet and playwright.

Ja•ru•zel•ski (yär′ə zel′skē), **Woj•ciech (Witold)** (voi′-cheKH), born 1923, Polish general and political leader: prime minister 1981–85; president 1989–90.

Jas•pers (yäs′pərs), **Karl,** 1883–1969, German philosopher.

Jau•rès (zhô res′), **Jean Léon** (zhäN), 1859–1914, French socialist and writer.

Jav•its (jav′its), **Jacob K(oppel),** 1904–86, U.S. politician: senator 1957–81.

Jaw•len•sky (you len′skē), **Alexej von,** 1864?–1941, German painter, born in Russia.

Jay (jā), **John,** 1745–1829, first Chief Justice of the U.S. 1789–95.

Jean (zhäN), born 1921, Grand Duke of Luxembourg since 1964.

Jeanne d'Arc (zhän dARK′), French name of JOAN OF ARC.

Jeans (jēnz), **Sir James (Hopwood),** 1877–1946, English astrophysicist and author.

Jebb (jeb), **Sir Richard Clav•er•house** (klav′ər hous′), 1841–1905, Scottish scholar of classical Greek.

Jef•fers (jef′ərz), **(John) Robinson,** 1887–1962, U.S. poet.

Jef•fer•son (jef′ər sən), **1. Joseph,** 1829–1905, U.S. actor. **2. Thomas,** 1743–1826, 3rd president of the U.S. 1801–09.

Jef•frey (jef′rē), **Francis** (*"Lord Jeffrey"*), 1773–1850, Scottish jurist, editor, and critic.

Jef•freys (jef′rēz), **1. George** (*1st Baron Jeffreys of Wem*), 1648–89, English jurist. **2. Sir Harold,** born 1891, British geophysicist and astronomer.

Jef•fries (jef′rēz), **James J.,** 1875–1953, U.S. boxer: world heavyweight champion 1899–1905.

Jel•li•coe (jel′i kō′), **John Rushworth, 1st Earl,** 1859–1935, British admiral.

Jen•ghis (or **Jen•ghiz**) **Khan** (jeng′gis kän′, -giz, jen′-), GENGHIS KHAN.

Jen•kin•son (jeng′kin sən), **Robert Banks, 2nd Earl of Liverpool,** 1770–1828, British statesman: prime minister 1812–27.

Jen•ner (jen′ər), **1. Edward,** 1749–1823, English physician: discoverer of smallpox vaccine. **2. Sir William,** 1815–98, English physician and pathologist.

Jen•ney (jen′ē), **William Le Baron,** 1832–1907, U.S. engineer and architect: pioneer in skyscraper construction.

Jen•sen (yen′zən *for 1;* yen′sən *for 2*), **1. J. Hans D.,** 1907–73, German physicist: Nobel prize 1963. **2. Johannes Vilhelm,** 1873–1950, Danish poet and novelist: Nobel prize 1944.

Je•ri•tza (yer′i tsä′), **Maria,** 1887–1982, Austrian operatic soprano.

Je•rome (jə rōm′), **1. Saint** (*Eusebius Hieronymus*), A.D. c340–420, Christian ascetic and Biblical scholar: chief preparer of the Vulgate. **2. Jerome K(lapka),** 1859–1927, English humorist and playwright.

Jes•per•sen (yes′pər sən, jes′-), **(Jens) Otto (Harry),** 1860–1943, Danish philologist.

Je•sus (jē′zəs, -zəz), **1.** Also called **Je′sus Christ′, Je′sus of Naz′areth.** born 4? B.C., crucified A.D. 29?, the source of the Christian religion. **2.** (*"the Son of Sirach"*) the author of the Apocryphal book of Ecclesiasticus, who lived in the 3rd century B.C.

Jev•ons (jev′ənz), **William Stanley,** 1835–82, English economist.

Jew•ett (jōō′it), **Sarah Orne,** 1849–1909, U.S. writer.

Jiang Qing (jyäng′ ching′), 1914–91, wife of Mao Zedong.

Jiang Ze•min (jyäng′ zœ′ min′), born 1926, Chinese Communist leader: general secretary of the Communist Party since 1989.

Ji•mé•nez (hē me′neth, -nes), **Juan Ramón,** 1881–1958, Spanish poet: Nobel prize 1956.

Ji•mé′nez de Cis•ne′ros (the thēs ne′rôs), **Francisco,** 1436–1517, Spanish cardinal and statesman. Also called **Ximenes.**

Ji•mé′nez de Que•sa′da (ke sä′thä), **Gonzalo,** 1497?–1579, Spanish explorer and conqueror in South America.

Jin•nah (jin′ə), **Mohammed Ali** (*"Quaid-i-Azam"*), 1876–1948, Muslim leader in India: first governor general of Pakistan 1947–48.

Jo•a•chim (yō′ä khim, yō ä′-), **Joseph,** 1831–1907, Hungarian violinist and composer.

Joan (jōn), (*"Fair Maid of Kent"*) 1328–85, wife of Edward, the Black Prince, and mother of Richard II.

Joan′ of Arc′ (ärk′), **Saint** (*"the Maid of Orléans"*),

1412?–31, French martyr who raised the siege of Orléans. French, **Jeanne d'Arc.**

Jobs (jōbz), **Steven Paul,** born 1955, U.S. computer inventor and entrepreneur.

Jodl (yōd′l), **Alfred,** 1892?–1946, German general: signed the surrender of Germany on behalf of the German high command in World War II.

Jo•el (jō′əl), **Billy** (*William Martin*), born 1949, U.S. singer and songwriter.

Jof•fre (zhôf′ʀᵉ), **Joseph Jacques Césaire,** 1852–1931, French general in World War I.

Jof•frey (jof′rē), **Robert** (*Abdullah Jaffa Bey Khan*), 1930–88, U.S. ballet dancer, choreographer, and dance company director.

Jo•han•an ben Zak•ka•i (jō han′ən ben zak′ā ī′), died A.D. c80, Palestinian rabbi who was a leading Pharisaic teacher: disciple of Hillel.

John[1] (jon), **1.** the apostle John, believed to be the author of the fourth Gospel, three Epistles, and the book of Revelation. **2.** (*John Lackland*) 1167?–1216, king of England 1199–1216: signer of the Magna Carta 1215 (son of Henry II). **3. Augustus Edwin,** 1878–1961, British painter. **4. Elton** (*Reginald Dwight*), born 1947, English singer and songwriter.

John[2] (jon), **1. John I, Saint,** died A.D. 526, Italian ecclesiastic: pope 523–526. **2. John II,** (*Mercurius*) died A.D. 535, Italian ecclesiastic: pope 533–535. **3. John III, a.** (*Catelinus*) died A.D. 574, Italian ecclesiastic: pope 561–574. **b.** (*John Sobieski*) 1624–96, king of Poland 1674–96. **4. John IV,** died A.D. 642, pope 640–642. **5. John V,** died A.D. 686, pope 685–686. **6. John VI,** died A.D. 705, Greek ecclesiastic: pope 701–705. **7. John VII,** died A.D. 707, Greek ecclesiastic: pope 705–707. **8. John VIII,** died A.D. 882, Italian ecclesiastic: pope 872–882. **9. John IX,** died A.D. 900, Italian ecclesiastic: pope 898–900. **10. John X,** died A.D. 929?, Italian ecclesiastic: pope 914–928. **11. John XI,** died A.D. 936, Italian ecclesiastic: pope 931–936. **12. John XII,** (*Octavian*) died A.D. 964, Italian ecclesiastic: pope 955–964. **13. John XIII,** died A.D. 972, Italian ecclesiastic: pope 965–972. **14. John XIV,** died A.D. 984, pope 983–984. **15. John XV,** died A.D. 996, Italian ecclesiastic: pope 985–996. **16. John XVII,** (*Sicco*) died 1003, pope 1003. **17. John XVIII,** (*Fasanus*) died 1009, Italian ecclesiastic: pope 1003–09. **18. John XIX,** died 1032, pope 1024–32. **19. John XXI,** (*Petrus Hispanus*) died 1277, Portuguese ecclesiastic: pope 1276–77. **20. John XXII,** (*Jacques Duèse*) c1244–1334, French ecclesiastic: pope 1316–34. **21. John XXIII,** (*Angelo Giuseppe Roncalli*) 1881–1963, Italian ecclesiastic: pope 1958–63.

John′ of Aus′tria, ("*Don John*") 1547?–78, Spanish naval commander and general: victor at the battle of Lepanto.

John′ of Damas′cus, Saint, A.D. c675–749, priest, theologian, and scholar of the Eastern Church, born in Damascus.

John′ of Gaunt′ (gônt), (*Duke of Lancaster*) 1340–99, founder of the English royal house of Lancaster (son of Edward III).

John′ of Ley′den (lād′n), (*Jan Beuckelszoon* or *Bockhold*) 1509–36, Dutch Anabaptist.

John′ of Salis′bur•y (sôlz′ber ē, -bə rē), c1115–80, English prelate and scholar.

John′ of the Cross′, Saint (*Juan de Yepis y Álvarez*), 1542–91, Spanish mystic, writer, and theologian: cofounder with Saint Theresa of the order of Discalced Carmelites. Spanish, **San Juan de la Cruz.**

John′ Paul′, 1. John Paul I, (*Albino Luciani*) 1912–78, Italian ecclesiastic: pope 1978. **2. John Paul II,** (*Karol Wojtyła*) born 1920, Polish ecclesiastic: pope since 1978.

Johns (jonz), **Jasper,** born 1930, U.S. painter.

John•son (jon′sən), **1. Andrew,** 1808–75, 17th president of the U.S. 1865–69. **2. Charles Spurgeon,** 1893–1956, U.S. educator and sociologist. **3. Earvin** (*"Magic"*), born 1959, U.S. basketball player. **4. Eyvind,** 1900–76, Swedish writer: Nobel prize 1974. **5. Gerald White,** 1890–1980, U.S. writer. **6. Howard (Deering),** 1896?–1972, U.S. businessman: founder of restaurant and motel chain. **7. Jack** (*John Arthur*), 1878–1946, U.S. heavyweight prizefighter: world champion 1908–15. **8. James Weldon,** 1871–1938, U.S. poet and essayist. **9. Lyndon Baines,** 1908–73, 36th president of the U.S. 1963–69. **10. Philip C(ortelyou),** born 1906, U.S. architect. **11. Reverdy,** 1796–1876, U.S. lawyer and politician: senator 1845–49, 1863–68. **12. Richard Mentor,** 1780–1850, vice president of the U.S. 1837–41. **13. Samuel** (*"Dr. Johnson"*), 1709–84, English lexicographer and writer. **14. Virginia E(shelman),** born 1925, U.S. psychologist: researcher on human sexual behavior (wife of William H. Masters). **15. Walter Perry** (*"Big Train"*), 1887–1946, U.S. baseball player. **16. Sir William,** 1715–74, British colonial administrator in America, born in Ireland.

John•ston (jon′stən, -sən), **1. Albert Sidney,** 1803–62, Confederate general. **2. Joseph Eggleston,** 1807–91, Confederate general. **3. Mary,** 1870–1936, U.S. writer.

Join•ville (zhwaɴ vēl′), **Jean de** (zhäɴ), 1224?–1317, French chronicler.

Jo•kai (yô′koi), **Mau•rus** (mou′rŏŏs) or **Mór** (môr), 1825–1904, Hungarian novelist.

Jo•li•et (jō′lē et′, -lē ā′), **Louis,** 1645–1700, French-Canadian explorer of the Mississippi.

Jo•liot-Cu•rie (zhōl yō′kyŏŏr′ē, -kyŏŏ rē′), **1. Irène,** (*Irène Curie*), 1897–1956, French nuclear physicist (daughter of Pierre and Marie Curie): Nobel prize for chemistry 1935. **2.** her husband, **(Jean) Frédéric** (zhäɴ), (*Jean Frédéric Joliot*), 1900–58, French nuclear physicist: Nobel prize for chemistry 1935.

Jo•li•vet (zhô lē ve′), **André,** 1905–74, French composer.

Jol•son (jōl′sən), **Al** (*Asa Yoelson*), 1886–1950, U.S. singer and entertainer, born in Russia.

Jones (jōnz), **1. Anson,** 1798–1858, president of the Republic of Texas. **2. Casey,** (*John Luther Jones*), 1864–1900, U.S. locomotive engineer: folk hero of ballads, stories, and plays. **3. Daniel,** 1881–1967, English phonetician. **4. Ernest,** 1879–1958, Welsh psychoanalyst. **5. (Everett) LeRoi,** original name of Imamu Amiri BARAKA. **6. Henry Arthur,** 1851–1929, English dramatist. **7. Howard Mumford,** 1892–1980, U.S. educator and critic. **8. In•i•go** (in′ə gō′), 1573–1652, English architect. **9. John Paul** (*John Paul*), 1747–92, American naval commander in the Revolutionary War, born in Scotland. **10. John Winston,** 1791–1848, U.S. politician: Speaker of the House 1843–45. **11. Mary Harris** (*"Mother Jones"*), 1830–1930, U.S. labor leader, born in Ireland. **12. Robert Edmond,** 1887–1954, U.S. set designer. **13. Robert Tyre** (*"Bobby"*), 1902–71, U.S. golfer. **14. Rufus Matthew,** 1863–1948, U.S. Quaker, teacher, author, and humanitarian. **15. Sir William,** 1746–94, English jurist, linguist, and Sanskrit scholar. **16. Spike** (*Lindley Armstrong Jones*), 1911–65, U.S. musician.

Jong (jong), **Erica,** born 1942, U.S. novelist and poet.

Jon•son (jon′sən), **Ben,** 1573?–1637, English dramatist and poet.

Jooss (yōs), **Kurt,** 1901–79, German ballet dancer and choreographer.

Jop•lin (jop′lin), **1. Janis,** 1943–70, U.S. singer. **2. Scott,** 1868–1917, U.S. ragtime pianist and composer.

Jor•daens (yôr′däns), **Jacob,** 1593–1678, Flemish painter.

Jor•dan (jôr′dn), **1. David Starr,** 1851–1931, U.S. biologist and educator. **2. Marie Ennemond Camille,** 1838–1922, French mathematician.

Jo•seph[1] (jō′zəf, -səf), (*Hinmaton-yalaktit*), c1840–1904, leader of the Nez Percé.

Jo•seph[2] (jō′zəf, -səf), **1. Joseph I,** 1678–1711, king of Hungary 1687–1711; king of Germany 1690–1711; emperor of the Holy Roman Empire 1705–11 (son of Leopold I). **2. Joseph II,** 1741–90, emperor of the Holy Roman Empire 1765–90 (son of Francis I).

Jo•se•phine (jō′zə fēn′, -sə-), **Empress** (*Marie Joséphine Rose Tascher de la Pagerie*), BEAUHARNAIS, Joséphine de.

Jo•seph•son (jō′zəf sən, -səf-), **Brian David,** born 1940, British physicist: Nobel prize 1973.

Jo•se•phus (jō sē′fəs), **Flavius,** A.D. 37?–c100, Jewish historian.

Jos•quin des Prés (zhus′kan də prā′, zhus KAN′), DES PRÉS, Josquin.

Jou•bert (zhōō bâr′), **Joseph,** 1754–1824, French moralist and essayist.

Jou•haux (zhōō ō′), **Léon,** 1879–1954, French labor leader and politician: Nobel peace prize 1951.

Joule (jōōl, joul), **James Prescott,** 1818–89, English physicist.

Jo•vi•an (jō′vē ən), (*Flavius Claudius Jovianus*) A.D. 331?–364, Roman emperor 363–364.

Jow•ett (jou′it), **Benjamin,** 1817–93, British educator and Greek scholar.

Joyce (jois), **1. James (Augustine Aloysius),** 1882–1941, Irish writer. **2. William** (*"Lord Haw-Haw"*), 1906–46, U.S. and English Nazi propagandist in Germany.

Juan Car•los I (wän kär′lōs, hwän), **King** (*Juan Carlos Alfonso Victor María de Borbón y Borbón*), born 1938, king of Spain since 1975.

Juá•rez (wär′ez, hwär′-), **Benito (Pablo),** 1806–72, president of Mexico 1857–72.

Ju•dah ha-Le•vi (or **Ha•le′vi**) (jo͞o′də hä lē′vī, -lā′vē), (*Judah ben Samuel Halevi*) 1085–1140, Spanish rabbi, physician, poet, and philosopher.

Ju′dah ha-Na•si′ (or **Ha•na•si**) (hä nä sē′), A.D. c135–c210, Jewish rabbi and scholar.

Ju•das (jo͞o′dəs), *n.* **1.** Judas Iscariot, the disciple who betrayed Jesus. **2.** Also, **Jude** (jo͞od). one of the 12 apostles (not Judas Iscariot). **3.** a brother of James and possibly of Jesus.

Ju′das Maccabae′us (jo͞o′dəs), MACCABAEUS, Judas.

Ju•gur•tha (jo͞o gûr′thə), died 104 B.C., king of Numidia 113–104.

Jul•ian (jo͞ol′yən), (*Flavius Claudius Julianus*) (*"the Apostate"*) A.D. 331–363, Roman emperor 361–363.

Ju•li•an•a (jo͞o′lē an′ə), born 1909, queen of the Netherlands 1948–80 (daughter of Wilhelmina I).

Jul•ius (jo͞ol′yəs), **1. Julius I, Saint,** died A.D. 352, Italian ecclesiastic: pope 337–352. **2. Julius II** (*Giuliano della Rovere*), 1443–1513, Italian ecclesiastic: pope 1503–13. **3. Julius III** (*Giammaria Ciocchi del Monte* or *Giovanni Maria del Monte*), 1487–1555, Italian ecclesiastic: pope 1550–55.

Jul′ius Cae′sar (jo͞ol′yəs), CAESAR, Gaius Julius.

Jung (yo͝ong), **Carl Gustav,** 1875–1961, Swiss psychiatrist and psychologist.

Jun•ius (jo͞on′yəs), **Franciscus,** 1589–1677, English philologist, born in Germany.

Jun•kers (yo͝ong′kərs), **Hugo,** 1859–1935, German aircraft designer and builder.

Ju•not (zho͞o nō′), **Andoche** (*Duc d'Abrantès*), 1771–1813, French marshal.

Jus•tin•i•an I (ju stin′ē ən), (*Flavius Anicius Justinianus*) (*"Justinian the Great"*) A.D. 483–565, Byzantine emperor 527–565.

Jus•tin Mar•tyr (jus′tin mär′tər), **Saint,** A.D. c100–163?, early church historian and philosopher.

Ju•var•ra (yo͞o vär′ə), **Filippo,** 1678–1736, Italian architect.

Ju•ve•nal (jo͞o′və nl), (*Decimus Junius Juvenalis*) A.D. c60–140, Roman satirical poet.

Ka•ba•lev•sky (kä′bə lef′skē), **Dmitri,** born 1904, Russian composer.

Ká•dár (kä′där), **Já•nos** (yä′nôsh), 1912–89, Hungarian political leader: general secretary of the Communist party 1956–88.

Kaf•ka (käf′kä, -kə), **Franz,** 1883–1924, Austrian writer, born in Prague.

Ka•ga•wa (kä′gä wä′), **Toyohiko,** 1888–1960, Japanese social reformer and religious leader.

Kah•lo (kä′lō), **Frida,** 1910–54, Mexican painter.

Kahn (kän), **1. Herman,** 1922–83, U.S. physicist and social theorist. **2. Louis Isadore,** 1901–74, U.S. architect, born in Estonia. **3. Philippe,** born 1952, French mathematician and computer software developer in U.S.

Kai•ser (kī′zər), **Henry J(ohn),** 1882–1967, U.S. industrialist.

Kalb (kalb, kälp), **Johann,** (*"Baron de Kalb"*), 1721–80, German general in the American Revolutionary Army.

Ka•li•da•sa (kä′li dä′sə), fl. 5th century A.D., Hindu dramatist and poet.

Ka•li•nin (kə lē′nin), **Mikhail Ivanovich,** 1875–1946, Russian revolutionary: president of the U.S.S.R. 1923–46.

Ka•me•ha•me•ha I (kä mā′hä mā′hä, kə mā′ə mā′ə), (*"the Great"*) 1737?–1819, king of the Hawaiian Islands 1810–19.

Ka•mer•lingh On•nes (kä′mər ling ô′nəs), **Heike,** 1853–1926, Dutch physicist: Nobel prize 1913.

Kan•din•sky (kan din′skē), **Was•si•ly** or **Va•si•li** (vas′ə lē, və sil′ē), 1866–1944, Russian painter.

K'ang Hsi or **Kang Xi** (käng′ shē′), (*Shêng-tsu*) 1654?–1722, Chinese emperor of the Ch'ing dynasty 1662–1722.

K'ang Yu-wei (käng′ yo͞o′wā′), 1858–1927, Chinese scholar and reformer.

Kant (kant, känt), **Immanuel,** 1724–1804, German philosopher.

Kan•to•ro•vich (kan tôr′ə vich, kan′tə rō′vich), **Leonid Vitalyevich,** 1912–86, Russian mathematician and economist: Nobel prize for economics 1975.

Ka•pell (kə pel′), **William,** 1922–53, U.S. pianist.

Ka•pi•la (kä′pi lə), fl. early 6th century B.C., Hindu philosopher: reputed founder of the Sandkhya system of Hindu philosophy.

Ka•pi•tsa or **Ka•pi•tza** (käp′yit sə), **Pyotr L(eonidovich),** 1894–1984, Russian physicist: Nobel prize 1978.

Kap•lan (kap′lən), **Mordecai Menahem,** 1881–1983, U.S. religious leader and educator, born in Lithuania: founder of the Reconstructionist movement in Judaism.

Kap•teyn (käp tin′), **Jacobus Cornelis,** 1851–1922, Dutch astronomer.

Ka•ra•jan (kar′ə yən, kär′ə yän′), **Herbert von,** 1908–89, Austrian conductor.

Karl•feldt (kärl′felt), **Erik Axel,** 1864–1931, Swedish poet: Nobel prize posthumously 1931.

Kar•loff (kär′lôf, -lof), **Boris** (*William Henry Pratt*), 1887–1969, British actor in the U.S.

Kar•mal (kär mäl′), **Babrak,** born 1929, Afghan political leader: president 1979–86.

Kar•pov (kär′pôf, -pof), **Anatoly,** born 1951, Russian chess player.

Kar•rer (kär′ər), **Paul,** 1889–1971, Swiss chemist, born in Russia: Nobel prize 1937.

Karsh (kärsh), **Yousuf,** born 1908, Canadian photographer, born in Armenia.

Kas•a•vu•bu (kas′ə vo͞o′bo͞o, kä′sä-), **Joseph,** 1917?–69, African political leader: first president of the Democratic Republic of the Congo (now Zaire) 1960–65.

Ka•spar•ov (kə spär′ôf, -of; *Russ.* ku spär′əf), **Gary** (*Garry*), born 1963, Armenian chess player.

Kast•ler (kast ler′), **Alfred,** 1902–84, French physicist, born in Germany: Nobel prize 1966.

Ka•ta•yev (ku tä′yif), **Valentin Petrovich,** 1897–1986, Russian writer.

Katz (kats), **Sir Bernard,** born 1911, British biophysicist, born in Germany: Nobel prize for medicine 1970.

Kauf•man (kôf′mən), **George S(imon),** 1889–1961, U.S. dramatist.

Ka•un•da (kä o͞on′dä, -o͝on′də), **Kenneth (David),** born 1924, Zambian political leader: president since 1964.

Kaut•sky (kout′skē), **Karl Johann,** 1854–1938, German socialist writer and editor.

Ka•wa•ba•ta (kä′wə bä′tə, -tä), **Yasunari,** 1899–1972, Japanese writer: Nobel prize 1968.

Kay (kā), **1. Alan,** born 1940, U.S. computer scientist. **2. Ulysses Simpson,** born 1917, U.S. composer.

Ka•yi•ban•da (kä′yi bän′də), **Grégoire,** 1924–76, president of the Republic of Rwanda 1962–73.

Ka•zan (kə zan′, -zän′), **Elia,** born 1909, U.S. film and stage director and novelist, born in Turkey.

Ka•zant•za•kis (kaz′ən zak′is, kä′zən zä′kis), **Nikos,** 1883–1957, Greek poet and novelist.

Kean (kēn), **Edmund,** 1787–1833, English actor.

Kea•ton (kēt′n), **Buster** (*Joseph Francis Keaton*), 1895–1966, U.S. film comedian and director.

Keats (kēts), **John,** 1795–1821, English poet.

Ke•ble (kē′bəl), **John,** 1792–1866, English clergyman and poet.

Kee•ler (kē′lər), **Ruby,** born 1909, U.S. dancer and actress.

Ke•fau•ver (kē′fô vər), **Estes,** 1903–63, U.S. political leader: U.S. senator 1949–63.

Keil•lor (kē′lər), **Garrison,** born 1942, U.S. writer and radio announcer.

Kei•ta (kā′tä), **Modibo,** 1915–77, African statesman: president of Mali 1960–68.

Kei•tel (kīt′l), **Wilhelm,** 1882–1946, German marshal: chief of the Nazi supreme command 1938–45.

Keith (kēth), **Sir Arthur,** 1866–1955, Scottish anthropologist.

Kek•ko•nen (kek′ə nen), **Urho Kaleva,** 1900–86, Finnish statesman: president 1956-81.

Kel•ler (kel′ər), **Helen (Adams),** 1880–1968, U.S. lecturer and author: blind and deaf from infancy.

Kel•logg (kel′ôg, -og), **1. Frank Billings,** 1856–1937, U.S. statesman: Secretary of State 1925–29; Nobel peace prize 1929. **2. W(ill) K(eith),** 1860–1951, U.S. manufacturer of prepared cereals and philanthropist.

Kel•ly (kel′ē), **1. Ellsworth,** born 1923, U.S. painter and sculptor. **2. Emmett (Leo),** 1898–1979, U.S. circus clown and pantomimist. **3. Gene** (*Eugene Curran Kelly*), born 1912, U.S. dancer, choreographer, and director. **4. George (Edward),** 1887–1974, U.S. playwright and actor. **5. Grace,** 1929–82, U.S. actress and Princess of Monaco 1956–82 (wife of Prince Rainier III).

Kel•vin (kel′vin), **William Thomson, 1st Baron,** 1824–1907, English physicist and mathematician.

Ke•mal A•ta•türk (kə mäl′ at′ə tûrk′, ä′tə-), (*Mustafa Kemal*) ("*Kemal Pasha*") 1881–1938, Turkish general: president of Turkey 1923–38.

Kem•ble (kem′bəl), **1. Frances Anne** or **Fanny** (*Mrs. Butler*), 1809–93, English actress and author. **2.** her uncle, **John Philip,** 1757–1823, English actor.

Kemp (kemp), **Jack F.,** born 1935, U.S. politician: congressman 1970–88; secretary of housing and urban development since 1989.

Kem•pis (kem′pis), **Thomas à,** 1379?–1471, German ecclesiastic and author.

Ken•dall (ken′dl), **Edward Calvin,** 1886–1972, U.S. biochemist: Nobel prize for medicine 1950.

Ken•drew (ken′dro͞o), **John C(owdery),** born 1917, English scientist: Nobel prize for chemistry 1962.

Ken•nan (ken′ən), **George Frost,** born 1904, U.S. author and diplomat.

Ken•ne•dy (ken′i dē), **1. Anthony M.,** born 1936, associate justice of the U.S. Supreme Court since 1988. **2. Edward Moore** (*Ted*), born 1932, U.S. politician: senator from Massachusetts since 1962. **3. John Fitzgerald,** 1917–63, 35th president of the U.S. 1961–63. **4. Joseph Patrick,** 1888–1969, U.S. financier and diplomat (father of Edward Moore, John Fitzgerald, and Robert Francis). **5. Robert Francis,** 1925–68, U.S. political leader and government official: attorney general 1961–64; senator from New York 1965–68.

Ken•ny (ken′ē), **Elizabeth** ("*Sister Kenny*"), 1886–1952, Australian nurse: researcher in poliomyelitis therapy.

Kent (kent), **1. James,** 1763–1847, U.S. jurist. **2. Rockwell,** 1882–1971, U.S. illustrator and painter.

Ken•ton (ken′tn), **Stan(ley Newcomb),** 1912–79, U.S. jazz composer, pianist, and bandleader.

Ken•yat•ta (ken yä′tə), **Jomo,** 1893?–1978, president of Kenya 1964–78.

Ken•yon (ken′yən), **John Samuel,** 1874–1959, U.S. phonetician and educator.

Kep•ler (kep′lər), **Johann,** 1571–1630, German astronomer.

Ke•ren•sky (kə ren′skē), **Aleksandr Feodorovich,** 1881–1970, Russian revolutionary leader: premier 1917; in the U.S. after 1946.

Kern (kûrn), **Jerome (David),** 1885–1945, U.S. composer.

Ker•ou•ac (ker′o͞o ak′), **Jack** (*Jean-Louis Lefris de Kérouac*), 1922–69, U.S. novelist.

Kes•sel•ring (kes′əl ring), **Albert,** 1885–1960, German field marshal.

Ket•ter•ing (ket′ər ing), **Charles Franklin,** 1876–1958, U.S. engineer and inventor.

Key (kē), **Francis Scott,** 1780–1843, U.S. lawyer: author of *The Star-Spangled Banner.*

Keynes (kānz), **John Maynard, 1st Baron,** 1883–1946, English economist and writer.

Key•ser•ling (kī′zər ling), **Hermann Alexander, Count,** 1880–1946, German philosopher and writer.

Kha•cha•tu•ri•an (kä′chə to͝or′ē ən, kach′ə-), **Aram Ilich,** 1903–78, Armenian composer in Soviet Union.

Kha•da•fy (kə dä′fē), **Muammar (Muhammad) al-** or **el-,** QADDAFI.

Khaf•re (kaf′rā, käf′-), (*Chephren*) fl. late 26th century B.C., Egyptian king of the fourth dynasty (son of Cheops).

Kha•lid (KHä lēd′, kä-), (*Khalid ibn Abdul-Aziz al Saud*) 1913–82, king of Saudi Arabia 1975–82.

Kha•ma (kä′mə), **Sir Seretse,** 1921–80, Botswanan political leader: president 1966–80.

Kha•me•nei (KHä′mə nā′, kä′-), **Ayatollah Mohammed Ali,** born 1939, chief Islamic leader of Iran since 1989.

Khan (KHän, kän, kan), **Ghulam Ishaq,** born 1915, president of Pakistan since 1988.

Khay•yám (kī yäm′, -yam′), **Omar,** OMAR KHAYYÁM.

Kho•mei•ni (KHō mā′nē, kō-), **Ayatollah Ruhollah,** 1900?–89, chief Islamic leader of Iran 1979–89.

Kho•ra•na (kō rä′nə, kô-), **Har Gobind,** born 1922, U.S. biochemist and researcher in genetics, born in India: Nobel prize for medicine 1968.

Khru•shchev (kro͞osh′chef, -chôf, kro͞osh′-), **Nikita S(ergeyevich),** 1894–1971, Russian political leader: premier of the U.S.S.R. 1958–64.

Khu•fu (ko͞o′fo͞o), CHEOPS.

Khwa•riz•mi (KHwär′iz mē′), **al-** (al), (*Muhammed ibn-Musa al-Khwarizmi*), A.D. c780–c850, Arab mathematician and astronomer.

Kidd (kid), **1. Michael,** born 1919, U.S. dancer and choreographer. **2. William** (*"Captain Kidd"*), 1645?–1701, Scottish navigator and privateer: hanged for piracy.

Kie•pu•ra (kē po͝or′ə), **Jan (Wiktor)** (yän), 1904?–66, Polish tenor.

Kier•ke•gaard (kēr′ki gärd′, -gôr′), **Sören Aabye,** 1813–55, Danish philosopher and theologian.

Kil•ly (kē lē′), **Jean-Claude** (zhäɴ klōd′), born 1943, French skier.

Kil•mer (kil′mər), **(Alfred) Joyce,** 1886–1918, U.S. poet.

Kil•pat•rick (kil pa′trik), **Hugh Judson,** 1836–81, Union general in the U.S. Civil War.

Kim Il Sung (kim′ il′ so͝ong′, sung′), born 1912, premier of North Korea 1948–72; president since 1972.

King (king), **1. Billie Jean (Moffitt),** born 1943, U.S. tennis player. **2. Martin Luther, Jr.,** 1929–68, U.S. Baptist minister: civil-rights leader: Noble peace prize 1964. **3. Riley B.** (*"B.B."*), born 1925, U.S. blues singer and guitarist. **4. William Lyon Mackenzie** 1874–1950, prime minister of Canada 1921–26, 1926–30, 1935–48. **5. William Rufus DeVane,** 1786–1853, vice president of the U.S. 1853.

Kings•ley (kingz′lē), **1. Charles,** 1819–75, English clergyman, novelist, and poet. **2. Sidney,** born 1906, U.S. playwright.

Kin•sey (kin′zē), **Alfred Charles,** 1894–1956, U.S. zoologist: directed studies of human sexual behavior.

Kip•ling (kip′ling), **(Joseph) Rud•yard** (rud′yərd), 1865–1936, English author: Nobel prize 1907.

Kip•nis (kip′nis), **Alexander,** 1891–1978, Russian singer in the U.S.

Kir•by-Smith (kûr′bē smith′), **Edmund,** 1824–93, Confederate general in the American Civil War.

Kirch•hoff (kēr′kôf, -kof, kērкн′hôf), **Gustav Robert,** 1824–87, German physicist.

Kirch•ner (kērsh′nər, kērk′-, kērкн′-), **Ernst Ludwig,** 1880–1938, German expressionist artist.

Kirk•pat•rick (kûrk pa′trik), **Jeane (Jordan),** born 1926, U.S. diplomat: ambassador to the U.N. 1981–85.

Kis•sin•ger (kis′ən jər), **Henry A(lfred),** born 1923, U.S. Secretary of State 1973–77, born in Germany: Nobel peace prize 1973.

Kitch•e•ner (kich′ə nər), **Horatio Herbert** (*1st Earl Kitchener of Khartoum and of Broome*), 1850–1916, English field marshal and statesman.

Kit•tredge (ki′trij), **George Lyman,** 1860–1941, U.S. literary scholar.

Klé•ber (klā bᴇʀ′), **Jean Baptiste** (zhäɴ), 1753–1800, French general.

Klee (klā), **Paul,** 1879–1940, Swiss painter.

Klei•ber (klī′bər), **Erich,** 1890–1956, Austrian conductor.

Klein (klīn), **Felix,** 1849–1925, German mathematician.

Kleist (klīst), **(Bernd) Heinrich (Wilhelm) von,** 1777–1811, German poet, dramatist, and story writer.

Klem•pe•rer (klem′pər ər), **Otto,** 1885–1973, German conductor.

Klimt (klimt), **Gustav,** 1862–1918, Austrian painter.

Kline (klīn), **Franz (Josef),** 1910–62, U.S. painter.

Kluck (klŏŏk), **Alexander von,** 1846–1934, German general.

Knight (nīt), **1. Eric,** 1897–1943, U.S. novelist, born in England. **2. Frank Hyneman,** 1885–1972, U.S. economist.

Knopf (knopf), **Alfred A(braham),** 1892–1984, U.S. publisher.

Knowles (nōlz), **John,** born 1926, U.S. novelist.

Knox (noks), **1. Henry,** 1750–1806, American Revolutionary general. **2. John,** c1510–72, Scottish religious reformer and historian. **3. Philander Chase,** 1853–1921, U.S. lawyer and politician: Secretary of State 1909–13.

Knut (kə nōōt′, -nyōōt′), CANUTE.

Knuth (knōōth), **Donald Ervin,** born 1938, U.S. computer sciences educator.

Koch (kôKH), **1. Edward I.,** born 1924, U.S. politician: mayor of New York City 1977–89. **2. Robert,** 1843–1910, German bacteriologist and physician: Nobel prize 1905.

Ko•cher (kō′kər; *Ger.* kō′KHəR), **Emil Theodor,** 1841–1917, Swiss physiologist, pathologist, and surgeon: Nobel prize 1909.

Ko•dá•ly (kō′dī, -dä ē), **Zoltán,** 1882–1967, Hungarian composer.

Koest•ler (kest′lər, kes′-), **Arthur,** 1905–83, British novelist, born in Hungary.

Koff•ka (kof′kə), **Kurt,** 1886–1941, German psychologist in the U.S.

Kohl (kōl), **Helmut,** born 1930, chancellor of West Germany 1982–90; chancellor of Germany since 1990.

Koi•vis•to (koi′vis tō), **Mau•no** (mou′nō), born 1923, president of Finland since 1982.

Ko•ko (kō′kō), born 1973, female gorilla, trained to communicate with humans by means of a sign language.

Ko•kosch•ka (kō kôsh′kə), **Oskar,** 1886–1980, Austrian painter and dramatist.

Kol•be (kôl′bə), **Ge•org** (gā ôRK′), 1877–1947, German sculptor.

Kol•chak (kôl chäk′), **Aleksandr Vasilyevich,** 1874–1920, Russian counterrevolutionary and admiral.

Kolff (kōlf, kolf), **Willem J(ohan),** born 1911, U.S. physician and inventor, born in the Netherlands: developed the artificial kidney machine.

Koll•witz (kôl′vits), **Kä•the** (ke′tə), 1867–1945, German graphic artist and sculptor.

Ko•men•ský (kō′men skē, kə men′-), **Jan Amos** (yän), Czech name of John Amos COMENIUS.

Koop•mans (kōōp′mənz), **Tjalling Charles,** 1910–85, U.S. economist, born in the Netherlands: Nobel prize 1975.

Kor•but (kôr′bət), **Olga,** born 1955, Russian gymnast.

Kor•da (kôr′də), **Sir Alexander** (*Sándor Kellner*), 1893–1956, British film producer, born in Hungary.

Korn•berg (kôrn′bûrg), **Arthur,** born 1918, U.S. biochemist: Nobel prize for medicine 1959.

Korn•gold (kôrn′gōld′), **Erich Wolfgang,** 1897–1957, Austrian composer, conductor, and pianist in the U.S.

Kor•zyb•ski (kôr zip′skē, -zhip′-), **Alfred (Habdank Skarbek),** 1879–1950, U.S. writer on general semantics, born in Poland.

Kos•ci•us•ko (kos′kē us′kō, kos′ē-, kosh cho͝osh′-), **Thaddeus** (*Tadeusz Andrzej Bonawentura Kościuszko*), 1746–1817, Polish patriot: general in the American Revolutionary army.

Kos•sel (kôs′əl), **Albrecht,** 1853–1927, German chemist: Nobel prize for medicine 1910.

Kos•suth (kos′o͞oth, kə so͞oth′), **La•jos** (lo′yôsh), 1802–94, Hungarian patriot.

Kos•te•la•netz (kos′tə lä′nits), **André,** 1901–80, U.S. orchestra conductor and pianist, born in Russia.

Ko•sy•gin (kə sē′gin), **Aleksei Nikolayevich,** 1904–80, Russian premier of the U.S.S.R. 1964–80.

Kou•fax (kō′faks), **Sanford** (*Sandy*), born 1935, U.S. baseball player.

Kous•se•vitz•ky (ko͞o′sə vit′skē), **Serge** (*Sergei Alexandrovich Kusevitsky*), 1874–1951, Russian conductor in the U.S.

Krae•pe•lin (krep′ə lēn′), **Emil,** 1856–1926, German psychiatrist.

Krafft-E•bing (kraft′eb′ing, -ā′bing, kräft′-), **Richard, Baron von,** 1840–1902, German neurologist.

Kra•mer (krā′mər), **John Albert** (Jack), born 1921, U.S. tennis player and promoter.

Kra•nach (*Ger.* KRÄ′NÄKH), CRANACH.

Kranz (kranz, krants), **Judith,** born 1928, U.S. novelist.

Krauss (krous), **Clemens,** 1893–1954, Austrian conductor and pianist.

Krebs (kreps, krebz), **Sir Hans Adolf,** 1900–81, German biochemist in England: Nobel prize for medicine 1953.

Krei•sky (krī′skē), **Bruno,** 1911–90, Austrian diplomat and political leader: chancellor 1970–83.

Kreis•ler (krīs′lər), **Fritz,** 1875–1962, Austrian violinist and composer in the U.S.

Kreut•zer (kroit′sər), **Rodolphe,** 1766–1831, French violinist.

Kreym•borg (krām′bôrg), **Alfred,** 1883–1966, U.S. poet, playwright, and critic.

Krish•na Men•on (krish′nə men′ən), **Vengalil Krishnan,** 1897–1974, Indian politician and statesman.

Kroe•ber (krō′bər), **Alfred Louis,** 1876–1960, U.S. anthropologist.

Krogh (krōg, krōKH), **(Schack) Auguste (Steenberg),** 1874–1949, Danish physiologist: Nobel prize for medicine 1920.

Kro•pot•kin (krə pot′kin), **Prince Pëter Alekseevich,** 1842–1921, Russian author and anarchist.

Kru•ger (kro͞o′gər), **Stephanus Johannes Paulus** (*"Oom Paul"*), 1825–1904, South African statesman: president of the Transvaal 1883–1900.

Krupp (krup), **Alfred,** 1812–87, German industrialist and manufacturer of armaments.

Krup•ska•ya (kro͞op′skə yə), **Nadezhda Konstantinovna,** 1869–1939, Russian social worker (wife of V.I. Lenin).

Krutch (kro͞och), **Joseph Wood,** 1893–1970, U.S. critic, biographer, naturalist, and teacher.

Ku•be•lík (ko͝ob′ə lik), **1. Jan** (yän), 1880–1940, Czech violinist and composer in Hungary. **2.** his son, **(Jeronym) Rafael,** born 1914, Czech conductor.

Ku•blai Khan (ko͞o′blī kän′) also **Ku′bla Khan′** (ko͞o′blə), 1216–94, khan c1260–94: founder of the Mongol dynasty in China (grandson of Genghis Khan).

Kuhn (ko͞on), **1. Richard,** 1900–1967, German chemist, born in Austria: declined 1938 Nobel prize at insistence of Nazi government. **2. Walt,** 1877?–1949, U.S. painter.

Kui•per (kī′pər), **Gerard Peter,** 1905–73, U.S. astronomer, born in the Netherlands.

Kum•mer (ko͝om′ər), **Ernst Eduard,** 1810–93, German mathematician.

Kun (ko͝on), **Béla,** 1885–1937, Hungarian Communist leader.

Kung (ko͝ong, go͝ong), **1. H. H.** (*K'ung Hsiang-hsi, Kong Xiangxi*), 1881–1967, Chinese financier and statesman. **2. Prince,** 1833–98, Chinese statesman of the late Ch'ing dynasty.

K'ung Ch'iu (ko͝ong′ chyo͞o′), personal name of Confucius.

K'ung Fu-tzu (ko͝ong′ fo͞o′dzu′), Chinese name of Confucius.

Ku•ni•yo•shi (ko͞o′nē yō′shē), **Yasuo,** 1893–1953, U.S. painter, born in Japan.

Ku•prin (ko͞o′prin; *Russ.* ko͞o pryēn′), **Alexander Ivanovich,** 1870–1938, Russian novelist and short-story writer.

Kur•cha•tov (ko͝or chä′tôf, -tof; *Russ.* ko͝or chä′təf), **Igor Vasilievich,** 1903–60, Russian nuclear physicist.

Ku•ro•ki (ko͝o′rô kē′), **Tamemoto, Count,** 1844–1923, Japanese general.

Ku•ro•sa•wa (ko͝or′ə sä′wə), **Akira,** born 1910, Japanese film director.

Ku•ru•su (ko͝o ro͞o′so͝o), **Saburo,** 1888–1954, Japanese diplomat.

Kusch (ko͝osh), **Polykarp,** born 1911, U.S. physicist, born in Germany: Nobel prize 1955.

Ku•tu•zov (ko͝o to͞o′zôf, -zof), **Mikhail Ilarionovich,** 1745–1813, Russian field marshal and diplomat.

Kuyp (koip, kīp), **Aelbert,** Cuyp, Aelbert.

Kuz•nets (ko͝oz′nits, ko͞oz′-), **Simon (Smith),** 1901–85, U.S. economist, born in Russia: Nobel prize 1971.

Kyd (kid), **Thomas,** 1558–94, English dramatist.

L

La•biche (lᴀ bĕsh′), **Eugène Marin,** 1815–88, French dramatist.

La Bru•yère (lᴀ bʀʏ yeʀ′), **Jean de** (zhäɴ), 1645–96, French moralist and author.

La•can (lə käɴ, -kän′), **Jacques,** 1901–81, French philosopher and psychoanalyst.

La Chaise (lᴀ shez′), **Père François d'Aix de,** 1624–1709, French Roman Catholic priest: confessor to Louis XIV.

La•chaise (lə shez′, lä), **Gaston,** 1882–1935, U.S. sculptor, born in France.

La•clos (lᴀ klō′), **Pierre Ambroise François Choderlos de,** 1741–1803, French general and writer.

La•coste (lə kôst′, -kost′), **René,** born 1905, French tennis player.

La•cre•telle (lᴀ kʀə tel′), **Jacques de,** 1888–1985, French novelist.

Lad•is•laus (lad′is lôs′) also **Lad•is•las** (-ləs, -läs), **Saint,** c1040–95, king of Hungary 1077–95.

Laën•nec (lā nek′), **René Théophile Hyacinthe,** 1781–1826, French physician who invented the stethoscope.

La Farge (lə färzh′, färj′), **1. John,** 1835–1910, U.S. painter. **2. Oliver Hazard Perry** ("*Oliver II*"), 1901–63, U.S. novelist and anthropologist.

La Fa•yette (laf′ē et′, lä′fā-), **Marie Madeleine Pioche de la Vergne, Comtesse de,** 1634–93, French novelist.

La•fa•yette (laf′ē et′, lä′fā-), **Marie Joseph Paul Yves Roch Gilbert du Motier, Marquis de,** 1757–1834, French statesman and general.

La•fitte or **Laf•fite** (lä fēt′), **Jean** (zhäɴ), c1780–c1825, French privateer in the Americas.

La Fol•lette (lə fol′it), **Robert Marion,** 1855–1925, U.S. politician.

La Fon•taine (lä′ fon ten′, -tān′), **1. Henri,** 1854–1943, Belgian statesman: Nobel peace prize 1913. **2. Jean de** (zhäɴ), 1621–95, French poet and fabulist.

La Fres•naye (lᴀ fʀe nā′), **Roger de,** 1885–1925, French painter.

La•ger•kvist (lä′gər kvist′), **Pär,** 1891–1974, Swedish writer: Nobel prize 1951.

La•ger•löf (lä′gər lœf′), **Selma (Ottiliana Lovisa),** 1858–1940, Swedish writer: Nobel prize 1909.

La•grange (lə grānj′, -gränj′, -gräɴzh′), **Joseph Louis, Comte,** 1736–1813, French mathematician and astronomer.

La Guar•di•a (lə gwär′dē ə), **Fi•o•rel•lo H(enry)** (fē′ə-rel′ō), 1882–1947, U.S. politican: mayor of New York City 1933–45.

Laing (lang), **R(onald) D(avid),** 1927–89, British psychiatrist.

Laj•oi•e (lash′ə wā′), **Napoleon** (*"Nap"*), 1875–1959, U.S. baseball player.

Lake (lāk), **Simon,** 1866–1945, U.S. engineer and naval architect.

La•lo (lᴀ lō′), **(Victor Antoine) Edouard,** 1832–92, French composer.

Lam (läm, lam), **Wifredo** or **Wilfredo,** 1902–82, Cuban painter in Europe.

La•mar (lə mär′), **1. Joseph R.,** 1857–1916, U.S. jurist: associate justice of the U.S. Supreme Court 1911–16. **2. Lucius Quintus Cincinnatus,** 1825–93, U.S. politician and jurist: associate justice of the U.S. Supreme Court 1888–93.

La•marck (lə märk′, lä-), **Jean Baptiste Pierre Antoine de Monet de,** 1744–1829, French naturalist.

La•mar•tine (lä′mär tēn′, lam′ər-), **Alphonse Marie Louis de Prat de,** 1790–1869, French poet.

Lamb (lam), **1. Charles** (*"Elia"*), 1775–1834, English essayist and critic. **2. Mary Ann,** 1764–1847, English author who wrote in collaboration with her brother Charles Lamb. **3. William, 2nd Viscount Melbourne,** 1779–1848, English prime minister 1834, 1835–41. **4. Willis E(ugene), Jr.,** born 1913, U.S. physicist: Nobel prize 1955.

Lam•bert (lam′bərt; *for 2 also* läm′bârt), **1. Constant,** 1905–51, English composer and conductor. **2. Johann Heinrich,** 1728–77, German scientist and mathematician.

L'A•mour (lä mŏŏr′), **Louis,** 1908–88, U.S. novelist.

La•mou•reux (lᴀ mōō rœ′), **Charles,** 1834–99, French violinist and conductor.

Lam•pe•du•sa (lam′pi dōō′sə, -zə), **Giuseppe (Tomasi) di,** 1896–1957, Italian novelist.

La•my (lä mē′), **John Baptist** (*Jean Baptiste l'Amy*), 1814–88, U.S. Roman Catholic clergyman, born in France: archbishop of Santa Fe, New Mexico 1875–88.

Lan•cas•ter (lang′kas tər), **Burt,** born 1913, U.S. actor.

Land (land), **Edwin Herbert,** 1909–91, U.S. inventor and businessman.

Lan•dau (län dou′), **Lev Davidovich,** 1908–68, Russian physicist: Nobel prize 1962.

Lan•di•ni (län dē′nē) also **Lan•di•no** (-nō), **Francesco,** c1325–97, Italian organist and composer.

Lan•dis (lan′dis), **Kenesaw Mountain,** 1866–1944, U.S. jurist: first commissioner of baseball 1920–44.

Lan•do (län′dō) also **Lan•dus** (-dəs), died A.D. 914, Italian ecclesiastic: pope 913–914.

Lan•don (lan′dən), **Alfred** (*"Alf"*) **Mossman,** 1887–1987, U.S. politician.

Lan•dor (lan′dər, -dôr), **Walter Savage,** 1775–1864, English writer.

Lan•dow•ska (lan dôf′skə, -dof′-), **Wanda,** 1879–1959, Polish harpsichordist.

Land•seer (land′sēr, -syər), **Sir Edwin Henry,** 1802–73, English painter, esp. of animals.

Land•stei•ner (land′stī′nər), **Karl,** 1868–1943, Austrian pathologist in the U.S.: Nobel prize for medicine 1930.

Lan•dy (lan′dē), **John Michael,** born 1930, Australian track-and-field athlete.

Lan•franc (lan′frangk), 1005?–89, Italian Roman Catholic prelate and scholar in England: archbishop of Canterbury 1070–89.

Lang (lang), **1. Andrew,** 1844–1912, Scottish writer and scholar. **2. Cosmo Gordon,** 1864–1945, English clergyman: archbishop of Canterbury 1928–42. **3. Fritz,** 1890–1976, U.S. film director, born in Austria. **4. Pearl,** born 1922, U.S. dancer and choreographer.

Lange (lang), **1. Christian Louis,** 1869–1938, Norwegian historian: Nobel peace prize 1921. **2. David (Russell),** born 1942, prime minister of New Zealand 1984–89. **3. Dorothea,** 1895–1965, U.S. photographer.

Lang•er (lang′ər), **Susanne (Knauth),** 1895–1985, U.S. philosopher.

Lang•land (lang′lənd), **William,** 1332?–c1400, English poet. Also called **Langley.**

Lang•ley (lang′lē), **1. Edmund of,** YORK, Edmund of Langley, 1st Duke of. **2. Samuel Pierpont,** 1834–1906, U.S. astronomer, physicist, and pioneer in aeronautics. **3. William,** LANGLAND, William.

Lang•muir (lang′myŏŏr), **Irving,** 1881–1957, U.S. chemist: Nobel prize 1932.

Lang•ston (lang′stən), **John Mercer,** 1829–97, U.S. public official, diplomat, and educator.

Lang•ton (lang′tən), **Stephen,** c1165–1228, English theologian, historian, and poet: archbishop of Canterbury.

Lang•try (lang′trē), **Lillie** (*Emily Charlotte Le Breton*) (*"the Jersey Lily"*), 1852–1929, English actress.

La•nier (lə nēr′), **Sidney,** 1842–81, U.S. poet and literary scholar.

Lan•kes•ter (lang′kə stər, -kes tər), **Sir Edwin Ray,** 1847–1929, English zoologist and writer.

Lans•downe (lanz′doun), **1. Henry Charles Keith Petty-Fitzmaurice, 5th Marquis of,** 1845–1927, British statesman: viceroy of India 1888–94, foreign secretary 1900–05. **2. William Petty Fitzmaurice, 2nd Earl of Shelburne, 1st Marquis of,** 1737–1805, British statesman: prime minister 1782–83.

Lan•sing (lan′sing), **Robert,** 1864–1928, U.S. lawyer and statesman: Secretary of State 1915–20.

Lan•za (län′zə), **Mario** (*Alfredo Cocozza*), 1921–59, U.S. singer and actor.

Lao She (lou′ shu′), (*Shu Qingchun, Shu Ch'ing-ch'un*) 1899–1966, Chinese novelist.

Lao-tzu or **Lao-tse** or **Lao•zi** (lou′dzu′), (*Li Erh, Li Er*) 6th-century B.C. Chinese philosopher: reputed founder of Taoism.

La Pé•rouse (LA pā ROOZ′), **Jean François de Galaup,** 1741–88, French naval officer and explorer.

La•place (lə pläs′), **Pierre Simon, Marquis de,** 1749–1827, French astronomer and mathematician.

Lard•ner (lärd′nər), **Ring(gold Wilmer),** 1885–1933, U.S. short-story writer and journalist.

Lar•kin (lär′kin), **Philip,** 1922–85, English poet, novelist, and editor.

La•roche (lə rōsh′), **Guy** (gē), 1923–89, French fashion designer.

La Roche•fou•cauld (lä rôsh′fo͞o kō′, rōsh′-), **François, 6th Duc de,** 1613–80, French moralist and composer of epigrams and maxims.

La•rousse (lə ro͞os′, lä-), **Pierre Athanase,** 1817–75, French grammarian, lexicographer, and encyclopedist.

Lar•ro•cha (lä rō′chä), **Alicia de,** born 1923, Spanish concert pianist.

Lar•tigue (lar tēg′), **Jacques Henri,** 1894–1986, French photographer and painter.

La Salle (lə sal′, säl′), **(René) Robert Cavelier, Sieur de,** 1643–87, French explorer of North America.

Las Ca•sas (läs kä′säs), **Bartolomé de,** 1474–1566, Spanish Dominican missionary and historian in the Americas.

Las•ker (läs′kər), **Emanuel,** 1868–1941, German chess player, mathematician, and author.

Las•ki (las′kē), **Harold Joseph,** 1893–1950, English political scientist.

Las•salle (lə sal′), **Ferdinand,** 1825–64, German socialist and writer.

Lat•i•mer (lat′ə mər), **Hugh,** c1470–1555, English Protestant Reformation bishop, reformer, and martyr.

La Tour (lä to͝or′), **Georges de,** 1593–1652, French painter.

La•trobe (lə trōb′), **Benjamin Henry,** 1764–1820, U.S. architect and engineer, born in England.

Laud (lôd), **William,** 1573–1645, archbishop of Canterbury and opponent of Puritanism: executed for treason.

Lau•der (lô′dər), **Sir Harry (MacLennan),** 1870–1950, Scottish balladeer and composer.

Lau•e (lou′ə), **Max Theodor Felix von,** 1879–1960, German physicist: Nobel prize 1914.

Laugh•ton (lôt′n), **Charles,** 1899–1962, U.S. actor, born in England.

Lau•rel (lôr′əl, lor′-), **Stan** (*Arthur Stanley Jefferson*), 1890–1965, U.S. motion-picture actor and comedian, born in England.

Lau•ren•cin (lô rän san′), **Marie,** 1885–1956, French painter, lithographer, and stage designer.

Lau•ri•er (lôr′ē ā′, lôr′ē ā′), **Sir Wilfrid,** 1841–1919, prime minister of Canada 1896–1911.

Lau•tré•a•mont (lō trā a môn′), **Comte de** (*Isidore Lucien Ducasse*), 1846–70, French poet, born in Uruguay.

Lau•trec (lō trek′), Toulouse-Lautrec, Henri.

La•val (lə val′), **Pierre,** 1883–1945, French premier of the Vichy government 1942–44.

La•va•lle•ja (lä′vä ye′hä), **Juan Antonio,** 1784–1853, Uruguayan revolutionary: leader in war of independence against Brazil 1825.

La•va•ter (lä′vä tər, lä vä′tər), **Johann Kaspar,** 1741–1801, Swiss poet, theologian, and physiognomist.

La•ver (lā′vər), **Rod(ney George),** born 1938, Australian tennis player.

La•ve•ran (LAVᵉ RÄN′), **Charles Louis Alphonse,** 1845–1922, French physician and bacteriologist: Nobel prize for medicine 1907.

La Vé•ren•drye (*Fr.* LA vā RÄN drē′), **Pierre Gaultier de Varenne, Sieur de,** 1685–1749, Canadian explorer of North America.

La•voi•sier (läv′wäz yā′, ləv wäz′-), **Antoine Laurent,** 1743–94, French chemist.

Law (lô), **1. Andrew Bon•ar** (bon′ər), 1858–1923, English statesman, born in Canada: prime minister 1922–23. **2. John,** 1671–1729, Scottish financier.

Lawes (lôz), **1. Henry** (*"Harry"*), 1596–1662, English composer. **2. Lewis E(dward),** 1883–1947, U.S. penologist.

Law•rence (lôr′əns, lor′-), **1. D(avid) H(erbert),** 1885–1930, English novelist. **2. Ernest O(rlando),** 1901–58, U.S. physicist: Nobel prize 1939. **3. Gertrude,** 1901?–52, English actress. **4. Jacob,** born 1917, U.S. painter and educator. **5. James,** 1781–1813, U.S. naval officer in the War of 1812. **6. Saint,** died A.D. 258?, early church martyr. **7. Sir Thomas,** 1769–1830, English painter. **8. T(homas) E(dward)** (*T. E. Shaw*) (*"Lawrence of Arabia"*), 1888–1935, English soldier and writer.

Law•son (lô′sən), **Robert,** 1892–1957, U.S. illustrator and author, esp. of children's books.

Lax•alt (lak′sôlt), **Paul,** born 1922, U.S. politician: senator 1974–87.

Lax•ness (läks′nes), **Halldór Kiljan,** born 1902, Icelandic writer: Nobel prize 1955.

Lay•a•mon (lā′ə mən, lä′yə-), fl. c1200, English poet and chronicler.

Layard (lârd, lā′ərd), **Sir Austen Henry,** 1817–94, English archaeologist, writer, and diplomat.

Laz•a•rus (laz′ər əs), **Emma,** 1849–87, U.S. poet.

La•zear (lə zēr′), **Jesse William,** 1866–1900, U.S. physician and bacteriologist.

Lea (lē), **Homer,** 1876–1912, U.S. soldier and author: adviser 1911–12 to Sun Yat-sen in China.

Lea•cock (lē′kok), **Stephen (Butler),** 1869–1944, Canadian humorist and economist.

Lead•bel•ly (led′bel′ē), LEDBETTER, Huddie.

Leaf (lēf), **Mun•ro** (mun rō′), 1905–76, U.S. author and illustrator of books for children.

Lea•hy (lā′hē), **William Daniel,** 1875–1959, U.S. admiral.

Lea•key (lē′kē), **1. Louis Seymour Bazett,** 1903–72,

British anthropologist. **2. Mary (Douglas),** born 1913, British anthropologist (wife of Louis Leakey). **3.** their son, **Richard (Erskine Frere),** born 1944, Kenyan anthropologist.

Lean (lēn), **David,** 1908–91, British film director.

Lear (lēr), **Edward,** 1812–88, English writer of humorous verse and landscape painter.

Lea•vis (lē′vis), **F(rank) R(aymond),** 1895–1978, English critic and teacher.

Leav•itt (lev′it), **Henrietta,** 1868–1921, U.S. astronomer.

Le•besgue (lə beg′), **Henri Léon,** 1875–1941, French mathematician.

Le•brun (lə brœɴ′, -brœn′), **1. Albert,** 1871–1950, president of France 1932–40. **2. Le Brun. Charles,** 1619–90, French painter.

le Car•ré (lə ka rā′), **John** (*David John Moore Cornwell*), born 1931, English author of spy novels.

Leck•y (lek′ē), **William Edward Hartpole,** 1838–1903, Irish essayist and historian.

Le•conte de Lisle (lə kôɴt də lēl′), **Charles Marie,** 1818–94, French poet.

Le Cor•bu•sier (lə kôr′bʏ zyā′), (*Charles Édouard Jeanneret*), 1887–1965, Swiss architect in France.

Le•cuo•na (lə kwō′nə; *Sp.* le kwô′nä), **Ernesto,** 1896–1963, Cuban composer.

Led•bet•ter (led′bet ər), **Huddie** (*"Leadbelly"*), 1885?–1949, U.S. folk singer.

Led•er•berg (led′ər bûrg′), **Joshua,** born 1925, U.S. geneticist: Nobel prize for medicine 1958.

Le•doux (lə do͞o′), **Claude-Nicolas,** 1736–1806, French architect.

Le Duc Tho (lā′ duk′ tō′), 1911–90, Vietnamese statesman: declined 1973 Nobel peace prize.

Lee (lē), **1. Ann,** 1736–84, British mystic: founder of Shaker sect in U.S. **2. Charles,** 1731–82, American Revolutionary general, born in England. **3. Doris Emrick,** born 1905, U.S. painter. **4. Fitzhugh,** 1835–1905, U.S. general and statesman (grandson of Henry Lee; nephew of Robert E. Lee). **5. Francis Lightfoot,** 1734–97, American Revolutionary statesman. **6. Gypsy Rose** (*Rose Louise Hovick*), 1914–70, U.S. entertainer. **7. Harper,** born 1926, U.S. novelist. **8. Henry** (*"Light-Horse Harry"*), 1756–1818, American Revolutionary general (father of Robert E. Lee). **9. Kuan Yew** (kwän yo͞o), born 1923, Singapore political leader: prime minister since 1959. **10. Richard Henry,** 1732–94, American Revolutionary statesman (brother of Francis L. Lee). **11. Robert E(dward),** 1807–70, Confederate general in the Civil War (son of Henry Lee). **12. Sir Sidney,** 1859–1926, English biographer and critic. **13. Tsung-Dao** (dzo͝ong′dou′), born 1926, Chinese physicist in the U.S.: Nobel prize 1957.

Lee Teng-hui (lē′ tung′hwē), born 1924, president of the Republic of China since 1988.

Lee•u•wen•hoek (lā′vən ho͝ok′, -wən-), **Anton van,** 1632–1723, Dutch naturalist and microscopist.

Le Gal•lienne (lə gal′yən, -gal yen′), **1. Eva,** 1899–1991, U.S. actress and producer, born in England. **2.** her father, **Richard,** 1866–1947, English writer.

Le•gen•dre (lə zhäɴ′dʀᵊ), **Adrien Marie,** 1752–1833, French mathematician.

Lé•ger (lā zhā′), **1. Alexis Saint-Léger,** St.-John Perse. **2. Fernand,** 1881–1955, French artist.

Le•guí•a (le gē′ä), **Augusto Bernardino,** 1863–1932, president of Peru 1908–12, 1919–30.

Le•Guin (lə gwin′), **Ursula K(roeber),** born 1929, U.S. science-fiction writer.

Le•hár (lā′här), **Franz,** 1870–1948, Hungarian composer of operettas.

Leh•man (lē′mən, lā′-), **Herbert H(enry),** 1878–1963, U.S. banker and statesman.

Leh•mann (lā′mən, -män), **1. Lilli,** 1848–1929, German operatic soprano. **2. Lotte,** 1888–1976, German operatic soprano in the U.S.

Lehm•bruck (lem′bro͝ok, lām′-), **Wilhelm,** 1881–1919, German sculptor.

Leib•niz or **Leib•nitz** (līb′nits, līp′-), **Gottfried Wilhelm von,** 1646–1716, German philosopher and mathematician.

Lei•bo•witz (lē′bə wits), **René,** born 1913, French conductor and composer, born in Poland.

Lei•dy (lī′dē), **Joseph,** 1823–91, U.S. paleontologist, parasitologist, and anatomist.

Leif′ Er′icson (lēf, lāf), Ericson, Leif.

Leigh•ton (lāt′n), **Frederick** (*Baron Leighton of Stretton*), 1830–96, English painter and sculptor.

Leins•dorf (līnz′dôrf, līns′-), **Erich,** born 1912, U.S. orchestra conductor, born in Austria.

Le Jeune (*Fr.* lə zhœn′), **Claude** (*Claudin*), 1530?–1600?, Flemish composer.

Le•jeune (lə jo͞on′, -zhœn′), **John Archer,** 1867–1942, U.S. Marine Corps general.

Le•loir (lə lwär′), **Luis Federico,** 1906–87, Argentine biochemist, born in France: Nobel prize for chemistry 1970.

Le•ly (lē′lē, lā′-), **Sir Peter** (*Pieter van der Faes*), 1618–80, Dutch painter in England.

Le•maî•tre (lə me′tʀᵊ), **1. Francois Élie Jules,** 1835–1915, Frenchcritic and dramatist. **2. Abbé Georges Édouard,** 1894–1966, Belgian astrophysicist and priest.

Le•mass (lə mas′), **Seán Francis** (shôn), 1899–1971, prime minister of Ireland 1959–66.

Le•May (lə mā′), **Curtis** (Emerson), 1906–90, U.S. Air Force officer: chief of the Strategic Air Command 1948–61; Chief of Staff of the Air Force 1961–65.

Lem•mon (lem′ən), **Jack,** born 1925, U.S. actor.

Le Nain (lə naɴ′), **Antoine** (*"the Elder"*), 1588?–1648, and his two brothers **Louis** (*"the Roman"*), 1593?–1648, and **Mathieu,** 1607–77, French painters.

Le•nard (lā′närd, -närt), **Philipp,** 1862–1947, German physicist, born in Czechoslovakia: Nobel prize 1905.

Len•clos (län klō′), **Anne,** (*Ninon de Lenclos*), 1620–1705?, French courtesan and wit.

L'En•fant (län fän′), **Pierre Charles,** 1754–1825, U.S. engineer and architect, born in France: designer of Washington, D.C.

Len•glen (leng′glən, -lən; *Fr.* län glen′), **Suzanne,** 1899–1938, French tennis player.

Le•nin (len′in), **V(ladimir) I(lyich)** (*Vladimir Ilyich Ulyanov*) (*"N. Lenin"*), 1870–1924, Russian revolutionary leader: Soviet premier 1918–24.

Le•noir (lən wär′), **Jean Joseph Étienne** (zhän), 1822–1900, French inventor.

Le•nô•tre (lə nō′tr°), **André,** 1613–1700, French architect and landscape designer.

Len•ya (len′yə, lān′-), **Lotte** (*Karoline Blamauer*), 1900–81, Austrian actress and singer, in the U.S. after 1935 (wife of Kurt Weill).

Le•o (lē′ō, lā′ō), **1. Leo I, Saint** (*"Leo the Great"*), A.D. c390–461, Italian ecclesiastic: pope 440–461. **2. Leo III, Saint,** A.D. c750–816, Italian ecclesiastic: pope 795–816. **3. Leo X** (*Giovanni de'Medici*), 1475–1521, Italian ecclesiastic: pope 1513–21 (son of Lorenzo de'Medici). **4. Leo XIII** (*Giovanni Vincenzo Pecci*), 1810–1903, Italian ecclesiastic: pope 1878–1903.

Leon•ard (len′ərd), **1. Elmore,** born 1925, U.S. novelist. **2. William Ellery (Channing),** 1876–1944, U.S. poet, essayist, and teacher.

Le•o•nar•do da Vin•ci (lē′ə när′dō də vin′chē, dä vin′-, lā′-), 1452–1519, Italian artist, architect, and engineer.

Le•on•ca•val•lo (lā′ôn kə vä′lō, lā ōn′-), **Ruggiero,** 1858–1919, Italian operatic composer and librettist.

Le•o•ne (le ô′ne), **Giovanni,** born 1908, Italian political leader: prime minister 1963, 1968; president 1971–78.

Le•o•ni (lā ō′nē), **Raúl,** 1905–72, Venezuelan statesman: president 1964–69.

Le•on•i•das (lē on′i dəs), died 480 B.C., Greek hero: king of Sparta 489?–480.

Le•o•nov (lē ō′nôf, -nof), **1. Aleksey Arkhipovich,** born 1934, Russian cosmonaut: first man to walk in space 1965. **2. Leonid Maksimovich,** born 1899, Russian writer.

Le•on•ti•ef (lē on′tē ef′, -əf), **Wassily,** born 1906, U.S. economist, born in Russia: Nobel prize 1973.

Le•on•to•vich (lē on′tə vich), **Eugenie Konstantin,** born 1900, U.S. actress, director, and playwright, born in Russia.

Le•o•par•di (lē′ə pär′dē, lā′-), **Count Giacomo,** 1798–1837, Italian poet.

Le•o•pold (lē′ə pōld′), **1. Leopold I, a.** 1640–1705, king of Hungary 1655–1705; emperor of the Holy Roman Empire 1658–1705. **b.** 1790–1865, king of Belgium 1831–65. **2. Leopold II, a.** 1747–92, emperor of the Holy Roman Empire 1790–92 (son of Francis I). **b.** 1835–1909, king of

Belgium 1865–1909 (son of Leopold I). **3. Leopold III,** 1901–83, king of Belgium 1934–51 (son of Albert I).

Lep•i•dus (lep′i dəs), **Marcus Aemilius,** died 13 B.C., Roman politician: member of the second triumvirate.

Lep•si•us (lep′sē o͝os′), **Karl Richard,** 1810–84, German philologist and Egyptologist.

Ler•mon•tov (lâr′mən tôf′, -tof′), **Mikhail Yurievich,** 1814–41, Russian poet and novelist.

Ler•ner (lûr′nər), **Alan Jay,** 1918–86, U.S. lyricist and librettist.

Le Sage or **Le•sage** (lə säzh′), **Alain René,** 1668–1747, French novelist and dramatist.

Le•sche•tiz•ky (lesh′ə tit′skē), **Theodor,** 1830–1915, Polish pianist and composer.

Les•seps (les′əps), **Ferdinand Marie, Vicomte de,** 1805–94, French engineer and diplomat: promoter of the Suez Canal.

Les•sing (les′ing), **1.** 1729–81, German critic and dramatist. **2. Doris (May),** born 1919, British writer. **3. Gotthold Ephraim,** 1729–81, German critic and dramatist.

Let•si•e III (let sē′ə), (*Sessie Mohato*), born 1963, king of Lesotho since 1990.

Leu•tze (loit′sə), **Emanuel Gottlieb,** 1816–68, German painter in the U.S.

Le Vau (lə vō′), **Louis,** 1612–70, French architect.

Le•ver (lē′vər), **Charles James** (*"Cornelius O'Dowd"*), 1806–72, Irish novelist and essayist.

Le•ver•hulme (lē′vər hyo͞om′ *or, often,* -yo͞om′), **Viscount** (*William Hesketh Lever*), 1851–1925, English soap manufacturer, originator of an employee profit-sharing plan, and founder of a model industrial town.

Le•ver•ri•er (lə ver′ē ā′), **Urbain Jean Joseph,** 1811–77, French astronomer.

Lev•er•tov (lev′ər tôf′, -tof′), **Denise,** born 1923, U.S. poet, born in England.

Lé•vesque (lə vek′, lā-), **René,** 1922–87, Canadian political leader: premier of Quebec 1976–85.

Le•vi (le′vē), **Carlo,** 1902–75, Italian painter and writer.

Lev•in (lev′in), **Ira,** born 1929, U.S. novelist and playwright.

Le•vine (lə vēn′ *for 1*; lə vīn′ *for 2*), **1. Jack,** born 1915, U.S. painter. **2. James,** born 1943, U.S. conductor and pianist.

Lé•vi-Strauss (lā′vē strous′), **Claude,** born 1908, French anthropologist, born in Belgium: founder of structural anthropology.

Le•vy (lē′vē, lev′ē), **Uriah Phillips,** 1792–1862, U.S. naval commander.

Lew•es (lo͞o′is), **George Henry,** 1817–78, English writer and critic.

Lew•is (lo͞o′is), **1. C(ecil) Day,** DAY-LEWIS, Cecil. **2. C(live) S(taples)** (*"Clive Hamilton"*), 1898–1963, English novelist and essayist. **3. Gilbert Newton,** 1875–1946, U.S. chemist. **4. (Harry) Sinclair,** 1885–1951, U.S. writer: Nobel prize 1930. **5. Isaac Newton,** 1858–1931, U.S. soldier and inventor. **6. Jerry** (*Joseph Levitch*), born 1926, U.S. comedian and actor. **7. Jerry Lee,** born 1935, U.S. country-and-western and rock-'n'-roll singer, musician, and songwriter. **8. John (Aaron),** born 1920, U.S. jazz pianist, composer, and musical director. **9. John L(lewellyn),** 1880–1969, U.S. labor leader. **10. Matthew Gregory** (*"Monk Lewis"*), 1775–1809, English novelist, dramatist, and poet. **11. Meriwether,** 1774–1809, U.S. explorer: leader of the Lewis and Clark expedition 1804–06. **12. (Percy) Wyndham,** 1884–1957, English writer and painter, born in the U.S.

Lew•i•sohn (lo͞o′ə sən, -zən, -sōn′), **Ludwig,** 1882?–1955, U.S. novelist and critic, born in Germany.

Ley•poldt (lī′pōlt), **Frederick,** 1835–84, U.S. editor and publisher, born in Germany.

Lhe•vinne (lā vēn′), **Josef,** 1874–1944, Russian pianist.

L'Hos•pi•tal or **L'Hô•pi•tal** (lō′pi tal′), **Guillaume François Antoine de,** 1661–1704, French mathematician.

Liang Ch'i-ch'ao or **Liang Qi•chao** (lyäng′ chē′chou′), 1873–1929, Chinese scholar, journalist, and reformer.

Lib•by (lib′ē), **Willard Frank,** 1908–80, U.S. chemist: Nobel prize 1960.

Lib•e•ra•ce (lib′ə rä′chē) (*Wladziu Valentino Liberace*), 1919–87, U.S. pianist and entertainer.

Li•be•ri•us (lī bēr′ē əs), died A.D. 366, pope 352–366.

Lich•ten•stein (lik′tən stēn′), **Roy,** born 1923, U.S. artist.

Lid•del Hart (lid′l härt′), **Sir Basil (Henry),** 1895–1970, English military authority and writer.

Lie (lē), **1. Jonas,** 1880–1940, U.S. painter, born in Norway. **2. (Marius) Sophus,** 1842–99, Norwegian mathematician. **3. Trygve Halvdan,** 1896–1968, Norwegian statesman: Secretary General of the United Nations 1946–53.

Lieb•er•mann (*Ger.* lē′bər män′), **1. Max,** 1847–1935, German painter and etcher. **2. Rolf,** born 1910, Swiss composer.

Lie•big (lē′big, -bikh), **Justus, Baron von,** 1803–73, German chemist.

Lieb•knecht (lēp′knekht, -nekt), **1. Karl,** 1871–1919, German socialist leader. **2.** his father, **Wilhelm,** 1826–1900, German journalist and political leader.

Li•far (lyi fär′), **Serge,** 1905–86, Russian ballet dancer and choreographer, in Paris after 1923.

Li Hung-chang (lē′ ho͝ong′jäng′) also **Li Hong•zhang** (lē′ hông′zhäng′), 1823–1901, Chinese statesman.

Lil•i•en•thal (lil′ē ən thôl′; *for 2 also Ger.* lē′lē ən täl′), **1. David E(ly),** 1899–1981, U.S. public administrator. **2. Otto,** 1848–96, German aeronautical engineer and inventor.

Li•li•u•o•ka•la•ni (lē lē′o͞o ō kä lä′nē), **Lydia Kamekeha,** 1838–1917, last queen of the Hawaiian Islands 1891–93.

Lil•lo (lil′ō), **George,** 1693?–1739, English dramatist.

Li•món (lē môn′), **José,** 1908–72, Mexican dancer and choreographer in the U.S.

Lin•a•cre (lin′ə kər), **Thomas,** 1460?–1521, English humanist, translator, scholar, and physician.

Lin Biao (lin′ byou′), 1907–71, Chinese marshal and Communist leader: defense minister 1959–71; leader of abortive coup 1971.

Lin•coln (ling′kən), **1. Abraham,** 1809–65, 16th president of the U.S. 1861–65. **2. Benjamin,** 1733–1810, American Revolutionary general.

Lind (lind), **Jenny** (*Johanna Maria Lind Goldschmidt*) (*"The Swedish Nightingale"*), 1820–87, Swedish soprano.

Lind•bergh (lind′bûrg, lin′-), **1. Anne (Spencer) Morrow,** born 1906, U.S. writer (wife of Charles Augustus Lindbergh). **2. Charles Augustus,** 1902–74, U.S. aviator: made the first solo nonstop transatlantic flight 1927.

Lin•de•gren (lin′də grən), **Erik (Johan),** 1910–68, Swedish poet and literary critic.

Lind•ley (lind′lē, lin′-), **John,** 1799–1865, English botanist.

Lind•say (lind′zē, lin′-), **1. Howard,** 1889–1968, U.S. playwright, producer, and actor. **2. John V(liet)** (vlēt), born 1921, U.S. politician: mayor of New York City 1966–74. **3. (Nicholas) Va•chel** (vā′chəl), 1879–1931, U.S. poet.

Lind•sey (lind′zē, lin′-), **Ben(jamin Barr),** 1869–1943, U.S. jurist and authority on juvenile delinquency.

Lin•nae•us (li nē′əs), **Carolus** (*Carl von Linné*), 1707–78, Swedish botanist.

Lin Sen (lin′ sun′), 1867–1943, Chinese statesman.

Lin•ton (lin′tn), **Ralph,** 1893–1953, U.S. anthropologist.

Li•nus (lī′nəs), **Saint,** died A.D. 76?, pope 67?–76?.

Lin Yu•tang (lin′ yo͞o′täng′), (*Lin Yü-t'ang*), 1895–1976, Chinese author and philologist.

Liou•ville (lyo͞o vēl′, lē′o͞o vil′), **Joseph,** 1809–82, French mathematician.

Lip•chitz (lip′shits), **Jacques,** 1891–1973, U.S. sculptor, born in Lithuania.

Li Peng (lē′ pung′), born 1924, Chinese Communist leader: premier since 1987.

Lip•mann (lip′mən), **Fritz Albert,** 1899–1986, U.S. biochemist, born in Germany: Nobel prize for medicine 1953.

Li Po (lē′ pō′, bō′), A.D. 701?–762, Chinese poet of the T'ang dynasty. Also called **Li Tai Po.**

Lip•pi (lip′ē), **Filippino,** 1457–1504, and his father, **Fra Filippo** or **Fra Lippo,** 1406?–69, Italian painters.

Lipp•mann (lip′mən; *also* lēp män′ *for 1*), **1. Gabriel,** 1845–1921, French physicist: Nobel prize 1908. **2. Walter,** 1889–1974, U.S. journalist.

Lip•pold (lip′ōld), **Richard,** born 1915, U.S. sculptor.

Lips•comb (lip′skəm), **William Nunn, Jr.,** born 1919, U.S. chemist: Nobel prize 1976.

Lip•ton (lip′tən), **1. Seymour,** born 1903, U.S. sculptor. **2. Sir Thomas Johnstone,** 1850–1931, Scottish merchant and yacht racer.

Lis•gar (lis′gär), **Sir John Young,** 1807–76, Canadian political leader: governor general 1869–72.

Lisle (lēl), **1.** LECONTE DE LISLE. **2.** ROUGET DE LISLE.

List (list), **Friedrich,** 1789–1846, U.S. political economist and journalist, born in Germany.

Lis•ter (lis′tər), **Joseph, 1st Baron Lister of Lyme Regis,** 1827–1912, English surgeon: founder of modern antiseptic surgery.

Liszt (list), **Franz,** 1811–86, Hungarian composer and pianist.

Li Tai Po (lē′ tī′ pō′, bō′) also **Li Tai•bo** (tī′bō′), LI PO.

Lit•tré (lē trā′), **Maximilien Paul Émile,** 1801–88, French lexicographer and philosopher.

Lit•vi•nov (lit vē′nôf, -nof), **Maksim Maksimovich,** 1876–1951, Russian Communist leader and diplomat.

Liu Pang or **Liu Bang** (lyōō′ bäng′), 247–195 B.C., Chinese emperor: founder of the Han dynasty 202 B.C.

Liu Shao•qi or **Liu Shao-ch'i** (lyōō′ shou′chē′), 1898–1973, Chinese Communist leader: head of state 1959–66.

Liv•ing•ston (liv′ing stən), **Robert R.,** 1746–1813, U.S. statesman.

Liv•ing•stone (liv′ing stən), **David,** 1813–73, Scottish missionary and explorer in Africa.

Liv•y (liv′ē), (*Titus Livius*) 59 B.C.–A.D. 17, Roman historian.

Li Xian•nian (lē′ shyän′nyän′), born 1907, Chinese Communist leader: president 1983–88.

Li Yüan or **Li Yuan** (lē′ yyän′), (*Kao Tsu* or *Gao Zu*), A.D. 565–635, Chinese emperor 618–27: founder of the Tang dynasty.

Lle•ras Ca•mar•go (ye′RäS kä mäR′gô), **Alberto,** 1906–89, Colombian journalist, writer, and political leader: president 1945–46, 1958–62.

Llew•el•lyn (lōō el′in), **Richard** (*Richard David Vivian Llewellyn Lloyd*), 1907?–83, Welsh novelist.

Lloyd (loid), **1. Harold (Clayton),** 1894–1971, U.S. actor. **2. (John) Selwyn (Brooke),** 1904–78, British statesman.

Lloyd George (loid′ jôrj′), **David, 1st Earl of Dwy•for** (dōō′vôr), 1863–1945, British prime minister 1916–22.

Lloyd-Web•ber (loid′web′ər), **Andrew,** born 1948, British composer.

Lo•ba•chev•sky (lō′bə chef′skē), **Nikolai Ivanovich,** 1793–1856, Russian mathematician.

Locke (lok), **1. Alain LeRoy,** 1886–1954, U.S. educator and author. **2. David Ross** (*"Petroleum V. Nasby"*), 1833–88, U.S. humorist and journalist. **3. John,** 1632–1704, English philosopher.

Lock•er-Lamp•son (lok′ər lam′sən), **Frederick** (*Frederick Locker*), 1821–95, English poet.

Lock•hart (lok′härt, lok′ərt), **John Gibson,** 1794–1854, Scottish biographer and novelist.

Lock•wood (lok′wŏŏd′), **Belva Ann Bennett,** 1830–1917, U.S. lawyer and women's-rights activist.

Lock•yer (lok′yər), **Sir Joseph Norman,** 1836–1920, English astronomer and author.

Lodge (loj), **1. Henry Cabot,** 1850–1924, U.S. senator 1893–1924. **2.** his grandson, **Henry Cabot, Jr.,** 1902–85, U.S. statesman. **3. Sir Oliver Joseph,** 1851–1940, English physicist and writer. **4. Thomas,** 1558?–1625, English poet and dramatist.

Loeb (lōb), **Jacques,** 1859–1924, German physiologist in the U.S.

Loef•fler (lef′ler), **Charles Martin Tornov,** 1861–1935, U.S. violinist and composer, born in France.

Loes•ser (les′ər), **Frank (Henry),** 1910–69, U.S. composer and lyricist, esp. of musicals and film songs.

Loewe (lō), **Frederick,** 1904–88, U.S. composer, born in Austria.

Loe•wi (lō′ē; *Ger.* lœ′vē), **Otto,** 1873–1961, German pharmacologist in the U.S.: Nobel prize for medicine 1936.

Loe•wy (lō′ē), **Raymond Fernand,** 1893–1986, U.S. industrial designer, born in France.

Löff•ler (lef′lər), **Friedrich August Johannes,** 1852–1915, German bacteriologist.

Loft•ing (lôf′ting, lof′-), **Hugh,** 1886–1947, U.S. author of books for children, born in England.

Lo•gan (lō′gən), **1. John** or **James** (*Tah-gah-jute*), c1725–80, leader of the Cayuga tribe. **2. Joshua,** 1908–88, U.S. playwright, director, and producer.

Lo•max (lō′maks), **John Avery,** 1867–1948, and his son, **Alan,** born 1915, U.S. folklorists.

Lom•bard (lom′bärd, -bərd, lum′-), **1. Carol** (*Jane Peters*), 1909–42, U.S. actress. **2. Peter** (*Petrus Lombardus*), c1100–64?, Italian theologian: bishop of Paris 1159–64?.

Lom•bar•di (lom bär′dē, lum-), **Vince(nt Thomas),** 1913–70, U.S. football coach.

Lom•bar•do (lom bär′dō, lum-), **Guy (Albert),** 1902–77, U.S. bandleader, born in Canada.

Lom•bro•so (lom brō′sō), **Cesare,** 1836–1909, Italian physician and criminologist.

Lo•mo•no•sov (lom′ə nô′sôf, -sof), **Mikhail Vasilevich,** 1711–65, Russian philosopher, poet, scientist, and grammarian.

Lon•don (lun′dən), **Jack,** 1876–1916, U.S. writer.

Long (lông, long), **1. Crawford Williamson,** 1815–78, U.S. surgeon: first to use ether as an anesthetic. **2. Huey Pierce,** 1893–1935, U.S. politician. **3. Russell B(illiu),** born 1918, U.S. lawyer and politician: U.S. senator 1948–87 (son of Huey Pierce Long). **4. Stephen Harriman,** 1784–1864, U.S. army officer and explorer.

Long•den (lông′dən, long′-), **John Eric** (*Johnny*), born 1907, U.S. jockey and thoroughbred horse trainer.

Long•fel•low (lông′fel′ō, long′-), **Henry Wads•worth** (wodz′wərth), 1807–82, U.S. poet.

Lon•gi•nus (lon jī′nəs), **Dionysius Cassius,** A.D. 213?–273, Greek philosopher and rhetorician.

Long•street (lông′strēt′, long′-), **James,** 1821–1904, Confederate general in the U.S. Civil War.

Long•worth (lông′wûrth, long′-), **Nicholas,** 1869–1931, U.S. politician: Speaker of the House 1925–31.

Lönn•rot (len′rot, -ro͞ot), **E•lias** (e′lyäs), 1802–84, Finnish scholar and editor.

Loos (lo͞os), **1. Adolf,** 1870–1933, Austrian architect and writer. **2. Anita,** 1893–1981, U.S. writer.

Lo•pat•ni•kov or **Lo•pat•ni•koff** (lō pat′ni kôf′, -kof′), **Nicolai Lvovich,** 1903–76, U.S. composer, born in Russia.

Lo•pe de Ve•ga (lō′pā də vā′gə), VEGA, Lope de.

Ló•pez (lō′pez), **Osvaldo,** (*Osvaldo López Arellano*), born 1921, Honduran air force general: president of Honduras 1963–75.

Ló•pez de A•ya•la (lō′pes dā ä yä′lä), **Pedro,** 1332–1407, Spanish writer and statesman.

Ló•pez de Le•gaz•pe (lō′pes dā lə gäs′pā) also **Ló•pez de Le•gas•pi** (lə gäs′pē), **Miguel,** 1510?–72, Spanish conqueror and colonizer of the Philippines 1565: founder of Manila 1571.

Ló•pez y Fuen•tes (lô′pes ē fwen′tes), **Gregorio,** 1895–1966, Mexican writer.

Lor•ca (lôr′kə), GARCÍA LORCA, Federico.

Lo•ren (lôr′ən, lə ren′), **Sophia** (*Sophia Scicoloni*), born 1934, Italian actress.

Lo•rentz (lôr′ənts, -ents, lōr′-), **Hendrik Antoon,** 1853–1928, Dutch physicist: Nobel prize 1902.

Lo•renz (lôr′ənz, -ents, lōr′-), **Konrad (Zacharias),** 1903–89, Austrian ethologist: Nobel prize for medicine 1973.

Lo•ren•zet•ti (lôr′ən zet′ē), **Ambrogio,** c1319–48, and his brother, **Pietro,** c1305–48, Italian painters.

Lor•raine (lə rān′, lô-, lō-; *Fr.* lô REN′) also **Lor•rain** (*Fr.* lô RAN′), **Claude** (*Claude Gelée*), 1600–82, French painter.

Lor•re (lôr′ē), **Peter** (*László Loewenstein*), 1904–64, U.S. film actor, born in Hungary.

Lo•thair (lō thâr′, -târ′), **1. Lothair I,** A.D. 795?–855, emperor of the Holy Roman Empire 840–855 (son of Louis I). **2. Lothair II** (*"the Saxon"*), c1070–1137, emperor of the Holy Roman Empire and king of the Germans 1125–37.

Lo•ti (lô tē′), **Pierre** (*Louis Marie Julien Viaud*), 1850–1923, French novelist.

Lo•tze (lōt′sə), **Rudolf Hermann,** 1817–81, German philosopher.

Lou•is[1] (lo͞o′is), **1. Joe** (*Joseph Louis Barrow*), 1914–81, U.S. boxer: world heavyweight champion 1937–49. **2. Morris** (*Morris Bernstein*), 1912–62, U.S. painter.

Lou•is[2] (lo͞o′ē; *Fr.* lwē), **1. Louis I** (*"the Pious"*), A.D. 778–840, emperor of the Holy Roman Empire 814–840 (son of Charlemagne). **2. Louis II, a. de Bourbon,** CONDÉ, Prince de. **b.** (*"the German"*) A.D. 804?–876, king of Germany 843–876 (son of Louis I), founder of the German kingdom. **3. Louis IX, Saint,** 1214?–70, king of France 1226–70. **4. Louis XI,** 1423–83, king of France 1461–83 (son of

Charles VII). **5. Louis XII** (*"the Father of the People"*), 1462–1515, king of France 1498–1515. **6. Louis XIII,** 1601–43, king of France 1610–43 (son of Henry IV of Navarre). **7. Louis XIV** (*"the Great"; "the Sun King"*), 1638–1715, king of France 1643–1715 (son of Louis XIII). **8. Louis XV,** 1710–74, king of France 1715–74 (great-grandson of Louis XIV). **9. Louis XVI,** 1754–93, king of France 1774–92 (grandson of Louis XV). **10. Louis XVII** (*"Louis Charles of France"*), 1785–95, titular king of France 1793–95 (son of Louis XVI). **11. Louis XVIII** (*Louis Xavier Stanislas*), 1755–1824, king of France 1814–15, 1815–24 (brother of Louis XVI).

Lou′is Napo′leon (lo͞o′ē; *Fr.* lwē), NAPOLEON (def. 3).

Lou′is Phi•lippe′ (fi lēp′), (*"Citizen King"*) 1773–1850, king of France 1830–48.

Louns•bur•y (lounz′ber′ē, -bə rē), **Thomas Raynesford,** 1838–1915, U.S. linguist and educator.

L'Ou•ver•ture (*Fr.* lo͞o VER TYR′), TOUSSAINT L'OUVERTURE.

Louys (lwē), **Pierre,** 1870–1925, French poet and novelist.

Love•craft (luv′kraft′, -kräft′), **H(oward) P(hillips),** 1890–1937, U.S. writer.

Love•joy (luv′joi′), **Elijah P(arish),** 1802–37, U.S. abolitionist and newspaper editor.

Love•lace (luv′lās′), **Richard,** 1618–56, English poet.

Lov•ell (lov′əl), **Sir Alfred Charles Bernard,** born 1931, English astronomer.

Lov•er (luv′ər), **Samuel,** 1797–1868, Irish novelist, painter, and songwriter.

Low (lō), **1. David,** 1891–1963, English political cartoonist, born in New Zealand. **2. Juliette,** 1860–1927, U.S. founder of the Girl Scouts. **3. Seth,** 1850–1916, U.S. political reformer, educator, and politician.

Low•ell (lō′əl), **1. Abbott Lawrence,** 1856–1943, political scientist and educator: president of Harvard University 1909–33. **2. Amy,** 1874–1925, U.S. poet and critic. **3. James Russell,** 1819–91, U.S. poet, essayist, and diplomat. **4. Percival,** 1855–1916, U.S. astronomer (brother of Amy Lowell). **5. Robert,** 1917–77, U.S. poet.

Lowes (lōz), **John Livingston,** 1867–1945, U.S. educator.

Lowndes (loundz), **William Thomas,** 1798–1843, English bibliographer.

Loy•o•la (loi ō′lə), **Saint Ignatius of** (*Iñigo López de Loyola*), 1491–1556, Spanish ecclesiastic: founder of the Society of Jesus.

Lub•bock (lub′ək), **Sir John, 1st Baron Avebury,** 1834–1913, English author, natural scientist, and statesman.

Lu•bitsch (lo͞o′bich), **Ernst,** 1892–1947, German film director, in the U.S. after 1922.

Lüb•ke (lʏp′kə), **Heinrich,** 1894–1972, German statesman: president of West Germany 1959–69.

Lu•can (lo͞o′kən), (*Marcus Annaeus Lucanus*) A.D. 39–65, Roman poet, born in Spain.

Lu•cas (lo͞o′kəs), **George,** born 1945, U.S. film director.

Luce (lo͞os), **1. Clare Boothe,** born 1903, U.S. writer and diplomat (wife of Henry Robinson Luce). **2. Henry Robinson,** 1898–1967, U.S. editor and publisher.

Lu•cian (lo͞o′shən), **1.** A.D. 117–c180, Greek rhetorician and satirist. **2.** (*"Lucian of Antioch"; "Lucian the Martyr"*) A.D. c240–312, theologian and Biblical critic, born at Samosata, in Syria.

Lu•cil•i•us (lo͞o sil′ē əs), **Gaius,** c180–102? B.C., Roman satirist.

Lu•cre•tius (lo͞o krē′shəs), (*Titus Lucretius Carus*) 97?–54 B.C., Roman poet and philosopher.

Lu•cul•lus (lo͞o kul′əs), **Lucius Licinius,** c110–57? B.C., Roman general and epicure.

Lu•den•dorff (lo͝od′n dôrf′), **Erich Friedrich Wilhelm von,** 1865–1937, German general.

Lud•wig (lud′wig, lo͝od′vig, -wig), **1. Emil,** (*Emil Cohn*), 1881–1948, German biographer. **2. Christa,** born 1928, German mezzo-soprano.

Luen•ing (lo͞o′ning), **Otto,** born 1900, U.S. composer, conductor, and flutist.

Lu•gar (lo͞o′gər), **Richard G(reen),** born 1932, U.S. politician: senator since 1977.

Lu•go•nes (lo͞o gō′nəs), **Leopoldo,** 1874–1938, Argentine poet and diplomat.

Lu•go•si (lo͞o gō′sē), **Bela,** 1884–1956, U.S. actor, born in Hungary: best known for his roles in horror films.

Lui•set•ti (lo͞o set′ē), **Angelo** (*"Hank"*), born 1916, U.S. basketball player.

Lu•kacs (lo͞o′käch), **George** (*György Lukács*), 1885–1971, Hungarian literary critic.

Lu•kas (lo͞o′kəs), **Paul,** 1895–1971, U.S. actor, born in Hungary.

Luke (lo͝ok), *n.* an early Christian disciple and companion of Paul, a physician and probably a gentile: traditionally believed to be the author of the third Gospel and the Acts.

Luks (luks), **George Benjamin,** 1867–1933, U.S. painter.

Lul•ly (lo͞o′lē, lo͞o lē′), **1. Jean Baptiste** (zhäɴ), 1632–87, French composer, born in Italy. **2.** Catalan, **Lull** (lo͝ol). **Raymond** or **Ramón** (*"Doctor Illuminatus"*), 1235?–1315, Spanish theologian, philosopher, and author. Italian, **Lul•li** (lo͝ol′lē).

Lu•mum•ba (lo͞o mo͞om′bə), **Patrice (Emergy),** 1925–61, African political leader: premier of the Democratic Republic of the Congo (now Zaire) 1960–61.

Lund•berg (lund′bərg), **George A(ndrew),** 1895–1966, U.S. sociologist and author.

Lunt (lunt), **Alfred,** 1893–1977, U.S. actor (husband of Lynn Fontanne).

Lur•çat (lʏʀ sa′), **Jean** (zhäɴ), 1892–1966, French painter and tapestry designer.

Lu•ri•a (lo͝or′ē ə), **Salvador Edward,** 1912–91, U.S. biologist, born in Italy: Nobel prize for medicine 1969.

Lu•rie (lo͝or′ē), **Alison,** born 1926, U.S. novelist.

Lu•ther (lo͞o′thər), **Martin,** 1483–1546, German leader of the Protestant Reformation.

Lu•thu•li (lo͞o to͞o′lē, -tyo͞o′-), **Albert John,** 1898–1967, African leader in the Republic of South Africa and former Zulu chief: Nobel peace prize 1960.

Lut•yens (luch′ənz, lut′yənz), **Sir Edwin Landseer,** 1869–1944, English architect.

Lux•em•burg (luk′səm bûrg′), **Rosa** (*"Red Rosa"*), 1870–1919, German socialist leader, born in Poland.

Lu Xun (lo͞o′ sho͞on′), (*Zhou Shuren*) 1881–1936, Chinese writer.

Lwoff (lwôf), **André,** born 1902, French microbiologist: Nobel prize for medicine 1965.

Lyau•tey (lyō tā′), **Louis Hubert Gonzalve,** 1854–1934, French marshal: resident general of Morocco 1912–16, 1917–25.

Ly•cur•gus (lī kûr′gəs), fl. 9th century B.C., Spartan lawgiver.

Lyd•gate (lid′gāt′, -git), **John,** c1370–1451?, English poet.

Ly•ell (lī′əl), **Sir Charles,** 1797–1875, English geologist.

Lyl•y (lil′ē), **John,** 1554?–1606, English writer of romances and plays.

Lynch (linch), **John** (*Jack*), born 1917, prime minister of Ireland 1966–73, 1977–79.

Lynd (lind), **Robert Staughton,** 1892–1970, and his wife **Helen (Merrell),** 1896–1982, U.S. sociologists.

Ly•nen (lē′nen), **Feodor,** 1911–79, German biochemist: Nobel prize in medicine 1964.

Lynn (lin), **Loretta** (*Loretta Webb*), born 1935, U.S. singer and songwriter.

Ly•on (lī′ən), **Mary,** 1797–1849, U.S. pioneer in advocating and providing advanced education for women: founder of Mount Holyoke College.

Ly•ons (lī′ənz), **Joseph Aloysius,** 1879–1939, Australian statesman: prime minister 1932–39.

Ly•san•der (lī san′dər), died 395 B.C., Spartan naval commander.

Ly•sen•ko (li seng′kō), **Trofim Denisovich,** 1898–1976, Russian biologist and agronomist.

Lys•i•as (lis′ē əs), c450–c380 B.C., Athenian orator.

Ly•sim•a•chus (lī sim′ə kəs), 361?–281 B.C., Macedonian general: king of Thrace 306–281.

Ly•sip•pus (lī sip′əs), fl. c360–c320 B.C., Greek sculptor.

Lyt•ton (lit′n), **1. Edward George Earle Lytton Bulwer-, 1st Baron Lytton,** 1803–73, English novelist, dramatist, and politician. **2.** his son, **Edward Robert Bulwer Lytton, 1st Earl Lytton** (*"Owen Meredith"*), 1831–91, English statesman and poet.

Ma (mä), **Yo-Yo,** born 1955, U.S. cellist, born in France.

Maa•zel (mä zel′), **Lorin,** born 1930, U.S. conductor and violinist.

Ma•buse (*Fr.* mᴀ ʙʏᴢ′), **Jan,** (*Jan Gossaert* or *Gossart*), 1478?–1533?, Flemish painter.

Ma•ca•pa•gal (mä′kə pə gäl′), **Diosdado,** born 1910, Philippine statesman: president 1961–65.

Mac•Ar•thur (mə kär′thər), **Douglas,** 1880–1964, U.S. general.

Ma•cau•lay (mə kô′lē), **1. Dame Rose,** c1885–1958, English novelist. **2. Thomas Babington, 1st Baron,** 1800–59, English historian and statesman.

Mac•beth (mək beth′, mak-), died 1057, king of Scotland 1040–57: subject of a tragedy by Shakespeare.

Mac•Bride (mək brīd′), **Seán** (shôn), 1904–88, Irish politician and diplomat, born in France: Nobel peace prize 1974.

Mac•ca•bae•us (mak′ə bē′əs), **Judas** or **Judah** (*"the Hammer"*), died 160 B.C., Judean patriot.

Mac•don•ald (mək don′əld), **1. George,** 1824–1905, Scottish novelist and poet. **2. Sir John Alexander,** 1815–91, Canadian statesman, born in Scotland.

Mac•Don•ald (mək don′əld), **James Ramsay,** 1866–1937, British prime minister 1924, 1929–35.

Mac•don•ough (mək don′ə), **Thomas,** 1783–1825, U.S. naval officer: defeated British on Lake Champlain 1814.

Mac•Dow•ell (mək dou′əl), **Edward Alexander,** 1861–1908, U.S. composer.

Mach (mäk, mäᴋʜ), **Ernst,** 1838–1916, Austrian physicist.

Ma•cha•do de As•siz (mä shä′do͝o di ä sēs′), **Joaquim Maria,** 1839–1908, Brazilian writer.

Ma•cha•do y Mo•ra•les (mə chä′dō ē mə rä′les), **Gerardo,** 1871–1939, president of Cuba 1925–33.

Ma•cha•do y Ru•iz (mə chä′dō ē ro͞o ēs′), **Antonio,** 1875–1939, Spanish writer.

Ma•chel (mə shel′), **Samora Moisés,** 1933–86, Mozambique political leader: president 1975–86.

Mach•en (mak′ən), **Arthur,** 1863–1947, Welsh novelist and essayist.

Mach•i•a•vel•li (mak′ē ə vel′ē), **Niccolò di Bernardo,** 1469–1527, Italian political philosopher.

Mac•in•tosh (mak′in tosh′), **Charles,** 1766–1843, Scottish chemist, inventor, and manufacturer.

Mac•I•ver (mək ī′vər, mə kī′-, mə kē′-), **1. Loren,** born 1909, U.S. painter. **2. Robert Morrison,** 1882–1970, U.S. sociologist, born in Scotland.

Mack (mak), **Connie** (*Cornelius McGillicuddy*), 1862–1956, U.S. baseball player and manager.

Ma•cke (mä′kə), **August,** 1887–1914, German painter.

Mack•en•sen (mä′kən zən), **August von,** 1849–1945, German field marshal.

Mac•ken•zie (mə ken′zē), **1. Sir Alexander,** 1764–1820, Scottish explorer in Canada. **2. Alexander,** 1822–92, prime minister of Canada 1873–78. **3. William Lyon,** 1795–1861, Canadian political leader and journalist, born in Scotland.

Ma•cker•ras (mə ker′əs), **Charles,** born 1925, Australian conductor.

Mack•in•tosh (mak′in tosh′), **Charles Rennie,** 1868–1928, Scottish architect and designer.

Mac•Laine (mə klān′), **Shirley** (*Shirley Beaty*), born 1934, U.S. actress, dancer, and author.

Mac•lau•rin (mək lôr′in, mə klôr′-), **Colin,** 1698–1746, Scottish mathematician.

Mac•Leish (mak lēsh′, mə klēsh′), **Archibald,** 1892–1982, U.S. poet.

Mac•Len•nan (mak len′ən, mə klen′-), **(John) Hugh,** 1907–90, Canadian novelist and essayist.

Mac•leod (mə kloud′), **John James Rickard,** 1876–1935, Scottish physiologist: a discoverer of insulin: Nobel prize for medicine 1923.

Mac•Ma•hon (mak ma ôn′), **Marie Edmé Patrice Maurice, Count de** (*Duke of Magenta*), 1808–93, president of France 1873–79.

Mac•Man•us (mək man′əs), **Seu•mas** (shā′məs), 1869–1960, Irish poet and short-story writer.

Mac•mil•lan (mək mil′ən), **Harold,** 1894–1986, British prime minister 1957–63.

Mac•Mil•lan (mək mil′ən), **Donald Baxter,** 1874–1970, U.S. arctic explorer.

Mac•Mon•nies (mək mun′ēz), **Frederick William,** 1863–1937, U.S. sculptor.

Mac•Neice (mək nēs′), **Louis,** 1907–63, Irish poet.

Ma•con (mā′kən), **Nathaniel,** 1758–1837, U.S. politician: Speaker of the House 1801–07.

Mac•pher•son (mək fûr′sən), **James,** 1736–96, Scottish author.

Mac•rea•dy (mək rē′dē, mə krē′-), **William Charles,** 1793–1873, English actor.

Ma•cy (mā′sē), **R(owland) H(ussey),** 1823–77, U.S. retail merchant.

Ma•da•ria•ga (mä′thä ryä′gä), **Salvador de** (*Salvador de Madariaga y Rojo*), 1886–1978, Spanish diplomat, historian, and writer in England.

Ma•der•no (mä der′nô), **Carlo,** 1556–1629, Italian architect.

Ma•de•ro (mə dâr′ō, mä-), **Francisco Indalecio,** 1873–1913, Mexican president 1911–13.

Mad•i•son (mad′ə sən), **1. Dolly** or **Dolley** (*Dorothea Payne*), 1768–1849, wife of James Madison. **2. James,** 1751–1836, 4th president of the U.S. 1809–17.

Ma•don•na (mə don′ə), (*Madonna Louise Ciccone*), born 1958, U.S. singer.

Mae•ce•nas (mē sē′nəs, mī-), **Gaius Cilnius,** c70–8 B.C., Roman statesman: friend and patron of Horace and Virgil.

Mae•ter•linck (mā′tər lingk′, met′ər-), **Comte Maurice,** 1862–1947, Belgian poet, dramatist, and essayist: Nobel prize 1911.

Ma•gel•lan (mə jel′ən), **Ferdinand,** c1480–1521, Portuguese navigator.

Ma•gen•die (mA zhäN dē′), **François,** 1783–1855, French physiologist.

Ma•gritte (ma grēt′), **René,** 1898–1967, Belgian painter.

Mag•say•say (mäg sī′sī), **Ramón,** 1907–57, Philippine statesman: president 1953–57.

Ma•han (mə han′), **Alfred Thayer,** 1840–1914, U.S. naval officer and writer on naval history.

Ma•hat′ma Gan′dhi (mə hät′mə, -hat′-), GANDHI, Mohandas Karamchand.

Ma•hen•dra (mä hen drä′), (*Mahendra Bir Bikram Shah Deva*) 1920–72, king of Nepal 1955–72.

Mah•fouz (mä fo͞oz′), **Naguib,** born 1911, Egyptian writer: Nobel prize 1988.

Mah•ler (mä′lər), **Gustav,** 1860–1911, Austrian composer.

Mah•mud II (mä mo͞od′), 1785–1839, sultan of Turkey 1809–39.

Mahmud′ of Ghaz′ni (guz′nē), A.D. 971?–1030, Muslim Amir of Ghazni 997–1030.

Ma•hom•et (mə hom′it), MUHAMMAD (def. 1).

Maid′ of Or′lé•ans (ôr′lē ənz; *Fr.* ÔR lā äN′), JOAN OF ARC.

Mail•er (mā′lər), **Norman,** born 1923, U.S. writer.

Mail•lart (mA YAR′), **Robert,** 1872–1940, Swiss engineer.

Mail•lol (mä yôl′, -yōl′, ma-), **Aristide,** 1861–1944, French sculptor.

Mai•mon•i•des (mī mon′i dēz′), (*Moses ben Maimon*) (*"RaMBaM"*), 1135–1204, Jewish philosopher and jurist.

Main•bo•cher (man′bō shā′), (*Main Rousseau Bocher*), 1891–1976, U.S. fashion designer.

Main•te•non (maNt° nôN′), **Marquise de** (*Françoise d'Aubigné*), 1635–1719, second wife of Louis XIV.

Mait•land (māt′lənd), **Frederic William,** 1850–1906, English legal historian.

Ma•jor (mā′jər), **John,** born 1943, British prime minister since 1990.

Ma•kar•i•os III (mə kar′ē əs, -ōs′), (*Michael Christodoulos Mouskos*), 1913–77, Cypriot statesman and Greek Orthodox prelate: archbishop and patriarch of Cyprus 1950–77; president 1960–77 (in exile 1974).

Ma•ka•ro•va (mə kär′ə və), **Natalia,** born 1940, Russian ballerina, in the U.S. and England since 1970.

Ma•kem•ie (mə kem′ē, -kā′mē), **Francis,** 1658?–1708, American Presbyterian clergyman, born in Ireland: founded the first Presbyterian church in America.

Ma•khlouf (mäKH lo͞of′, mä klo͞of′), **Saint Shar•bel** (shär′-bəl), 1828–98, Lebanese monk: canonized 1977.

Mal•a•mud (mal′ə məd, -mo͝od′), **Bernard,** 1914–86, U.S. writer.

Ma•lan (mä län′), **Daniel François,** 1874–1959, South African editor and political leader: prime minister 1948–54.

Mal•colm X (mal′kəm eks′), (*Malcolm Little*), 1925–65, U.S. civil-rights activist and religious leader.

Male•branche (mAl brANsh′), **Nicolas de,** 1638–1715, French philosopher.

Ma•len•kov (mä′lən kôf′, -kof′; *Russ.* mə lyin kôf′), **Georgi Maximilianovich,** 1902–88, Russian political leader: premier of the Soviet Union 1953–55.

Mal•e•vich (mal′ə vich′), **Kasimir Severinovich,** 1878–1935, Russian painter, founded Suprematist school of art.

Mal•herbe (mAl erb′), **François de,** 1555–1628, French poet and critic.

Ma•li•bran (mä′li brän′), **Maria Felicita,** 1808–36, Spanish opera singer, born in France.

Ma•lik (mä′lik, mal′ik), **Adam,** 1917–84, Indonesian politician and diplomat.

Ma•li•nov•sky (mal′ə nôf′skē, -nof′-), **Rodion Yakovlevich,** 1898–1967, Russian army officer: minister of defense of the U.S.S.R. 1957–67.

Ma•li•now•ski (mal′ə nôf′skē, -nof′-), **Bronislaw Kasper,** 1884–1942, social anthropologist, born in Poland.

Ma•li•pie•ro (mä′lē pye′rô), **Gian Francesco,** 1882–1973, Italian composer.

Mal•lar•mé (mal′är mā′), **Stéphane,** 1842–98, French poet.

Mal•lo•ry (mal′ə rē), **Stephen Russell,** 1813?–73, U.S. lawyer and politician.

Ma•lone (mə lōn′), **Edmond,** 1741–1812, Irish Shakespearean scholar.

Mal•o•ry (mal′ə rē), **Sir Thomas,** c1400–71, English author.

Mal•pi•ghi (mal pē′gē, mäl-), **Marcello,** 1628–94, Italian anatomist.

Mal•raux (mal rō′), **André,** 1901–76, French writer, art historian, and politician.

Mal•thus (mal′thəs), **Thomas Robert,** 1766–1834, English economist.

Mam•et (mam′it), **David (Alan),** born 1947, U.S. playwright.

Ma'•mun (or **Ma•moun**), **al-** (al′mä mo͞on′, -ma-), (*abu-al-'Abbās 'Abdullāh*) A.D. 786–833, caliph of Baghdad 813–833 (son of Harun al-Rashid).

Man•ci•ni (man sē′nē), **Henry,** born 1924, U.S. composer.

Man•de•la (man del′ə), **1. Nelson (Rolihlahla),** born 1918, South African antiapartheid activist. **2.** his wife, **Winnie,** born 1936?, South African antiapartheid activist.

Man•de•ville (man′də vil′), **Sir John,** died 1372, pseudonymous English travel writer.

Ma•nes (mā′nēz), A.D. 216?–276?, Persian prophet: founder of Manicheanism.

Ma•net (ma nā′), **Édouard,** 1832–83, French painter.

Man•e•tho (man′ə thō′), fl. c250 B.C., Egyptian high priest of Heliopolis: author of a history of Egypt.

Mang•rum (mang′grəm), **Lloyd,** 1914–73, U.S. golf player.

Man•i•low (man′l ō′), **Barry,** born 1946, U.S. singer and songwriter.

Man•kie•wicz (mang′kə wits), **Joseph L(eo),** born 1909, U.S. motion-picture director, producer, and writer.

Mann (man, män *for 1, 3;* man *for 2*), **1. Heinrich,** 1871–1950, German novelist and dramatist, in the U.S. after 1940 (brother of Thomas Mann). **2. Horace,** 1796–1859, U.S. educational reformer. **3. Thomas,** 1875–1955, German novelist, in the U.S. 1938–52: Nobel prize 1929.

Man•ner•heim (mä′nər hām′), **Baron Carl Gustaf Emil von,** 1867–1951, Finnish soldier and statesman.

Man•nes (man′is), **Leopold Damrosch,** 1899–1964, U.S. composer and chemist.

Mann•heim (man′hīm, män′-), **Karl,** 1893–1947, German sociologist.

Man•ning (man′ing), **Henry Edward,** 1808–92, English prelate and ecclesiastical writer: cardinal 1875–92.

Ma•no•le•te (mä′nō let′ā), (*Manuel Laureano Rodríguez y Sánchez*), 1917–47, Spanish matador.

Man•sart (mäɴ sar′; *Eng.* man′särt, -sərt), **1. Jules Hardouin** (*Jules Hardouin*), 1646–1708, French architect: chief architectural director for Louis XIV. **2.** his granduncle, **(Nicolas) François,** 1598–1666, French architect.

Mans•field (manz′fēld′), **1. Katherine** (*Kathleen Beauchamp Murry*), 1888–1923, English short-story writer. **2. Michael Joseph** (*Mike*), born 1903, U.S. politician: senator 1953–77. **3. Richard,** 1857–1907, U.S. actor, born in Germany.

Man•sur, al- (al′man so͝or′), (*ʿAbdullāh al-Mansūr*), A.D. 712?–775, Arab caliph 754–775: founder of Baghdad 764.

Man•te•gna (män tān′yä), **Andrea,** 1431–1506, Italian painter.

Man•tle (man′tl), **1. Mickey (Charles),** born 1931, U.S. baseball player. **2. (Robert) Burns,** 1873–1948, U.S. journalist.

Man•to•va•ni (män′tə vä′nē), **Annunzio Paolo,** born 1905, British conductor, born in Italy.

Ma•nu•ti•us (mə no͞o′shē əs, -nyo͞o′-), **Aldus** (*Teobaldo Mannucci* or *Manuzio*), 1450–1515, Italian printer and classical scholar.

Man•zo•ni (män zō′nē, mänd-), **Alessandro (Francesco Tommaso Antonio),** 1785–1873, Italian novelist and poet.

Man•zù (män dzo͞o′), **Giacomo,** 1908–91, Italian sculptor.

Mao Dun or **Mao Tun** (mou′ do͝on′) (*Shen Yanbing*), 1896–1981, Chinese writer.

Mao Ze•dong (mou′ zə do͝ong′, dzə-) also **Mao Tse-tung** (mou′ tsə to͝ong′, dzə do͝ong′), 1893–1976, chairman of the People's Republic of China 1949–59 and of the Chinese Communist party 1943–76.

Map (map) also **Mapes** (māps, mā′pēz), **Walter,** c1140–1209?, Welsh ecclesiastic, poet, and satirist.

Ma•rat (mA RA′), **Jean Paul** (zhäN), 1743–93, French Revolutionary leader, born in Switzerland.

Mar•ble (mär′bəl), **Alice,** 1913–90, U.S. tennis player.

Marc (märk), **Franz,** 1880–1916, German painter.

Mar•ceau (mär sō′), **Marcel,** born 1923, French mime.

Mar•cel (mär sel′), **1. Gabriel, 2.** 1887–1973, French philosopher, dramatist, and critic.

Mar•cel•li•nus (mär′sə lī′nəs), **Saint,** died A.D. 304, pope 296–304.

Mar•cel•lo (mäR chel′lô), **Benedetto,** 1686–1739, Italian composer.

Mar•cel•lus[1] (mär sel′əs), **Marcus Claudius,** 268?–208 B.C., Roman general and consul.

Mar•cel•lus[2] (mär sel′əs), **1. Marcellus I, Saint,** died A.D. 309, pope 308–309. **2. Marcellus II,** (*Marcello Cervini*) 1501–55, Italian ecclesiastic: pope 1555.

March (märch), **1. Francis Andrew,** 1825–1911, U.S. philologist and lexicographer. **2. Fredric** (*Frederick McIntyre Bickel*), 1897–1975, U.S. actor. **3. Peyton Conway,** 1864–1955, U.S. army officer (son of Francis Andrew March).

Mar•cian (mär′shən), A.D. 392?–457, emperor of the Eastern Roman Empire 450–457. Also called **Mar•ci•a•nus** (mär′shē ā′nəs).

Mar•ci•a•no (mär′sē ä′nō, -an′ō), **Rocky** (*Rocco Francis Marchegiano*), 1924–69, U.S. boxer: world heavyweight champion 1952–56.

Mar•cion (mär′shən, -shē ən, -sē ən), A.D. c100–c160, Christian Gnostic.

Mar•co•ni (mär kō′nē), **Guglielmo,** 1874–1937, Italian electrical engineer and inventor in the field of wireless telegraphy: Nobel prize for physics 1909.

Mar•co Po•lo (mär′kō pō′lō), POLO, Marco.

Mar•cos (mär′kōs), **Ferdinand E(dralin),** 1917–1989, Philippine politician: president 1965–86.

Mar•cus (mär′kəs), **Saint,** died A.D. 336, pope 336. Also called **Mark.**

Mar′cus Au•re′li•us (ô rē′lē əs, ô rēl′yəs), A.D. 121–180, Stoic philosopher: emperor of Rome 161–180. Also called **Mar′cus Aure′lius An•to•ni′nus** (an′tə nī′nəs).

Mar•cu•se (mär ko͞o′zə), **Herbert,** 1898–1979, U.S. political and social philosopher, born in Germany.

Mar′ga•ret of An′jou (mär′gə rit, -grit; an′jo͞o), 1430–82, queen of Henry VI of England.

Mar′garet of Na•varre′ (nə vär′), 1492–1549, queen of Navarre 1544–49 and author. Also called **Mar′garet of An•gou•lême′** (äng′go͞o lem′).

Mar′garet of Va•lois′ (val wä′), (*"Queen Margot"*)

1533–1615, 1st wife of Henry IV of France: queen of Navarre.

Mar′garet Rose′, born 1930, English princess (daughter of George VI; sister of Elizabeth II).

Mar•gre•the II (mär grā′tə), born 1940, queen of Denmark since 1972.

Ma•ri•a de Me•di•ci (*It.* mä rē′ä de me′dē chē). MARIE DE MÉDICIS.

Ma•ri•a Lu•i•sa (*Ger.* mä rē′ä lo͞o ē′sä). MARIE LOUISE.

Ma•ri•a The•re•sa (mə rē′ə tə rā′sə, -zə), 1717–80, archduchess of Austria; queen of Hungary and Bohemia 1740–80 (wife of Francis II).

Ma•rie (mə rē′), (*Marie Alexandra Victoria of Saxe-Coburg*) 1875–1938, queen of Romania 1914–27.

Marie′ An•toi•nette′ (an′twə net′, an′tə-), (*Josèphe Jeanne Marie Antoinette*) 1755–93, queen of France 1774–93: wife of Louis XVI (daughter of Maria Theresa).

Ma•rie de France (mA rē′ də fräns′), fl. 12th century, French poet in England.

Marie′ de Mé•di•cis′ (də mā′də sēs′, med′i chē), 1573–1642, queen of Henry IV of France: regent 1610–17.

Marie′ Lou•ise′ (lo͞o ēz′), 1791–1847, 2nd wife of Napoleon I: empress of France.

Ma•riette (mA Ryet′), **Auguste Édouard,** 1821–81, French Egyptologist.

Mar•in (mär′in), **John,** 1870–1953, U.S. painter and etcher.

Ma•ri•net•ti (mar′ə net′ē), **Emilio Filippo Tommaso,** 1876–1944, Italian poet.

Ma•ri•ni (mə rē′nē), **1. Giambattista.** Also, **Ma•ri′no.** (*"il Cavalier Marino"*) 1569–1625, Italian poet. **2. Marino,** 1901–80, Italian sculptor and painter.

Ma•ri•nus (mə ri′nəs), **1. Marinus I.** Also called **Martin II.** died A.D. 884, pope 882–884. **2. Marinus II.** Also called **Martin III.** died A.D. 946, pope 942–946.

Mar•i•on (mar′ē ən, mâr′-), **Francis,** (*"the Swamp Fox"*), 1732?–95, American Revolutionary general.

Mar•is (mar′is), **Roger (Eugene),** 1934–85, U.S. baseball player.

Mar•i•sol (mar′i sol′), (*Marisol Escubar*) born 1930, Venezuelan artist, in U.S. since 1950.

Ma•ri•tain (mar′i taN′), **Jacques,** 1882–1973, French philosopher.

Mar•i•us (mâr′ē əs, mar′-), **Gaius,** c155–86 B.C., Roman general and consul.

Ma•ri•vaux (mar′ə vō′), **Pierre Carlet de Chamblain de,** 1688–1763, French dramatist and novelist.

Mark (märk), one of the four Evangelists: traditionally believed to be the author of the second Gospel.

Mark An•to•ny (märk an′tə nē), ANTONY, Mark.

Mar•ke•vich (mär kā′vich), **Igor,** 1912–83, Russian conductor and composer.

Mark•ham (mär′kəm), **(Charles) Edwin,** 1852–1940, U.S. poet.

Mar•ko•va (mär kō′və), **Alicia,** (*Lilian Alicia Marks*), born 1910, English ballet dancer.

Marl•bor•ough (märl′bûr ō, -bur ō -brə, môl′-), **John Churchill, 1st Duke of,** CHURCHILL, John.

Mar•lowe (mär′lō), **1. Christopher,** 1564–93, English dramatist. **2. Julia** (*Sarah Frances Frost Sothern*), 1866–1950, U.S. actress born in England (wife of E. H. Sothern).

Mar•quand (mär kwond′), **J(ohn) P(hillips),** 1893–1960, U.S. novelist.

Mar•quette (mär ket′), **Jacques** (*"Père Marquette"*), 1637–75, French Jesuit missionary and explorer in America.

Mar•quis (mär′kwis), **Don(ald Robert Perry),** 1878–1937, U.S. humorist.

Mar•ry•at (mar′ē ət), **Frederick,** 1792–1848, English naval officer and novelist.

Mar•sal•is (mär sal′is), **Wynton,** born 1961, U.S. classical and jazz trumpeter.

Marsh (märsh), **1. Dame (Edith) Ngai•o** (nī′ō), 1899–1982, New Zealand writer of detective novels. **2. Reginald,** 1898–1954, U.S. painter and illustrator.

Mar•shall (mär′shəl), **1. Alfred,** 1842–1924, English economist. **2. George C(atlett),** 1880–1959, U.S. general and statesman: Nobel peace prize 1953. **3. John,** 1755–1835, Chief Justice of the U.S. 1801–35. **4. Thomas Riley,** 1854–1925, vice president of the U.S. 1913–21. **5. Thurgood,** born 1908, associate justice of the U.S. Supreme Court 1967–91.

Mar•sil′i•us of Pad′u•a (mär sil′ē əs; pad′yo͞o ə), c1280–1343?, Italian scholar and political theorist. Italian, **Mar•si•glio de•i Mai•nar•di•ni** (mär sē′lyô de′ē mī′när-dē′nē).

Mars•ton (mär′stən), **John,** c1575–1634, English dramatist and satirist.

Mar•tel (mär tel′), **Charles,** CHARLES MARTEL.

Mar•tí (mär tē′), **José,** 1853–95, Cuban patriot and writer.

Mar•tial (mär′shəl), (*Marcus Valerius Martialis*) A.D. 43?–104?, Roman epigrammatist, born in Spain.

Mar•tin[1] (mär′tn), **1. Archer John Porter,** born 1910, English biochemist: Nobel prize for chemistry 1952. **2. Glenn Luther,** 1886–1955, U.S. airplane designer and manufacturer. **3. Homer Dodge,** 1836–97, U.S. painter. **4. Mary,** 1913–91, U.S. actress and singer. **5. Saint,** A.D. 316?–397, French prelate: bishop of Tours 370?–397.

Mar•tin[2] (mär′tn), **1. Martin I, Saint,** died A.D. 655, Italian ecclesiastic: pope 649–655. **2. Martin IV,** (*Simon de Brie* or *Simon de Brion*) c1210–85, French ecclesiastic: pope 1281–85. **3. Martin V,** (*Oddone Colonna*) 1368–1431, Italian ecclesiastic: pope 1417–31.

Mar•tin du Gard (mar tan dy gar′), **Roger,** 1881–1958, French novelist: Nobel prize 1937.

Mar•ti•neau (mär′tn ō′), **1. Harriet,** 1802–76, English writer and economist. **2.** her brother, **James,** 1805–1900, English theologian.

Mar•ti•nel•li (mär′tn el′ē), **Giovanni,** 1885–1969, U.S. operatic tenor, born in Italy.

Mar•ti•ni (mär tē′nē), **Simone,** 1283–1344, Italian painter.

Mar•ti•non (MAR tē nôN′), **Jean** (zhäN), 1910–76, French composer.

Mar•tins (mär′tnz), **Peter,** born 1946, U.S. dancer, choreographer, and ballet master, born in Denmark.

Mar•tin•son (mär′tn sən), **Harry Edmund,** 1904–78, Swedish novelist and poet: Nobel prize 1974.

Mar•vell (mär′vəl), **Andrew,** 1621–78, English poet.

Marx (märks), **Karl (Heinrich),** 1818–83, German economist, philosopher, and socialist.

Marx′ Broth′ers, a family of U.S. comedians, including **Julius Henry** (*"Groucho"*), 1890–1977, **Arthur** (*Adolph Marx*) (*"Harpo"*), 1888–1964, **Leonard** (*"Chico"*), 1887–1961, and **Herbert** (*"Zeppo"*), 1901–79.

Mar•y[1] (mâr′ē), (*Princess Victoria Mary of Teck*) 1867–1953, Queen of England 1910–36 (wife of George V).

Mar•y[2] (mâr′ē), **1. Mary I,** (*Mary Tudor*) (*"Bloody Mary"*) 1516–58, queen of England 1553–58 (wife of Philip II of Spain; daughter of Henry VIII). **2. Mary II,** 1662–94, queen of England 1689–94: joint ruler with her husband William III (daughter of James II).

Mar′y, Queen′ of Scots′, (*Mary Stuart*) 1542–87, queen of Scotland 1542–67.

Ma•sac•cio (mə sä′chē ō′, -chō), (*Tommaso Guidi*) 1401–28?, Italian painter.

Ma•sa•ryk (mas′ə rik), **1. Jan** (yän), 1886–1948, Czech statesman (son of Tomáš). **2. To•máš Gar•rigue** (tô′mäsh gä′RIK), 1850–1937, 1st president of Czechoslovakia 1918–35.

Mas•ca•gni (mä skän′yē), **Pietro,** 1863–1945, Italian composer.

Mase•field (mās′fēld′, māz′-), **John,** 1878–1967, English poet: poet laureate 1930–67.

Mas•i•nis•sa or **Mas•si•nis•a** or **Mas•si•nis•sa** (mas′ə-nis′ə), 238–149 B.C., king of Numidia c210–149.

Ma•son (mā′sən), **1. Charles,** 1730–87, English astronomer and surveyor. **2. George,** 1725–92, American statesman. **3. Lowell,** 1792–1872, U.S. hymnist and educator.

Mas•pe•ro (mas pə rō′), **Sir Gaston Camille Charles,** 1846–1916, French Egyptologist.

Mas•sa•soit (mas′ə soit′), c1580–1661, North American Indian leader: negotiator of peace treaty with the Pilgrims 1621.

Mas•sé•na (mas ā nä′), **André, duc de Rivoli** and **Prince d'Essling,** 1758–1817, French marshal under Napoleon I.

Mas•se•net (mas′ə nā′), **Jules Émile Frédéric,** 1842–1912, French composer.

Mas•sey (mas′ē), **1. Vincent,** 1887–1967, Canadian

statesman: governor general 1952–59. **2. William Ferguson,** 1856–1925, New Zealand statesman, born in Ireland: prime minister 1912–25.

Mas•sine (mä sēn′), **Léonide,** 1896–1979, U.S. ballet dancer and choreographer, born in Russia.

Mas•sin•ger (mas′ən jər), **Philip,** 1583–1640, English dramatist.

Mas•si•nis•a or **Mas•si•nis•sa** (mas′ə nis′ə), MASINISSA.

Mas•sys (mä′sis) also **Matsys** or **Metsys, Quentin,** 1466?–1530, Flemish painter.

Mas•ters (mas′tərz, mä′stərz), **1. Edgar Lee,** 1869–1950, U.S. author. **2. William Howell,** born 1915, U.S. physician: researcher on human sexual behavior.

Mas•ter•son (mas′tər sən, mä′stər-), **William Barclay** (*"Bat"*), 1853–1921, U.S. frontier law officer.

Mas•tro•ian•ni (mä′strō yä′nē), **Marcello,** born 1924, Italian actor.

Ma•sur (mə zŏŏr′), **Kurt,** born 1927, German conductor.

Ma•ta Ha•ri (mä′tə här′ē, mat′ə har′ē), (*Gertrud Margarete Zelle*) 1876–1917, Dutch dancer in France: executed as a spy by the French.

Math•er (math′ər, math′-), **1. Cotton,** 1663–1728, American clergyman and author. **2.** his father, **Increase,** 1639–1723, American clergyman.

Math•ew•son (math′yōō sən), **Christopher** (*"Christy"*), 1880–1925, U.S. baseball player.

Ma•thi•as (mə thī′əs), **Robert Bruce** (*Bob*), born 1930, U.S. track-and-field athlete.

Ma•til•da (mə til′də), 1102–67, empress of the Holy Roman Empire 1114–25; queen of England 1141 (daughter of Henry I of England). Also called **Maud.**

Ma•tisse (mə tēs′, ma-), **Henri,** 1869–1954, French painter.

Mat•sys (mät′sis), **Quentin.** MASSYS, Quentin.

Mat•ta E•chaur•ren (mä′tə e chou′ren), **Roberto Antonio Sebastián,** born 1911, Chilean painter.

Mat•ta•thi•as (mat′ə thī′əs), died 167? B.C., Jewish priest in Judea (father of Judas Maccabaeus).

Mat•te•ot•ti (mat′ē ot′ē), **Giacomo,** 1885–1924, Italian socialist leader.

Mat•thew (math′yōō), *n.* one of the four Evangelists; one of the 12 apostles.

Mat•thews (math′yōōz), **1. (James) Brander,** 1852–1929, U.S. writer and educator. **2. Sir Stanley,** born 1915, British soccer player.

Mat•thi•as (mə thī′əs), **1.** a disciple chosen to take the place of Judas Iscariot as one of the apostles. **2.** 1557–1619, king of Hungary 1608–18; king of Bohemia 1611–17; emperor of the Holy Roman Empire 1612–19 (son of Maximilian II).

Maud (môd), MATILDA

Mauds•lay (môdz′lē), **Henry,** 1771–1831, English mechanical engineer.

Maugham (môm), **W(illiam) Somerset,** 1874–1965, English writer.

Maul•din (môl′dən), **William Henry** (*Bill*), born 1921, U.S. political cartoonist.

Mau•pas•sant (mō′pə sänt′, mō′pə säɴ′), **(Henri René Albert) Guy de** (gē də), 1850–93, French writer.

Mau•per•tuis (mō pᴇʀ twē′), **Pierre Louis Moreau de,** 1698–1759, French mathematician, astronomer, and biologist.

Mau•riac (mô ʀyäk′), **François,** 1885–1970, French novelist: Nobel prize 1952.

Mau•rice (môr′is, mor′-, mô rēs′), 1521–53, German general: elector of Saxony 1547–53. German, **Moritz.**

Mau′rice of Nas′sau (môr′is, mor′-, mô rēs′), 1567–1625, Dutch statesman.

Mau•rois (môr wä′), **André** (*Émile Salomon Wilhelm Herzog*), 1885–1967, French writer biographer and novelist.

Mau•ry (môr′ē, mor′ē), **Matthew Fontaine,** 1806–73, U.S. naval officer and scientist.

Mau•ser (mou′zər), **Peter Paul,** 1838–1914, and his brother, **Wilhelm,** 1834–82, German inventors of firearms.

Maw•son (mô′sən), **Sir Douglas,** 1882–1958, Australian antarctic explorer, born in England.

Max•im (mak′sim), **1. Hiram Percy,** 1869–1936, U.S. inventor. **2. Sir Hiram Stevens,** 1840–1916, English inventor, born in the U.S. **3.** his brother, **Hudson,** 1853–1927, U.S. inventor.

Max•i•mil•ian[1] (mak′sə mil′yən), 1832–67, archduke of Austria: emperor of Mexico 1864–67.

Max•i•mil•ian[2] (mak′sə mil′yən), **1. Maximilian I,** 1459–1519, emperor of the Holy Roman Empire 1493–1519. **2. Maximilian II,** 1527–76, emperor of the Holy Roman Empire 1564–76.

Max•well (maks′wel, -wəl), **1. Elsa,** 1883–1963, U.S. professional hostess and author. **2. James Clerk** (klärk), 1831–79, Scottish physicist.

Ma•ya•kov•ski or **Ma•ya•kov•sky** (mä′yə kôf′skē, -kof′-), **Vladimir Vladimirovich,** 1893–1930, Russian poet.

May•er (mī′ər *for 1, 3;* mā′ər *for 2),* **1. Julius Robert von,** 1814–78, German physicist. **2. Louis B(urt),** 1885–1957, U.S. motion-picture producer, born in Russia. **3. Maria Goeppert,** 1906–72, U.S. physicist, born in Poland: Nobel prize 1963.

May•hew (mā′hyo͞o), **1. Jonathan,** 1720–66, American Congregational clergyman. **2. Thomas,** 1593–1682, American colonist, born in England: settler and governor of Martha's Vineyard.

May•o (mā′ō), **Charles Horace,** 1865–1939, and his brother **William James,** 1861–1939, U.S. surgeons.

Mays (māz), **Willie (Howard),** born 1931, U.S. baseball player.

Maz·a·rin (maz′ə raɴ′, -rēn′), **Jules** (*Giulio Mazarini*), 1602–61, French cardinal and statesman, born in Italy.

Maz·zi·ni (mät sē′nē, mäd zē′-), **Giuseppe,** 1805–72, Italian patriot.

M'Ba (əm bä′), **Léon,** 1902–67, African statesman: president of Gabon 1961–67.

Mboy·a (əm boi′ə), **Tom** (*Thomas Joseph Mboya*), 1930–69, African political leader in Kenya.

Mc·A·doo (mak′ə do͞o′), **William Gibbs,** 1863–1941, U.S. lawyer and statesman: Secretary of the Treasury 1913–18.

Mc·Au·liffe (mə kô′lif), **Anthony Clement,** 1898–1975, U.S. Army general.

Mc·Car·thy (mə kär′thē), **1. Joseph R(aymond),** 1909–57, U.S. politician. **2. Joseph Vincent,** 1887–1978, U.S. baseball manager. **3. Mary (Therese),** 1912–89, U.S. novelist.

Mc·Clel·lan (mə klel′ən), **George Brinton,** 1826–85, Union general in the American Civil War.

Mc·Clos·key (mə klos′kē), **John,** 1810–85, U.S. Roman Catholic clergyman: first U.S. cardinal 1875.

Mc·Cloy (mə kloi′), **John Jay,** 1895–1989, U.S. lawyer, banker, and government official.

Mc·Clure (mə klo͝or′), **Samuel Sidney,** 1857–1949, U.S. editor and publisher, born in Ireland.

Mc·Cor·mack (mə kôr′mik), **1. John,** 1884–1945, U.S. tenor, born in Ireland. **2. John William,** 1891–1980, U.S. politician.

Mc·Cor·mick (mə kôr′mik), **1. Cyrus Hall,** 1809–84, U.S. inventor. **2. Robert Rutherford,** 1880–1955, U.S. newspaper publisher.

Mc·Crae (mə krā′), **John,** 1872–1918, Canadian physician, soldier, and poet.

Mc·Cul·lers (mə kul′ərz), **Carson,** 1917–67, U.S. author.

Mc·Don·ald (mək don′ld), **David John,** 1902–79, U.S. labor leader: president of the United Steelworkers of America 1952–65.

Mc·Doug·all (mək do͞o′gəl), **William,** 1871–1938, U.S. psychologist and writer, born in England.

Mc·Dow·ell (mək dou′əl), **Ephraim,** 1771–1830, U.S. surgeon.

Mc·Fee (mək fē′), **William,** 1881–1966, English writer.

Mc·Gov·ern (mə guv′ərn), **George (Stanley),** born 1922, U.S. politician: Democratic presidential candidate 1972, senator 1963–81.

Mc·Graw (mə grô′), **John Joseph,** 1873–1934, U.S. baseball player and manager.

Mc·Guf·fey (mə guf′ē), **William Holmes,** 1800–73, U.S. educator.

Mc·In·tire (mak′in tīᵊr′), **Samuel,** 1757–1811, U.S. architect and woodcarver.

Mc·In·tyre (mak′in tīᵊr′), **James Francis Aloysius,** 1886–1979, U.S. Roman Catholic clergyman: cardinal from 1953; archbishop of Los Angeles 1948–70.

Mc•Ken•na (mə ken′ə), **Sio•bhan** (shə vôn′, -von′), 1923–86, Irish actress.

Mc•Ken•zie (mə ken′zē), **Robert Tait** (tāt), 1867–1938, Canadian physician, educator, and sculptor.

Mc•Kim (mə kim′), **Charles Follen,** 1847–1909, U.S. architect.

Mc•Kin•ley (mə kin′lē), **William,** 1843–1901, 25th president of the U.S. 1897–1901.

Mc•Kis•sick (mə kis′ik), **Floyd Bixler,** 1922–91, U.S. lawyer and civil-rights leader: chairman of Congress of Racial Equality 1963–66, director 1966–68.

Mc•Lar•en (mə klar′ən), **Norman,** 1914–87, Canadian film director and animator, born in Scotland.

Mc•Lu•han (mə klo͞o′ən), **Marshall,** 1911–80, Canadian cultural historian and mass-communications theorist.

Mc•Mas•ter (mək mas′tər, -mä′stər), **John Bach,** 1852–1932, U.S. historian and educator.

Mc•Mil•lan (mək mil′ən), **Edwin Mattison,** 1907–91, U.S. physicist: Nobel prize for chemistry 1951.

Mc•mur•ty (mək mûr′tē), **Larry Jeff,** born 1936, U.S. novelist.

Mc•Nair (mək nâr′), **Lesley James,** 1883–1944, U.S. army officer.

Mc•Na•ma•ra (mak′nə mar′ə), **Robert Strange,** born 1916, U.S. business executive and government official.

Mc•Naugh•ton (mək nôt′n), **Andrew George Latta,** 1887–1966, Canadian army officer, statesman, diplomat, and scientist.

Mc•Nutt (mək nut′), **Paul Vo•ries** (vôr′ēz, vōr′-), 1891–1955, U.S. diplomat and government official.

Mc•Part•land (mək pärt′lənd), **Marian,** born 1920, British jazz pianist and composer, in the U.S. since 1946.

Mc•Pher•son (mək fûr′sən, -fēr′-), **Aimee Semple,** 1890–1944, U.S. evangelist, born in Canada.

Mc•Rey•nolds (mək ren′ldz), **James Clark,** 1862–1946, U.S. jurist: associate justice of the U.S. Supreme Court 1914–41.

Mead (mēd), **Margaret,** 1901–78, U.S. anthropologist.

Meade (mēd), **1. George Gordon,** 1815–72, Union general in the American Civil War. **2. James Edward,** born 1907, British economist: Nobel prize 1977.

Mean•y (mē′nē), **George,** 1894–1980, U.S. labor leader.

Med•a•war (med′ə wər), **Peter Brian,** born 1915, English zoologist and anatomist, born in Brazil: Nobel prize for medicine 1960.

Med•i•ci (med′i chē), **1. Catherine de′,** Catherine de Médicis. **2. Cosmo** or **Cosimo de′** (*"the Elder"*), 1389–1464, Italian banker and statesman. **3. Cosmo** or **Cosimo de′** (*"the Great"*), 1519–74, first grand duke of Tuscany. **4. Giovanni de′,** Leo X. **5. Giulio de′,** Clement VII. **6. Lorenzo de′** (*"the Magnificent"*), 1449–92, ruler of Florence 1478–92. **7. Maria de′,** Marie de Médicis.

Me•dill (mə dil′), **Joseph,** 1823–99, U.S. journalist.

Meh•ta (mā′tə), **Zubin,** born 1936, Indian orchestra conductor, in the U.S. since 1961.

Mé•hul (mā YL′), **Étienne Nicolas** or **Étienne Henri,** 1763–1817, French composer.

Meigh•en (mē′ən), **Arthur,** 1874–1960, Canadian statesman: prime minister 1920–21, 1926.

Meil•hac (me YAK′), **Henri,** 1831–97, French dramatist: collaborator with Ludovic Halévy.

Meil•let (me yā′), **Antoine,** 1866–1936, French linguist.

Mei•nong (mī′nông), **Alexius,** 1853–1920, Austrian psychologist and philosopher.

Me•ir (mā ēr′, mī′ər), **Golda** (*Goldie Mabovitch, Goldie Myerson*), 1898–1978, prime minister of Israel 1969–74, born in Russia.

Meis•so•nier (mes′ən yā′, mā′sən-), **Jean Louis Ernest** (zhäN), 1815–91, French painter.

Meit•ner (mīt′nər), **Lise,** 1878–1968, Austrian nuclear physicist.

Me•lanch•thon (mə langk′thən), **Philipp** (*Philipp Schwarzert*), 1497–1560, German Protestant reformer.

Mel•ba (mel′bə), **(Dame) Nellie** (*Helen Porter Mitchell Armstrong*), 1861–1931, Australian soprano.

Mel•bourne (mel′bərn), **2nd Viscount,** LAMB, William.

Mel•chers (mel′chərz), **Gari,** 1860–1932, U.S. painter.

Mel•chi•a•des (mel kī′ə dēz′), **Saint,** died A.D. 314, pope 310–314. Also called **Miltiades.**

Mel•chior (mel′kyôr, -kē ôr′), **Lauritz (Lebrecht Hommel),** 1890–1973, U.S. tenor, born in Denmark.

Mel•e•a•ger (mel′ē ā′jər), fl. 1st century B.C., Greek epigrammatist.

Mé•liès (mā lyes′), **Georges** (zhôRzh), 1861–1938, French film director.

Mel•lers (mel′ərz), **Wilfrid Howard,** born 1914, English musicologist and composer.

Mel•lon (mel′ən), **Andrew William,** 1855–1937, U.S. financier.

Mel•ville (mel′vil), **Herman,** 1819–91, U.S. novelist.

Mem•ling (mem′ling) also **Mem•linc** (-lingk), **Hans,** c1430–94?, German painter of the Flemish school.

Me•nan•der (mə nan′dər), 342?–291 B.C., Greek writer of comedies.

Men•ci•us (men′shē əs), c380–289 B.C., Chinese philosopher. Also called **Mengtzu.**

Menck•en (meng′kən), **H(enry) L(ouis),** 1880–1956, U.S. editor and critic.

Men•del (men′dl), **Gregor Johann,** 1822–84, Austrian monk and botanist.

Men•de•le•ev or **Men•de•ley•ev** (men′dl ā′əf, -ā′yef), **Dmitri Ivanovich,** 1834–1907, Russian chemist.

Men•del•sohn (men′dl sən), **Erich,** 1887–1953, German architect in England and in the U.S.

Men•dels•sohn (men′dl sən), **1. Felix** (*Jacob Ludwig Fe-*

lix Mendelssohn-Bartholdy), 1809–47, German composer. **2.** his grandfather, **Moses,** 1729–86, German philosopher.

Men•de•res (men′de res′), **Adnan,** 1899–1961, Turkish political leader: premier 1950–60.

Men•dès-France (men′dis fräns′; *Fr.* mäN des fRäNs′), **Pierre,** 1907–82, French statesman and economist: premier 1954–55.

Men•do•za (men dō′zə), **Pedro de,** 1487–1537, Spanish soldier and explorer: founder of the first colony of Buenos Aires 1536?.

Men•e•lik II (men′l ik), 1844–1913, emperor of Ethiopia 1889–1913.

Me•nem (men′əm), **Carlos Saul,** born 1932, Argentine political leader: president since 1989.

Me•nén•dez de A•vi•lés (me nen′des dā ä′vē lās′), **Pedro,** Spanish admiral and colonizer: founder of St. Augustine, Florida 1565.

Me•ne•ptah (men′ep tä′, mə nep′tə), MERNEPTAH.

Me•nes (mē′nēz), fl. c3200 B.C., traditionally the first king of Egypt and founder of the first dynasty.

Meng•er (meng′ər), **Karl,** 1840–1921, Austrian economist.

Men•gis•tu Hai•le Ma•ri•am (meng gis′tōō hī′lē mär′ē-əm), born 1937, head of state of Ethiopia 1977–87; president 1987–91.

Meng•tzu (mung′dzu′), MENCIUS.

Men•ning•er (men′ing ər), **Karl Augustus,** 1893–1990, U.S. psychiatrist.

Me•not•ti (mə not′ē), **Gian Carlo** (jän), born 1911, U.S. composer, born in Italy.

Men•u•hin (men′yōō in), **Ye•hu•di** (ye hōō′dē), born 1916, U.S. violinist.

Men•zies (men′zēz), **Sir Robert Gordon,** 1894–1978, prime minister of Australia 1939–41 and 1949–66.

Mer•ca•tor (mər kā′tər), **Gerhardus** (*Gerhard Kremer*), 1512–94, Flemish cartographer and geographer.

Mer•cer (mûr′sər), **Johnny,** 1909–76, U.S. songwriter.

Mer•cier (mer syā′), **Désiré Joseph,** 1851–1926, Belgian cardinal and patriot.

Mer•e•dith (mer′i dith), **1. George,** 1828–1909, English novelist and poet. **2. Owen,** pen name of Edward Robert Bulwer LYTTON.

Mer•gen•tha•ler (mûr′gən thô′lər), **Ottmar,** 1854–99, U.S. inventor of the Linotype, born in Germany.

Mé•ri•mée (mā′rē mā′, mer′ə mā′), **Prosper,** 1803–70, French writer.

Mer•man (mûr′mən), **Ethel** (*Ethel Zimmerman*), 1909–84, U.S. singer and actress.

Mer•nep•tah (mer′nep tä′, mər nep′tə) also **Meneptah,** king of ancient Egypt c1225–c1215 B.C. (son of Ramses II).

Mer•rick (mer′ik), **David** (*David Margulies*), born 1912, U.S. theatrical producer.

Mer•rill (mer′əl), **Robert** (*Robert Miller*), born 1919, U.S. baritone.

Mer•senne (mər sen′), **Marin,** 1588–1648, French mathematician.

Mer•ton (mûr′tn), **1. Robert King,** born 1910, U.S. sociologist. **2. Thomas,** 1915–68, U.S. poet and religious writer, born in France.

Mes•mer (mez′mər, mes′-), **Franz** or **Friedrich Anton,** 1733–1815, Austrian physician.

Mes•sa•li•na (mes′ə lī′nə, -lē′-), **Valeria,** died A.D. 48, third wife of Claudius I.

Mes•siaen (mes yäɴ′), **Olivier Eugène Prosper Charles,** born 1908, French composer.

Mes•sier (mes′ē ā′), **Charles,** 1730–1817, French astronomer.

Met•a•com•et (met′ə kom′it), PHILIP[1], King.

Me•ta•sta•sio (me′tä stä′zyô), (*Pietro Antonio Domenico Bonaventura Trapassi*) 1698–1782, Italian poet and dramatist.

Me•tax•as (mə tak′səs), **Joannes,** 1871–1941, Greek general and dictator 1936–40.

Metch•ni•koff (mech′ni kôf′, -kof′), **Élie** (*Ilya Ilyich Mechnikov*), 1845–1916, Russian zoologist and bacteriologist in France: Nobel prize for medicine 1908.

Me•tho•di•us (mə thō′dē əs), **Saint** (*Apostle of the Slavs*), A.D. c825–885, Greek missionary in Moravia (brother of Saint Cyril).

Met•sys (met′sis), **Quentin,** MASSYS, Quentin.

Met•ter•nich (met′ər nɪᴋʜ, -nik), **Prince Klemens Wenzel Nepomuk Lothar von,** 1773–1859, Austrian statesman and diplomat.

Mey•er (mī′ər), **1. Adolf,** 1866–1950, U.S. psychiatrist, born in Switzerland. **2. Albert (Gregory),** 1903–65, U.S. Roman Catholic clergyman. **3. Julius Lothar,** 1830–95, German chemist.

Mey•er•beer (mī′ər bēr′, -bâr′), **Giacomo** (*Jakob Liebmann Beer*), 1791–1864, German composer.

Mey•er•hof (mī′ər hof′, -hōf′), **Otto,** 1884–1951, German physiologist: Nobel prize for medicine 1922.

Meyn•ell (men′l), **Alice Christiana (Thompson),** 1850–1922, English poet and essayist.

Mi•an•to•no•mo (mī an′tə nō′mō, mē-), died 1643, leader of the Narragansetts.

Mi•chael (mī′kəl), born 1921, king of Romania 1927–30, 1940–47 (son of Carol II). Romanian, **Mi•hai** (mē hī′).

Michael VIII Pa•lae•ol•o•gus (pā′lē ol′ə gəs, pal′ē-), 1234–1282, Byzantine ruler 1259–82, first of the Palaeologus emperors.

Mi•chaux (mē shō′), **Henri,** 1899–1984, French poet and painter, born in Belgium.

Mi•chel•an•ge•lo (mī′kəl an′jə lō′, mik′əl-), (*Michelangelo Buonarroti*), 1475–1564, Italian artist, architect, and poet.

Mi•che•let (mēshᵊ lā′), **Jules,** 1798–1874, French historian.

Mi•chel•son (mī′kəl sən), **Albert Abraham,** 1852–1931, U.S. physicist, born in Prussia (now Poland): Nobel prize 1907.

Mich•e•ner (mich′ə nər, mich′nər), **1. (Daniel) Roland,** 1900–91, Canadian public official and diplomat: governor general 1967–74. **2. James A(lbert),** born 1907, U.S. novelist.

Mic•kie•wicz (mits kyā′vich), **Adam,** 1798–1855, Polish poet.

Mid•dle•ton (mid′l tən), **Thomas,** c1570–1627, English dramatist.

Mid•ler (mid′lər), **Bette** (bet), born 1945, U.S. singer and actress.

Mi•do•ri (mi dôr′ē), born 1971, U.S. violinist, born in Japan.

Miel•zi•ner (mēl zē′nər, mel-), **Jo,** 1901–76, U.S. stage designer, born in France.

Mies van der Ro•he (mēz′ van dər rō′ə, fän, mēs′), **Ludwig,** 1886–1969, U.S. architect, born in Germany.

Miff•lin (mif′lin), **Thomas,** 1744–1800, American politician and Revolutionary general: president of the Continental Congress 1783–84; governor of Pennsylvania 1790–99.

Mi•fu•ne (mi fo͞o′nē), **Toshiro,** born 1920, Japanese film actor, born in China.

Mi•khai•lo•vitch or **Mi•hai•lo•vić** (mi hī′lə vich), **Draja** or **Draža,** 1893–1946, Yugoslav military leader.

Mi•ko•yan (mē′kô yän′), **Anastas Ivanovich,** 1895–1978, Soviet official, born in Armenia: president of the Soviet Union 1964–65.

Mi•la•nov (mil′ə nôf′, -nof′), **Zinka** (*Zinka Kunc*), 1906–89, Yugoslavian soprano, in the U.S.

Miles (mīlz), **Nelson Appleton,** 1839–1925, U.S. army officer.

Mi•lhaud (mē yō′, mē ō′), **Darius,** 1892–1974, French composer, in U.S. from 1940.

Mill (mil), **1. James,** 1773–1836, English philosopher, historian, and economist, born in Scotland. **2.** his son **John Stuart,** 1806–73, English philosopher and economist.

Mil•lais (mi lā′), **Sir John Everett,** 1829–96, English painter.

Mil•lay (mi lā′), **Edna St. Vincent,** 1892–1950, U.S. poet.

Mil•ler (mil′ər), **1. Arthur,** born 1915, U.S. playwright. **2. Glenn,** 1904–44, U.S. bandleader. **3. Henry,** 1891–1980, U.S. novelist. **4. Joaquin** (*Cincinnatus Heine Miller*), 1841–1913, U.S. poet. **5. Joe** (*Joseph* or *Josias Miller*), 1684–1738, English actor, after whom *Joe Miller's Jestbook* was named. **6. William,** 1782–1849, U.S. religious leader: founder of the Adventist Church.

Mille•rand (mēl RÄN′), **Alexandre,** 1859–1943, president of France 1920–24.

Mil•les (mil′əs), **Carl** (*Carl Wilhelm Emil Anderson*), 1875–1955, U.S. sculptor, born in Sweden.

Mil•let (mi lā′), **1. Francis Davis,** 1846–1912, U.S. painter, illustrator, and journalist. **2. Jean François** (zhäN), 1814–75, French painter.

Mil•li•kan (mil′i kən), **Robert Andrews,** 1868–1953, U.S. physicist: Nobel prize 1923.

Mills (milz), **Robert,** 1781–1855, U.S. architect and engineer.

Milne (miln), **A(lan) A(lexander),** 1882–1956, English writer.

Milne-Ed•wards (miln′ed′wərdz), **Henri,** 1800–85, French zoologist.

Mil•ner (mil′nər), **Alfred,** 1st Viscount, 1854–1925, British statesman and colonial administrator.

Milnes (milnz), **Sherrill,** born 1935, U.S. baritone.

Mi•losz (mē′losh, -lôsh), **Czeslaw,** born 1911, U.S. poet and novelist, born in Poland: Nobel prize 1980.

Mil•ti•a•des (mil ti′ə dēz′), **1.** c540–488? B.C., Athenian general. **2.** MELCHIADES.

Mil•ton (mil′tn), **John,** 1608–74, English poet.

Mi•lyu•kov (mil′yə kôf′, -kof′), **Pavel Nikolaevich,** 1859–1943, Russian statesman and historian.

Mind•szen•ty (mind′sen tē), **Joseph** (*Joseph Pehm*), 1892–1975, Hungarian Roman Catholic clergyman: primate of Hungary 1945–74.

Min•gus (ming′gəs), **Charles** (*Charlie*), 1922–79, U.S. jazz bass player and composer.

Min•kow•ski (ming kôf′skē, -kof′-), **Hermann,** 1864–1909, German mathematician.

Min•nel•li (mi nel′ē), **Liza,** born 1946, U.S. singer and actress (daughter of Judy Garland).

Mi•not (mi′nət), **George Richards,** 1885–1950, U.S. physician: Nobel prize 1934.

Min•to (min′tō), **Gilbert John Elliot-Murray-Kynynmond, 4th Earl of,** 1845–1914, British colonial administrator: governor general of Canada 1898–1904; viceroy of India 1905–10.

Mi•nu•ci•us Fe•lix (mi no͞o′shē əs fē′liks, -shəs, -nyo͞o′-), **Marcus,** Roman writer of the 2nd century A.D. whose dialogue *Octavius* is the earliest known work of Latin-Christian literature.

Min•u•it (min′yo͞o it), **Peter,** 1580–1638, Dutch colonial administrator in America 1626–31.

Mi•ra•beau (mir′ə bō′), **Honoré Gabriel Victor Riqueti, Count de,** 1749–91, French Revolutionary statesman and orator.

Mi•ran•da (mi ran′də), **Francisco de,** 1750–1816, Venezuelan revolutionist and patriot.

Mi•ró (mē rō′), **1. Gabriel,** 1879–1930, Spanish novelist, short-story writer, and essayist. **2. Jo•an** (zho͞o än′, hwän), 1893–1983, Spanish painter.

Mi•shi•ma (mi shē′mə, mē′shē mä′), **Yukio** (*Kimitake Hiraoka*), 1925–70, Japanese writer.

Mis•tral (mē stral′, -sträl′), **1. Frédéric,** 1830–1914, French Provençal poet: Nobel prize 1904. **2. Gabriela** (*Lu-*

cila Godoy Alcayaga), 1889–1957, Chilean poet and educator: Nobel prize for literature 1945.

Mitch•ell (mich′əl), **1. Arthur,** born 1934, U.S. ballet dancer, choreographer, and ballet company director. **2. John,** 1870–1919, U.S. labor leader. **3. Margaret,** 1900–49, U.S. novelist. **4. Maria,** 1818–89, U.S. astronomer. **5. Silas Weir** (wēr), 1829–1914, U.S. physician and novelist. **6. William,** 1879–1936, U.S. general: pioneer in the field of aviation.

Mit•ford (mit′fərd), **Mary Russell,** 1787–1855, English novelist, poet, playwright, and essayist.

Mith•ri•da•tes VI (mith′ri dā′tēz), (*"the Great"*) 132?–63 B.C., king of Pontus 120–63.

Mi•tro•pou•los (mi trop′ə ləs), **Dimitri,** 1897–1960, Greek symphony orchestra conductor in the U.S.

Mit•ter•rand (mē′tə rän′, mē′tə räɴ′, -rand′), **François (Maurice Marie),** born 1916, president of France since 1981.

Mö•bi•us or **Moe•bi•us** (mœ′bē əs, mā′-, mō′-), **August Ferdinand,** 1790–1868, German mathematician.

Mo•bu•tu Se•se Se•ko (mō bo͞o′to͞o ses′ā sek′ō, mə-), (*Joseph-Désiré Mobutu*), born 1930, president of Zaire since 1965.

Moc•te•zu•ma (*Sp.* môk′te so͞o′mä), MONTEZUMA II.

Mo•der•sohn-Beck•er (mō′dər zōn bek′ər), **Paula,** 1876–1907, German painter.

Mo•di•glia•ni (mō dē′lē ä′nē, mō′dēl yä′-), **Amedeo,** 1884–1920, Italian painter in France.

Mof•fo (mof′ō), **Anna,** born 1932, U.S. soprano.

Mo•ham•med (mo͝o ham′id, -hä′mid, mō-), MUHAMMAD (def. 1).

Mohammed II, (*"the Conqueror"*) 1430–81, sultan of Turkey 1451–81: conqueror of Constantinople 1453.

Moham′med Za•hir′ Shah′ (zä hēr′), born 1914, king of Afghanistan 1933–73.

Mo•holy-Nagy (mə hō′lē noj′), **László** or **Ladislaus,** 1895–1946, Hungarian painter, designer, and photographer, in the U.S. after 1936.

Moi•se•i•vich or **Moi•se•i•witsch** (moi sā′i vich), **Benno,** 1890–1963, English pianist, born in Russia.

Moi•se•yev (moi sā′yev, -yəf), **Igor Alexandrovich,** born 1906, Russian dancer and choreographer.

Mois•san (mwᴀ säɴ′), **Henri,** 1852–1907, French chemist: Nobel prize 1906.

Mo•lière (mōl yâr′), (*Jean Baptiste Poquelin*) 1622–73, French playwright.

Mo•li•na (mō lē′nə, mə-), **Tirso de,** TIRSO DE MOLINA.

Mo•li•nos (mə lē′nōs), **Miguel de,** c1640–c95, Spanish priest and mystic: chief exponent of quietism.

Mol•let (mō lā′), **Guy,** 1905–75, French political leader.

Mol•nár (mōl′när), **Fe•renc** (fer′ənts), 1878–1952, Hungarian playwright, novelist, and short-story writer.

Mo•lo•tov (mol′ə tôf′, -tof′, mō′lə-), **Vyacheslav**

Mikhailovich (*Vyacheslav Mikhailovich Skryabin*), 1890–1986, Russian statesman: commissar of foreign affairs 1939–49, 1953–56.

Molt•ke (môlt′kə), **1. Helmuth Karl,** 1800–91, Prussian field marshal. **2.** his nephew, **Helmuth Johannes, Count von,** 1848–1916, German general.

Momm•sen (mom′sən), **Theodor,** 1817–1903, German classical historian: Nobel prize for literature 1902.

Monck or **Monk** (mungk), **George** (*1st Duke of Albemarle and Earl of Torrington*), 1608–70, English general.

Mon•dale (mon′dāl′), **Walter Frederick** (*"Fritz"*), born 1928, U.S. vice president 1977–81.

Mon•dri•an (môn′drē än′, mon′-), **Piet** (*Pieter Cornelis Mondriaan*), 1872–1944, Dutch painter.

Mo•net (mō nā′), **Claude,** 1840–1926, French painter.

Mo•ne•ta (mō nā′tə; *It.* mô ne′tä), **Ernesto Teodoro,** 1833–1918, Italian journalist: Nobel peace prize 1907.

Mo•niz (mô nēsh′), **Antonio Caetano de Abreu Freire Egas,** 1874–1955, Portuguese neurosurgeon: Nobel prize 1949.

Monk (mungk), **1. Thelonious (Sphere),** 1917–1982, U.S. jazz pianist and composer. **2. George,** MONCK, George.

Mon•mouth (mon′məth), **James Scott, Duke of,** 1649–85, illegitimate son of Charles II of England and pretender to the throne of James II.

Mon•net (mō nā′; *Fr.* mô ne′), **Jean** (zhäN), 1888–1979, French economist: originator of the European Common Market.

Mo•nod (mô nō′), **Jacques,** 1910–76, French chemist: Nobel prize 1965.

Mon•roe (mən rō′), **1. James,** 1758–1831, 5th president of the U.S. 1817–25. **2. Marilyn** (*Norma Jean Baker* or *Mortenson*), 1926–62, U.S. film actress.

Mon•sar•rat (mon′sə rat′), **Nicholas,** 1910–79, English novelist in Canada.

Mon•ta•gu (mon′tə gyōō′), **1. Ashley** (*Montague Francis Ashley Montagu*), born 1905, U.S. anthropologist and writer, born in England. **2. Charles, 1st Earl of Halifax,** 1661–1715, British statesman: prime minister 1714–15. **3. Lady Mary Wortley** (*Mary Pierrepont*), 1689–1762, English author.

Mon•ta•gue (mon′tə gyōō′), **William Pepperell,** 1873–1953, U.S. philosopher.

Mon•taigne (mon tān′; *Fr.* môN ten′yᵊ), **Michel Eyquem, Seigneur de,** 1533–92, French essayist.

Mon•ta•le (môn tä′le), **Eugenio,** 1896–1981, Italian poet: Nobel prize 1975.

Mon•tal•vo (môn täl′vō), **Garci Ordóñez de,** 15th-century Spanish writer.

Mont•calm (mont käm′, môN-), **Louis Joseph,** 1712–59, French general in Canada.

Mon•tes•quieu (mon′tə skyōō′; *Fr.* môN tes kyœ′), (*Charles Louis de Secondat, Baron de la Brède et de Montesquieu*) 1689–1755, French philosophical writer.

Mon•tes•so•ri (mon′tə sôr′ē, -sōr′ē), **Maria,** 1870–1952, Italian educator.

Mon•teux (mon tœ′, môɴ-), **Pierre,** 1875–1964, U.S. symphony orchestra conductor born in France.

Mon•te•ver•di (mon′tə vâr′dē), **Claudio,** 1567–1643, Italian composer.

Mon•tez (mon′tez, mon tez′), **Lola** (*Marie Dolores Eliza Rosanna Gilbert*), 1818?–61, British dancer, born in Ireland: gained notoriety as mistress of Franz Liszt, Alexandre Dumas *père,* and Louis I of Bavaria (1786–1868).

Mon•te•zu•ma II (mon′tə zo͞o′mə) also **Moctezuma,** c1470–1520, last Aztec emperor of Mexico 1502–20.

Mont•fort (mont′fərt; *Fr.* môɴ fôʀ′), **1. Simon de,** c1160–1218, French leader of the crusade against the Albigenses. **2.** his son **Simon de, Earl of Leicester,** 1208?–65, English soldier and statesman.

Mont•gol•fi•er (mont gol′fē ər; *Fr.* môɴ gôl fyā′), **Jacques Étienne,** 1745–99, and his brother **Joseph Michel,** 1740–1810, French aeronauts: inventors of the first practical balloon 1783.

Mont•gom•er•y (mont gum′ə rē, -gum′rē), **1. Bernard Law, 1st Viscount Montgomery of Alamein** (*"Monty"*), 1887–1976, British field marshal. **2. Richard,** 1736–75, American Revolutionary general.

Mon•ther•lant (môɴ teʀ läɴ′), **Henry de,** 1896–1972, French author.

Mont•mo•ren•cy (mont′mə ren′sē; *Fr.* môɴ mô ʀäɴ sē′), **Anne, Duc de,** 1493–1567, French marshal: constable of France 1537.

Moo•dy (mo͞o′dē), **1. Dwight Lyman,** 1837–99, U.S. evangelist. **2. Helen Wills,** Wills, Helen Newington. **3. William Vaughn** (vôn), 1869–1910, U.S. poet and playwright.

Moon (mo͞on), **Sun Myung,** born 1920, Korean religious leader: founder of the Unification Church.

Moore (mo͝or, môr, mōr), **1. Archibald Lee** (*Archie*), born 1916?, U.S. boxer. **2. Clement Clarke,** 1779–1863, U.S. scholar and writer. **3. Douglas Stuart,** 1893–1969, U.S. composer. **4. George,** 1852–1933, Irish writer. **5. G(eorge) E(dward),** 1873–1958, English philosopher. **6. Henry,** 1898–1986, English sculptor. **7. Marianne (Craig),** 1887–1972, U.S. poet and critic. **8. Stanford,** 1913–82, U.S. biochemist: Nobel prize for chemistry 1972. **9. Thomas,** 1779–1852, Irish poet.

Mo•ran (mə ran′), **Thomas,** 1837–1926, U.S. landscape painter, born in England.

Mo•ra•vi•a (mô rä′vē ə, -rä′-, mō-), **Alberto** (*Alberto Pincherle*), 1907–90, Italian writer.

More (môr, mōr), **1. Hannah,** 1745–1833, English writer on religious subjects. **2. Paul Elmer,** 1864–1937, U.S. essayist, critic, and editor. **3. Sir Thomas,** 1478–1535, English statesman and author: canonized in 1935.

Mo•reau (mô rō′), **1. Gustave,** 1826–98, French painter.

2. **Jeanne** (zhän), born 1928, French film actress. 3. **Jean Victor** (zhäɴɴ), 1763–1813, French general.

Mo•rel (mô rel′), **Jean** (zhäɴ), 1903–75, French orchestra conductor.

Mo•re•los y Pa•vón (mô rā′lôs ē pä vôn′), **José María,** 1765–1815, Mexican priest and revolutionary leader.

Mor•ga•gni (môr gan′yē), **Giovanni Battista,** 1682–1771, Italian anatomist.

Mor•gan (môr′gən), 1. **Charles Langbridge,** 1894–1958, English novelist and critic. 2. **Daniel,** 1736–1802, American Revolutionary general. 3. **Sir Henry,** 1635?–88, Welsh buccaneer in the Americas. 4. **John Hunt,** 1826–64, Confederate general. 5. **J(ohn) P(ierpont),** 1837–1913, U.S. financier and philanthropist. 6. his son **John Pierpont,** 1867–1943, U.S. financier. 7. **Lewis Henry,** 1818–81, U.S. ethnologist and anthropologist. 8. **Thomas Hunt,** 1866–1945, U.S. zoologist: Nobel prize for medicine 1933.

Mor•gen•thau (môr′gən thô′), 1. **Henry,** 1856–1946, U.S. financier and diplomat, born in Germany. 2. **Henry, Jr.,** 1891–1967, U.S. statesman: Secretary of the Treasury 1934–45.

Mo•ri•ni (mô rē′nē), **Erika,** born 1906, U.S. violinist, born in Austria.

Mor•i•son (môr′ə sən, mor′-), **Samuel Eliot,** 1887–1976, U.S. historian.

Mo•ri•sot (mô ʀē zō′), **Berthe** (beʀt), 1841–95, French painter.

Mor•ley (môr′lē), 1. **Christopher Darlington,** 1890–1957, U.S. writer. 2. **Edward Williams,** 1838–1923, U.S. chemist and physicist. 3. **John, Viscount Morley of Blackburn,** 1838–1923, English statesman, journalist, biographer, and critic. 4. **Thomas,** 1557–1603?, English composer.

Mor•nay (môr nā′), **Philippe de** (*"Pope of the Huguenots"*), 1549–1623, French statesman and Protestant leader. Also called **Duplessis-Mornay.**

Mo•ro (môr′ō, mor′ō), **Aldo,** 1916–78, Italian author and statesman: prime minister 1963–68, 1974–76.

Mor•phy (môr′fē), **Paul Charles,** 1837–84, U.S. chess player.

Mor•ris (môr′is, mor′-), 1. **Gouverneur,** 1752–1816, U.S. statesman. 2. **Robert,** 1734–1806, U.S. financier and statesman, born in England. 3. **William,** 1834–96, English artist, poet, and socialist writer.

Mor•ri•son (môr′ə sən, mor′-), **Toni,** born 1931, U.S. novelist.

Morse (môrs), **Samuel F(inley) B(reese),** 1791–1872, U.S. artist and developer of the telegraph.

Mor•ton (môr′tn), 1. **Jelly Roll** (*Ferdinand Morton*), 1885–1941, U.S. jazz pianist and composer. 2. **Levi Parsons,** 1824–1920, vice president of the U.S. 1889–93; governor of New York 1895–96. 3. **William Thomas Green,**

1819–68, U.S. dentist: first to demonstrate the use of ether as an anesthetic.

Mos•by (mōz′bē), **John Singleton,** 1833–1916, Confederate cavalry colonel.

Mose•ley (mōz′lē), **Henry Gwyn Jeffreys,** 1887–1915, English physicist: pioneer in x-ray spectroscopy.

Mo•ses[1] (mō′ziz, -zis), the Hebrew prophet who led the Israelites out of Egypt and delivered the Law during their years of wandering in the wilderness.

Mo•ses[2] (mō′ziz, -zis), **1. Anna Mary Robertson** (*"Grandma Moses"*), 1860–1961, U.S. painter. **2. Robert,** 1888–1981, U.S. public official: New York City Commissioner of Parks 1934–60.

Mo•shoe•shoe II (mō shwā′shwā), (*Constantine Bereng Seeiso*) born 1938, king of Lesotho 1966–90.

Mos•sa•degh (mō′sä dek′), **Mohammed,** 1880–1967, Iranian statesman: premier 1951–53.

Möss•bau•er (môs′bou ər, mos′-), **Rudolf L.,** born 1929, German physicist: Nobel prize 1961.

Moth•er•well (muth′ər wel′, -wəl), **Robert,** 1915–91, U.S. painter.

Mot•ley (mot′lē), **John Lothrop,** 1814–77, U.S. historian and diplomat.

Mott (mot), **1. John Raleigh,** 1865–1955, U.S. religious leader: Nobel peace prize 1946. **2. Lucretia Coffin,** 1793–1880, U.S. advocate of women's rights and the abolition of slavery. **3. Sir Nevill Francis,** born 1905, British physicist: developer of solid-state circuitry; Nobel prize 1977.

Mot•tel•son (mot′l sən, -sôn′), **Ben R(oy),** born 1926, Danish physicist, born in the U.S.: Nobel prize 1975.

Mo•tze or **Mo-tse** (mô′dzu′), (*Mo Ti*) fl. 5th century B.C., Chinese philosopher.

Mount•bat•ten (mount bat′n), **Louis, 1st Earl Mountbatten of Burma,** 1900–79, British admiral: viceroy of India 1947; governor general of India 1947–48.

Mous•sorg•sky (mŏŏ sôrg′skē, -zôrg′-), **Modest Petrovich,** MUSSORGSKY, Modest Petrovich.

Mo•zart (mōt′särt), **Wolfgang Amadeus,** 1756–91, Austrian composer.

Mpha•hle•le (əm pä hlā′lā, -lā′lā), **Ezekiel,** born 1919, South African writer.

Mu•ba•rak (mŏŏ bär′ək), **(Mohammed) Hosni,** born 1928, president of Egypt since 1981.

Muel•ler (myŏŏ′lər, mul′ər, mil′-), **Paul,** 1899–1965, Swiss chemist: Nobel prize for medicine 1948.

Mu•ga•be (mŏŏ gä′bē, -bā), **Robert (Gabriel),** born 1924, prime minister of Zimbabwe 1980–87; president since 1987.

Mu•ham•mad (mŏŏ ham′əd, -hä′məd), **1.** Also, **Mohammed.** A.D. 570–632, Arab prophet: founder of Islam. **2. Elijah** (*Elijah Poole*), 1897–1975, U.S. leader of the Black Muslims 1934–75.

Muham′mad Ah′med (am′əd), (*"the Mahdi"*) 1844–85, Muslim leader in Anglo-Egyptian Sudan.

Muh•len•berg (myo͞o′lən bûrg′), **1. Frederick Augustus Conrad,** 1750–1801, U.S. clergyman and statesman: first Speaker of the House 1789–91, 1793–95. **2. Henry Melchior,** 1711–87, American Lutheran clergyman, born in Germany.

Muir (myo͝or), **John,** 1838–1914, U.S. naturalist, explorer, and writer, born in Scotland.

Mul•ler (myo͞o′lər, mul′ər, mil′-), **Hermann Joseph,** 1890–1967, U.S. geneticist: Nobel prize for medicine 1946.

Mül•ler (myo͞o′lər, mul′ər), **1. Friedrich Max,** 1823–1900, English Sanskrit scholar and philologist, born in Germany. **2. Johann** (*"Regiomontanus"*), 1436–76, German mathematician and astronomer. **3. Johannes Peter,** 1801–58, German physiologist and comparative anatomist. **4. Wilhelm,** 1794–1827, German poet.

Mul•li•ken (mul′i kən), **Robert Sanderson,** 1896–1986, U.S. chemist and physicist: Nobel prize for chemistry 1966.

Mul•ro•ney (mul rō′nē), **(Martin) Brian,** born 1939, prime minister of Canada since 1984.

Mum•ford (mum′fərd), **Lewis,** 1895–1990, U.S. author and social scientist.

Munch (mo͝ongk), **Edvard,** 1863–1944, Norwegian painter.

Münch (mʏnsh), **Charles,** 1891–1968, French conductor in the U.S.

Münch•hau•sen (mʏnкн′hou′zən), **Karl Friedrich Hieronymus, Baron von,** 1720–97, German soldier, adventurer, and teller of tales. English, **Mun•chau•sen** (mun′-chou′zən, munch′hou′-).

Mu•ni (myo͞o′nē), **Paul** (*Muni Weisenfreund*), 1895–1967, U.S. actor, born in Austria.

Mun•ro (mən rō′), **H(ector) H(ugh)** (*"Saki"*), 1870–1916, Scottish novelist and short-story writer, born in Burma.

Mu•ra•sa•ki Shi•ki•bu (mo͝or′ə sä′kē shē′kē bo͞o′), **Lady,** 978?–1031?, Japanese poet and novelist.

Mu•rat (myo͝o ra′, -rä′), **Joachim,** 1767?–1815, French marshal: king of Naples 1808–15.

Mu•ril•lo (myo͝o ril′ō, mo͞o rē′ō, myo͞o-), **Bartolomé Esteban,** 1617–82, Spanish painter.

Mur•phy (mûr′fē), **1. Frank,** 1890–1949, U.S. statesman and jurist: associate justice of the U.S. Supreme Court 1940–49. **2. Isaac,** 1861–96, U.S. thoroughbred racehorse jockey. **3. William Parry,** born 1892, U.S. physician: Nobel prize for medicine 1934.

Mur•ray (mûr′ē, mur′ē), **1. Sir (George) Gilbert (Aimé),** 1866–1957, English classical scholar. **2. Sir James Augustus Henry,** 1837–1915, Scottish lexicographer and philologist. **3. Lindley,** 1745–1826, English grammarian, born in the U.S. **4. Philip,** 1886–1952, U.S. labor leader: president of the CIO 1940–52.

Mur•row (mûr′ō, mur′ō), **Edward R(oscoe),** 1908–65, U.S. news broadcaster and commentator.

Mu•si•al (myōō′zē əl, -zhē əl, -zhəl), **Stanley Frank** (*"Stan the Man"*), born 1920, U.S. baseball player.

Mu•sil (mōō′sil, -zil), **Robert,** 1880–1942, Austrian writer.

Mus•kie (mus′kē), **Edmund (Sixtus),** born 1914, U.S. politician: senator 1959–80; Secretary of State 1980–81.

Mus•set (mʏ sā′), **(Louis Charles) Alfred de,** 1810–57, French poet, dramatist, and novelist.

Mus•so•li•ni (mŏŏs′ə lē′nē, mōō′sə-), **Benito** (*"Il Duce"*), 1883–1945, Italian Fascist leader: premier of Italy 1922–43.

Mus•sorg•sky (mŏŏ sôrg′skē, -zôrg′-), **Modest Petrovich,** 1839–81, Russian composer.

Mus•ta•fa Ke•mal (mŏŏs′tä fä kə mäl′), Kemal Atatürk.

Mu•ti (mōō′tē), **Riccardo,** born 1941, Italian symphonic conductor.

Mu•tsu•hi•to (mōō′tsŏŏ hē′tō), 1852–1912, emperor of Japan 1867–1912.

Muy•bridge (mī′brij), **Eadweard** (*Edward James Muggeridge*), 1830–1904, U.S. photographer, born in England.

Myr•dal (mēr′däl, -dôl, mûr′-), **1. Alva (Reimer),** 1902–86, Swedish sociologist and diplomat: Nobel peace prize 1982 (wife of Gunnar Myrdal). **2. (Karl) Gunnar,** 1898–1987, Swedish sociologist and economist: Nobel prize for economics 1974.

My•ron (mī′rən), fl. c450 B.C., Greek sculptor.

N

Na•bo•kov (nə bô′kəf, nab′ə kôf′, -kof′), **Vladimir Vladimirovich,** 1899–1977, U.S. writer born in Russia.

Nab•o•nas•sar (nab′ō nas′ər), died 733? B.C., king of Babylon 747?–733?. Assyrian, **Nab′u-nas′ir.**

Nab•o•ni•dus (nab′ō nī′dəs), died 539? B.C., last king of Babylonia 556–539.

Na•der (nā′dər), **Ralph,** born 1934, U.S. consumer advocate.

Na•guib (nə gēb′), **Mohammed,** born 1901, Egyptian general and political leader: premier 1952–54; president 1953–54.

Na•gur•ski (nə gûr′skē) **Bron•is•law** (bron′ə slof′), (*"Bronko"*), 1908–90, U.S. football player.

Nagy (nod′yᵉ, noj), **Imre,** 1896–1958, Hungarian political leader: premier 1953–55, 1956.

Nai•smith (nā′smith), **James,** 1861–1939, U.S. physical-education teacher and originator of basketball, born in Canada.

Na•ka•so•ne (nä′kä sô′ne), **Yasuhiro,** born 1918, Japanese political leader: prime minister 1982–87.

Na•nak (nä′nək), (*"Guru"*) 1469–1539, Indian founder of Sikhism.

Nan•sen (nan′sən, nän′-), **Fridtjof,** 1861–1930, Norwegian arctic explorer, zoologist, and statesman: Nobel peace prize 1922.

Na•pi•er (nā′pē ər, nə pēr′), **1. Sir Charles James,** 1782–1853, British general. **2. John,** 1550–1617, Scottish mathematician: inventor of logarithms.

Na•po•le•on (nə pō′lē ən, -pōl′yən), **1. Napoleon I** (*Napoleon Bonaparte*) (*"the Little Corporal"*), 1769–1821, French general born in Corsica: emperor of France 1804–15. **2. Napoleon II** (*François Charles Joseph Bonaparte*) (*Duke of Reichstadt*), 1811–32, titular king of Rome (son of Napoleon I). **3. Napoleon III** (*Louis Napoleon*) (*Charles Louis Napoleon Bonaparte*), 1808–73, president of France 1848–52, emperor of France 1852–70 (nephew of Napoleon I).

Nar•mer (när′mər), a king of Egypt identified by modern scholars as the Menes of tradition and depicted as the unifier of Upper and Lower Egypt.

Nar•vá•ez (nän vä′eth, -vä′es), **Pánfilo de,** 1478?–1528, Spanish soldier and adventurer in America.

Nash (nash), **1. John,** 1752–1835, English architect and city planner. **2. Ogden,** 1902–71, U.S. poet. **3.** Also, **Nashe. Thomas** (*"Pasquil"*), 1567–1601, English dramatist and satirist.

Nas•ser (nä′sər, nas′ər), **Gamal Abdel,** 1918–70, president of Egypt 1956–58; president of the United Arab Republic 1958–70.

Nast (nast), **Thomas,** 1840–1902, U.S. illustrator and cartoonist.

Na•than (nā′thən), **1. George Jean,** 1882–1958, U.S. drama critic. **2. Robert,** 1894–1985, U.S. novelist and poet.

Na•than•iel (nə than′yəl), *n.* BARTHOLOMEW.

Na•thans (nā′thənz), **Daniel,** born 1928, U.S. biologist: Nobel prize for medicine 1978.

Na•tion (nā′shən), **Carry** or **Carrie (Amelia Moore),** 1846–1911, U.S. temperance leader.

Na•tsu•me (nä′tso͞o me′), **Soseki** (*Kinnosuke Natsume*), 1867–1916, Japanese novelist.

Nat•ta (nät′tä), **Giulio,** 1903–79, Italian chemist and engineer: Nobel prize for chemistry 1963.

Nav•ra•ti•lo•va (nav′rə ti lō′və, näv′-), **Martina,** born 1956, U.S. tennis player, born in Czechoslovakia.

Na•zi•mo•va (nə zim′ə və), **Alla,** 1879–1945, Russian actress in the U.S.

Neck•er (ne kâr′, nek′ər), **Jacques,** 1732–1804, French statesman, born in Switzerland.

Né•el (nā el′), **Louis Eugène Félix,** born 1904, French physicist: Nobel prize 1970.

Nef•er•ti•ti (nef′ər tē′tē) also **Nef•re•te•te** (nef′ri-), fl. early 14th century B.C., Egyptian queen: wife of Akhenaton.

Neh•ru (nā′ro͞o, nâr′o͞o), **Jawaharlal,** 1889–1964, Hindu political leader: first prime minister of the republic of India 1947–64 (father of Indira Gandhi).

Neil•son (nēl′sən), **William Allan,** 1869–1946, U.S. educator and lexicographer, born in Scotland.

Nel•son (nel′sən), **1. Viscount Horatio,** 1758–1805, British admiral. **2. Willie,** born 1933, U.S. singer.

Nem•e•rov (nem′ə rôf′, -rof′), **Howard,** 1920–91, U.S. poet and novelist: U.S. poet laureate 1988–90.

Nen•ni (nen′nē), **Pietro,** 1891–1980, Italian socialist leader and author.

Ne•pos (nē′pos, nep′os), **Cornelius,** 99?–24? B.C., Roman biographer and historian.

Ne•ri (nâr′ē; *It.* ne′rē), **Saint Philip** (*Filippo Neri*), 1515–95, Italian priest: founder of Congregation of the Oratory.

Nernst (nârnst, nûrnst; *Germ.* nernst), **Walther Herman,** 1864–1941, German physicist and chemist: Nobel prize for chemistry 1920.

Ne•ro (nēr′ō), (*Lucius Domitius Ahenobarbus*) (*"Nero Claudius Caesar Drusus Germanicus"*) A.D. 37–68, emperor of Rome 54–68.

Ne•ru•da (nə ro͞o′də, -dä), **Pablo** (*Neftali Ricardo Reyes Basoalto*), 1904–73, Chilean poet and diplomat: Nobel prize for literature 1971.

Ner•va (nûr′və), **Marcus Cocceius,** A.D. 32?–98, emperor of Rome 96–98.

Nes•to•ri•us (ne stôr′ē əs, -stōr′-), died A.D. 451?, Syrian ecclesiastic: patriarch of Constantinople 428–431; condemned as a heretic.

Neu•tra (noi′trə), **Richard Joseph,** 1892–1970, U.S. architect, born in Austria.

Nev•el•son (nev′əl sən), **Louise,** 1900–88, U.S. sculptor, born in Russia.

Nev•ille (nev′əl), **Richard,** WARWICK, Earl of.

Nev•in (nev′in), **Ethelbert Woodbridge,** 1862–1901, U.S. composer.

Nev•ins (nev′inz), **Allan,** 1890–1971, U.S. historian.

Nev•sky (nev′skē, nef′-), **Alexander,** ALEXANDER NEVSKY.

New•ber•y (nōō′ber ē, -bə rē, nyōō′-), **John,** 1713–67, English publisher.

New•bolt (nōō′bōlt, nyōō′-), **Sir Henry John,** 1862–1938, English poet, novelist, naval historian, and critic.

New•comb (nōō′kəm, nyōō′-), **Simon,** 1835–1909, U.S. astronomer.

New•com•en (nōō kum′ən, nyōō-), **Thomas,** 1663–1729, English inventor.

New•house (nōō′hous′, nyōō′-), **Samuel I(rving),** 1895–1979, U.S. publisher.

Ne Win (ne′ win′), **U** (ōō), (*Maung Shu Maung*), born 1911, Burmese soldier and political leader: prime minister 1958–60, 1962–74; president 1974–81.

New•man (nōō′mən, nyōō′-), **1. Barnett,** 1905–70, U.S. painter. **2. John Henry, Cardinal,** 1801–90, English theologian and author. **3. Paul,** born 1925, U.S. actor and director.

New•ton (nōōt′n, nyōōt′n), **Sir Isaac,** 1642–1727, English physicist and mathematician.

Nex•ö (nek′sœ), **Martin Andersen,** 1869–1954, Danish novelist.

Ney (nā), **Michel, Duke of Elchingen,** 1769–1815, French military leader: marshal of France 1805–15.

Ngo Dinh Diem (ngō′ dēn′ dyem′, dzyem′, nō′ dēn′), 1901–1963, president of South Vietnam 1956–63.

Ngu•yen Van Thieu (ngōō′yen′ vän′ tyōō′, nōō′yen′), born 1923, president of South Vietnam 1967–75.

Ni•ar•chos (nē är′kōs), **Stavros Spyros,** born 1909, Greek businessman.

Nich•o•las[1] (nik′ə ləs, nik′ləs), **1. of Cusa,** 1401–1464, German cardinal, mathematician, and philosopher. **2. Grand Duke,** 1856–1929, Russian general in World War I. **3. Saint,** fl. 4th century A.D., bishop in Asia Minor: patron saint of Russia; protector of children and prototype of Santa Claus.

Nich•o•las[2] (nik′ə ləs, nik′ləs), **1. Nicholas I,** 1796–1855, czar of Russia 1825–55. **2. Nicholas II,** 1868–1918, czar of Russia 1894–1917: executed 1918.

Nich•ol•son (nik′əl sən), **1. Ben,** 1894–1982, British painter. **2. Jack,** born 1937, U.S. actor. **3. Sir Francis,** 1655–1728, English colonial administrator in America.

Nick•laus (nik′ləs), **Jack (William),** born 1940, U.S. golfer.

Nic•o•lay (nik′ə lā′), **John George,** 1832–1901, U.S. biographer.

Ni•co•let (nik′ə lā′; *Fr.* nē kô le′), **Jean** (zhäɴ), 1598–1642, French explorer in America.

Ni•colle (nē kôl′), **Charles,** 1866–1936, French physician: Nobel prize 1928.

Nic•ol•son (nik′əl sən), **1. Sir Harold George,** 1886–1968, English diplomat, biographer, and journalist (husband of Victoria Mary Sackville-West). **2. Marjorie Hope,** born 1894, U.S. scholar, educator, and author.

Nie•buhr (nē′bŏŏr), **1. Barthold Georg,** 1776–1831, German historian. **2. Reinhold,** 1892–1971, U.S. theologian and philosopher.

Niel•sen (nēl′sən), **Carl August,** 1865–1931, Danish composer.

Nie•mey•er (nē′mī ər), **Oscar,** born 1907, Brazilian architect.

Nie•moel•ler or **Nie•möl•ler** (nē′mœ ləʀ), **Martin,** 1892–1984, German Lutheran clergyman: resisted Nazism.

Niepce (nyeps), **Joseph Nicéphore,** 1765–1833, French inventor.

Nier (nēr), **Alfred Otto Carl,** born 1911, U.S. physicist.

Nie•tzsche (nē′chə, -chē), **Friedrich Wilhelm,** 1844–1900, German philosopher.

Night•in•gale (nīt′n gāl′, nī′ting-), **Florence,** 1820–1910, English nurse.

Ni•jin•sky (ni zhin′skē, -jin′-), **Vaslav,** 1890–1950, Polish ballet dancer and choreographer.

Ni•kon (nē′kôn; *Russ.* nyē′kən), 1605–81, patriarch of Russian Orthodox Church 1652–66.

Nils•son (nil′sən), **(Märta) Birgit,** born 1918, Swedish soprano.

Ni•mei•ry or **Ni•mei•ri** (nə mâr′ē), **Gaafar Muhammad al-,** born 1930, Sudanese political leader: president 1969–85.

Nim•itz (nim′its), **Chester William,** 1885–1966, U.S. admiral.

Nir•en•berg (nir′ən bûrg′), **Marshall Warren,** born 1927, U.S. biochemist: pioneered studies on the genetic code; Nobel prize for medicine 1968.

Niv•en (niv′ən), **David,** 1910–83, U.S. actor, born in Scotland.

Nix•on (nik′sən), **Richard M(ilhous),** born 1913, 37th president of the U.S., 1969–74 (resigned).

Nkru•mah (ən krōō′mə, əng krōō′-), **Kwame,** 1909–72, president of Ghana 1960–66.

No•bel (nō bel′), **Alfred Bernhard,** 1833–96, Swedish engineer, manufacturer, and philanthropist.

No•bi•le (nō′bē lā′), **Umberto,** 1885–1978, Italian aeronautical engineer and arctic explorer.

No•el-Ba•ker (nō′əl bā′kər, nōl′-), **Philip John,** 1889–1982, British statesman and author: Nobel peace prize 1959.

No•gu•chi (nə gōō′chē, nō-), **1. Hideyo,** 1876–1928, Japanese physician and bacteriologist in the U.S. **2. Isamu,** 1904–88, U.S. sculptor.

Nor•dau (nôr′dou), **Max Simon,** 1849–1923, Hungarian author, physician, and Zionist leader.

Nor•den•skjöld (nôr′dn shōld′, -shəld), **1. Baron Nils Adolf Erik,** 1832–1901, Swedish arctic explorer, geographer, and geologist; born in Finland. **2.** his nephew **Nils Otto Gustaf,** 1869–1928, Swedish arctic and antarctic explorer.

Nor•di•ca (nôr′di kə), **Lillian** (*Lillian Norton*), 1859–1914, U.S. soprano.

Nor•doff (nôr′dof, -dôf), **Charles Bernard,** 1887–1947, U.S. novelist.

Nor•man (nôr′mən), **Jessye,** born 1945, U.S. soprano.

No•ro•dom Si•ha•nouk (nôr′ə dom′ sē′ə no͝ok′, -dəm), **Prince,** born 1922, Cambodian statesman: premier 1952–60; chief of state 1960–70 and 1975–76.

Nor•ris (nôr′is, nor′-), **1. Charles Gilman,** 1881–1945, U.S. novelist and editor. **2. Frank,** 1870–1902, U.S. novelist. **3. George William,** 1861–1944, U.S. senator 1913–43. **4. Kathleen (Thompson),** 1880–1966, U.S. novelist and short-story writer.

Nor•rish (nôr′ish, nor′-), **Ronald George Wreyford,** 1897–1978, British chemist: Nobel prize 1967.

Nor•stad (nôr′stad, -städ), **Lauris,** 1907–88, U.S. Air Force general: Supreme Allied Commander of NATO 1956–63.

North (nôrth), **1. Frederick, 2nd Earl of Guilford** (*"Lord North"*), 1732–92, English statesman: prime minister 1770–82. **2. Sir Thomas,** 1535?–1601?, English translator.

North•cliffe (nôrth′klif), **Viscount,** HARMSWORTH, Alfred Charles William.

Nor•throp (nôr′thrəp), **John Howard,** born 1891, U.S. biochemist: Nobel prize for chemistry 1946.

Nor•ton (nôr′tn), **1. Charles Eliot,** 1827–1908, U.S. scholar. **2. Peter,** born 1943, U.S. computer scientist and author: pioneer inventor of utilities programs. **3. Thomas,** 1532–84, English author.

Nos•tra•da•mus (nos′trə dā′məs, -dä′-, nō′strə-), (*Michel de Nostredame*), 1503–66, French astrologer.

No•va•lis (nō vä′lis), (pen name of *Friedrich von Hardenberg*), 1772–1801, German poet.

Noyes (noiz), **1. Alfred,** 1880–1958, English poet. **2. John Humphrey,** 1811–86, U.S. social reformer: founder of the Oneida Community.

Nu (no͞o), **U** (o͞o), (*Thauin Nu*), born 1907, Burmese political leader: prime minister 1948–56, 1957–58, 1960–62.

Nu•ma Pom•pil•i•us (no͞o′mə pom pil′ē əs, nyo͞o′-), died 673? B.C., 2nd legendary Sabine king of Rome 715–673?.

Nu•re•yev (no͝o rā′ef, -ev), **Rudolf (Hametovich),** born 1938, Austrian ballet dancer, born in Russia.

Nur•mi (nûr′mē; *Fin.* no͝or′mi), **Paavo Johannes,** 1897–1973, Finnish athlete.

Nut•ting (nut′ing), **Wallace,** 1861–1941, U.S. antiquary, author, and illustrator.

Nye (nī), **Edgar Wilson** (*"Bill Nye"*), 1850–96, U.S. humorist.

Nye•re•re (*Swahili.* nye RE′RE; *Eng.* ni râr′ē), **Julius Kambarage,** born 1921, African statesman: president of Tanzania 1964–85.

Ny•kvist (nīk′vist, nik′-), **Sven,** born 1922, Swedish cinematographer.

O

Oak•ley (ōk′lē), **Annie** (*Phoebe Anne Oakley Mozee*), 1860–1926, U.S. sharpshooter.

Oates (ōts), **1. Joyce Carol,** born 1938, U.S. writer. **2. Titus,** 1649–1705, English conspirator and Anglican priest: instigator of the Popish Plot scare.

O•ber•lin (ō′bər lin, -lᴀɴ′), **Jean Frédéric** (zhäɴ), 1740–1826, Alsatian clergyman.

O•ber•on (ō′bə ron′), **Merle** (*Estelle Thompson*), 1911–79, British actress, born in Tasmania.

O•berth (ō′bərt), **Hermann Julius,** born 1894, German physicist: pioneer in rocketry.

O•bo•te (ō bō′tā), **(Apollo) Milton,** born 1924, Ugandan political leader: president 1966–71 and 1980–85.

O'Boyle (ō boil′), **Patrick Aloysius,** born 1896, U.S. Roman Catholic clergyman: archbishop of Washington, D.C., 1947–73.

O•brecht (ō′breᴋʜt), **Jacob,** 1430–1505, Dutch composer and conductor.

O•bre•gón (ô′ᴠʀᴇ gôn′), **Álvaro,** 1880–1928, Mexican general and statesman: president 1920–24.

O'Ca•sey (ō kā′sē), **Sean** (shôn), 1880–1964, Irish playwright.

Oc•cam or **Ock•ham** (ok′əm), **William of,** died 1349?, English scholastic philosopher.

O•cho•a (ō chō′ə), **Severo,** born 1905, U.S. biochemist, born in Spain: Nobel prize for medicine 1959.

Ochs (oks), **Adolph Simon,** 1858–1935, U.S. newspaper publisher.

Ock•ham (ok′əm), **William of,** Occam.

O'Con•nell (ō kon′l), **Daniel,** 1775–1847, Irish nationalist leader and orator.

O'Con•nor (ō kon′ər), **1. Frank** (*Michael Donovan*), 1903–66, Irish writer. **2. (Mary) Flannery,** 1925–64, U.S. author. **3. John Joseph, Cardinal,** born 1920, U.S. Roman Catholic clergyman: archbishop of New York since 1984. **4. Sandra Day,** born 1930, associate justice of the U.S. Supreme Court since 1981. **5. Thomas Power,** 1848–1929, Irish journalist and political leader.

Oc•ta•vi•a (ok tā′vē ə), **1.** died 11 B.C., wife of Mark Antony and sister of Augustus. **2.** A.D. c42–62 Roman empress, wife of Nero.

Oc•ta•vi•an (ok tā′vē ən), Augustus.

O•dets (ō dets′), **Clifford,** 1906–63, U.S. dramatist.

O•det•ta (ō det′ə), (*Odetta Holmes*), born 1930, U.S. folk singer.

O•do•a•cer (ō′dō ā′sər) also **O′do•va′car** (-vā′kər), A.D. 434?–493, first barbarian ruler of Italy 476–493.

Oer•sted (ûr′sted; *Dan.* œʀ′stlth), **Hans Christian,** 1777–1851, Danish physicist.

O'Fao·láin (ō fā′lən, ō fal′ən), **Seán** (shôn), 1900–91, Irish writer.

Of·fen·bach (ô′fən bäk′, of′ən-), **Jacques,** 1819–80, French composer.

O'Fla·her·ty (ō fla′hər tē), **Liam,** 1896–1984, Irish novelist.

Og·burn (og′bûrn), **William Fielding,** 1886–1959, U.S. sociologist and educator.

Og·den (ôg′dən, og′-), **Charles Kay,** 1889–1957, British psychologist and linguist.

O·gil·vie (ō′gəl vē), **John,** 1797–1867, Scottish lexicographer.

O·gle·thorpe (ō′gəl thôrp′), **James Edward,** 1696–1785, British general: founder of the colony of Georgia.

Oh (ō), **Sa·da·ha·ru** (sä′də här′o͞o), born 1940, Chinese baseball player in Japan.

O'Har·a (ō hâr′ə, ō har′ə), **John (Henry),** 1905–70, U.S. author.

O. Hen·ry (ō hen′rē), pen name of William S. PORTER.

O'Hig·gins (ō hig′inz), **1. Ambrosio** (*Marqués de Osorno*), 1720?–1801, Irish soldier and administrator in South America. **2. Bernardo** (*Liberator of Chile*), 1778–1842, Chilean general and statesman.

Oh·lin (ō′lin, o͞o lēn′), **Bertil,** 1899–1979, Swedish economist: Nobel prize 1977.

Ohm (ōm), **Georg Simon,** 1787–1854, German physicist.

Oi·strakh (oi′sträk, -sträкн), **David,** 1908–74, Russian violinist.

O'Keeffe (ō kēf′), **Georgia,** 1887–1986, U.S. painter.

O'Kel·ley (ō kel′ē), **Seán Thomas** (shôn), 1882–1966, president of Ireland 1945–59.

O·ken (ō′kən), **Lorenz** (*Lorenz Ockenfuss*), 1779–1851, German naturalist and philosopher.

O·laf or **O·lav** (ō′läf, ō′ləf), **1. Olaf** (or **Olav**) **I** (*Olaf Tryggvason*), A.D. 969–1000, king of Norway 995–1000. **2. Olaf** (or **Olav**) **II, Saint** (*Olaf Haraldsson*), A.D. 995–1030, king of Norway 1016–29: patron saint of Norway. **3. Olaf V,** OLAV V.

O·lav V (ō′läf, ō′ləf) 1903–91, king of Norway 1957–91.

Ol·bers (ōl′bərz, ôl′-), **Heinrich Wilhelm Matthäus,** 1758–1840, German astronomer and physician.

Old·cas·tle (ōld′kas′əl, -kä′səl), **Sir John (Lord Cobham),** 1377–1417, English leader of a Lollard conspiracy.

Old·field (ōld′fēld′), **Berna Eli** (*"Barney"*), 1878–1946, U.S. racing-car driver.

Olds (ōldz), **Ransom Eli,** 1864–1950, U.S. automobile pioneer and manufacturer.

Ol·ga (ol′gə, ōl′-; *Russ.* ôl′gə), **Saint,** died A.D. 968?, regent of Kiev until 955: saint of the Russian Orthodox Church.

Ol·i·phant (ol′ə fənt), **Margaret Wilson,** 1828–97, Scottish novelist.

Ol·i·ver (ol′ə vər), **Joseph** (*"King"*), 1885?–1938, U.S. cornet player, bandleader, and composer: pioneer in jazz.

O·liv·i·er (ō liv′ē ā′), **Laurence (Kerr)** (*Baron Olivier of Brighton*), 1907–89, English actor and director.

Olm·sted (ōm′stid, -sted), **Frederick Law,** 1822–1903, U.S. landscape architect.

Ol·sen (ōl′sən), **Kenneth Harry,** born 1926, U.S. computer entrepreneur.

O·lym·pi·o (ə lim′pē ō′), **Sylvanus,** 1902–63, African statesman: first president of the Republic of Togo 1961–63.

O·mar Khay·yám (ō′mär kī yäm′, -yam′, ō′mər), died 1123?, Persian poet and mathematician.

O·nas·sis (ō nas′is, ō nä′sis), **1. Aristotle Socrates,** 1906–75, Greek businessman, born in Turkey. **2. Jacqueline (Lee Bouvier Kennedy)** (*"Jackie"*), born 1929, wife of John F. Kennedy (1953–63) and Aristotle Onassis (1968–75).

O·ña·te (ô nyä′te), **Juan de,** 1550?–1624, Spanish explorer who colonized New Mexico.

O'Neill (ō nēl′), **1. Eugene (Gladstone),** 1888–1953, U.S. playwright: Nobel prize 1936. **2. Thomas P(hilip)** (*"Tip"*), born 1912, U.S. politician: congressman 1953–87; Speaker of the House 1977–87.

O·net·ti (ō net′ē), **Juan Carlos,** born 1909, Uruguayan novelist and short-story writer.

On·ions (un′yənz), **Charles Talbut,** 1873–1965, English lexicographer and philologist.

On·sa·ger (on′sä gər, ôn′-), **Lars,** 1903–76, U.S. chemist, born in Norway: Nobel prize 1968.

Oost (ōst), **Jacob van,** 1600?–71, and his son, **Jacob van,** 1639?–1713, Flemish painters.

O·pech·an·ca·nough (ō pech′ən kä′nō), c1545–1644, Algonquian leader, brother of Powhatan: led Jamestown massacre 1622.

O·phüls (ō′fəls), **Max** (*Max Oppenheimer*), 1902–57, German film director, in Germany, France, and the U.S.

Op·pen·heim (op′ən hīm′), **E(dward) Phillips,** 1866–1946, English novelist.

Op·pen·heim·er (op′ən hī′mər), **J(ulius) Robert,** 1904–67, U.S. nuclear physicist.

Or·czy (ôrt′sē), **Emmuska, Baroness,** 1865–1947, English novelist, born in Hungary.

Orff (ôrf), **Carl,** 1895–1982, German composer.

Or·i·gen (ôr′i jen′, -jən, or′-), (*Origenes Admantius*) A.D. 185?–254?, Alexandrian writer and Christian theologian.

Or·lan·do (ôr lan′dō), **Vittorio Emanuele,** 1860–1952, Italian statesman.

Or·lé·ans, d' (dôr lā äN′), **Louis Philippe Joseph, Duc** (*Philippe Égalité*), 1747–93, French political leader.

Or·lich (ôr′lich, -lēch), **Francisco J.,** 1906–69, Costa Rican engineer and statesman: president 1962–66.

Or·man·dy (ôr′mən dē), **Eugene,** 1899–1985, U.S. conductor and violinist, born in Hungary.

O•ro•si•us (ô rō′zhē əs), **Paulus,** fl. 5th century A.D., Spanish theologian and historian.

O•roz•co (ô rôs′kō), **José Clemente,** 1883–1949, Mexican painter.

Orr (ôr), **Robert Gordon** (*Bobby*), born 1948, Canadian ice-hockey player.

Or•te•ga Sa•a•ve•dra (ôr tā′gə sä′ä ved′rə), **(José) Daniel,** born 1945, president of Nicaragua 1985–90.

Or•te•ga y Gas•set (ôr tā′gə ē gä set′), **José,** 1883–1955, Spanish philosopher and statesman.

Or•ton (ôr′tn), **Joe,** born 1933, English playwright.

Or•well (ôr′wel, -wəl), **George** (*Eric Arthur Blair*), 1903–50, English novelist and essayist.

Os•born (oz′bərn, -bôrn), **Henry Fairfield,** 1857–1935, U.S. paleontologist.

Os•borne (oz′bərn, -bôrn, -bōrn), **1. John (James),** born 1929, English playwright. **2. Thomas Mott,** 1859–1926, U.S. prison reformer.

Os•car II (os′kər), 1829–1907, king of Sweden 1872–1907; king of Norway 1872–1905.

Os•ce•o•la (os′ē ō′lə, ō′sā-), 1804–38, U.S. Indian leader: chief of the Seminole tribe.

Os•ler (ōs′lər, ōz′-), **Sir William,** 1849–1919, Canadian physician and professor of medicine.

Os•man (oz′mən, os′-, os män′), 1259–1326, Turkish emir 1299–1326: founder of the Ottoman dynasty.

Os•si•etz•ky (ô′sē ets′kē), **Carl von,** 1889–1938, German pacifist leader: Nobel peace prize 1935.

Ost•wald (ôst′vält), **Wilhelm,** 1853–1932, German chemist: Nobel prize 1909.

Os•wald (oz′wôld), **Lee Harvey,** 1939–63, designated by a presidential commission to be the lone assassin of John F. Kennedy.

O•tis (ō′tis), **1. Elisha Graves,** 1811–61, U.S. inventor. **2. Harrison Gray,** 1837–1917, U.S. army officer and newspaper publisher. **3. James,** 1725–83, American Revolutionary lawyer and public official.

Ot•ter•bein (ot′ər bin′), **Philip William,** 1726–1813, American clergyman, founder of the United Brethren, born in Germany.

Ot•to I (ot′ō), (*"the Great"*) A.D. 912–973, king of the Germans 936–973; emperor of the Holy Roman Empire 962–973.

Ot•way (ot′wā), **Thomas,** 1652–85, English dramatist.

Ou•spen•sky (o͞o spen′skē), **Peter Demianovich,** 1878–1947, Russian philosopher and author.

Ov•id (ov′id), (*Publius Ovidius Naso*) 43 B.C.–A.D. 17?, Roman poet.

Ow•en (ō′ən), **1. Sir Richard,** 1804–92, English zoologist and anatomist. **2. Robert,** 1771–1858, Welsh social reformer in Great Britain and the U.S. **3. Wilfred,** 1893–1918, English poet.

Ow•ens (ō′ənz), **Jesse** (*John Cleveland*), 1913–80, U.S. athlete.

O•ya•ma (ô′yä mä′), **Iwao,** 1842–1916, Japanese field marshal.

O•za•wa (ō zä′wə), **Seiji,** born 1935, Japanese conductor in the U.S.

O•zick (ō′zik), **Cynthia,** born 1928, U.S. author.

O•zu (ô′zo͞o), **Yasujiro,** 1903–63, Japanese film director.

P

Paa•si•ki•vi (pä′si ki vi), **Juho Kusti,** 1870–1956, Finnish statesman: president 1946–56.

Pach•el•bel (pä′kəl bel′ päкн′əl-), **Johann,** 1653–1706, German organist and composer.

Pach•mann (päk′mən, päкн′), **Vladimir de,** 1848–1933, Russian pianist.

Pa•cho•mi•us (pə kō′mē əs), **Saint,** A.D. 292?–348?, Egyptian ascetic: founder of the cenobitical form of monasticism.

Pack•wood (pak′wo͝od′), **Bob,** born 1932, U.S. politician: senator since 1969.

Pa•de•rew•ski (pad′ə ref′skē, -rev′-), **Ignacy Jan,** 1860–1941, Polish pianist, composer, and statesman.

Pa•ga•ni•ni (pag′ə nē′nē, pä′gə-), **Niccolò,** 1784–1840, Italian composer and violinist.

Page (pāj), **1. Thomas Nelson,** 1853–1922, U.S. novelist and diplomat. **2. Walter Hines,** 1855–1918, U.S. journalist, editor, and diplomat.

Pah•la•vi (pä′lə vē′), **1. Muhammad Re•za** (ri zä′), 1919–80, shah of Iran 1941–79. **2.** his father, **Reza Shah,** 1877–1944, shah of Iran 1925–41.

Paine (pān), **Thomas,** 1737–1809, U.S. patriot and political writer, born in England.

Pa•le•stri•na (pal′ə strē′nə), **Giovanni Pierluigi da,** 1526?–94, Italian composer.

Pa•ley (pā′lē), **1. Grace,** born 1922, U.S. short-story writer. **2. William,** 1743–1805, English philosopher and clergyman. **3. William S.,** 1901–90, U.S. broadcasting executive.

Pal•grave (pôl′grāv, pal′-), **Francis Turner,** 1824–97, English critic and poet.

Pal•la•dio (pə lä′dē ō′), **Andrea,** 1508–80, Italian architect.

Pal•me (päl′mə), **(Sven) Olof (Joachim),** 1927–86, Swedish political leader: prime minister 1969–76, 1982–86.

Palm•er (pä′mər), **1. Alice Elvira,** 1855–1902, U.S. educator. **2. Arnold,** born 1929, U.S. golfer. **3. Daniel David,** 1845–1913, Canadian originator of chiropractic medicine. **4. George Herbert,** 1842–1933, U.S. educator, philosopher, and author.

Palm•er•ston (pä′mər stən), **Henry John Temple, 3rd Viscount,** 1784–1865, British statesman: prime minister 1855–58, 1859–65.

Palm•gren (päm′grən), **Selim,** 1878–1951, Finnish pianist and composer.

Pan•dit (pun′dit), **Vijaya Lakshmi,** 1900–90, Indian stateswoman (sister of Jawaharlal Nehru).

Pa•ni•ni (pä′nē nē *for 1;* pä nē′nē *for 2*), **1.** fl. c400 B.C., Indian grammarian of Sanskrit. **2.** PANNINI, Giovanni Paolo.

Pank•hurst (pangk′hûrst), **Emmeline (Goulden),** 1858–1928, English suffragist leader.

Pan•ni•ni or **Pa•ni•ni** (pä nē′nē), **Giovanni (Paolo),** 1692?–1765, Italian painter.

Pa•nof•sky (pa nof′skē), **Erwin,** 1892–1968, U.S. art historian, born in Germany.

Pa•pan•dre•ou (pä′pən drā′o͞o), **1. Andreas (George),** born 1919, Greek political leader: premier 1981–89 (son of George Papandreou). **2. George,** 1888–1968, Greek statesman: premier 1944, 1963–65.

Pa•pas (pä′pəs), **Irene,** born 1926, Greek actress.

Pa•pen (pä′pən), **Franz von,** 1879–1969, German diplomat, statesman, and soldier.

Pa•pin•i•an (pə pin′ē ən), (*Aemilius Papinianus*), died A.D. 212, Roman jurist and writer.

Papp (pap), **Joseph** (*Yosl Papirofsky*), 1921–91, U.S. theatrical producer and director.

Pa•ré (PA RĀ′), **Ambroise,** 1510–90, French surgeon.

Pa•re•to (pə rā′tō, pä-), **Vilfredo,** 1848–1923, Italian sociologist and economist in Switzerland.

Park (pärk), **1. Mungo,** 1771–1806?, Scottish explorer in Africa. **2. Robert E.,** 1864–1944, U.S. sociologist.

Par•ker (pär′kər), **1. Charles Christopher, Jr.** (*"Bird"*), 1920–55, U.S. jazz saxophonist and composer. **2. Dorothy (Rothschild),** 1893–1967, U.S. author. **3. Sir Gilbert,** 1862–1932, Canadian novelist and politician in England. **4. Matthew,** 1504–75, English theologian. **5. Theodore,** 1810–60, U.S. preacher, theologian, and reformer.

Park•man (pärk′mən), **Francis,** 1823–93, U.S. historian.

Parks (pärks), **Gordon (Alexander Buchanan),** born 1912, U.S. photojournalist and film director.

Par•men•i•des (pär men′i dēz′), fl. c450 B.C., Greek Eleatic philosopher.

Par•nell (pär nel′, pär′nl), **Charles Stewart,** 1846–91, Irish political leader.

Par•nis (pär′nis), **Mollie** (*Mollie Parnis Livingston*), born 1905, U.S. fashion designer.

Parr (pär), **Catherine,** CATHERINE PARR.

Par•ran (par′ən), **Thomas, Jr.,** 1892–1968, U.S. public health official.

Par•ring•ton (par′ing tən), **Vernon Louis,** 1871–1929, U.S. literary historian and critic.

Par•rish (par′ish), **1. Anne,** 1888–1957, U.S. novelist and author of books for children. **2. (Frederick) Maxfield,** 1870–1966, U.S. painter.

Par•ry (par′ē), **William Edward,** 1790–1855, English arctic explorer.

Par•sons (pär′sənz), **1. Talcott,** 1902–79, U.S. sociologist and author. **2. Theophilus,** 1750–1813, U.S. jurist.

Par•tridge (pär′trij), **Eric (Honeywood),** 1894–1979, British lexicographer, born in New Zealand.

Pas•cal (pa skal′), **Blaise,** 1623–62, French philosopher and mathematician.

Pas•cin (pä skaN′), **Jules** (*Julius Pincas*), 1885–1930, French painter, born in Bulgaria.

Pas•sy (pA sē′), **1. Frédéric,** 1822–1912, French economist and statesman: Nobel peace prize 1901. **2.** his son, **Paul Édouard,** 1859–1940, French phonetician.

Pas•ter•nak (pas′tər nak′), **Boris Leonidovich,** 1890–1960, Russian poet, novelist, and translator: declined 1958 Nobel prize.

Pas•teur (pa stûr′), **Louis,** 1822–95, French chemist and bacteriologist.

Pa•tan•ja•li (pə tun′jə lē), fl. late 2nd century B.C., Indian scholar and philosopher: sometimes regarded as the founder of yoga.

Pa•ter (pā′tər), **Walter Horatio,** 1839–94, English critic and essayist.

Pa•ton (pāt′n), **Alan (Stewart),** 1903–88, South African novelist.

Pat•rick (pa′trik), **Saint,** A.D. 389?–461?, British missionary and bishop in Ireland: patron saint of Ireland.

Pat•ti (pat′ē, pä′tē), **Adelina** (*Adela Juana Maria Patti*), 1843–1919, Italian operatic soprano, born in Spain.

Pat•ton (pat′n), **George Smith,** 1885–1945, U.S. general.

Paul[1] (pôl), **1. Saint,** died A.D. c67, a missionary and apostle to the gentiles: author of several of the Epistles. **2. Alice,** 1885–1977, U.S. women's-rights activist.

Paul[2] (pôl), **1. Paul I, a.** (*Pavel Petrovich*), 1754–1801, emperor of Russia 1796–1801 (son of Peter III). **b.** 1901–64, king of Greece 1947–64. **2. Paul III** (*Alessandro Farnese*), 1468–1549, Italian pope 1534–49. **3. Paul V** (*Camillo Borghese*), 1552–1621, Italian pope 1605–21. **4. Paul VI** (*Giovanni Battista Montini*), 1897–1978, Italian pope 1963–78.

Paul-Bon•cour (pôl bôN ko͞or′), **Joseph,** 1873–1972, French lawyer and statesman: premier 1932–33.

Pau•li (pô′lē, pou′-), **Wolfgang,** 1900–58, Austrian physicist in the U.S.: Nobel prize 1945.

Paul•ing (pô′ling), **Linus Carl,** born 1901, U.S. chemist: Nobel prize in chemistry 1954; Nobel peace prize 1962.

Pau•li•nus (pô lī′nəs), **Saint,** died A.D. 644, Roman missionary in England with Augustine: 1st archbishop of York 633–644.

Pau•sa•ni•as (pô sā′nē əs), fl. A.D. c175, Greek traveler and geographer.

Pa•va•rot•ti (pav′ə rot′ē, pä′və rô′tē), **Luciano,** born 1935, Italian operatic tenor.

Pav•lov (pav′lof, -lôf), **Ivan Petrovich,** 1849–1936, Russian physiologist: Nobel prize for medicine 1904.

Pa•vlo•va (pav′lə və, päv lō′və, pav-), **Anna,** 1885–1931, Russian ballet dancer.

Pax•ton (pak′stən), **Sir Joseph,** 1801–65, English horticulturist and architect.

Payne (pān), **John Howard,** 1791–1852, U.S. actor and dramatist.

Paz (päz; *Sp.* päs), **Octavio,** born 1914, Mexican poet and essayist: Nobel prize 1990.

Paz Es•tens•so•ro (päs′ es′ten sôr′ō), **Victor,** born 1907, Bolivian economist and statesman: president 1952–56, 1960–64.

Pea•bod•y (pē′bod′ē, -bə dē), **1. Elizabeth Palmer,** 1804–94, U.S. educator: founded the first U.S. kindergarten. **2. Endicott,** 1857–1944, U.S. educator. **3. George,** 1795–1869, U.S. merchant and philanthropist in England.

Pea•cock (pē′kok′), **Thomas Love,** 1785–1866, English poet and novelist.

Peale (pēl), **1. Charles Willson,** 1741–1827, and his brother **James,** 1749–1831, U.S. painters. **2. Norman Vincent,** born 1898, U.S. Protestant clergyman and author. **3. Rembrandt,** 1778–1860, U.S. painter (son of Charles Willson Peale).

Pear•son (pēr′sən), **1. Drew** (*Andrew Russell Pearson*), 1897–1969, U.S. journalist. **2. Lester Bowles,** 1897–1972, Canadian diplomat and politician: Nobel prize for peace 1957; prime minister 1963–68.

Pea•ry (pēr′ē), **Robert Edwin,** 1856–1920, U.S. arctic explorer.

Peck (pek), **Gregory** (*Edward Gregory Peck*), born 1916, U.S. actor.

Pe•der•sen (pith′ər sən), **Charles J.,** 1904–89, U.S. chemist: Nobel prize 1987.

Peel (pēl), **Sir Robert,** 1788–1850, British statesman: founder of the London constabulary; prime minister 1834–35, 1841–46.

Peele (pēl), **George,** 1558?–97?, English dramatist.

Peerce (pērs), **Jan** (*Jacob Pincus Perelmuth*), 1904–84, U.S. opera singer.

Peg•ler (peg′lər), **(James) Westbrook,** 1894–1969, U.S. journalist.

Pei (pā), **I(eoh) M(ing),** born 1917, U.S. architect, born in China.

Peirce (pûrs, pērs), **1. Benjamin,** 1809–80, U.S. mathematician. **2. Charles Sanders,** 1839–1914, U.S. philosopher, mathematician, and physicist.

Pei•sis•tra•tus (pi sis′trə təs, pi-), Pisistratus.

Pe•la•gi•us (pə lā′jē əs), A.D. 360?–420?, British monk and theologian who lived in Rome: teachings opposed by St. Augustine.

Pe•lé (pā lā′, pā′lā), (*Edson Arantes do Nascimento*), born 1940, Brazilian soccer player.

Pel•ham-Hol•les (pel′əm hol′is), **Thomas, 1st Duke of Newcastle,** 1693–1768, British statesman: prime minister 1754–56, 1757–62.

Pel•le•tier (pel′i tēr′; *Fr.* pelᵊ tyā′), **Wilfrid,** 1896–1982, Canadian orchestra conductor.

Pe•lop•i•das (pə lop′i dəs), died 364 B.C., Theban general.

Pen•de•rec•ki (pen′də ret′skē), **Krzysztof,** born 1933, Polish composer.

Peng De•huai (peng′ du′hwī′), 1898–1974, Chinese Communist military leader: defense minister 1954–59.

Penn (pen), **1. Sir William,** 1621–70, English admiral. **2.** his son, **William,** 1644–1718, English Quaker: founder of Pennsylvania.

Pen•nell (pen′l), **Joseph,** 1860–1926, U.S. etcher and writer.

Pen•ney (pen′ē), **J(ames) C(ash),** 1875–1971, U.S. retail merchant.

Pen•zi•as (pent′sē əs, pen′zē-), **Arno Allan,** born 1933, U.S. astrophysicist, born in Germany: Nobel prize for physics 1978.

Pep•in (pep′in), (*"the Short"*) died A.D. 768, king of the Franks 751–768 (father of Charlemagne).

Pepys (pēps, peps, pē′pis, pep′is), **Samuel,** 1633–1703, English diarist and naval official.

Pe•ra•hia (pə ri′ə), **Murray,** born 1947, U.S. pianist.

Per•ce•val (pûr′sə vəl), **Spencer,** 1762–1812, British statesman: prime minister 1809–12.

Per•cy (pûr′sē), **1. Sir Henry** (*"Hotspur"*), 1364–1403, English military and rebel leader. **2. Thomas,** 1729–1811, English bishop, poet, and antiquary. **3. Walker,** 1916–90, U.S. novelist and essayist.

Per•el•man (per′əl mən, pûrl′-), **S(idney) J(oseph),** 1904–79, U.S. author.

Per•es (per′ez), **Shi•mon** (shi mōn′), born 1923, prime minister of Israel 1984–86.

Per•etz (per′its), **I(saac) L(oeb)** or **Yitzchok Leibush,** 1852–1915, Polish author: writer of plays, poems, and short stories in Yiddish.

Pé•rez de Cué•llar (per′ez də kwā′yär), **Javier,** born 1920, Peruvian diplomat: Secretary General of the United Nations since 1982.

Per•go•le•si (per′gə lā′zē), **Giovanni Battista,** 1710–36, Italian composer.

Pe•ri (pe′RĒ), **Jacopo,** 1561–1633, Italian composer.

Per•i•an•der (per′ē an′dər), died 585 B.C., tyrant of Corinth.

Per•i•cles (per′i klēz′), c495–429 B.C., Athenian statesman.

Per•kin (pûr′kin), **Sir William Henry,** 1838–1907, English chemist.

Per•kins (pûr′kinz), **1. Frances,** 1882–1965, U.S. sociologist. **2. Maxwell (Evarts),** 1884–1947, U.S. editor.

Perl•man (pûrl′mən), **It•zhak** (it′säk), born 1945, Israeli violinist.

Pe•rón (pə rōn′, pā-), **1. Eva Duarte de,** 1919–52, Argentine political figure (wife of Juan Perón). **2. Juan (Domingo),** 1895–1974, president of Argentina 1946–55, 1973–74.

Pe•rot (pə rō′), **H(enry) Ross,** born 1930, U.S. businessman and philanthropist.

Per•o•ti•nus (per′ə ti′nəs, -tē′-) also **Per′o•tin′** (-tēn′),

("*Magnus Magister*"), fl. late 12th to early 13th century, French composer.

Per•rault (pə rō′, pe-), **1. Charles,** 1628–1703, French poet, critic, and author of fairy tales. **2.** his brother, **Claude,** 1613–88, French architect, scientist, and physician.

Per•ret (pə rā′), **Auguste,** 1874–1954, French architect.

Per•rin (pe raɴ′), **Jean Baptiste** (zhäɴ), 1870–1942, French physicist.

Per•rot (pə rō′, pe-), **Nicolas,** 1644–1717, North American fur trader and explorer in the Great Lakes region, born in France.

Per•ry (per′ē), **1. Antoinette,** 1888–1946, U.S. actress, theatrical manager, and producer. **2. Bliss,** 1860–1954, U.S. educator, literary critic, and editor. **3. Frederick John** (*Fred*), born 1909, British tennis player. **4. Matthew Calbraith,** 1794–1858, U.S. commodore. **5.** his brother, **Oliver Hazard,** 1785–1819, U.S. naval officer. **6. Ralph Barton,** 1876–1957, U.S. philosopher and educator.

Perse (pers, pûrs), **St.-John** (sin′jən), St.-John Perse.

Per•shing (pûr′shing, -zhing), **John Joseph** ("*Black-jack*"), 1860–1948, U.S. general in World War I.

Per•si•chet•ti (pûr′si ket′ē), **Vincent,** born 1915, U.S. composer.

Per•sius (pûr′shəs, -shē əs), (*Aulus Persius Flaccus*), A.D. 34–62, Roman satirist.

Pe•ru•gi•no (per′o͞o jē′nō), (*Pietro Vannucci*), 1446–1524, Italian painter.

Per•utz (per′əts, pə ro͞ots′), **Max Ferdinand,** born 1914, English chemist, born in Austria: Nobel prize 1962.

Pe•ruz•zi (pə ro͞ot′sē), **Baldassare Tommaso,** 1481–1536, Italian architect and painter.

Pes•ta•loz•zi (pes′tl ot′sē), **Johann Heinrich,** 1746–1827, Swiss educator.

Pé•tain (pā taɴ′), **Henri Philippe Omer,** 1856–1951, marshal of France: premier of the Vichy government 1940–44.

Pe•ter[1] (pē′tər), died A.D. 67?, one of the 12 apostles and the reputed author of two of the Epistles. Also called **Simon Peter.**

Pe•ter[2] (pē′tər), **1. Peter I** ("*the Great*"), 1672–1725, czar of Russia 1682–1725. **2. Peter II,** 1923–70, king of Yugoslavia 1934–45. **3. Peter III,** 1728–62, czar of Russia 1762 (husband of Catherine II).

Pe•ters (pē′tərz), **Roberta,** born 1930, U.S. soprano.

Pe•ter•son (pē′tər sən), **1. Oscar,** born 1925, Canadian jazz pianist. **2. Roger Tory,** born 1908, U.S. ornithologist, author, and artist.

Pe′ter the Her′mit, c1050–1115, French monk: preacher of the first Crusade 1095–99.

Pe•ti•pa (pet′ē pä′, pet′ē pä′), **Marius,** 1819–1910, French ballet dancer and choreographer in Russia.

Pe•tö•fi (pet′ə fē′), **Sán•dor** (shän′dôr), (*Sándor Petrovics*), 1823–49, Hungarian poet and patriot.

Pe•trarch (pē′trärk, pe′-), (*Francesco Petrarca*), 1304–74, Italian poet and scholar.

Pe•trie (pē′trē), **Sir (William Matthew) Flinders,** 1853–1942, English Egyptologist and archaeologist.

Pe•tril•lo (pi tril′ō), **James Caesar,** 1892–1984, U.S. labor leader: president of the American Federation of Musicians 1940–58.

Pe•tro•ni•us (pi trō′nē əs), **Gaius** (*Gaius Petronius Arbiter*) (*"Arbiter Elegantiae"*), died A.D. 66?, Roman satirist.

Pet•ty (pet′ē), **Richard,** born 1937, U.S. racing-car driver.

Pevs•ner (pevz′nər, pefs′-), **Antoine,** 1886–1962, French sculptor and painter, born in Russia (brother of Naum Gabo).

Pfitz•ner (pfits′nər), **Hans Erich,** 1869–1949, German composer and conductor.

Phae•drus (fē′drəs, fed′rəs), fl. A.D. c40, Roman writer of fables.

Pham Van Dong (fäm′ vän′ dông′), born 1906, Vietnamese political leader: prime minister of North Vietnam 1955–76 and of unified Vietnam 1976–86.

Phei•dip•pi•des (fī dip′i dēz′), 5th-century B.C. Athenian runner sent to request aid from Sparta against the Persians before the battle at Marathon 490 B.C.

Phid•i•as (fid′ē əs), c500–432? B.C., Greek sculptor.

Phil•by (fil′bē), **Harold Adrian Russell** (*"Kim"*), born 1912, British double agent: defected to U.S.S.R. 1963.

Phil•ip[1] (fil′ip), **1.** one of the 12 apostles. **2.** one of the leaders of the Christian Hellenists in the early church in Jerusalem who afterwards became an evangelist and missionary. **3. King** (*Metacomet*), died 1676, sachem of the Wampanoag Indians 1662–76. **4. Prince, Duke of Edinburgh,** born 1921, consort of Elizabeth II.

Phil•ip[2] (fil′ip), **1. Philip I,** 1052–1108, king of France 1060–1108 (son of Henry I of France). **2. Philip II, a.** (*"Philip of Macedon"*) 382–336 B.C., king of Macedonia 359–336 (father of Alexander the Great). **b.** (*"Philip Augustus"*) 1165–1223, king of France 1180–1223. **c.** 1527–98, king of Spain 1556–98 (husband of Mary I). **3. Philip IV** (*"Philip the Fair"*), 1268–1314, king of France 1285–1314. **4. Philip V,** 1683–1746, king of Spain 1700–46. **5. Philip VI,** 1293–1350, king of France 1328–50: first ruler of the house of Valois.

Phil′ip of Swa′bi•a (swā′bē ə), 1180?–1208, king of Germany and uncrowned emperor of the Holy Roman Empire 1198–1208 (son of Frederick I).

Phil•ips (fil′ips), **Ambrose,** 1675?–1749, English poet and dramatist.

Phil′ip the Good′, 1396–1467, duke of Burgundy 1419–67.

Phil•lips (fil′ips), **1. David Graham,** 1867–1911, U.S. novelist. **2. Stephen,** 1868–1915, English poet and playwright. **3. Wendell,** 1811–84, U.S. orator and reformer.

Phi•lo Ju•dae•us (fī′lō jo͞o dē′əs), c20 B.C.–A.D. c50, Alexandrian Jewish theologian and philosopher.

Pho•ci•on (fō′shē ən, -on′), 402?–317 B.C., Athenian statesman and general.

Pho•ti•us (fō′shē əs), A.D. c820–891, patriarch of Constantinople 858–867, 877–882.

Phyfe (fīf), **Duncan,** 1768–1854, U.S. cabinetmaker, born in Scotland.

Pi•af (pē äf′, pē′äf), **Edith** (*Edith Giovanna Gassion*), 1914–63, French singer.

Pia•get (pē′ə zhā′, pyä-), **Jean** (zhäN), 1896–1980, Swiss cognitive psychologist.

Pia•ti•gor•sky (pyä′ti gôr′skē, pyat′i-), **Gregor,** 1903–76, U.S. cellist, born in Russia.

Pi•az•zi (pē ät′sē, -ä′zē), **Giuseppe,** 1746–1826, Italian astronomer.

Pi•card (pē kär′, -kärd′), **1. Charles Émile,** 1856–1941, French mathematician. **2. Jean** (zhäN), 1620–82, French astronomer.

Pi•cas•so (pi kä′sō, -kas′ō), **Pablo,** 1881–1973, Spanish painter and sculptor in France.

Pic•card (pē kär′, -kärd′), **1. Auguste,** 1884–1962, Swiss physicist, aeronaut, inventor, and deep-sea explorer. **2.** his son **Jacques,** born 1922, Swiss oceanographer and bathyscaphe designer, born in Belgium. **3. Jean Félix** (zhäN), 1884–1963, U.S. chemist and aeronautical engineer, born in Switzerland (brother of Auguste).

Pic•cin•ni or **Pic•ci•ni** or **Pi•cin•ni** (pē chē′nē), **Niccolò** (or **Nicola,**) 1728–1800, Italian composer.

Pick•ens (pik′ənz), **Andrew,** 1739–1817, American Revolutionary general.

Pick•er•ing (pik′ər ing), **Edward Charles,** 1846–1919, and his brother, **William Henry,** 1858–1938, U.S. astronomers.

Pick•ett (pik′it), **George Edward,** 1825–75, Confederate general.

Pick•ford (pik′fərd), **Mary** (*Gladys Marie Smith*), 1893–1979, U.S. motion-picture actress, born in Canada.

Pi•co del•la Mi•ran•do•la (pē′kō del′ə mə ran′dl ə), **Count Giovanni,** 1463–94, Italian humanist and writer.

Pid•geon (pij′ən), **Walter,** 1898–1984, U.S. actor, born in Canada.

Pierce (pērs), **1. Franklin,** 1804–69, 14th president of the U.S. 1853–57. **2. John Robinson,** born 1910, U.S. electrical engineer: helped develop communications satellites.

Pie•ro del•la Fran•ce•sca (pē âr′ō del′ə fran ches′kə, frän-), (*Piero de' Franceschi*), FRANCESCA, Piero della.

Pie•ro di Co•si•mo (pē âr′ō di kō′zə mō′), (*Piero di Lorenzo*), 1462–1521, Italian painter.

Pike (pīk), **1. James Albert,** 1913–69, U.S. Protestant Episcopal clergyman, lawyer, and author. **2. Zebulon Montgomery,** 1779–1813, U.S. general and explorer.

Pi•late (pī′lət), **Pon•tius** (pon′shəs, -tē əs), fl. early 1st century A.D., Roman procurator of Judea A.D. 26–36?.

Pills•bur•y (pilz′ber′ē, -bə rē), **Charles Alfred,** 1842–99, U.S. businessman.

Pil•sud•ski (pil so͞ot′skē), **Józef,** 1867–1935, president of Poland 1918–22; premier 1926–28, 1930.

Pinch•back (pinch′bak′), **Pinckney Benton Stewart,** 1837–1921, U.S. politician.

Pin•chot (pin′shō), **Gifford,** 1863–1946, U.S. political leader, forester, and teacher.

Pinck•ney (pingk′nē), **1. Charles,** 1757–1824, American Revolutionary leader and politician: senator 1798–1801. **2. Charles Cotesworth,** 1746–1825, and his brother **Thomas,** 1750–1825, U.S. patriots and statesmen.

Pin•dar (pin′dər), 522?–443? B.C., Greek poet.

Pind•ling (pind′ling), **Lynden Oscar,** born 1930, Bahamian political leader: prime minister since 1967.

Pi•nel (pē nel′), **Phillippe,** 1745–1826, French physician: reformer in the treatment and care of the mentally ill.

Pi•ne•ro (pə nēr′ō, -nâr′ō), **Sir Arthur Wing,** 1855–1934, English playwright and actor.

Pink•er•ton (ping′kər tən), **Allan,** 1819–84, U.S. detective, born in Scotland.

Pink•ham (ping′kəm), **Lydia (Estes),** 1819–83, U.S. businesswoman: manufactured patent medicine.

Pin•ter (pin′tər), **Harold,** born 1930, English playwright.

Pin•za (pin′zə), **Ezio,** 1895–1957, Italian basso, in the U.S.

Pin•zón (pin zōn′), **Martín Alonzo,** c1440–93?, and his brother, **Vicente Yáñez,** c1460–1524?, Spanish navigators with Christopher Columbus.

Pi•oz•zi (pē ot′sē), **Hester Lynch,** THRALE, Hester Lynch.

Pi•ran•del•lo (pir′ən del′ō), **Luigi,** 1867–1936, Italian dramatist, novelist, and poet: Nobel prize 1934.

Pi•ra•ne•si (pir′ə nā′zē), **Giambattista,** 1720–78, Italian architect and engraver.

Pire (*Fr.* pēr), **Dominique Georges Henri,** 1910–69, Belgian priest: Nobel peace prize 1958.

Pi•sa•nel•lo (pē′zä nel′ō), **Antonio** (*Antonio Pisano*), 1397–1455?, Italian painter and medalist.

Pi•sa•no (pi zä′nō), **1. Andrea,** c1270–c1348, Italian sculptor. **2. Giovanni,** c1245–c1320, and his father, **Nicola,** c1220–78, Italian sculptors and architects.

Pi•sis•trat•i•dae (pi′sə strat′i dē′, pis′ə-), Hippias and Hipparchus, the sons of Pisistratus.

Pi•sis•tra•tus or **Pei•sis•tra•tus** (pī sis′trə təs, pi-), c605-527 B.C., tyrant of Athens c560-527.

Pis•sar•ro (pi sär′ō), **Camille,** 1830–1903, French painter.

Pis•ton (pis′tən), **Walter,** 1894–1976, U.S. composer.

Pitch•er (pich′ər), **Molly** (*Mary Ludwig Hays McCauley*), 1754–1832, American Revolutionary heroine.

Pit•man (pit′mən), **Sir Isaac,** 1813–97, English inventor of a system of shorthand.

Pitt (pit), **1. William, 1st Earl of Chatham,** 1708–78, British statesman. **2.** his son **William,** 1759–1806, British prime minister 1783–1801, 1804–06.

Pit•ta•cus (pit′ə kəs), c650–570 B.C., democratic statesman and reformer from Mytilene.

Pi•us (pī′əs), **1. Pius II,** (*Enea Silvio de Piccolomini*) 1405–64, Italian pope 1458–64. **2. Pius V, Saint** (*Michele Ghislieri*) 1504–72, Italian pope 1566–72. **3. Pius VII,** (*Luigi Barnaba Chiaramonti*) 1740–1823, Italian pope 1800–23. **4. Pius IX,** (*Giovanni Maria Mastai-Ferretti*) 1792–1878, Italian pope 1846–78. **5. Pius X, Saint** (*Giuseppe Sarto*) 1835–1914, Italian pope 1903–14. **6. Pius XI,** (*Achille Ratti*) 1857–1939, Italian pope 1922–39. **7. Pius XII,** (*Eugenio Pacelli*) 1876–1958, Italian pope 1939–58.

Pi•zar•ro (pi zär′ō), **Francisco,** c1470–1541, Spanish conqueror of Peru.

Planck (plängk), **Max Karl Ernst,** 1858–1947, German physicist: Nobel prize 1918.

Plante (plänt), **Jacques,** 1929–86, Canadian ice-hockey player.

Plan•tin (plän tan′), **Christophe,** c1520–1589, French typographer.

Plath (plath), **Sylvia,** 1932–63, U.S. poet.

Pla•to (plā′tō), 427–347 B.C., Greek philosopher.

Plau•tus (plô′təs), **Titus Maccius,** c254–c184 B.C., Roman dramatist.

Play•er (plā′ər), **Gary,** born 1935, South African golfer.

Pla•za Las•so (plä′sä lä′sō), **Galo,** 1906–87, Ecuadorian statesman and diplomat, born in the U.S.: president 1948–52.

Ple•kha•nov (pli kä′nôf, -nof; *Russ.* plyi khä′nəf), **Georgi** (or **Georgy**) **Valentinovich,** 1857–1918, Russian philosopher and leader of the Mensheviks.

Plin•y (plin′ē), **1.** (*"the Elder"*) (*Gaius Plinius Secundus*) A.D. 23–79, Roman naturalist and writer. **2.** his nephew (*"the Younger"*) (*Gaius Plinius Caecilius Secundus*) A.D. 62?–c113, Roman writer and orator.

Pli•set•ska•ya (pli set′skä yə), **Maya (Mikhailovna)** born 1925, Russian ballet dancer.

Plo•ti•nus (plō tī′nəs), A.D. 205?–270?, Roman philosopher, born in Egypt: founder of Neoplatonism.

Plumb (plum), **J(ohn) H(arold),** born 1911, British historian.

Plu•tarch (plōō′tärk), A.D. c46–c120, Greek biographer.

Po•ca•hon•tas (pō′kə hon′təs), 1595?–1617, American Indian woman, daughter of Powhatan.

Po Chü-i (bô′ jy′ē′), A.D. 772–846, Chinese poet.

Pod•gor•ny (pod gôr′nē, pud-), **Nikolai Viktorovich,** 1903–83, Russian government official: president of the Soviet Union 1965–77.

Poe (pō), **Edgar Allan,** 1809–49, U.S. short-story writer and poet.

Po•ga•ny (pō gä′nē), **Willy** (*William Andrew*), 1882–1955, U.S. painter, stage designer, and illustrator; born in Hungary.

Poin•ca•ré (pwan ka rā′), **1. Jules Henri,** 1854–1912,

French mathematician. **2.** his cousin **Raymond,** 1860–1934, president of France 1913–20.

Poi•ret (pwä rā′), **Paul,** 1879–1944, French fashion designer.

Poi•ti•er (pwä′tē ā′), **Sidney,** born 1927, U.S. actor and director.

Po•li•tian (pō lish′ən), (*Angelo Poliziano*) 1454–94, Italian classical scholar and poet.

Polk (pōk), **James Knox,** 1795–1849, the 11th president of the U.S. 1845–49.

Pol•lai•uo•lo (pō′lī wō′lō) also **Pol′lai•o′lo** (-lī ō′-), **Pol′-laj•uo′lo** (-lī wō′-). **1. Antonio,** 1429–98, Italian sculptor, painter, and goldsmith. **2.** his brother **Piero,** 1443–96, painter, sculptor, and goldsmith.

Pol•lock (pol′ək), **1. Sir Frederick,** 1845–1937, English legal scholar and author. **2. Jackson,** 1912–56, U.S. painter.

Po•lo (pō′lō), **Marco,** c1254–1324, Venetian traveler.

Po•lyb•i•us (pə lib′ē əs), c205–c123 B.C., Greek historian.

Pol•y•carp (pol′ē kärp′), **Saint,** A.D. 69?–155, bishop of Smyrna and a Christian martyr.

Pol•y•cli•tus or **Pol•y•clei•tus** (pol′i klī′təs), also **Pol•y•cle•tus** (-klē′-), fl. c450–c420 B.C., Greek sculptor.

Po•lyc•ra•tes (pə lik′rə tēz′), died 522? B.C., Greek tyrant of Samos.

Pol•y•do•rus (pol′i dôr′əs, -dōr′-), fl. 1st century B.C., Greek sculptor.

Pol•yg•no•tus (pol′ig nō′təs), fl. c450 B.C., Greek painter.

Pom•pa•dour (pom′pə dôr′, -dōr′, -do͝or′), **Marquise de** (*Jeanne Antoinette Poisson*), 1721–64, mistress of Louis XV.

Pom•pe•ia (pom pē′ə, -pā′ə), fl. 1st century B.C., second wife of Julius Caesar, divorced in 62 B.C.

Pom•pey (pom′pē), (*Gnaeus Pompeius Magnus*) (*"the Great"*) 106–48 B.C., Roman general and statesman.

Pom•pi•dou (pom′pi do͞o′), **Georges Jean Raymond** (zhäɴ), 1911–74, prime minister of France 1962–68; president 1969–74.

Ponce de Le•ón (pons′ də lē′ən, pon′sā dā lē ōn′), **Juan,** c1460–1521, Spanish explorer.

Pon•ce•let (pôɴsᵊ le′), **Jean Victor** (zhäɴ), 1788–1867, French mathematician.

Pon•chiel•li (pông kyel′lē), **Amilcare,** 1834–86, Italian composer.

Pons (ponz, pôɴs), **Lily,** 1904–76, U.S. soprano, born in France.

Pon•selle (pon sel′), **Rosa (Melba),** 1897–1981, U.S. soprano.

Pon•ti•ac (pon′tē ak′), c1720–69, Ottawa Indian chief.

Pon′tius Pi′late (pon′shəs, -tē əs), PILATE, Pontius.

Pon•top•pi•dan (pon top′i dän′), **Hen•rik** (hen′rēk), 1857–1943, Danish novelist: Nobel prize 1917.

Pope (pōp), **1. Alexander,** 1688–1744, English poet. **2.**

John, 1822–92, Union general in the U.S. Civil War. **3. John Russell,** 1874–1937, U.S. architect.

Po•pé (pō pā′), died 1690?, Pueblo medicine man: led rebellion against the Spanish 1680.

Pop•pae•a Sa•bi•na (po pē′ə sə bī′nə, -bē′-), died A.D. 65?, second wife of the Roman emperor Nero.

Pop•per (pop′ər), **Sir Karl (Raimund),** born 1902, British philosopher, born in Austria.

Por•phy•ry (pôr′fə rē), (*Malchus*) A.D.c233–c304, Greek philosopher.

Por•ter (pôr′tər, pōr′-), **1. Cole,** 1893–1964, U.S. composer. **2. David,** 1780–1843, U.S. naval officer. **3.** his son, **David Dixon,** 1813–91, Union naval officer in the Civil War. **4. Gene** (*Gene Stratton Porter*), 1868–1924, U.S. novelist. **5. Sir George,** born 1920, British chemist: Nobel prize 1967. **6. Katherine Anne,** 1890–1980, U.S. writer. **7. Noah,** 1811–92, U.S. educator, writer, and lexicographer. **8. Rodney Robert,** 1917–85, British biochemist: Nobel prize for medicine 1972. **9. William Sydney** (*"O. Henry"*), 1862–1910, U.S. short-story writer.

Por•ti•na•ri (pôr′ti när′ē), **Cândido,** 1903–62, Brazilian painter.

Post (pōst), **1. Charles William,** 1854–1914, U.S. businessman: developed breakfast foods. **2. Emily Price,** 1873?–1960, U.S. writer on social etiquette. **3. Wiley,** 1899–1935, U.S. aviator.

Po•tëm•kin (pə tem′kin, -tyôm′-), **Prince Grigori Aleksandrovich,** 1739–91, Russian statesman.

Po•tok (pō′tôk, pō′-), **Chaim,** born 1929, U.S. novelist.

Pot•ter (pot′ər), **1. Beatrix,** 1866–1943, English writer and illustrator of children's books. **2. Paul,** 1625–54, Dutch painter.

Pou•lenc (po͞o laɴk′), **Francis,** 1899–1963, French composer.

Pound (pound), **1. Ezra Loomis,** 1885–1972, U.S. poet. **2. Louise,** 1872–1958, U.S. scholar and linguist. **3. Roscoe,** 1870–1964, U.S. legal scholar and writer.

Pous•sin (po͞o saɴ′), **Nicolas,** 1594–1655, French painter.

Pow•ell (pou′əl *for 1, 4, 5;* pō′əl, pou′- *for 2, 3*), **1. Adam Clayton, Jr.,** 1908–72, U.S. clergyman, politician, and civil-rights leader: congressman 1945–67, 1969–71. **2. Anthony,** born 1905, English author. **3. Cecil Frank,** 1903–69, English physicist: Nobel prize 1950. **4. John Wesley,** 1834–1902, U.S. geologist and ethnologist. **5. Lewis Franklin, Jr.,** born 1907, associate justice of the U.S. Supreme Court 1972–87.

Pow•ers (pou′ərz), **Hiram,** 1805–73, U.S. sculptor.

Pow•ha•tan (pou′ə tan′, pou′hat′n), c1550–1618, North American Indian chief in Virginia, father of Pocahontas.

Pow•ys (pō′is), **John Cowper,** 1872–1963, and his brothers **Llewelyn,** 1884–1939, and **Theodore Francis,** 1875–1953, English authors.

Pra•ja•dhi•pok (prə chä′ti pok′), 1893–1941, king of Siam 1925–35.

Pra•sad (prə säd′), **Rajendra,** 1884–1963, first president of the Republic of India 1950–62.

Pratt (prat), **Edwin John,** 1883–1964, Canadian poet.

Prax•it•e•les (prak sit′l ēz′), fl. c350 B.C., Greek sculptor.

Pre•ble (preb′əl), **Edward,** 1761–1807, U.S. naval officer.

Pregl (prā′gəl), **Fritz,** 1869–1930, Austrian chemist: Nobel prize 1923.

Pre•log (prel′ôg, -og), **Vladimir,** born 1906, Swiss chemist, born in Yugoslavia: Nobel prize 1975.

Prem•in•ger (prem′in jər), **Otto (Ludwig),** 1906–86, U.S. motion-picture actor, director, and producer, born in Austria.

Pren•der•gast (pren′dər gast′, -gäst′), **Maurice Brazil,** 1859–1924, U.S. painter.

Pres•cott (pres′kət, -kot), **1. William,** 1726–95, American Revolutionary military leader. **2. William Hickling,** 1796–1859, U.S. historian.

Pres•ley (pres′lē, prez′-), **Elvis (Aron),** 1935–77, U.S. singer.

Pre•to•ri•us (pri tôr′ē əs, -tōr′-), **Andries Wilhelmus Jacobus,** 1799–1853, and his son **Marthinus Wessels,** 1819–1901, Boer soldiers and statesmen in South Africa.

Prev•in (prev′in), **Andre,** born 1929, U.S. conductor and composer.

Pré•vost (prā vō′), **Marcel,** 1862–1941, French novelist and dramatist.

Pré•vost d'Ex•iles (prā vō′ deg zēl′), **Antoine François** (*"Abbé Prévost"*), 1697–1763, French novelist.

Price (prīs), **1. Bruce,** 1845–1903, U.S. architect. **2. (Mary) Le•on•tyne** (lē′ən tēn′), born 1927, U.S. soprano.

Pride (prīd), **Thomas,** died 1658, English soldier and regicide.

Priest•ley (prēst′lē), **1. J(ohn) B(oynton),** 1894–1984, English writer. **2. Joseph,** 1733–1804, English chemist, author, and clergyman.

Pri•go•gine (pri gō′zhin, -gō zhēn′), **Ilya,** born 1917, Belgian chemist, born in Russia: Nobel prize 1977.

Pri•mo de Ri•ve•ra (prē′mō ŧħā ri vâr′ə), **Miguel, Marqués de Estella** (*Miguel Prima de Rivera y Orbaneja*), 1870–1930, Spanish general and political leader: dictator of Spain 1923–29.

Prince (prins), **Harold S.,** born 1928, U.S. stage director and producer.

Pri•or (prī′ər), **Matthew,** 1664–1721 English poet.

Pris•ci•an (prish′ē ən, prish′ən), fl. A.D. c500, Latin grammarian.

Pro•clus (prō′kləs, prok′ləs), A.D. c411–485, Greek philosopher.

Pro•co•pi•us (prō kō′pē əs, prə-), A.D. c490–c562, Byzantine historian.

Pro•kho•rov (prō′kə rôf′, -rof′), **Aleksandr Mikhailovich,** born 1916, Russian physicist: Nobel prize 1964.

Pro•ko•fiev (prə kô′fē əf, -ef′, -kō′-), **Sergei Sergeevich,** 1891–1953, Russian composer.

Pro•per•ti•us (prō pûr′shē əs, -shəs), **Sextus,** c50–c15 B.C., Roman poet.

Pros•ser (pros′ər), **Gabriel,** 1775?–1800, U.S. leader of unsuccessful slave revolt.

Pro•tag•o•ras (prō tag′ər əs), c480–c421 B.C., Greek Sophist philosopher.

Prou•dhon (prōō dôɴ′), **Pierre Joseph,** 1809–65, French socialist and writer.

Proust (prōōst), **1. Joseph Louis,** 1754–1826, French chemist. **2. Marcel,** 1871–1922, French novelist.

Pru•d'hon (pʀōō dôɴ′), **Pierre Paul**, 1758–1823, French painter.

Prynne (prin), **William,** 1600–69, English Puritan leader and pamphleteer.

Ptol•e•my[1] (tol′ə mē), (*Claudius Ptolemaeus*) fl. A.D. 127–151, Alexandrian mathematician, astronomer, and geographer.

Ptol•e•my[2] (tol′ə mē), **1. Ptolemy I,** (surnamed *Soter*) 367?–280 B.C., ruler of Egypt 323–285: founder of Macedonian dynasty in Egypt. **2. Ptolemy II,** (surnamed *Philadelphus*) 309?–247? B.C., king of Egypt 285–247? (son of Ptolemy I).

Puc•ci•ni (pōō chē′nē), **Giacomo,** 1858–1924, Italian composer.

Pu•dov•kin (pōō dôf′kin, -dof′-), **Vsevolod Ilarionovich,** 1893–1953, Russian motion-picture director.

Pu•gin (pyōō′jin), **1. Augustus Charles,** 1762–1832, French architectural draftsman and archaeologist in England. **2.** his son, **Augustus Welby Northmore,** 1812–52, English architect and designer.

P'u-i (pōō′ē′), Pu-yi.

Pu•las•ki (pə las′kē), **Count Casimir,** 1748–79, Polish patriot: general in the American Revolutionary army.

Pu•litz•er (pŏŏl′it sər, pyōō′lit-), **Joseph,** 1847–1911, U.S. journalist and publisher, born in Hungary.

Pull•man (pŏŏl′mən), **George Mortimer,** 1831–97, U.S. inventor and railroad car designer.

Pu•pin (pōō pēn′, pyōō-), **Michael Idvorsky,** 1858–1935, U.S. inventor, physicist, and author, born in Hungary.

Pur•cell (pûr sel′ *for 1;* pûr′səl *for 2*), **1. Edward Mills,** born 1912, U.S. physicist: Nobel prize 1952. **2. Henry,** 1659–95, English composer.

Pur•chas (pûr′chəs), **Samuel,** 1575?–1626, English writer and editor of travel books.

Pu•sey (pyōō′zē), **1. Edward Bouverie,** 1800–82, English clergyman. **2. Nathan Marsh,** born 1907, U.S. educator: president of Harvard University 1953–71.

Push•kin (pŏŏsh′kin), **Alexander Sergeevich,** 1799–1837, Russian poet and dramatist.

Put•nam (put′nəm), **1. Herbert,** 1861–1955, U.S. librarian: headed Library of Congress 1899–1939. **2. Israel,** 1718–90, American Revolutionary general. **3. Rufus,**

1738–1824, American Revolutionary officer: engineer and colonizer in Ohio.

Pu•vis de Cha•vannes (po͝o vē′ də sha van′), **Pierre Cécile,** 1824–98, French painter.

Pu-yi (po͞o′yē′), **Henry,** 1906–67, last emperor of China 1908–12; puppet emperor of Manchukuo 1934–45.

Pyle (pīl), **1.** **2. Ernest** (*"Ernie"*), 1900–45, U.S. war correspondent and journalist. **3. Howard,** 1853–1911, U.S. illustrator and author.

Pym (pim), **John,** 1584–1643, English statesman.

Pyn•chon (pin′chən), **1. Thomas,** born 1937, U.S. novelist. **2. William,** 1590?–1662, English colonist in America.

Pyr•rho (pir′ō), c365–c275 B.C., Greek philosopher.

Pyr•rhus (pir′əs), c318–272 B.C., king of Epirus c300–272.

Py•thag•o•ras (pi thag′ər əs), c582–c500 B.C., Greek philosopher and mathematician.

Q

Qad•da•fi or **Qa•dha•fi** (kə dä′fē), **Mu•am•mar (Muhammad) al-** or **el-** (mo͞o ä′mär), born 1942, Libyan chief of state since 1969.

Qua•nah (kwä′nə), (*Quanah Parker*), 1845?–1911, Comanche leader.

Quan•trill (kwon′tril), **William Clarke,** 1837–65, Confederate guerrilla leader.

Quantz (kvänts), **Johann Joachim,** 1697–1773, German flutist and composer: teacher of Frederick the Great.

Qua•si•mo•do (kwä′sə mō′dō, -zə mō′-), **Salvatore,** 1901–68, Italian poet: Nobel prize 1959.

Quay (kwā), **Matthew Stanley,** 1833–1904, U.S. politician: senator 1887–99, 1901–4.

Quayle (kwāl), **James Danforth** (*Dan*), born 1947, vice president of the U.S. since 1989.

Quer•cia (kwâr′chä), **Jacopo Della,** 1374?–1438, Italian sculptor.

Ques•nay (kā nā′), **François,** 1694–1774, French economist and physician.

Que•zon y Mo•li•na (kā′zon ē mō lē′nə, -sōn), **Manuel Luis,** 1878–1944, 1st president of the Philippine Commonwealth 1933–44.

Quid•de (kvid′ə), **Ludwig,** 1858–1941, German historian and pacifist: Nobel peace prize 1927.

Quil•ler-Couch (kwil′ər ko͞och′), **Sir Arthur Thomas** ("*Q*"), 1863–1944, English novelist and critic.

Quin•cy (kwin′zē, -sē), **Josiah,** 1744–75, American patriot and writer.

Quin•til•ian (kwin til′yən, -ē ən), (*Marcus Fabius Quintilianus*) A.D. c35–c95, Roman rhetorician.

R

Raab (rab), **Julius,** 1891–1964, Austrian engineer and statesman: chancellor of Austria 1953–61.

Rabe (rāb), **David (William),** born 1940, U.S. playwright.

Rab•e•lais (rab′ə lā′, rab′ə lā′), **François,** c1490–1553, French satirist and humorist.

Ra•bi (rä′bē), **Isidor Isaac,** 1898–1988, U.S. physicist: Nobel prize 1944.

Ra•bin (rä bēn′), **Yit•zhak** (yit′säk), born 1922, Israeli military and political leader: prime minister 1974–77.

Ra•bi•no•witz (rə bin′ə vits, -wits), **Solomon,** ALEICHEM, Sholom.

Ra•cine (rə sēn′, ra-), **Jean Baptiste,** 1639–99, French dramatist.

Rack•ham (rak′əm), **Arthur,** 1867–1939, English illustrator and painter.

Rad•cliffe (rad′klif), **Ann (Ward),** 1764–1823, English writer of Gothic romances.

Ra•dek (rä′dek), **Karl,** 1885–1939?, Russian writer and politician.

Ra•detz•ky (rä dets′kē), **Count Joseph,** 1766–1858, Austrian field marshal.

Rad•ford (rad′fərd), **Arthur William,** 1896–1973, U.S. admiral: chairman of Joint Chiefs of Staff 1953–57.

Ra•dha•krish•nan (rä′də krish′nən), **Sir Sarvepalli,** 1888–1975, president of India 1962–67.

Ra•din (rād′n), **Paul,** 1883–1959, U.S. anthropologist, born in Poland.

Rae•burn (rā′bərn), **Sir Henry,** 1756–1823, Scottish painter.

Raf•fles (raf′əlz), **Sir Thomas Stamford,** 1781–1826, English colonial administrator in the East Indies.

Ra•fi•nesque (rä′fē nesk′), **Constantine Samuel,** 1783–1840, U.S. naturalist, born in Turkey.

Raf•san•ja•ni (räf′sän jä′nē), **Hojatolislam Ali Akbar Hashemi,** born 1935, president of Iran since 1989.

Rah•man (rä′män), **Prince Abdul,** ABDUL RAHMAN, Tunku.

Rai•mon•di (rī mōn′dē, -mon′-), **Marcantonio,** c1480–c1534, Italian engraver.

Rai•ney (rā′nē), **1. Gertrude** (*"Ma"*), 1886–1939, U.S. blues singer. **2. Joseph Hayne,** 1832–87, U.S. politician: first black congressman 1870–79.

Rai•nier III (rā nēr′, re-, rə-; *Fr.* RE nyā′), **Rainier Louis Henri Maxence Bertrand de Gri•mal•di** (GRē mAl dē′), **Prince of Monaco,** born 1923, reigning prince of Monaco since 1949.

Rain•wa•ter (rān′wô′tər, -wot′ər), **(Leo) James,** 1917–86, U.S. physicist: Nobel prize 1975.

Ra•leigh or **Ra•legh** (rô′lē, rä′-), **Sir Walter,** 1552?–1618, English explorer and writer.

Rama IX, (*Bhumibol Adulyadej*) born 1927, king of Thailand since 1950.

Ra•ma•krish•na (rä′mə krish′nə), **Sri** (srē, shrē), 1836–86, Hindu religious reformer and mystic.

Ra•man (rä′mən), **Sir Chandrasekhara Venkata,** 1888–1970, Indian physicist: Nobel prize 1930.

Ra•ma•nu•jan (rä mä′nōō jən), **Srinivasa,** 1887–1920, Indian mathematician.

Ram•bert (räm bâr′) **Dame Marie** (*Cyvia* or *Myriam Rambam*), 1888–1982, English ballet dancer, producer, and director, born in Poland.

Ra•meau (ra mō′), **Jean Philippe** (zhäɴ), 1683–1764, French composer and musical theorist.

Ra•mée (rə mā′), **Louise de la** (*"Ouida"*), 1839–1908, English novelist.

Ram•e•ses (ram′ə sēz′), Ramses.

Ra•món y Ca•jal (rä mōn′ ē kä häl′), **Santiago,** 1852–1934, Spanish histologist: Nobel prize for medicine 1906.

Ram•pal (räm päl′), **Jean-Pierre** (zhäɴ pyer′), born 1922, French flutist.

Ram•say (ram′zē), **1. Allan,** 1686–1758, Scottish poet. **2. George,** Dalhousie, George Ramsay, Earl of. **3. James Andrew Broun,** Dalhousie, James Andrew Broun Ramsay, 1st Marquis and 10th Earl of. **4. Sir William,** 1852–1916, English chemist: Nobel prize 1904.

Ram•ses (ram′sēz) also **Rameses, 1. Ramses II,** king of ancient Egypt 1292–1225 B.C. **2. Ramses III,** king of ancient Egypt 1198–1167 B.C.

Ram•sey (ram′zē), **Arthur Michael** (*Baron Ramsey of Canterbury*), born 1904, English clergyman and scholar: archbishop of Canterbury 1961–74.

Rand (rand), **Ayn** (īn), 1905–82, U.S. novelist and essayist, born in Russia.

Ran•dolph (ran′dolf, -dəlf), **1. A(sa) Philip,** 1889–1979, U.S. labor leader. **2. Edmund Jennings,** 1753–1813, U.S. statesman: first U.S. Attorney General 1789–94; Secretary of State 1794–95. **3. John,** 1773–1833, U.S. statesman and author.

Ran•jit Singh (run′jit sing′), (*"Lion of the Punjab"*) 1780–1839, Indian maharaja: founder of the Sikh kingdom of Punjab.

Rank (räŋgk), **Otto,** 1884–1939, Austrian psychoanalyst.

Ran•ke (räng′kə), **Leopold von,** 1795–1886, German historian.

Ran•kin (rang′kin), **Jeannette,** 1880–1973, U.S. women's-rights leader and pacifist: first woman elected to Congress; served 1917–19, 1941–43.

Ran•kine (rang′kin), **William John Macquorn,** 1820–70, Scottish engineer and physicist.

Ran•som (ran′səm), **John Crowe,** 1888–1974, U.S. poet, critic, and teacher.

Raph•a•el (raf′ē əl, rā′fē-, rä′fī el′), (*Raffaello Santi* or *Sanzio*) 1483–1520, Italian painter.

Rapp (rap; *Ger.* räp), **George,** 1757–1847, U.S. religious preacher, born in Germany: leader of the Harmonists.

Ra•shi (rä′shē), (*Solomon ben Isaac*) 1040–1105, French Hebrew scholar.

Rask (rask, räsk), **Rasmus Christian,** 1787–1832, Danish philologist.

Ras•mus•sen (ras′mo͝o sən), **Knud Johan Victor** (kno͞oth), 1879–1933, Danish arctic explorer.

Ra•spu•tin (ra spyo͞o′tin, -spyo͞ot′n), **Grigori Efimovich,** 1871–1916, Russian mystic.

Rath•bone (rath′bōn), **Basil,** 1892–1967, English actor, born in South Africa.

Ra•the•nau (rät′n ou′), **Walther,** 1867–1922, German industrialist.

Rat•ti•gan (rat′i gən), **Terence,** 1911–77, English playwright.

Rau (rou), **Santha Rama,** born 1923, Indian writer and astrologer.

Rau•schen•berg (rou′shən bûrg′), **Robert,** born 1925, U.S. artist.

Rau•schen•busch (rou′shən bo͝osh′), **Walter,** 1861–1918, U.S. clergyman and social reformer.

Ra•vel (rə vel′), **Maurice Joseph,** 1875–1937, French composer.

Raw•lings (rô′lingz), **Marjorie Kinnan,** 1896–1953, U.S. novelist and journalist.

Raw•lin•son (rô′lin sən), **1. George,** 1812–1902, English historian. **2.** his brother, **Sir Henry Creswicke,** 1810–95, English archaeologist, diplomat, and soldier.

Ray (rā), **1. John,** 1627?–1705, English naturalist. **2. Man,** 1890–1976, U.S. painter and photographer. **3. Satyajit,** 1921–92, Indian film director.

Ray•burn (rā′bûrn), **Sam,** 1882–1961, U.S. lawyer and political leader: Speaker of the House 1940–47, 1949–53, 1955–61.

Ray•leigh (rā′lē), **John William Strutt, 3rd Baron,** 1842–1919, English physicist: Nobel prize 1904.

Read (rēd), **1. George,** 1733–98, American political leader: served in the Continental Congress 1774–77. **2. Sir Herbert,** 1893–1968, English critic and poet.

Reade (rēd), **Charles,** 1814–84, English novelist.

Read•ing (red′ing), **Rufus Daniel Isaacs, 1st Marquis of,** 1860–1935, Lord Chief Justice of England 1913–21; viceroy of India 1921–26.

Rea•gan (rā′gən), **Ronald (Wilson),** born 1911, 40th president of the U.S. 1981–89.

Ré•au•mur (rā′ə myo͝or′), **René Antoine Ferchault de,** 1683–1757, French physicist and inventor.

Ré•ca•mier (rā′kam yā′), **Madame** (*Jeanne Françoise Julie Adélaïde Bernard*), 1777–1849, influential French salon hostess.

Red′ Cloud′, (*Mahpiua Luta*), 1822–1909, Lakota Indian leader.

Red•field (red′fēld′), **Robert,** 1897–1958, American anthropologist.

Red•ford (red′fərd), **Robert,** born 1937, U.S. actor and director.

Red•grave (red′grāv), **1. Sir Michael (Scudamore),** 1908–85, English actor. **2.** his daughter, **Vanessa,** born 1937, English actress.

Red′ Jack′et, (*Sagoyewatha*), c1756–1830, Seneca leader.

Red•mond (red′mənd), **John Edward,** 1856–1918, Irish political leader.

Re•don (rə don′, -dôN′), **O•di•lon** (ō′dē on′, -ôN′), 1840–1916, French painter and etcher.

Red′ Wing′, (*Tantangamini*), c1750–c1825, Sioux leader.

Reed (rēd), **1. Sir Carol,** 1906–76, British film director. **2. Ishmael (Scott),** born 1938, U.S. novelist and poet. **3. John,** 1887–1920, U.S. journalist and poet. **4. Stanley Forman,** 1884–1980, U.S. jurist: associate justice of the U.S. Supreme Court 1938–57. **5. Thomas Brackett,** 1839–1902, U.S. politician: Speaker of the House 1889–91, 1895–99. **6. Walter C.,** 1851–1902, U.S. army surgeon.

Re•ger (rā′gər), **Max,** 1873–1916, German composer and pianist.

Reg•u•lus (reg′yə ləs), **Marcus Atilius,** died 250? B.C., Roman general.

Rehn•quist (ren′kwist), **William H(ubbs),** born 1924, Chief Justice of the U.S. Supreme Court since 1986.

Reich (rīKH), **Wilhelm,** 1897–1957, Austrian psychoanalyst in the U.S.

Reich•stein (rīk′stīn′; *Ger.* RīKH′shtīn′), **Tadeus,** born 1897, Swiss chemist, born in Poland: Nobel prize for medicine 1950.

Reid (rēd), **1. Sir George Huston,** 1845–1918, Australian statesman, born in Scotland: prime minister 1904–05. **2. Thomas,** 1710–96, Scottish philosopher. **3. White•law** (hwīt′lô′, wīt′-), 1837–1912, U.S. diplomat and journalist.

Reik (rīk; *Ger.* Rīk), **Theodor,** 1888–1969, U.S. psychologist and author, born in Austria.

Rei•ner (rī′nər), **1. Carl,** born 1922, U.S. director, writer, and actor. **2. Fritz,** 1888–1963, Hungarian conductor in the U.S.

Rein•hardt (rīn′härt), **Max** (*Max Goldmann*), 1873–1943, German theater director and producer, born in Austria.

Ré•jane (rā zhan′), (*Gabrielle-Charlotte Réju*), 1856–1920, French actress.

Re•marque (ri märk′), **Erich Maria,** 1898–1970, German novelist, in the U.S. after 1939.

Rem•brandt (rem′brant, -bränt), (*Rembrandt Harmenszoon van Rijn* or *van Ryn*) 1606–69, Dutch painter.

Rem•ing•ton (rem′ing tən), **1. Eliphalet,** 1793–1861, U.S. arms manufacturer. **2. Frederic,** 1861–1909, U.S. painter and sculptor.

Rem•sen (rem′sən), **Ira,** 1846–1927, U.S. chemist and educator.

Re•nan (rə nan′, -näɴ′), **Ernest,** 1823–92, French philologist, historian, and critic.

Re•nault (rə nôlt′; *Fr.* ʀə nō′), **Louis,** 1843–1918, French jurist: Nobel peace prize 1907.

Re•noir (ren′wär, ren wär′), **1. Jean** (zhäɴ), 1894–1979, French film director and writer. **2.** his father, **Pierre Auguste,** 1841–1919, French painter.

Ren•wick (ren′wik), **James,** 1818–95, U.S. architect.

Re•shev•sky (rə shef′skē), **Samuel,** born 1911, U.S. chess player, born in Poland.

Res•nik (rez′nik), **Regina,** born 1922, U.S. mezzo-soprano.

Re•spi•ghi (re spē′gē), **Ottorino,** 1879–1936, Italian composer.

Res•ton (res′tən), **James (Barrett),** born 1909, U.S. journalist, born in Scotland.

Reuch•lin (ʀoiᴋʜ′lēn, ʀoiᴋʜ lēn′), **Johann,** 1455–1522, German humanist scholar.

Reu•ter (roi′tər), **Paul Julius, Baron de,** 1816–99, English founder of an international news agency, born in Germany.

Reu•ther (ro͞o′thər), **Walter Philip,** 1907–70, U.S. labor leader.

Rev•els (rev′əlz), **Hiram Rhoades** (rōdz), 1822–1901, U.S. clergyman, educator, and politician: first black senator 1870–71.

Re•vere (ri vēr′), **Paul,** 1735–1818, American silversmith and patriot.

Rex•roth (reks′rôth, -roth), **Kenneth,** 1905–82, U.S. poet, critic, and translator.

Rey•mont (ʀā′mônt), **Wła•dy•sław Sta•ni•sław** (vwä dē′swäf stä nē′swäf), (*"Ladislas Regmont"*), 1868–1925, Polish novelist: Nobel prize 1924.

Rey•naud (ʀe nō′), **Paul** (pôl), 1878–1966, French statesman: premier 1940.

Reyn•olds (ren′ldz), **Sir Joshua,** 1723–92, English painter.

Re•za Shah Pah•la•vi (ri zä′ shä′ pä′lə vē′, shô′), PAHLAVI[1] (def. 2).

Rhee (rē), **Syng•man** (sing′mən), 1875–1965, president of South Korea 1948–60.

Rhine (rīn), **Joseph Banks,** 1895–1980, U.S. psychologist: pioneer in parapsychology.

Rhodes (rōdz), **1. Cecil John,** 1853–1902, English capitalist and administrator in S Africa. **2. James Ford,** 1848–1927, U.S. historian.

Rhoe•cus (rē′kəs), fl. 6th century B.C., Greek sculptor and architect.

Rhys (rēs), **Jean,** 1894-1979, English novelist.

Rib•ben•trop (ʀib′ən tʀôp′), **Joachim von,** 1893–1946,

German leader in the Nazi party: minister of foreign affairs 1938–45; executed for war crimes.

Ri•car•do (ri kär′dō), **David,** 1772–1823, English economist.

Rice (rīs), **1. Dan** (*Daniel McLaren*), 1823–1900, U.S. circus clown, circus owner, and Union patriot. **2. Elmer,** 1892–1967, U.S. playwright. **3. Grantland,** 1880–1954, U.S. journalist.

Rich (rich), **Adrienne,** born 1929, U.S. poet.

Rich•ard (rich′ərd), **1. Richard I** (*"Richard the Lion-Hearted," "Richard Coeur de Lion"*), 1157–99, king of England 1189–99. **2. Richard II,** 1367–1400, king of England 1377–99 (son of Edward, Prince of Wales). **3. Richard III** (*Duke of Gloucester*), 1452–85, king of England 1483–85.

Rich•ards (rich′ərdz), **1. Dickinson Woodruff,** 1895–1973, U.S. physician: Nobel prize 1956. **2. I(vor) A(rmstrong),** 1893–1979, English literary critic in the U.S. **3. Theodore William,** 1868–1928, U.S. chemist: Nobel prize 1914.

Rich•ard•son (rich′ərd sən), **1. Henry Handel** (*Henrietta Richardson Robertson*), 1870–1946, Australian novelist. **2. Henry Hobson,** 1838–86, U.S. architect. **3. Sir Owen Williams,** 1879–1959, English physicist: Nobel prize 1928. **4. Sir Ralph (David),** 1902–83, English actor. **5. Samuel,** 1689–1761, English novelist. **6. Tony,** 1928–91, English motion-picture and theatrical director.

Rich•e•lieu (rish′ə lo͞o′, rēsh′-), **Armand Jean du Plessis, Duc de,** 1585–1642, French cardinal and statesman.

Ri•chet (ri shā′, rē-), **Charles Robert,** 1850–1935, French physician: Nobel prize 1913.

Ri•chier (rē shyā′), **Germaine,** 1904–59, French sculptor.

Rich•ler (rich′lər), **Mordecai,** born 1931, Canadian novelist.

Rich•ter (rik′tər), **1. Burton,** born 1931, U.S. physicist: Nobel prize 1976. **2. Conrad,** 1890–1968, U.S. novelist. **3. Sviatoslav (Teofilovich),** born 1915, Russian pianist.

Richt•ho•fen (rɪᴋʜt′hō′fən), **Baron Manfred von** (*"Red Baron"* or *"Red Knight"*), 1892–1918, German aviator.

Rick•en•back•er (rik′ən bak′ər), **Edward Vernon** (*"Eddie"*), 1890–1973, U.S. aviator and aviation executive.

Rick•ey (rik′ē), **(Wesley) Branch,** 1881–1965, U.S. baseball executive.

Rick•o•ver (rik′ō vər), **Hyman George,** 1900–86, U.S. naval officer, born in Poland: helped develop the nuclear submarine.

Rid•ley (rid′lē), **Nicholas,** c1500–55, English bishop, reformer, and martyr.

Rie•fen•stahl (ʀē′fən shtäl′), **Leni,** born 1902, German film director.

Rieg•ger (rē′gər), **Wallingford,** 1885–1961, U.S. composer.

Ri•el (rē el′), **Louis,** 1844–85, Canadian revolutionary.

Ri•en•zi (rē en′zē) also **Ri•en•zo** (-zō), **Cola di** (*Nicholas Gabrini*), 1313?–54, Italian patriot and tribune.

Ries•man (rēs′mən), **David,** born 1909, U.S. sociologist.

Riet•veld (rēt′felt), **Gerrit Thomas,** 1888–1964, Dutch architect.

Riis (rēs), **Jacob August,** 1849–1914, U.S. journalist and social reformer, born in Denmark.

Ri•ley (rī′lē), **James Whitcomb,** 1849–1916, U.S. poet.

Ril•ke (ril′kə), **Rainer Maria,** 1875–1926, Austrian poet, born in Prague.

Rim•baud (ram bō′, ʀaɴ-), **(Jean Nicolas) Arthur** (zhäɴ), 1854–91, French poet.

Rim•i•ni (rim′ə nē), **Francesca da,** FRANCESCA DA RIMINI.

Rim•mer (rim′ər), **William,** 1816–79, U.S. sculptor and painter, born in England.

Rim•sky-Kor•sa•kov (rim′skē kôr′sə kôf′, -kof′), **Nicolai Andreevich,** 1844–1908, Russian composer.

Rine•hart (rīn′härt), **Mary Roberts,** 1876–1958, U.S. novelist and playwright.

Ring•ling (ring′ling), **Albert** (1852–1916), and his brothers **Alfred** (1861–1919), **Charles** (1863–1926), **John** (1866–1936), and **Otto** (1858–1911), U.S. circus owners.

Ri•o•pelle (rē′ə pel′), **Jean Paul** (zhäɴ), born 1923, Canadian painter, in France since 1946.

Rip•ley (rip′lē), **George,** 1802–80, U.S. literary critic, author, and social reformer: associated with the founding of Brook Farm.

Rit•ter (rit′ər), **1. Joseph Elmer,** 1891–1967, U.S. cardinal. **2. Woodward Maurice** ("*Tex*"), 1907–74, U.S. country-and-western singer, songwriter, and film actor.

Ri•ve•ra (ri vâr′ə), **1. Diego,** 1886–1957, Mexican painter. **2. José Eustasio,** 1889–1928, Colombian poet and novelist. **3. (José) Fructuoso,** 1790?–1854, Uruguayan revolutionary and political leader: president of Uruguay 1830–34, 1839–42.

Riv•ers (riv′ərz), **1. Larry,** born 1923, U.S. painter. **2. William Halse** (hôls), 1865–1922, English physiologist and anthropologist.

Ri•zal (rē zäl′, -säl′), **José,** 1861–96, Philippine patriot, novelist, poet, and physician.

Riz•zio (rit′sē ō′, rēt′-), **David,** 1533?–66, Italian musician: private foreign secretary to Mary, Queen of Scots 1564–66.

Ro•bards (rō′bärdz), **Jason, Jr.,** born 1922, U.S. actor.

Robbe-Gril•let (rôb′grē yā′), **Alain,** born 1922, French writer.

Rob•bia (rō′bē ə), **Andrea della,** 1435–1525, and his uncle, **Luca della,** c1400–82, Italian sculptors.

Rob•bins (rob′inz), **1. Frederick C(hapman),** born 1916, U.S. physician: Nobel prize 1954. **2. Harold,** born 1916, U.S. novelist. **3. Jerome,** born 1918, U.S. choreographer.

Rob•ert (rob′ərt), **Henry Martyn,** 1837–1923, U.S. engineer and authority on parliamentary procedure.

Robert I, 1. ("*Robert the Devil*") died 1035, duke of Normandy 1028–35 (father of William I of England). **2.** Also called **Rob′ert the Bruce′, Rob′ert Bruce′.** 1274–1329, king of Scotland 1306–29.

Rob•erts (rob′ərts), **1. Sir Charles George Douglas,** 1860–1943, Canadian poet and novelist. **2. Elizabeth Mad•ox** (mad′əks), 1886–1941, U.S. poet and novelist. **3. Glenn** (*"Fireball"*), 1929–64, U.S. racing-car driver. **4. Oral,** born 1918, U.S. evangelist. **5. Owen Josephus,** 1875–1955, U.S. jurist: associate justice of the U.S. Supreme Court 1930–45.

Rob•ert•son (rob′ərt sən), **1. Pat** (*Marion Gordon*), born 1930, U.S. evangelist. **2. William,** 1721–93, Scottish historian. **3. Sir William Robert,** 1860–1933, British field marshal.

Robe•son (rōb′sən), **Paul,** 1898–1976, U.S. singer and actor.

Robes•pierre (rōbz′pēr, -pē âr′, rō′bəs pē âr′), **1. Maximilien François Marie Isidore de,** 1758–94, French revolutionary leader. **2.** 1758–94, French lawyer and revolutionary leader.

Rob•in•son (rob′in sən), **1. Bill** (*"Bojangles"*), 1878–1949, U.S. tap dancer. **2. Boardman,** 1876–1952, U.S. painter and illustrator, born in Nova Scotia. **3. Edward G.** (*Emanuel Goldenberg*), 1893–1973, U.S. actor, born in Romania. **4. Edwin Arlington,** 1869–1935, U.S. poet. **5. Jack Roosevelt** (*Jackie*), 1919–72, U.S. baseball player. **6. James Harvey,** 1863–1936, U.S. historian. **7. Mary,** born 1944, Irish political leader: president of the Republic of Ireland since 1990. **8. Ray** (*Walker Smith*) (*"Sugar Ray"*), 1921–89, U.S. boxer. **9. Sir Robert,** 1886–1975, English chemist: Nobel prize 1947.

Ro•bus (rō′bəs), **Hugo,** 1885–1963, U.S. sculptor.

Ro•cham•beau (rō′shäɴ bō′), **Jean Baptiste Donatien de Vimeur, Count de,** 1725–1807, French general in the American Revolution.

Roch•es•ter (roch′es tər, -ə stər), **John Wilmot, 2nd Earl of,** 1647–80, English poet and courtier.

Rock•e•fel•ler (rok′ə fel′ər), **1. John D(avison),** 1839–1937, and his son **John D(avison), Jr.,** 1874–1960, U.S. oil magnates and philanthropists. **2. Nelson A(ldrich),** 1908–79, vice president of the U.S. 1974–77 (son of John D. Rockefeller, Jr.).

Rock•ne (rok′nē), **Knute (Kenneth)** (no͞ot), 1888–1931, U.S. football coach, born in Norway.

Rock•well (rok′wel′, -wəl), **Norman,** 1894–1978, U.S. illustrator.

Rod•chen•ko (rod cheng′kō; *Russ.* rôt′chyin kə), **Aleksandr (Mikhailovich),** 1891–1956, Russian painter, photographer, and designer.

Rodg•ers (roj′ərz), **1. James Charles** (*Jimmie*), 1897–1933, U.S. country-and-western singer, guitarist, and songwriter. **2. Richard,** 1902–79, U.S. composer. **3. William Henry** (*Bill*), born 1947, U.S. track-and-field athlete.

Ro•din (rō dan′, -daɴ′), **(François) Auguste (René),** 1840–1917, French sculptor.

Rod•ney (rod′nē), **George Brydges, Baron,** 1718–92, British admiral.

Roeb•ling (rō′bling), **1. John Augustus,** 1806–69, U.S. engineer, born in Germany. **2.** his son, **Washington Augustus,** 1837–1926, U.S. engineer.

Roent•gen or **Rönt•gen** (rent′gən, -jən, runt′-), **Wilhelm Konrad,** 1845–1923, German physicist: discoverer of x-ray 1895; Nobel prize 1901.

Roe•rich (rûr′ik), **Nicholas Konstantinovich,** 1874–1947, Russian painter, archaeologist, and author; in the U.S. after 1920.

Roeth•ke (ret′kə), **Theodore,** 1908–63, U.S. poet and teacher.

Ro•ger-Du•casse (rô zhā′dʏ kas′), **Jean Jules Amable** (zhäɴ), 1873–1954, French composer. Also called **Ducasse.**

Rog•ers (roj′ərz), **1. Bruce,** 1870–1957, U.S. book designer and printer. **2. Carl (Ransom),** 1902–87, U.S. psychologist. **3. Ginger** (*Virginia Katherine McMath*), born 1911, U.S. actress and dancer. **4. James Gamble,** 1867–1947, U.S. architect. **5. Roy** (*Leonard Slye*), born 1912, U.S. actor and singer. **6. Samuel,** 1763–1855, English poet. **7. Will(iam Penn Adair),** 1879–1935, U.S. actor and humorist. **8. William P(ierce),** born 1913, U.S. lawyer: Attorney General 1957–61; Secretary of State 1969–73.

Ro•get (rō zhā′, rō′zhā), **Peter Mark,** 1779–1869, English physician and author of a thesaurus.

Roh Tae Woo (nō′ tā′ wōō′), born 1932, president of South Korea since 1988.

Ro•jas (rō′häs), **Fernando de,** c1475–1541?, Spanish writer.

Rolfe (rolf), **John,** 1585–1622, English colonist in Virginia (husband of Pocahontas).

Rol•land (rô läɴ′), **Romain,** 1866–1944, French writer: Nobel prize 1915.

Rol•lins (rol′inz), **Theodore Walter** (*"Sonny"*), born 1929, U.S. jazz saxophonist and composer.

Rol•lo (rol′ō), A.D. c860–931?, Norse chieftain: 1st duke of Normandy.

Röl•vaag (rōl′väg), **Ole Edvart,** 1876–1931, U.S. novelist and educator, born in Norway.

Ro•mains (rô maɴ′), **Jules** (*Louis Farigoule*), 1885–1972, French novelist, poet, and dramatist.

Ro•ma•nov or **Ro•ma•noff** (rō′mə nôf′, -nof′, rō mä′nəf), **Mikhail Feodorovich,** 1596–1645, emperor of Russia 1613–45: first ruler of the house of Romanov.

Rom•berg (rom′bûrg), **Sigmund,** 1887–1951, U.S. composer, born in Hungary.

Rome (rōm), **Harold (Jacob),** born 1908, U.S. lyricist and composer.

Rom•mel (rom′əl, rum′-), **Erwin** (*"the Desert Fox"*), 1891–1944, German field marshal.

Rom•ney (rom′nē, rum′-), **George,** 1734–1802, English painter.

Ro•mu•lo (rom′yo͞o lō′), **Carlos Pena,** 1901–85, Philippine diplomat, journalist, and educator.

Ron•sard (RÔN SAR′), **Pierre de,** 1524–85, French poet.

Ron•stadt (ron′stat), **Linda,** born 1946, U.S. singer.

Rönt•gen (rent′gən, -jən, runt′-), **1. Julius,** 1855–1932, Dutch pianist, conductor, and composer; born in Germany. **2. Wilhelm Konrad,** ROENTGEN, Wilhelm Konrad.

Roo•se•velt (rō′zə velt′, -vəlt, rōz′-; *spelling pron.* ro͞o′-), **1. (Anna) Eleanor,** 1884–1962, U.S. diplomat and author (wife of Franklin Delano Roosevelt). **2. Franklin Delano** (*"FDR"*), 1882–1945, 32nd president of the U.S. 1933–45. **3. Theodore** (*Teddy, "T.R."*), 1858–1919, 26th president of the U.S. 1901–09: Nobel peace prize 1906.

Root (ro͞ot), **1. Elihu,** 1845–1937, U.S. statesman: Nobel peace prize 1912. **2. John Wellborn,** 1851–91, U.S. architect.

Ro•sa (rō′zə), **Salvator,** 1615–73, Italian painter and poet.

Ros•ci•us (rosh′ē əs, rosh′əs), **Quintus,** c126–c62 B.C., Roman actor.

Rose (rōz), **Billy,** 1899–1966, U.S. theatrical producer.

Rose•ber•y (rōz′bə rē), **Archibald Philip Primrose, 5th Earl of,** 1847–1929, British statesman and author: prime minister 1894–95.

Rose•crans (rōz′krans), **William Starke,** 1819–98, U.S. general.

Ro•sen•berg (rō′zən bûrg′), **Julius,** 1918–53, and his wife, **Ethel Greenglass,** 1915–53, U.S. citizens executed for espionage.

Ro•sen•thal (rō′zən thôl′), **1. Jean,** 1912–69, U.S. theatrical lighting designer. **2. Emmanuel,** born 1904, French conductor and composer.

Ro•sen•wald (rō′zən wôld′), **Julius,** 1862–1932, U.S. businessman and philanthropist.

Ross (rôs, ros), **1. Betsy Griscom,** 1752–1836, maker of the first U.S. flag. **2. Diana,** born 1944, U.S. singer and actress. **3. Harold Wallace,** 1892–1951, U.S. publisher and editor. **4. Sir James Clark,** 1800–62, English explorer of the Arctic and the Antarctic. **5.** his uncle, **Sir John,** 1777–1856, Scottish Arctic explorer. **6. John** (*Coowescoowe* or *Kooweskoowe*), 1790–1866, Cherokee leader. **7. Sir Ronald,** 1857–1932, English physician: Nobel prize 1902.

Ross•by (rôs′bē, ros′-), **Carl-Gustaf Arvid,** 1898–1957, U.S. meteorologist, born in Sweden.

Ros•sel•li•ni (rô′sə lē′nē, ros′ə-), **Roberto,** 1906–77, Italian motion-picture director.

Ros•set•ti (rō set′ē, -zet′ē, rə-), **1. Christina Georgina,** 1830–94, English poet. **2.** her brother, **Dante Gabriel** (*Gabriel Charles Dante Rossetti*), 1828–82, English poet and painter.

Ros•si•ni (rō sē′nē, rô-), **Gioacchino Antonio,** 1792–1868, Italian composer.

Ros•tand (rô stäɴ′), **Edmond,** 1868–1918, French dramatist and poet.

Ro•stov•tzeff (rə stôf′tsef, -stof′-), **Michael Ivanovich,** 1870–1952, U.S. historian, born in Russia.

Ros•tro•po•vich (ros′trə pō′vich), **Msti•slav (Leopoldovich)** (mis′tə släv′), born 1927, Russian cellist and conductor, in the U.S. since 1974.

Ro•szak (rô′shäk, -shak), **Theodore,** 1907–81, U.S. sculptor, born in Poland.

Roth (rôth, roth), **Philip,** born 1933, U.S. novelist and short-story writer.

Roth•ko (roth′kō), **Mark,** 1903–70, U.S. painter, born in Russia.

Roth•schild (rôth′child, rôths′-, roth-, roths′-), **1. Lionel Nathan, Baron de** (*"Lord Natty"*), 1809–79, English banker: first Jewish member of Parliament (son of Nathan Meyer Rothschild). **2. Mayer Amschel,** 1743–1812, German banker: founder of the Rothschild family and international banking firm. **3.** his son, **Nathan Mayer, Baron de,** 1777–1836, English banker, born in Germany.

Rou•ault (ro͞o ō′), **Georges,** 1871–1958, French painter.

Rou•get de Lisle (ro͞o zhā′ də lēl′), **Claude Joseph,** 1760–1836, French army officer and composer: wrote the *Marseillaise.*

Rous (rous, ro͞os), **(Francis) Peyton,** 1879–1970, U.S. pathologist: Nobel prize for medicine 1966.

Rous•seau (ro͞o sō′), **1. Henri** (*"Le Douanier"*), 1844–1910, French painter. **2. Jean Jacques** (zhäɴ), 1712–78, French philosopher and social reformer, born in Switzerland. **3. (Pierre Étienne) Théodore,** 1812–67, French painter.

Rous•sel (ro͞o sel′), **Albert (Charles Paul Mari),** 1869–1937, French composer.

Rowe (rō), **Nicholas,** 1674–1718, British poet and dramatist: poet laureate 1715–18.

Row•land•son (rō′lənd sən), **Thomas,** 1756–1827, English caricaturist.

Ro•xas (rō′häs), **Manuel,** 1892–1948, Philippine statesman: 1st president of the Philippines 1946–48.

Ro•y (rō′ē), **Ram•mo•hun** (rä mō′hon), 1774–1833, Indian religious leader: founder of Brahmo Samaj.

Roy•all (roi′əl), **Anne Newport,** 1769–1854, U.S. writer, newspaper publisher, and reformer.

Royce (rois), **Josiah,** 1855–1916, U.S. philosopher and educator.

Ru•bens (ro͞o′bənz), **Peter Paul,** 1577–1640, Flemish painter.

Ru•bin•stein (ro͞o′bin stin′), **1. Anton,** 1829–94, Russian pianist and composer. **2. Arthur,** 1887–1982, U.S. pianist, born in Poland.

Rude (ʀʏd), **François,** 1784–1855, French sculptor.

Ru•dolf (ro͞o′dolf), **Max,** born 1902, U.S. conductor, born in Germany.

Ru•dolf (or **Ru•dolph**) **I** (ro͞o′dolf), 1218–91, Holy Roman emperor 1273–91: founder of the Hapsburg dynasty. Also called **Rudolph I of Hapsburg.**

Ru•dolph (ro͞o′dolf), **1. Paul (Marvin),** born 1918, U.S. architect. **2. Wilma (Glo•de•an)** (glō′dē ən), born 1940, U.S. track and field athlete.

Ruis•dael or **Ruys•dael** (rois′däl, -dāl, rīz′-, rīs′-), **Jacob van,** 1628?–82, and his uncle, **Salomon van,** 1601?–70, Dutch painters.

Ru•key•ser (ro͞o′kī zər), **Muriel,** 1913–80, U.S. poet.

Ruml (rum′əl), **Beardsley,** 1894–1960, U.S. economist and businessman.

Rum•sey (rum′zē), **James,** 1743–92, U.S. engineer and inventor.

Run•cie (run′sē), **Robert Alexander Kennedy,** born 1921, English clergyman: archbishop of Canterbury 1980–91.

Run•yon (run′yən), **(Alfred) Da•mon** (dā′mən), 1884–1946, U.S. journalist and short-story writer.

Ru•pert (ro͞o′pərt), **Prince,** 1619–82, German Royalist general and admiral in the English Civil War (nephew of Charles I of England).

Ru•rik (ro͝or′ik), died A.D. 879, Scandinavian prince: considered the founder of the Russian monarchy.

Rush (rush), **1. Benjamin,** 1745–1813, U.S. physician and political leader: author of medical treatises. **2.** his son, **Richard,** 1780–1859, U.S. lawyer, politician, and diplomat.

Rush•die (rush′dē), **Salman,** born 1947, British novelist.

Rusk (rusk), **(David) Dean,** born 1909, U.S. Secretary of State 1961–69.

Rus•ka (rus′kə, ro͝os′-), **Ernst (August Friedrich),** 1906–88, German physicist and engineer: developed the electron microscope; Nobel prize 1986.

Rus•kin (-kin), **John,** 1819–1900, English author, art critic, and social reformer.

Rus•sell (rus′əl), **1. Bertrand (Arthur William), 3rd Earl,** 1872–1970, English philosopher and mathematician: Nobel prize for literature 1950. **2. Charles Edward,** 1860–1941, U.S. journalist, sociologist, biographer, and political leader. **3. Charles Taze** (*"Pastor Russell"*), 1852–1916, U.S. founder of Jehovah's Witnesses. **4. Elizabeth Mary, Countess** (*Mary Annette Beauchamp*) (*"Elizabeth"*), 1866–1941, Australian novelist. **5. George William** (*"Æ"*), 1867–1935, Irish poet and painter. **6. Henry Norris,** 1877–1957, U.S. astronomer. **7. John Russell, 1st Earl** (*Lord John Russell*), 1792–1878, British prime minister 1846–52, 1865–66. **8. Lillian** (*Helen Louise Leonard*), 1861–1922, U.S. singer and actress. **9. William Felton** (*Bill*), born 1934, U.S. basketball player and coach.

Russ•wurm (rus′wûrm), **John Brown,** 1799–1851, Jamaican-born journalist in the U.S. and (after 1829) journalist and statesman in Liberia.

Rus•tin (rus′tin), **Bayard,** born 1910, U.S. civil-rights leader.

Ruth (rōōth), **George Herman** (*"Babe"*), 1895–1948, U.S. baseball player.

Ruth•er•ford (ruth′ər fərd, ruth′-), **1. Daniel,** 1749–1819, Scottish physician and chemist: discoverer of nitrogen. **2. Ernest** (*1st Baron Rutherford of Nelson*), 1871–1937, English physicist, born in New Zealand: Nobel prize for chemistry 1908. **3. Joseph Franklin,** 1869–1942, U.S. leader of Jehovah's Witnesses. **4. Dame Margaret,** 1892–1972, British actress.

Rut•ledge (rut′lij), **1. Ann,** 1816–35, fiancée of Abraham Lincoln. **2. Edward,** 1749–1800, U.S. lawyer and statesman. **3.** his brother, **John,** 1739–1800, U.S. jurist and statesman: associate justice of the U.S. Supreme Court 1789–91. **4. Wiley Blount** (blunt), 1894–1949, U.S. jurist: associate justice of the U.S. Supreme Court 1943–49.

Ruys•dael (rois′däl, -dāl, rīz′-, rīs′-), RUISDAEL.

Ru•žič•ka (rōō′zhich kə, rōō zich′-), **Leopold** 1887–1976, Swiss chemist, born in Yugoslavia: Nobel prize 1939.

Ry•der (rī′dər), **Albert Pinkham,** 1847–1917, U.S. painter.

Ryle (rīl), **Sir Martin,** 1918–84, British astronomer: Nobel prize for physics 1974.

Ry•sa•nek (rē′zä nek′), **Leonie,** born 1926, Austrian soprano.

S

Saa•di (sä dē′), (*Muslih ud-Din*) 1184?–1291?, Persian poet. Also, **Sadi.**

Saa•ri•nen (sär′ə nən, sar′-), **Eero,** 1910–61, and his father, **(Gottlieb) Eliel,** 1873–1950, U.S. architects, born in Finland.

Sa•a•ve•dra La•mas (sä′ä ve′thrä lä′mäs), **Carlos,** 1878?–1959, Argentine statesman and diplomat: Nobel peace prize 1936.

Sa•ba•tier (sä′bä tyä′), **Paul,** 1854–1941, French chemist: Nobel prize 1912.

Sa•bin (sā′bin), **Albert Bruce,** born 1906, U.S. physician, born in Russia: developed the Sabin vaccine.

Sa•bine (sā′bīn, -bin), **Wallace Clement (Ware),** 1868–1919, U.S. physicist: pioneered research in acoustics.

Sa•bin•i•a•nus (sə bin′ē ā′nəs), died A.D. 606, pope 604–606.

Sac•a•ja•we•a (sak′ə jə wē′ə) also **Sac•a•ga•we•a** (-gə-wē′ə, -jə-), 1787?–1812?, Shoshone guide and interpreter: accompanied Lewis and Clark expedition 1804–05.

Sac•co (sak′ō), **Nicola,** 1891–1927, Italian anarchist, in the U.S. after 1908: with Bartolomeo Vanzetti executed for robbery and murder.

Sa•cher-Ma•soch (zä′KHər mä′zōKH), **Leopold von,** 1836–95, Austrian novelist.

Sachs (zäks), **1. Hans,** 1494–1576, German Meistersinger. **2. Nelly (Leonie),** 1891–1970, German poet and playwright, in Sweden after 1940: Nobel prize 1966.

Sack•ville (sak′vil), **Thomas, 1st Earl of Dorset,** 1536–1608, English statesman and poet.

Sack′ville-West′, Dame Victoria Mary ("*Vita*"), 1892–1962, English poet and novelist.

Sa•dat (sə dät′, -dat′), **An•war el-** (än′wär el), 1918–81, president of Egypt 1970–81: Nobel peace prize 1978.

Sade (säd, sad), **Donatien Alphonse François, Comte de** (*Marquis de Sade*), 1740–1814, French novelist: notorious for his tales of sexual gratification through the infliction of pain.

Sa•gan (sā′gən *for 1;* SA gäN′ *for 2*), **1. Carl (Edward),** born 1934, U.S. astronomer and writer. **2. Françoise** (*Françoise Quoirez*), born 1935, French novelist.

Sage (sāj), **Russell,** 1816–1906, U.S. financier.

Sainte-Beuve (saNt bœv′), **Charles Augustin,** 1804–69, French literary critic.

Saint-Ex•u•pé•ry (saN teg zy pā rē′), **Antoine de,** 1900–45, French author and aviator.

Saint-Gau•dens (sānt gôd′nz), **Augustus,** 1848–1907, U.S. sculptor, born in Ireland.

Saint-Just (saN zhyst′), **Louis Antoine Léon de,** 1767–94, French revolutionist.

Saint-Saëns (sᴀɴ sᴀ̈ɴs′), **(Charles) Camille,** 1835–1921, French composer.

Saints•bur•y (sānts′bə rē), **George Edward Bateman,** 1845–1933, English critic and historian.

Saint-Si•mon (sᴀɴ sē môɴ′), **1. Comte de,** 1760–1825, French philosopher and social scientist. **2. Louis de Rouvroy,** 1675–1755, French soldier, diplomat, and author.

Sa•kel (zä′kəl), **Manfred (Joshua),** 1906–57, U.S. psychiatrist, born in Austria.

Sa•kha•rov (sä′kə rôf′, -rof′, sak′ə-), **Andrei (Dmitrievich),** 1921–89, Russian nuclear physicist and human-rights advocate: Nobel peace prize 1975.

Sa•ki (sä′kē), pen name of H. H. Mᴜɴʀᴏ.

Sal•a•din (sal′ə din), (*Salāh-ed-Din Yūsuf ibn Ayyūb*) 1137–93, sultan of Egypt and Syria 1175–93.

Sa•la•zar (sal′ə zär′, sä′lə-), **Antonio de Oliveira,** 1889–1970, premier of Portugal 1933–68.

Sa•lie•ri (səl yâr′ē, sal-), **Antonio,** 1750–1825, Italian composer and conductor.

Sa•li•nas de Gor•ta•ri (sä lē′näs dā gôr tär′ē), **Carlos,** born 1948, president of Mexico since 1988.

Sal•in•ger (sal′in jər), **J(erome) D(avid),** born 1919, U.S. novelist and short-story writer.

Salis•bur•y (sôlz′ber′ē, -bə rē, -brē), **Robert Arthur Talbot Gascoyne Cecil, 3rd Marquis of,** 1830–1903, British prime minister 1885–86, 1886–92, 1895–1902.

Salk (sôk, sôlk), **Jonas E(dward),** born 1914, U.S. bacteriologist: developed the Salk vaccine.

Sal•lust (sal′əst), (*Caius Sallustius Crispus*) 86–34 ʙ.ᴄ., Roman historian.

Sa•lo•me (sə lō′mē), the daughter of Herodias, who is said to have danced for Herod Antipas and was granted the head of John the Baptist.

Sal•o•mon (sal′ə mən), **Haym,** 1740?–85, American financier and patriot, born in Poland.

Sa•man (sä′män), a Persian noble who lived in the 8th century ᴀ.ᴅ., progenitor of the Samanid dynasty.

Sam•mar•ti•ni (säm′mäʀ tē′nē), **Giovanni Battista,** 1698–1775, Italian composer and organist.

Sam•o (sam′ō), died ᴀ.ᴅ. 658, first ruler of the Slavs 623–658.

Sam•o•set (sam′ə set′), died 1653?, North American Indian leader: aided Pilgrims during early years in New England.

Sam•u•el•son (sam′yo͞o əl sən, -yəl-), **Paul A(nthony),** born 1915, U.S. economist: Nobel prize 1970.

Sand (sand; *Fr.* säɴd, säɴ), **George** (*Amandine Aurore Lucile Dupin Dudevant*), 1804–76, French novelist.

San•dage (san′dij), **Allan R(ex),** born 1926, U.S. astronomer: codiscoverer of the first quasar 1961.

Sand•burg (sand′bûrg, san′-), **Carl,** 1878–1967, U.S. poet and biographer.

San·di·no (san dē′nō, sän-), **Augusto (César),** 1893–1934, Nicaraguan revolutionary leader.

Sán·dor (shän′dôr, shan′-), **György,** born 1912, U.S. pianist, born in Hungary.

Sang·er (sang′ər), **1. Frederick,** born 1918, English biochemist: Nobel prize for chemistry 1958. **2. Margaret Higgins,** 1883–1966, U.S. leader of birth-control movement.

San Juan de la Cruz (*Sp.* sän hwän′ de lä KROOTH′, -KROOS′), JOHN OF THE CROSS, Saint.

San·ka·ra (sung′kər ə), SHANKARA.

San Mar·tín (san′ mär tēn′), **José de,** 1778–1850, South American general and statesman.

San·so·vi·no (san′sō vē′nō, sän′-), **1. Andrea** (*Andrea Contucci*), 1460–1529, Italian sculptor and architect. **2.** his pupil **Jacopo** (*Jacopo Tatti*), 1486–1570, Italian sculptor and architect.

San·ta An·na (sän′tä ä′nä, san′tə an′ə), **Antonio López de,** 1795?–1876, Mexican general and revolutionist: dictator 1844–45; president 1833–35, 1853–55.

San·ta·na (san tan′ə, sän tä′nä), **Pedro,** 1801–64, Dominican revolutionary and political leader: president 1844–48, 1853–56, 1858–61.

San·tan·der (sän′tän deR′), **Francisco de Paula,** 1792–1840, South American soldier and statesman: president of New Granada 1832–37.

San·ta·ya·na (san′tē an′ə, -ä′nə), **George,** 1863–1952, U.S. philosopher and writer, born in Spain.

San·tos-Du·mont (san′təs do͞o mont′, -dyo͞o-; *Port.* säN′-to͞oz do͞o môNt′), **Alberto,** 1873–1932, Brazilian aeronaut in France: designer and builder of dirigibles and airships.

Sa·pir (sə pēr′), **Edward,** 1884–1939, U.S. anthropologist and linguist, born in Germany.

Sap·pho (saf′ō), c620–c565 B.C., Greek poet of Lesbos.

Sa·ra·gat (sär′ə gät′), **Giuseppe,** born 1898, Italian statesman: president 1964–71.

Sar·dou (sär do͞o′), **Victorien,** 1831–1908, French dramatist.

Sarg (särg), **Tony** (*Anthony Frederic Sarg*), 1882–1942, U.S. illustrator and marionette maker, born in Guatemala.

Sar·gent (sär′jənt), **1. Sir (Harold) Malcolm (Watts),** 1895–1967, English conductor. **2. John Singer,** 1856–1925, U.S. painter.

Sar·gon (sär′gon), fl. c2300 B.C., Mesopotamian ruler: founder of Akkadian kingdom.

Sargon II, died 705 B.C., king of Assyria 722–705.

Sa·rit Tha·na·rat (sä rēt′ tä nä rät′), 1908–63, Thai statesman: premier 1952–63.

Sar·mien·to (säR myen′tô), **Domingo Faustino,** 1811–88, Argentine writer, educator, and political leader: president 1868–74.

Sar·noff (sär′nôf, -nof), **David,** 1891–1971, U.S. businessman and broadcasting executive, born in Russia.

Sa·roy·an (sə roi′ən), **William,** 1908–81, U.S. writer.

Sar•raute (sə rōt′), **Nathalie,** born 1902, French novelist, born in Russia.

Sar•to (sär′tō), **Andrea del,** ANDREA DEL SARTO.

Sar•tre (SAR′TRᵊ), **Jean-Paul** (zhän pōl′), 1905–80, French philosopher, novelist, and dramatist: declined 1964 Nobel prize for literature.

Sas•set•ta (sä set′ə), **Stefano di Giovanni,** 1392?–1450, Italian painter.

Sas•soon (sa sōōn′), **Siegfried (Loraine),** 1886–1967, English poet and novelist.

Sa•tie (sä tē′), **Erik Alfred Leslie,** 1866–1925, French composer.

Sa•to (sä′tō), **Eisaku,** 1901–75, Japanese political leader: prime minister 1964–72; Nobel peace prize 1974.

Sa•ud (sä ōōd′), (*Saud ibn Abdul-Aziz*), 1901?–69, king of Saudi Arabia 1953–64 (son of ibn-Saud and brother of Faisal).

Saul (sôl), **1.** the first king of Israel. **2.** Also called **Saul′ of Tar′sus** (tär′səs). the original name of the apostle Paul.

Saus•sure (*Fr.* sō SYR′), **Ferdinand de,** 1857–1913, Swiss linguist.

Sav•age (sav′ij), **1. Michael Joseph,** 1872–1940, New Zealand statesman and labor leader: prime minister 1935–40. **2. Richard,** 1697?–1743, English poet.

Sav•o•na•ro•la (sav′ə nə rō′lə), **Girolamo,** 1452–98, Italian monk, reformer, and martyr.

Saxe (saks), **Comte Hermann Maurice de,** 1696–1750, French military leader: marshal of France 1744.

Saxe-Co•burg-Go•tha (saks′kō′bûrg gō′thə), **Albert Francis Charles Augustus Emanuel, Prince of,** ALBERT, Prince.

Sax•o Gram•mat•i•cus (sak′sō grə mat′i kəs), c1150–1206?, Danish historian and poet.

Say (sā), **1. Jean Baptiste** (zhäɴ), 1767–1832, French economist. **2. Thomas,** 1787–1834, U.S. entomologist.

Say•ers (sā′ərz, sârz), **Dorothy L(eigh),** 1893–1957, English novelist, essayist, and dramatist.

Scae•vo•la (sē′və lə, sev′ə-), **Gaius** (or **Caius**) **Mucius,** fl. 6th century B.C., Roman hero.

Sca•li•a (skə lē′ə), **Antonin,** born 1936, associate justice of the U.S. Supreme Court since 1986.

Scal•i•ger (skal′i jər), **1. Joseph Justus,** 1540–1609, French scholar and critic. **2.** his father, **Julius Caesar,** 1484–1558, Italian scholar, philosopher, and critic in France.

Scan•der•beg (skan′dər beg′), (*George Castriota*) 1403?–68, Albanian chief and revolutionary leader.

Scar•lat•ti (skär lä′tē), **1. Alessandro,** 1659–1725, Italian composer. **2.** his son, **Domenico,** 1685–1757, Italian harpsichordist, organist, and composer.

Scar•ron (SKA RÔN′), **Paul,** 1610–60, French writer.

Schaerf (shârf), **Adolf,** 1890–1965, Austrian statesman: president 1957–65.

Schal•ly (shal′ē), **Andrew Victor,** born 1926, U.S. physiologist, born in Poland: Nobel prize 1977.

Schar•wen•ka (shär veng′kə), **1. (Ludwig) Philipp,** 1847–1917, German composer. **2.** his brother, **(Franz) Xaver,** 1850–1924, German pianist and composer.

Schau•dinn (shou′din), **Fritz** 1871–1906, German zoologist.

Schech•ter (shek′tər), **Solomon,** 1847–1915, U.S. Hebraist, born in Romania.

Schee•le (shā′lə), **Karl Wilhelm,** 1742–86, Swedish chemist.

Schel•ling (shel′ing), **Friedrich Wilhelm Joseph von,** 1775–1854, German philosopher.

Schia•pa•rel•li (skyä′pə rel′ē *or, esp. for 1,* skap′ə-), **1. Elsa,** 1890–1973, French fashion designer, born in Italy. **2. Giovanni Virginio,** 1835–1910, Italian astronomer.

Schick (shik), **Béla,** 1877–1967, U.S. pediatrician, born in Hungary.

Schil•ler (shil′ər), **1. Ferdinand Canning Scott,** 1864–1937, English philosopher in the U.S. **2. Johann Christoph Friedrich von,** 1759–1805, German poet, dramatist, and historian.

Schip•pers (ship′ərz), **Thomas,** 1930–77, U.S. conductor.

Schir•mer (shûr′mər), **Gustav,** 1829–93, born in Germany, and his sons **Rudolph Edward,** 1859–1919, and **Gustave,** 1864–1907, U.S. music publishers.

Schir•ra (shi rä′), **Walter Marty, Jr.,** born 1923, U.S. astronaut.

Schle•gel (shlā′gəl), **1. August Wilhelm von,** 1767–1845, German poet, critic, and translator. **2.** his brother, **Friedrich von,** 1772–1829, German critic, philosopher, and poet.

Schle•icher (shlī′kər; *Ger.* shlī′ᴋʜəʀ), **August,** 1821–68, German linguist.

Schlei•den (shlīd′n), **Matthias Jakob,** 1804–81, German botanist.

Schlei•er•ma•cher (shlī′ər mä′kər, -ᴋʜər), **Friedrich Ernst Daniel,** 1768–1834, German theologian and philosopher.

Schles•in•ger (shles′in jər, shlā′zing ər), **1. Arthur Meier,** 1888–1965, U.S. historian. **2.** his son, **Arthur Meier, Jr.,** born 1917, U.S. historian and writer.

Schlie•mann (shlē′män′), **Heinrich,** 1822–90, German archaeologist: excavated ancient cities of Troy and Mycenae.

Schme•ling (shmel′ing, shmā′ling), **Max,** born 1905, German boxer.

Schmidt (shmit), **Helmut (Heinrich Waldemar),** born 1918, chancellor of West Germany 1974–82.

Schmitt (shmit), **1. Bernadotte Everly,** 1886–1969, U.S. historian. **2. Harrison (Hagan)** ("*Jack*"), born 1935, U.S. astronaut, geologist, and politician: U.S. senator 1977–83.

Schna•bel (shnä′bəl), **Artur,** 1882–1951, Austrian pianist.

Schnei•der•man (shnī′dər mən), **Rose,** 1884–1972, U.S. labor leader, born in Poland.

Schnitz•ler (shnits′lər), **Arthur,** 1862–1931, Austrian dramatist and novelist.

Schoen•heim•er (shōn′hī′mər), **Rudolf,** 1898–1941, U.S. biochemist, born in Germany.

Scho•field (skō′fēld′), **John McAllister,** 1831–1906, U.S. general.

Schom•burg (shom′bûrg), **Arthur Alfonso,** 1874–1938, U.S. scholar and collector of books on black literature and history, born in Puerto Rico.

Schön•bein (shœn′bīn), **Christian Friedrich,** 1799–1868, Swiss chemist.

Schön•berg (shœn′bûrg), **Arnold,** 1874–1951, U.S. composer, born in Austria.

Schon•gau•er (shōn′gou ər), **Martin,** c1430–91, German engraver and painter.

School•craft (skōōl′kraft′, -kräft′), **Henry Rowe,** 1793–1864, U.S. explorer, ethnologist, and author.

Scho•pen•hau•er (shō′pən hou′ər), **Arthur,** 1788–1860, German philosopher.

Schrei•ner (shrī′nər), **Olive** (*"Ralph Iron"*), c1862–1920, English author and feminist.

Schrief•fer (shrē′fər), **John Robert,** born 1931, U.S. physicist: Nobel prize 1972.

Schrö•ding•er (shrō′ding ər, shrā′-), **Erwin,** 1887–1961, Austrian physicist: Nobel prize 1933.

Schu•bert (shōō′bərt, -bert), **Franz,** 1797–1828, Austrian composer.

Schul•berg (shŏŏl′bərg), **Budd,** born 1914, U.S. novelist, short-story writer, and scenarist.

Schulz (shŏŏlts), **Charles M(onroe),** born 1922, U.S. cartoonist.

Schu•man (shōō′mən), **1. Robert,** 1886–1963, French political leader: premier of France 1947–48. **2. William (Howard),** born 1910, U.S. composer and teacher.

Schu•mann (shōō′män), **Robert,** 1810–56, German composer.

Schu′mann-Heink′ (hīngk), **Ernestine,** 1861–1936, U.S. contralto, born in Bohemia.

Schum•pe•ter (shŏŏm′pā tər), **Joseph Alois,** 1883–1950, U.S. economist, born in Austria.

Schurz (shûrz, shûrts, shŏŏrts), **Carl,** 1829–1906, U.S. general, statesman, and newspaperman, born in Germany.

Schusch•nigg (shŏŏsh′nik), **Kurt von,** (1897–1977), Austrian statesman in the U.S.: Chancellor of Austria 1934–38.

Schütz (shYts), **Heinrich,** 1585–1672, German composer.

Schuy•ler (skī′lər), **Philip John,** 1733–1804, American statesman and general in the Revolutionary War.

Schwann (shvän, shwän), **Theodor,** 1810–82, German zoologist.

Schwartz (shwôrts), **Delmore,** 1913–1966, U.S. poet, short-story writer, and critic.

Schwarz (shwôrts), **Gerard,** born 1947, U.S. conductor.

Schwarz•en•eg•ger (shwôrt′sə neg′ər), **Arnold,** born 1947, U.S. actor, born in Austria.

Schwarz•kopf (shwôrts′kôpf, -kopf, shwärts′-), **1. Elisabeth,** born 1915, German soprano, born in Poland. **2. H. Norman,** born 1934, U.S. general.

Schweit•zer (shwīt′sər, shvīt′-), **Albert,** 1875–1965, Alsatian writer, missionary, doctor, and musician in Africa: Nobel peace prize 1952.

Schwin•ger (shwing′gər), **Julian Seymour,** born 1918, U.S. physicist: Nobel prize 1965.

Schwit•ters (shvit′ərs), **Kurt,** 1887–1948, German artist and writer.

Scip•i•o (sip′ē ō′, skip′-), **1.** (*Publius Cornelius Scipio Africanus Major*) (*"Scipio the Elder"*), 237–183 B.C., Roman general who defeated Hannibal. **2.** his adopted grandson, (*Publius Cornelius Scipio Aemilianus Africanus Numantinus Minor*) (*"Scipio the Younger"*), c185–129 B.C., Roman general: besieger and destroyer of Carthage.

Sco•pas (skō′pəs), fl. 4th century B.C., Greek sculptor and architect.

Scopes (skōps), **John Thomas,** 1901–70, U.S. high-school teacher convicted for teaching the Darwinian theory of evolution.

Scott (skot), **1. Barbara Ann,** born 1928, Canadian figure skater. **2. Dred,** 1795?–1858, a black slave whose suit for freedom (1857) was denied by the U.S. Supreme Court. **3. Duncan Campbell,** 1862–1947, Canadian poet and public official. **4. Robert Falcon,** 1868–1912, British naval officer and Antarctic explorer. **5. Sir Walter,** 1771–1832, Scottish novelist and poet. **6. Winfield,** 1786–1866, U.S. general.

Scot•to (skot′ō), **Renata,** born 1933, Italian soprano.

Sco•tus (skō′təs), **John Duns,** DUNS SCOTUS, John.

Scria•bin (skrē ä′bin), **Aleksandr Nikolaevich,** 1872–1915, Russian composer and pianist.

Scribe (skrēb), **Augustin Eugène,** 1791–1861, French dramatist.

Scripps (skrips), **Edward Wyllis,** 1854–1926, U.S. newspaper publisher.

Scul•lin (skul′in), **James Henry,** 1876–1953, Australian statesman: prime minister 1929–31.

Sea•borg (sē′bôrg), **Glenn T(heodor),** born 1912, U.S. chemist: Nobel prize 1951.

Sea•bur•y (sē′ber′ē, -bə rē), **1. Samuel,** 1729–96, American clergyman: first bishop of the Protestant Episcopal Church. **2. Samuel,** 1873–1958, U.S. jurist (great-great-grandson of Samuel Seabury).

Searle (sûrl), **Ronald (William Fordham),** born 1920, British cartoonist and artist.

Sears (sērz), **Richard Warren,** 1863–1914, U.S. mail-order retailer.

Se•at•tle (sē at′l), (*Seatlh*), c1790–1866, Suquamish leader: Seattle, Washington, named after him.

Se•bas•tian (si bas′chən), **Saint,** died A.D. 288?, Roman martyr.

Sec•chi (sek′ē), **Pietro Angelo,** 1818–78, Italian Jesuit and astronomer.

Sed•don (sed′n), **Richard John,** 1845–1906, New Zealand statesman, born in England: prime minister 1893–1906.

Sedg•wick (sej′wik), **Ellery,** 1872–1960, U.S. journalist and editor.

See•ger (sē′gər), **1. Alan,** 1888–1916, U.S. poet. **2. Peter** (*Pete*), born 1919, U.S. folk singer.

Se•fe•ri•a•des (se fer′ē ä′thēs), **Giorgos Stylianou** (*George Seferis*), 1900–71, Greek poet and diplomat: Nobel prize for literature 1963.

Se•gal (sē′gəl), **George,** born 1924, U.S. sculptor.

Se•gar (sē′gär), **Elzie (Crisler),** 1894–1938, U.S. comic-strip artist: creator of "Popeye."

Se•ghers (zā′gərs), **Anna** (*Netty Radvanyi*), born 1900, German novelist.

Se•gni (sen′yē), **Antonio,** 1891–1972, Italian teacher, lawyer, and statesman: president 1962–64.

Se•go•vi•a (sə gō′vē ə), **Andrés,** 1893–1987, Spanish guitarist.

Se•grè (sə grā′; *It.* se gʀe′), **Emilio,** 1905–89, U.S. physicist, born in Italy: Nobel prize 1959.

Sei•fert (sī′fərt), **Jaroslav,** 1901–86, Czech poet: Nobel prize 1984.

Sel•den (sel′dən), **1. George Baldwin,** 1846–1922, U.S. inventor of a gasoline-powered car. **2. John,** 1584–1654, English historian, Orientalist, and politician.

Se•ler (zā′lər), **Eduard,** 1859–1922, German archaeologist: first to decipher Mayan calendar and inscriptions.

Se•leu•cus I (si lo͞o′kəs), (*Seleucus Nicator*) 358?–281? B.C., Macedonian general: founder of the Seleucid dynasty.

Sel•fridge (sel′frij), **Harry Gordon,** 1857?–1947, British retail merchant, born in the U.S.

Sel•kirk (sel′kûrk), **Alexander** (originally *Alexander Selcraig*), 1676–1721, Scottish sailor marooned on a Pacific island: supposed prototype of Robinson Crusoe.

Sel•lers (sel′ərz), **Peter,** 1925–80, English actor.

Sel•ye (zel′ye, -yā), **Hans,** 1907–82, Canadian physician and medical educator, born in Austria.

Selz•nick (selz′nik), **David O(liver),** 1902–65, U.S. motion-picture producer.

Se•më•nov (sim yô′nəf), **Nikolai Nikolaevich,** born 1896, Russian chemist: Nobel prize 1956.

Sem•mel•weis (zem′əl vīs′), **Ignaz Philipp,** 1818–65, Hungarian obstetrician.

Semmes (semz), **Raphael,** 1809–77, Confederate admiral in the American Civil War.

Sen•dak (sen′dak), **Maurice (Bernard),** born 1928, U.S. author and illustrator of children's books.

Sen•e•ca (sen′i kə), **Lucius Annaeus,** c4 B.C.–A.D. 65, Roman philosopher and dramatist.

Se•ne•fel•der (zā′nə fel′dər), **Aloys,** 1771–1834, German inventor of lithography.

Sen•ghor (saɴ gôr′), **Léopold Sédar,** born 1906, African poet, teacher, and statesman: president of the Republic of Senegal 1960–80.

Sen•nach•er•ib (sə nak′ər ib), died 681 B.C., king of Assyria 705–681.

Sen•nett (sen′it), **Mack** (*Michael Sinnott*), 1884–1960, U.S. motion-picture director and producer, born in Canada.

Se•quoy•a or **Se•quoy•ah** (si kwoi′ə), 1770?–1843, Cherokee Indian, credited with the invention of a syllabary for writing Cherokee.

Ser•kin (sûr′kin), **1. Rudolf,** 1903–91, U.S. pianist, born in Bohemia. **2. Peter,** born 1947, U.S. pianist (son of Rudolf).

Ser•ra (ser′ə), **Junípero** (*Miguel José Serra*), 1713–84, Spanish missionary in California and Mexico.

Sert (seʀt), **José María,** 1876–1945, Spanish painter.

Ser•to•ri•us (sər tôr′ē əs, -tōr′-), **Quintus,** died 72 B.C., Roman general and statesman.

Ser•ve•tus (sər vē′təs), **Michael** (*Miguel Serveto*), 1511–53, Spanish theologian, accused of heresy and burned at the stake.

Ser•vice (sûr′vis), **Robert W(illiam),** 1874–1958, Canadian writer, born in England.

Ses•shu (ses sho͞o′), 1420?–1506, Japanese Zen Buddhist monk and painter.

Ses•sions (sesh′ənz), **Roger Huntington,** 1896–1985, U.S. composer.

Se•ton (sēt′n), **1. Saint Elizabeth Ann (Bayley)** (*"Mother Seton"*), 1774–1821, U.S. religious leader: canonized 1975. **2. Ernest Thompson,** 1860–1946, English writer and illustrator in the U.S.

Seu•rat (so͝o rä′), **Georges,** 1859–91, French painter.

Seuss (so͞os), **Dr.,** Geisel, Theodor Seuss.

Se•ver•sky (sə ver′skē), **Alexander Procofieff de,** 1894–1974, U.S. airplane designer, manufacturer, and writer; born in Russia.

Se•ve•rus (sə vēr′əs), **Lucius Septimius,** A.D. 146–211, Roman emperor 193–211.

Sé•vi•gné (sā vē nyā′), **Marie de Rabutin-Chantal, Marquise de,** 1626–96, French writer, esp. of letters.

Sew•all (so͞o′əl), **Samuel,** 1652–1730, American jurist, born in England.

Sew•ard (so͞o′ərd), **William Henry,** 1801–72, U.S. Secretary of State 1861–69.

Sex•ton (sek′stən), **Anne (Harvey),** 1928–74, U.S. poet.

Sey•mour (sē′môr, -mōr), **Jane,** c1510–37, third wife of Henry VIII of England and mother of Edward VI.

Sfor•za (sfôrt′sə), **1. Count Carlo,** 1873–1952, Italian anti-Fascist leader. **2. Lodovico** (*"the Moor"*), 1451–1508, duke of Milan 1494–1500.

Shack•le•ton (shak′əl tən), **Sir Ernest Henry,** 1874–1922, English explorer of the Antarctic.

Shad•well (shad′wel′, -wəl), **Thomas,** 1642?–92, English dramatist: poet laureate 1688–92.

Shaftes•bur•y (shafts′bə rē, shäfts′-), **1. Anthony Ashley Cooper, 1st Earl of,** 1621–83, English statesman. **2. Anthony Ashley Cooper, 3rd Earl of,** 1671–1713, English moral philosopher (grandson of Anthony Ashley Cooper, 1st Earl of Shaftesbury). **3. Anthony Ashley Cooper, 7th Earl of,** 1801–85, English philanthropist.

Shah Ja•han (or **Je•han**) (shä′ jə hän′), 1592?–1666, Mogul emperor in India 1628?–58: built the Taj Mahal.

Shahn (shän), **Ben,** 1898–1969, U.S. painter, born in Lithuania.

Shairp (shârp, shärp), **John Campbell** (*"Principal Shairp"*), 1819–85, English critic, poet, and educator.

Shake•speare (shāk′spēr), **William,** 1564–1616, English poet and dramatist.

Shal•ma•ne•ser III (shal′mə nē′zər), died 824? B.C., Assyrian ruler 859–824?.

Sha•mir (shä mēr′), **Yit•zhak** (yit′säk), born 1915, Israeli prime minister since 1986.

Sham•mai (shä′mī), fl. 1st century B.C., Hebrew rabbi: founder of Beth Shammai, school of hermeneutics.

Shan•kar (shäng′kär), **Ra•vi** (rä′vē), born 1920?, Indian sitarist.

Shan•ka•ra (shung′kər ə), A.D. 789?–821?, Hindu Vedantist philosopher and teacher.

Shan•non (shan′ən), **Claude Elwood,** born 1916, U.S. applied mathematician.

Sha•pi•ro (shə pēr′ō), **Karl (Jay),** born 1913, U.S. poet.

Shap•ley (shap′lē), **Harlow,** 1885–1972, U.S. astronomer.

Sha•rett or **Sha•ret** (shä ret′), **Moshe** (*Moshe Shertok*), 1894–1965, Israeli statesman, born in Russia: prime minister 1953–55.

Sharp (shärp), **William** (*"Fiona Macleod"*), 1855–?1905, Scottish poet and critic.

Shas•tri (shäs′trē), **Lal Bahadur,** 1904–66, Indian statesman: prime minister 1964–66.

Shaw (shô), **1. Artie** (*Arthur Arshawsky*), born 1910, U.S. clarinetist and bandleader. **2. George Bernard,** 1856–1950, Irish writer: Nobel prize 1925. **3. Henry Wheeler** (*"Josh Billings"*), 1818–85, U.S. humorist. **4. Irwin,** 1913–84, U.S. dramatist and author. **5. Richard Norman,** 1831–1912, English architect, born in Scotland.

Shawn (shôn), **Ted** (*Edwin M.*), 1891–1972, U.S. dancer and choreographer (husband of Ruth St. Denis).

Shays (shāz), **Daniel,** 1747–1825, American Revolutionary War soldier: leader of a popular insurrection in Massachusetts 1786–87.

Sha•zar (shä zär′, sha-), **Zalman** (*Shneor Zalman Ru-*

bashev), 1889–1974, Israeli statesman, born in Russia: president 1963–73.

Shcha•ran•sky (shə ran′skē), **(Natan) Anatoly,** born 1948, Russian mathematician and human-rights activist, in Israel since 1986.

Shear•er (shēr′ər), **Moira** (*Moira Shearer King*), born 1926, British ballerina.

Shear•ing (shēr′ing), **George,** born 1919, British jazz pianist, in the U.S.

Shee•ler (shē′lər), **Charles,** 1883–1965, U.S. painter and photographer.

Sheen (shēn), **Fulton (John),** 1895–1979, U.S. Roman Catholic clergyman, writer, and teacher.

Shel•don (shel′dən), **Sidney,** born 1917, U.S. novelist.

Shel•ley (shel′ē), **1. Mary Wollstonecraft (Godwin),** 1797–1851, English author (wife of Percy Bysshe Shelley). **2. Percy Bysshe** (bish), 1792–1822, English poet.

Shen•stone (shen′stən), **William,** 1714–63, English poet.

Shep•ard (shep′ərd), **1. Alan Bartlett, Jr.,** born 1923, U.S. astronaut: first American in space, May 5, 1961. **2. Sam(uel),** born 1943, U.S. dramatist and actor.

Sher•a•ton (sher′ə tn), **Thomas,** 1751–1806, English cabinetmaker and furniture designer.

Sher•i•dan (sher′i dn), **1. Philip Henry,** 1831–88, U.S. general. **2. Richard Brinsley,** 1751–1816, Irish dramatist and political leader.

Sher•man (shûr′mən), **1. James Schoolcraft,** 1855–1912, U.S. vice president 1909–12. **2. John,** 1823–1900, U.S. statesman (brother of William T.). **3. Roger,** 1721–93, American statesman. **4. William Tecumseh,** 1820–91, Union general in the Civil War.

Sher•riff (sher′if), **Robert Cedric,** 1896–1975, English playwright and novelist.

Sher•ring•ton (sher′ing tən), **Sir Charles Scott,** 1861–1952, English physiologist: Nobel prize for medicine 1932.

Shev•ard•na•dze (shev′ərd näd′zə), **Eduard A.,** born 1928, Soviet diplomat, born in Georgian Republic: Soviet foreign minister 1985–91; chairman of State Council of Georgian Republic since 1992.

Shih Huang Ti or **Shi Huang Di** (shœ′ hwäng′ dē′), 259–210 B.C., Chinese emperor c247–210 B.C.

Shi•ma•za•ki (shē′mä zä′kē), **Tō•son** (tô′sôn), (*Haruki Shimazaki*), 1872–1943, Japanese author.

Shir•er (shīər′ər), **William Lawrence,** born 1904, U.S. journalist, news broadcaster, and writer.

Shir•ley (shûr′lē), **James,** 1596–1666, English dramatist.

Shock•ley (shok′lē), **William Bradford,** 1910–89, U.S. physicist: Nobel prize 1956.

Shoe•mak•er (sho͞o′mā′kər), **William Lee** (*Willie*), born 1931, U.S. jockey.

Sholes (shōlz), **Christopher Latham,** 1819–90, U.S. inventor of the typewriter.

Sho•lo•khov (shô′lə kôf′, -kof′), **Mikhail,** 1905–84, Russian novelist: Nobel prize 1965.

Sho•lom A•lei•chem (shô′ləm ä lā′KHem), ALEICHEM, Sholom.

Shore (shôr, shōr), **1. Dinah** (*Frances Shore*), born 1917, U.S. singer and performer. **2. Jane,** 1445?–1527, mistress of Edward IV of England.

Shor•ter (shôr′tər), **Frank,** born 1947, U.S. marathon runner.

Sho•sta•ko•vich (shos′tə kō′vich), **Dimitri Dimitrievich,** 1906–75, Russian composer.

Shot•well (shot′wel′, -wəl), **James Thomson,** 1874–1965, U.S. diplomat, historian, and educator.

Shri•ver (shrī′vər), **(Robert) Sargent, Jr.,** born 1915, U.S. businessman and government official: first director of the U.S. Peace Corps 1961–66.

Shu•bert (sho͞o′bərt), **Lee** (*Levi Shubert*), 1875–1953, and his brothers **Sam S.,** 1876–1905, and **Jacob J.,** 1880–1963, U.S. theatrical managers.

Shultz (sho͝olts), **George P(ratt),** born 1920, U.S. government official and diplomat: Secretary of State 1982–89.

Shute (sho͞ot), **Nevil** (*Nevil Shute Norway*), 1899–1960, British novelist and aeronautical engineer.

Shver•nik (shvâr′nik), **Nikolai,** 1888–1970, Russian government official: president of the Soviet Union 1946–53.

Si•ad Bar•re (sē äd′ bä rā′), **Muhammad,** born 1919, Somali army officer and political leader: president since 1969.

Si•be•li•us (si bā′lē əs, -bāl′yəs), **Jean** (zhän, yän), (*Johan Julius Christian Sibelius*), 1865–1957, Finnish composer.

Sick•ert (sik′ərt), **Walter Richard,** 1860–1942, English painter.

Sid•dons (sid′nz), **Sarah (Kemble),** 1755–1831, English actress.

Sid•ney or **Syd•ney** (sid′nē), **Sir Philip,** 1554–86, English poet, statesman, and soldier.

Sieg•bahn (sēg′bän), **Karl Manne Georg,** 1886–1978, Swedish physicist: Nobel prize 1924.

Sie•mens (sē′mənz), **1. (Ernst) Werner von,** 1816–92, German inventor and electrical engineer. **2. Sir William** (*Karl Wilhelm Siemens*), 1823–83, British inventor, born in Germany.

Sien•kie•wicz (shen kyā′vich), **Henryk,** 1846–1916, Polish novelist: Nobel prize 1905.

Sie•pi (sē ep′ē), **Cesare,** born 1923, Italian basso.

Sie•vers (zē′fərs), **Eduard,** 1850–1932, German philologist.

Sig•is•mund (sij′is mənd, sig′is-), 1368–1437, Holy Roman emperor 1411–37.

Si•gnac (sē nyAK′), **Paul,** 1863–1935, French painter.

Si•gno•rel•li (sēn′yə rel′ē), **Luca,** c1445–1523, Italian painter.

Sigs•bee (sigz′bē), **Charles Dwight,** 1845–1923, U.S. naval officer: captain of the *Maine* in 1898.

Si•ha•nouk (sē′ə no͝ok′), **Prince Norodom,** NORODOM SIHANOUK.

Si•kor•sky (si kôr′skē), **Igor,** 1889–1972, U.S. aeronautical engineer, born in Russia.

Sil•lan•pää (sil′län pa′), **Frans Eemil,** 1888–1964, Finnish author: Nobel prize 1939.

Sil•li•man (sil′ə mən), **Benjamin,** 1779–1864, U.S. scientist and educator.

Sil•li•toe (sil′i tō′), **Alan,** born 1928, English fiction writer and poet.

Sills (silz), **Beverly** (*Belle Silverman*), born 1929, U.S. opera singer and administrator.

Si•lo•ne (si lō′nē), **Ignazio** (*Secondo Tranquilli*), 1900–78, Italian author.

Sil•vers (sil′vərz), **Phil,** 1912–85, U.S. actor and comedian.

Sil•ves•ter (sil ves′tər), SYLVESTER.

Si•me•non (sēmə nôN′), **Georges (Joseph Christian),** 1903–89, French novelist, born in Belgium.

Sim•e•on ben Yo•hai (sim′ē ən ben yō′KHī), fl. 2nd century A.D., Palestinian rabbi.

Sim′eon Sty•li′tes (stī lī′tēz), **Saint,** A.D. 390?–459, Syrian monk and stylite.

Sim•mel (zim′əl), **Georg,** 1858–1918, German sociologist and philosopher.

Simms (simz), **William Gilmore,** 1806–70, U.S. author.

Si•mon (sī′mən; *Fr.* sē môN′ *for* 4), **1.** (*"Simon the Canaanite"* or *"Simon the Zealot"*) one of the 12 apostles. **2.** (*"Simon Magus"*) the Samaritan sorcerer who was converted by the apostle Philip. **3. Carly,** born 1945, U.S. singer and songwriter. **4. Claude,** born 1913, French novelist: Nobel prize 1985. **5. Herbert Alexander,** born 1916, U.S. social scientist and economist: Nobel prize 1978. **6. Neil,** born 1927, U.S. playwright. **7. Paul,** born 1941, U.S. singer and songwriter.

Si•mon•i•des (sī mon′i dēz′), 556?–468? B.C., Greek poet. Also called **Simon′ides of Ce′os** (sē′os).

Si•mo•nov (sē′mə nôf′, -nof′), **Konstantin M.,** 1915–79, Russian journalist and playwright.

Si′mon Pe′ter, PETER[1].

Si•mon•son (sī′mən sən), **Lee,** 1888–1967, U.S. set designer.

Sim•pli•ci•us (sim plish′ē əs), **Saint,** died A.D. 483, pope 468–483.

Simp•son (simp′sən), **1. Louis,** born 1923, U.S. poet and teacher. **2. Wallis Warfield,** WINDSOR, Wallis Warfield, Duchess of.

Sims (simz), **William Sowden,** 1858–1936, U.S. admiral, born in Canada.

Si•nan (si nän′), 1489?–1587, Turkish architect, esp. of mosques.

Si•na•tra (si nä′trə), **Frank** (*Francis Albert*), born 1915, U.S. singer.

Sin•clair (sin klâr′, sing-), **1. Harry Ford,** 1876–1956, U.S. oil businessman: a major figure in the Teapot Dome scandal. **2. May,** 1865?–1946, British novelist. **3. Upton (Beall),** 1878–1968, U.S. novelist and reformer.

Sing•er (sing′ər), **1. Isaac Bashevis,** 1904–91, U.S. writer in Yiddish, born in Poland: Nobel prize 1978. **2. Isaac Merrit,** 1811–75, U.S. inventor.

Si•quei•ros (sē kâr′ōs), **David Alfaro,** 1896–1974, Mexican painter.

Si•ric•a (sə rik′ə), **John J(oseph),** born 1904, U.S. jurist.

Si•ri•ci•us (si rish′ē əs), **Saint,** died A.D. 399, pope 384–399.

Sis•ley (sis′lē, sēs lā′), **Alfred,** 1839–99, French painter.

Sis•mon•di (sis mon′dē; *Fr.* sēs môɴ dē′), **Jean Charles Léonard Simonde de** (zhäɴ), 1773–1842, Swiss historian and economist.

Sit•ter (sit′ər), **Willem de,** 1872–1934, Dutch astronomer and mathematician.

Sit′ting Bull′, 1834–90, Lakota Indian leader.

Sit•well (sit′wəl, -wel), **1. Dame Edith,** 1887–1964, English poet and critic. **2.** her brother, **Sir Osbert,** 1892–1969, English poet and novelist. **3.** her brother, **Sir Sacheverell,** 1897–1988, English poet, novelist, and art critic.

Skeat (skēt), **Walter William,** 1835–1912, English philologist.

Skel•ton (skel′tn), **1. John,** c1460–1529, English poet. **2. Red** (*Richard Skelton*), born 1910, U.S. comedian.

Skin•ner (skin′ər), **1. B(urrhus) F(rederic),** 1904–90, U.S. psychologist. **2. Cornelia Otis,** 1901–79, U.S. actress. **3.** her father, **Otis,** 1858–1942, U.S. actor.

Ško•da (skō′də), **Emil von,** 1839–1900, Czech engineer and industrialist.

Skou•ras (skŏŏr′əs), **Spyros (Panagiotes),** 1893–1971, U.S. film-studio executive, born in Greece.

Sla•ter (slā′tər), **Samuel,** 1768–1835, U.S. industrialist, born in England.

Slat•kin (slat′kin), **Leonard,** born 1944, U.S. conductor.

Sla•ven•ska (slä ven′skä), **Mia** (*Mia Corak*), born 1917, U.S. dancer and choreographer, born in Yugoslavia.

Slay•ton (slāt′n), **Donald Kent** (*"Deke"*), born 1924, U.S. astronaut.

Sle•zak (slā′zäk), **Leo,** 1873–1946, Austrian tenor.

Sloan (slōn), **John,** 1871–1951, U.S. painter.

Slo•cum (slō′kəm), **Joshua,** 1844–c1910, U.S. mariner, author, and lecturer, born in Nova Scotia.

Smalls (smôlz), **Robert,** 1839–1915, U.S. captain in the Union navy and politician, born a slave in South Carolina: congressman 1875–79, 1882–87.

Sme•ta•na (smet′n ə), **Be•dřich** (bed′ər zhiᴋʜ, -zhik), 1824–84, Czech composer.

Smith (smith), **1. Adam,** 1723–90, Scottish economist. **2. Bessie,** 1894?–1937, U.S. singer. **3. Charles Henry** (*"Bill*

Arp"), 1826–1903, U.S. humorist. **4. David,** 1906–65, U.S. sculptor. **5. Edmond Kirby,** 1824–93, Confederate general in the Civil War. **6. Francis Hopkinson,** 1838–1915, U.S. novelist, painter, and engineer. **7. George,** 1840–76, English archaeologist and Assyriologist. **8. Ian Douglas** born 1919, Rhodesian political leader: prime minister 1964–79. **9. John,** 1580–1631, English adventurer and colonist in Virginia. **10. Joseph,** 1805–44, U.S. religious leader: founded the Mormon Church. **11. Kate,** 1909–86, U.S. singer. **12. Logan Pearsall,** 1865–1946, U.S. essayist in England. **13. Maggie,** born 1934, English actress. **14. Margaret Chase,** born 1897, U.S. politician. **15. Oliver,** born 1918, U.S. set designer and theatrical producer. **16. Red** (*Walter Wellesley Smith*), 1905–82, U.S. sports journalist. **17. Sydney,** 1771–1845, English clergyman, writer, and wit. **18. William,** 1769–1839, English geologist.

Smith•son (smith′sən), **James,** 1765–1829, English chemist and mineralogist.

Smol•lett (smol′it), **Tobias George,** 1721–71, English novelist.

Smuts (smuts, smœts), **Jan Christiaan,** 1870–1950, prime minister of South Africa 1919–24, 1939–48.

Snead (snēd), **Samuel Jackson** (*"Slamming Sammy"*), born 1912, U.S. golfer.

Snef•ru (snef′ro͞o), fl. c2920 B.C., Egyptian ruler of the 4th dynasty.

Snell (snel), **Peter (George),** born 1938, New Zealand track-and-field athlete.

Snor•ri Stur•lu•son (snôr′ē stûr′lə sən), 1179–1241, Icelandic historian and poet.

Snow (snō), **Sir Charles Percy** (*C. P. Snow*), 1905–80, English novelist and scientist.

Soa•res (swär′əsh), **Mário,** born 1924, president of Portugal since 1986.

So•bhu•za II (sô bo͞o′zə), 1899–1982, king of Swaziland 1921–82.

So•bies•ki (sô byes′kē), **John,** JOHN[2] (def. 3b).

So•ci•nus (sō si′nəs), **Faustus** (*Fausto Sozzini*), 1539–1604, and his uncle **Laelius** (*Lelio Sozzini*), 1525–62, Italian Protestant theologians and reformers.

Soc•ra•tes (sok′rə tēz′), 469?–399 B.C., Athenian philosopher.

Sod•dy (sod′ē), **Frederick,** 1877–1956, English chemist: Nobel prize 1921.

Sö•der•blom (sŒ′dər blo͝om′), **Nathan,** 1866–1931, Swedish theologian: Nobel peace prize 1930.

So•ler (sō lâr′; *Sp.* sô leʀ′), **Padre Antonio,** 1729–83, Spanish organist and composer.

So•le•ri (sō lâr′ē), **Paolo,** born 1919, U.S. architect, born in Italy.

So•lon (sō′lən), c638–c558 B.C., Athenian statesman.

Sol•ti (shōl′tē), **Sir Ge•org** (gā′ôrg, jôrj), born 1912, British conductor, born in Hungary.

Sol•vay (sol′vā; *Fr.* sôl vā′), **Ernest,** 1838–1922, Belgian chemist.

Sol•zhe•ni•tsyn (sōl′zhə nēt′sin, sôl′-), **Aleksandr (Isayevich),** born 1918, Russian novelist, in the U.S. since 1974: Nobel prize 1970.

Som•mer•feld (zô′mər felt′), **Arnold** (Johannes Wilhelm), 1868–1951, German physicist.

So•mo•za (sə mō′zə, -mō′sə), **Anastasio** (*Anastasio Somoza García*), 1896–1956, Nicaraguan political leader: president 1937–47, 1950–56 (father of Anastasio and Luis Somoza Debayle).

Somo′za De•bay′le (də bi′lā), **1. Anastasio,** 1925–80, Nicaraguan army officer, businessman, and political leader: president 1967–72, 1974–79 (brother of Luis Somoza Debayle). **2. Luis,** 1922–67, Nicaraguan political leader: president 1957–63.

Sond•heim (sond′him), **Stephen (Joshua),** born 1930, U.S. composer and lyricist.

Soong (sŏŏng), **1. Charles Jones,** 1866–1918, Chinese merchant (father of Ai-ling, Ch'ing-ling, Mei-ling, and Tse-ven Soong). **2. Ai-ling,** 1888–1973, wife of H. H. Kung. **3. Ching-ling** or **Ch'ing-ling,** 1892–1981, widow of Sun Yat-sen. **4. Mei-ling** or **Mayling,** born 1898, wife of Chiang Kai-shek. **5. Tse-ven** or **Tzu-wen** (*T.V.*), 1894–1971, Chinese financier.

Soph•o•cles (sof′ə klēz′), 495?–406? B.C., Greek dramatist.

So•ro•kin (sə rō′kin, sô-), **Pitirim Alexandrovitch,** 1889–1968, U.S. sociologist, born in Russia.

So•ter (sō′tər), **Saint,** pope A.D. 166?–175?.

Soth•ern (suth′ərn), **E(dward) H(ugh),** 1859–1933, U.S. actor, born in England (husband of Julia Marlowe).

Souf•flot (sōō flō′), **Jacques Germain,** 1713–80, French architect.

Sou•pha•nou•vong (sōō pä′nōō vông′), **Prince,** born 1902, Laotian political leader: president since 1975 (half brother of Prince Souvanna Phouma).

Sou•sa (sōō′zə, -sə), **John Philip,** 1854–1932, U.S. band conductor and composer.

Sou•ter (sōō′tər), **David H.,** born 1939, associate justice of the U.S. Supreme Court since 1990.

South•amp•ton (south amp′tən, -hamp′-), **Henry Wriothesley, 3rd Earl of,** 1573–1624, English nobleman, soldier, and patron of writers, including William Shakespeare.

Sou•they (sou′thē, suth′ē), **Robert,** 1774–1843, English poet and prose writer: poet laureate 1813–43.

Sou•tine (sōō tēn′), **Chaim,** 1894–1943, Lithuanian painter in France.

Sou•van•na Phou•ma (sōō vän′nä pōō′mä), **Prince,** 1901–84, Laotian statesman: premier 1951–54, 1956–58, 1960, and 1962–75.

So•yin•ka (shô ying′kə), **Wo•le** (wō′lā), born 1934, Nigerian playwright, novelist, and poet: Nobel prize 1986.

Spaak (späk; *Fr.* spAK), **Paul Henri,** 1889–1972, Belgian statesman: prime minister of Belgium, 1938–39, 1946–49; first president of the General Assembly of the United Nations 1946–47; Secretary General of NATO 1957–61.

Spaatz (späts), **Carl,** 1891–1974, U.S. general.

Spa•cek (spā′sik), **Sissy** (*Mary Elizabeth Spacek*), born 1949, U.S. actress.

Spal•ding (spôl′ding), **Albert,** 1888–1953, U.S. violinist.

Spal•lan•za•ni (spä′lən zä′nē), **Lazzaro,** 1729–99, Italian biologist.

Spark (spärk), **Muriel (Sarah) (Camberg),** born 1918, British novelist, born in Scotland.

Sparks (spärks), **Jared,** 1789–1866, U.S. historian and editor.

Spar•ta•cus (spär′tə kəs), died 71 B.C., Thracian slave, gladiator, and insurrectionist against Rome.

Spas•sky (spas′kē), **Boris (Vasilyevich),** born 1937, Russian chess player.

Spea•ker (spē′kər), **Tris(tram E.),** 1888–1958, U.S. baseball player.

Speer (spēr; *Ger.* shpāR), **Albert,** 1905–81, German Nazi leader: appointed by Hitler as official Nazi architect.

Spell•man (spel′mən), **Francis Joseph, Cardinal,** 1889–1967, U.S. Roman Catholic clergyman: archbishop of New York 1939–67.

Spe•mann (shpā′män), **Hans,** 1869–1941, German zoologist: Nobel prize for medicine 1935.

Spen•cer (spen′sər), **1. Charles, 3rd Earl of Sunderland,** 1674–1722, British statesman: prime minister 1718–21. **2. Herbert,** 1820–1903, English philosopher. **3. Platt Rogers,** 1800–64, U.S. calligrapher and teacher of penmanship.

Spen•der (spen′dər), **Stephen,** born 1909, English poet and critic.

Spe•ner (shpā′nəR), **Philipp Jakob,** 1635–1705, German theologian: founder of Pietism.

Speng•ler (speng′glər, shpeng′-), **Oswald,** 1880–1936, German philosopher.

Spen•ser (spen′sər), **Edmund,** c1552–99, English poet.

Sper•ry (sper′ē), **Elmer Ambrose,** 1860–1930, U.S. inventor and manufacturer.

Spiel•berg (spēl′bûrg), **Steven,** born 1947, U.S. film director, writer, and producer.

Spin•garn (spin′gärn), **Joel Elias,** 1875–1939, U.S. literary critic, publisher, and editor.

Spi•no•za (spi nō′zə), **Baruch** or **Benedict de,** 1632–77, Dutch philosopher.

Spit•te•ler (*Ger.* shpit′l əR), **Carl** (*"Felix Tandem"*), 1845–1924, Swiss poet, novelist, and essayist: Nobel prize 1919.

Spitz (spits), **Mark (Andrew),** born 1950, U.S. swimmer: winner of seven gold medals in 1972 summer Olympic Games.

Spock (spok), **Benjamin (McLane),** 1903–91, U.S. physician and educator.

Spode (spōd), **Josiah,** 1733–97, and his son, **Josiah,** 1754–1827, English potters.

Spohr (shpôr), **Ludwig** or **Louis,** 1784–1859, German violinist and composer.

Spot′ted Tail′, (*Sinte-galeshka*), 1833?–81, Brulé Sioux leader.

Sprague (sprāg), **Frank Julian,** 1857–1934, U.S. electrical engineer and inventor.

Spring•steen (spring′stēn), **Bruce,** born 1949, U.S. singer and songwriter.

Spur•geon (spûr′jən), **Charles Haddon,** 1834–92, English Baptist preacher.

Spy•ri (shpē′rē, spē′-), **Johanna,** 1827–1901, Swiss author.

Squan•to (skwon′tō), died 1622, North American Indian of the Narragansett tribe: interpreter for the Pilgrims.

Squibb (skwib), **Edward Robinson,** 1819–1900, U.S. pharmaceutical manufacturer and medical reformer.

Staël-Hols•tein (stäl′ôl sten′), **Anne Louise Germaine Necker, Baronne de,** (*Madame de Staël*) 1766–1817, French writer.

Staf•ford (staf′ərd), **Sir Edward William,** 1819–1901, New Zealand political leader, born in Scotland: prime minister 1856–61, 1865–69, 1872.

Stagg (stag), **Amos Alonzo,** 1862–1965, U.S. football coach.

Stahl (shtäl), **Georg Ernst,** 1660–1734, German chemist and physician.

Sta•lin (stä′lin, -lēn, stal′in), **Joseph V.** (*Iosif Vissarionovich Dzhugashvili*), 1879–1953, premier of the U.S.S.R. 1941–53.

Stan•dish (stan′dish), **Myles** or **Miles,** c1584–1656, American settler, born in England.

Stan•ford (stan′fərd), **(Amasa) Leland,** 1824–93, U.S. railroad developer, politician, and philanthropist: governor of California 1861–63; senator 1885–93.

Stan•hope (stan′hōp′, stan′əp), **James, 1st Earl Stanhope,** 1673–1721, British soldier and statesman: prime minister 1717–18.

Stan•is•laus I (stan′is lôs′, -lous′) (*Stanislaus Leszczynski*) 1677–1766, king of Poland 1704–09, 1733–35.

Stan•i•slav•sky or **Stan•i•slav•ski** (stan′ə släv′skē, -släf′-), **Konstantin** (*Konstantin Sergeevich Alekseev*), 1863–1938, Russian actor, producer, and director.

Stan•ley (stan′lē), **1. Edward George Geoffrey Smith, 14th Earl of Derby,** 1799–1869, British prime minister. **2. Francis Edgar,** 1849–1918, and his twin brother, **Freelan,** 1849–1940, U.S. inventors and manufacturers: developed steam-powered car. **3. Sir Henry Morton** (*John Rowlands*), 1841–1904, British journalist and explorer in Africa. **4. Wendell M(eredith),** 1904–71, U.S. biochemist: Nobel prize 1946.

Stan•ton (stan′tn), **1. Edwin McMasters,** 1814–69, U.S. Secretary of War 1862–67. **2. Elizabeth Cady,** 1815–1902, U.S. social reformer.

Stark (stärk; *for 2 also* shtärk), **1. Harold Raynsford,** 1880–1972, U.S. admiral. **2. Johannes,** 1874–1957, German physicist: Nobel prize 1919. **3. John,** 1728–1822, American Revolutionary War general.

Star•ker (shtär′kər), **Janos,** born 1924, U.S. cellist, born in Hungary.

Stas•sen (stas′ən), **Harold Edward,** born 1907, U.S. politician.

Sta•ti•us (stā′shē əs), **Publius Papinius,** A.D. c45–c96, Roman poet.

Stat•ler (stat′lər), **Ellsworth Milton,** 1863–1928, U.S. hotel-chain developer.

Stau•ding•er (shtou′ding ər), **Hermann,** 1881–1965, German chemist: Nobel prize 1953.

St. Clair (sānt′ klâr′, sing′klâr, sin′-), **Arthur,** 1736–1818, American Revolutionary War general, born in Scotland: 1st governor of the Northwest Territory, 1787–1802.

St. Den•is (sānt′ den′is), **Ruth,** 1880?–1968, U.S. dancer.

Steele (stēl), **Sir Richard,** 1672–1729, English essayist, dramatist, and political leader; born in Ireland.

Steen (stān), **Jan,** 1626–79, Dutch painter.

Stef•ans•son (stef′ən sən), **Vil•hjal•mur** (vil′hyoul′mər), 1879–1962, U.S. arctic explorer and author, born in Canada.

Stef•fens (stef′ənz), **(Joseph) Lincoln,** 1866–1936, U.S. author, journalist, and editor.

Stei•chen (stī′kən), **Edward,** 1879–1973, U.S. photographer.

Steig (stīg), **William,** born 1907, U.S. artist.

Stein (stīn), **1. Gertrude,** 1874–1946, U.S. author in France. **2. William Howard,** 1911–80, U.S. biochemist: Nobel prize for chemistry 1972.

Stein•beck (stīn′bek), **John (Ernst),** 1902–68, U.S. novelist: Nobel prize 1962.

Stein•berg (stīn′bûrg), **1. Saul,** born 1914, U.S. painter and cartoonist. **2. William,** 1899–1978, U.S. conductor, born in Germany.

Stein•em (stī′nəm), **Gloria,** born 1934, U.S. women's-rights activist.

Stei•ner (stī′nər, shtī′-), **1. Jakob,** 1796–1863, Swiss mathematician. **2. Rudolf,** 1861–1925, Austrian philosopher.

Stei•nitz (stī′nits, shtī′-), **William** (*Wilhelm Steinitz*), 1836–1900, U.S. chess player, born in Czechoslovakia.

Stein•man (stīn′mən), **David Barnard,** 1886–1960, U.S. civil engineer: specialist in bridge design and construction.

Stein•metz (stīn′mets), **Charles Proteus,** 1865–1923, U.S. electrical engineer, born in Germany.

Stein•way (stīn′wā′), **Henry Engelhard** (*Heinrich Engelhard Steinweg*), 1797–1871, U.S. piano manufacturer, born in Germany.

Stel•la (stel′ə), **Frank (Philip),** born 1936, U.S. painter.

Sten•dhal (sten däl′, stan-), (*Marie Henri Beyle*), 1783–1842, French novelist and critic.

Steng•el (steng′gəl), **Charles Dillon** (*"Casey"*), 1891–1975, U.S. baseball player and manager.

Ste•phen (stē′vən), **1. Saint,** died A.D. c35, first Christian martyr. **2. Saint,** c975–1038, first king of Hungary 997–1038. **3.** (*Stephen of Blois*) 1097?–1154, king of England 1135–54. **4. Sir Leslie,** 1832–1904, English critic, biographer, and philosopher.

Ste•phens (stē′vənz), **1. Alexander Hamilton,** 1812–83, vice-president of the Confederacy 1861–65. **2. James,** 1882–1950, Irish poet and novelist.

Ste•phen•son (stē′vən sən), **1. George,** 1781–1848, English inventor and engineer. **2.** his son **Robert,** 1803–59, English engineer.

Stern (stûrn), **1. Isaac,** born 1920, U.S. violinist, born in Russia. **2. Otto,** 1888–1969, U.S. physicist, born in Germany: Nobel prize 1943.

Stern•berg (stûrn′bûrg), **George Miller,** 1838–1915, U.S. bacteriologist and medical researcher.

Sterne (stûrn), **Laurence,** 1713–68, English novelist and clergyman.

Steu•ben (sto͞o′bən, styo͞o′-, shtoi′-, sto͞o ben′, styo͞o-), **Friedrich Wilhelm Ludolf Gerhard Augustin von,** 1730–94, Prussian major general in the American Revolutionary army.

Ste•vens (stē′vənz), **1. George (Cooper),** 1905–75, U.S. film director. **2. John Cox,** 1749–1838, and his son **Robert Livingston,** 1787–1856, U.S. engineers and inventors. **3. John Paul,** born 1920, associate justice of the U.S. Supreme Court since 1975. **4. Risë,** born 1913, U.S. mezzo-soprano. **5. Thaddeus,** 1792–1868, U.S. abolitionist and political leader. **6. Wallace,** 1879–1955, U.S. poet.

Ste•ven•son (stē′vən sən), **1. Ad•lai Ewing** (ad′lā), 1835–1914, U.S. vice president 1893–97. **2.** his grandson, **Adlai E(wing),** 1900–65, U.S. statesman and diplomat: ambassador to the U.N. 1960–65. **3. Robert Louis** (*Robert Lewis Balfour*), 1850–94, Scottish novelist, essayist, and poet.

Ste•vin (stə vīn′), **Simon,** 1548–1620, Dutch mathematician and physicist.

Stew•art (sto͞o′ərt, styo͞o′-), **1. Dugald,** 1753–1828, Scottish philosopher. **2. James,** born 1908, U.S. actor. **3. Potter,** 1915–85, U.S. jurist: associate justice of the U.S. Supreme Court 1958–81.

Stie•gel (stē′gəl; *Ger.* shtē′gəl), **Henry William,** 1729–85, German iron and glass manufacturer in America.

Stieg•litz (stēg′lits), **Alfred,** 1864–1946, U.S. photographer.

Stil•i•cho (stil′i kō′), **Flavius,** A.D. 359?–408, Roman general and statesman.

Still (stil), **1. Andrew Taylor,** 1828–1917, U.S. founder of osteopathy. **2. William Grant,** 1895–1978, U.S. composer.

Stil•well (stil′wel, -wəl), **Joseph W.** (*"Vinegar Joe"*), 1883–1946, U.S. general.

Stim•son (stim′sən), **Henry L(ewis),** 1867–1950, U.S. statesman.

Sting (sting), (*Gordon Matthew Sumner*), born 1951, British actor and musician.

Stin•nes (shtin′əs), **Hugo,** 1870–1924, German industrialist.

St. John (sānt′ jon′; *for 1 also* sin′jən), **Henry, 1st Viscount Bolingbroke,** BOLINGBROKE, 1st Viscount.

St.-John Perse (sin′jən pûrs′), (*Alexis Saint-Léger Léger*), 1887–1975, French diplomat and poet: Nobel prize for literature 1960.

St. Lau•rent (SAN lô RÄN′), **1. Louis Stephen,** 1882–1973, prime minister of Canada 1948–57. **2. Yves (Mathieu)** (ēv), born 1936, French fashion designer.

Stock•hau•sen (shtôk′hou′zən), **Karlheinz,** born 1928, German composer.

Stock•ton (stok′tən), **Frank R.** (*Francis Richard Stockton*), 1834–1902, U.S. novelist and short-story writer.

Sto•ker (stō′kər), **Bram** (*Abraham Stoker*), 1847–1912, British novelist, born in Ireland: creator of Dracula.

Stokes (stōks), **1. Carl B(urton),** born 1927, U.S. politician: the first black mayor of a major U.S. city (Cleveland, Ohio, 1967–71). **2. Sir Frederick Wilfrid Scott,** 1860–1927, British inventor and engineer. **3. Sir George Gabriel,** 1819–1903, British physicist and mathematician, born in Ireland.

Sto•kow•ski (stə kou′skē, -kôf′-, -kôv′-), **Leopold Antoni Stanislaw,** 1882–1977, U.S. orchestra conductor, born in England.

Stone (stōn), **1. Edward Durell,** 1902–78, U.S. architect. **2. Harlan Fiske,** 1872–1946, Chief Justice of the U.S. 1941–46. **3. Irving** (*Irving Tennenbaum*) 1903–89, U.S. author. **4. I(sidor) F(einstein),** 1907–89, U.S. political journalist. **5. Lucy,** 1818–93, U.S. suffragist.

Stop•pard (stop′ərd), **Tom** (*Thomas Straussler*), born 1937, British playwright, born in Czechoslovakia.

Storm (shtōʀm), **Theodore Woldsen,** 1817–88, German poet and novelist.

Sto•ry (stôr′ē, stōr′ē), **1. Joseph,** 1779–1845, U.S. jurist. **2. William Wetmore,** 1819–95, U.S. sculptor and poet.

Stout (stout), **Robert,** 1844–1930, New Zealand jurist and statesman: prime minister 1884–87.

Stowe (stō), **Harriet (Elizabeth) Beecher,** 1811–96, U.S. abolitionist and novelist.

Stra•bo (strā′bō), 63? B.C.–A.D. 21?, Greek geographer and historian.

Stra•chey (strā′chē), **(Giles) Lytton,** 1880–1932, English biographer and literary critic.

Stra•di•va•ri (strad′ə vâr′ē, -vär′ē), **Antonio,** 1644?–

1737, Italian violinmaker of Cremona. Latin, **Strad/i•var′i•us** (-vâr′ē əs).

Straf•ford (straf′ərd), **1st Earl of** (*Thomas Wentworth*), 1593–1641, English statesman: chief adviser of Charles I of England.

Strand (strand), **1. Mark,** born 1934, U.S. poet, born in Canada: U.S. poet laureate 1990–91. **2. Paul,** 1890–1976, U.S. photographer and documentary-film producer.

Stras•berg (sträs′bərg, stras′-), **Lee,** 1901–82, U.S. theatrical director, teacher, and actor, born in Austria.

Strat•ton (strat′n), **Charles Sherwood** (*"General Tom Thumb"*), 1838–83, U.S. midget who performed in the circus of P. T. Barnum.

Straus (strous, shtrous), **1. Isidor,** 1845–1912, U.S. retail merchant and politician, born in Bavaria: congressman 1894–95 (brother of Nathan and Oscar Solomon Straus). **2. Nathan,** 1848–1931, U.S. retail merchant, born in Bavaria. **3. Oscar,** 1870–1954, French composer, born in Austria. **4. Oscar Solomon,** 1850–1926, U.S. diplomat, jurist, and government official, born in Bavaria: Secretary of Commerce and Labor 1906–09.

Strauss (strous, shtrous), **1. David Friedrich,** 1808–74, German theologian, philosopher, and author. **2. Johann,** 1804–49, Austrian composer. **3.** his son **Johann** (*"The Waltz King"*), 1825–99, Austrian composer. **4. Levi,** 1829?–1902, U.S. pants manufacturer: developed Levis. **5. Ri•chard** (riᴋʜ′ärt), 1864–1949, German composer.

Stra•vin•sky (strə vin′skē), **Igor Fëdorovich,** 1882–1971, U.S. composer, born in Russia.

Streep (strēp), **Meryl,** born 1949, U.S. actress.

Strei•sand (strī′sənd), **Barbra (Joan),** born 1942, U.S. actress, singer, and film director.

Stre•se•mann (shtʀā′zə män′), **Gustav,** 1878–1929, German statesman: Nobel peace prize 1926.

Strick•land (strik′lənd), **William,** 1787–1854, U.S. architect and engineer.

Strind•berg (strind′bûrg, strin′-), **Johan August,** 1849–1912, Swedish novelist and dramatist.

Stroess•ner (stres′nər), **Alfredo,** born 1912, Paraguayan general and statesman: president 1954–89.

Stroz•zi (strot′sē), **Bernardo** (*"Il Cappuccino"*), 1581–1644, Italian painter and engraver.

Stru•ve (stro͞o′və, shtro͞o′-), **1. Friedrich Georg Wilhelm von,** 1793–1864, Russian astronomer, born in Germany. **2. Otto,** 1897–1963, U.S. astronomer, born in Russia.

Stu•art (sto͞o′ərt, styo͞o′-), **1.** a member of the royal family that ruled in Scotland from 1371 to 1714 and in England from 1603 to 1714. **2. Charles Edward** (*"the Young Pretender"* or *"Bonnie Prince Charlie"*), 1720–80, grandson of James II. **3. Gilbert (Charles),** 1755–1828, U.S. painter. **4. James Ewell Brown** (*"Jeb"*), 1833–64, Confederate general in the Civil War. **5. James Francis Edward.** Also called **James III.** (*"the Old Pretender"*), 1688–1766, English prince. **6. Jesse Hilton,** 1907–84, U.S. writer. **7.**

John, 3rd Earl of Bute, 1713–92, British statesman: prime minister 1762–63.

Stubbs (stubz), **William,** 1825–1901, English historian and bishop.

Stu•de•ba•ker (stoo͞/də bā/kər, styoo͞/-), **Clement,** 1831–1901, U.S. wagon maker and pioneer automobile designer.

Stur•gis (stûr/jis), **Russell,** 1836–1909, U.S. architect and author.

Stur•lu•son (stûr/lə sən), SNORRI STURLUSON.

Stutz (stuts), **Harry Clayton,** 1876–1930, U.S. automobile manufacturer.

Stuy•ve•sant (stī/və sənt), **Peter,** 1592–1672, last Dutch governor of New Netherland 1646–64.

Styne (stīn), **Jule,** born 1905, U.S. composer and producer.

Sty•ron (stī/rən), **William,** born 1925, U.S. author.

Suá•rez (swär/ez, -eth), **Francisco,** 1548–1617, Spanish theologian and philosopher.

Suck•ling (suk/ling), **Sir John,** 1609–42, English poet.

Su•cre (soo͞/krā), **Antonio José de,** 1793–1830, Venezuelan general and South American liberator: 1st president of Bolivia 1826–28.

Sue (soo͞; *Fr.* sy), **Eugène** (*Marie Joseph Sue*), 1804–57, French writer.

Sue•to•ni•us (swi tō/nē əs), (*Gaius Suetonius Tranquillus*) A.D. 75–150, Roman historian.

Su•har•to (soo͞ här/tō), **Raden,** born 1921, president of Indonesia since 1968.

Sui (swē), a dynasty ruling in China A.D. 589–618.

Su•kar•no (soo͞ kär/nō), **Achmed,** 1901–1970, president of Indonesia 1945–67.

Su•lei•man I (soo͞/lə män/, -lā-, soo͞/lā män/), (*"the Magnificent"*) 1495?–1566, sultan of the Ottoman Empire 1520–66.

Sul•la (sul/ə), (*Lucius Cornelius Sulla Felix*) 138–78 B.C., Roman general and statesman: dictator 82–79.

Sul•li•van (sul/ə vən), **1. Annie** (*Anne Mansfield Sullivan Macy*), 1866–1936, U.S. teacher of Helen Keller. **2. Sir Arthur (Seymour),** 1842–1900, English composer. **3. Ed(ward Vincent),** 1902–74, U.S. journalist and television host. **4. Harry Stack,** 1892–1949, U.S. psychiatrist. **5. John L(awrence),** 1858–1918, U.S. boxer. **6. Louis Henri,** 1856–1924, U.S. architect.

Sul•ly (sul/ē; *for 1 also* sə lē/), **1. Maximilien de Béthune, Duc de,** 1560–1641, French statesman. **2. Thomas,** 1783–1872, U.S. painter, born in England.

Sul•ly-Pru•dhomme (sə lē/prə dōm/), **René François Armand,** 1839–1907, French poet: Nobel prize 1901.

Sum•ner (sum/nər), **1. Charles,** 1811–74, U.S. statesman. **2. James Batcheller,** 1887–1955, U.S. biochemist: Nobel prize 1946. **3. William Graham,** 1840–1910, U.S. sociologist and economist.

Sun•day (sun′dā, -dē), **William Ashley** (*"Billy Sunday"*), 1862–1935, U.S. evangelist.

Sung (so͝ong) also **Song,** a dynasty in China, A.D. 960–1279.

Sun Yat-sen (so͝on′ yät′sen′), 1866–1925, Chinese political and revolutionary leader.

Sup•pé (so͞o′pā; *Ger.* zo͞op′ā), **Franz von,** 1819–95, Austrian composer.

Sur•ratt (sə rat′), **Mary Eugenia (Jenkins),** 1820–65, alleged conspirator in the assassination of President Lincoln.

Sur•rey (sûr′ē, sur′ē), **Earl of** (*Henry Howard*), 1517?–47, English poet.

Sur•tees (sûr′tēz), **Robert Smith,** 1805–64, English editor and writer.

Suth•er•land (suth′ər lənd), **1. Earl Wilbur, Jr.,** 1915–74, U.S. biochemist: Nobel prize for medicine 1971. **2. George,** 1862–1942, U.S. politician and jurist: associate justice of the U.S. Supreme Court 1922–38. **3. Dame Joan,** born 1926, Australian soprano.

Sut•ter (sut′ər), **John Augustus,** 1803–80, U.S. frontiersman.

Sutt•ner (zo͝ot′nər, so͝ot′-), **Bertha von,** 1843–1914, Austrian writer: Nobel peace prize 1905.

Su•vo•rov (so͞o vôr′ôf, -of), **Aleksandr Vasilevich,** 1729–1800, Russian field marshal.

Sved•berg (sved′bərg, -bar′yᵊ, sfed′-), **The(odor),** 1884–1971, Swedish chemist: Nobel prize 1926.

Sver•drup (sver′drəp, sfer′-), **Otto Neumann,** 1855?–1930, Norwegian explorer of the Arctic.

Swam•mer•dam (sväm′ər däm′, sfäm′-), **Jan,** 1637–80, Dutch anatomist and entomologist.

Swan (swon), **Sir Joseph Wilson,** 1828–1914, British chemist, electrical engineer, and inventor.

Swan•son (swon′sən), **Gloria** (*Gloria Josephine May Swenson*), 1899–1983, U.S. film actress.

Swart (swôrt), **Charles Robberts,** 1894–1982, South African statesman: president 1961–67.

Swe•den•borg (swēd′n bôrg′), **Emanuel** (*Emanuel Swedberg*), 1688–1772, Swedish scientist, philosopher, and mystic.

Swee•linck or **Swe•linck** (svā′lingk), **Jan Pie•ters** (yän pē′tərs) or **Jan Pie•ters•zoon** (-sōn′), 1562–1621, Dutch organist and composer.

Sweet (swēt), **Henry,** 1845–1912, English philologist and linguist.

Swift (swift), **1. Gustavus Franklin,** 1839–1903, U.S. meat packer. **2. Jonathan** (*"Isaac Bickerstaff"*), 1667–1745, English satirist and clergyman, born in Ireland.

Swin•burne (swin′bərn), **Algernon Charles,** 1837–1909, English poet and critic.

Swin•ner•ton (swin′ər tən), **Frank (Arthur),** 1884–1982, English novelist and critic.

Swith•in or **Swith•un** (swith′in, swith′-), **Saint,** died A.D. 862, English ecclesiastic: bishop of Winchester 852?–862.

Syl•ves•ter or **Sil•ves•ter** (sil ves′tər), **1. Sylvester I, Saint,** died A.D. 335, pope 314–335. **2. Sylvester II,** (*Gerbert*) died 1003, French ecclesiastic: pope 999–1003.

Sy•ming•ton (sī′ming tən), **(William) Stuart,** 1901–88, U.S. politician: senator 1952–77.

Sym•ma•chus (sim′ə kəs), **Saint,** died A.D. 514, pope 498–514.

Sym•onds (sim′əndz), **John Addington,** 1840–93, English poet, essayist, and critic.

Sy•mons (sī′mənz), **Arthur,** 1865–1945, English poet and critic, born in Wales.

Synge (sing), **1. John Millington,** 1871–1909, Irish dramatist. **2. Richard Laurence Millington,** born 1914, English biochemist: Nobel prize for chemistry 1952.

Szell (sel), **George,** 1897–1970, U.S. pianist and conductor, born in Hungary.

Szent-Györ•gyi (sent jûr′jē, -jôr′-), **Albert,** 1893–1986, U.S. biochemist, born in Hungary: Nobel prize for medicine 1937.

Szi•ge•ti (sig′i tē, si get′ē), **Joseph,** 1892–1973, U.S. violinist, born in Hungary.

Szi•lard (sil′ärd), **Leo,** 1898–1964, U.S. physicist, born in Hungary.

Szold (zōld), **Henrietta,** 1860–1945, U.S. Zionist.

T

Tac•i•tus (tas′i təs), **Publius Cornelius,** A.D. c55–c120, Roman historian.

Taft (taft), **1. Lorado,** 1860–1936, U.S. sculptor. **2. Robert A(lphonso),** 1889–1953, U.S. lawyer and political leader (son of William Howard). **3. William Howard,** 1857–1930, 27th president of the U.S. 1909–13.

Tag•gard (tag′ərd), **Genevieve,** 1894–1948, U.S. poet.

Ta•glia•vi•ni (täl′yə vē′nē), **Ferruccio,** born 1913, Italian tenor.

Ta•gore (tə gôr′, -gōr′), **Sir Rabindranath,** 1861–1941, Indian poet: Nobel prize 1913.

Taine ((tān, ten),), **Hippolyte Adolphe,** 1828–93, French literary critic and historian.

T'ai Tsung (tī′ dzŏŏng′) also **Tai Zong** (tī′ zông′), A.D. 597–649, Chinese emperor of the T'ang dynasty 627–649.

Tal•bot (tôl′bət), **1. Charles, Duke of Shrewsbury,** 1660–1718, British statesman: prime minister 1714. **2. William Henry Fox,** 1800–77, English pioneer in photography.

Tal•i•es•in (tal′ē es′in), fl. A.D. c550, Welsh bard.

Tal•ley•rand-Pé•ri•gord (tal′ə rand′per′i gôr′), **Charles Maurice de, Prince de Bénévent,** 1754–1838, French statesman.

Tal•lis or **Tal•lys** or **Tal•ys** (tal′is), **Thomas,** c1505–85, English organist and composer, esp. of church music.

Ta•ma•yo (tä mä′yō), **Rufino,** 1899–91, Mexican painter.

Tam•er•lane (tam′ər lān′) also **Tam•bur•laine** (tam′bər-), (*Timur Lenk*) 1336?–1405, Tartar conqueror in S and W Asia. Also called **Timur.**

Tamm (täm), **Igor Evgenievich,** 1895–1971, Russian physicist: Nobel prize 1958.

Ta•na•ka (tə nä′kə), **Baron Giichi,** 1863–1929, Japanese military and political leader: prime minister 1927–29.

Tan•cred (tang′krid), 1078?–1112, Norman leader in the 1st Crusade.

Tan•dy (tan′dē), **Jessica,** born 1909, English actress, in the U.S.

Ta•ney (tô′nē), **Roger Brooke,** 1777–1864, Chief Justice of the U.S. 1836–64.

Tan•guy (täɴ gē′), **Yves** (ēv), 1900–55, French painter, in the U.S. after 1939.

Ta•ni•za•ki (tä′nē zä′kē), **Junichiro,** 1886–1965, Japanese novelist.

Tan•ner (tan′ər), **Henry Ossawa,** 1859–1937, U.S. painter, in France after 1891.

Tà•pies (tä′pyes), **Antoni** or **Antonio,** born 1923, Spanish painter.

Tap•pan (tap′ən), **Arthur,** 1786–1865, and his brother **Lewis,** 1788–1873, U.S. businessmen, philanthropists, and abolitionists.

Tar•bell (tär′bel′), **Ida M(inerva),** 1857–1944, U.S. author.

Tarde (tärd), **Gabriel,** 1843–1904, French sociologist.

Tar•dieu (tᴀʀ dyœ′), **André Pierre Gabriel Amédée,** 1876–1945, French statesman.

Tar•king•ton (tär′king tən), **(Newton) Booth,** 1869–1946, U.S. novelist and playwright.

Tarl•ton (tärl′tn), **Richard,** died 1588, English actor.

Tar•quin•i•us (tär kwin′ē əs) also **Tar′quin, 1.** (*Lucius Tarquinius Priscus*) died 578 B.C., king of Rome 616–578. **2.** (*Lucius Tarquinius Superbus*) (*"the Proud"*) died 498 B.C., king of Rome 534–510.

Tar•ski (tär′skē), **Alfred,** born 1902, U.S. mathematician and logician, born in Poland.

Tar•ti•ni (tär tē′nē), **Giuseppe,** 1692–1770, Italian violinist and composer.

Tas•man (taz′mən), **Abel Janszoon,** 1602?–59, Dutch explorer.

Tas•so (tas′ō, tä′sō), **Torquato,** 1544–95, Italian poet.

Tate (tāt), **1. Sir Henry,** 1819–99, English merchant and philanthropist: founder of an art gallery. **2. (John Orley) Allen,** 1899–1979, U.S. poet and critic. **3. Nahum,** 1652–1715, English poet and playwright, born in Ireland: poet laureate 1692–1715.

Ta•tum (tā′təm), **1. Art,** 1910–56, U.S. jazz pianist. **2. Edward Lawrie,** 1909–75, U.S. biochemist: Nobel prize for medicine 1958.

Tau•ber (tou′bər), **Richard,** 1892–1948, Austrian tenor, in England after 1940.

Tauch•nitz (touᴋʜ′nits), **Karl Christoph Traugott,** 1761–1836, and his son, **Karl Christian Philipp,** 1798–1884, German printers and publishers.

Taus•sig (tou′sig), **Frank William,** 1859–1940, U.S. economist.

Taw•ney (tô′nē, tä′-), **Richard Henry,** 1880–1962, English historian, born in Calcutta.

Tay•lor (tā′lər), **1. Bayard** (*James Bayard*), 1825–78, U.S. poet and travel writer. **2. Brook,** 1685–1731, English mathematician. **3. Cecil (Percival),** born 1933, U.S. jazz pianist and composer. **4. David Watson,** 1864–1940, U.S. naval architect. **5. Elizabeth,** born 1932, U.S. actress, born in England. **6. Edward,** 1644?–1729, American physician, clergyman, and poet, born in England. **7. Edward Thompson** (*"Father Taylor"*), 1793–1871, U.S. Methodist clergyman. **8. Frederick Winslow,** 1856–1915, U.S. inventor. **9. James,** born 1948, U.S. singer, guitarist, and songwriter. **10. Jeremy,** 1613–67, English prelate and theological writer. **11. John W.,** 1784–1854, U.S. politician: Speaker of the House 1820–21, 1825–27. **12. (Joseph) Deems,** 1885–1966, U.S. composer, music critic, and author. **13. Maxwell (Davenport),** 1901–87, U.S. army general. **14. Myron Charles,** 1874–1959, U.S. lawyer, industrialist, and diplomat. **15. Paul (Belville),** born

1930, U.S. choreographer. **16. Tom,** 1817–80, English playwright and editor.

Tchai•kov•sky (chī kôf′skē, -kof′-, chi-), **Peter Ilyich** or **Pëtr Ilich,** 1840–93, Russian composer.

Tche•rep•nin (chə rep′nin), **1. Alexander** (*Aleksandr Nikolaevich*), 1899–1977, Russian pianist and composer, in the U.S. **2.** his father, **Nicholas** (*Nikolai Nikolaevich*), 1873–1945, Russian composer and conductor.

Teach (tēch), **Edward** (*"Blackbeard"*), died 1718, English pirate and privateer in the Americas.

Tea•gar•den (tē′gär′dn), **Weldon John,** (*Jack*), 1905–64, U.S. jazz trombonist and singer.

Teas•dale (tēz′dāl′), **Sara,** 1884–1933, U.S. poet.

Te•bal•di (tə bäl′dē, -bôl′-), **Renata,** born 1922, Italian soprano.

Te•cum•seh (ti kum′sə) also **Te•cum•tha** (-thə), 1768?–1813, Shawnee Indian chief and military leader.

Ted•der (ted′ər), **Arthur William,** 1st Baron, 1890–1967, British Royal Air Force marshal and educator, born in Scotland.

Teil•hard de Char•din (te YAR də SHAR daN′), **Pierre,** 1881–1955, French Jesuit priest, paleontologist, and philosopher.

Tek•a•kwith•a (tek′ə kwith′ə), **Kateri** or **Catherine,** 1656–80, Mohawk Indian convert to Roman Catholicism.

Te•le•mann (tā′lə män′), **Georg Philipp,** 1681–1767, German composer.

Te•les•pho•rus (tə les′fər əs), pope A.D. 125?–136?.

Tel•ler (tel′ər), **Edward,** born 1908, U.S. physicist, born in Hungary.

Tél•lez (tel′yeth), **Gabriel,** TIRSO DE MOLINA.

Tem•in (tem′in), **Howard M(artin),** born 1934, U.S. virologist: Nobel prize for medicine 1975.

Tem•ple (tem′pəl), **1. Shirley** (*Shirley Temple Black*), born 1928, U.S. film actress and diplomat. **2. Sir William,** 1628–99, English essayist and diplomat.

Teng Hsiao-ping or **Teng Hsiao-p'ing** (*Chin.* dung′ shyou′ping′), DENG XIAOPING.

Ten•iers (ten′yərz, tə nērz′), **1. David** (*"the Elder"*), 1582–1649, Flemish painter and engraver. **2.** his son, **David** (*"the Younger"*), 1610–90, Flemish painter.

Ten•nant (ten′ənt), **Smithson,** 1761–1815, English chemist: discoverer of osmium and iridium.

Ten•niel (ten′yəl), **Sir John,** 1820–1914, English caricaturist and illustrator.

Ten•ny•son (ten′ə sən), **Alfred, Lord** (*1st Baron*), 1809–92, English poet: poet laureate 1850–92.

Ten•zing (ten′zing), (*Norgay*) 1913?–86, Nepalese mountain climber: scaled Mt. Everest 1953.

Ter Borch or **Ter•borch** (tər bôrk′, -bôrKH′), also **Ter•burg** (-bûrg′, -bŏŏrKH′), **Gerard,** 1617–81, Dutch painter.

Ter•ence (ter′əns), (*Publius Terentius Afer*) c190–159? B.C., Roman playwright.

Te•re•sa (tə rē′sə, -zə, -rā′sə), **1. Mother** (*Agnes Gonxha Bojaxhiu*), Roman Catholic nun, born 1910 in Skopje: Nobel peace prize 1979. **2. Saint,** THERESA, Saint.

Te•resh•ko•va (ter′əsh kō′və), **Valentina Vladimirovna,** born 1937, Russian cosmonaut: first woman in space 1963.

Ter•hune (tər hyōōn′), **Albert Payson,** 1872–1942, U.S. novelist and short-story writer.

Ter•kel (tûr′kəl), **Studs,** born 1912, U.S. writer.

Ter•ry (ter′ē), **Ellen (Alicia** or **Alice),** 1848?–1928, English actress.

Ter•tul•li•an (tər tul′ē ən, -tul′yən), (*Quintus Septimius Florens Tertullianus*) A.D. c160–c230, Carthaginian theologian.

Tes•la (tes′lə), **Nikola,** 1856–1943, U.S. physicist, electrical engineer, and inventor, born in Croatia.

Te•traz•zi•ni (te′trə zē′nē), **Luisa,** 1874–1940, Italian soprano.

Tet•zel or **Te•zel** (tet′səl), **Johann,** 1465?–1519, German monk: antagonist of Martin Luther.

Thack•er•ay (thak′ə rē), **William Makepeace,** 1811–63, English novelist, born in India.

Tha•ïs (thā′is), fl. late 4th century B.C., Athenian courtesan: mistress of Alexander the Great and Ptolemy I.

Thal•berg (thôl′bûrg), **Irving (Grant),** 1899–1936, U.S. motion-picture producer.

Tha•les (thā′lēz), c640–546? B.C., Greek philosopher, born in Miletus.

Thant (tänt, thänt, thant), **U** (ōō), U THANT.

Tharp (thärp), **Twyla,** born 1941, U.S. dancer and choreographer.

Thatch•er (thach′ər), **Margaret (Hilda),** born 1925, British prime minister 1979–90.

Thay•er (thā′ər, thâr), **1. Sylvanus,** 1785–1872, U.S. army officer and educator. **2. William Roscoe,** 1859–1923, U.S. historian and author.

Thei•ler (tī′lər), **Max,** 1899–1972, South African medical scientist, in the U.S. after 1922: Nobel prize for medicine 1951.

The•mis•to•cles (thə mis′tə klēz′), 527?–460? B.C., Athenian statesman.

The•o•bald (thē′ə bôld′), **Lewis,** 1688–1744, English author.

The•oc•ri•tus (thē ok′ri təs), fl. c270 B.C., Greek poet.

The•o•do•ra (thē′ə dôr′ə, -dōr′ə), A.D. 508–548, Byzantine empress: consort of Justinian I.

The•od•o•ric (thē od′ə rik), A.D. 454?–526, king of the Ostrogoths: ruler of Italy 493–526.

The•o•do•si•us I (thē′ə dō′shē əs, -shəs), (*"the Great"*) A.D. 346?–395, Roman emperor 379–395.

The•o•phras•tus (thē′ə fras′təs), 372?–287 B.C., Greek philosopher.

The•o•rell (tā′ō rel′), **Axel Hugo Teodor,** 1903–82, Swedish biochemist: Nobel prize for medicine 1955.

The•re•sa or **Te•re•sa** (tə rē′sə, -zə, -rā′sə), **Saint,** 1515–82, Spanish Carmelite mystic. Also called **There′sa of A′vi•la** (ä′vē lə).

Thé•rèse de Li•sieux (tā ʀez də lē zyœ′), **Saint** (*Marie Françoise Thérèse Martin*) (*"the Little Flower"*), 1873–97, French Carmelite nun.

The•roux (thə ro͞o′), **Paul,** born 1941, U.S. writer.

Thes•pis (thes′pis), fl. 6th century B.C., Greek poet.

Thiers (tyâr′), **Louis Adolphe,** 1797–1877, French statesman: president 1871–73.

Thieu (tyo͞o), **Nguyen Van,** NGUYEN VAN THIEU.

Thom•as (tom′əs), **1.** an apostle who demanded proof of Christ's Resurrection. **2. Augustus,** 1857–1934, U.S. playwright, journalist, and actor. **3. (Charles Louis) Ambroise,** 1811–96, French composer. **4. Clarence,** born 1948, U.S. jurist: associate justice of the U.S. Supreme Court since 1991. **5. Dyl•an (Marlais)** (dil′ən), 1914–53, Welsh poet. **6. George Henry,** 1816–70, Union general in the U.S. Civil War. **7. Lowell (Jackson),** 1892–1981, U.S. newscaster, world traveler, and writer. **8. Martha Carey,** 1857–1935, U.S. educator and women's-rights advocate. **9. Michael Tilson,** born 1944, U.S. conductor. **10. Norman (Mattoon),** 1884–1968, U.S. socialist leader and political writer. **11. Seth,** 1785–1859, U.S. clock designer and manufacturer. **12. William Isaac,** 1863–1947, U.S. sociologist.

Thom′as of Er′celdoune (ûr′səl do͞on′) (*"Thomas the Rhymer"*), c1220–97?, Scottish poet.

Thom•as of Wood•stock (tom′əs əv wo͝od′stok′), **Duke of Gloucester,** 1355–97, English prince (son of Edward III).

Thomp•son (tomp′sən, tom′-), **1. Benjamin, Count Rumford,** 1753–1814, English physicist and diplomat, born in the U.S. **2. Dorothy,** 1894–1961, U.S. journalist. **3. Francis,** 1859–1907, English poet. **4. J(ames) Walter,** 1847–1928, U.S. advertising executive. **5. Sir John Sparrow David,** 1844–94, Canadian statesman: prime minister 1892–94. **6. Randall,** 1899–1984, U.S. composer and teacher. **7. Sylvia,** 1902–68, English novelist, born in Scotland.

Thom•sen (tom′sən), **Christian Jürgensen,** 1788–1865, Danish archaeologist.

Thom•son (tom′sən), **1. Elihu,** 1853–1937, U.S. inventor, born in England. **2. Sir George Paget,** 1892–1975, English physicist (son of Sir Joseph John): Nobel prize 1937. **3. James,** 1700–48, English poet, born in Scotland. **4. James** (*"B.V."*), 1834–82, English poet. **5. John Arthur,** 1861–1933, Scottish scientist and author. **6. Sir Joseph John,** 1856–1940, English physicist: Nobel prize 1906. **7. Virgil,** 1896–1989, U.S. composer and music critic. **8. Sir William,** KELVIN, 1st Baron.

Tho•reau (thə rō′, thôr′ō, thōr′ō), **Henry David,** 1817–62, U.S. naturalist and author.

Thorn•dike (thôrn′dīk′), **1. Ashley Horace,** 1871–1933, U.S. literary historian and teacher. **2. Edward Lee,** 1874–1949, U.S. psychologist and lexicographer. **3. (Everett) Lynn,** 1882–1965, U.S. historian and scholar (brother of Ashley Horace Thorndike). **4. Dame Sybil,** 1882–1976, English actress.

Thorn•ton (thôrn′tn), **William,** 1759–1828, U.S. architect, born in the British Virgin Islands.

Thorpe (thôrp), **James Francis** (*"Jim"*), 1888–1953, U.S. athlete.

Thor•vald•sen or **Thor•wald•sen** (to͝or′väl′sən, thôr′-), **Albert Bertal,** 1770–1844, Danish sculptor.

Thot•mes (thōt′mēz, -mes) also **Thoth•mes** (thōth′-), Thutmose.

Thrale (thrāl), **Hester Lynch** (*Hester Lynch Piozzi*), 1741–1821, Welsh writer and friend of Samuel Johnson.

Thras•y•bu•lus (thras′ə byo͞o′ləs), died c389 B.C., Athenian patriot and general.

Thu•cyd•i•des (tho͞o sid′i dēz′), c460–c400 B.C., Greek historian.

Thu•nen (to͞o′nən), **Johann Heinrich von,** 1783–1850, German economic theorist.

Thur•ber (thûr′bər), **James (Grover),** 1894–1961, U.S. writer, caricaturist, and illustrator.

Thur•low (thûr′lō), **Edward, 1st Baron,** 1731–1806, British statesman: Lord Chancellor 1778–92.

Thut•mo•se (tho͞ot mō′sə, -mōs′) also **Thut•mo•sis** (-mō′sis), **1. Thutmose I,** fl. c1500 B.C., Egyptian ruler. **2. Thutmose II,** fl. c1495 B.C., Egyptian ruler, son of Thutmose I, half brother of Thutmose III. **3. Thutmose III,** fl. c1475 B.C., Egyptian ruler.

Thwing (twing), **Charles Franklin,** 1853–1937, U.S. educator and Congregational clergyman.

Thys•sen (tis′ən), **Fritz,** 1873–1951, German industrialist.

Tib•bett (tib′it), **Lawrence (Mervil),** 1896–1960, U.S. baritone.

Ti•be•ri•us (tī bēr′ē əs), (*Tiberius Claudius Nero Caesar*) 42 B.C.–A.D. 37, Roman emperor 14–37.

Ti•bul•lus (ti bul′əs), **Albius,** c54–c19 B.C., Roman poet.

Tick•ell (tik′əl), **Thomas,** 1686–1740, English poet and translator.

Tick•nor (tik′nər, -nôr), **George,** 1791–1871, U.S. literary historian and educator.

Tieck (tēk), **Ludwig,** 1773–1853, German writer.

Tie•po•lo (tē ep′ə lō′), **Giovanni Battista,** 1696–1770, and his son, **Giovanni Domenico,** 1727–1804, Italian painters.

Tif•fa•ny (tif′ə nē), **1. Charles Lewis,** 1812–1902, U.S. jeweler. **2.** his son **Louis Comfort,** 1848–1933, U.S. painter and decorator, esp. of glass.

Tig•lath-pi•le•ser III (tig′lath pi lē′zər, -pī-), died 727 B.C., king of Assyria 745–727.

Til·den (til′dən), **1. Samuel Jones,** 1814–86, U.S. statesman. **2. William Tatem, Jr.,** 1893–1953, U.S. tennis player.

Til·dy (til′dē), **Zoltán,** 1889–1961, Hungarian statesman: premier 1945–46; president 1946–48.

Til·lich (til′ik, -iᴋʜ), **Paul Johannes,** 1886–1965, U.S. philosopher and theologian, born in Germany.

Til·lot·son (til′ət sən), **John,** 1630–94, English clergyman: archbishop of Canterbury 1691–94.

Til·ly (til′ē), **Count Johan Tserclaes von,** 1559–1632, German general in the Thirty Years' War.

Ti·mo·shen·ko (tim′ə sheng′kō), **Semion Konstantinovich,** 1895–1970, Russian general.

Tim·rod (tim′rod), **Henry,** 1828–67, U.S. poet.

Ti·mur (ti mŏŏr′), Tᴀᴍᴇʀʟᴀɴᴇ.

Tin·ber·gen (tin′bûr gən), **1. Jan** (yän), born 1903, Dutch economist: Nobel prize 1969. **2.** his brother **Nikolaas,** 1907–88, British ethologist, born in the Netherlands: Nobel prize for medicine 1973.

Tin·dal (tin′dl), **Matthew,** c1655–1733, English deist.

Tin·dale or **Tin·dal** (tin′dl), **William,** Tʏɴᴅᴀʟᴇ, William.

Ting (ting), **Samuel C(hao) C(hung),** born 1936, U.S. physicist: Nobel prize 1976.

Ting·ley (ting′lē), **Katherine Augusta Westcott,** 1847–1929, U.S. theosophist leader.

Tin·to·ret·to (tin′tə ret′ō), **Il** (ēl), (*Jacopo Robusti*), 1518–94, Venetian painter.

Tip·pett (tip′it), **Sir Michael (Kemp),** born 1905, British composer.

Ti·pu Sa·hib (tip′ōō sä′ib, -ēb), 1750–99, sultan of Mysore 1782–99.

Tir·pitz (tûr′pits, tēr′-), **Alfred von,** 1849–1930, German admiral and statesman.

Tir·so de Mo·li·na (tēr′sō dā mə lē′nə), (*Gabriel Téllez*) 1571?–1648, Spanish dramatist.

Tisch·en·dorf (tish′ən dôrf′), **Lobegott Friedrich Konstantin von,** 1815–74, German Biblical critic.

Ti·se·li·us (tē sā′lē ŏŏs′), **Arne,** 1902–71, Swedish biochemist: Nobel prize 1948.

Tis·sot (tē sō′), **James Joseph Jacques,** 1836–1902, French painter.

Ti·tian (tish′ən), (*Tiziano Vecellio*) c1477–1576, Italian painter.

Ti·to (tē′tō), **Marshal** (*Josip Broz*), 1891–1980, president of Yugoslavia 1953–80.

Ti·tov (tē′tôf, -tof), **Herman** or **Gherman Stepanovich,** born 1935, Russian cosmonaut.

Ti·tus (tī′təs), (*Titus Flavius Sabinus Vespasianus*) ᴀ.ᴅ. 40?–81, Roman emperor 79–81.

To·bey (tō′bē), **Mark,** 1890–1976, U.S. painter.

Toch (tôᴋʜ), **Ernst,** 1887–1964, Austrian composer.

Tocque·ville (tōk′vil, tok′-), **Alexis Charles Henri Maurice Clérel de,** 1805–59, French statesman and author.

Todd (tod), **1. Alexander Robertus** (*Baron of Trumpington*), born 1907, Scottish chemist: Nobel prize 1957. **2. David,** 1855–1939, U.S. astronomer and teacher.

Todt (tōt), **Fritz,** 1891–1942, German military engineer.

To•gliat•ti (tōl yä′tē), **Palmiro,** 1893–1964, Italian Communist party leader.

To•go (tô′gô), **1. Heihachiro, Marquis** 1847–1934, Japanese admiral. **2. Shigenori,** 1882–1950, Japanese political leader and diplomat.

To•jo (tō′jō), **Hideki,** 1885–1948, Japanese general and politician.

To•klas (tō′kləs), **Alice B.,** 1877–1967, U.S. author in France: friend and companion of Gertrude Stein.

To•land (tō′lənd), **Gregg,** 1904–48, U.S. cinematographer.

Tol•kien (tōl′kēn, tol′-), **J(ohn) R(onald) R(euel),** 1892–1973, English novelist and philologist, born in South Africa.

Tol•stoy or **Tol•stoi** (tōl′stoi, tol′-, tōl stoi′, tol-), **Leo** or **Lev Nikolaevich, Count,** 1828–1910, Russian novelist and social critic.

Tom•baugh (tom′bô), **Clyde William,** born 1906, U.S. astronomer: discovered the planet Pluto 1930.

Tom•ma•si•ni (tom′ə sē′nē, -zē′-), **Vicenzo,** 1880–1950, Italian composer.

Tomp•kins (tomp′kinz), **Daniel D.,** 1774–1825, vice president of the U.S. 1817–25.

Tor•me (tôr mā′), **Mel,** born 1925, U.S. jazz singer.

Tor•que•ma•da (tôr′kə mä′də), **Tomás de,** 1420–98, Spanish inquisitor general.

Tor•ri•cel•li (tôr′i chel′ē), **Evangelista,** 1608–47, Italian physicist.

Tor•vill (tôr′vil), **Jayne,** born 1958, British ice dancer.

Tos•ca•ni•ni (tos′kə nē′nē), **Arturo,** 1867–1957, Italian conductor.

Tou•louse-Lau•trec (tŏŏ lōōz′lō trek′; *often* -lōōs′-), **Henri Marie Raymond de,** 1864–1901, French painter and lithographer.

Tous•saint L'Ou•ver•ture (*Fr.* tŏŏ saɴ′ lŏŏ ver tʏʀ′), (*Francis Dominique Toussaint*) 1743–1803, Haitian military and political leader.

Toyn•bee (toin′bē), **Arnold J(oseph),** 1889–1975, English historian.

Tra•cy (trā′sē), **Spencer,** 1900–67, U.S. actor.

Tra•jan (trā′jən), (*Marcus Ulpius Nerva Trajanus*) A.D. 53?–117, Roman emperor 98–117.

Trau•bel (trou′bəl), **Helen,** 1903–72, U.S. soprano.

Tree (trē), **Sir Herbert Beerbohm,** (*Herbert Beerbohm*), 1853–1917, English actor and theater manager.

Tre•vel•yan (tri vel′yən, -vil′-), **1. George Macaulay,** 1876–1962, English historian. **2.** his father, **Sir George Otto,** 1838–1928, English biographer, historian, and statesman.

Trev•or-Ro•per (trev′ər rō′pər), **Hugh (Redwald),** born 1914, British historian.

Tril•lin (tril′in), **Calvin,** born 1935, U.S. humorous author.

Tril•ling (tril′ing), **Lionel,** 1905–75, U.S. critic and author.

Trol•lope (trol′əp), **Anthony,** 1815–82, English novelist.

Tromp (tromp), **Cornelis,** 1629–91, and his father, **Maarten Harpertszoon,** 1597–1653, Dutch admirals.

Trot•sky (trot′skē), **Leon** (*Lev,* or *Leib, Davidovich Bronstein*), 1879–1940, Russian Communist revolutionary.

Tro•yon (trwa yôn′), **Constant,** 1813–65, French painter.

Tru•betz•koy or **Tru•bets•koi** (troo͞′bit skoi′), **N(ikolai) S(ergeievich),** 1890–1938, Russian linguist in Austria.

Tru•deau (troo͞ dō′), **Pierre Elliott,** born 1919, Canadian prime minister 1968–79, 1980–84.

Truf•faut (troo͞ fō′), **François,** 1932–84, French film director.

Tru•ji•llo (troo͞ hē′ō), **Rafael Leonidas** (*Rafael Leonidas Trujillo Molina*), Dominican general and politician: president 1930–38, 1942–52.

Tru•man (troo͞′mən), **Harry S,** 1884–1972, 33rd president of the U.S. 1945–53.

Trum•bull (trum′bəl), **1. John,** 1756–1843, U.S. painter (son of Jonathan). **2. Jonathan,** 1710–85, U.S. statesman.

Trump (trump), **Donald (John),** born 1946, U.S. businessman.

Trum•pel•dor (trum′pəl dôr′), **Joseph,** 1880–1920, Zionist leader, born in Russia.

Truth (troo͞th,), **Sojourner** (*Isabella Van Wagener*), 1797?–1883, U.S. abolitionist and women's-rights advocate, born a slave.

Ts'ao Hsüeh-ch'in (tsou′ shye′chin′), (*Ts'ao Chan*) c1717–63, Chinese novelist.

Tseng Kuo-fan (dzung′ gwô′fän′), 1811–72, Chinese general and statesman.

Tshom•be (chom′bā), **Moise Kapenda,** 1919–69, African political leader in the Republic of the Congo (now Zaire): prime minister 1964–65.

Tsiol•kov•sky (tsyôl kôf′skē, -kof′-), **1. Konstantin Eduardovich, 2.** 1857–1935, Russian inventor and rocket expert.

Tsi•ra•na•na (tsē rä′nä nä), **Philibert,** 1910–78, president of the Malagasy Republic (now Madagascar) 1959–72.

Tub•man (tub′mən), **1. Harriet** (*Araminta*), 1820?–1913, U.S. abolitionist: escaped slave. **2. William Vacanarat Shadrach,** 1895–1971, president of Liberia 1944–71.

Tuch•man (tuk′mən), **Barbara (Wertheim),** 1912–89, U.S. historian and writer.

Tuck•er (tuk′ər), **1. Richard,** 1915–75, U.S. tenor. **2. Sophie** (*Sophie Abruza*), 1884–1966, U.S. singer and entertainer, born in Russia.

Tu•dor (to͞o′dər, tyo͞o′-), **Antony,** 1909–87, English dancer and choreographer.

Tu Fu (do͞o′ fo͞o′), A.D. 712–770, Chinese poet.

Tul·ly (tul′ē), CICERO, Marcus Tullius.

Tun·ney (tun′ē), **James Joseph** (*"Gene"*), 1898–1978, U.S. boxer: world heavyweight champion 1926–28.

Tu·po·lev (to͞o pō′ləf, to͞o′pə ləf), **Andrei Nikolayevich,** 1888–1972, Russian engineer and aircraft designer.

Tup·per (tup′ər), **Sir Charles,** 1821–1915, Canadian statesman: prime minister 1896.

Tu·ra (to͝or′ə), **Co·si·mo** (kô′zē mô), c1430–98?, Italian painter.

Tu·reck (to͝or′ek, tyo͝or′-), **Rosalyn,** born 1914, U.S. pianist.

Tu·renne (to͞o ren′), **Henri de la Tour d'Auvergne de,** 1611–75, French marshal.

Tur·ge·nev or **Tur·ge·niev** (tûr gen′yəf, -gān′-), **Ivan Sergeevich,** 1818–83, Russian novelist.

Tur·got (to͝or gō′), **Anne Robert Jacques,** 1727–81, French statesman, financier, and economist.

Tu·ring (to͝or′ing), **Alan Mathison,** 1912–54, British mathematician and computer theoretician.

Tur·ner (tûr′nər), **1. Frederick Jackson,** 1861–1932, U.S. historian. **2. Joseph Mallord William,** 1775–1851, English painter. **3. Lana,** born 1920, U.S. actress. **4. Nat,** 1800–31, U.S. leader of uprising of slaves. **5. Robert Edward, III** (*Ted*), born 1938, U.S. businessman and sportsman.

Tur·pin (tûr′pin), **1. Ben,** 1874–1940, U.S. silent-film comedian. **2. Richard** (*Dick*), 1706–39, English highwayman.

Tus·saud (to͞o sō′), **Marie Grosholtz** (*"Madame Tussaud"*), 1760–1850, Swiss wax modeler in France and England: wax museum founder.

Tut·ankh·a·men or **Tut·ankh·a·mon** or **Tut·ankh·a·mun** (to͞ot′äng kä′mən), fl. c1350 B.C., king of Egypt.

Tu·tu (to͞o′to͞o), **Desmond (Mpilo),** born 1931, South African Anglican clergyman and civil-rights activist: Nobel peace prize 1984.

Twain (twān), **Mark,** pen name of Samuel Langhorne CLEMENS.

Tweed (twēd), **William Marcy** (*"Boss Tweed"*), 1823–78, U.S. politician.

Twi·ning (twī′ning), **Nathan Farragut,** 1897–1982, U.S. Air Force general: chairman of the Joint Chiefs of Staff 1957–60.

Twor·kov (twôr′kof), **Jack,** 1900–82, U.S. painter, born in Poland.

Ty·ler (tī′lər), **1. Anne,** born 1931, U.S. novelist. **2. John,** 1790–1862, 10th president of the U.S. 1841–45. **3. Moses Coit,** 1835–1900, U.S. historian and educator. **4. Wat** or **Walter,** died 1381, English leader of the peasants' revolt of 1381.

Tyn·dale or **Tindale** or **Tindal** (tin′dl), **William,** c1492–1536, English religious reformer, translator of the Bible into English, and martyr.

Tyn·dall (tin′dl), **John,** 1820–93, English physicist.

Tyr•tae•us (tûr tē′əs), fl. 7th century B.C., Greek poet.

Tyr•whitt-Wil•son (tir′it wil′sən), **Gerald Hugh, 14th Baron Berners,** 1883–1950, English composer, painter, and author.

Ty•son (tī′sən), **Mike,** born 1966, U.S. heavyweight boxer.

Tz'u Hsi or **Tzu Hsi** (tso͞o′ shē′), 1835–1908, empress dowager of China: regent 1862–73, 1875–89, 1898–1908.

U

Uc·cel·lo (o͞o chel′ō), **Paolo** (*Paolo di Dono*), 1397–1475, Italian painter.

U·dall (yo͞o′dôl, yo͝od′l), **1. Nicholas,** 1505–56, English translator and playwright, esp. of comedy. **2. Stewart Lee,** born 1920, U.S. politician: Secretary of the Interior 1961–69.

Uh·de (o͞o′də), **Fritz Karl Hermann von,** 1848–1911, German painter.

Uh·land (o͞o′länt′), **Johann Ludwig,** 1787–1862, German poet and writer.

U·la·no·va (o͞o lä′nə və), **Galina (Sergeyevna),** born 1910, Russian ballerina.

Ul·bricht (o͝ol′briкнt), **Walter,** 1893–1973, chief of state of East Germany 1960–73.

Ul·fi·las (ul′fi ləs) also **Ul·fi·la** (-lə), **Wulfila,** A.D. c311–c382, Christian missionary: translated Bible into Gothic.

Ull·man (o͝ol′mən), **Liv** (lēv), born 1938, Norwegian actress, born in Japan.

Ul·pi·an (ul′pē ən), (*Domitius Ulpianus*) died A.D. 288?, Roman jurist.

U·na·mu·no (o͞o′nə mo͞o′nō), **Miguel de,** 1864–1936, Spanish philosopher and writer.

Un·cas (ung′kəs), (*"the Circler"*) 1588?–1683?, Mohegan leader.

Und·set (o͝on′set), **Sigrid,** 1882–1949, Norwegian novelist: Nobel prize 1928.

Un·ser (un′sər), **Albert** (*Al*), born 1939, and his brother **Robert** (*Bobby*), born 1934, U.S. racing-car drivers.

Un·ter·mey·er (un′tər mī′ər), **Louis,** 1885–1977, U.S. poet.

Up·dike (up′dīk′), **John,** born 1932, U.S. author.

Up·john (up′jon′), **Richard,** 1802–78, and his son, **Richard Michell,** 1828–1903, U.S. architects, born in England.

Urban (ûr′bən), **1. Urban I, Saint,** pope A.D. 222–230. **2. Urban II,** (*Odo* or *Otho*) c1042–99, French ecclesiastic: pope 1088–99. **3. Urban III,** (*Uberto Crivelli*) Italian ecclesiastic: pope 1185–87. **4. Urban IV,** (*Jacques Pantaléon*) died 1264, French ecclesiastic: pope 1261–64. **5. Urban V,** (*Guillaume de Grimoard*) c1310–70, French ecclesiastic: pope 1362–70. **6. Urban VI,** (*Bartolomeo Prignano*) c1318–89, Italian ecclesiastic: pope 1378–89. **7. Urban VII,** (*Giovanni Battista Castagna*) 1521–90, Italian ecclesiastic: pope 1590. **8. Urban VIII,** (*Maffeo Barberini*) 1568–1644, Italian ecclesiastic: pope 1623–44.

U·rey (yo͝or′ē), **Harold Clayton,** 1893–1981, U.S. chemist: Nobel prize 1934.

Ur·is (yo͝or′is), **Leon,** born 1924, U.S. novelist.

Ur-Nam·mu (o͝or′nä′mo͞o), king of the Sumerian city-state of Ur c2000 B.C.

Ur•quhart (ûr′kərt, -kärt), **Sir Thomas,** 1611–60, Scottish author and translator.

Ussh•er (ush′ər), **James,** 1581–1656, Irish prelate and scholar.

U•ta•ma•ro (o͞o′tə mär′ō), **Kitagawa,** 1753–1806, Japanese painter, draftsman, and designer of prints.

U Thant (o͞o′ tänt′, thänt′, thant′), 1909–74, Burmese statesman: Secretary General of the United Nations 1962–71.

U•tril•lo (yo͞o tril′ō, -trē′ō, o͞o-), **Maurice,** 1883–1955, French painter.

V

Vá•clav (väts′läf), Czech form of WENCESLAUS.

Va•la•don (VA LA dôN′), **Suzanne,** 1865–1938, French painter (mother of Maurice Utrillo).

Val•de•mar I (väl′də mär′), WALDEMAR I.

Va•len•ci•a (və len′shē ə, -shə, -sē ə), **Guillermo León,** 1909–71, Colombian diplomat and statesman: president 1962–66.

Va•lens (vā′lənz), **Flavius,** A.D. c328–378, emperor of the Eastern Roman Empire 364–378.

Val•en•tine (val′ən tīn′), **Saint,** died A.D. c270, Christian martyr at Rome.

Val•en•tin•i•an (val′ən tin′ē ən) also **Val•en•tin•i•a•nus** (-tin′ē ā′nəs), **1. Valentinian I,** A.D. 321?–375, emperor of the Western Roman Empire 364–375. **2. Valentinian II,** A.D. c371–392, emperor of the Western Roman Empire 375–392. **3. Valentinian III,** A.D. 419?–455, emperor of the Western Roman Empire 425–455.

Val•en•ti•no (val′ən tē′nō), **Rudolph** (*Rodolpho d'Antonguolla*), 1895–1926, U.S. motion-picture actor, born in Italy.

Va•le•ra (və lâr′ə, -lēr′ə), **Eamon De,** DE VALERA, Eamon.

Va•le•ra y Al•ca•lá Ga•lia•no (bä le′RÄ ē äl′kä lä′ gä-lyä′nô), **Juan,** 1824–1905, Spanish novelist, critic, diplomat, and statesman.

Va•le•ri•an (və lēr′ē ən), (*Publius Licinius Valerianus*), died A.D. c260, Roman emperor 253–60.

Va•lé•ry (VA lā RĒ′), **Paul,** 1871–1945, French poet and philosopher.

Val•la (väl′ə), **Lorenzo,** 1407–57, Italian humanist and critic.

Val•le•jo (və lā′ō, -yā′hō), **1. César,** 1895–1938, Peruvian poet. **2. Mariano Guadalupe,** 1808–90, American military and political leader in California.

Val•mi•ki (väl mē′kē), Hindu poet and reputed author of the Ramayana.

Van Al•len (van al′ən), **1. James Alfred, 2.** born 1914, U.S. physicist.

Van•brugh (van brōō′ *or, esp. Brit.,* van′brə), **John,** 1664–1726, English dramatist and architect.

Van Bu•ren (van byŏŏr′ən), **Martin,** 1782–1862, 8th president of the U.S. 1837–41.

Van•cou•ver (van kōō′vər), **George,** 1758–98, English explorer.

Van•den•berg (van′dən bûrg′), **1. Arthur Hendrick,** 1884–1951, U.S. statesman. **2. Hoyt Sanford,** 1899–1954, U.S. general: Chief of Staff of Air Force 1948–53.

Van•der•bilt (van′dər bilt), **1. Cornelius,** 1794–1877, U.S. financier. **2. Harold Stirling,** 1884–1970, U.S. business executive.

van der Roh•e (van dər rō′ə, fän), **Ludwig Mies,** MIES VAN DER ROHE, Ludwig.

Van Der Zee or **Van Der•Zee** (van′ dər zē′), **James,** 1886–1983, U.S. photographer.

Van De•van•ter (van′ di van′tər), **Willis,** 1859–1941, U.S. jurist: associate justice of the U.S. Supreme Court 1910–37.

van Dong•en (van dong′ən), **Kees** (kās), (*Cornelius Theodorus Marie*), 1877–1968, French painter, born in the Netherlands.

Van Do•ren (van dôr′ən, dōr′-), **1. Carl,** 1885–1950, U.S. writer. **2.** his brother, **Mark,** 1894–1972, U.S. writer and critic.

Van Dru•ten (van drōōt′n), **John William,** 1901–57, U.S. playwright, born in England.

Van Dyck or **Van•dyke** (van dīk′), **Sir Anthony,** 1599–1641, Flemish painter.

Vane (vān), **Sir Henry** (*Sir Harry Vane*), 1613–62, British statesman and author.

Van Fleet (van flēt′), **James Alward,** born 1892, U.S. army general.

van Gogh (van gō′, gôKH′), **Vincent,** 1853–90, Dutch painter.

Va•nier (van′yā, van yā′), **Georges P.,** 1888–1967, Canadian soldier and diplomat: governor-general 1959–67.

Van Loon (van lōōn′, lōn′), **Hendrik Willem,** 1882–1944, U.S. author, born in the Netherlands.

Van Paas•sen (vän pä′sən), **Pierre,** (*Pieter Anthonie Laurusse*), 1895–1968, U.S. journalist, author, and clergyman; born in the Netherlands.

Van Rens•se•laer (van ren′sə lēr′, ren′sə lēr′), **1. Kiliaen,** 1595–1644, Dutch merchant and landowner in America (ancestor of Stephen Van Rensselaer). **2. Stephen,** 1765–1839, U.S. political leader and major general.

Van•sit•tart (van sit′ərt), **Sir Robert Gilbert, 1st Baron Vansittart of Denham,** 1881–1957, British statesman and diplomat.

van't Hoff (vänt hôf′), **Jacobus Hendricus,** 1852–1911, Dutch chemist: Nobel prize 1901.

Van Vech•ten (van vek′tən), **Carl,** 1880–1964, U.S. author.

Van Vleck (van vlek′), **John H(asbrouck),** 1899–1980, U.S. physicist: Nobel prize 1977.

Van Zee•land (vän zā′länt), **Paul,** 1893–1973, Belgian statesman: premier 1935–37.

Van•zet•ti (van zet′ē), **Bartolomeo,** 1888–1927, Italian anarchist, in the U.S. after 1908. Compare SACCO, Nicola.

Var•don (vär′dn), **Harry,** 1870–1937, British golfer.

Va•rèse (və rāz′, -rez′), **Edgard,** 1885–1965, U.S. composer, born in France.

Var•gas (vär′gəs), **Getulio Dornelles,** 1883–1954, Brazilian statesman.

Var•ro (var′ō), **Marcus Terentius,** c116–27? B.C., Roman scholar and author.

Va•sa•ri (və zär′ē, -sär′ē), **Giorgio,** 1511–74, Italian painter, architect, and art historian.

Vas•co da Ga•ma (vas′kō də gam′ə, gä′mə), GAMA, Vasco da.

Vas•sa (vas′ə), **Gustavus** (*Olaudah Equiano*), c1745–1801?, African slave, sold in the West Indies, and, after gaining freedom, abolitionist and writer in England.

Vas•sar (vas′ər), **Matthew,** 1792–1868, U.S. merchant, philanthropist, and supporter of education for women; born in England: founder of Vassar College.

Vat•tel (fät′l), **Emmerich,** 1714–67, Swiss jurist and diplomat.

Vau•ban (vō bäɴ′), **Sébastien le Prestre de,** 1633–1707, French military engineer and marshal.

Vaughan (vôn), **1. Henry,** 1622–95, English poet and mystic. **2. Sarah (Lois),** 1924–90, U.S. jazz singer.

Vaughan′ Wil′liams, Ralph (*usu.* rāf), 1872–1958, English composer.

Vau•que•lin (vōkᵉ laɴ′), **Louis Nicolas,** 1763–1829, French chemist: discoverer of chromium and beryllium.

Veb•len (veb′lən), **1. Oswald,** 1880–1960, U.S. mathematician. **2. Thorstein,** 1857–1929, U.S. economist and sociologist.

Veeck (vek), **William Louis, Jr.,** 1914–86, U.S. baseball team owner and promoter.

Ve•ga (vā′gə), **Lope de,** (*Lope Félix de Vega Carpio*), 1562–1635, Spanish dramatist and poet.

Ve•las•co I•bar•ra (be läs′kô ē vär′rä), **José María,** 1893–1979, Ecuadorean political leader: president 1934–35, 1944–47, 1952–56, 1960–61, 1968–72.

Ve•láz•quez (və läs′kes, -las′kəs), **Diego Rodríguez de Silva y,** 1599–1660, Spanish painter.

Ven•dôme (väɴ dōm′), **Louis Joseph de,** 1654–1712, French general and marshal.

Ve•ni•ze•los (ve′nē ze′lôs), **Eleutherios,** 1864–1936, prime minister of Greece 1910–15, 1917–20, 1928–33.

Ver•cin•get•o•rix (vûr′sin jet′ə riks, -get′-), died 45? B.C., Gaulish chieftain conquered by Caesar.

Ver•di (vâr′dē), **Giuseppe,** 1813–1901, Italian composer.

Ve•re•shcha•gin (ver′ə shä′gin), **Vasili Vasilievich,** 1842–1904, Russian painter.

Ver•gil (vûr′jil), VIRGIL.

Ve•rís•si•mo (və rē′si mo͝o), **Érico Lopes,** born 1905, Brazilian novelist.

Ver•laine (vər lān′, -len′), **Paul,** 1844–96, French poet.

Ver•meer (vər mēr′), **Jan** (yän), (*Jan van der Meer van Delft*), 1632–75, Dutch painter.

Verne (vûrn), **Jules,** 1828–1905, French novelist.

Ver•ner (vûr′nər, vâr′-), **Karl Adolph,** 1846–96, Danish linguist.

Ver•net (vâr nā′), **1. Claude Joseph,** 1714–89, French painter. **2.** his grandson **(Émile Jean) Horace,** 1789–1863, French painter.

Ver•nier (vûr′nē ər, vern yā′), **Pierre,** 1580–1637, French mathematician and inventor.

Ver•non (vûr′nən), **Edward** (*"Old Grog"*), 1684–1757, British admiral.

Ve•ro•ne•se (ver′ə nā′zē), **Paolo** (*Paolo Cagliari*), 1528–88, Venetian painter.

Ver•ra•za•no or **Ver•raz•za•no** (ver′ə zä′nō, -əd zä′-, -ət sä′-), **Giovanni da,** c1480–1527?, Italian navigator and explorer.

Ver•roc•chio (və rō′kē ō′), **Andrea del,** 1435–88, Italian goldsmith, sculptor, and painter.

Ver•woerd (fər vōōrt′), **Hendrik Frensch,** 1901–66, South African political leader: prime minister 1958–66.

Ve•sa•li•us (vi sā′lē əs, -sāl′yəs), **Andreas,** 1514–64, Flemish anatomist.

Ve•sey (vē′zē), **Denmark,** 1767–1822, black freedman, born probably on St. Thomas, Danish West Indies: hanged as alleged leader of a slave insurrection, in Charleston, S.C.

Ves•pa•sian (ve spā′zhən, -zhē ən), (*Titus Flavius Sabinus Vespasianus*), A.D. 9–79, Roman emperor 70–79.

Ves•puc•ci (ve spōō′chē, -spyōō′-), **Amerigo,** (*Americus Vespucius*), 1451–1512, Italian explorer after whom America was named.

Vick•ers (vik′ərz), **Jon,** born 1926, Canadian tenor.

Vi•co (vik′ō, vē′kō), **Giovanni Battista,** 1668–1744, Italian philosopher and jurist.

Vic•tor (vik′tər), **1. Victor I, Saint,** pope A.D. 189–198. **2. Victor II,** (*Gebhard*) 1018–57, German ecclesiastic: pope 1055–57. **3. Victor III,** (*Dauferius*) 1027–87, Italian ecclesiastic: pope 1086–87.

Vic′tor Em•man′u•el (i man′yōō əl), **1. Victor Emmanuel I,** 1759–1824, king of Sardinia 1802–21. **2. Victor Emmanuel II,** 1820–78, king of Sardinia 1849–78; first king of Italy 1861–78. **3. Victor Emmanuel III,** 1869–1947, king of Italy 1900–46.

Vic•to•ri•a (vik tôr′ē ə, -tōr′-), **1.** 1819–1901, queen of Great Britain 1837–1901; empress of India 1876–1901. **2. Guadalupe,** (*Manuel Félix Fernández*), 1789-1843, Mexican military and political leader: first president of the republic 1824–29.

Vic•to•ri•o (vik tôr′ē ō′, -tōr′-), 1809?–80, leader of the Chiricahua Apache tribe.

Vi•dal (vi dal′), **Gore** (*Eugene Luther*), born 1925, U.S. novelist.

Vi•dor (vē′dôr, -dōr), **King (Wallis),** 1895–1982, U.S. motion-picture director and producer.

Vie•reck (vēr′ek), **Peter,** born 1916, U.S. poet and historian.

Vi•ë•tor (fē′ā tôr′), **Wilhelm,** 1850–1918, German philologist and phonetician.

Vieux•temps (*Fr.* vyœ tän′), **Henri François Joseph,** 1820–81, Belgian violinist and composer.

Vi•gée-Le•brun (vē zhā lə brœn′), **(Marie Anne) Élisabeth,** 1755–1842, French painter.

Vi•gil•i•us (vi jil′ē əs), died A.D. 555, pope 537–555.

Vi•gno•la (vē nyô′lä), **Giacomo da** (*Giacomo Barocchio* or *Barozzi*), 1507–73, Italian architect.

Vi•gny (vē nyē′), **Alfred Victor de,** 1797–1863, French poet, novelist, and dramatist.

Vi•go (vē′gō; *Fr.* vē gō′), **Jean** (zhän) (*Jean Almereyda*), 1905–34, French film director.

Vil•la (vē′ə), **Francisco,** (*Doroteo Arango*) (*"Pancho Villa"*), 1877–1923, Mexican general and revolutionist.

Vil•la-Lo•bos (vē′lä lō′bôs, -bōs, vil′ə-), **Heitor,** 1881–1959, Brazilian composer.

Vil•lard (vi lär′, -lärd′), **1. Henry** (*Ferdinand Heinrich Gustav Hilgard*) 1835–1900, U.S. railroad executive and publisher, born in Bavaria. **2. Oswald Garrison,** 1872–1949, U.S. journalist and author.

Vil•lars (vē lar′), **Claude Louis Hector de,** 1653–1734, marshal of France.

Vi•lle•da Mo•ra•les (bē ye′thä mô rä′les), **Ramón,** 1909?–71, Honduran diplomat and statesman: president 1957–63.

Vil•lel•la (vi lel′ə), **Edward,** born 1936, U.S. ballet dancer.

Ville•neuve (vēl nœv′), **Pierre Charles Jean Baptiste Silvestre de** (zhän), 1763–1806, French admiral.

Vil•liers (vil′ərz, vil′yərz), **1. Frederic,** 1852–1922, English artist and war correspondent. **2. George,** BUCKINGHAM, 1st Duke of. **3. George,** BUCKINGHAM, 2nd Duke of.

Vil•lon (vē yôn′), **1. François,** 1431–63?, French poet. **2. Jacques** (*Gaston Duchamp*), 1875–1963, French painter.

Vin•cent (vin′sənt), **Saint,** died A.D. 304, Spanish martyr: patron saint of winegrowers.

Vin•cent de Paul (vin′sənt də pôl′), **Saint,** 1576–1660, French priest noted for his aid to the poor.

Vin•ci (vin′chē), **Leonardo da,** LEONARDO DA VINCI.

Vin•son (vin′sən), **Frederick Moore,** 1890–1953, Chief Justice of the U.S. 1946–53.

Viol•let-le-Duc (vyô le′lə dyk′), **Eugène Emmanuel,** 1814–79, French architect and writer,

Vir•chow (fir′khō), **Rudolf,** 1821–1902, German pathologist, anthropologist, and political leader.

Vir•gil (vûr′jəl), (*Publius Vergilius Maro*) 70–19 B.C., Roman poet: author of the epic poem *The Aeneid.*

Vir′gin Queen′, Queen Elizabeth I of England.

Vir•ta•nen (vər tä′nən), **Artturi Ilmari,** 1895–1973, Finnish biochemist: Nobel prize 1945.

Vis•con•ti (vis kon′tē), an Italian family that ruled Milan and Lombardy from 1277 to 1447.

Vi•shin•sky or **Vy•shin•sky** (vi shin′skē), **Andrei Yanuarievich,** 1883–1954, Soviet statesman.

Vish•nev•ska•ya (vish nef′skä yə), **Galina (Pavlovna),** born 1926, Russian operatic soprano, in the U.S. (wife of Mstislav Rostropovich).

Vis•ser 't Hooft (vis′ərt hōft′), **Willem Adolf,** 1900–85, Dutch Protestant clergyman and writer: leader in ecumenical movement.

Vi•tal•ian (vi tāl′yən, -tā′lē ən), died A.D. 672, pope 657–672.

Vi•to•ria (vi tôr′ē ə, -tōr′-), **Francisco de,** c1480–1546, Spanish scholar and theologian.

Vi•tru•vi•us Pol•li•o (vi trōō′vē əs pol′ē ō′), **Marcus,** fl. 1st century B.C., Roman architect, engineer, and author.

Vi•try (vē trē′), **Philippe de,** 1290?–1361, French music theorist, composer, and poet.

Vi•val•di (vi väl′dē), **Antonio,** 1678–1741, Italian composer.

Vi•ve•ka•nan•da (vē′vi kə nun′də), (*Narendranath Datta*) 1863–1902, Hindu religious leader and teacher.

Vi•via•ni (vē vyä nē′), **René,** 1863–1925, French statesman: premier of France 1911–15.

Vlad•i•mir (vlad′ə mēr′, vlə dē′mir) **Saint,** (*"Vladimir the Great"*) A.D. c956-1015, grand prince of Kiev 980-1015: first Christian ruler of Russia. Also called **Vladimir I.**

Vla•minck (vlä mangk′), **Maurice de,** 1876–1958, French painter.

Vo•gel (vō′gəl), **Sir Julius,** 1835–99, New Zealand statesman, born in England: prime minister 1873–75, 1876.

Voit (foit), **Carl** or **Karl von,** 1831–1908, German physiologist.

Vol•stead (vol′sted, vōl′-), **Andrew Joseph,** 1860–1946, U.S. legislator.

Vol•ta (vōl′tə, vol′-), **Count Alessandro,** 1745–1827, Italian physicist.

Vol•taire (vōl târ′, vol-), (*François Marie Arouet*), 1694–1778, French writer and philosopher.

Von Bé•ké•sy (von bā′kə shē), **Ge•org** (gā′ôrg), 1899–1972, U.S. physicist, born in Hungary: Nobel prize for medicine 1961.

von Braun (von broun′, fən), BRAUN, Wernher von.

Von Kár•mán (von kär′män, -mən), **Theodore,** 1881–1963, U.S. scientist and aeronautical engineer, born in Hungary.

Von•ne•gut (von′i gət), **Kurt, Jr.,** born 1922, U.S. novelist.

Von Neu•mann (von noi′män, -mən), **John,** 1903–57, U.S. mathematician, born in Hungary.

Von Sta•de (von shtä′də, stä′-, fən), **Frederica,** born 1945, U.S. mezzo-soprano.

von Stern•berg (von stûrn′bûrg), **Josef** or **Joseph** (*Josef Stern*), 1894–1969, U.S. film director, born in Austria.

Von Stro•heim (von strō′hīm, shtrō′-, fən), **Erich,** 1885–1957, U.S. actor and film director, born in Austria.

Vo•ro•shi•lov (vôr′ə shē′ləf), **Kliment Efremovich,** 1881–1969, president of the Soviet Union 1953–60.

Vor•ster (fôr′stər), **Balthazar Johannes,** 1915–83, South

African political leader: prime minister 1966–78; president 1978–79.

Voz•ne•sen•sky (voz′nə sen′skē), **Andrei (Andreievich),** born 1933, Russian poet.

Vries (vrēs), **Hugo de,** DE VRIES, Hugo.

Vuil•lard (vwē yär′), **(Jean) Édouard,** 1868–1940, French painter.

Vy•shin•sky (vi shin′skē), **Andrei Yanuarievich,** VISHINSKY, Andrei Yanuarievich.

Waals (väls), **Johannes Diderick van der,** 1837–1923, Dutch physicist: Nobel prize 1910.

Wace (wäs, wās), **Robert** (*"Wace of Jersey"*), c1100–c1180, Anglo-Norman poet.

Wag•ner (wag′nər *for 1, 4, 5;* väg′nər *for 2, 3*), **1. Honus** (*John Peter*), 1874–1955, U.S. baseball player. **2. Otto,** 1841–1918, Austrian architect. **3. Richard,** 1813–83, German composer. **4. Robert F(erdinand),** 1877–1953, U.S. politician. **5.** his son, **Robert F(erdinand), Jr.,** 1910–91, U.S. politician: mayor of New York City 1954–65.

Wag•ner-Jau•regg (väg′nər your′ek), **Julius,** 1857–1940, Austrian psychiatrist: Nobel prize for medicine 1927.

Waite (wāt), **Morrison Remick,** 1816–88, Chief Justice of the U.S. 1874–88.

Waks•man (waks′mən), **Selman Abraham,** 1888–1973, U.S. microbiolgist: Nobel prize for medicine 1952.

Wal•cott (wôl′kət, -kot), **Joe** (*Arnold Cream*) (*"Jersey Joe"*), born 1914, U.S. boxer: world heavyweight champion 1951–52.

Wald (wôld), **1. George,** born 1906, U.S. biochemist: Nobel prize for medicine 1967. **2. Lillian,** 1867–1940, U.S. social worker.

Wal•de•mar (or **Val•de•mar**) **I** (väl′də mär′), (*"the Great"*) 1131–82, king of Denmark 1157–82.

Wald•heim (wôld′hīm′, vält′-), **Kurt,** born 1918, Secretary General of the United Nations 1972–82; president of Austria 1986–92.

Wal•do (wôl′dō, wol′-), **Pierre** or **Peter,** died c1217, French religious reformer, declared a heretic.

Wa•łę•sa (və wen′sə), **Lech** (lek), born 1943, Polish labor leader: president since 1990; Nobel peace prize 1983.

Wa•ley (wā′lē), **Arthur** (*Arthur David Schloss*), 1889–1966, British translator of Chinese and Japanese literature.

Walk•er (wô′kər), **1. Alice,** born 1944, U.S. writer. **2. David,** 1785–1830, U.S. abolitionist. **3. James John** (*Jimmy*), 1881–1946, U.S. politician: mayor of New York City 1926–32. **4. John,** born 1952, New Zealand track-and-field athlete. **5. Sarah Breedlove,** 1867–1919, U.S. businesswoman and philanthropist.

Wal•lace (wol′is, wô′lis), **1. Alfred Russel,** 1823–1913, English naturalist. **2. George Corley,** born 1919, U.S. politician: governor of Alabama 1963–67, 1971–79, and 1983–87. **3. Henry (Agard),** 1888–1965, vice president of the U.S. 1941–45. **4. Lewis** (*"Lew"*), 1827–1905, U.S. general and novelist. **5. Sir William,** 1272?–1305, Scottish military leader and patriot. **6. (William Roy) DeWitt,** 1889–1981, and his wife, **Lila Bell (Acheson),** 1889–1984, U.S. magazine publishers.

Wal•lach (wol′ək; *Ger.* väl′äкн), **Otto,** 1847–1931, German chemist: Nobel prize 1910.

Wal•len•da (wo len′də, vä-), **Karl,** 1905–78, German circus aerialist.

Wal•len•stein (wol′ən stīn′), **1. Albrecht Eusebius Wenzel von,** 1583–1634, Austrian general in the Thirty Years' War. **2. Alfred,** 1898–1983, U.S. cellist and conductor.

Wal•ler (wol′ər, wô′lər), **1. Edmund,** 1607–87, English poet. **2. Thomas** (*"Fats"*), 1904–43, U.S. jazz pianist and songwriter.

Wal•lis (wol′is, wô′lis), **1. Harold Brent** (*Hal*), 1899–1986, U.S. film producer. **2. John,** 1616–1703, English mathematician.

Wal•pole (wôl′pōl′, wol′-), **1. Horace, 4th Earl of Orford** (*Horatio Walpole*), 1717–97, English author (son of Sir Robert Walpole). **2. Sir Hugh Seymour,** 1884–1941, English novelist, born in New Zealand. **3. Sir Robert, 1st Earl of Orford,** 1676–1745, British prime minister 1715–17, 1721–42.

Wal•pur•gis (väl po͝or′gis), **Saint,** A.D. c710–780, English missionary and abbess in Germany: feast day May 1.

Wal•ras (VAl RA′), **(Marie Esprit) Léon,** 1834–1910, French economist.

Wal•sing•ham (wôl′sing əm), **Sir Francis,** c1530–90, English statesman: Secretary of State to Elizabeth I, 1573–90.

Wal•ter (väl′tər), **1. Bruno** (*Bruno Schlesinger*), 1876–1962, German conductor, in U.S. after 1939. **2. Thomas U•stick** (yo͞o′stik), 1804–87, U.S. architect.

Wal•ters (wôl′tərz), **Barbara,** born 1931, U.S. news broadcaster and commentator.

Wal•ther von der Vo•gel•wei•de (väl′tər fôn dər fō′gəl vī′də), c1170–c1230, German minnesinger and poet.

Wal•ton (wôl′tn), **1. Ernest Thomas Sinton,** born 1903, Irish physicist: Nobel prize 1951. **2. Izaak,** 1593–1683, English writer. **3. Sir William (Turner),** 1902–83, English composer.

Wan•a•ma•ker (won′ə mā′kər), **John,** 1838–1922, U.S. merchant and philanthropist.

Wang Ching-wei (or **Jing•wei**) (wäng′ jing′wā′), 1883–1944, Chinese political leader.

Wang•chuk (wäng′cho͝ok), **Jigme Dorji,** 1929–72, king of Bhutan 1952–72.

Wang Yang-ming (wäng′ yäng′ming′), (*Wang Shou-jen, Wang Shouren*) 1472–1529, Chinese scholar and philosopher.

Wan•kel (wäng′kəl, wang′-, väng′-), **Felix,** born 1902–88, German engineer: inventor of rotary engine.

War•beck (wôr′bek), **Perkin,** 1474–99, Flemish imposter who pretended to the throne of England.

War•burg (wôr′bûrg; *Ger.* väR′bo͝oRk), **Otto Heinrich,** 1883–1970, German physiologist: Nobel prize for medicine 1931.

Ward (wôrd), **1. (Aaron) Montgomery,** 1843–1913, U.S. mail-order retailer. **2. Ar•te•mas** (är′tə məs), 1727–1800, American general in the American Revolution. **3. Ar•te•**

mus (är′tə məs), (*Charles Farrar Browne*), 1834–67, U.S. humorist. **4. Barbara** (*Baroness Jackson of Lodsworth*), 1914–81, English economist and author. **5. Mrs. Humphry** (*Mary Augusta Arnold*), 1851–1920, English novelist, born in Tasmania. **6. Sir Joseph George,** 1856–1930, New Zealand statesman, born in Australia: prime minister 1906–12, 1928–30. **7. Lester Frank,** 1841–1913, U.S. sociologist. **8. Nathaniel** (*"Theodore de la Guard"*), 1578?–1652, English clergyman, lawyer, and author in America.

War•field (wôr′fēld′), **David,** 1866–1951, U.S. actor.

War•hol (wôr′hôl, -hol), **Andy,** 1930?–87, U.S. artist.

War•ner (wôr′nər), **Jack L(eonard),** 1892–1978, U.S. film producer, born in Canada.

War•ren (wôr′ən, wor′-), **1. Earl,** 1891–1974, Chief Justice of the U.S. Supreme Court 1953–69. **2. Joseph,** 1741–75, American physician, statesman, and patriot. **3. Mercy Otis,** 1728–1814, U.S. historian and poet (sister of James Otis). **4. Robert Penn,** 1905–89, U.S. novelist and poet: named the first U.S. poet laureate 1986–87.

War•wick (wôr′ik, wor′-), **Earl of** (*Richard Neville, Earl of Salisbury*) (*"the Kingmaker"*), 1428–71, English military leader and statesman.

Wash•ing•ton (wosh′ing tən, wô′shing-), **1. Booker T(aliaferro),** 1856–1915, U.S. reformer and educator. **2. Dinah,** 1924–63, U.S. singer. **3. George,** 1732–99, U.S. general: 1st president of the U.S. 1789–97. **4. Martha** (*Martha Dandridge*), 1732–1802, wife of George.

Was•ser•mann (wä′sər mən), **August von,** 1866–1925, German physician and bacteriologist.

Wa•ters (wô′tərz, wot′ərz), **Ethel,** 1896–1977, U.S. singer and actress.

Wat•son (wot′sən), **1. James Dewey,** born 1928, U.S. biolgist: Nobel prize for medicine 1962. **2. John** (*"Ian Maclaren"*), 1850–1907, Scottish clergyman and novelist. **3. John Broadus,** 1878–1958, U.S. psychologist. **4. John Christian,** 1867–1941, Australian statesman, born in Chile: prime minister 1904. **5. Thomas Augustus,** 1854–1934, U.S. electrical experimenter, associated with Alexander Graham Bell. **6. Thomas John,** 1874–1956, U.S. industrialist. **7. Thomas Sturges** (*Tom*), born 1949, U.S. golfer. **8. Sir William,** 1858–1935, English poet.

Wat′son-Watt′, Sir Robert Alexander, 1892–1973, Scottish physicist.

Wat′son-Went′worth, Charles, 2nd Marquis of Rock•ing•ham (rok′ing əm), 1730–82, British statesman: prime minister 1765–66, 1782.

Watt (wot), **James,** 1736–1819, Scottish engineer and inventor.

Wat•teau (wo tō′, vä-), **Jean Antoine** (zhäɴ), 1684–1721, French painter.

Wat•ter•son (wot′ər sən, wô′tər-), **Henry** (*"Marse Henry"*), 1840–1921, U.S. journalist and political leader.

Watts (wots), **1. André,** born 1946, U.S. concert pianist, born in Germany. **2. George Frederick,** 1817–1904, English painter and sculptor. **3. Isaac,** 1674–1748, English theologian and hymnist.

Watts-Dun•ton (wots′dun′tn), **(Walter) Theodore** (*Walter Theodore Watts*), 1832–1914, English poet, novelist, and critic.

Waugh (wô), **1. Alec** (*Alexander Raban*), 1898–1981, English novelist, traveler, and lecturer (son of Arthur, brother of Evelyn). **2. Arthur,** 1866–1943, English literary critic, publisher, and editor (father of Alec and Evelyn). **3. Eve•lyn (Arthur St. John)** (ēv′lin, ē′və-), 1903–66, English novelist. **4. Frederick Judd,** 1861–1940, U.S. painter and illustrator.

Wa•vell (wā′vəl), **Archibald Percival, 1st Earl,** 1883–1950, British field marshal and author: viceroy of India 1943–47.

Wayne (wān), **1. Anthony** (*"Mad Anthony"*), 1745–96, American Revolutionary War general. **2. John** (*Marion Michael Morrison*) (*"Duke"*), 1907–79, U.S. film actor.

Wea•ver (wē′vər), **1. James Baird,** 1833–1912, U.S. politician: congressman 1879–81, 1885–89. **2. Robert Clifton,** born 1907, U.S. economist and government official: first Secretary of Housing and Urban Development, 1966–68.

Webb (web), **(Martha) Beatrice (Potter),** 1858–1943, and her husband, **Sidney (James), 1st Baron Passfield,** 1859–1947, English economists and socialists.

We•ber (vā′bər *for 1–3, 5;* web′ər *for 4*), **1. Ernst Heinrich,** 1795–1878, German physiologist. **2. Baron Karl Maria Friedrich Ernst von,** 1786–1826, German composer. **3. Max,** 1864–1920, German sociologist and political economist. **4. Max,** 1881–1961, U.S. painter, born in Russia. **5. Wilhelm Eduard,** 1804–91, German physicist (brother of Ernst Heinrich).

We•bern (vā′bərn), **Anton von,** 1883–1945, Austrian composer.

Web•ster (web′stər), **1. Daniel,** 1782–1852, U.S. statesman and orator. **2. John,** c1580–1625?, English dramatist. **3. Margaret,** 1905–72, British stage director, producer, and actress, born in the U.S. **4. Noah,** 1758–1843, U.S. lexicographer and essayist. **5. William H(edgcock),** born 1924, U.S. judge and government official: director of the FBI 1978–91.

Weed (wēd), **Thur•low** (thûr′lō), 1797–1882, U.S. journalist and politician.

Week•ley (wēk′lē), **Ernest,** 1865–1954, English etymologist and lexicographer.

Weems (wēmz), **Mason Locke** (*"Parson Weems"*), 1759–1825, U.S. clergyman and biographer.

We•ge•ner (vā′gə nər), **Alfred Lothar,** 1880–1930, German meteorologist and geophysicist.

Wei (wā), any of several dynasties that ruled in North China, esp. one ruling A.D. 220–265 and one ruling A.D. 386–534.

Weid•man (wīd′mən), **1. Charles Edward, Jr.,** 1901–75,

U.S. dancer, choreographer, and teacher. **2. Jerome,** born 1913, U.S. author.

Wei•er•strass (vī′ər sträs′, -shträs′), **Karl Theodor,** 1815–97, German mathematician.

Weill (wīl, vīl), **Kurt,** 1900–50, German composer, in the U.S. after 1935.

Wei•ser (wī′zər), **(Johann) Conrad,** 1696–1760, American colonial Indian agent and interpreter, born in Germany.

Weis•mann (vīs′män′, wīs′mən), **August,** 1834–1914, German biologist.

Weiss•mul•ler (wīs′mul′ər), **Peter John** (*Johnny*), 1904–84, U.S. swimmer and film actor.

Weiz•mann (vīts′män′, wīts′mən), **Cha•im** (ḵī′im), 1874–1952, 1st president of Israel 1948–52, born in Russia.

Weiz•säck•er (vīts′zek′ər), **Carl Friedrich von,** born 1912, German physicist and cosmologist.

Welch (welch, welsh), **1. Joseph Nye,** 1890–1960, U.S. trial lawyer. **2. Robert, Jr.,** 1899–1985, U.S. candy manufacturer: founder of the John Birch Society 1958. **3. William Henry,** 1850–1934, U.S. medical pathologist and educator.

Weld (weld), **Theodore Dwight,** 1803–95, U.S. abolitionist leader.

Welk (welk), **Lawrence,** 1903–92, U.S. musician and bandleader.

Wel•ler (wel′ər), **Thomas Huckle,** born 1915, U.S. physician: Nobel prize for medicine 1954.

Welles (welz), **1. (George) Orson,** 1915–85, U.S. actor, director, and producer. **2. Gideon,** 1802–78, U.S. journalist, legislator, and government official: Secretary of the Navy 1861–69. **3. Sumner,** 1892–1961, U.S. diplomat and government official.

Welles•ley (welz′lē), **Robert Col•ley** (kol′ē), **1st Marquis,** 1760–1842, British statesman and administrator, born in Ireland: governor general of India 1797–1805.

Wel•lesz (vel′es), **E•gon** (ā′gōn), 1885–1974, Austrian musicologist and composer.

Wel•ling•ton (wel′ing tən), **1st Duke of** (*Arthur Wellesley*), 1769–1852, British general and statesman, born in Ireland: prime minister 1828–30.

Wells (welz), **1. Henry,** 1805–78, U.S. businessman: pioneered in banking, stagecoach services, and express shipping. **2. H(erbert) G(eorge),** 1866–1946, English novelist and historian. **3. Horace,** 1815–48, U.S. dentist: pioneered use of nitrous oxide as an anesthetic. **4. Ida Bell** (*Ida Bell Wells-Barnett*), 1862–1931, U.S. journalist and civil-rights leader.

Wel•ty (wel′tē), **Eudora,** born 1909, U.S. writer.

Wen•ces•laus or **Wen•ces•las** (wen′sis lôs′), **1.** 1361–1419, emperor of the Holy Roman Empire 1378–1400; as **Wenceslaus IV,** king of Bohemia 1378–1419. **2. Saint**

("*Good King Wenceslaus*"), A.D. 903?–c935, duke of Bohemia 928–935. Czech, **Václav.** German, **Wen•zel** (ven′tsəl).

Went•worth (went′wûrth′), **1. Thomas, 1st Earl of Strafford.** STRAFFORD, 1ST EARL OF. **2. William Charles,** 1793–1872, Australian political leader, author, and journalist.

Wer•fel (vâr′fəl), **Franz,** 1890–1945, Austrian novelist, poet, and dramatist, born in Prague.

Wer•ner (wûr′nər, vâr′-), **Alfred,** 1866–1919, Swiss chemist: Nobel prize 1913.

Wes•ley (wes′lē, wez′-), **1. Charles,** 1707–88, English evangelist and hymnist. **2.** his brother **John,** 1703–91, English theologian and evangelist: founder of Methodism.

West (west), **1. Benjamin,** 1738–1820, U.S. painter, in England after 1763. **2. Mae,** 1892?–1980, U.S. actress. **3. Nathanael** (*Nathan Wallenstein Weinstein*), 1902?–40, U.S. novelist. **4. Dame Rebecca** (*Cicily Isabel Fairfield Andrews*), 1892–1983, English novelist, journalist, and critic, born in Ireland.

Wes•ter•marck (wes′tər märk′, ves′-), **Edward Alexander,** 1862–1939, Finnish sociologist.

West•ing•house (wes′ting hous′), **George,** 1846–1914, U.S. inventor and manufacturer.

West•more•land (west′môr′lənd, -mōr′-), **William Childs,** born 1914, U.S. army officer: commander of U.S. forces in Vietnam and Thailand 1964–68.

Wes•ton (wes′tən), **Edward,** 1886–1958, U.S. photographer.

Wey•den (vīd′n), **Roger** or **Rogier van der,** 1400?–64, Flemish painter.

Wey•gand (vā gäɴ′), **Maxime,** 1867–1965, French general.

Weyl (vīl), **Hermann,** 1885–1955, German mathematician, in the U.S. after 1933.

Whar•ton (hwôr′tn, wôr′-), **Edith,** 1862–1937, U.S. novelist.

Wheat•ley (hwēt′lē, wēt′-), **Phillis,** 1753?–84, American poet, born in Africa.

Wheat•stone (hwēt′stōn′, wēt′-; *esp. Brit.* -stən), **Sir Charles,** 1802–75, English physicist and inventor.

Whee•ler (hwē′lər, wē′-), **1. Burton Kendall,** 1882–1975, U.S. political leader. **2. Joseph,** 1836–1906, U.S. Confederate officer and political leader. **3. William Almon,** 1819–87, vice president of the U.S. 1877–81.

Whee•lock (hwē′lok, wē′-), **Eleazar,** 1711–79, U.S. clergyman and educator: founded Dartmouth College.

Wheel•wright (hwēl′rīt′, wēl′-), **John,** 1592?–1679, English clergyman in America.

Whip•ple (hwip′əl, wip′-), **1. Fred Lawrence,** born 1906, U.S. astronomer. **2. George Hoyt,** 1878–1976, U.S. pathologist: Nobel prize for medicine 1934.

Whis•tler (hwis′lər, wis′-), **James (Abbott) McNeill,** 1834–1903, U.S. painter and etcher.

White (hwīt, wīt), **1. Byron R(aymond)** ("*Whizzer*"), born

1917, associate justice of the U.S. Supreme Court since 1962. **2. Edward Douglass,** 1845–1921, Chief Justice of the U.S. Supreme Court 1910–21. **3. Edward H(iggins), II,** 1930–67, U.S. astronaut: first American to walk in space 1965. **4. E(lwyn) B(rooks),** 1899–1985, U.S. humorist and poet. **5. George Leonard,** 1838–95, U.S. choral conductor. **6. Gilbert,** 1720–93, English clergyman, naturalist, and writer. **7. Patrick (Victor Martindale),** 1912–90, Australian writer, born in England: Nobel prize 1973. **8. Stanford,** 1853–1906, U.S. architect. **9. Stewart Edward,** 1873–1946, U.S. novelist. **10. T(erence) H(anbury),** 1896–1964, English novelist. **11. Walter Francis,** 1893–1955, U.S. civil-rights leader and writer: executive secretary of the NAACP 1931–55. **12. William A(l•an•son)** (al′ən sən), 1870–1937, U.S. neurologist, psychiatrist, and writer. **13. William Allen,** 1868–1944, U.S. journalist.

White•field (hwit′fēld′, wit′-), **George,** 1714–70, English Methodist evangelist.

White•head (hwīt′hed′, wīt′-), **Alfred North,** 1861–1947, English philosopher and mathematician, in the U.S. after 1924.

White•man (hwīt′mən, wīt′-), **Paul** (*"Pops"*), 1891–1967, U.S. orchestra conductor.

Whit•man (hwit′mən, wit′-), **1. Marcus,** 1802–47, U.S. missionary and pioneer. **2. Walt(er),** 1819–92, U.S. poet.

Whit•ney (hwit′nē, wit′-), **1. Eli,** 1765–1825, U.S. manufacturer and inventor. **2. John Hay,** 1904–82, U.S. diplomat and newspaper publisher. **3. Josiah Dwight,** 1819–96, U.S. geologist. **4. William Dwight,** 1827–94, U.S. philologist and lexicographer.

Whit•ta•ker (hwit′ə kər, wit′-), **Charles Evans,** 1901–73, U.S. jurist: associate justice of the U.S. Supreme Court 1957–62.

Whit•ti•er (hwit′ē ər, wit′-), **John Greenleaf,** 1807–92, U.S. poet.

Whit•ting•ton (hwit′ing tən, wit′-), **Richard** (*"Dick"*), 1358?–1423, Lord Mayor of London, England.

Whit•tle (hwit′l, wit′l), **Sir Frank,** born 1907, English engineer and inventor.

Whit•worth (hwit′wûrth′, wit′-), **Kathrynne Ann** (*Kathy*), born 1939, U.S. golfer.

Whorf (hwôrf, wôrf), **Benjamin Lee,** 1897–1941, U.S. linguist.

Wie•land (vē′länt′), **1. Christoph Martin,** 1733–1813, German writer. **2. Heinrich,** 1877–1957, German chemist: Nobel prize 1927.

Wien (vēn), **Wilhelm,** 1864–1928, German physicist: Nobel prize 1911.

Wie•ner (wē′nər), **Norbert,** 1894–1964, U.S. mathematician: pioneer in cybernetics.

Wie•sel (wi zel′), **El•ie** (el′ē), (*Eliezer*), born 1928, U.S. author, born in Romania: Nobel peace prize 1986.

Wig•gin (wig′in), **Kate Douglas,** 1856–1923, U.S. writer.

Wig•gles•worth (wig′əlz wûrth′), **Michael,** 1631–1705, U.S. theologian and author, born in England.

Wight•man (wīt′mən), **Hazel Hotchkiss,** 1886–1974, U.S. tennis player.

Wig•man (vig′män), **Mary,** 1886–1973, German dancer and choreographer.

Wig•ner (wig′nər), **Eugene Paul,** born 1902, U.S. physicist, born in Hungary: Nobel prize 1963.

Wil•ber•force (wil′bər fôrs′, -fōrs′), **William,** 1759–1833, British statesman, philanthropist, and writer.

Wil•bur (wil′bər), **Richard,** born 1921, U.S. poet: U.S. poet laureate 1987–88.

Wil•cox (wil′koks), **Ella Wheeler,** 1850–1919, U.S. poet.

Wilde (wīld), **Oscar (Fingal O'Flahertie Wills),** 1854–1900, Irish writer.

Wil•der (wīl′dər), **1. Billy** (*Samuel Wilder*), born 1906, U.S. film director, producer, and writer; born in Austria. **2. Laura Ingalls,** 1867–1957, U.S. writer of children's books. **3. Thornton (Niven),** 1897–1975, U.S. novelist and playwright.

Wil•hel•mi•na I (wil′ə mē′nə, wil′hel-), 1880–1962, queen of the Netherlands 1890–1948.

Wilkes (wilks), **1. Charles,** 1798–1877, U.S. rear admiral and explorer. **2. John,** 1727–97, English political leader.

Wil•kins (wil′kinz), **1. Sir George Hubert,** 1888–1958, Australian Antarctic explorer. **2. Maurice Hugh Frederick,** born 1916, English biophysicist, born in New Zealand: Nobel prize for medicine 1962. **3. Roy,** 1901–81, U.S. civil-rights leader.

Wil•kin•son (wil′kin sən), **1. Geoffrey,** born 1921, British chemist: Nobel prize 1973. **2. James,** 1757–1825, U.S. military officer, politician, and adventurer.

Wil•laert (wil′ärt, vil′-), **Adrian,** c1480–1562, Flemish composer.

Wil•lard (wil′ərd), **1. Emma (Hart),** 1787–1870, U.S. educator and poet. **2. Frances Elizabeth Caroline,** 1839–98, U.S. educator, reformer, and author. **3. Jess,** 1883–1968, U.S. boxer: world heavyweight champion 1915–19.

Wil•liam (wil′yəm), **1. William I, a.** (*"the Conqueror"*) 1027–87, duke of Normandy 1035–87; king of England 1066–87. **b.** (*William I of Orange*) (*"the Silent"*) 1533–84, Dutch leader born in Germany: 1st stadholder of the Netherlands 1578–84. **c.** (*Wilhelm Friedrich Ludwig*) 1797–1888, King of Prussia 1861–88; emperor of Germany 1871–88. **2. William II, a.** (*William Rufus*) (*"the Red"*) 1056?–1100, King of England 1087–1100 (son of William I, duke of Normandy). **b.** (*Frederick Wilhelm Viktor Albert*) 1859–1941, king of Prussia and emperor of Germany 1888–1918. **3. William III,** (*William III of Orange*) 1650–1702, stadholder of the Netherlands 1672–1702; king of England 1689–1702, joint ruler with his wife, Mary II. **4. William IV,** 1765–1837, king of Great Britain and Ireland 1830–37 (brother of George IV).

Wil′liam of Malmes′bur•y (mämz′ber′ē, -bə rē, -brē), c1090–1143?, English historian.

Wil•liams (wil′yəmz), **1. Bert** (*Egbert Austin Williams*), 1876?–1922, U.S. comedian and songwriter. **2. Betty (Smyth),** born 1943, Northern Irish peace activist: Nobel peace prize 1976. **3. Emlyn,** born 1905, Welsh playwright and actor. **4. Esther,** born 1923, U.S. actress and swimmer. **5. G. Mennen,** born 1911, U.S. politician and diplomat. **6. Hank,** 1923–53, U.S. singer and songwriter. **7. John Towner,** born 1932, U.S. composer and conductor. **8. Roger,** 1603?–83, English clergyman in America: founder of Rhode Island colony 1636. **9. Tennessee** (*Thomas Lanier Williams*), 1914–83, U.S. dramatist. **10. Theodore Samuel** (*Ted*), born 1918, U.S. baseball player. **11. William Carlos,** 1883–1963, U.S. poet and novelist.

Wil′liam the Con′queror, William I.

Wil•ling•don (wil′ing dən), **Freeman Freeman-Thomas, 1st Marquis of,** 1866–1941, British colonial official: governor general of Canada 1926–31; viceroy and governor general of India 1931–36.

Will•kie (wil′kē), **Wendell Lewis,** 1892–1944, U.S. executive, lawyer, and political leader.

Wills (wilz), **Helen Newington,** born 1906, U.S. tennis player.

Will•stät•ter (vil′shtet′ər), **Richard,** 1872–1942, German chemist: Nobel prize 1915.

Wil•mot (wil′mət), **David,** 1814–68, U.S. politician and jurist: congressman 1845–51; senator 1861–63.

Wil•son (wil′sən), **1. Sir Angus (Frank Johnstone),** 1913–91, English writer. **2. Charles Thomson Rees,** 1869–1959, Scottish physicist: Nobel prize 1927. **3. Edmund,** 1895–1972, U.S. literary and social critic. **4. Henry** (*Jeremiah Jones Colbath* or *Colbaith*), 1812–75, vice president of the U.S. 1873–75. **5. James,** 1742–98, U.S. jurist, born in Scotland: associate justice of the U.S. Supreme Court 1789–98. **6. Sir (James) Harold,** born 1916, British prime minister 1964–70, 1974–76. **7. John** (*"Christopher North"*), 1785–1854, Scottish poet, journalist, and critic. **8. Robert W(oodrow),** born 1936, U.S. radio astronomer: Nobel prize for physics 1978. **9. Sloan,** born 1920, U.S. journalist and novelist. **10. (Thomas) Woodrow,** 1856–1924, 28th president of the U.S. 1913–21: Nobel peace prize 1919.

Win•chell (win′chəl), **Walter,** 1897–1972, U.S. newspaper columnist and radio and television broadcaster.

Winck•el•mann (ving′kəl män′), **Johann Joachim,** 1717–68, German archaeologist and art historian.

Win•daus (vin′dous), **Adolf,** 1876–1959, German chemist: Nobel prize 1928.

Wind•sor (win′zər), **1.** (since 1917) a member of the present British royal family. **2. Duke of,** Edward VIII. **3. Wallis Warfield, Duchess of** (*Bessie Wallis Warfield Spencer Simpson*), 1896–1986, U.S. socialite: wife of Edward VIII of England.

Wins•low (winz′lō), **Edward,** 1595–1655, English colonist in America: governor of Plymouth Colony 1633, 1639, 1644.

Win•sor (win′zər), **Justin,** 1831–97, U.S. librarian and historian.

Win•ters (win′tərz), **Y•vor** (ī′vôr), 1900–68, U.S. poet and critic.

Win•throp (win′thrəp), **1. John,** 1588–1649, English colonist in America: 1st governor of the Massachusetts Bay colony. **2.** his son, **John,** 1606–76, colonial governor of Connecticut 1657, 1659–76. **3. John** or **Fitz-John,** 1638–1707, American soldier and statesman: colonial governor of Connecticut 1698–1707 (son of the younger John Winthrop). **4. John,** 1714–79, American astronomer, mathematician, and physicist. **5. Robert Charles,** 1809–94, U.S. politician: Speaker of the House 1847–49.

Wirtz (wûrts), **William Willard,** born 1912, U.S. lawyer and government official: Secretary of Labor 1962–69.

Wise (wīz), **1. Isaac Mayer,** 1819–1900, U.S. rabbi, born in Bohemia; founder of Reform Judaism in the U.S. **2. Stephen Samuel,** 1874–1949, U.S. rabbi and Zionist leader, born in Hungary.

Wise•man (wīz′mən), **Nicholas Patrick Stephen,** 1802–65, Irish cardinal and author, born in Spain.

Wiss•ler (wis′lər), **Clark,** 1870–1947, U.S. anthropologist.

Wis•ter (wis′tər), **Owen,** 1860–1938, U.S. novelist.

With•er (wiꟸ′ər) also **With•ers** (-ərz), **George,** 1588–1667, English poet and pamphleteer.

With•er•spoon (wiꟸ′ər spo͞on′), **John,** 1723–94, U.S. theologian and statesman, born in Scotland.

Witt (vit), **Katarina,** born 1965, German figure skater.

Wit•te (vit′ə), **Sergei Yulievich,** 1849–1915, Russian statesman.

Wit•te•kind (vit′ə kint′), died A.D. 807?, Westphalian chief: leader of the Saxons against Charlemagne.

Witt•gen•stein (vit′gən shtīn′, -stīn′), **Ludwig (Josef Johann),** 1889–1951, Austrian philosopher.

Wode•house (wo͝od′hous′), **Sir P(elham) G(renville),** 1881–1975, U.S. novelist and humorist, born in England.

Wöh•ler (wûr′lər, vûr′-), **Friedrich,** 1800–82, German chemist.

Wolf (vôlf), **1. Friedrich August,** 1759–1824, German classical scholar. **2. Hugo,** 1860–1903, Austrian composer.

Wolfe (wo͝olf), **1. Charles,** 1791–1823, Irish poet. **2. James,** 1727–59, English general. **3. Thomas (Clayton),** 1900–38, U.S. novelist.

Wolff (vôlf *for 1, 3;* wo͝olf *for 2*), **1. Christian von, Baron.** Also, **Wolf.** 1679–1754, German philosopher and mathematician. **2. Hugh,** born 1953, U.S. conductor, born in France. **3. Kaspar Friedrich,** 1733–94, German anatomist and physiologist.

Wolf-Fer•ra•ri (vôlf′fə rär′ē), **Ermanno,** 1876–1948, Italian composer.

Wölff•lin (*Ger.* vœlf′lin), **1. Eduard,** 1831–1908, Swiss classical scholar. **2.** his son **Heinrich,** 1864–1945, Swiss art historian.

Wolf•ram von Esch•en•bach (vôl′främ fən esh′ən-bäкн′, wo͝ol′frəm von esh′ən bäk′), c1170–c1220, German poet.

Wol•las•ton (wo͝ol′ə stən), **William Hyde,** 1766–1828, English chemist and physicist.

Wolse•ley (wo͝olz′lē), **Garnet Joseph, 1st Viscount,** 1833–1913, British field marshal.

Wol•sey (wo͝ol′zē), **Thomas,** 1475?–1530, English cardinal and statesman.

Won•der (wun′dər), **Stevie** (*Steveland Judkins Morris*), born 1950, U.S. singer and songwriter.

Wood (wo͝od), **1. Grant,** 1892–1942, U.S. painter. **2. Leonard,** 1860–1927, U.S. military doctor and political administrator.

Wood•hull (wo͝od′hul′), **Victoria Claflin,** 1838–1927, U.S. social reformer, newspaper publisher, and women's-rights advocate.

Wood•ruff (wo͝od′rəf), **Hiram,** 1817–67, Canadian driver, trainer, and breeder of harness-racing horses.

Wood•son (wo͝od′sən), **Carter Godwin,** 1875–1950, U.S. historian and publisher: pioneer in modern black studies.

Wood•ward (wo͝od′wərd), **1. Joanne,** born 1930, U.S. actress. **2. Robert Burns,** 1917–79, U.S. chemist: Nobel prize 1965.

Woolf (wo͝olf), **Virginia** (*Adeline Virginia Stephen Woolf*), 1882–1941, English novelist, essayist, and critic.

Wooll•cott (wo͝ol′kət), **Alexander,** 1887–1943, U.S. essayist and journalist.

Wool•ley (wo͝ol′ē), **Sir (Charles) Leonard,** 1880–1960, English archaeologist and explorer.

Wool•worth (wo͝ol′wûrth′), **Frank Winfield,** 1852–1919, U.S. merchant.

Woos•ter (wo͝os′tər), **David,** 1711–77, American Revolutionary War general.

Worces•ter (wo͝os′tər), **Joseph Emerson,** 1784–1865, U.S. lexicographer.

Words•worth (wûrdz′wûrth′), **William,** 1770–1850, English poet: poet laureate 1843–50.

Work (wûrk), **Henry Clay,** 1832–84, U.S. songwriter.

Wot•ton (wot′n), **Henry,** 1568–1639, English poet and diplomat.

Wouk (wōk), **Herman,** born 1915, U.S. novelist.

Wo•vo•ka (wə vō′kə), c1856–1932, Northern Paiute religious leader: revived the ghost dance religion 1889.

Woz•ni•ak (woz′nē ak′), **Stephen** (*Steve*), born 1950, U.S. computer inventor and entrepreneur.

Wren (ren), **1. Sir Christopher,** 1632–1723, English architect. **2. Percival Christopher,** 1885–1941, English novelist.

Wright (rīt), **1. Frances** or **Fanny,** 1795–1852, U.S. abolitionist and social reformer, born in Scotland. **2. Frank**

Lloyd, 1867–1959, U.S. architect. **3. Joseph** (*"Wright of Derby"*), 1734–97, English painter. **4. Joseph,** 1855–1935, English philologist and lexicographer. **5. Mary Kathryn** (*"Mickey"*), born 1935, U.S. golfer. **6. Orville,** 1871–1948, and his brother **Wilbur,** 1867–1912, U.S. aeronautical inventors. **7. Richard,** 1908–60, U.S. novelist. **8. Russel,** 1904–76, U.S. industrial designer. **9. Willard Huntington** (*"S. S. Van Dine"*), 1888–1939, U.S. journalist, critic, and author.

Wrig•ley (rig′lē), **William, Jr.,** 1861–1932, U.S. chewing-gum manufacturer and baseball team owner.

Wul•fi•la (wo͝ol′fə lə), ULFILAS.

Wundt (vo͝ont), **Wilhelm Max,** 1832–1920, German physiologist and psychologist.

Wy•att or **Wy•at** (wī′ət), **1. James,** 1746–1813, English architect. **2. Sir Thomas,** 1503?–42, English poet and diplomat.

Wych•er•ley (wich′ər lē), **William,** c1640–1716, English dramatist.

Wyc•liffe or **Wyc•lif** (wik′lif), **John,** c1320–84, English religious reformer and Biblical translator.

Wy•eth (wī′əth), **1. Andrew Newell,** born 1917, U.S. painter. **2.** his son **James Browning,** born 1946, U.S. painter. **3.** his father, **Newell Convers,** 1882–1945, U.S. illustrator and painter.

Wyld (wīld), **Henry Cecil Kennedy,** 1870–1945, English lexicographer and linguist.

Wy•ler (wī′lər), **William,** 1902–81, U.S. film director, born in Germany.

Wy•lie (wī′lē), **1. Elinor** (*Elinor Morton Hoyt*), 1885–1928, U.S. poet and novelist. **2. Philip,** 1902–71, U.S. novelist and critic.

Wynd•ham (win′dəm), **John** (*John Benyon Harris*), 1903–69, British science-fiction writer.

Wynn (win), **Ed** (*Isaiah Edwin Leopold*), 1886–1966, U.S. comedian.

Wythe (with), **George,** 1729–1806, U.S. jurist and statesman.

Xan•thip•pe (zan tip′ē), fl. late 5th century B.C., wife of Socrates.

Xa•vi•er (zā′vē ər, zav′ē-, zā′vyər), **Saint Francis** (*Francisco Javier*), 1506–52, Spanish Jesuit missionary.

Xe•noc•ra•tes (zə nok′rə tēz′), 396–314 B.C., Greek philosopher.

Xe•noph•a•nes (zə nof′ə nēz′), c570–c480 B.C., Greek philosopher.

Xen•o•phon (zen′ə fən, -fon′), 434?–355? B.C., Greek historian.

Xerx•es I (zûrk′sēz), 519?–465 B.C., king of Persia 486?–465 (son of Darius I).

Xi•me•nes (*Sp.* hē me′nes), JIMÉNEZ DE CISNEROS.

Y

Yale (yāl), **Elihu,** 1648–1721, English colonial official, born in America: governor of Madras 1687–92.

Yal•ow (yal′ō), **Rosalyn (Sussman),** born 1921, U.S. medical physicist: Nobel prize for medicine 1977.

Ya•ma•ga•ta (yä′mə gä′tə), **Prince Aritomo,** 1838–1922, Japanese field marshal and statesman.

Ya•ma•gu•chi (yä′mə go͞o′chē), **Kristi,** born 1971, U.S. figure skater.

Ya•ma•mo•to (yä′mə mō′tō), **Isoroku,** 1884–1943, Japanese naval officer.

Ya•ma•ni (yä mä′nē), **Sheik Ahmed Zaki,** born 1930, Saudi Arabian government official: minister of petroleum and natural resources 1962–86.

Ya•ma•sa•ki (yä′mə sä′kē), **Minoru,** 1912–86, U.S. architect.

Ya•ma•shi•ta (yä′mə shē′tə), **Tomoyuki,** (*"the Tiger of Malaya"*), 1885–1946, Japanese general.

Yang Chen Ning (yäng′ chen′ ning′), born 1922, Chinese physicist in the U.S.: Nobel prize 1957.

Yang Shang•kun (yäng′ shäng′ko͞on′), born 1907, Chinese Communist leader: president since 1988.

Ya•ni (yä′nē), (*Wang Yani*), born 1975, Chinese painter.

Yea•ger (yā′gər), **Charles (Elwood)** (*"Chuck"*), born 1923, U.S. aviator and test pilot: the first person to fly faster than the speed of sound (1947).

Yeats (yāts), **William Butler,** 1865–1939, Irish poet and dramatist: Nobel prize 1923.

Ye Jian•ying (yu′ jyän′ying′) also **Yeh Chien-ying** (jyun′-), 1898–1986, Chinese marshal and Communist leader: defense minister 1971–78.

Yel•tsin (yelt′sin), **Boris Nikolayevich,** born 1931, president of the Russian Federation since 1991.

Yen Hsi-shan (yun′ shē′shän′), 1882–1960, Chinese general.

Yer•kes (yûr′kēz), **1. Charles Tyson,** 1837–1905, U.S. financier. **2. Robert Mearns,** 1876–1956, U.S. psychologist and psychobiologist.

Ye•se•nin (yə sā′nin), **Sergey Aleksandrovich,** 1895–1925, Russian poet.

Yev•tu•shen•ko (yev′to͝o sheng′kō), **Yevgeny Alexandrovich,** born 1933, Russian poet.

Yong Lo (yông′ lô′), (*Zhu Di*) Yung Lo.

York (yôrk), **1. 1st Duke of** (*Edmund of Langley*), 1341–1402, progenitor of the house of York (son of Edward III). **2. Alvin Cullum** (*Sergeant*), 1887–1964, U.S. soldier.

Yo•shi•hi•to (yō′shē hē′tō), 1879–1926, emperor of Japan 1912–26 (son of Mutsuhito).

You•lou (yo͞o′lo͞o), **Fulbert,** 1917–72, African political leader: president of the Republic of Congo (now People's Republic of the Congo) 1959–63.

Young (yung), **1. Andrew (Jackson, Jr.),** born 1932, U.S. clergyman, civil-rights leader, politician, and diplomat: mayor of Atlanta, Georgia, since 1981. **2. Art(hur Henry),** 1866–1944, U.S. cartoonist and author. **3. Brigham,** 1801–77, U.S. Mormon leader. **4. Charles,** 1864–1922, U.S. army colonel: highest-ranking black officer in World War I. **5. Denton T.** (*Cy*), 1867–1955, U.S. baseball player. **6. Edward,** 1683–1765, English poet. **7. Ella,** 1867–1956, Irish poet and mythologist in the U.S. **8. Owen D.,** 1874–1962, U.S. lawyer, industrialist, government administrator, and financier. **9. Stark,** 1881–1963, U.S. drama critic, novelist, and playwright. **10. Thomas,** 1773–1829, English physician, physicist, and Egyptologist. **11. Whitney M., Jr.,** 1921–71, U.S. social worker and educator.

Young•er (yung′gər), **Thomas Coleman** (*"Cole"*), 1844–1916, U.S. outlaw, associated with Jesse James.

Young′ Pretend′er, Stuart, Charles Edward.

Yous•ke•vitch (yo͞os kā′vich), **Igor,** born 1912, U.S. ballet dancer, born in Russia.

Yp•si•lan•ti (ip′sə lan′tē), **Alexander,** 1792–1828, and his brother **Demetrios,** 1793–1832, Greek patriots and revolutionary leaders.

Y•sa•ye (*Fr.* ē za ē′), **Eugène,** 1858–1931, Belgian violinist, composer, and conductor.

Yu•ka•wa (yo͞o kä′wä), **Hideki,** 1907–81, Japanese physicist: Nobel prize 1949.

Yung Lo (yo͝ong′ lô′), (*Chu Ti*) 1360–1424, Chinese emperor 1403–25. Also called **Ch'eng Tsu.**

Z

Zach·a·ri·as (zak′ə rī′əs) also **Zach·a·ry** (zak′ə rē), **Saint,** died 752, Greek ecclesiastic, born in Italy: pope 741–752.

Zad·kine (zäd kēn′), **Ossip,** 1890–1967, Russian sculptor, in France.

Zagh·lul Pa·sha (zäg′lo͞ol pä′shä), **Saad,** c1860–1927, Egyptian political leader: first prime minister 1924–27.

Za·har·i·as (zə hâr′ē əs, -har′-), **Mildred Didrikson** (*"Babe"*), 1914–56, U.S. track-and-field athlete and golfer.

Za·mo·ra (thä mô′ʀä, sä-), **Alcalá,** (*Niceto Alcalá Zamora y Torres*), 1877–1949, Spanish statesman: 1st president of the Republic 1931–36.

Zang·will (zang′wil), **Israel,** 1865–1926, English novelist and playwright.

Zan·uck (zan′ək), **Darryl F(rancis),** 1902–79, U.S. motion-picture producer.

Za·pa·ta (sä pä′tä), **Emiliano,** 1877?–1919, Mexican revolutionary and agrarian reformer.

Zar·a·thus·tra (zar′ə tho͞o′strə), ZOROASTER.

Zá·to·pek (zä′tə pek′), **Emil,** born 1922, Czechoslovakian long-distance runner.

Zee·man (zā′män′), **Pieter,** 1865–1943, Dutch physicist: Nobel prize 1902.

Zeng·er (zeng′ər, -gər), **John Peter,** 1697–1746, American journalist, printer, and publisher, born in Germany.

Ze·no (zē′nō), **1.** ZENO OF CITIUM. **2.** ZENO OF ELEA.

Ze·no·bi·a (zə nō′bē ə), (*Septimia Bathzabbai*) died after A.D. 272, queen of Palmyra in Syria A.D. 267–272.

Ze′no of Ci′ti·um (sish′ē əm), c340–c265 B.C., Greek philosopher, born in Cyprus. Also called **Ze′no the Sto′ic.**

Ze′no of E′le·a (ē′lē ə), c490–c430 B.C., Greek philosopher.

Zeph·y·ri·nus (zef′ə rī′nəs), **Saint,** pope A.D. 198?–217.

Zep·pe·lin (zep′ə lin), **Count Ferdinand von,** 1838–1917, German general and manufacturer of the zeppelin.

Zer·ni·ke (zâr′ni kə, zûr′-), **Frits,** 1888–1966, Dutch physicist: Nobel prize 1953.

Zeux·is (zo͞ok′sis), fl. c430–c400 B.C., Greek painter.

Zhao Zi·yang (jou′ zœ′yäng′), born 1919, Chinese Communist leader: premier 1980–87; general secretary of the Communist Party 1987–89.

Zhiv·kov (zhif′kôf), **Todor,** born 1911, Bulgarian political leader: prime minister 1962–71; president 1971–89.

Zhou En·lai or **Chou En-lai** (jō′ en lī′), 1898–1976, Chinese Communist leader: premier 1949–76.

Zhu De (jo͞o′ du′), 1886–1976, Chinese military and Communist leader.

Zhu·kov (zho͞o′kôf, -kof), **Georgi Konstantinovich,** 1896–1974, Soviet marshal.

Z·ia-ul-Haq (zē′ä o͝ol häk′), **Mohammed,** 1924–88, Pakistani army general and political leader: president 1978–88.

Zieg·feld (zig′feld), **Florenz,** 1867–1932, U.S. theatrical producer.

Zie·gler (zē′glər, tsē′-), **Karl,** 1897–1973, German chemist: Nobel prize 1963.

Zim·ba·list (zim′bə list) **1. Efrem,** 1889–1985, U.S. violinist and composer, born in Russia. **2.** his son, **Efrem, Jr.,** born 1923, U.S. actor.

Zin·del (zin del′), **Paul,** born 1936, U.S. playwright and novelist.

Zi·no·viev (zi nō′vē ef′, -nōv′yef), **Grigori Evseevich,** 1883–1936, Russian Bolshevik leader.

Zins·ser (zin′sər), **Hans,** 1878–1940, U.S. bacteriologist.

Zin·zen·dorf (tsin′tsən dôrf′), **Count Nikolaus Ludwig von,** 1700–60, German religious leader: reformer and organizer of the Moravian Church.

Žiž·ka (zhish′kä), **Jan** (yän), c1370–1424, Bohemian Hussite military leader.

Zna·nie·cki (znä nyets′kē), **Florian,** 1882–1958, Polish sociologist.

Zog I (zōg) also **Zo·gu I** (zō′go͞o), (*Ahmed Bey Zogu*) 1895–1961, king of Albania 1928–39.

Zo·la (zō′lə, -lä), **Émile,** 1840–1902, French novelist.

Zo·rach (zôr′äk, -äkн, -ak, zōr′-), **William,** 1887–1966, U.S. sculptor and painter, born in Lithuania.

Zorn (sôrn), **Anders Leonhard,** 1860–1920, Swedish painter, etcher, and sculptor.

Zo·ro·as·ter (zôr′ō as′tər, zōr′-, zôr′ō as′tər, zōr′-), fl. 6th century B.C., Persian religious teacher. Also called **Zarathustra.**

Zor·ri·lla y Mo·ral (sôr ēl′yä ē mô räl′), **José,** 1817–93, Spanish poet and dramatist.

Zo·ser (zō′sər), fl. c2800 B.C., Egyptian ruler of the 3rd dynasty.

Zo·si·mus (zō′sə məs), **Saint,** died 418, pope 417–418.

Zsig·mon·dy (zhig′môn dē), **Richard,** 1865–1929, German chemist, born in Austria: Nobel prize 1925.

Zuc·ca·ri (tso͞o′kə rē) also **Zuc·ca·ro** or **Zuc·che·ro** (-rō), **Federico,** 1543?–1609, and his brother **Taddeo,** 1529–66, Italian painters.

Zuk·er·man (zo͝ok′ər mən), **Pinchas,** born 1948, Israeli violinist.

Zu·kor (zo͞o′kər), **Adolph,** 1873–1976, U.S. film producer, born in Hungary.

Zu·lo·a·ga (zo͞o′lō ä′gä, so͞o′-), **Ignacio,** 1870–1945, Spanish painter.

Zur·ba·rán (zo͝or′bä rän′, so͝or′-), **Francisco de,** 1598–1663?, Spanish painter.

Zweig (zwīg, swīg, tsvīk), **1. Arnold,** 1887–1968, German writer. **2. Stefan,** 1881–1942, Austrian writer.

Zwick·y (tsvik′ē, zwik′ē), **Fritz,** 1898–1974, Swiss astrophysicist, born in Bulgaria, in the U.S. after 1925.

Zwing•li (zwing′glē, swing′-, tsving′-), **Ulrich** or **Huldreich,** 1484–1531, Swiss Protestant reformer.

Zwor•y•kin (zwôr′i kin), **Vladimir Kosma,** 1889–1982, U.S. engineer and inventor, born in Russia.